Bea Eisenhour

MARYHELEN VANNIER, ED. D.

Professor and Director, Women's Division,
Department of Health and Physical Education,
Southern Methodist University, Dallas, Texas

HALLY B. W. POINDEXTER, ED. D.

Professor of Health and Physical Education,
University of Houston and Rice Universities,
Houston, Texas

Illustrated by WILLIAM OSBURN
and JAMES BONNER

W. B. SAUNDERS COMPANY
Philadelphia, London, Toronto

INDIVIDUAL AND TEAM SPORTS FOR GIRLS AND WOMEN

Third Edition

VANNIER
and
POINDEXTER

W. B. Saunders Company: West Washington Square
Philadelphia, Pa. 19105

1 St. Anne's Road
Eastbourne, East Sussex BN21 3UN, England

833 Oxford Street
Toronto, Ontario M8Z 5T9, Canada

Library of Congress Cataloging in Publication Data

Vannier, Maryhelen

Individual and team sports for girls and women.

Includes index.

1. Sports for women. I. Poindexter, Hally Beth, joint author. II. Title.

GV709.V3 1976 796'.019'4 73–86388

ISBN 0–7216–8992–2

Cover illustration courtesy of the authors.

Individual and Team Sports for Girls and Women ISBN 0-7216-8992-2

Last digit is the print number: 9 8 7 6 5 4 3 2

This book is dedicated to

all persons who are students or teachers of the processes of skill development in aquatics, gymnastics, and sports.

PREFACE

The Third Edition represents a major revision of content and methodology, designed to enhance skill development in aquatics, gymnastics, and individual and team sports. In the fifteen years since the First Edition was published, social evolutionary and revolutionary changes have reflected the strong emerging partnership and leadership roles of women in American society. In no other social institutions are the immediate effects felt more strongly than in the schools, with their educational programs of physical education and recreational and competitive athletics. Encouraged by social awareness and acceptance and supported by new federal statutes, girls, women, boys, and men are assured of equal opportunities to learn, participate in, and excel in a wide variety of sports and games.

In the past decade a variety of methodological approaches, delivery systems, and teaching strategies which expedite and enhance the teaching-learning process have evolved. Through research and empirical evidence it is obvious that learning experiences, individually or group designed, may be enhanced through such varied approaches as core-content curriculum, competency- or performance-based models, and humanistic models. The importance of skill and technique is basic to any approach or strategy. This edition strives to present material to facilitate the teaching-learning-participation process applicable to any curriculum model in physical education.

First, it is a presentation of purposes, values, and opportunities for the individual who is striving for a full expressive life which includes physical skill development and sports participation; second, it is a presentation of theoretical and practical considerations for the development of a learning environment; and third, it is a book of content materials and methods helpful in the successful learning and teaching of a variety of sports skills.

This book was written with four groups in mind: (1) the physical education major student preparing to be a teacher; (2) the beginning or experienced teacher searching for productive and interesting ways to teach others the skills and strategies of sports; (3) the individual player desirous of refining and mastering the numerous skills of the sport in which she seeks to excel; and (4) the playground, camp, or community recreation leader seeking to expand recreational sport or athletic offerings with new materials and fresh approaches. Reflecting the new approaches to learning, the book is designed so that it may be used as an individual, self-paced experience, by a teacher using group core instructions, or as a learning resource in a competency-based program.

In each of the sport chapters the reader will find a brief historical treatment of the sport, a description of the nature and purpose of the game, a listing of needed facilities and equipment, a summary of rules and scoring, an analysis of basic skills and techniques, suggested teaching units for beginners and more advanced players, suggested teaching progressions with sample plans, and a presentation of some game strategies with the duties and specific responsibilities of each player. Furthermore, there is a unique analysis of skill difficulties and their corrections which is presented both verbally and visually for easy reference. Each chapter also includes suggested skill and knowledge tests for individual or teacher assessment, terminology, discussion questions and selected references, and recommended audiovisual materials.

The official rulebooks and guides of national sport organizations and of the National Association for Girls and Women in Sport are important supplements to this book. In addition to complete rules of each sport, which are not fully covered in this book, these publications emphasize officiating techniques and present articles on sport conditioning and coaching strategies.

The authors recognize that no single book can serve the variety of needs and expectations of all learners and teachers of sports. Just as the authors have combined their professional knowledge and experiences in the development of the content of this textbook, it is hoped that the reader will read, question, discuss, and modify the material to fit her own learning environment.

Maryhelen Vannier

Hally B. W. Poindexter

ACKNOWLEDGMENTS

The authors are indebted to many persons who have made this book possible. Martha Sue Wood, Shirley Corbitt, and Barbara Camp of the Department of Health and Physical Education of Southern Methodist University gave valuable suggestions for the revision of selected individual sports chapters. Eva Jean Lee of Rice University, Martha Hawthorne of Northeastern State University (Louisiana), Ruth Nelson of the University of Houston, and Judy Glazener of Channelview Independent School District, Channelview, Texas, faithfully reviewed and modified many aspects of the book. We would also like to thank the many students and professional colleagues who have "field tested" many ideas and offered suggestions over the years.

We are also grateful to Wallace Pennington, editor, of the W. B. Saunders Company and also to William Osburn and James Bonner, assisted by Ellen Cole and Barbara Fennison, who so ably illustrated the book. Our eternal thanks and appreciation go to our families and professional colleagues for their understanding and support during the preparation of the manuscript.

CONTENTS

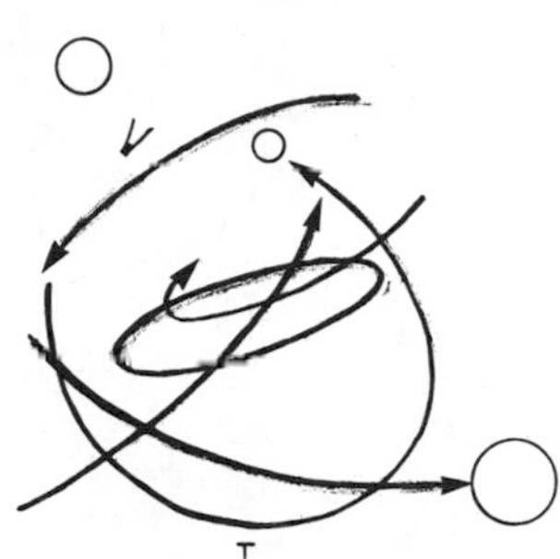

PART I

ORIENTATION

REFLECTIONS*

Sport holds a mirror to a woman's life
all that she can know
of joy
or sadness
finds its counterpart in sport
she learns not only how she moves
but how she feels
and thinks
and struggles
how she is tormented
triumphs
and then finds peace
as she absorbs the
mood
drama
and emotion
which are the essences of her sport
so she discovers
all the inward stresses
that move her being

LaFerne E. Price

---

*From LaFerne E. Price: *The Wonder of Motion—a sense of life for woman.* 2nd ed. University of North Dakota Press, Grand Forks, North Dakota, 1974. Reprinted by permission of the author.

CHAPTER 1

THE UNIQUE CONTRIBUTIONS OF SPORTS TO LIFE

Never before in our history have girls' and women's interest and participation in individual and team sports been greater. Current research focusing on the physiological, psychological, and sociological aspects of sports discloses that many of the potential values and benefits traditionally considered to be of importance to male participants only are equally beneficial for females. Former taboos and social stigmas surrounding female sports participation are rapidly disappearing. Television and newspaper coverage of the Olympic games and of national and local sporting events such as swimming, track and field, ice skating, skiing, tennis, golf, gymnastics, basketball, and volleyball has given impetus to women's sports and has done much to change the distorted public image of the female athlete. More women are competing now in intercollegiate sports, as individuals or as representatives of clubs or athletic groups; more high school girls are playing in expanded interscholastic and after-school sports programs; and selected elementary school programs offer competition for girls in the upper grades. More women are becoming educated spectators of both male and female sporting events through television and expanded local sports groups.

Equality of opportunity for women to learn, participate in, and compete in sports has become a national concern. Federal legislation designed to assure equal funding, facilities, and leadership in schools and colleges for males and females is opening avenues for sports instruction and participation never before explored by women.

VALUES OF SPORTS PARTICIPATION – TRADITIONAL VERSUS CURRENT

Lord Wellington's often quoted phrase, "The Battle of Waterloo was won on the playing fields of Eton," is an obvious reference to the positive relationship of sports participation and the development of character and leadership qualities. He surmised that his officers, who as young men had been educated in traditional British sports at the distinguished preparatory school, had been imbued with the same qualities of courage, character and leadership they needed to direct the decisive victory over Napoleon. Similar claims by President Theodore Roosevelt referring to the character-building qualities of American football and by numerous well intentioned educators and political officials have led the American public to believe sports participation is the panacea for the correction of societal ills.

A large number of people contend that the root of the problem is that we are becoming a nation of spectators rather than one of participants. They note that in sports greater numbers are becoming increasingly content to watch fewer play. They support their arguments with the statistics of those rejected for military service because of physical defects and the failure of American children to meet the assessed fitness levels of some European and Asian groups. The latter statistics, coupled with some poor showings in the Olympic games, give rise to concern over our lagging international prestige as a strong and viable nation. Others cite the increases in obesity, heart diseases, mental illnesses, and death from degenerative diseases as the result of lessening individual physical effort. These individuals and others relate the discipline and drug problems of youth, the alcoholic syndrome of middle age, and the tragedies of aging to poor preparation in use of leisure time.

All of the well intentioned critics must recognize that sports and games are but vehicles for the use of individuals and groups. They can serve people only as they choose to be served. Sports and games serve best if people actively participate in them. It is not possible for sports educators or sport participants to assume a greater burden of responsibility. Involvement in sports and games as a player or spectator *can* lead to personal, social, and cultural development, but the benefits are individual matters dependent upon one's personal involvement and experience. For individual and group participants sports can provide an environment for: (1) developing improved health and physical fitness; (2) increasing physical skill development; (3) improving social interaction; (4) developing self-understanding, desirable social values and attitudes; (5) developing specialized knowledge and appreciation of sports; and (6) fostering appreciation of the play concept while developing knowledge for leisure time use.

DEVELOPING IMPROVED HEALTH AND PHYSICAL FITNESS

Total individual fitness—physical, nutritional, and spiritual—eludes definition, for it is a complex blending of positive health practices, proper exercises, and emotional and social balance. Physical fitness, a vital part of total fitness, is an equally difficult concept to define. A highly individual quality, it may be explored by citing the components one strives for in physical fitness development. These include:

1. Muscular strength—the maximum force of a muscle or group of muscles against resistance.
2. Muscular endurance—the ability to continue muscular exertion.
3. Muscular power—the ability to utilize maximum force in the shortest possible time.
4. Cardiorespiratory endurance—the ability to maintain demanding efforts of the cardiovascular and respiratory systems.
5. Flexibility—the degree of range of motion around the joints.
6. Agility—the ability to change positions in space in relation to time.
7. Coordination—the ability to integrate different movements into a patterned skilled movement.
8. Speed—a complex pattern of cue perception, impulsion, and total movement within the shortest period of time.
9. Balance—the complex abilities of controlling body position in dynamic (moving body or base), static (stationary), or rotational positions.
10. Maximum oxygen uptake—the capacity of the body to utilize oxygen at the cellular level.

Exercise, sports, and games, properly planned and regularly pursued, are the foundations upon which physical fitness is developed and maintained.

The physiological benefits of continuing and recurrent exercise are numerous. However, many beneficial claims have not been supported by experimental evidence; other claims remain controversial. Those listed below are considered supportable as meaningful outcomes of regular exercise:

1. Increased muscular strength, developed by the principle of "overload" and specific to the muscles involved.
2. Increased muscular endurance of muscles actively involved in exercise.
3. Increased functional capacity of the heart muscle, due to increase in size and muscular efficiency of contraction.
4. Increased connective tissue growth between muscle fibers and in tendons and ligaments. This serves to protect tissues and joints and affords better anchorage of muscle to bone.
5. Increased myoglobin stores which increase muscular endurance.
6. Increased enzyme activity which facilitates energy metabolism.
7. Stimulation and increase in bone formation. This occurs by stimulation of cells by weight-bearing compression and pull of muscles and by increased blood flow through bones.
8. Increase in relative number of open capillaries in heart and active muscles.

9. Increased blood volume, due to increased plasma and red blood cell production to serve increased number of capillaries in skeletal muscles and to carry away heat of energy metabolism.
10. Lowered triglyceride (blood fat) volume.
11. Lowered resting breathing (ventilation) rate and increased amount of air taken in with each breath.
12. Improved capacity to utilize oxygen.
13. Increased capacity to contract an oxygen debt, which is a measure of ability to execute high-energy tasks.
14. Improved movement skills so that one moves more efficiently using a minimal number of muscles with less muscular tension and consequently, less energy cost.
15. Improved systemic circulatory, respiratory, and digestive functions.
16. Utilization of energy stores and thus, reduction of body weight and dimensions when coupled with controlled food intake.
17. More efficient body heat dissipation and removal of waste products through improved circulation, perspiration, and elimination.
18. Expedited recovery from coronary disability, surgery, childbirth, and many illnesses.

Perhaps less supportable by experimental evidence at this time, but as obvious as the physiological benefits to those who exercise and play regularly, are the psychological results. Feelings of emotional exuberance, vitality, and well-being are frequently expressed by the sportswoman. Many attest to relieved tensions and greater tolerance for psychological anxieties and stresses, to more restful and revitalizing sleep, to fewer physical manifestations of headaches and pains of tension, and to a greater everyday joy through a youthful zest for living. To these persons, health is one of life's sought-for and self-produced major goals. Such health-conscious persons are self-motivated to:

1. Have periodic medical and dental checkups.
2. Watch what, when, and how much they eat daily.
3. Be careful to keep their total daily caloric intake of food balanced with a daily amount of vigorous physical activity.
4. Limit alcohol consumption.
5. Avoid tobacco and drug use.
6. Get adequate sleep and rest.
7. Work efficiently according to a devised time and energy short-cut plan so that they have time for daily recreational activity.
8. Carry out personal hygiene patterns.
9. Exercise on a planned schedule for development or maintenance of a personal skill and fitness program.

IMPROVING MOVEMENT SKILLS

One of the primary and direct benefits of sports skill practice and participation is the improvement of specific neuromuscular skills. Through specifically designed teaching and practice one can improve the golf swing, the track start, strategic play in basketball, or any other single or complex motor pattern. The complex process of learning and improving neuromuscular skills and motor responses is the primary concern of the field of motor learning. Some of the considerations and principles which guide individual learners and teachers in planning and directing learning are considered in Chapter 2.

It is generally agreed that movement behavior is modifiable; that is, an individual can learn and improve her proficiency in motor skill execution. The process involves a motivated learner—one who has a desire to learn, who understands the demands of the task, who improves perception of the cues needed to initiate and continue the task, and who practices the skills of the task. An individual's motor ability is a reflection of her heredity and her environmental experiences. Her genetic heritage produces the cognitive, physical, and neuromuscular base from which she begins. This base is expanded and modified by the experiences afforded her by her environment. An individual learns in a variety of ways, and often these ways are unlike those which are important to other learners. However, in motor skill development, physical practice of the act is necessary to the development of the skill. *Motor skills are best learned through the involvement of the learner in performing the skill;* however, *practice makes perfect only if one practices perfectly.*

Skills develop in a hierarchical fashion, one upon the others, much like the sound construction of a cement-block building. The learner begins with the base of fundamental movement skills of walking, running, jumping, twisting, turning, hopping, hanging, climbing, and falling which she gained largely through the maturational processes with few intentional attempts at formal learning. The next level, *technique development,* includes the proper form and execution of a simple or complex skill. This is a level at which both understanding of the principles and goal of the task, and instruction, are necessary for execution of the skill. The third level of the hierarchy involves putting the skilled techniques together in a form or *pattern* to make more complex skills or to incorporate strategy with the simple and complex forms. The final level, *individual style,* is the highly developed point on the developmental skill scale where the individual utilizes her distinct body type, minimizes her weaknesses, and capitalizes on her strengths in executing the techniques and patterns of the sport skills. This is the epitome of skill development, and the achievement of this level indicates a degree of personal excellence in learning and executing motor skills.

IMPROVING SOCIAL INTERACTION

Sports participation affords opportunities for social interaction. This interaction may take many forms, depending upon the needs expressed by the player or group. Social environments are structured by many institutions—schools, churches, and clubs—but nowhere is the opportunity for social contact more evident than when people gather to play and compete in sports.

Interaction can foster fun and the development of many desirable attitudes, values, and social skills. However, the potential values of interaction must not be left to chance development but must be planned and directed by conscious leadership.

DEVELOPING SELF-UNDERSTANDING AND DESIRABLE SOCIAL VALUES AND ATTITUDES

The varied situations that arise in sports and games participation provide opportunities for the development of attitudes, values, and skills deemed important in our society. Values and attitudes are established early in life and resist change. If alterations are to take place, they must be planned for and directed by competent leaders. There is nothing inherently "good" or "bad" in sport; it is the way the participant views the value of the sport and the manner in which the sport is conducted that determine whether or not the sport or game is a developmental experience. Consider a few of the possibilities for behavior modification through a well planned and well directed program.

1. Self-understanding is basic to an integrated personality. Sports give a clear estimate of more than one dimension of the individual. They mirror actions through which a participant can realistically see herself and be seen as herself. The player is able to assess her skill in comparison to others, to react to challenges, to measure her communication through both verbal and nonverbal actions, and to gain insight into her emotional responses to interpersonal conflicts, group problems, and ultimately, to victory and defeat.
2. Success and failure in sports can be building blocks in personality and ego development. Earned success in sport or defeat in a well played game can do much to structure confidence and establish a realistic self-concept. Sports can offer an opportunity for almost everyone to achieve her own level of success and excellence in one or many activities.
3. The desire to win can foster cooperation as group members engage in a united team effort. Substituting the dominant *I* for the cooperative *we,* one can learn the lesson of give and take. During adolescence, the desire to belong to a club, gang, or team may result in the kind of behavior modification desirable for group membership. It may be as a team member that one recognizes leaders as positive behavior modifiers and team members as the stable reflectors of group values. It is not beyond reason that one may come to understand and appreciate fully the importance of such frequently repeated phrases as *all for one and one for all* and *where there is unity there is strength.*
4. The values of honesty, integrity, fair play, sportsmanship, and consideration for others can be fostered in team and individual sports. Consider the participant who learns respect and consideration for the rights of others as she maintains quiet on the putting green, takes turns retrieving arrows from the target, or spots for her partner in gymnastics. Honesty can be fostered and

assessed in unofficiated games, where one is responsible for keeping her own golf score or calling balls on her side of the net during a tennis match. Sports thus provide a testing arena for behavior patterns which our society considers good, fair, and proper. Alert leadership assures the learner that sportsmanship is valued above poor conduct, that honesty is rewarded (if only by self-esteem), and that dishonesty is ultimately penalized.

Without question, the varied situations which arise when one is participating in sports and games can provide opportunities for developing cooperation, competition, decision making, creativity, self-insight, self-discipline, and an appreciation of excellence. Sport is a universal language and a democratic common denominator that can provide an opportunity for every player—regardless of racial, religious, or national differences—to strive to be the best competitor, the best player, or the best sport.

DEVELOPING SPECIALIZED KNOWLEDGE AND APPRECIATION OF SPORTS

Sport is an American sociocultural phenomenon. While only active participants or students of sport may concentrate on the specialized body of knowledge of sport history, strategy, performers' records, and the myriad details of a sport, the public is generally interested and involved in many aspects of sports. Business interests are obviously concerned with spectator and participant views and habits.

The appreciation and meaning of sport are different among those who are in the business of sport, those who are sport spectators, and those who are recreational participants. Appreciation of the effort and consequences of the "big play," the record-breaking run, and the well executed dive have various meanings to individuals. To some they are acts of beauty of physical execution and expressions of the true meaning of "poetry in motion." To others the acts are vicariously enjoyed and related to their personal lives, and to others, the performances represent models for practice and participation in preparation for their own "big play." Whether viewed by the artist, writer, spectator, or participant, sport is considered an avenue of human expression and a worthwhile endeavor.

Fostering Appreciation of the Play Concept and Use of Free Time

Ask a child why she plays a game and she will usually reply, "It's fun." A close examination of the reasons most people of all ages participate in sports and games reveals that they "play to have fun." Having fun in physically exerting and challenging sports and games is a desirable outcome of participation.

America is entering an age of expanding free time to be spent away from work, school, or other responsibilities. This rapidly approaching era was brought about basically by the invention of the wheel, the machine, and the subsequent Industrial Revolution with its resulting labor-saving devices. Although there are many assets to the new age of increased freedom, liabilities are also numerous. Many seers warn us that too many are living at too fast a pace, both in work and play and that too few are finding the release and recreation inherent in the leisure age. Others contend that free time has afforded "idle time for the work of the devil." Certainly there is evidence that Americans are as frenzied in their free time activities as in their work pursuits. All people have free time, but only an elite minority partakes of leisure through which they strive to better themselves culturally.

People voluntarily do in their free time those things which bring them joy and satisfaction. They will choose to play only when they have an interest in doing so, a feeling that they can gain something of value from such activity, or when they possess enough skill to receive real satisfaction from participation. This is an admonition to teachers of sports and games to develop the love of movement, teach for value development, and provide the opportunity for learning physical skills so that students will want to continue participation after school hours and for years to come. As individuals analyze themselves and as nations define their images, both come to the conclusions that play—the voluntary act engaged in, in a time and space pattern, with the outcome uncertain and of no economic benefit—is a meaningful enterprise.

DISCUSSION QUESTIONS

1. As an individual interested in sports and sport education, what is the major *personal goal* you are seeking through sports participation and competition? How do you feel sports can serve to further this goal?
2. It has often been said that sports serve culture and society in many different ways. From your background and readings, how do you feel sports serve people (a) during time of war; (b) during economic crises; (c) during periods of prosperity; (d) during periods of international tension? How does sport help increase international prestige?
3. Review a current issue of *The Sportwoman* or *Womensports* and identify an article in which the woman about whom it is written makes statements regarding the value of sports in her life. Analyze two such articles and discuss them with the class.
4. Numerous research studies are in process that concern the physiological aspects of sports participation for women. What are some of the findings that are altering the misconceptions about the effects of strenuous activity on the female?
5. Contrast the benefits one can receive from being a spectator of sports with those received from being a regular sports participant.

SELECTED AUDIOVISUAL AIDS

Run Dick, Run Jane. Featuring Dr. Kenneth Cooper. (16 mm., 28 min., sound, color.) (Purchase: Department of Motion Picture Production, Brigham Young University, Provo, Utah 84601) (Rental: Modern Talking Pictures, 4084 Westheimer, Houston, Texas 77027) (Loan: local chapter of American Heart Association)

SUGGESTED READINGS

Caillois, Roger: *Man, Play, and Games.* Glencoe, Illinois, The Free Press, 1961.

Cratty, Bryant: *Social Dimensions of Physical Activity.* Englewood Cliffs, New Jersey, Prentice-Hall, 1967.

Division of Girls' and Women's Sports: *Research Reports: Women in Sports.* (Vol. 1 and 2) Washington, D.C., American Association for Health, Physical Education, and Recreation, 1971, 1973.

Gerber, Ellen W., Felshin, Jan, Berlin, Pearl, and Wyrick, Waneen: *The American Woman in Sport.* Addison-Wesley Publishing Co., Reading, Massachusetts, 1974.

Jokl, Ernst: *Medical Sociology and Cultural Anthropology of Sport and Physical Education.* Springfield, Illinois, Charles C Thomas, 1964.

Klafs, Carl E., and Lyon, M. Joan: *The Female Athlete.* St. Louis, The C. V. Mosby Co., 1973.

Mathews, Donald K., and Fox, Edward L.: *The Physiological Basis of Physical Education and Athletics.* Philadelphia, W. B. Saunders Co., 1971.

Metheny, Eleanor: Symbolic Forms of Movement: The Feminine Image in Sports, *Connotations of Movement in Sport and Dance.* Dubuque, Iowa, W. C. Brown Co., 1965.

Miller, Donna Mae, and Russell, Kathryn: *Sport: A Contemporary View.* Philadelphia, Lea and Febiger, 1971.

Neal, Patsy: *Coaching Methods For Women.* Reading, Massachusetts, Addison-Wesley Publishing Co., 1969.

Loy, John, and Kenyon, Gerald: *Sport, Culture and Society.* New York, The Macmillan Co., 1960.

Poindexter, Hally Beth, and Mushier, Carole L.: *Coaching Competitive Team Sports for Girls and Women.* Philadelphia, W. B. Saunders Co., 1973.

Sage, George: *Sport and American Society.* Reading, Massachusetts, Addison-Wesley Publishing Co., 1970.

Siedentop, Daryl: *Physical Education Introductory Analysis.* Dubuque, Iowa, Wm. C. Brown Co., 1972.

Slusher, Howard: *Man, Sport and Existence: A Critical Analysis.* Philadelphia, Lea and Febiger, 1967.

Vannier, Maryhelen, Foster, Mildred, and Gallahue, David: *Teaching Physical Education in Elementary Schools.* 5th Ed. Philadelphia, W. B. Saunders Co., 1973.

Vannier, Maryhelen, and Poindexter, Hally Beth: *Physical Activities For College Women.* 2nd Ed. Philadelphia, W. B. Saunders Co., 1969.

Vannier, Maryhelen: *Recreation Leadership.* 3rd Ed. Philadelphia, Lea and Febiger, 1976.

Quest, Perspectives For Sports. The National Association For Physical Education of College Women, Washington, D. C., AAHPER, January, 1973.

Weiss, Paul: *Sport: A Philosophic Inquiry.* Carbondale, Illinois, Southern Illinois University Press, 1969.

CHAPTER 2

LEARNING AND TEACHING

Learning theorists continue to explore the mechanics and manner by which humans learn and how learning can be accomplished more efficiently. Educators still define the qualities of good teaching and good methods which facilitate the learning process. Although the search will continue indefinitely, each new theory and list of competencies brings us closer to understanding the teaching-learning act. It seems that good sports teachers are special kinds of people with distinct competencies in the cognitive, motor, and affective areas. More specifically, they have a great deal of knowledge about sports; they have studied how sports skills are learned and how they are improved. They know about the beneficial effects of exercise and sports participation; they know students, as individuals and in groups; they know the ways to interest students in learning. Further, they appreciate sports and have experienced a variety of activities through personal participation. They *know, can do,* and *can teach.*

How Learning Takes Place

Learning is a relatively permanent change in performance brought about by understanding, experience, and practice. Motor skill learning results in a change of motor behavior. Skill development is an integral part of motor learning, when skill is defined as the learned ability to produce predetermined results with maximum certainty with a minimum of expenditure of time or energy, or both.* Motor learning is a sensory experience and involves both mental and physical activity.

---

*See Barbara Knapp: *Skill in Sport.* London, Routledge and Kegan Paul, 1963, p. 4.

Individuals learn at different rates and acquire different skills although they may be exposed to identical or similar learning environments. Learners do not bring the same genetic backgrounds, experiences, or levels of motivation to the learning arena; consequently, practice and learning experiences have differing effects on different individuals. For clarity in understanding the many aspects of learning, human learning is frequently categorized according to: (1) motor skills; (2) concepts, meanings, and generalizations; (3) motives, interests, and attitudes; (4) social and emotional control; (5) esthetic appreciations; and (6) ability to solve problems. Theorists and practitioners agree that learning is a lifelong task involving constant human adjustment.

There are numerous theories that attempt to explain the psychological and physiological phenomena of human learning. All theories focus on the nature of the learning process, the role of the individual in learning, and conditions that facilitate the learning process. Although it is difficult to categorize learning theories, there are two major theories—stimulus-response (connectionism) and cognitive (field theories). A third group, which explains learning through neurological and physiological phenomena, and a fourth, information theories which use cybernetics and information system analogs to explain the learning process, are emerging now.

Stimulus-Response Theories. The stimulus-response theories are among the oldest concepts of learning. Those using this approach see the learner as passive and governed by stimuli supplied by the external environment. They believe man can be manipulated and behavior can be controlled through proper control of environmental stimuli. Exponents believe that one builds a coordinated whole by the gradual addition of new elements to those already acquired. One of the most influential exponents of bond connectionism was Edward L. Thorndike, whose laws of learning exemplified his approach and emphasized the importance of trial and error learning. These include the following:

The Law of Readiness states that learning will take place most efficiently and effectively when the learner is prepared to respond to learning experiences. This has been interpreted to mean that the learner is "ripe" for learning when her maturational development, previous experiences, and motivation have reached a level of *readiness* for the learning experience.

The Law of Exercise indicates that practicing a particular response under *favorable* conditions strengthens the relationship between the stimulus and the response and makes the future repetition of the response more likely. The implication is that practice and proper responses occur through *trial* and *error* experiences.

The Law of Effect suggests that pleasurable experiences tend to strengthen a stimulus-response connection more than unpleasant experiences. This concept led to extensive investigation in the area of positive and negative reinforcement.

As Thorndike emphasized reinforcement of the total stimulus-response bond, B. F. Skinner is primarily concerned with reinforcement of the response. He contends that through "operant conditioning" learning can proceed through reinforcement of the (operant) desirable behavior or correct response. His "shaping of behavior concept" is a viable behavioristic approach utilized by many teachers who determine the desired action and then condition the students by rewarding them when they respond with the desirable act or a close approximation of the act. Such a notion is basic to the use of the teaching machine.

Cognitive Theories. Cognitive theories grew from the concept of perception. Gestalt, field, and association theorists adhere to the idea that through understanding and insight the learner organizes stimuli and perceptions into a pattern or a whole. They advocate developing skills by taking the total reaction of the beginner and eventually refining the response through an understanding of the whole situation. Learning becomes a matter of the individual's ability to organize the stimulus field. Cognitive theorists reject trial and error and automatic skill response in favor of the process of approximation and corrections. Increased skill is due to differentiation of the whole of the parts.

Neurological Theories. Some of these theories, specifically designed to explain motor learning, are based upon the concept of nervous system development as a primary factor in motor improvement. Franklin Henry postulates a memory drum theory; Hebb describes a recruitment theory, and Kappers defines a neurological explanation through neurobiotaxis. These and other neurological theories remain speculative and have yet to satisfy a complete explanation of the psychological and physiological processes of learning.

Cybernetic, Information, and Systems Model Theories. These emphasize man's total performance, capacities, limitations, and adaptive abilities. Learning is thought of as a series of events occurring in a certain order. Cybernetic theorists emphasize feedback loops as the basic element of the nervous sytem. The concept of self-regulatory movement and the feedback principle imply that an organism's behavior is automatically controlled, regulated, and adapted from previous response. Models are used to conceptualize how the nervous system handles information.

PRINCIPLES OF LEARNING APPLICABLE TO MOTOR SKILL

Development

Principles are the end products of expert opinions, research, experience and philosophy. They serve as guides to help develop a philosophy and appropriate techniques and methods for successful teaching and learning. Selected principles most helpful to teachers of motor and sports skills are noted.

1. Individual learning involves both heredity and environment. One's heredity sets limitations on potential development, but environment and experience offer avenues for the full development of potential. The learner brings only her genetic background and her previous experience to the learning environment. She must be "taken where she is" and helped to a higher developmental skill level.

2. The only real learning is *self-learning*. One learns only as she is involved in the learning act. Every person learns in her own unique way, dependent upon her background, her perception of cues, and the importance she attaches to the task. The role of the teacher becomes one of motivating, and of providing a variety of methods for approaching the learning task.

3. The rate of learning varies with the individual. A rapid initial rate of learning does not indicate that the learner will continue to learn at a rapid rate, nor does it indicate that she will learn more than others. It appears that there are hierarchies of learning, and that a learner may attain one level with great speed but have greater difficulty at other levels.

4. Motor learning is ultimately a doing act. Although a learner receives much information from visual, auditory, and proprioceptive cues that facilitate her learning, she must experience the motor act for learning to be most meaningful.

5. Individuals learn tasks which are meaningful to them more rapidly and with greater retention than they do tasks to which they cannot relate. An individual must be interested in a particular task before the most effective learning can occur.

6. Students master only the material they deem important for their purposes. Their retention of meaningful material is greater than their retention of material which they feel is unimportant.

7. Practice makes perfect only if one practices a perfect act. Replication of incorrect motor skills tends to make faulty movements habitual.

8. Overlearning motor skills results in greater retention of the skills. The value of overlearning increases as the time for forgetting increases; however, to be effective, overlearning should be practiced as seriously as the initial learning of the task.

9. Once learned, the knowledge and skills of motor acts are never completely forgotten. Although interference from other activities and from lack of practice may dim the performance of motor skills, once the criteria of performance have been met, they are never completely forgotten.

10. An individual's readiness to learn a motor skill is dependent upon her physiological maturity, neuromuscular abilities, previous experience, and motivation. There is undoubtedly a "best time" in every individual's life to acquire certain motor skills. Although skills may be learned before or after the "ideal period of readiness," such learning is less economical in terms of learning time.

11. Motivation is an integral part of the learning process. A desire to accomplish a task affects control of behavior and is manifested in the individual's physiological condition, interests, attitudes, and aspirations. A motivated learner learns more readily than one who is not motivated.

12. Learning under intrinsic motivation is preferable to learning under extrinsic motivational forces. The student who wants to learn a task for its own sake, rather than for extrinsic, materialistic reasons seems to have a more effective and sustaining motivation than does the extrinsically motivated individual.

13. A learner's level of aspiration is a determinant in achieving success or failure. Since success results in a rise in aspiration level and failure results in a lower-

ing of aspiration, it seems that the learner should experience reasonable amounts of success in learning experiences if her motivation is to continue as a positive force for learning.

14. Teachers are motivators and reinforcers. Since both motivation and positive reinforcement are supportive for learning, the teacher should develop competencies in fulfilling these roles.

15. Reinforcement is an event or condition which strengthens the probability of a response. Reinforcement is a valuable tool in motivation and consequently, in learning. The most meaningful reinforcement occurs immediately following the act that is to be encouraged.

16. Knowledge of performance—feedback—is helpful in improving performance patterns. Whether the learner is aware of the results or whether the teacher becomes the feedback mechanism, it seems that higher levels of achievement are reached when feedback is immediate and specific.

17. Transfer, the influence of a task already learned on one to be learned, underlies all motor learning. Transfer of useful elements from one skill or sport to another is influenced by factors of practice, training, and motivation to transfer the skills. Transfer is most likely when the elements are identical; transfer of similar elements from one experience to another will occur only if conscious effort is made.

18. Mental practice and rehearsal of a skill is most meaningful to motor learning when the task is clearly understood and some physical practice has preceded mental practice.

19. Tasks should be sequentially structured for beginners so that success can be achieved at each step and the learner will be motivated to progress.

TEACHING METHODS

The purpose of effective teaching is to facilitate the learning process. There is no single best method of instruction appropriate for all teachers, all students, and all skills. When one considers the individual differences of learners—their structural characteristics, functional motor abilities, background and experience, intelligence and motivation—it becomes obvious that the teacher must use a variety of strategies to reach all learners at various skill levels. *Students are different and learn in different ways;* the same student may learn through different methods. *Teachers are different;* their backgrounds and personalities vary as much as the individuals whom they teach. The ways in which they are effective are as varied as the methods they use. A teaching method which has proven to be successful for one teacher may be a failure when used by another. Ways of teaching are patterns which must be tailored to fit the teacher and the situation.

Careful planning begins by: (1) planning course objectives for or with the students, (2) planning individual or group learning experiences for each class on a weekly and daily basis, and (3) planning for evaluation of the accomplishment of the learning experiences. When teaching large groups, the teacher must remember that it is the *individual* in the group who is the learner; consequently, the teacher and students together should establish individual goals and class objectives, determine learning alternatives, experiences, and evaluative techniques.

Each of the many teaching methods is valuable, but there are times when one may be superior to others. A method is selected on the basis of its effectiveness in obtaining desired results through socially approved ways. Among the many successful techniques are:

- Chalk talks
- Drills
- Scrimmages
- Independent study and practice
- Lectures
- Questions and answers
- Reports
- Demonstrations and participation
- Supervised practice
- Role playing
- Audiovisual materials
- Experiments
- Class discussions
- Workshops
- Forums
- Assignments
- Field trips
- Debates
- Workbooks
- Projects
- Combinations of all listed

TEACHING MOTOR SKILLS

Motor skill improvement results from correct practice of the movement patterns and utilizing them within the total skill and in the proper environment. There are numerous conditions which influence skill practice and sports performance, but only selected areas which have obvious influence on teaching methodology will be discussed.

Learning Curves. A learning curve is a graphic display of an individual's or team's performance on a given task over a period of time. When viewed as a whole, a performance curve may serve to illustrate the effectiveness of selected teaching methods, motivational techniques or other variables injected into the learning process. Although a single performance may not reflect the true learning of an individual or team because of the mental or physical state of the performer or the environmental influences, over a period of time the plotted curve should reflect the relatively stable learning effect. Learning is ultimately reflected in behavior. The learner may display periods of rapid skill increase (negatively accelerated curve) of a relatively simple skill; she may display slower learning (positively accelerated) with more difficult tasks; a linear relationship may reflect some improvement with each trial; or a combination of the curves (**S** curve) may develop, due to the varied complexity of the skills. Plateaus are manifested by a stabilizing period with lack of obvious progress. They may occur at any point on the learning curve for variable periods of time before progress is once again noted. Plateaus may not appear, but when they are evidenced, numerous reasons are given for this "flat" in learning. Some suggest that there really is no plateau in the *learning,* and if the learner continues the task it will soon become obvious that learning has continued. Some researchers contend a plateau is a period of fatigue or poor motivation; others suggest that as one develops a complex skill there are different hierarchies, or levels, to be mastered, and after a period of learning the plateau reflects a period of synthesis and integration necessary before moving to mastery of the next level. Whatever the causes, plateaus can be overcome if the learner continues motivated and persistent practice of the task elements.

Levels of Skill. There is increasing evidence that there is a change in factors or ability patterns as one practices and improves. Abilities important for early success in a complex skill are not necessarily the same as those contributing to success at a higher skill level. Assuming the above to be worthy of consideration, the performer's level of skill will require different methods and learning considerations on the part of the instructor.

At a *beginning skill level* the learner often makes inappropriate and random movements resulting in great energy expenditure and fatigue. She may be overstimulated and further induce fatigue. The beginner experiences many trials and errors but eventually limits the error responses as she achieves success; however, she can select error responses which can be persistent and handicapping to further learning unless she and the instructor identify and correct the errors.

The beginner's lack of understanding and experience in the skill indicate a need for special methodological consideration. The beginner needs to be acquainted with facilities and equipment and given the "big picture" of the purpose and nature of the activity. A demonstration film, a well played game or an effective demonstration of the complex whole may serve this purpose. Demonstrations are usually effective for beginners, for they learn well by mimicry gained through visual cues. The demonstration may be repeated at a slower rate for clarity and understanding, but practice by the learner should be at a speed approximating that at which the skill will be used. The instructor should *avoid* lengthy verbal descriptions and precise detail of form and execution when working with beginners. Use of teaching cues and aids facilitates learning when traditional methods fail. Changing the routine of methodology may also serve as a motivating force.

Beginners need to experience the skill as rapidly as possible and get involved in "doing." If the skill is too complex as a whole, the simpler skills can be taught by the "whole method"; later the necessary refinement can be accomplished. Finally, beginners need reinforcement and feedback. Constructive guidance is more effective than criticism in reducing muscular tension and gaining self-confidence.

The *more advanced learner* of motor skills is familiar with and conditioned for the skill. She makes fewer random movements and becomes less fatigued. Her energy is used for practice and performance and is not dissipated through tension and unproductive movements. The more advanced learner is less easily distracted by outside stimuli, and she has little difficulty concentrating and recognizing cues for action or alteration of performance. Her vocabulary of the skill has increased and is helpful in understanding instruction, mental planning, and in retention. Skills become generalized at higher levels, allowing for more adaptation and variation of performance in different settings. Greater variations among individuals are noticed, and each person finds her most efficient form, practice procedure, and style of play. For the teacher this means the advanced performer can experience meaningful drill on *parts* of the total skill, for she is able to fill in the other parts of the act mentally. This is conducive to rapid learning.

The more advanced performer can endure longer practice sessions without fatiguing; she is capable of some self-analysis, but she is much more able to synthesize instructor analysis and that of mechanical aids. Because her patterns are habituated, she must rehearse them until they are automatic before using them in experiences requiring peak performance. She can benefit from mental rehearsal more than the beginner can, for she has a good image of her movements and the skills she must execute. She should utilize mental practice to prevent lapses in performance, although she must often review skills physically to maintain a high level of performance. In essence, advanced learning emphasizes the perception of what to do, and much of the adjustment is transferable from previous motor and nonmotor experiences. Verbal and kinesthetic cues are important at higher levels of performance, and the perception of cues results in movement adaptations acquired from feedback.

Rate and Degree of Learning. There are many factors which influence both the rate and degree of learning. A teacher is quick to sense that everyone learns in her own unique way and at her own rate. Some grasp the basic skills quickly but then make little progress after a brilliant beginning; others start slowly, as if chiseling out each painful step up the skill ladder. Yet once the basic level is captured, they progress rapidly and consistently. Obviously, learning is dependent upon the nature and difficulty of the task, the degree of the learner's desire for mastery, and the conditions of practice and learning methods. Some of the factors which influence the rate and quality of learning are very personal to the learner. One's own personal drives, needs, and level of aspiration can be determinants in the speed of learning, just as one's degree of innate ability and type of body build can influence the ultimate level of skill achievement. The presence of spectators, size of the group, degree of group interaction, and the kinds and amounts of tension, anxiety, and stress created by the learning or competitive situation all have an influence on learning. Since each individual reacts to these factors in different ways, a teacher must be alert to ways to create the best possible learning environment for all.

Readiness to learn a skill is a concept basic to rate and quality of learning. Motor learning readiness is dependent on physiological age, previous learning, and experience and motivation and is a determinant of what skills can best be learned at a given time. Most elementary school age children experience activities of the gross motor variety, with the intricacies of fine motor responses needed for activities such as golf and fencing left for a more physiologically mature age.

Practice Factors. There are many considerations for planning practices that potentially influence learning and performance.

Practice Schedules. Research results have produced inconclusive evidence on the most desirable length of practice periods, frequency of practice periods and the best time of day for practice. The answers seem to vary with the age of the learner, the complexity and strenuousness of the skill, the level of learning achieved, the experiential background of the learner, the motivation of the learner, and the environmental conditions. Limited research and considerable practical evidence indicate that beginners profit more from shorter practice periods spaced over an extended period of time. Daily practices, or even more than once a day, may be desirable if the activity is not too exhausting. Highly motivated learners can endure longer practice periods, as can those of more advanced skill levels. Difficult tasks seem to require periods of synthesis which may be best accomplished by short, frequent practices spaced over a relatively long period of time. Much practice is needed in varied situations with complex skills so that automatic performance will result in varying environments. Practice sessions of relatively constant length seem to produce more learning than regular increases and decreases in succeeding sessions. Short rest periods during practice sessions tend to increase the amount of learning.

Learning Mechanical Principles. Teaching mechanical principles of the skill may be of little value to those with low skill levels, since they are unable to incorporate theoretical knowledge into performance. Knowledge of mechanical principles may be helpful for more advanced learners and for the teacher in analyzing the complete act.

Speed and Accuracy. Skills which require speed plus accuracy (precision) should be taught with emphasis on both speed and accuracy. The speed of execution should approximate the normal pattern of the skill without causing deterioration of accuracy or endangering the safety of the performer. In the past, attempts have been made to emphasize accuracy in the skill initially and to add speed of execution later. Others have emphasized speed, with accuracy developed later. It has been determined that breaking a skill into speed and accuracy components is actually increasing learning time, because two skills, rather than one, must be learned. As soon as possible and as often as possible, the skill should be taught and practiced under gamelike conditions.

Mental Practice. Mental practice is a valuable supplement to physical practice. Its greatest effectiveness is for those more advanced in skill. Thinking through and mentally performing a well rehearsed skill can help when physical practice is not possible and when establishing a motor pattern. The effectiveness of this technique varies with the nature of the skill practiced and the learner's ability to successfully practice mentally.

Feedback. Feedback is the term used for the knowledge of results. Research has investigated the improvement of learning as the learner was made aware of the effectiveness of her performance. Current investigators are studying the precise variations in feedback that alter performance. Knowledge of results is gained in a myriad of ways—through teacher analysis and comments, peer evaluation, video tape assessment, self-analysis and kinesthesis. Although the area has presented research problems, it seems that little or no learning takes place without knowledge of results. Some further findings indicate that:

1. Learning is proportionately greater as the quality and precision of knowledge of results increases.
2. When feedback is delayed, performance declines.
3. When knowledge of results is withdrawn, performance declines.
4. Continuous and complete knowledge of results fosters greater learning than does feedback which is incomplete.
5. Definitive information, such as shot percentages and action films, which makes it possible to compare the learner's performance with those of better ability, seems to increase learning.
6. Incorrect feedback retards learning and performance.

Transfer. Transfer of learning implies the ability to apply previous learning from one skill to another task. Although some theorists believe in learning every act or skill specifically, most feel that some transfer of isolated skills or concepts must occur, otherwise every new experience would require complete learning. It appears that identical elements within different tasks transfer, and there may be previously developed bases of both motor and nonmotor knowledge and ability which help in the learning of new skills. Transfer may be *positive,* that is, a learner responds to a new task using an already learned pattern, or *negative,* in which the learner is asked to make a different response from that already learned. The greatest possibility for positive transfer occurs when the learner is aware of the opportunity for transfer. It may occur more easily if the instructor points out similarities in the two responses (softball throw and tennis serve), and the learner's attention is directed to cues that enhance transfer opportunities.

Reinforcement. Reinforcement is an event or condition which strengthens the probability of a response. Every practice session affords opportunities for meaningful reinforcement. Immediate reinforcement has been found to be most valuable; progressive delays result in less effectiveness. Random reinforcement is a more effective form of motivator than constant reinforcement. Techniques of reinforcement such as constructive criticism, the pat on the back, and the "job well done" are considered important motivational and feedback tools.

The Three Ds of Teaching Motor Skills

Although individuals can and do learn motor skills without the benefits of a teacher, the most efficient skill learning results from understanding proper techniques of skill execution, guidance in accomplishing the skill, and feedback, which involves error correction. It is much more difficult to unlearn an incorrect habituated skill and relearn the proper execution than it is to learn the skill correctly from the beginning.

In addition to the many functions of the teacher—motivator, behavior modifier, and counselor—a primary function of the physical educator and coach is to facilitate the learning of motor skills. In this task the teacher utilizes the three Ds of teaching—demonstration, diagnosis, and direction.

Demonstration. Much of what we learn comes to us through our eyes and ears. Students mimic movement patterns and by copying what they see and hear, they develop movements and skills. The teacher should be able to demonstrate skills as perfectly as possible, for it is important that the students duplicate correct movement patterns. Mastery of many skills is part of a physical educator's professional preparation, but no one person is expected to master all skills. Consequently, if the teacher is unable to execute the skill efficiently, a film may be used, or a student with skill proficiency may be prepared to demonstrate before the class. Demonstrations are superior to lengthy verbal instructions for the beginner, but verbal explanations may be a part of the total demonstration-discussion session.

Diagnosis. Some students in every class will have difficulty in learning skills. There are many reasons for this, ranging from fear of injury, poor coordination, obesity, or lack of sufficient strength to poor general physical condition. The teacher must become an expert in diagnosing difficulties before help can be given. Some teachers excel in this area and find they can identify the problem and redirect movement patterns with a few verbal cues. Ability to diagnose learning difficulties comes largely from (1) ability to perform the skill correctly, (2) knowledge of what each part of the correct movement pattern is, (3) experience, and (4) recognition of the fact that such detection is a vital part of the teaching-learning process which every physical educator must master.

Direction. Directing is the process of planning and implementing group and individual learning experiences that help the student move from the technique level to *her own style* level. The teacher uses a variety of teaching methods, aids, and motivational techniques to help the student over the rough spots and on to attainment of success in motor skills.

It is not possible to isolate skill learning from attitude development or behavioral changes. *How* the student *feels* about the teacher and about what she is learning is often as important as *what* she learns. The teacher's presence, encouragement, patience, and faith in the student's ability to master what she sets out to do help longed-for goals become realities.

TEACHING GAME RULES

One of the best ways to teach game rules is in relation to skills to be mastered. For example, the knowledge of rules for serving a volleyball and techniques for doing so correctly should be developed simultaneously, just as should the teaching of the basketball free throw and the reasons a player is awarded it. All players must know and understand that game rules are necessary for safe and proper play. Planned game situations, showing how rules are broken and what happens when they are, afford excellent ways to help players learn them. Pencil and paper tests aid the instructor in identifying those who have a hazy or false concept of the laws of any game. All such tests should be discussed with the group and the correct answers given for all questions. Oral review, for several days, of certain test sections may be followed successfully by another revised written rule test.

The instructor should help her class know each rule and why it is a rule, as well as the penalty for breaking it. When players discover that rules have been devised for their protection and for the improvement of the quality of the game, they are often more interested in learnlng them. The use of student officials increases a desire for rule mastery, especially when it is considered an honor among peer groups to be chosen for such a leadership position. Physical education majors are usually required to complete an officiating course for many sports as part of their professional preparation, and frequently they call games in the intramural program in order to fulfill requirements of the course. Student players and officials often help teams and classmates learn game rules more quickly than can the teacher.

All practice and competitive games should be played according to the rules. Games and scrimmages should be stopped in classes or at practice periods at *teachable moments* when rule infractions occur. In class situations the teacher may ask the group to interpret the rule infraction, rather than calling out the penalty or awarding the offended player her earned privilege. Students should be encouraged to discuss rule interpretation in class; however, part of the student's responsibility is that of respecting officials and *their* interpretations during competition.

The use of clinics and workshops is also often a successful way to teach rules to large groups. Films, slide tape presentations, or situational demonstrations all may be used successfully as means of summarizing materials for a class, a clinic, or other groups.

TEACHING GAME STRATEGY

Strategy is an integral part of successful play in both individual and team sports. When strategic tactics are applied to basic sport and game techniques the true purposes and satisfactions of the games can be achieved. Strategy of individual and team play involves overcoming psychological barriers, combating environmental conditions, and countering the physical and psychological strategies of an opponent or team. Scouting of opponents in interscholastic and intercollegiate competition has become commonplace and allows an opponent to prepare for *known* offensive and defensive patterns.

Ultimately, practice and playing experience appear to be the best environments for developing strategic play. Practicing under conditions of tension, anxiety, and fatigue in the environment of a noisy gymnasium or on a cold and windy playing field best prepare the player for meeting these conditions in competition. Obviously, a player should be well conditioned to cope with the physical demands of the sport if she is to benefit from and utilize learned strategies.

The techniques of offensive and defensive game tactics can be presented in many ways. Frequently a teacher introduces basic plays by use of chalk board diagrams, play books, or magnetized boards on which player positions can be changed to simulate game situations. Numerous films, filmstrips, slide-tape presentations, and printed materials are available or may be developed. Ultimately, drills of desired plays and variations of offensive and defensive tactics must be practiced and rehearsed so that they become readily available responses when playing. As the drills and scrimmages progress the teacher finds it is possible to give short verbal cues—"toss," for the player who has been coached in the techniques of lifting the ball high enough for an effective tennis serve but who suddenly experiences difficulty in execution under competitive stress—as reminders until playing positions and strategic responses become habituated. Practices, scrimmages, and competitive games which utilize sound strategies aid in the development of the calm and efficient responses seen among excellent players and teams.

INDIVIDUALIZING INSTRUCTION

One of the greatest challenges a dedicated teacher faces is that of finding ways to meet the needs of *each* student in large classes. Although making groups or classes smaller does not necessarily individualize instruction, small groups can produce a better environment in which the teacher can discover each individual. Only the ingenuity of each instructor can solve the problem, for there is no magic formula for individualizing instruction in classes of forty or more students. Many instructors develop plans which utilize paraprofessionals, team teaching, student teachers, and student officials, as well as individualized instructional materials, to augment their own contact with students. The teacher's role often becomes one of finding the right combination of people, materials, and techniques which are meaningful in facilitating learning for each student. For some, learning is more easily motivated in group settings; for others, the best environment is independent study. Some students learn best through visual cues; for others, verbal stimulation is more meaningful. Still others find the kinesthetic-tactile approach to be of greater value, and for a large number, a multisensory approach is indicated.

In an endeavor to become acquainted quickly with students, some teachers require all of them to wear name tags. Others begin each semester's class by having each student tell interesting facts about herself or by calling the roll for the first few class meetings instead of using the number system as a means of becoming familiar with each person's name and face. Some take squad or individual pictures and then put them on roll or other record cards as a means of quickly identifying students. Still others make a real effort to become personally acquainted with each student through conferences, group discussions, and individual counseling.

The master teacher recognizes the individuality of every student and utilizes her skill, knowledge, and teaching techniques to help each person to develop and progress toward the attainment of her learning goals. This is the challenge of teaching!

DISCUSSION QUESTIONS

1. Explain the concept, "The only learning is self-learning." What implications does this have for the teacher of sports skills?
2. Identify three principles of learning applicable to motor skill development. Discuss each of the principles and explain its influence on determining teaching methods in a physical education class.
3. Learning is often assessed by performance curves. These learning curves tell much about the task being learned. Chart your progress in a specific activity over a period of time. Discuss the implications of the learning curve. What is a plateau? How does performance differ from learning?
4. Explain the difference between intrinsic and extrinsic motivation. What role does motivation play in learning?
5. Take the point of view of a selected learning theorist. Explain the implications of the specific theory on the principles of motor skill learning.

SUGGESTED READINGS

Broer, Marion: *Efficiency of Human Movement.* 3rd Ed. Philadelphia, W. B. Saunders Co., 1973.
Cratty, Bryant: *Movement Behavior and Motor Learning.* 3rd Ed. Philadelphia, Lea & Febiger, 1973.
Johnson, Warren (ed.): *Science and Medicine of Exercise and Sports.* New York, Harper and Row, 1960.
Knapp, Barbara: *Skill in Sport.* London, Routledge and Kegan Paul, 1963.
Lawther, John: *The Learning of Physical Skills.* Englewood Cliffs, New Jersey, Prentice-Hall, 1968.
Mosston, M.: *Teaching Physical Education.* Columbus, Ohio, Charles E. Merrill, 1966.
Oxendine, Joseph: *Psychology of Motor Learning.* New York, Appleton-Century-Crofts, 1968.
Plagenhoef, Stanley: *Patterns of Human Motion.* Englewood Cliffs, New Jersey, Prentice-Hall, Inc., 1971.
Quest: Learning models and the acquisition of motor skills. The National Association for Physical Education of College Women, and National College Physical Education Association for Men, January, 1972.
Robb, Margaret: *The Dynamics of Motor Skill Acquisition.* Englewood Cliffs, New Jersey, Prentice-Hall, 1972.
Sage, George H.: *Introduction to Motor Behavior. A Neuropsychological Approach.* Reading, Massachusetts, Addison-Wesley, 1971.
Singer, Robert: *Motor Learning and Human Performance.* 2nd ed. New York, The Macmillan Co., 1975.
Singer, Robert: *Coaching, Athletics and Psychology.* New York, McGraw-Hill Book Co., 1972.
Skinner, B. F.: *The Technology of Teaching.* New York, Appleton-Century-Crofts, 1968.
Stallings, Loretta: *Motor Skills, Development and Learning.* Dubuque, Iowa, Wm. C. Brown Co., 1973.
Whiting, H. T. A.: *Acquiring Ball Skill.* Philadelphia, Lea and Febiger, 1969.

CHAPTER 3

CLASS ORGANIZATION AND MANAGEMENT

Organization and good class management are basic to effective teaching. No matter what the size of the class, how formal or informal the class structure, or what methods and strategies of teaching are used, structuring the necessary routine functions frees more time and creates a better environment for learning. Involvement of students in class management can aid in development of their motivation, facilitate cooperative discipline, and afford opportunities for decision making. Many organizational and management policies are established by the school district or school; some are left to the discretion of the teacher. In colleges and universities, many class policies are determined by the instructor and the students. In all cases, consideration must be given to any policies and procedures which protect the health and safety of the student and provide her with better learning opportunities from the moment she enters the physical education and athletic complex until she safely departs. Policies must be established and implemented to deal with locker room behavior, costumes for participation, attendance and excuses, issuing equipment, ability grouping, evaluation and grading, class discipline, and student leadership roles.

Many procedures may be followed in the implementation of established policies. Obviously, the teacher in a given situation is best qualified to judge the maturity of her students and their abilities to develop and effect management policies. Many teachers feel good organization begins with a sound teaching plan designed within a realistic time block. For example, a fifty-minute period for a beginning class in a team or individual sport might follow the following plan:

Undressing	5 minutes
Roll check	2 minutes
Announcements	1 minute
Conditioning exercises (student as well as teacher directed)	5 minutes
Teacher demonstration and instruction	5 minutes
Drill and practice of specific skills	12 minutes
Team play or other culminating experience	12 minutes
Showering and dressing	8 minutes
	50 minutes

Careful planning will assure that each teaching period results in productive learning for each student. The class must be a controlled one, although it may be conducted informally, with evidence present of good rapport and group unity which have been developed through cooperative teacher-student planning, class discussion, and frequent evaluation of learning results. Such procedures help students gain leadership skills and increase their interest and motivation in what they are learning. Students who become self-motivated respond quickly to patterns of dressing, roll check, and equipment issue so that they can get about the business of participation and learning. These same students do much to exert peer pressure on students who might otherwise be disruptive in class.

Sound management techniques can aid each individual in developing responsibility for her own actions; they can encourage more understanding and cooperative teacher-pupil relationships. Although teacher and student attainment and personal goals need not be the same, each must understand the *why* of what is being done, whether it is why an anchor point is used in archery, why the hands are placed on a racket in a certain position, or why certain court behavior is inappropriate in competitive play. Both the teacher and the learner must know the overall program and daily objectives which they are striving to attain by working together, whether these be to increase physical fitness, to learn recreational skills for leisure time use, or to develop a specific neuromuscular skill.

At the end of a class, a teacher may evaluate the events of the day by reflecting on the following positive points:

1. Administrative details used minimal time.
2. Students were motivated—assembled and proceeded quickly.
3. Students dressed—no disciplinary problems—morale high.
4. Instruction well planned—scientific approach—had direction.
5. Teacher saw leadership qualities emerge in students.

ROLL CHECKING

Checking attendance is a necessary procedure, but it should be accomplished speedily and accurately to save instructional time. It may be successfully accomplished by any of the following methods:

1. Assigning each student a floor number and recording the numbers of the uncovered spaces.
2. Assigning each student a number which is called out as the instructor moves down a squad line or around a squad sitting in a circle composed of ten or less and recording the unspoken number.
3. Giving each student a name on a tag board and recording absentees shown by the unturned discs.
4. Having squad leaders check and report absentees in their lines.
5. Calling each person's name.
6. Signing in on roll sheet by each student or by squad leader.

LOCKER ROOM

Locker assignments are made very early in the year. At that time students are given clear explanations about the use of lockers, locks, storage of clothing and valuables and behavior in the locker room. In overcrowded conditions it may be necessary to design "traffic rules" to facilitate the passage of classes as periods change. Supervision of the locker room early in the semester, and perhaps throughout the year, helps students establish good housekeeping and behavior habits and diminishes discipline problems that otherwise might present hazards to students.

COSTUMES

Class costumes should be chosen to enhance the comfort and safety of the participants. Administrative policies establish the style, color, and standards of cleanliness of uniforms. Stylish one-piece designs are usually preferred in high schools, and shorts and blouses, tunics, or kilts and blouses are more frequently selected for college students. Some programs successfully use varied colors to distinguish squads or fitness test levels; others prefer a single color for all students. Uniforms may be purchased and laundered by the student or furnished and laundered by the school on a semester-fee basis.

Some teachers and school systems now are de-emphasizing conformity and uniformity and are allowing students of both sexes to wear gym costumes of their own choosing rather than requiring everyone to wear the same type of clothing. The costume may be prescribed only in terms of specific color for shorts and blouse or T-shirt.

Justification usually given for requiring regulation clothing is that it is less expensive over a period of time, does not discriminate according to socioeconomic status, can help build class morale, leads to better appearance of the class, and provides for more comfort and safety. On the other hand, some teachers now claim that far too many students are "turned off" to physical education by the required uniform policy (as well as by the showering requirement) and that it is what the student is and does that is important, not what she wears. There is merit in both arguments; consequently, whether or not to require standardized clothing is the individual teacher's decison.

Footwear must be comfortable and provide secure footing for the specific activity. Leather or canvas top tennis or basketball shoes with rubber soles are usually required. Cleated shoes, either leather or canvas topped, reduce the possibility of slipping when participating in field sports. Light weight cotton or wool socks are usually preferred over the heavier, bulkier sock.

Towels are a necessity for the success of the showering program. Most students find it inconvenient to bring towels from home each day and prefer to pay a small fee for linen service.

Jewelry can be dangerous to the wearer and to her classmates during participation. Policies concerning the wearing and storage of valuables during class must be enforced.

Special dress and equipment are required for safe participation in many sports. Comfortable swimsuits, goalkeeper's equipment in hockey, softball gloves and masks, and jackets for fencing are but a few of the items which may be needed. Some schools furnish warm-up suits for comfort and protection during the colder months. Instructional equipment should be furnished by the school, and it is often desirable to extend its use to recreational settings until the students can afford to purchase their own equipment.

Teachers have an obligation to dress appropriately for the activities which they are teaching. Some prefer to dress in apparel similar to that of the class; others prefer distinctive colors and styles. The key is that the teacher must always appear appropriately dressed—attractive, neat, and clean. Her influence is often greatest as a model on whom others fashion their behavior.

ATTENDANCE AND CLASS EXCUSES

Students enrolled in physical education classes and in attendance at school are expected to attend and participate in class activities. A physician's excuse, accepted by the school administration, is the only acceptable reason for a permanent excuse from participation. Usually these students can benefit from adaptive instruction and modified recreational activities.

Those students with temporary disabling injuries or those recuperating from illness should attend and participate to the degree approved by the physician. Students with colds, minor injuries, or menstrual disorders should dress and be encouraged to participate in appropriate milder forms of activity. Students should not be excused from physical education classes to participate in other curricular or extracurricular activities on any basis other than that accepted by general school policy for all instructional areas. Policies concerning attendance and excuses should be explained and posted for student reference.

USE OF SPACE AND ASSISTANTS

Since learning of motor skills is largely a "doing" act, it is imperative that all class members take an active part in as much of each class program as possible. The teacher must devise ways to utilize allotted space to best advantage. The use of squads and squad leaders affords students the opportunity to work at their own skill levels and enables the teacher to move from group to group, giving individual help when needed. All student leaders should be carefully selected and given leadership training, as well as additional skill instruction so that they can best assist their squads. Ideally, such chosen assistants should either dress differently from their peers, or wear some awarded emblem which distinguishes them. The use of such young leaders will only prove successful, however, if (1) it is a real honor to be selected, (2) all who are chosen are really outstanding, and (3) this picked group receives extra help in skill mastery and training in the techniques of leading others successfully.

ISSUING EQUIPMENT

A well-organized lesson clearly takes into account the availability of equipment and the procedures for setting up for class. Class or squad leaders or responsible students can assume much of the responsibility of getting equipment from the central storage area, setting up standards, nets, or other appropriate equipment, and checking for safety hazards prior to class. The teacher supervises the preparation and always checks safety devices and potential hazards. Well-organized equipment issue is one more way to save valuable instructional time.

GROUPING CLASS MEMBERS

Properly grouped teams and squads can result in better student motivation and cooperative learning. Consequently, more rapid and more meaningful learning can result. Experienced physical educators have little difficulty distinguishing between good and bad form, beginning and more advanced skills, and stronger and weaker players. Many kinds of grouping techniques may be tried within a class. Individuals may be classified according to age, grade in school, skill level, fitness level, height and weight, and individual needs. Homogeneous grouping has the following advantages:

1. It enables the teacher to observe more quickly the needs of each individual in each subgroup.
2. It provides a better opportunity for individual skill development.
3. It offers more equitable competition.
4. It maintains interest and motivation at one's own skill level.
5. It provides an environment of equals for those with lesser skills and affords "strength in numbers."
6. It can prevent cliques and provide a setting where each student can become a contributing team member.

However, if this type of grouping is used, the teacher should watch carefully for lagging interest and lack of leadership in the low ability groups. She may also find it a challenge to know when to change group membership so that improvement is most likely to be made and whether to spend the major part of her instructional time with the highly skilled, average, or slow learners, realizing that as an educator she must provide equal opportunities for all in each group. To avoid helping good students become better at the expense of the slower students is one of the greatest challenges a highly skilled performer faces when she becomes a teacher of students with average or below average skills.

Heterogeneous grouping has the following advantages:

1. It helps mix the above and below average with the average and provides opportunities for students to help each other.
2. It is more realistic and life-like, thus preparing students to cooperate and compete with those of like and unlike abilities.
3. It provides a learning laboratory where the less skilled can see the results and techniques of highly skilled performance.

All methods of grouping have their advantages, disadvantages, and problems. Before any grouping and regrouping of students, the teacher must keep uppermost in her own mind the needs of each separate class group as an entity and of each individual within it. The skillful instructor will provide, through a balanced, graded program and the use of various teaching techniques, rich educational experiences to fill these needs in light of the realistic situation in which she works in terms of its equipment, facilities, time limits, available teaching assistants, and student leaders.

DRILLS

Technique drills play a vital part in skill mastery. Drills should be designed to approximate as closely as possible the game skills and the settings in which they will be used. Group and partner formations and suggested specific drills are discussed in detail in each sport chapter.

EVALUATION

Measurement and evaluation serve to assess the status and progress of a student in the skills, knowledge, and attitudes considered important objectives in sport learning. Records and test scores enable a student to view her accomplishments, strengths, and weaknesses in relation to her own potential and in relation to other class members. Measurement techniques are vital to the teacher in evaluating her techniques and methods of accomplishing learning objectives. To both the student and teacher, evaluation serves as a motivator for improving performance.

Tests may be teacher made, pupil made or standardized, but they should be reliable and valid; that is, they measure what they purport to measure with consistency. A meaningful test should be easily understood, economically administered in terms of both time and money, and easily scored and assessed. The results of the tests should be given to students, for only as the results are fed back can they be used to determine progress and to guide further learning.

Some of the many areas and techniques of measurement and evaluation which may be helpful follow:

1. Knowledge tests
   a. Essay tests
   b. Objective tests
      (1) True-false, right-wrong, same-opposite, yes-no
      (2) Short answer, completion questions, association
      (3) Multiple choice of choosing most correct answer, selecting all correct answers in a question of four or more parts, choosing the wrong answer
      (4) Matching key words with phrases
   c. Situational tests using pictured playing areas requiring students to mark appropriate plays, player positions, or outcomes
2. Sport skill tests
   a. Isolated game skills for speed and accuracy
   b. Ability rating scales in which each player is ranked in relationship to others on a team or in a class; a diagnostic check list for rating each student's ability to perform isolated techniques making up a specific skill (e.g., if the racket is held correctly for a tennis serve, the ball contacted at the right place, etc.)
   c. Game incidence charts showing how many goals were made out of a designated number of trials, number of successful blocks made in volleyball, number of successful traps completed in soccer, etc. Such checklist charts show up both skill and game strategy strong and weak points
   d. Jury of experts who assess players' abilities on predetermined attributes
3. Physical fitness tests of endurance, speed, strength, agility, motor capacity
4. Attitude tests
5. Social development tests

6. Posture tests
7. Cardiovascular tests
8. Somatotyping

DISCUSSION QUESTIONS

1. List the organizational areas that you would discuss with a class the first few meetings of the semester. Visit a local school physical education class and report on administrative class procedures.
2. Bring to class pictures taken from advertisements appearing in any issue of the *Journal of Health, Physical Education, Recreation* of the uniforms you would like your class to be required to wear. Discuss the desirable qualities of these uniforms.
3. List and discuss five qualities you would want your selected student leaders to have.
4. Devise a ten-lesson training period for your selected student assistants for a unit on field hockey or advanced swimming.
5. Show in a diagram assigned class space and duties for five homogeneously grouped squads in a class of 40 students for instruction in basketball. Design a similar plan for 40 persons in a gymnastics class with six teaching stations.

SUGGESTED READINGS

Bucher, Charles, Koenig, Constance, and Barnhard, Milton: *Methods and Materials in Secondary School Physical Education.* 2nd ed. St. Louis, The C. V. Mosby Co., 1972.

Clarke, H. Harrison: *Application of Measurement to Health and Physical Education.* 4th ed. Englewood Cliffs, New Jersey, Prentice-Hall, 1969.

Daughtrey, Greyson: *Methods in Physical Education and Health for Secondary Schools.* 2nd Ed. Philadelphia, W. B. Saunders Co., 1973.

Davis, Elwood, and Wallis, Earl: *Toward Better Teaching in Physical Education.* Englewood Cliffs, New Jersey, Prentice-Hall, 1961.

Insley, Gerald: *Practical Guidelines for the Teaching of Physical Education.* Reading, Massachusetts, Addison-Wesley, 1973.

Mathews, Donald: *Measurement in Physical Education.* 4th Ed. Philadelphia, W. B. Saunders Co., 1973.

McGee, Rosemary, and Drews, Fred: *Proficiency Testing for Physical Education.* Washington, D.C., American Association for Health, Physical Education and Recreation, 1974.

Rethlingshafer, Dorothy: *Motivation as Related to Personality.* New York, McGraw-Hill Book Co., 1963.

Vannier, Maryhelen, Foster, Mildred, and Gallahue, David. *Teaching Physical Education in Elementary Schools.* 5th Ed. Philadelphia, W. B. Saunders Co., 1967.

Vannier, Maryhelen and Fait, Hollis: *Teaching Physical Education in Secondary Schools.* 4th Ed. Philadelphia, W. B. Saunders Co., 1975.

CHAPTER 4

EQUIPMENT AND ITS CARE

Physical education teachers are best qualified to requisition equipment and materials for purchase. Only they know the type and amount of equipment which best serves the instructional, recreational, and intramural programs. Athletic coaches should determine their own needs. They must operate within a designated annual budget, allocating funds for the instructional area and for teaching methods and procedures. Administrative policies will determine the manner of purchasing. Many schools and colleges place their orders on bid, accepting the lowest bid for the specified items; other institutions patronize local suppliers to assure prompt, personalized service.

Sports equipment is of three types: *permanent,* which lasts over many years, such as tennis posts and diving boards; *semi-permanent,* which must be replaced after several seasons of hard use, such as archery targets and tennis nets; and *expendable,* such as badminton shuttlecocks and tennis balls, which often must be restocked yearly. Instructors have an obligation not only to make the best use of what materials they have, but also to increase the life span and usefulness of these materials.

THE PURCHASE OF EQUIPMENT

Regardless of whether one does her own buying or this is handled by the school's purchasing agent, the following suggestions will prove helpful in obtaining the best value from allotted funds:

1. All orders should be made on a purchase order blank and kept on file.
2. When buying uniforms or other articles of clothing, factors to keep in mind are: attractiveness of appearance, comfort, quality, durability, guarantee, and manner and expense of laundering or cleaning needed.

3. Buy quality products in quantity; take advantage of legitimate discounts and off-season sales.
4. Buy multi-purpose equipment when possible.
5. Avoid salesmen's gifts, for their acceptance usually entails an obligation or hidden cost.
6. See and test what you buy; avoid ordering only from catalogs unless they offer proven products.
7. Use all allotted funds. Check regularly the amount of money still available. Buy throughout the year rather than purchasing unneeded items at the close of the fiscal year in order to use up all of your budget.
8. Make a yearly inventory and running seasonal check of all equipment. Buy needed items at the close of each sport season.
9. Buy from local merchants only when they can offer values equal to those from larger, better known firms.

THE CARE OF EQUIPMENT

Ten basic principles for good equipment maintenance are:

1. There must be a definite policy regarding the care of instructional and athletic equipment.
2. All players must be instructed in the care of athletic equipment.
3. One person should be directly responsible for the care of athletic equipment.
4. An accurate record must be kept of all equipment. This record should show, among other things, condition and age.
5. All equipment must be marked for size and identification.
6. There must be a definite system regarding the issuance, use, and return of athletic equipment.
7. If an equipment manager is utilized, there must be a clear understanding of her duties and responsibilities.
8. Athletic equipment must be cleaned or laundered frequently. Equipment should be dried and properly stored after use.
9. All equipment should be stored, repaired, and maintained in accordance with manufacturer's recommendations.
10. Proper methods of out-of-season storage should be utilized.

Costumes. Woolen, cotton, and rayon uniforms should be cleaned and stored in dry, well ventilated places. Moth protection will insure their utility over a longer period of time.

Leather Goods. Leather is best protected by cleaning with saddle soap and treating with neat's-foot oil or a leather conditioner. A light coat of oil should be applied to softball gloves, and a light coat of petroleum jelly to the leather of lacrosse sticks. Wet balls should be dried out gradually at normal room temperature and stored in a cool dry place. Too much heat causes cracking as the ball dries and too much moisture allows mould to grow. Saddle soap will keep the leather clean and soft. Stored balls should be only partially inflated, and when they are inflated, the needle should be moistened with glycerin before inserting it carefully into the valve. The pressure gauge on the pump insures that the ball is inflated to the manufacturer's specifications. The strain of overinflation will shorten the life of the ball.

Rubber Balls. Many schools are now buying rubber instead of leather balls, since they are less expensive and are proving as serviceable. Proper cleaning with a mild soap and warm water plus careful storage in a cool, dry area will increase the length of their usefulness. Cleaning fluids should never be used on this equipment. *Plastic balls* used in the practice of hockey and golf need only be wiped after use.

Wooden Equipment. Bats, hockey and lacrosse sticks, and other similar wooden equipment should be carefully wiped, rough spots sandpapered out, and waxed before storing.

Archery Equipment. Targets should be laid out flat for storage and be stacked or laid singly on a platform several inches from the floor. Powdered sulfur spread among the butts will keep rodents and insects away.* Target faces can be reinforced by cardboard or heavy paper backings. A thin coating of paraffin will increase the life of corrugated cardboard targets.

Bows should be unbraced, hung vertically on wooden pegs, and stored in a cool, humid place. Fiberglas bows need only to be wiped clean and dried; wax should be applied to wooden bows at the end of the season to protect their finish, and those with leather handles should be saddlesoaped. Strings should be beeswaxed at least once weekly and frayed strings replaced.

Arrows should always be stored in a rack instead of in a box to protect the fletching from damage. An arrow tray can be made by drilling holes through three boards which are nailed in three layers about 8 inches apart to two upright boards. Arrows numbered on the shaft in sets of six to correspond to numbered holes in the tray will enable students to replace them quickly. A thin coating of wax, applied at the end of the season, will protect the finish of wooden arrows. Fiberglas should be carefully wiped, and aluminum should be wiped with a light oil when stored. Finger tabs and leather quivers should be saddlesoaped regularly.

Tennis and Badminton Equipment. Wooden tennis and badminton rackets should be in presses and hung on a wall. Head covers are recommended for expensive rackets. Although steel and Fiberglas rackets do not need to be in presses, they should never be stacked together but rather stood upright in a box or metal container. Tennis balls should be dried thoroughly and kept in separate boxes with the correct number for each class. Shuttlecocks, both plastic and feathered, must be stored in a moist environment, for dryness causes them to become brittle. A commercial humidifier or a breadbox may be used for this purpose. Many schools now using plastic shuttles for large classes are finding them inexpensive and satisfactory, especially for beginners. Regardless of the type used, students need careful instruction in handling shuttlecocks properly. Cotton or woolen practice balls used for beginners are often economical, al-

---

*Grace Robertson: Elementary care and repair of archery tackle. *Archery-Riding Guide.* Washington, D.C., AAHPER, DGWS, June 1958–June 1960, p. 33.

though these students should use regular shuttles as soon as they have learned basic game strokes.

Nets. Outdoor tennis nets are tarred, chemically treated, or made of metal. They should be stored on pegs (never rolled or folded) in a cool, dry place. Indoor badminton and volleyball nets may be rolled or folded when not in use. Rips and breaks should be mended immediately. All nets should be loosened when not in use to relieve tension.

Mats. Rubber and plastic mat covers should be carefully cleaned with soap, water, and disinfectant. Uncovered mats should first be vacuumed and then carefully scrubbed with either commercial mat cleaner or soap and water by washing only a small area at a time and wiping it dry. Mats should never be dragged across the floor but should be carried and hung on pegs or racks. They should never be rolled but always kept flat.

Metal Equipment. This type of equipment should be lightly oiled or painted in order to prevent rust. Steel tapes, jumping standards, and other such equipment may be cleaned with steel wool and lightly oiled or sprayed with petroleum-base rust-resistant products instead of painting them.

All cloth materials such as fencing jackets, goalkeeper's chest protector, shin guards, and fencing gloves should be washed, dried, and stored in a well ventilated area.

Care of specific items of equipment is mentioned in each activity chapter.

REPAIRING OF EQUIPMENT

Numerous firms specialize in repairing sports equipment and give relatively inexpensive service. Prompt attention should be paid to all items needing repair to extend the life of the equipment and to protect the safety of students. Simple repairs, such as sewing ripped balls, replacing foil blades, repairing torn nets, replacing arrow tips and fletching, and rewrapping golf club and racket handle grips can be made by the teacher or students. A liquid fabric cement called Lam-A-Fab can be used to repair minor rips and tears in cloth or canvas.* All broken racket strings should be repaired at once. Some damaged and broken equipment, such as splintered arrows, cracked bats, and broken racket frames should not be repaired. It should be discarded in the interest of player safety.

The Equipment Room. This room should be dry, well ventilated, kept locked, and located near the gymnasium floor and instructor's office. A half door or small window through which equipment can be issued is recommended.

A good equipment room is the first essential in proper care of athletic equipment. A sloppy, carelessly kept room can take a greater toll on the

*Edward Voltmer and Arthur Esslinger: *The Organization and Administration of Physical Education.* 4th Ed. New York, Appleton-Century-Crofts, 1967, p. 48.

life of sports equipment than many hours of hard service on the playing fields. The following list should be considered in planning an equipment room:

1. The room should be large, free from sweaty walls and pipes, and not located near the shower room.
2. It should be protected against moths, roaches, and other insects.
3. It should house all of the equipment of the department and provide space for handling and repair.
4. It should be properly lighted and heated.
5. It should have deep shelves large enough to hold cartons and bulky articles.
6. It should have narrow shelves for smaller articles.
7. Nothing should be stored on the floor.
8. Racks should be available for hanging equipment up to dry.

Checking Equipment In and Out. If no attendant is available for this task, a student employee or class leader can be assigned this responsibility. Large laundry sacks for carrying bats, mesh ball bags, carts for rackets, foils, and golf clubs, or targets placed on a stand with rollers will enable squad leaders or others to move needed equipment to playing areas quickly. Each instructor should (1) carefully study what equipment she has and know what condition it is in, (2) devise best ways for getting it out to each class (here a student committee can often come up with some fine ideas), and then (3) strive to decrease the time needed for getting a properly equipped group ready for instruction.

Marking Equipment. All equipment should be stenciled. Uniforms should be stamped according to size (large, medium, or small or 38, 34, 32), name of the school, and date of purchase (Central High, 8/15/75). Although stealing is rarely a serious problem where limited equipment is issued, it does exist in some school and college instructional and athletic programs. Every department must work out the solution to this difficulty, determining written policies to combat it, and call upon each teacher and coach to enforce the policies. Students usually cooperate when they come to realize that they are really hurting themselves and others by their "borrowing habits" in that the budget is limited and the purchase of new equipment is impossible if part of it must be used to replace missing items. Stress should be placed upon personal integrity and the fact that those who "take" equipment without permission are short-changing themselves in the long run.

When teaching any sport, the instructor should devote time to instructing students on the desirable features of different brands and types of equipment. This helps them in the purchase of personal items and gives them an appreciation for the school equipment that has been supplied to them.

IMPROVISED EQUIPMENT

"Where there is a will there is, indeed, a way," as any creative teacher knows when faced with a lack of or poor equipment. Although it is neither advisable nor possible to make many pieces of instructional equipment, in many phases of the program, certain pieces of equipment can be made by either the school's mechanical arts or home economics department. Teachers rarely have the time to undertake construction tasks by themselves. Imaginative leaders, with student assistance, can add much to this list of suggested things that can be devised safely from inexpensive or cost-free materials:

Archery. Arm guards may be made from heavy cardboard and rubber bands; quivers from mailing tubes or tennis ball cans; target backstops from bales of hay or heavy cardboard; archery strings from Barbour's No. 12 Irish linen or heavy carpet thread; finger tabs from shoe tongues or inner tubes; golf tees, Coke bottle tops with nails driven through them, or spools for toe markers; points of aim from used ice picks; bow sights from adhesive tape and big-headed pins; tassels from discarded yarn for wiping arrows.

Bowling. Make bowling alley backstops from discarded mats and crating for use in gymnasium.

Softball. Use discarded lumber for home plate and bases, covering them with heavy canvas. Make batting tees with a heavy wooden base and a hard rubber tube. Make a backstop with old lumber and inexpensive chicken wire.

Basketball. Make outdoor backboards and goal posts from discarded lumber. Goals can be made of heavy iron rings or be cut from heavy metal cans.

Golf. Putting greens can be made from scrap carpeting; cane poles and pennants serve as flagsticks.

Stunts and Gymnastics. A balance beam and Swedish box from old lumber; broomsticks for balancing and body flexibility stunts; a chinning bar, ladder walk, rope climb from discarded materials. Mats from old mattresses or from surplus stores.

Soccer, Hockey, Speedball, Lacrosse. Goal posts from discarded lumber and chicken wire.

Swimming. Buoys from rope and unsinkable wood.

Tennis, Badminton, Volleyball, Racketball and Table Tennis. Net posts and practice backboards from old lumber; heavy ropes for nets. Paddles for racketball and table tennis from scrap plywood.

Track and Field. Starting blocks, jump standards, broad jump takeoff board, etc. can all be made from discarded lumber.

Storage Equipment. Numerous types of carts, bins, and lockers can be built of scrap lumber, hardware cloth or Fiberglas sheets.

DISCUSSION QUESTIONS

1. In chart form, list the equipment needs for a class of 40 beginning students in basketball, soccer, golf, and badminton. How would you store the equipment? How would you transport it to the instructional area?

2. Write a short paper on how the methods used in the storage of athletic equipment in your school could be improved.
3. How is the problem of student "borrowing" of equipment handled in your own and other schools? Give your reactions to these methods. How do you plan to solve this problem if it occurs?
4. Bring to class any article of athletic equipment you have repaired. What did you learn from this experience which will prove profitable for your classmates?
5. Bring to class any piece of athletic equipment you have made from discarded or inexpensive material. Explain its use, safety features, and ways in which it helps in teaching the activity.

SELECTED AUDIOVISUAL AIDS

Basic Net Mending. (16 min., sound, color.) Fish and Wildlife Service, Department of Visual Information, Washington, D.C. (Free)

The Inside Story of a Golf Ball. (10 min., sound, b & w.) United States Rubber Company, Advertising Department, 1230 Avenue of the Americas, New York, New York. (Free)

The Spalding Story. (30 min., sound, color.) Spalding and Brothers, 4850 N. Harlem, Chicago, Illinois or 1505 Hi-Line Drive, Dallas, Texas. (Free)

Working for Fun. (31 min., sound, color.) MacGregor Company, Advertising Department, 14861 Spring Grove Avenue, Cincinnati, Ohio. (Free)

You Asked for It—How Bowling Balls Are Made. (5 min., sound, b & w.) Brunswick-Balke-Collender Company, 623–633 South Wabash Avenue, Chicago, Illinois. (Free)

SUGGESTED READINGS*

Ashton, Dudley: *Administration of Physical Education for Women.* New York, The Ronald Press, 1968.

Equipment and Supplies for Athletics, Physical Education and Recreation. Washington, D.C., AAHPER, 1960.

Bourguardez, Virginia, and Heilman, Charles: *Sports Equipment: Selection, Care, and Repair.* New York, A. S. Barnes, 1950.

Carter, Joel: *How to Make Athletic Equipment.* New York, The Ronald Press, 1960.

Daughtrey, Greyson: *Methods in Physical Education and Health for Secondary Schools.* 2nd Ed. Philadelphia, W. B. Saunders Co., 1973.

Gillson, Frederick: *Make-It-Yourself Games Book.* New York, Emerson Publishing Co., 1963.

Planning Areas and Facilities for Health, Physical Education and Recreation. Chicago, The Athletic Institute, 1965.

Vannier, Maryhelen and Fait, Hollis: *Teaching Physical Education in Secondary Schools.* 4th Ed. Philadelphia, W. B. Saunders Co., 1975.

*Contact sporting goods manufacturers for information on the maintenance of special equipment.

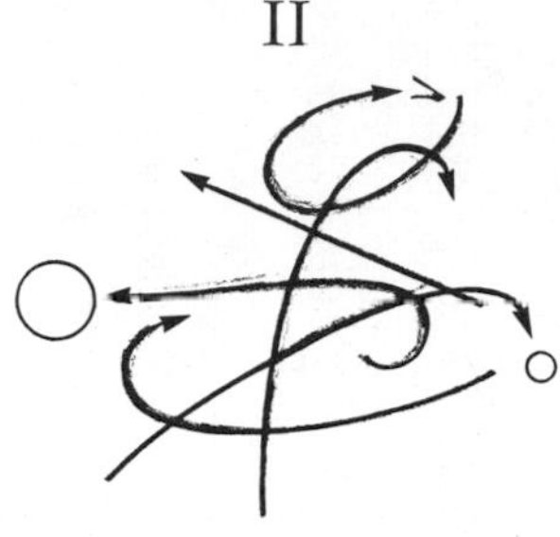

PART II

INDIVIDUAL SPORTS

"Personality is not so much like a structure as like a river—it continuously flows, and to be a person is to be engaged in a perpetual process of becoming."

Harry Emerson Fosdick

CHAPTER 5

ARCHERY

Archery is a year-round sport for both sexes of all ages, the physically strong or the muscularly weak. Engaged in either indoors or outdoors as an individual or group activity, it can improve posture and develop chest, arms, and back strength while developing neuromuscular skill and techniques for a lasting competitive or recreational sport. It is a sport that appeals to young and old alike, for it offers recreational and competitive target and field events for school, college, and club groups as well as sport archery for hunting and fishing. It is a sport of continuing challenges; when one has mastered target shooting there are opportunities for hunting small game or joining an African safari for big game. Some toxophilites develop the craftsmanship to make their own equipment.

The origin of archery is in antiquity, when the crudely fashioned bow and arrow served primitive man as a protective weapon and as a means of providing food. Archery allowed man to make a step toward civilized acts when he no longer had to engage in hand-to-hand combat to kill his prey. This ancient sport of Robin Hood, William Tell, and Hiawatha has strong romantic appeal, especially to youth. The evolution of archery displays the colorful panorama of Egyptian, Greek, Turkish, Japanese, English, and French armies standing shoulder to shoulder, or mounted on heavily padded horses shooting hundreds of arrows in unision at the approaching enemy. Museums in almost every nation have exhibits of these ancient weapons—the short heavy bow of only 4½ feet with even shorter arrows, the oddly-shaped C bow from which 6 foot long arrows were shot, or the highly polished English or Oriental crossbows, the unattractive but deadly weapons of the Indian hunters, or the poisoned arrows of uncivilized tribes.

Since the beginning of the 17th century, after gunpowder gained prominence as a means of warfare in most of the world, archery continued to gain popularity as a sport, and the bow and arrow became symbolic of love, power, and religion in various parts of the world. In the United States today more than 6 million people of varying ages participate in target and field archery in schools, colleges, camps, forests and parks. For more than 25 years the Camp Archery Association has granted proficiency certificates to youth in Y's, schools, and summer camps. The National Archery Association, organized in America in 1879, and the National Field Archery Association, founded in 1939, sponsor annual tournaments. The International Federation of Archery sponsors a world championship tournament every two years, and archery has achieved the status of an event in the Olympic Games.

NATURE AND PURPOSE OF THE SPORT

The skills basic to the sport of archery are used in many archery activities. The most common form of target archery leads to the development of field archery, flight shooting, archery games, clout shooting, and bow hunting and bow fishing.

Target Archery. The purpose of *target archery* is to hit the target, preferably the "gold," with a prescribed number of arrows shot from specified distances. This is called a round. There are rounds designed for both sexes and all ability levels. In school competition the *Scholastic Round* and the *Junior Scholastic Round* are used most often. The *Range Round* and *Miniature Round* are suggested for indoor use. In college competition the *Columbia Round* is ordinarily used. Some collegiate events specify "classes" designed for a specified number of arrows at a single distance.

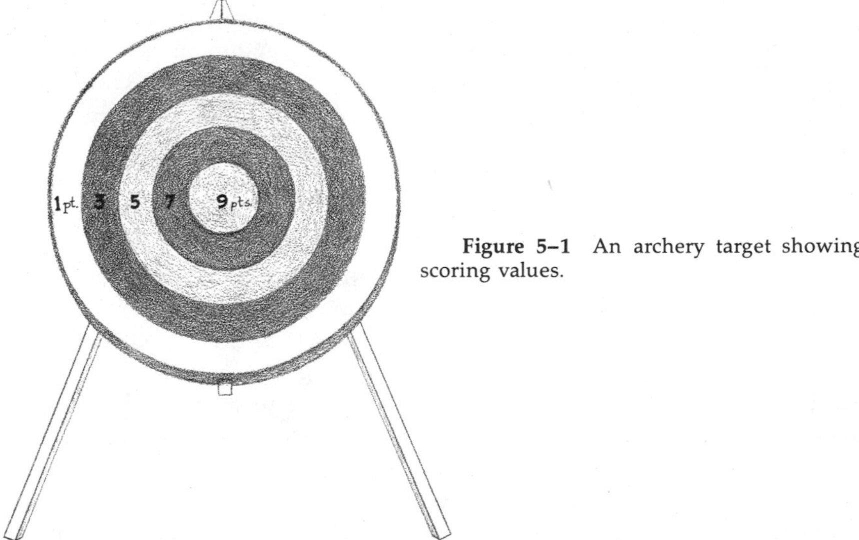

Figure 5–1 An archery target showing scoring values.

Some competitive rounds are:

FITA (International Archery Federation) *Round*—36 arrows at 70, 60, 50, and 30 meters for ladies.
American Round—30 arrows from 60 yards, 50 yards and 40 yards respectively.
Junior American Round—30 arrows from 50 yards, 40 yards and 30 yards respectively.
Columbia Round—24 arrows from 50, 40, and 30 yards respectively.
Junior Columbia Round—24 arrows from 40 yards, 30 yards and 20 yards respectively.
*Scholastic Round**—24 arrows from 40 yards and 30 yards respectively.
*Junior Scholastic Round**—24 arrows from 30 yards and 20 yards respectively.
*Range Round**—60 arrows from a single distance; either 50 yards or 40 yards or 30 yards or 20 yards on regulation targets.
*Miniature Round**—60 arrows from 15 yards on a *two-foot* target, scaled to the same proportions as is the regulation target.

Flight Shooting. Participants in flight shooting release a designated number of arrows from a shooting line in an attempt to send the arrows as far as possible. Competition is held for regular flight (bow held in the hands) and free-style flight, or foot archery, with the bow held by the feet and pulled by the hands and arms.

Field Archery. Field archery includes hunting with bow, roving (shooting at various inanimate objects while walking in fields or woods), and shooting at established targets while walking over a designated course. In these activities the distances shot are unknown and the instinctive aiming method is generally used.

Clout Shooting. Participants direct 36 arrows at a target 48 feet in diameter which is placed on the ground. The target, laid out in concentric circles, has values similar to those of a regular target. Men shoot from 180 yards, women from 120 or 140 yards.

Archery Games. Archery games are increasing in popularity, since they are great fun for the participants and serve as motivating activities during instructional units. Several such games are described below.

Archery Golf. Played on a golf course with a nine-inch cloth-ball target located by the side of each green. The archer shoots as many arrows down the fairway and into the target as needed. The archer taking the least number of shots is the winner. Teela-Wooket Archery Camp has developed rules for the game, since no official rules presently exist.

Tick-Tack-Toe. Three rows of balloons are placed on the target matt. The game may be played as a team game or as an individual game with the winner being the first to hit three balloons in any line. A variation requires that all balloons be broken.

Wand Shooting. Place a one-inch strip of masking tape on the target face from top to bottom. One point is given for each arrow landing on the tape. The game may be played as an individual or team game with a prede-

*Not official rounds of the National Archery Association.

termined number of points (perhaps two for a team) which must be achieved to be declared a winner.

Bingo. The target face is designed to look like a bingo card. The first player or team to hit five squares in any straight line is declared winner.

William Tell. The target face represents a boy with an apple on his head. Any team member hitting the boy's face is declared out; the first team to hit the apple is declared the victor.

Safari Hunt. This game may be played on a target range or over a field range. Figures of lions, tigers, cheetahs, elephants, and other game animals are placed on the target face or on the range. A determined number of arrows are shot from 15, 20, and 25 yards on the target range and from assigned positions on the field range. The winning individual or team scores the largest number of hits on the animals.

GAME RULES AND SCORING

Target Archery

In target archery there are various competitive rounds, yet all are governed by the same basic rules and scoring.

Basic Rules

1. Archers must straddle the shooting line when shooting.
2. Lady Paramount's whistle signals the beginning of shooting an end.
3. Archers must be three yards back of line when not shooting.
4. When a round requires shooting from several range distances, begin shooting from the greatest distance.
5. An arrow leaving the bow is considered shot if the archer cannot reach it with her bow.
6. All shooting stops on two blasts of Lady Paramount's whistle.
7. The target face is usually 48 inches in diameter.
8. An end consists of six arrows.

Scoring

1. Score values are gold—9 points; red—7 points; blue—5 points; black—3 points; white—1 point.
2. An arrow that cuts two colors is given the higher value.
3. An arrow that passes through the scoring face so it is not visible from the front counts 7 points if witnessed.
4. An arrow rebounding from the scoring face shall count 7 points if witnessed.
5. Arrows in the petticoat have no scoring value.

Scores are recorded by listing the highest values first. Each score is recorded. No recorded score indicates a miss or hit outside of the scoring area. Ties are resolved in favor of the archer who shoots the highest score at the longest distance. If a tie still exists, the archer with the greatest number of gold points, red points, etc., is declared winner.

Name	Audrey Bullett		
Round	Jr. Col. Round		
Date	May 20, 1975		
At 40 yds.		Hits	Score
	9 7 7 7 5	5	35
	9 7 7 7 7 5	6	42
	9 7 7 7 7	5	37
	9 9 7 7 7 7	6	46
		22	160
At 30 yds.			
	9 7 7 7 7 5	6	42
	7 7 7 7 7 5	6	40
	9 9 9 9 5 5	6	46
	7 7 7 5 5 5	6	36
		24	764
At 20 yds.			
	9 9 9 9 7 7	6	50
	9 9 9 9 9 9 Low	(6)	(54)
	9 9 9 9 9 7	6	52
	9 9 9 9 7 7	6	50
		24	206
Total Score		70	530

Name	Mary McGowan		
Round	Jr. Col. Round		
Date	May 20, 1975		
At 40 yds.		Hits	Score
	9 5 5 3 3	5	25
	7 5 5 5 3 1	6	26
	5 5 1 1	4	12
	9 5 3	3	17
		18	80
At 30 yds.			
	9 9 7 5 5 3	6	38
	9 7 7 5 5 5	6	38
	7 7 7 7 3 3	6	34
	7 7 5 5 5 3	6	32
		24	142
At 20 yds.			
	9 7 7 7 5 3	6	38
	7 7 7 7 5 3	6	36
	9 7 7 7 5 5	6	40
	9 7 7 5 5 3	6	36
		24	150
Total Score		66	372

Name	Joan Lord		
Round	Jr. Col. Round		
Date	May 20, 1975		
At 40 yds.		Hits	Score
	9 9 7 7 5 3	6	40
	7 7 7 5 5 5	6	36
	7 7 7 5 3 1	6	30
	9 9 7 5 5 5	6	40
		24	146
At 30 yds.			
	9 9 9 9 9 7	6	52
	9 9 9 9 9 7	6	52
	9 9 7 7 7 5	6	44
	9 9 9 9 9 7	6	52
		24	200
At 20 yds.			
	9 9 9 7 7 1	6	42
	9 9 9 9 9 7	6	52
	9 9 9 9 9 7	6	52
	9 9 9 9 7 7	6	50
		24	196
Total Score		72	542

Name	Nancy Hoag		
Round	Jr. Col. Round		
Date	May 20, 1975		
At 40 yds.		Hits	Score
	7 7 7 5 5	5	31
	7 7 5 3 1 1	6	24
	7 7 7 7 5 5	6	38
	9 9 9 7 7 3	6	44
		23	137
At 30 yds.			
	7 7 7 7 5 3	6	36
	9 9 7 7 7 5	6	44
	9 9 9 7 7 5	6	46
	9 9 7 7 7 7	6	46
		24	172
At 20 yds.			
	9 7 7 7 7 7	6	44
	9 7 7 7 7 5	6	42
	9 9 9 7 5 5	6	44
	9 9 9 9 7 7	6	50
		24	180
Total Score		71	489

Team Score 279–1933

Figure 5–2 Sample score sheet.

Field Archery

The National Field Archery Association is the organization concerned with the rules and development of field archery. Ranges are usually constructed in fields or rugged areas. The archer moves to designated areas to shoot at stationary targets. There are several suggested rounds, such as the Field Round, Flint Round, Hunter's Round, and Big Game Round. Target sizes vary, usually from 12 to 24 inches, and shooting distances differ at each target. The standard target face has two concentric circles with a hit in the inner circle scoring five points and one in the outer circle scoring three points. Field archery tournaments are both freestyle (sight shooters) and bare bow, using instinctive technique. An end in the field consists of four arrows.

The Flint Round is an appropriate test for beginners. Simplified rules and scoring include the following.

1. Seven targets will be set; archers will go around twice for a total of 14 targets.
2. Archers shoot in groups of four, with the target captain calling scores and pulling arrows. One person is the scorer.
3. Archers stand behind the shooting stake and shoot four arrows if it is a one position shot, or one arrow from each of four designated positions. These four positions are of the "walk-up" type, getting closer to the target in the Flint Round but may be fan-shaped in other rounds.

Table 1. THE FLINT ROUND

Target No.	Shooting Distance	No. Arrows	Target Size
1	25 yards	4	12″
2	20 feet	4	6″
3	30 yards	4	12″
4	15 yards	4	6″
5	20 yards	4	12″
6	10 yards	4	6″
7	30, 25, 20, and 15 yds.	Walk up, shoot one at each distance	12″

4. Center circle, including the spot, scores five points; the outer circle scores 3 points.
5. An arrow cutting two rings is given the higher value. Skids or glances into the target are not counted. Arrows passing through the face, but still in the butt (object against which the face is placed), may be pushed back and scored as hits in the circle through which they entered.
6. Witnessed bounceouts believed to have hit a scoring area will be reshot. Arrows passing through the target in the scoring area and witnessed will be scored.

Advanced archers shoot the Field Round, which consists of fourteen targets, twice around, with distances ranging from 20 feet to 80 yards.

NEEDED FACILITIES AND EQUIPMENT

An archer's equipment is called *tackle.* Essential equipment for a beginner includes a bow, bowstring, arrows, arm guard, finger tab or glove, and a quiver. Some instructors would include a bowsight among the essentials for a target archer. There are numerous accessories, including bow cases, chest guards, slings, clickers, "kiss" buttons, and items that aid in the comfort and increase the accuracy of the archer.

The Bow. Modern technology has provided new materials and supe-

Table 2. MODIFIED FLINT ROUND

Target No.	Shooting Distance	No. Arrows	Target Size
1	17 yards	4	8″
2	20 feet	4	6″
3	20 yards	4	8″
4	14 yards	4	6″
5	15 yards	4	8″
6	10 yards	4	6″
7	20, 17, 15, and 10 yds.	Walk up, shoot one from each distance	8″

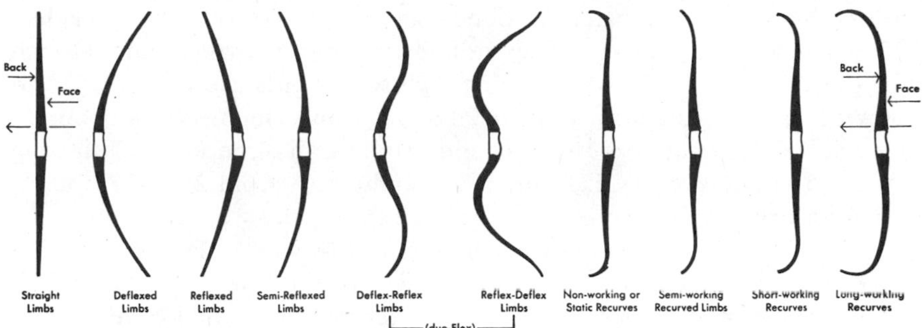

Figure 5–3 Bow designs. (From DGWS Archery-Riding Guide, 1964–66.)

rior designs to enhance the accuracy of all archers. The old yew, osage orange, and lemonwood bows of a straight end design have been designated museum items and are rarely found in instructional equipment. However, wood is still the basic material in many of the most expensive bows. Fiberglas, laminated Fiberglas, and composite materials of laminated wood and Fiberglas are the most common materials used in the construction of the various modern bow designs. Basically, there are three bow designs: the straight end, the working recurve, and the static recurve bows. The straight end bow has lost popularity to the recurve designs, for the recurved limbs provide cast, or speed, with which the bow propels the arrow. The major difference between the working recurve and the static recurve is that the working recurve flows into the bow on a draw, whereas the static recurve remains at a sharp angle to the bow limb on the draw.

The most popular instructional bow is the fiberglass working recurve. It is easily cared for and is less expensive than the laminated bow. Such bows provide a quality of smoothness of draw and release not common to the less expensive wooden bows. Prices range from approximately $6.00 to $300.00, and an individual should consult an authority and experiment with several designs and materials prior to making a serious investment.

The recently developed compound bow with draw length of 22 to 33 inches and draw weights of 15 to 50 pounds in the target model and 35 to 70 pounds in hunter models has cable adjustments which may be set to an individual's draw length. Once set, the tension is assured for speed and reliability of arrow release. The design is receiving wide acceptance among serious archers.

Bow *lengths* vary, with the archer's preference the main consideration. Beginners usually shoot with a 56 to 64 inch bow. The average bow length for women collegiate archers approximates 66 inches; men average 69 inches. Bow hunters often prefer a shorter bow, since it is less cumbersome in the field.

Bow *weight* is determined by the number of pounds of force needed to pull the bowstring a specified distance. The poundage marked on the bow is generally established at a 28-inch draw. If arrows are shorter, and the draw is less, *subtract* approximately 2 pounds per inch; if the arrow is longer than 28 inches, and the draw is correspondingly longer, *add* two pounds per inch for the greater draw. Most beginning high school girls use 15 to 25 pound bows; collegiate women archers use 24 to 30 pounds; men, 34 to 42 pounds. Heavier bows are used for hunting and fishing with some women selecting 30 to 45 pound weights. Field archery weights vary from 25 to 32 pounds for most experienced women archers.

Bow Parts. The parts of the bow are illustrated in Figure 5–5. The *riser* of the bow includes the center portion of the bow, with the handle, grip, arrow rest and arrow plate. The center portion should have enough weight, in addition to mass, to balance the force and weight exerted by the archer. Proper weighting increases the stability of the bow arm and thus, the control of the arrow and release. Most fiberglass and composite bows have built-up molded handles and grips designed to aid in balancing and distributing the force of the pull equally to the upper and lower limbs during the draw.

The *arrow rest* is a shelf attached to the bow or molded in the handle on the side of the bow. It secures the arrow during the draw and aim, but its greatest value is in assuring that the arrow leaves the bow at the same spot on every release. Approximately 10 per cent of all archers will be left-handed, and either special bows for the left-handed or bows with arrow rests on each side must be available. *Arrowplates* are inserted into the bow to protect it against the friction of released arrows. Horn or plastic inserts are very durable, but leather deadens the sound of the arrow on release and is considered superior by hunters.

Bowstrings. The best string to use depends upon the weight, length, style, and model of the bow. Both double and single loop strings should be purchased only for specific bow types. Strings made of Fortisan and Dacron or of Dacron with a nylon serving are considered superior to those made of linen or latex. The *serving* is the reinforced center of the string and should be thick enough to hold the arrow when nocked. Strings should be kept well waxed. The best strings are those which distribute stress from the draw evenly to the limbs of the bow. When a single loop bowstring is attached, the timber hitch knot should be used to tie the string at the lower nock.

Bow tip protectors prevent scuffing of the bow tip and help to hold the bowstring in place during stringing or storage. Manufactured tips are made of plastic or pliable rubber; however, the archer can secure the bowstring in the nock by twisting a small rubber band around the string at the nock.

Nocking Point. A nocking point is essential to the development of consistency and accuracy. It serves as a specific spot and indicator so that the arrow is always placed on the string at exactly the same point when nocked. Once a proper nocking point is determined, the arrow will be at right angles to the string at full draw. This angle is necessary for proper arrow trajectory following release. The average nocking point is approximately one-eighth of an inch above 90 degrees as measured from the arrow shelf to the bowstring.

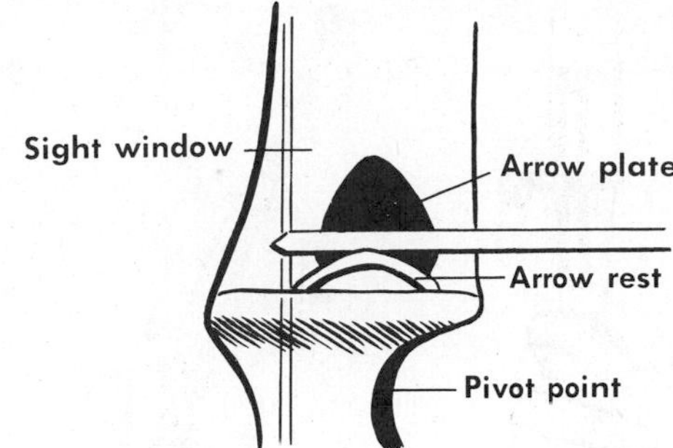

Figure 5–4 Arrow rest. (From Pszczola, Lorraine: *Archery*. Philadelphia, W. B. Saunders Co., 1971.)

Commercial nocking points are available; however, dental tape or plastic tape is equally effective. The tape should be built up sufficiently so that the arrow may be nocked below it, but rest securely against the base of the tape. Check the nocking point frequently for slippage.

Bowsights. A bowsight is a mechanical device secured to the bow to aid the archer in aiming directly at the target. It may be attached to either the face or the back of the bow directly above the arrow rest. Single setting sights are used for target shooting, and multiple pin settings may be used for

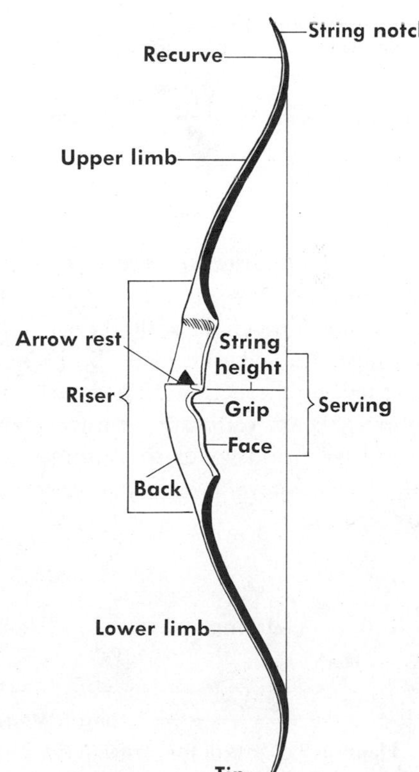

Figure 5–5 Bow with labelled parts.

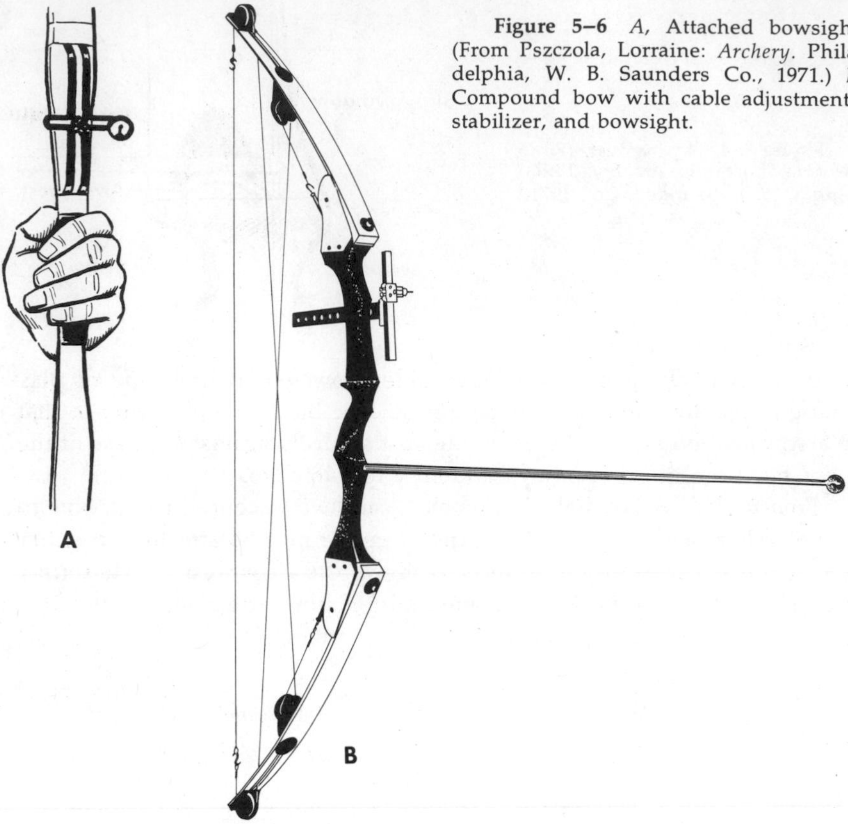

Figure 5–6 *A,* Attached bowsight. (From Pszczola, Lorraine: *Archery*. Philadelphia, W. B. Saunders Co., 1971.) *B,* Compound bow with cable adjustments, stabilizer, and bowsight.

hunting when distances are not established. Bowsights may be self-constructed for a few pennies or purchased for $2.00 to $20.00 for simple sights and as much as $100.00 for telescopic sights. Sights are constructed so adjustments can be made both *vertically,* for elevation, and *horizontally,* for windage corrections. There are numerous designs of metal or plastic; some sights are calibrated, some sit away from the bow on extension bars, some have hoods over the aiming device, and some are prismatic. Telescopic sights have a variety of apertures such as pin, post, peep and cross hair sighting.

Figure 5–7 Parts of the arrow. (From Pszczola, Lorraine: *Archery*. Rev. Ed. Philadelphia, W. B. Saunders Co., 1976.)

The beginner may make a bowsight in one of the following ways:

1. Mount a tongue depressor on the back of the bow above the arrow rest; clamp a bobby pin over the tongue blade so that it extends into the sight window view (arrow side). The bobby pin may be moved up and down, and the tip is used for target alignments.
2. Mount a strip of cork, sponge rubber, or self-adhesive material about six inches long and one fourth of an inch thick that is cut to fit the width of the back of the bow. Once the material is glued to the bow above the arrow rest, a beaded pin is inserted so the pin head protrudes into the sight view. The pin may be moved up and down and in and out as required to correct directional errors.

Arrows. The arrow is the scoring device in all archery events and in hunting and fishing. It is false economy to purchase poor quality arrows, because they do not reflect the true skill of the archer. Arrows are made from wood, fiberglass, or aluminum. Wooden arrows are the least expensive, but they have the disadvantages of splintering and warping easily. Fiberglass arrows are durable and easily maintained and are often the choice of field archers. Aluminum arrows are the most expensive but are considered superior, because they can be manufactured to specific degrees of flexibility and balance, resulting in a true arrow flight. Arrows should be matched in *length, weight,* and *spine,* since matched arrows travel consistently to the target with consistent releases. Arrows vary in weight, usually 250 to 300 grams; matched arrows vary only five grains from one another. Spine (the flexibility or stiffness of the arrow) is within 0.2 degree in matched arrows. Arrows must be spined to match the weight of the bow for greatest accuracy. Arrows vary in length from approximately 22 to 30 inches. Women commonly use arrows 24 to 28 inches long. Proper arrow length is very important, because an arrow that is too short may cause injury while one that is too long results in inaccuracy. Correct length can be determined by placing a yardstick against the archer's breastbone while she extends both arms and hands. The distance reached indicates the length of arrow needed. One may also place an arrow against the breastbone and extend arms toward the tip. The arrow is the proper length if the pile extends just beyond the fingertips of each hand. Some archers prefer to measure their arm spread from fingertip to fingertip and refer to an arrow-length chart based upon arm spread. Thirty-eight per cent of the total measurement is the recommended arrow length.

The structure of the arrow should be familiar to all archers. The tip of the arrow is the *pile.* These arrow points are fashioned in various shapes for the specific projectile of the arrow. Target piles are bullet or parallel style; the parallel field point is used for field archery; and hunting points are of many types, including blunt, broadhead, and fishing points. The blunt bird hunting point often has wire loops surrounding it, thus enlarging the striking portion of the arrow to approximately six inches.

The *shaft* is the longest portion of the arrow, and it continues into the *shaftment,* the portion which runs from the crest to the base of the arrow.

The *nock* is the notched end that fits the string of the bow. The vanes at the end of the arrow are called the *fletching* and are made of feathers or plastic. Generally, there are three feathers, although occasionally there are four. The fletching serves to stabilize the arrow through the wind currents it en-

Types of Armguards.

Training

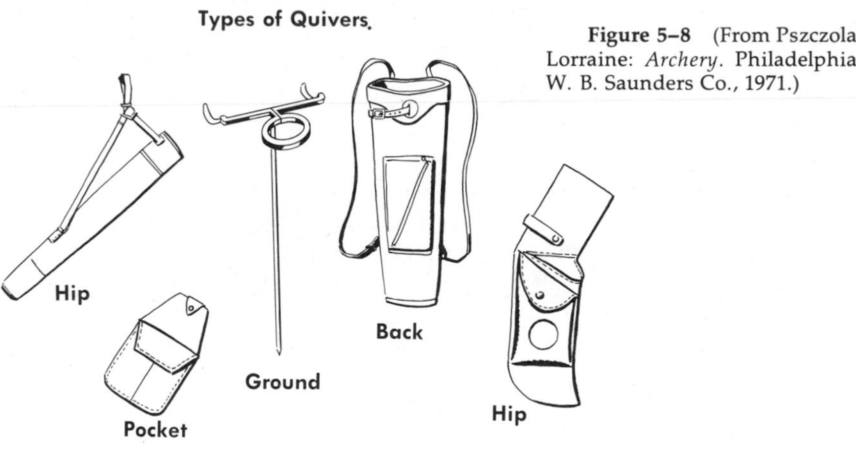

Figure 5–8 (From Pszczola, Lorraine: *Archery*. Philadelphia, W. B. Saunders Co., 1971.)

Types of Finger Protection.

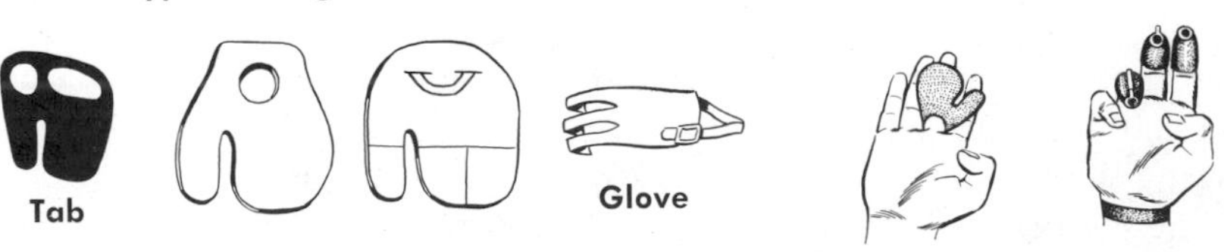

Illustration continued on opposite page.

Figure 5–8 *Continued.*

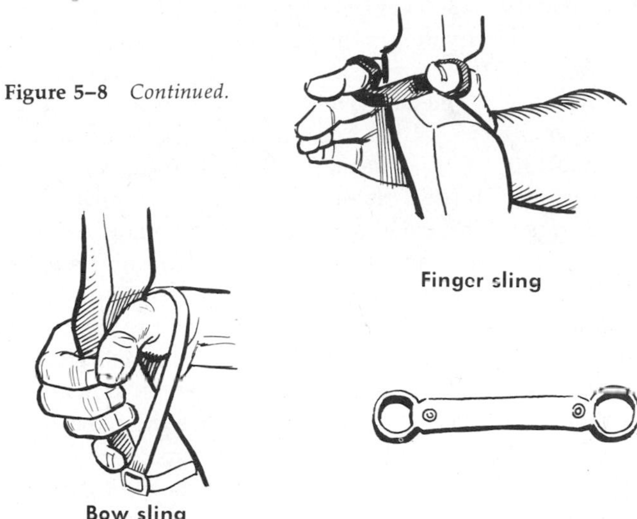

counters in flight; the feathers maintain rotation around the axis, thus resisting wind control. On an arrow with three vanes, two are of similar color and are called hen feathers. The third, more colorful, vane is the index feather, or cock, and is set at right angles to the groove in the arrow's nock. All the feathers are evenly spaced and of the same shape, height, and length. Size and design vary according to the size, weight, and purpose of the arrow. Target arrow vanes are usually small and are designed to resist wind alterations and result in freer flight; hunting arrows may have longer fletchings to increase flight time. A flu-flu fletch is often used to hunt birds and small game, because the large, full feathers slow the arrow flight quickly and ease arrow retrieval.

Finger Protection. Finger tabs or finger gloves are used to protect the middle three fingers of the drawing hand from friction of the string on release. They also aid in a smooth release. Leather tabs are less expensive than gloves and are used in most instructional classes. The index finger is placed through the smaller hole, and the second and third fingers are placed through the larger hole. The fingers contact the rough surface, and the tab is bent so the smooth surface contacts the bowstring. Some archers prefer the smooth leather glove which fits over the shooting fingers and is secured around the wrist or hand.

Arm Guards. Guards should cover the inner forearm, below the elbow and near the wrist, of the bow arm for protection against the string recoil and to offer the security and confidence needed to maintain a steady bow. A training guard which is much longer than the regular arm guard is manufactured. Guards are made of leather, aluminum or plastic and may be reinforced inside by metal ribs to assure firmness. They buckle or lace over the back of the forearm.

Quivers. Quivers hold arrows as well as other accessories. The type of archery activity determines the kind of quiver necessary. Target archers use back and hip quivers as well as ground quivers. Ground quivers are usually made of metal, have a pointed tip at the bottom, and are circle-shaped at the top, with a hook near the circle on which to rest the bow.

Back, hip, and pocket quivers made of leather and plastic are used by field archers. Hunters also use arm and bow quivers.

Slings. These devices keep the bow under control and in or near the archer's hand after the arrow is released. The sling allows the archer to use a relaxed hand on the bow. The *bow* sling is attached to the bow just below the grip; the archer inserts her hand into the large loop as she holds the bow. The loop fits around the archer's wrist and gives security to the hand on the bow. The *finger* sling is a device which attaches the index finger and the thumb to enclose the bow and secure the hand to the bow. Numerous materials are used—leather strips with slits at either end, nylon cord with finger loops, heavy rubber bands, and other homemade as well as custom-made designs.

There are numerous other accessories that may be needed as an archer increases in her skill. Such items are clickers, draw checkers, and kiss buttons which aid in shooting accuracy for the serious competitor.

The Target Range. The outdoor range should be on well mowed, level ground in a remote spot (preferably inside a fenced or roped-off area when located in a heavily populated play space). The target backdrop may be a nylon backstop, a hill, a cliff, or bales of hay. An open area may be used as long as there is an open space of no less than 30 yards behind the farthest target. The total range should be at least 75 yards long and marked with white shooting lines parallel to the line of the target at 20, 30, 40, and 50 yards. For a permanent range, place targets 10 feet apart, as measured from target center to center; cement blocks can be recessed into the ground, directly in front of each target, to indicate specific shooting positions.

An indoor range area of 30 to 50 feet, with 10 targets, 36 inches in diameter, placed side by side, will accommodate as many as forty shooters. All room exits and entrances must be kept locked while shooting is in progress. Targets should be placed three feet from the back wall on stands or suspended by wires or ropes. Angle the base of the target slightly toward the shooting line. Matts should be fireproofed if they are made of straw or excelsior. Backstops made of nylon netting, canvas, Fiberglas, or of heavy canvas mats will protect the wall and arrows. Floor quivers made of tennis ball cans nailed to square boards are practical in this setting. A 20-foot range and a 30-foot range can be set up in such an area.

Field Archery Course.* Field archery courses may be laid out on relatively rough, undeveloped land. The Flint Round is suggested as a beginning course. (See page 47.)

---

*For information on construction and complete rules, consult the National Field Archery Association, Route 2, Box 514, Redlands, California 92373.

Targets. Although bales of hay or heavy cardboard boxes stuffed with hay or straw can be used, rye straw, Indian grass and Johnson grass tightly wound in a coil and held together by tarred twine offer the best backing. The matt should be 48 inches in diameter (36 inches may be used indoors), 4 to 6 inches thick, and placed so that the center of the gold is 51 inches from the ground. The face is tilted slightly toward the sky.

Target stands are made of three soft pine, cedar, or cypress boards, 6 feet long, 3 inches wide and 1 inch thick, which are bolted into a tripod. On windy days ropes or ground hooks should be used to secure the target. Portable metal stands are convenient for class use but have a detrimental effect on arrows which strike the stand.

Preferably, the target face is made of oil cloth, but it may be of canvas or paper composition materials. The face should be painted in nonglare, yet bright, colors with a gold center 9⅗ inches in diameter and four concentric rings, each 4⅘ inches in width, colored red, light blue, black, and white. The outer edge, or petticoat, beyond the outer white ring should be 1 inch wide. If the target has a skirt, it encloses the edge of the mat and is tied with a drawstring in back.

Accessory Equipment on the Range. There are innumerable items that will be helpful on the target range. They include toe markers, points of aim, tongue depressors and pins, adhesive tape, extra bowstrings and towels or tassels for wiping arrows. *Score cards* should be kept to help motivate individuals and class groups. An alert instructor can note an individual's difficulty "in the making" and an individual's improvement by daily observation of the scores. Charts may be kept by teachers or students to show progress, plateaus in performance and ultimate achievement in a given period of time. A *first aid kit* with a supply of adhesive bandages, tweezers, antiseptic, and tincture of benzoin, which aids in toughening the fingers of the shooting hand, should be available.

ARCHERY SAFETY AND ETIQUETTE

Courtesy and safety are inseparable in archery. The penetrating power of an arrow is greater than that of a bullet and consequently, a bow and an arrow are dangerous weapons. Safety practices protect the archer as well as her fellow shooters. For self-protection:

1. Check all tackle for cracks, frayed strings, and imperfect arrows. Never shoot with a damaged bow, worn strings, or splintered arrows or with those improperly fletched.
2. Be properly equipped with glove or tab and arm guard. Wear suitable clothing that does not interfere with shooting.
3. Make certain arrows are long enough to avoid pulling the arrow within the bow.
4. Be sure bow is properly braced.

For the protection of others:

1. Everyone, when shooting, stands astride the shooting line.
2. Nock the arrow only after the signal is given to shoot. Nock only in the direction of the target.
3. One blast of the whistle signifies the beginning of shooting; one blast signals to stop shooting; two blasts indicate an emergency, and all shooting and activity stop.
4. After shooting, step back to the safety line until a signal is given for retrieving arrows.
5. If an arrow falls from the bow, retrieve it *only* if it can be reached by the use of the bow without changing your body position.
6. Release an arrow *only* if you can see the unobstructed target and a clear area behind it.
7. No one points an arrow at anybody; no one shoots for distance except on a specially marked field; no one shoots straight up into the air.
8. In drawing arrows from the target, be certain there is no one behind who might be injured by the sudden withdrawal of an arrow.
9. Target mates help one another look for lost arrows; all return together.
10. When different target ranges are used for a group, always use one shooting line and place the targets at the desired distances from the line.
11. Treat archery tackle with respect and never leave equipment unguarded where others might use it without proper instruction and caution.

PURCHASE AND CARE OF EQUIPMENT

Archery tackle should be bought for specific uses. Guidance by an expert will be helpful, whether purchasing modestly priced or individually constructed bows and arrows. Whether selecting a recurved fiberglass target bow or a yew hunting bow, make sure that:

1. The bow is straight. Before bracing the bow, place the lower nock on the ground, face of the bow toward the archer; place index finger under string at upper nock. If the bow is straight, the bowstring will bisect the bow the full length. When fully strung, the string should still bisect the bow.
2. Thickness of the bow tapers from approximately 1 1/8 inches at the handle to about 5/8 inch, no more than 3 inches from the handle on each limb. Bows should be at least a third wider than they are thick.
3. The bow has more bend in the upper limb than in the lower, and the limbs bend uniformly from handle to tip. The distance of the string from the bow is approximately 1/4 inch greater in the upper limb when measured at about the middle of each limb.
4. The bow is the proper weight, length, and construction for the archer and her purpose.

Bows may be protected by light cases when traveling or when stored for a period of time. After each use they should be unbraced, wiped thoroughly and placed horizontally on two pegs (one at either end) or hung vertically by the bowstring near the upper nock. *Never* let a bow stand. Store in a cool, slightly humid, ventilated area. Wooden bows should be waxed occasionally and refinished every few years.

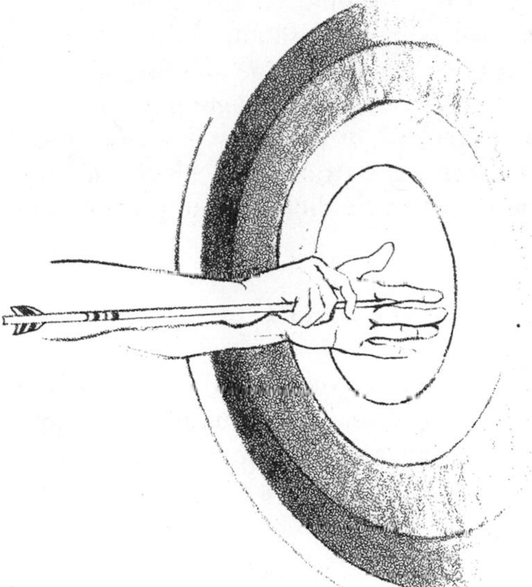

Figure 5–9 Removing the arrow from the target.

Bowstrings should be waxed frequently with paraffin on the serving and beeswax on the remainder of the string.

When selecting *arrows,* make certain they are (1) the proper length, (2) of a matched set (weight, fletching, spine), (3) marked with the same crest, and (4) the correct arrow for the archer's purpose.

After use, arrows should be dried and stored vertically, tips down, to avoid bending the shaft. Destroy cracked or splintered arrows; vanes, points, and nocks, however, can be replaced with a do-it-yourself kit. Wooden arrows that are warped may be heated and bent to original shape. Aluminum arrows may be straightened by the manufacturer or by the hobbyist with an arrow tube straightener. When storing arrows for a long period of time, spray the feathers with moth repellent.

When retrieving arrows from the target, place the back of one hand against the target with the index and second fingers close to the arrow. The other hand grasps the arrow close to the target and twists the arrow out at the angle it entered the target. The target hand exerts pressure on the face to prevent tearing. If the arrow is so deep in the target that the feathers are lodged, draw the arrow through the back of the target. If the arrow is in the dirt or grass with feathers out, remove straight backwards; if the feathers are caught, grasp the tip and pull forward. Hold arrows near the pile, fanned out so that the feathers do not touch.

Arm guards, gloves, and *quivers* are largely a matter of personal choice. They may be home made or bought reasonably. All leather equipment should be dried slowly when wet and cleaned occasionally with saddle soap or commercial leather cleaners.

Targets should be stored flat, face downward in a cool, humid area. Rodent repellent should be used on straw matts. Do not roll targets, because they lose shape and firmness. In dry weather when targets are in use, it is wise to spray a light mist of water on them to avoid extreme drying and breaking of the straw. Loose and soft conditions can be corrected by tightening the strings with which the target is bound. Repairing the condition is far more difficult than preventing it.

TEACHING UNITS

Suggested course content for beginning and advanced archery students follows. The selection of aiming techniques (gap, POA,* etc.) is dependent on the available equipment and the instructor's choice. POA is not included in the suggested units.

Beginning Students

- Brief History
- Selection of proper tackle
- Care of equipment
- Safety precautions
- Fundamentals
  - Placement of quiver
  - Use of glove or finger tab
  - Use of arm guard
  - Stringing
  - Stance
  - Bow hold
  - Nocking
  - Holding and drawing
  - Anchor points
  - Aiming (gap methods and bowsight)
  - Release
  - Follow-through
- Scoring
- Target shooting beginning at 20 feet, progressing to 20 and 30 yards
- Archery games (balloon shoot, etc.)
- Evaluation

Advanced Students

- Brief review of safety and etiquette
- Review of fundamentals
- Shooting at distances of 20, 30, 40 and 50 yards
- Introduce accessories to increase skill—slings, clickers, draw checkers, and kiss buttons
- Use of a commercial bowsight
- Review instinctive techniques for those who wish bare bow competition and hunting
- Field archery
- Flight shooting
- Clout shooting
- Prepare for competition, technically and psychologically
- Competitive events
- Evaluation

Programs for Inclement Weather

An indoor range is highly desirable, but where this is not possible, the following topics can be introduced to the group or in individual "modules" of written materials, filmstrips, loop films, etc., so that a person may advance at her own rate.

---

*Point of aim.

Historical materials (evolution of archery and its role in literature and art)
Care and repair of equipment
Terminology—puzzles, crosswords, etc.†
Tournament organization and etiquette

BASIC SKILLS

Many skills are basically the same for both target and field archery. Differences will be noted in the discussion that follows.

Prior to developing shooting skills, the beginner should determine her dominant eye. Although some archers shoot with both eyes open, the dominant eye aligns with linear objects, and consequently, the shooting (string hand side) arm should be on the same side as the dominant eye.

A simple method for determining dominance is to extend both arms in front of the body; the palms are facing away from the body and the fingers and thumbs overlap so that there is a small opening between the two hands. With both eyes open, focus on an object through the opening. Close the left eye; if the object remains in the opening, the right eye is dominant. To verify this, close the right eye and see if the object moves from focus. Occasionally a person may have "nondominance," and she may then shoot from the more natural side.

---

†Dorothy Hanpeter: Terminology teaser. *Archery-Riding Guide.* Washington, D.C., AAHPER, June 1964–June 1966, pp. 35–37.

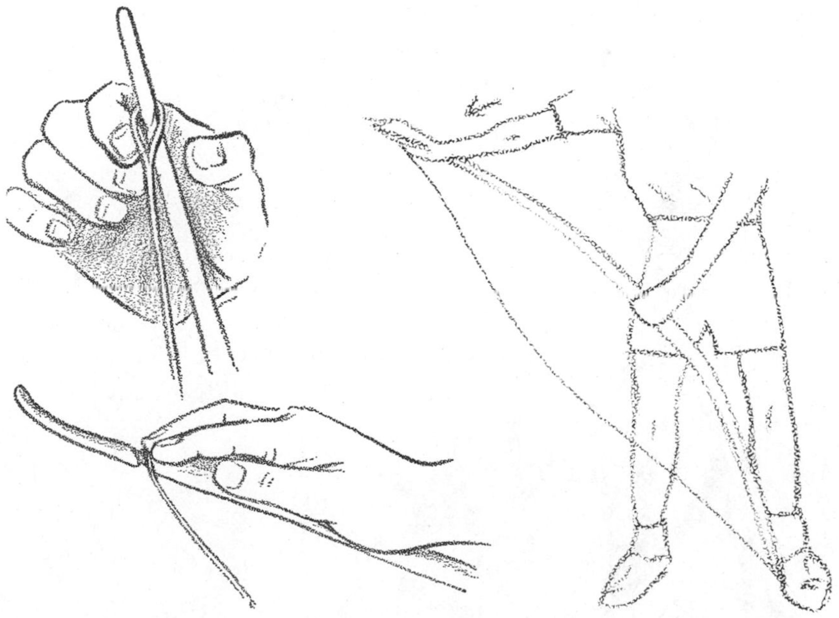

Figure 5–10 Bracing the bow.

Bracing and Unbracing the Bow. Bracing, or stringing, the bow is the process of bending the limbs and placing the loop of the string into the notch of the upper limb of the bow. Commercial stringers are most desirable, since they not only lessen the labor of stringing, but also equalize the stress on the bow while it is being strung and lessen the risk of twisting the lower limb or limb tip.

The *push-pull method* is frequently used on light-weight bows. The lower end of the bow, just above the nock, is placed against the inside arch of the left foot with the back of the bow facing the body. Be certain the loop of the string is in the lower nock. The bow tip does not touch the ground. The heel of the right hand is placed near the bow tip while the left hand, on the handle, pulls the bow toward the body. The heel of the right hand presses the upper limb of the bow down while the thumb and index finger slide up the bow to slip the loop into the nock.

To unstring the bow, the same hand and body positions are used. Using the principle of push-pull, leverage is applied. The upper hand *pushes* as the string is lifted from its nock by the index and middle fingers and is slipped down the bow as the left hand *pulls* the bow toward the body.

The *step-in method* of bracing is used on recurve bows, but it must be used with caution to avoid twisting the lower limb. A commercial bow stringer (when one is available) is the preferred method. With the right leg between the string and the face of the bow, face forward, the lower end of the bow rests on the instep of the left foot. As the right hand pushes the bow forward at the top of the upper limb, the bow handle is forced against the back of the right thigh, while being held by the instep of the foot. The left hand guides the string into the nock.

Figure 5–11 Step-in method of stringing.

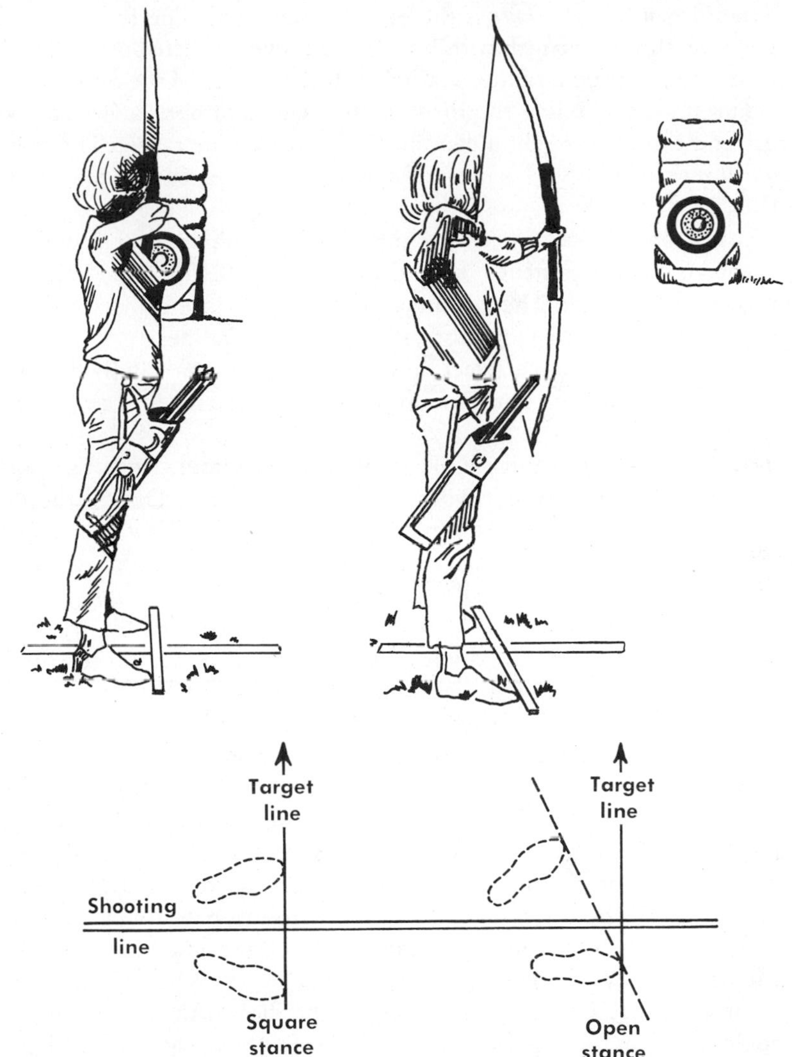

Figure 5–12 (From Pszczola, Lorraine: *Archery*. Philadelphia, W. B. Saunders Co., 1971.)

The Basic Techniques of Shooting. The act of shooting should be thought of and practiced as a whole; however, an understanding of each part of the total aids in analyzing performance for the beginner and improving performance for the more skillful archer. Each of the following affects the flight of the arrow; 1) stance, 2) bow hold, 3) nocking, 4) gripping the string and drawing, 5) anchoring, 6) aiming, 7) releasing, and 8) follow-through.

Stance. The stance refers to the positioning of the feet so that the body is comfortably balanced and properly aligned with the target. The two basic stances are the *square stance* and the *open stance.* The advantage of the more traditional *square stance* is the ease of alignment. The feet are spread apart at least shoulder width with body weight evenly distributed. The toes are placed on an imaginary line aligned with the center of the target. (Some archers prefer that the line run through the insteps of both feet.) The body is erect, and the forward shoulder and the head face the target. The body is relaxed; there is no sway or weight shift at any time during the draw or release.

The less natural *open stance* is achieved by moving the foot closer to the target approximately 6 inches back, thus allowing the hip and shoulder to open toward the target. The advantage is in giving more room for the bow arm and consequently, giving more stability and steadiness.

The decision of stance selection is largely a matter of individual comfort, balance, and secure bow arm. Archers must experiment to find their best position.

Bow Hold. The term *grip* is actually a misnomer, since the bow is never truly "gripped" except when nocking the arrow. During the draw, aim, and release, the bow is actually *pushed* by the bow hand against the force of the draw. The design of the handle affects the grip used on the bow. The smaller standard handle encourages a palm grip or hold and a *low wrist position.* The bow is braced against the palm, toward the fleshy portion near the base of the thumb. Although this position is used successfully by some, it is not recommended for the beginner, since as the bow is braced against the fleshy part of the palm, the wrist is dropped, and it becomes difficult to hold the elbow and shoulder in proper position.

The more desirable, extended, *high wrist position* is achieved by "shaking hands" with the bow. The forefinger and thumb of the bow hand lightly encircle the bow so that a V is formed by the thumb and forefinger at the balance or pivot point of the bow where pressure is exerted. The forefinger wraps around the bow for stability, and the thumb may touch the finger, thus closing a circle. The remaining fingers are relaxed and extended slightly toward the target. The bow is *not gripped; it is braced.* When the bow is extended toward the target in preparation for the draw, the bow arm is raised to shoulder height. The wrist is cocked slightly above, or directly behind, the hand. The arm is extended with elbow down and rotated slightly

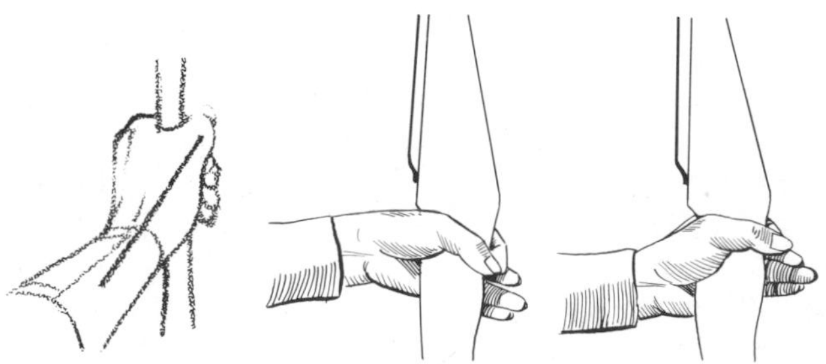

Figure 5–13 High and low hold positions on the grip.

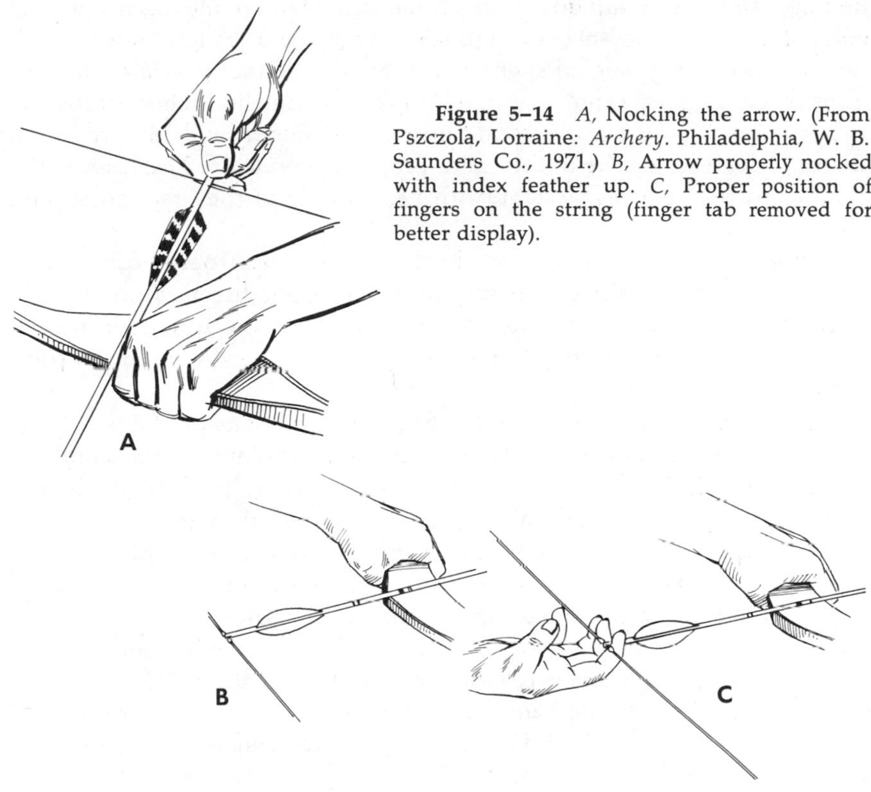

Figure 5–14 *A,* Nocking the arrow. (From Pszczola, Lorraine: *Archery*. Philadelphia, W. B. Saunders Co., 1971.) *B,* Arrow properly nocked with index feather up. *C,* Proper position of fingers on the string (finger tab removed for better display).

outward. The forward shoulder is down and rotated back to avoid leaning toward the target.

Nocking. The bow is held in a horizontal position with the back of the bow hand facing up. The arrow may be grasped by the thumb and index finger at the end of the arrow nock or on the shaft forward to the fletching. With the index feather up and away from the bow, the arrow is placed across the arrow rest, and the nock is placed on the string. Beginners will nock the arrow at a 90 degree angle to the string, but experienced archers use a nocking point $^1/_8$ to $^1/_4$ inch above 90 degrees. Arrows should be placed below a *nocking point,* a commercially manufactured or homemade device, which assures consistent arrow placement and thus eliminates one more possible variable toward successful shooting. (See Equipment.)

The index finger of the bow hand *may* be used to support the arrow until the string is grasped by the drawing hand.

Gripping the String and Drawing. After the arrow is nocked on the serving, the first three fingers of the drawing hand reach under the string and reach upward to contact the string. The index finger is placed above the arrow with the other two fingers below it. The arrow is *contacted* by the fingers directly above and below, but the arrow is *not squeezed or controlled* by the fingers. The fingers are at right angles to the string.

Either shallow or deep finger contact may be used. In each case the little finger and the thumb do not touch the string but are moved toward the palm of the hand; they may even touch. To achieve a shallow "hook" position, the string is contacted slightly in front of or in the groove of the first joint of the fingers. Using the deep hook position the archer grasps the string *between* the first and second finger joints. Either hold can produce a smooth release when the fingers relax properly on release. The back of the hand and wrist remains straight, with flexion only in the first and second finger joints.

The Draw. As the draw is made, the bow is raised from a horizontal to a vertical shooting position. The bow may be brought directly from the side of the body to a vertical position by the extended bow arm, or it may be raised above the head as the arm extends, and thus, lowered into a vertical position.

After the bow is positioned, the fingers act as hooks on the bowstring as the force of pull against the bow is exerted by the upper arm, shoulder, and back muscles. At the completion of a full draw the shoulder blades are close together, and the line from the tip of the arrow through the hand and elbow is straight. Often the elbow is slightly above the arrow tip. Taking a deep breath as the pull begins often facilitates a smooth draw.

Anchor Positions. Drawing an arrow to the same position with the same length of draw is imperative for developing consistency of the propelling force of the arrow release. The more reference or "check points" an archer has on string and hand position prior to release, the more consistent her performance will be. There are basically two anchor positions: *high* and *low.* The *low anchor* is most widely used by target archers and freestyle shooters. The string is drawn so that it bisects the face; that is, the string touches the tip of the nose and the middle of the chin. The forefinger of the drawing hand is under the jawbone. This position assures consistency of the position of the head and the aiming eye. Some archers purse their lips or "kiss" the string or have a kiss button (plastic disc) on the string that touches the lips on the draw and anchor.

The *high anchor* is preferred by some hunters, field archers and instinctive shooters, because they feel that the high position places the sighting eye so that the aim can be directly along the shaft. This position approximates that for aiming a gun. The anchor points vary, but a common high anchor places the tip of the index finger at the corner of the sighting eye. Others

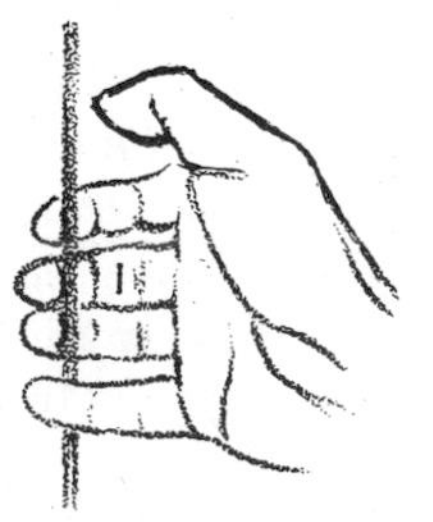

Figure 5–15 Placement of fingers in drawing the bowstring (archer's view).

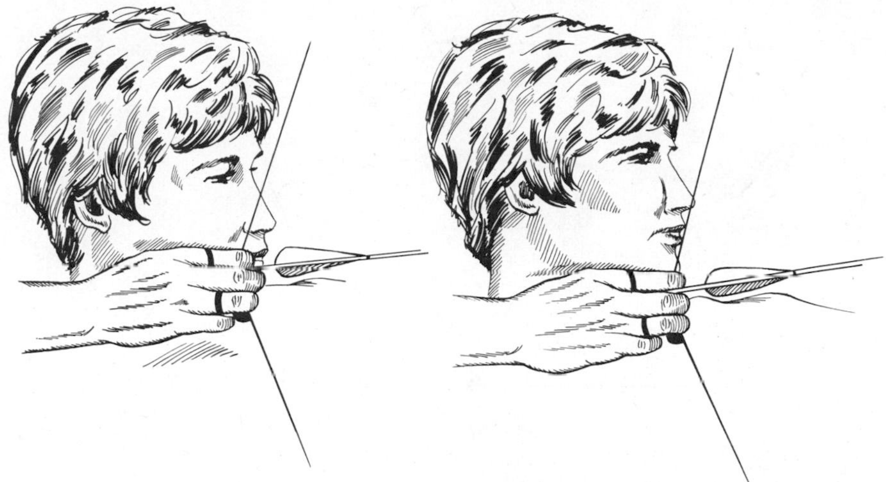

Figure 5–16 High and low anchor positions.

bring the string to the side of the face so that it touches the corner of the mouth with the upper surface of the forefinger resting snugly under the right cheekbone. Field archers often tip the bow and head 15 to 30 degrees to insure that the aiming eye is over the arrow.

No matter what anchor position is used, the anchor remains the same, and adjustments for distance and directional corrections are made in aiming techniques.

Aiming. Basically there are three methods of aiming—(1) instinctive, (2) bowsight, and (3) point of aim. A fourth technique, the gap method, is similar to point of aim and is discussed briefly.

The *instinctive* or bare bow technique implies shooting without a sight or point of aim marker. Beginning archers are usually introduced to this method until they become proficient in the fundamentals and are able to group arrows. Continued use of the instinctive method requires excellent eyesight, depth perception and developed kinesthetic awareness. This difficult bare bow technique used by hunters, field archers, and some target archers requires extensive experience until the bow arm automatically adjusts to the target as the archer concentrates and focuses on the target area, rather than on the arrow tip or hand. The secret of instinctive shooting is developing the knowledge of "how much and where" that comes from practice and familiarity with one's equipment.

The *bowsight* technique should be used by all serious target archers, since it allows the archer to aim directly at the target from every distance and is by far the most accurate aiming technique. Bowsights may be used in "freestyle" tournaments but are forbidden in those designated for bare bow. Sight design and construction are discussed on page 51.

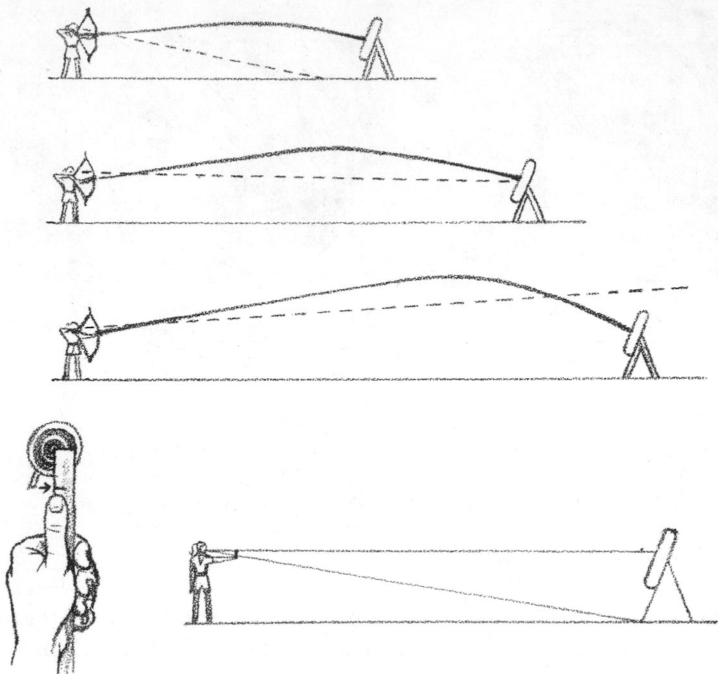

Figure 5–17 Determining the point of aim.

The sight is placed on the back of the bow, or on the front, if it is smoother, above the arrow rest. Bowsight settings must be established for every shooting distance. The right-handed archer sights from the right of the string through the sight to the small spot in the center of the gold. For the beginner to establish a setting, she must shoot a large number of ends from each distance. After arrows begin to group on the target face, corrections can be made. The greater the distance from the target, the lower the bowsight. Pin adjustments are always made in the direction of arrow grouping errors with the bow held in vertical shooting position. For example, the sight settings are moved down and to the left if arrows were grouped left and low. Once settings are established, the distance can be marked on the sight bar or the side of the bow. A rule of thumb in establishing other settings is that an archer generally lowers her sight approximately 3/4 inch for each additional ten yards from the target and, conversely, raises it 3/4 inch for each ten yards closer to the target. Most authorities recommend sighting with the dominant eye (right for right-handed shooters) and closing the other eye; however, some archers are successful in keeping both eyes open while letting the dominant eye guide the sighting.

Point of aim method (POA) is considered an outmoded technique with limitations and, if used, should serve only as a temporary procedure until bowsights are available. POA involves using a spot on the ground, target, or background at which the archer sights over her arrow tip. The aim point is dependent on the height of the shooter, bow weight, length and design of the drawn arrow, environmental conditions, and distance to the target. For shooting long distances the point of aim should be well above the target, for medium distances, on or near the target, and in front of the target for short-range shooting. The point of aim should be lowered when arrows go over the target and raised when they go below it. There is only one distance, *point blank range,* when the tip of the arrow can be aimed directly at the target center. This distance may not coincide with an established shooting distance.

After a POA is found for a specific distance it should be recorded on a range finder for future use. A short stick or tongue depressor can serve as a range finder when it is held by the extended bow arm in a precise shooting position with the top of the thumbnail (which approximates arrow position when placed on top of the index finger) matching the point of aim. The arm must be held steady for accurate placement. The top edge of the stick is aligned with the eye to the center of the gold, and the inside edge of the stick bisects the target. To use the range finder, stand on the shooting line with range finder in hand as it was when the distance was recorded, with bow arm extended. Align the top of the stick with the center of the gold and the inside line so that it bisects the target. Look down the stick until the marking for the specific distance is found. Note a spot on the ground, target, or background where the sighting will be directed over the arrow point.

Gap method of aiming is similar to POA, since the archer sights over the tip of the arrow to a selected spot. It differs from POA in that once the bow arm is set, the eyes focus on the target rather than on the point of aim. The distance between the aiming point and the desired point of arrow entry is called the gap. Pregap technique determines the gap from a shooting position prior to the draw; postgap technique determines the gap from a full draw position. Beginning archers often find the gap methods helpful in learning instinctive shooting. The principle of this technique is that it sets the shooter's arm on a plane with the target and in proper position so that at draw, her concentration can be entirely on the spot she intends to hit.

Release. The release is the simple act of relaxing the fingers and forearm to loose the string so that the arrow can fly to its predetermined target. All of the preparation of the draw and aim are realized through the release. *Concentration* is the key to establishing the timing of the neuromuscular sequence, and *relaxation* is the critical factor for a smooth release that does not alter the established flight path. The back muscles are contracted, and as the hand steadies and the eyes sight, a message is sent to the central nervous system. The back muscles contract slightly, and as the fingers release, the hand is pulled back along the neck.

Follow-Through. What body movements occur *after* the release of the arrow do not affect arrow flight; however, the body, arm, and head positions at release should be maintained until the arrow reaches the target. This "after hold" position allows the archer (or her teacher) to concentrate on her form and the possible mistakes which might have occurred prior to the release which are reflected in the follow-through. The points to be checked are: (1) erect body with shoulders back and down; (2) head toward target with eyes focused on target spot; (3) bow arm extended toward the target and the bow hand easily holding, but not gripping, the bow so that the bow moves naturally after the release; and (4) the string hand and arm move back with the hand relaxed as it passes the side of the neck.

CLASS ORGANIZATION

Ideally, each student should have her own tackle, but regardless of the amount of equipment and the size of the class, a partner system should be used with beginners. If equipment is very limited, three lines, one person shooting and two behind the line and the shooter, can be used. If equipment is shared, the partners should use the same arrow lengths and bow weight, if possible. The partner not shooting will aid in checking the shooter's form.

Prior to formal instruction in shooting, check eye dominance (see page 68) and alert those who shoot with the right hand and have left eye dominance, or vice versa, that they should attempt to draw with the hand corresponding to eye dominance; otherwise, arrows tend to cluster in the direction of the dominant eye. A review of safety precautions, including proper attire and removal of jewelry, pencils, and the like should also take place.

At the first session it is best to have the bows already strung so that students can immediately begin shooting techniques. Bracing the bow is introduced later but is best accomplished by a commercial bow stringer. Tackle should be numbered, with corresponding numbers on the storage racks. A student should use the same equipment each class period. Students should be responsible for returning equipment at the end of the class. Left-handed archers will be grouped at the right end of the shooting line so that they can easily watch the demonstrations of the instructor. The line may change to a semicircle for demonstrations, since it is easier for all to see and hear from this formation. All instruction is at the shooting line. Initially, this line may be only twenty feet from the targets, but as archers progress, a single line is determined so that targets may be placed at 20, 30, 40, 50, or more yards from the archers. (See Figure 5–18.)

Before any shooting is done, the use of the whistle should be explained. *One* blast from the whistle means either begin shooting or retrieve arrows. The blast to retrieve arrows is blown only after all shooting is completed and the archers have stepped back from the shooting line. Two or more blasts indicate an emergency, and all shooters stop, return arrows to the quivers, and step back from the shooting line.

Squad organization may prove best for large classes, since groups can be rotated for various shooting distances, archery games, and testing.

Table 3. Shooting Chart Summary – Common Causes of Shooting Errors

Arrows grouping high	Arrows grouping low	Arrows grouping right	Arrows grouping left
1. Straightening the bow arm at release	1. Dropping the bow arm on release	1. Moving bow arm to right	1. Hunched bow shoulder
2. Raising the bow arm on or before release	2. Failing to bring the arrow to full draw before release	2. Turning bow hand to right before or during release	2. Flinching the bow arm
3. Leaning away from target	3. Creeping or pushing the arrow forward on release	3. Top of bow tilted to the right	3. Moving bow arm to left
4. Releasing before arrow is lowered to aiming position	4. Dropping the bow shoulder toward the target	4. Body weight on the toes rather than distributed	4. Tilting top of bow to left
5. Dropping the elbow or hand of the drawing arm on release	5. Anchoring too high	5. Jerking or plucking string to right on release	5. Cocking bow wrist to right on release
6. Opening the mouth, causing the anchor point to be lowered	6. Pursing the lips or lifting the chin, causing anchor to be raised	6. Gap and POA too far to right; bowsight extended too far left.	6. Weight on heels and body leaning backward
7. Overdrawing by bringing the string beyond the anchor point	7. Drawing upward rather than straight back	7. Extreme right errors occur when left-handed archer sights with right eye	7. Gripping bow with fingers and pressing on right side of bow
8. Jerking hand back and inward on release	8. Dropping right elbow, breaking alignment of drawing arm	8. Wind blowing from left to right	8. Arrow shaft away from bow on release
9. Arrow nocked low	9. Using only wrist and hand pull rather than shoulder and back		9. Moving string hand too far to the right so release is away from the face.
10. Gap aiming – gap is too small POA – placed too high Sight – placed too low	10. Gap aiming – gap too large POA – placed too low Sight – placed too high		10. Squeezing arrow with fingers and "controlling" it left
11. Tail wind	11. Head wind		11. Gap and POA too far to left; bowsight not far enough to left
			12. Extreme left errors result when right-handed archer sights with left eye
			13. Wind blowing from right to left

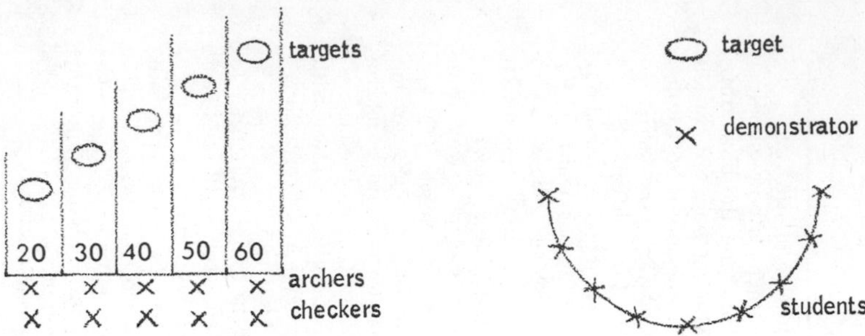

Figure 5–18 Suggested class organizations.

Homogeneous pupil grouping is favored by some instructors, but many feel that placing a novice with a more experienced or skilled archer produces faster learning. Equal ability grouping provides more incentive in class tournaments.

TEACHING PROGRESSION

As soon as all tackle has been properly fitted to each student and safety rules have been introduced, the instructional objective is immediate participation and immediate success. In the initial stages there should be no insistence on perfect form. The class must gain a clear understanding of the basic steps in shooting: the stance, bow hold, nock, grip of string, draw, anchor, aim, release, and follow-through. Introduction to each of these steps may be first without an arrow but accomplished mimetically, step-by-step, as the instructor explains and demonstrates. First, she faces the group; then she turns her back so that they can replicate her movements. The draw will be made without the string in the first trials. Thereafter, a group at the shooting line repeats these steps in their first attempts at shooting toward a target. The instructor may break down the complete movement by using key words until the archer is familiar with the progression. This should *not* be continued for a long period of time, since each archer will set her own timing, particularly during the aim. The following key words may be used:

Count 1 (Stance)	Establish the stance
Count 2 (Bow hold)	Hold bow properly with arm straight at the side
Count 3 (Nock)	Nock arrow on the serving
Count 4 (Grip)	Grasp string in preparation for the draw
Count 5 (Draw)	Raise bow to vertical position and draw string
Count 6 (Anchor)	Anchor (either high or low) and hold
Count 7 (Aim)	Initially, make a general sighting toward the target; later, the gap method or bowsight is used
Count 8 (Release)	Loose the string so that the arrow flies free
Count 9 (Follow-through)	Hold position, allowing for natural recoil, until arrow hits target

Following the first experiences of shooting at close range with little concern for form or aiming techniques, the high anchor and gap aiming are introduced, followed by bowsight aiming and a low anchor. Individual progress will vary, and throughout the unit, time must be given to each individual to correct form and faults. A suggested outline for a beginner's unit follows.

Lesson I

1. Equip each archer with necessary and proper tackle
2. Explain the safety rules
3. Demonstrate and explain the basic steps of shooting. Demonstrate the steps without the use of an arrow; the bowstring is not drawn, but the hand executes the acts of draw, anchor, and follow-through mimetically
4. Have the class execute the basic steps in shooting without an arrow, as demonstrated
5. Class members join their assigned partners with one on the line and the other back. With complete tackle, the instructor "talks" the shooters through the basic steps as they shoot six arrows. Change partner positions and repeat. Target distance is 20 feet
6. Stress bow hold, anchor, and hook position of the drawing hand at end of period review

Lesson II

1. Review safety precautions
2. Describe and demonstrate the nine basic steps of shooting
3. Shoot from 20 feet (at least a round of three ends)
4. Explain predraw gap aiming and high anchor position. Demonstrate
5. Move to 10 yards and shoot several ends using pregap aim and high anchor position. Explain the relationship to instinctive shooting
6. Explain scoring

Lesson III

1. Issue a self-checklist and progress chart record to each student, and explain its use by the individual
2. Shoot two ends from 10 yards; two ends from 20 yards
3. Instructor begins individual analysis of form. Aid each to identify faults in others so that all can serve as student coaches when partner is shooting

Lesson IV

1. Introduce bowsight aiming and low anchor position. If possible, use simple pin sights initially. Explain method of setting sight following arrow clusters
2. Shoot three ends at 20 yards
3. Adjust sights as necessary, checking anchor position. Shoot two ends from 20 yards. Mark sightings
4. Stress the importance of consistent anchor position and relaxed release with afterhold (follow-through)

Lesson V

1. Continue shooting at 20 yards for three ends
2. Using sight, move to 30 yards and shoot until consistent sighting is established
3. Instructor must be alert to errors of each individual. (Note error and correction chart on p. 71)

Lesson VI

1. Shoot and score three ends at 20 yards; at 30 yards
2. Check individual analysis charts and progress charts to pinpoint weaknesses. Verify with the "coaching partners"

Lesson VII

1. A complete review of form prior to moving to the 30-yard target for those who have been scoring consistently at 10 and 20 yards. Not all students will be ready to progress
2. Establish sighting for 30 yards
3. Continue to work on individual form and skill

Lesson VIII

1. Introduce novelty events or clout shooting for those making normal progress
2. Instructor is available to confer and work with any student who expresses difficulty or seeks help to improve form and score

Lesson IX

1. Review of materials covered in the unit. Teacher-student evaluation and question-and-answer session
2. Skill test and beginning of class tournament. Allow an opportunity for students to give written evaluations of their own progress and comments about the conduct of the course

Lesson X

1. Written examination of knowledge concepts
2. Each student turns in her self-checklist and progress chart
3. Completion of class tournament

SKILL DIFFICULTIES AND THEIR CORRECTION

Stringing the Bow

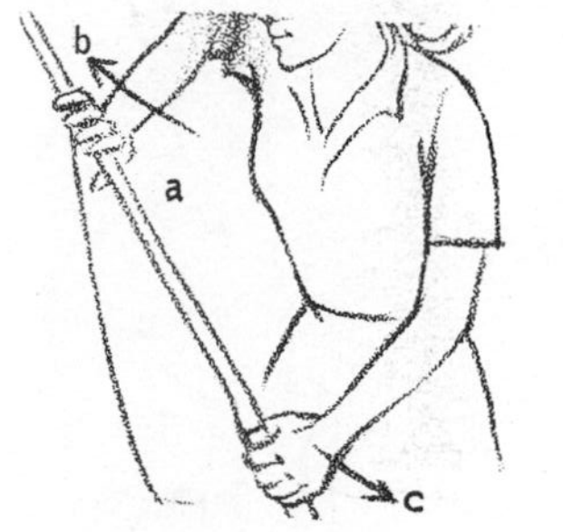

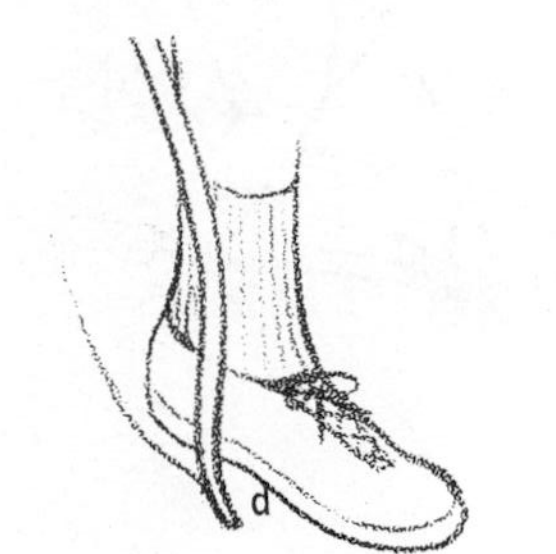

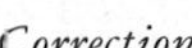
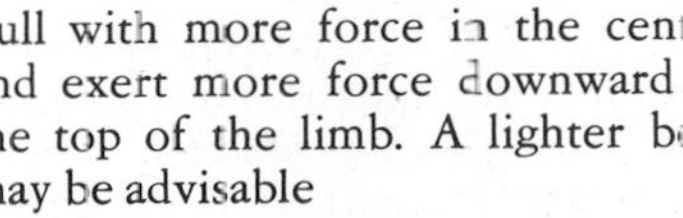
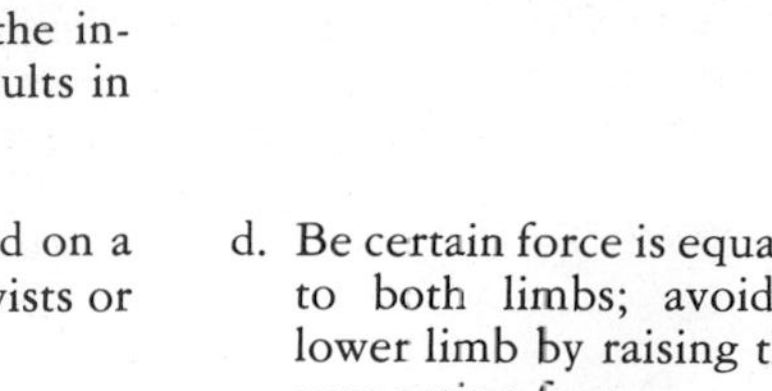
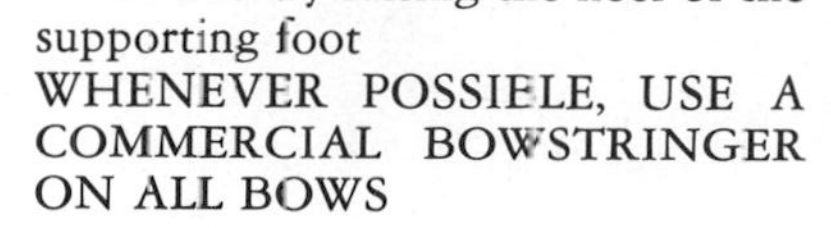

Difficulty	*Correction*
a. Inability to bend the bow far enough to put string in nock	a. Pull with more force in the center and exert more force downward at the top of the limb. A lighter bow may be advisable
b. Turning the bow away from the body and losing leverage and power	b. Suggest that the elbow of the arm at the center of the bow remain close to the body as the hand turns the bow toward the body
c. Pushing the bow end into the ground when using the push-pull method rather than bracing it against the instep of the foot. This often results in tip cracks or breaks	c. Press tip of lower limb against instep, as illustrated, with tip off the ground
d. Using the step-through method on a heavier bow, the lower limb twists or breaks	d. Be certain force is equally distributed to both limbs; avoid turning the lower limb by raising the heel of the supporting foot WHENEVER POSSIBLE, USE A COMMERCIAL BOWSTRINGER ON ALL BOWS

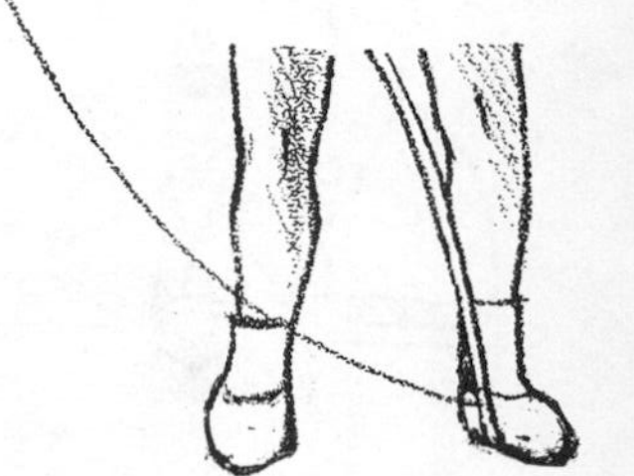

Stance

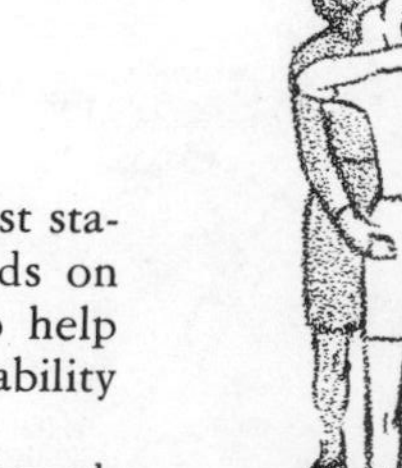

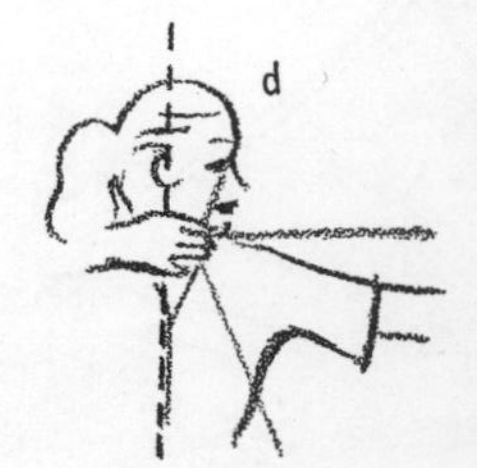

Difficulty	*Correction*
a. Body weight unequally distributed, either on the front foot or the rear foot, causing erratic arrow flight	a. Ask student to achieve the most stable base; instructor holds hands on student's hips as she draws to help her "feel" a weight shift and stability
b. Stance is too narrow or too wide, making stability difficult to maintain	b. Insist upon a comfortable, but broad, stable base. Demonstrate and have student try both square and open stances
c. Improper body alignment with the target	c. Place body at right angles to the target, feet astride; and then move forward foot slightly back if open stance is desired
d. Stance limits proper draw or results in string's slapping arm	d. Suggest that archer open her stance to allow more bow room and arm stability

Holding the Bow

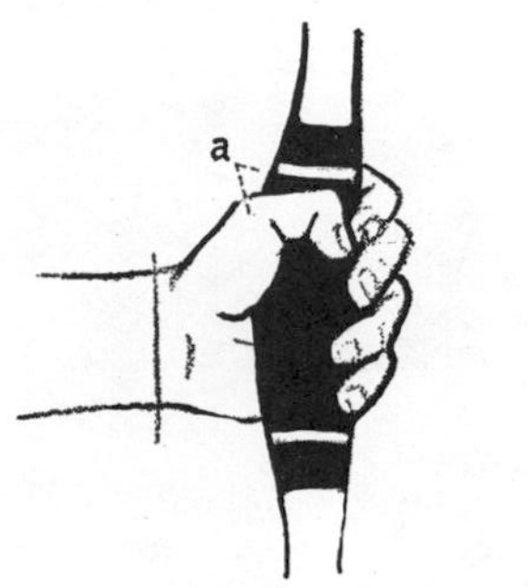

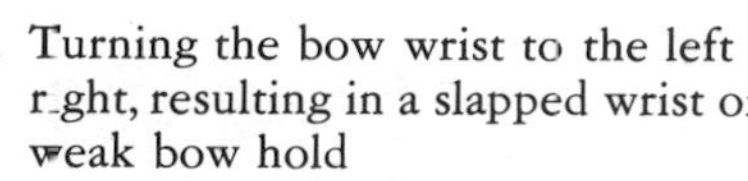

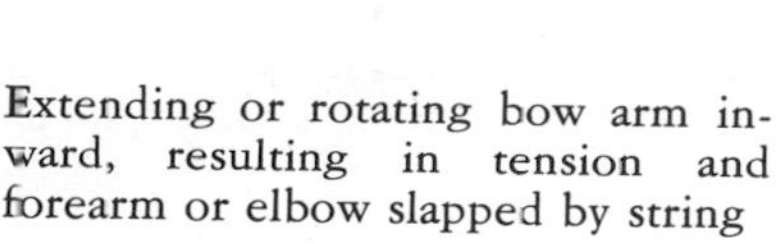

Difficulty	*Correction*
a. Actually "gripping" the bow tightly, which results in tension and resistance to the draw	a. Student should review section on holding the bow, stressing that forefinger and thumb are on the handle with other fingers extended *forward.* Bow rests in the "V" of the hand and pressure is exerted on the belly of the bow on the draw
b. Turning the bow wrist to the left or right, resulting in a slapped wrist or a weak bow hold	b. Practice drawing string only a short distance while concentrating on a straight wrist and forearm behind the hand. Increase the draw while continuing to feel the pressure of the bow against the "V" of the thumb and forefinger. (Low wrist position is common with smaller grip; high wrist position is encouraged with all bows and particularly with larger gripped recurves)
c. Extending or rotating bow arm inward, resulting in tension and forearm or elbow slapped by string	c. The clue is, "elbow down and slightly out"; emphasize pull of the string more than push of the bow arm

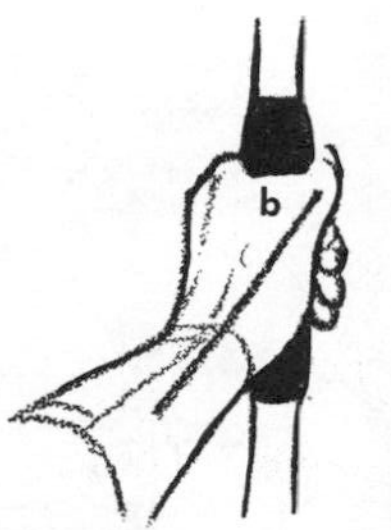

Nocking the Arrow

Difficulty	*Correction*
a. Index feather not perpendicular when nocked, often resulting in damaged feather and erratic flight	a. Check ridge on arrow nock; turn arrow on arrow rest so that index feather is up. When looking down at the back of her hand, index feather is up.
b. Failing to nock the arrow at a 90 degree angle (or slightly above for advanced archers) on the serving, resulting in erratic flight trajectory	b. Place a nocking point on the string so that the arrow is consistently placed below it. (Use tape, commercial nocking point, etc.)

Gripping the String and Drawing

Difficulty	*Correction*
a. Squeezing or pinching the arrow so it falls from the arrow rest	a. Concentrate on pulling the string, not the arrow. The arrow is *contacted* by the fingers above and below, but it is not held if properly nocked and string is drawn correctly. Imagine the arrow is a drinking straw that must not be bent
b. Fingers fail to grip the string at right angles, resulting in a pull to the right or left	b. The fingers are in "hook" position. Suggest that the student make a "Boy Scout salute" with thumb and little

	finger touching over the palm, and the other three fingers straight. Make a hook by flexing the tips of the three fingers. The fingers are hooked on the string, usually with the string in the crease of the first joint
c. Draw is executed by fingers and arm, resulting in inconsistent release and fatigue	c. Instructor illustrates the use of back, shoulder, and upper arm muscles; show how close the shoulder blades come on a full draw
d. Hunching forward shoulder or leaning away from target, resulting in low or high arrow flight	d. Instructor or partner holds a small rod parallel to normal shoulder alignment and calls attention to hunching, if it occurs. A rod or stick may also be used to illustrate leaning away from the target, but holding at the waist and hips helps to develop kinesthetic awareness in the archer
e. Dropping head forward and tipping bow to sight	e. Target archers should be reminded to look at the tip of the arrow and then at the target in gap shooting and at the sight in bowsight shooting. Do not look along the arrow to aim it like a gun. Check for eye dominance if archer finds it difficult to keep head up and forward

Anchor Position

Difficulty	*Correction*
a. Anchor is drawn to right of proper anchor point, resulting in arrow's going to left of target	a. Whether high or low anchor point is used, be certain it is consistent. Low anchor is suggested for beginners at target, and the string should bisect the nose and chin. When high anchor is used, be certain the point of anchor is *always the same*
b. Anchor is too high on the face for proper aim	b. See a above. Practice draw and anchor in a mirror to see if the anchor is really where you "feel" it and want it
c. Archer opens mouth, thus drawing deeper with arrow flight higher; conversely, pursing lips results in less draw and lower flight	c. Stress *consistency* in anchor position and facial set. Get a "shooting face" with clenched teeth and tight lips or pursed lips. Practice in front of a mirror
d. Moving head toward string	d. Stand erect and use back muscles, pulling shoulder blades together.

Aiming

Difficulty	*Correction*
a. Aiming with nondominant eye	a. Review section noting how one determines eye dominance. Close nonsighting eye if aiming is not consistent
b. Failure to hold long enough to get correct sighting before release	b. Practice draw and anchor without release until it is comfortable with little tension. *Concentration* is the key word in holding the position until sight and steadiness are attained
c. Numerous difficulties arise in aiming, such as tipping head to sight along the arrow, for there are several techniques and often, the principles are misunderstood. An inexperienced archer has difficulty releasing at the proper time when the sighting or aim is momentarily established. Tension can destroy the aim	c. The instructor suggests that the student review the materials on "aiming." Once knowledge is gained, stress practice and relaxation

Release

Difficulty	Correction
a. Moving the string hand forward and collapsing the bow arm when shooting the arrow	a. Remind the student to hold shooting position a bit longer after arrow leaves the bow
b. Holding the string too far back in fingers resulting in loss of arrow or jerky release.	b. Remind student to hook the string at the first joint
c. String hand jerks or flies away from the string, resulting in erratic arrow flight	c. Remind the archer that the fingers simply relax to loose the string. Place bow hand on anchor point, back of hand toward face, and palm forward; then place hook of bow hand against the other hand as if pulling the string. Release by relaxing; check to see that the release is in a straight line with a follow-through

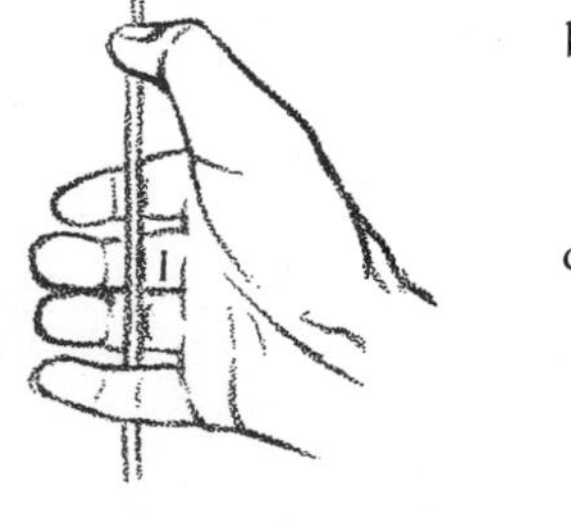

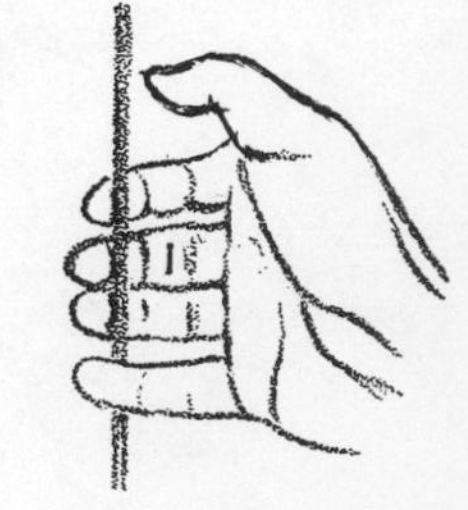

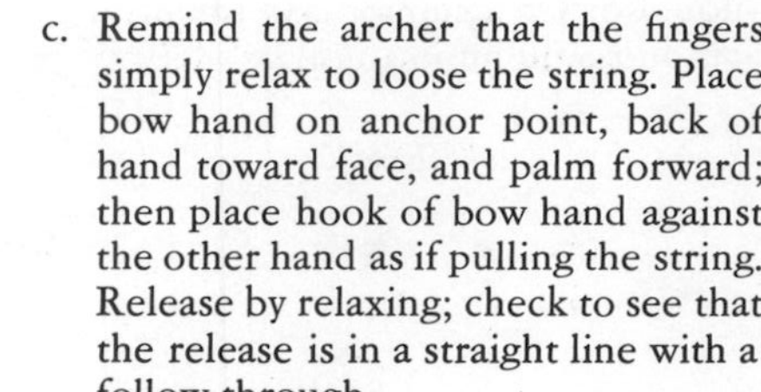

d. Moving the string hand forward (creeping) at the moment of release	d. Remind the student to hold the anchor position and to follow through after release. Review the bow hold position; the arm is extended so the pull is against the bow hand
e. Tension in bow hand and arm, resulting in throwing bow arm to left or right.	e. Relax bow hand as soon as string is released. A natural movement of the bow slightly down and to the side is expected. Shoulder remains steady. Arm guards give a sense of security and safety. Concentrate on contraction of back muscles. If tension and unsteadiness continue, try a lighter bow

Follow-Through

Difficulty	*Correction*
a. Failure to hold follow-through or "after hold" position often indicates poor muscular contraction in back and shoulder	a. Suggest that the student hold, as if posing for a picture, until the arrow reaches the target
b. Failure to follow through may indicate that archer is moving to see the arrow flight, shooting too fast, dropping the bow arm, or relaxing her string hand.	b. Again, stress the "pose." Although movements after the release do not affect the arrow flight, if a follow-through does not occur, it indicates errors in technique. Hold until the instructor or partner can analyze for corrections

EVALUATING THE RESULTS

Evaluative tools are useful for the student who wishes to assess her progress, whether she is in an individual, self-paced program or in a group instructional class. Assessment techniques should also serve as motivating forces for the student and teacher. Sound evaluation serves as the basis of student grades. The following means for evaluating the knowledge, affective, and motor skill development are suggested:

1. Written objective tests of rules, equipment, shooting techniques and safety precautions.
2. Results of archery tournaments.
3. A progress chart of daily scores kept by each archer on her individual record card.
4. An analysis technique form chart based upon correct shooting fundamentals as assessed by the instructor and by one's shooting partner in class.
5. Use of the Hyde Archery Test* for college women. The test uses the Columbia Round, and the scales are sufficiently wide in range to provide a means for evaluating the success of both beginning and advanced archers. Test administration and test scales are noted in several measurement books.†

TERMINOLOGY

AAC—The American Archery Council.

AIAA—American Indoor Archery Association.

Anchor point or **anchor spot**—The point under the jawbone where the target archer's index finger is consistently placed at the draw position prior to release. A higher point, placing the tip of the index finger at the corner of the sighting eye *or* on a spot underneath the cheekbone with the string at the corner of the mouth for field archery and hunting.

Arm guard—A protective piece of leather, plastic, or composition material worn on the bow arm to prevent abrasion by the released string.

Arrow plate—An insert of hard, protective material placed above the arrow rest; the arrow rubs against it when drawn and on release.

Arrow rest—A small ledge on which the arrow rests slightly above the grip.

Back—The side of the bow away from the string and toward the target when shooting.

Belly—A once frequently used term, now obsolete, for the *face* of the bow.

Bow arm—The archer's arm that holds the bow while shooting.

Bow bracer—A device designed to brace a bow efficiently and safely.

Bowsight—A mechanical aiming device that may be adjusted so that the archer may aim the point of her arrow directly at the center of the target.

Bow weight—The force, expressed in pounds, required to draw a bow a given distance (usually 28 inches).

Brace height—The manufacturer's recommended distance from the pivot point of the bow to the string when the bow is braced.

Broadhead—An arrow point used in hunting; it has several flat blades with sharp edges.

Brush button—A small rubber object placed at each end of the bowstring when hunting to eliminate string noise on release.

Butt—Another name for "target," usually straw mat, hay, or excelsior.

---

*Hyde, Edith I.: An Achievement Scale in Archery. *Research Quarterly,* 8:2, May, 1937.

†Mathews, Donald K.: *Measurement in Physical Education.* 4th ed. Philadelphia, W. B. Saunders Co., 1973

Cant—To tilt the bow to the right or left when drawn.
Cast—The ability of a bow to release an arrow; refers to the speed that a bow imparts to the arrow.
Closed stance—Position of the feet on the shooting line so that the line to the target runs from the toe of the foot away from the target, through the instep of the target foot, and thus to the target center.
Clout—Competition in which arrows are shot in the air with trajectory to fall on a distant ground target.
Cock feather—An obsolete term for "index feather"; the vane or feather at right angles to the nock. It is usually a different color from that of the other feathers or vanes.
Composite bow A bow made of two or more materials; often the center is wood and the back and face are of fiberglass.
Creeping—Allowing the string hand to edge forward while aiming or at the moment of release.
Crest—Colorful painted bands on the arrow shaft below the fletching that aid in identification.
Cross hair sight—A bowsight made of a circle of glass on which two lines cross at right angles.
Dead release—Releasing the string with no follow-through. Generally, the hand follows the string or remains inert; this error in release is due to restricted use of the muscles of the back.
Draw—Spreading the bow and string from brace height to anchor position.
Drawing fingers—The middle three fingers of the string hand.
Drift—The movement of the arrow to either side of the target because of wind conditions.
End—A specified number of arrows, usually six, that are shot before retrieving and scoring.
Face—The side of the bow facing the archer when shooting.
Finger tab—A small piece of leather or composition material designed to be worn on the string hand for finger protection and smoother release.
Finger sling—A leather or composition strip designed to loop over the thumb and index finger of the bow hand and aid the archer in maintaining a relaxed grip during the release and follow-through. It keeps the bow from falling from a relaxed hand.
Fletching—The three or four feathers or vanes on the arrow.
Flinch—A movement of the bow arm at release as a result of fear of being slapped by the bowstring.
Flu-flu—Feathers arranged in spiral fashion to resist windage effects while hunting or field shooting.
Grip—The center of the bow where it is contacted by the bow hand.
Group—A cluster of arrows that are in approximately the same place on the target.
Heeling—Pushing against the bow with the palm or fleshy part of the hand, rather than with the more correct position of the "V" between the thumb and index finger of the bow hand.
Hit—An arrow which scores.
Holding—Holding an arrow at full draw while steadying or aiming, prior to release.
Index feather—The feather or vane at right angles to the slit in the nock.
Instinctive aiming system—Aiming and shooting without sighting devices. Often called bare bow method.
Jig—A device for holding feathers or vanes while fletching an arrow; also, a device for holding a string in place while making a bowstring.
Lady paramount—Presiding woman official in tournaments.
Limbs—The upper and lower portions of the bow above and below the grip and riser.
Long bow—A relatively straight bow with no built-in curves.
Loop—The reinforced ends of the bowstring that fit into the bow notches.
Loose—The release of the arrow toward the predetermined target.
NAA—National Archery Association of the United States of America; the association governs target archery.
NFAA—National Field Archery Association; the association governs field archery in the United States.
Nock—The device at the base of the arrow which has a slit into which the string is fitted during nocking.
Nocking—The act of placing the arrow on the string.
Nocking point—A specific point on the string, marked with a nock locator, thread, or marking pencil, where an archer's arrow should be placed prior to each release.
Open stance—Position of feet on the shooting line so that the line to the target runs from the instep of the away foot through the toe of the target foot and thus, to the target center.

Overbowed—Shooting with a bow which is too heavy for the strength and endurance of the archer.
Overdraw—Unsafe act of drawing an arrow point back so far that it passes the face of the bow; drawing the bow beyond its safe distance.
Overstrung—A bow with a brace height greater than desirable; usually the result of too short a string.
Peeking—An undesirable habit of moving the head or eyes toward the arrow or target during release and arrow flight.
Peep sight—A bowsight or string sight designed with a small hole through which the archer looks at the target center.
Petticoat—The part of the target face that extends beyond the scoring area.
Pivot point—The fulcrum or spot on the grip where the "V" of the hand is located during the draw and release.
Plucking—Snapping the string hand out to the side and away from the anchor point when releasing the arrow.
Pointblank range—Shooting distance at which the aim and the arrow flight follow the same path.
Point of aim—An outmoded technique which involves using a spot on the ground, target, or background at which the archer sights over the arrow tip.
Point—The arrowhead or end of the arrow which enters the target.
Post sight—A bowsight which projects a bar, with a right angle projection upward or downward. The end of the angled bar is the point which is aligned with the aiming spot on the target.
Quiver—One of many types of devices for holding arrows—on the ground, on the bow, and on a person.
Range—Indoor or outdoor area designated for shooting. Also, a distance to be shot.
Recurved bow—A bow with limbs that have a reverse curve (toward the back of the bow). The recurve design provides quality cast and smoothness.
Release—A term which has replaced "loose"; it is the release of the string by the fingertips which sends the arrow on its flight.
Riser—The rigid portion of the bow directly above and below the grip.
Round—Shooting a prescribed number of arrows at a given target from specified distances.
Serving—The reinforcing thread at the center and ends of the bowstring which serves to protect the string from wear.
Shaft—The main portion of the arrow.
Shooting glove—A full glove or partial glove used for protection of the string fingers.
Shooting line—A line designating the distance from the target; the archer straddles the line in target archery and stands behind the line and posts in field archery events.
Sight window—An area on the upper limb of the bow, above the grip, and cut away to allow the arrow to be released closer to the center of the bow.
Spine—The flexibility or stiffness of an arrow.
Square stance—Foot placement on the shooting line so the toes of both feet are on an imaginary line aligned with the center of the target.
String fingers—The three fingers used to hook and draw the string.
String notch—Often referred to as "notch," it is the groove near the tip of each limb into which the string fits when the bow is braced.
Tackle—Archery equipment.
Target captain—The person assigned to a target and designated to call the value and pull arrows for archers on the target.
Target face—The scoring area on the material placed on a butt or matt.
Tassel—Cloth used to wipe soiled or wet arrows.
Timber!—Term used as a warning in field archery.
Timber hitch—A knot used to tie a single looped string to the lower notch.
Torque—An undesirable twist imparted to the bow during bracing, drawing, anchoring, releasing, or follow-through.
Toxophilite—An ardent student or practitioner of archery.
Underbowed—Shooting with a bow which is too light for the strength and potential of the archer.
Understrung bow—A bow with too little brace height, usually the result of too much string length.

Vane—Thin plastic fletching.

Wrist sling—A light leather, string, or composition device attached to the bow below the grip and looped around the archer's wrist to prevent the bow from falling during release and follow-through. It aids in relaxing the hand and fingers of the bow arm.

DISCUSSION QUESTIONS

1. Explain the differences between the long bow and the recurve bow. Which type is considered to provide the better quality draw? What is meant by cast of the bow? By torque?
2. Use of a bowsight is considered superior to point of aim technique in target archery. Discuss several sights, and explain how one satisfactory sight may be made for class use for a small amount of money and a little time. What archers prefer bare bow techniques of aiming?
3. Discuss your teaching methods and strategies for teaching the basic technique of shooting with its eight important components. Discuss or outline the progression you would follow with a group of beginning target archers.
4. Plan an archery tournament for 60 participants. What (a) entry qualifications, (b) safety regulations, (c) methods of officiating, (d) type of tournament, and (e) kinds of awards would you suggest?
5. Demonstrate the techniques for correcting the common errors of consistent grouping (a) below the target, (b) to the right and high, (c) to the left and low. Explain how bowsight adjustments must be made for such corrections.
6. Plan a period of archery games for your class. Consider the safety of all archers, placement of the activities, number of persons participating at one time, and the value of the games selected.
7. With several other class members, plan an instructional unit which would be appropriate for the beginning archer. The module should be self-paced, with audio and visual materials. Although a unit on the history of archery or recreational values of archery may be selected, also develop an instructional unit related to techniques or beginning tournament archery or safety.

SELECTED AUDIOVISUAL AIDS

Archery. (Super 8 film loops, 3⅔ min. each, silent, color.) Ealing Film Loops, 2225 Massachusetts Avenue, Cambridge, Massachusetts 02140. (Purchase)

Archery for Beginners. (16 mm., 12 min., silent, b&w.) Shick Film Service, 6157 Yarmouth Avenue, Reseda, California 91335. (Rental)

Archery—an Introduction. (16 mm., 18 min., sound, color.) Ben Pearson Film Library, 421 North Altadena Drive, Pasadena, California 91107. (Rental)

Archery for Girls. (16 mm., 11 min., sound, b&w.) Shick Film Service, 6157 Yarmouth Avenue, Reseda, California 91335. (Rental)

Archery Fundamentals (16 mm., 10 min., sound, b&w, color.) Shick Film Service and Bailey-Film Associates, 11559 Santa Monica Boulevard, Los Angeles, California 90025. (Rental)

Archery with Larry Hughes. (16 mm., 8 min., silent, b&w.) Shick Film Service, 6157 Yarmouth Avenue, Reseda, California 91335. (Rental)

The Art of Archery. (16 mm., 12½ min., sound, color.) Grayling Film Service, R.D. #1, Grayling, Michigan 49738. (Rental)

Bowfishing Fun. (16 mm., 11 min., sound, color.) Grayling Film Service, R.D. #1, Grayling, Michigan 49738. (Rental)

Introduction to Field Archery. (16 mm., 12 min., sound, color.) Harold C. Ambrosch Productions, Box 3, Rancho Mirago, California 92270. (Rental)

Straight as an Arrow. (16 mm., 20 min., sound, color) Easton Aluminum, 7800 Haskell Avenue, Van Nuys, California, 91406. (Rental)

Fins, Feathers, and Fur. (16 mm., 25 min., sound, color.) Grayling Film Service, R.D. #1, Grayling, Michigan 49738. (Rental)

SUGGESTED READINGS

Archery-Golf Guide. Current ed. American Alliance for Health, Physical Education and Recreation; National Association for Girls and Women in Sport, 1201 Sixteenth St., N.W., Washington, D.C. 20036.
Barrett, Jean A.: *Archery.* Pacific Palisades, California, Goodyear Publishing Co., 1969.
Burke, Edmund: *The History of Archery.* New York, William Morrow and Co., 1957.
Elmer, Robert P. and Gillelan, G. Howard: *Modern ABC's of Bow and Arrow.* Harrisburg, Pennsylvania, Stackpole Books, 1967.
Elmer, Robert P.: *Target Archery.* New York, Knopf and Co., 1946.
Keaggy, Dave J., Sr.: *Power Archery.* Second ed., Power Archery Products, Paradise Valley, Arizona, 1968.
Klann, Margaret L.: *Target Archery.* Reading, Massachusetts, Addison-Wesley Co., 1970.
Miller, Myrtle: *Practical Aids for Archery Instructors.* Roxbury, Vermont, Teelawooket Archery Camp.
National Archery Association: *The Archer's Handbook.* Ranks, Pennsylvania, Clayton Shenk, 1968.
National Field Archery Association: *Official Handbook of Field Archery,* Redlands, California, 1965.
Pszczola, Lorraine: *Archery.* Rev. Ed. Philadelphia, W. B. Saunders Co., 1976.

PERIODICALS AND PAMPHLETS

Archery Skill Test Manual. American Alliance for Health, Physical Education, and Recreation, Washington, D.C. 20036
Archery. Official publication of the National Field Archery Association. Route 2, Box 514, Redlands, California 92373. (Monthly)
Archery World. Official publication of the National Archery Association, Market Communications, Inc., 534 North Broadway, Milwaukee, Wisconsin 53202. (Bimonthly)
Bow and Arrow. Gallant Publishing Co., 34249 Camino Capistrano, Capistrano Beach, California 92624. (Bimonthly)
Bowhunter. Blue J Publishing Co., Inc., P.O. Box 5377, Ft. Wayne, Ind. 46805.

ORGANIZATIONS

American Indoor Archery Association (AIAA). P.O. Box 174, Grayling, Michigan 49738.
Archery Manufacturers Organization. R.D. #1 Box 119, Bechtelsville, Pennsylvania 19505.
National Archery Association (NAA). 1951 Geraldson Drive, Lancaster, Pennsylvania 17601.
National Field Archery Association (NFAA). Route 2, Box 514, Redlands, California 92373.
Professional Archers Association (PAA). Route 1, Box 32, Hickory Corners, Michigan 49060.

CHAPTER 6

BADMINTON

Badminton developed from the ancient game of battledore and shuttlecock played in Siam and China over 2000 years ago. The influence of ancient heritage is still reflected in the national sport status given badminton in India, Malaysia, Indonesia, and Thailand. A modified version of the ancient sport known as "Poona" caught the attention and enthusiasm of British Army officers stationed in India. They brought the game to England around 1870. The Duke of Beaufort gave real impetus to the game at his estate, Badminton House, in the rural hamlet of Badminton in Gloucestershire. The racket sport spread rapidly throughout the world and reached America via Canada.

Increased popularity in the United States can be noted from 1929, resulting in the formation of the American Badminton Association in 1936. The ABA speaks through its official publication, *Badminton, U.S.A.,** and the association has sponsored an annual National Championship since 1937 and the Junior National Championships since 1947.

International competition is held in men's singles and doubles, women's singles and doubles, and mixed doubles. The All-England Tournament, with a 75 year tradition, remains the oldest and most prestigious annual championship. The Thomas Cup for men, first held in 1949, and the Uber Cup for women, initiated in 1957, are held every three years and represent the highest levels of international competition. Women's competition gained impetus in 1970 with the inauguration of the National Intercollegiate Badminton Championships of the Association for Intercollegiate Athletics for Women.

---

*For information regarding this magazine, write to Beatrice Massman, Editor, 333 Saratoga Road, Buffalo, New York 14226.

Badminton may be a leisurely activity for the inexperienced or a challenging and exciting competitive experience for the skilled performer. The badminton racket is light and easily handled, and the air resistance to the cone shaped shuttle allows players to regulate the speed of the game through style and manner of hitting. Youngsters and beginners quickly learn to hit the shuttle across the net while advanced players demonstrate strategy and skill of shuttle placement coupled with agility and endurance for long rallies and grueling matches. Badminton can be played outdoors with heavier shuttles, but tournament play must be conducted indoors because of the sensitivity of the shuttle to air flow. Accidents and injuries are minimal, court area is moderately small, and equipment costs are reasonable enough to assure badminton as a game for all ages in schools, camps, playgrounds, and back lawns.

NATURE AND PURPOSE OF THE GAME

Badminton is a racket game played by two (singles) or four (doubles) players on a level rectangular court. The object of the game is to serve the shuttle strategically and thereafter direct it with speed or accuracy to an unprotected point on the opponent's court so that the opponent is unable to return it across the net or into the proper court area. Conversely, the opponent attempts to prevent the shuttle from falling to the court on her side of the net and to return it to an unprotected spot in her opponent's court.

GAME RULES AND SCORING*

A game of women's singles is 11 points, whereas a game of men's singles, men's and women's doubles, or mixed doubles is 15 to 21 points as arranged. A match is the best of three games unless otherwise determined. The winner of the toss has the option of serving first, receiving first, or choosing side of court. Players change ends at the beginning of the second game and the third game, if played. In the third game players change courts when the leading score in a game is 6 in a game of 11; 8 in a game of 15; or 11 in a game of 21. The side winning a game serves first in the following game.

"Setting" is a method of increasing game points when the score is tied. In a game of 11 points, when the score is 9-All the player who first

---

*See American Badminton Association *Official Rules* or NAGWS *Tennis-Badminton-Squash Guide* for complete rules.

reached 9 has the option of setting the game to 3. When the score is 10-All the player first reaching ten points has the option of setting the game to 2 points. In games of 15 or 21 points the option of setting by the side first reaching the score is 13-All, 5 points; 14-All, 3 points; 19-All, 5 points; and 20-All, 3 points. After a game is set the score is called love-All, and the side which first scores 2, 3, or 5 points, as set, is declared winner.

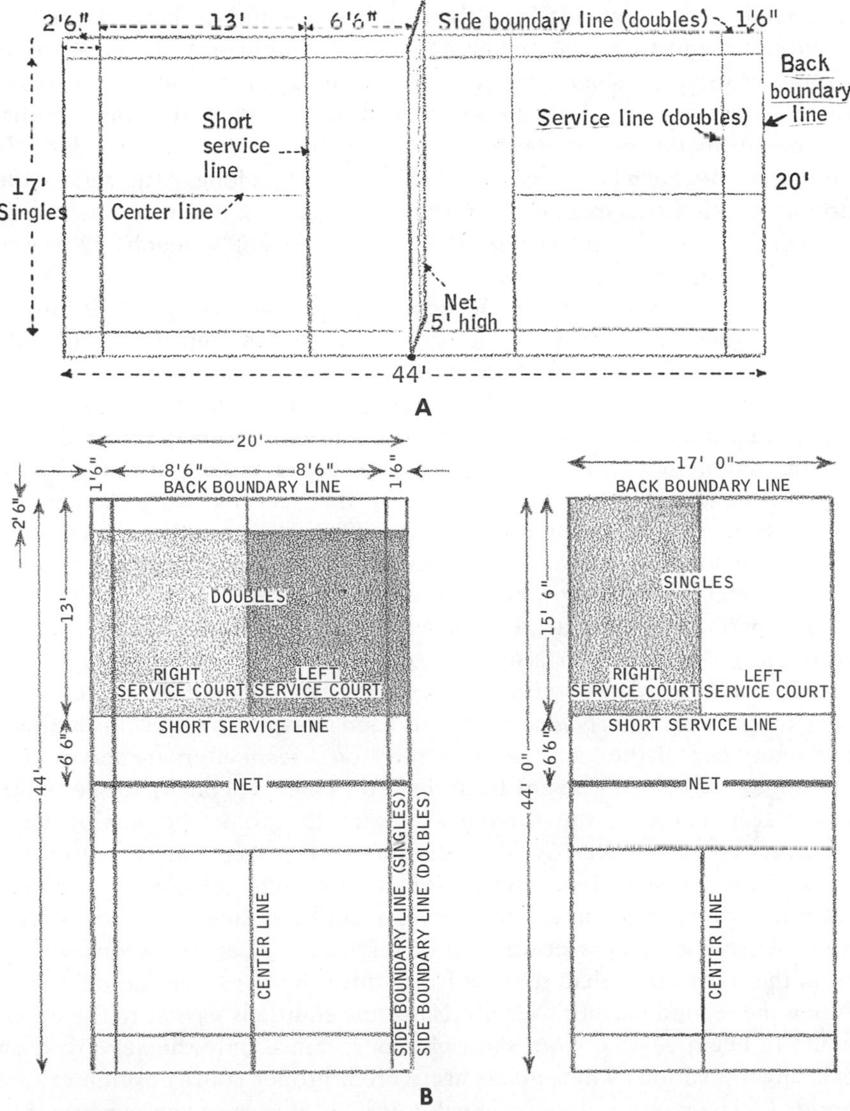

Figure 6–1 *A,* Badminton court. *B,* Badminton singles and doubles court. (From Vannier, Maryhelen, and Poindexter, Hally Beth: *Physical Activities for College Women.* 3rd Ed. Philadelphia, W. B. Saunders Co., 1975.)

A side rejecting the option of setting at the first opportunity *may* set at the second opportunity. Setting is not permitted in handicap games.

The singles court is 17 feet wide and 44 feet long overall; the doubles court is 20 feet wide and 44 feet long overall. (See Fig. 6–1.) Each is divided by a net 5 feet, 1 inch from the floor at each side of the court, tapering to 5 feet in the center of the court. The singles service court extends from the short service line (6½ feet from the net) to the baseline and from the center court line to the singles side boundary line. The doubles service court extends from the short service line to the back doubles service line and from the center line to the doubles side boundary line. Comparatively, the singles court service boundaries are long and narrow; for doubles they are short and wide. Following service the singles court extends from the net to the back boundary line and to each singles side boundary line. Each court is 17 feet wide and 22 feet long. After service the doubles playing area extends from the net to the back boundary line and to each doubles side boundary line. This is a total area of 20 feet by 22 feet on each side of the net.

Points are scored only by the serving side. The serving side is known as the "in" side; the receiving side is the "out" side. A fault by the "in" side results in loss of service. A fault by the "out" side results in a point for the server and continued service. In the singles game the server begins her serve from the right court and serves the shuttle diagonally across the net to the opponent's right service court. Thereafter court position of both players for the serve is determined by the server's score. When the server's score is an even number of points (0, 2, 4, 6, etc.) the service is delivered from the right court to the receiver's right court; when the server's score is uneven (1, 3, 5, 7, etc.) the serve is delivered from the left court to the opponent's left court. Each player must move to the proper court to accommodate the server's score.

In doubles, only one player serves at the beginning of the game. Actually, the serving side begins with one hand down. However, throughout the remainder of the game both partners on a team alternate serves. Service in doubles always begins from the right court diagonally to the opponent's right court. If the serving side wins the point the serving team members change court positions, and the same player continues to serve from the left court. Receiving players *do not* exchange courts. A player continues to serve from alternate courts until her side loses her service right. After one hand is down (loss of service), her partner begins service from the court other than the one from which the last serve was delivered. When the second partner's service is lost the shuttle is passed to the opponents to begin service from the right court. Since only the serving team exchanges positions when points are scored, proper court position can be verified; players are in their original positions (at start of game) when *their* score is an even number. When players are in courts different from original positions, *their* scores are uneven numbers.

Basic Playing Rules

1. The serve must be executed underhand and in such a manner that the shuttle is struck no higher than the server's waist. The racket head must be completely below the server's hand at the moment of contact.
2. Only one attempt at service is allowed unless the shuttle is cleanly missed.
3. The feet of both the server and the receiver must be within their respective courts, not touching any line. The feet must remain stationary within these courts until the shuttle is contacted by the server.
4. A service that strikes the top of the net and continues into the proper service court is a legal serve.
5. The server may not serve until the opponent is ready. She is deemed ready if she attempts to return the serve.
6. Only the player served to may return the service.
7. The shuttle must be struck cleanly by the racket head or frame only once before passing to the opponent's court.
8. The shuttle remains in play when it strikes the top of the net and continues over the net.
9. A player who attempts to hit a shuttle on service or during play and who cleanly misses may repeat the serve or attempt to strike the shuttle in play before it contacts the playing surface.
10. A let shall be called and the point replayed with no penalty if the following errors are discovered *before* the next service:
    a. player serves out of turn
    b. player serves from wrong court
    c. player stands in wrong court to receive

    If either server or receiver is not in the correct court and the discovery is not made until after the next serve, the play shall stand.
11. A let shall be called if any player is accidentally hindered from making a return by outside objects including spectators.

Faults

A fault is an infraction of the rules for which a penalty is assessed against the offender. A fault by the individual or team serving results in loss of service; a fault by the individual or team receiving results in a point for the serving team. A *let* may be called with no penalty assessed, and the serving player serves again. In addition to faults in executing the above general rules, the following are common faults of play:

1. The shuttle is hit into the wrong service area or out of the service area by the server.
2. The shuttle is hit out of bounds; it hits the ceiling, walls, or other obstruction.
3. The shuttle fails to cross to opponent's court or falls into hitter's court.
4. A player hits the shuttle twice in succession or the shuttle is hit by a player and her partner successively.
5. A player intentionally balks an opponent before or during service.
6. A player obstructs an opponent.
7. A player reaches across the net to make a return. It is legal to follow through with the racket across the net if net contact is not made.
8. The shuttle strikes a player or a player's clothing.
9. A player touches the net or net posts with her racket, person, or clothing while the shuttle is in play.
10. The shuttle is carried or slung when struck.

FACILITIES AND EQUIPMENT

The rectangular court is marked with lines ($1\frac{1}{2}$ inches wide) of white, yellow, or other distinct color. An unobstructed ceiling height of at least

26 feet is essential above the court, and at least 4 feet of clear space should surround the court. The walls surrounding the court should be a dark color to offer a contrasting background to the shuttle in flight.

Net posts are placed on the side boundary lines equidistant from the back boundary lines. If the net posts cannot be placed on the side boundary lines, vertical markers must be placed from each sideline to the top of the net to orient the player to the court. The net is 2½ feet in depth, is tautly strung to a height of 5 feet, one inch, at the side boundaries, and tapers to 5 feet in the middle of the court. The net is made of small diameter cord of dark color with mesh openings from ⅝ inch to ¾ inch in size. It is edged on top with 3-inch tape doubled over the small sturdy support rope or cable. When not in use, nets should be folded and stored in a cool, dry place.

Badminton rules do not dictate size, shape, or weight of the racket. Generally, rackets weigh 3¾ to 5½ ounces and are approximately 26 inches in length. Leather- or composition-wrapped handles range in size from 3½ to 4½. Proper balance is a more important factor than weight in racket selection; however, a lighter racket allows for more speed in stroking, and a heavier racket provides more power. The head and shaft of the racket are constructed of laminated wood, tubular metal, or a combination of wooden head and metal shaft. Racket heads are strung with gut or nylon. Gut strings offer great resiliency but lack the durability of braided nylon. Gut-strung rackets must be protected from moisture, and wooden racket heads should be stored in presses to prevent warping. Nylon-strung metal frames need no special care; however, a rack or a cart on wheels facilitates storage and ease of racket distribution for class use.

A variety of shuttlecocks are available for indoor and outdoor use. Plastic and nylon shuttles are more durable and less expensive than feathered shuttles and are widely used for instructional and recreational purposes. Some nylon shuttles are approved for Class B tournament play. The official Class A tournament shuttlecock is made of 14 to 16 matched goose feathers inserted into a cork base which is covered with lightweight leather. Flight speed of feathered shuttles is dependent upon the lead shot weight added to the base and the design of the tips of the feathers. The usual weight for indoor use is approximately 79 grains with rounded end feathers and 76 grains with feathers with pointed ends. A common measure of acceptability for play is that an average player can drive the shuttle from back line to back line. Shuttles going beyond are too heavy; those falling short are too light. Students should be encouraged to straighten the feathers before each serve; avoid kicking or stepping on the shuttle. Plastic or nylon shuttles should be stored in a cool, dry area, whereas feathered shuttles should be kept at between 60 and 65 degrees with a humidity of 70 to 75 per cent. A damp towel placed around the cardboard tube is usually sufficient moisture to prevent the feathers from becoming brittle.

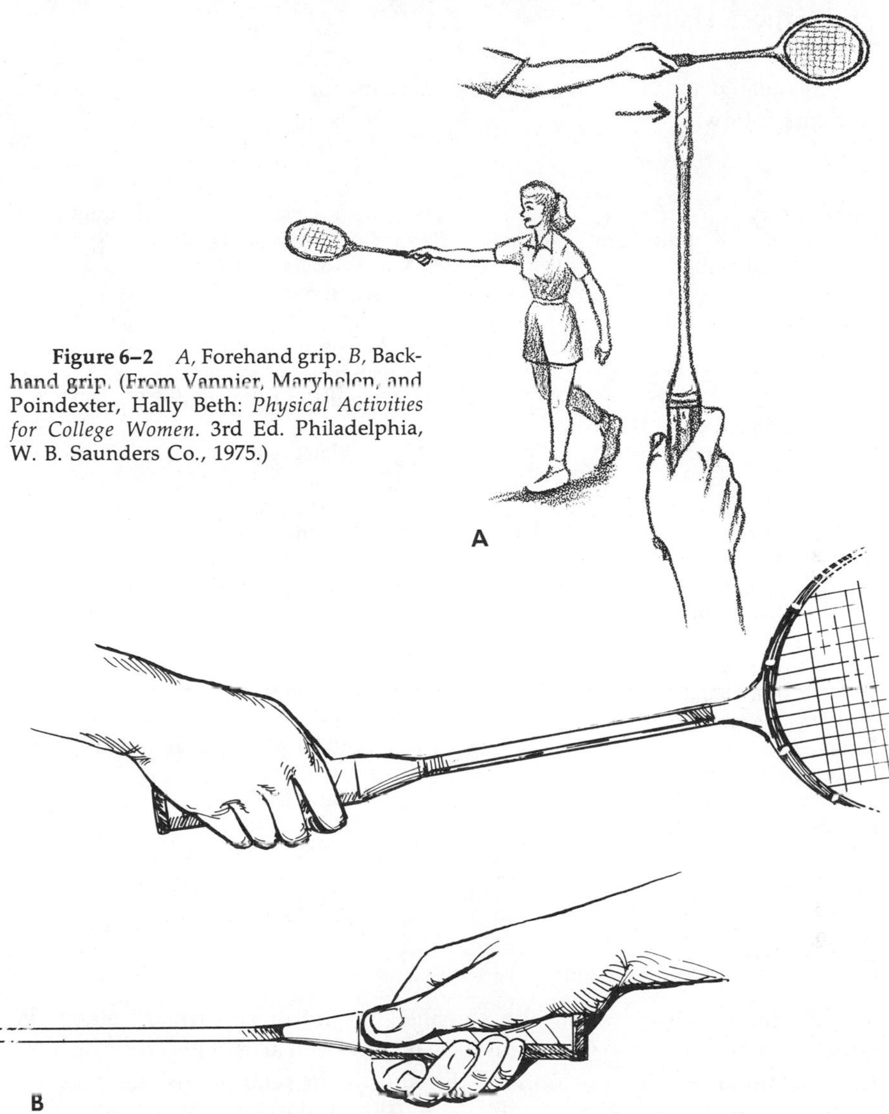

Figure 6–2 *A,* Forehand grip. *B,* Backhand grip. (From Vannier, Maryhelen, and Poindexter, Hally Beth: *Physical Activities for College Women.* 3rd Ed. Philadelphia, W. B. Saunders Co., 1975.)

Comfortable and properly fitting shorts, blouses, socks, and rubber-soled shoes are necessary for instructional and recreational play. Sweat bands and towels are useful accessories. White clothing is traditional for tournament play, although pastel shades are acceptable in some areas. Special care should be taken to select lightweight shoes with hard rubber soles that allow a slight slide following a quick stop or change of direction. Two pairs of socks, a thin pair under a thicker, shock absorbing pair, are suggested for competitive play.

TEACHING UNITS

Suggested areas to be included in units for beginners and advanced students follow:

Beginners	*Advanced*
Brief history	Selection and care of personal equipment
Care and use of equipment	Review of fundamental skills
Fundamental skills	Advanced skills
Grip	Flick serve
Positioning	Drive serve
Footwork	Half paced smash
Low, short serve	Backhand smash
High, deep serve	Round-the-head stroke
Underhand clear	Net play
Forehand	Hairpin net
Backhand	Push shot
Overhead clear	Net smash
Forehand	Underhand dropshot
Backhand	Sidearm strokes
Drop shot (overhead)	Singles strategy—stress speed and pace variance
Forehand Smash	
Drive	Doubles strategy
Forehand	Up and back
Backhand	Side by side
Hairpin net stroke	Rotation
Rules	Mixed doubles play—up and back formation
Basic singles and doubles strategy	
Tournament play	Tournament play
Evaluation	Evaluation

BASIC SKILLS

Badminton strokes may be classified by the three primary planes in which they are hit—overhead, underhand, and sidearm. They may be further classified by the position of the shuttle in relation to the player's body, that is, forehand, backhand, and around the head. The trajectory, depth of flight, and ultimate court placement of the shuttle further define the shots as serves, clears, smashes, drop shots, drives, net strokes, and pushes. The following chart illustrates the classification of the majority of strokes.

Proper execution of a stroke is dependent upon the correctness of the grip, proper body and court position for stroking, and skillful execution of the mechanics of the shot.

The Grip. A proper grip affords the advantage of full racket length while maintaining complete racket control. The force and power of a

Table 4. STROKE CLASSIFICATION CHART

Plane	Side of Body	Stroke
Underhand	Forehand	Serve 1. short, low 2. high, deep 3. drive serve* 4. flick serve* Clear Drop Hairpin net
	Backhand	Serve 1. backhand low* 2. flick* Clear Drop* Hairpin net
Sidearm	Forehand	Drive Drop Clear Hairpin net Push (net)
	Backhand	Drive Drop Clear Hairpin net Push (net)
Overhead	Forehand	Clear Drop Smash Half paced smash*
	Backhand	Clear Drop Smash* Half paced smash*
	Round the Head*	Clear* Drop* Smash* Half paced smash*

*Advanced technique.

swing can be imparted only through an effective grip. The following descriptions are for the right-handed player; a left-handed player need only reverse the terms "left" and "right" for clarity.

Forehand Grip. The forehand grip is used for all strokes on the racket side of the body and by many players for the round-the-head stroke. Many players use the same grip for forehand and backhand strokes.

To achieve the proper grip, hold the racket shaft in the left hand with the racket face at right angles to the floor. The right hand grasps the handle with a handshake grip so the "V" formed by the thumb and forefinger is on the top bevel of the handle. The fingers are spread slightly apart around the handle, and the thumb is angled diagonally up along the handle. The thumb exerts pressure against the index finger. To facilitate wrist movement, the handle rests at the base of the fingers (rather than in the palm), with the butt end of the racket resting against the heel of the hand. The first two fingers and thumb hold the racket firmly as the third and fourth fingers curl lightly but firmly around the handle. This allows the wrist and hand to remain firm yet supple, insuring forearm rotation. Undue tension resulting from gripping too tightly should be avoided, for it restricts the necessary forearm rotation.

Backhand Grip. A large number of players prefer a grip with more power potential when the racket is extended across the body. The hand shifts counterclockwise to the left so the closed "V" of the thumb and index finger is pointed to the inside of the left bevel of the handle. The forefinger rests on the top plate of the handle, and the three remaining fingers extend diagonally up the back plate of the handle. As the body positions for a backhand stroke the grip will result in a slightly pronated forearm with a slightly flexed wrist.

Footwork. Good footwork serves to position the body quickly and efficiently in any court area in preparation for a stroke. Proper footwork makes it possible to return to the center of the court prior to an opponent's return.

The *ready position* is an efficient waiting position from which the player can move quickly in any direction with minimal effort. After receiving service in singles the ready position should be astride the center line and two or three feet behind the middle of the court. Some players prefer to stand deeper in the court, for they find it easier to move forward than

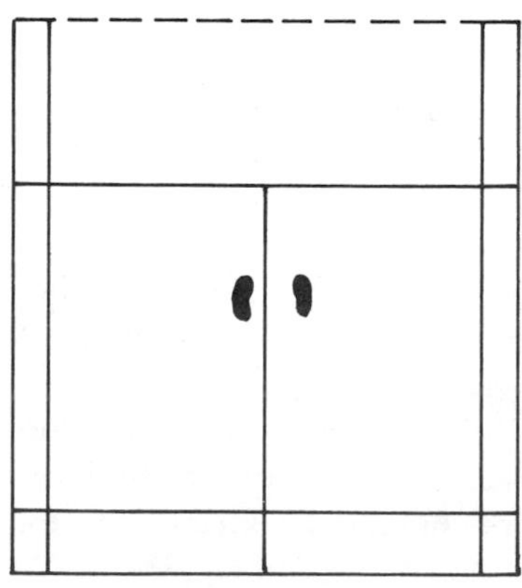

Figure 6–3 Ready position.

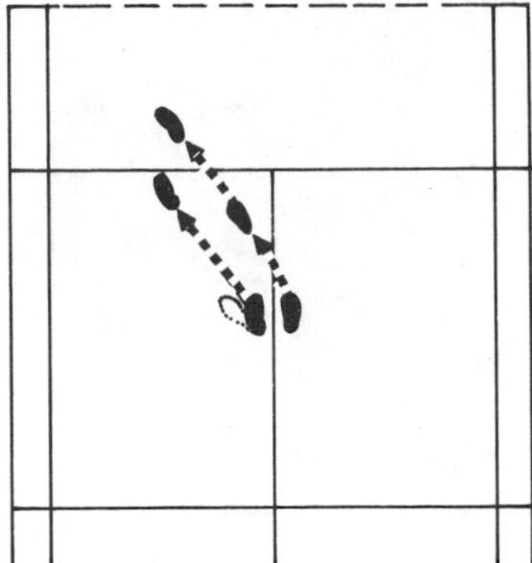

Figure 6–4 Moving to left front.

backward. Tall players may stand closer to the net. While awaiting an opponent's stroke the player stands facing the net, eyes on the shuttle and weight slightly forward and distributed over both feet. The dominant foot (generally the right foot for a right-handed player) is slightly forward in stride position to protect the more vulnerable backhand. The racket is held in front of the body and extended about shoulder height. The angle between the forearm and racket shaft is between 90 and 120 degrees.

Moving to the Stroke. Several concepts underlie good footwork. First, a player moves to a spot to await the shuttle in flight *only after* an opponent has executed a shot. A player should avoid shifting her weight forward in anticipation of a net retrieve until the opponent has hit the shuttle. Second, the last step before contacting the shuttle should be taken with the racket foot (right foot for right-handed player, left foot for left-handed player) if at all possible. This step is important for maintaining balance and proper shift of weight on the stroke and for the return to ready position.

There are six basic areas or directions in which a player must move. Unless the shuttle is within three or four feet of the ready position and can be approached with a jab step, some pattern of footwork is needed.

Moving to Left Front. This position is used for backhand underhand net or clear strokes. A small backward or diagonal pivot step on the left foot turns the body in the direction of intended movement. The right foot crosses over, followed by a step with the left foot (or a shuffle step, left-right-left, for shorter distances). The final step is on the right foot with the toe of that foot facing the left net post. The hips and body are low with the upper body bent forward from the waist. The right shoulder is forward in preparation for the stroke. Following the stroke the player begins the return to waiting position by a push off the right foot or a step up with the left foot to relieve the right foot of weight. The right shoulder turns, and the body opens to the net as the return to center position is accomplished by small balanced backward steps initiated by the right foot.

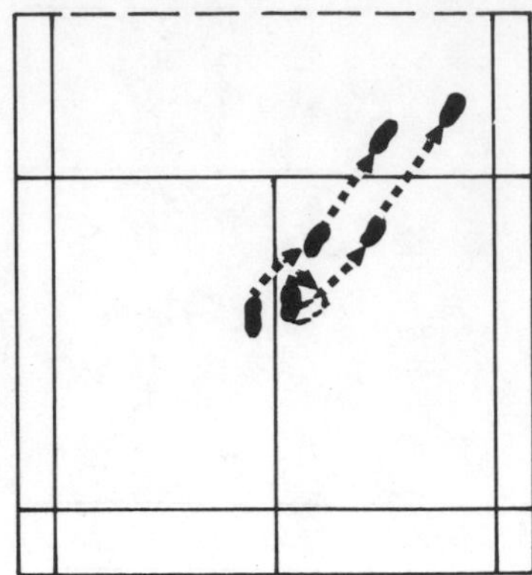

Figure 6–5 Moving to right front.

Moving to Right Front. This position is for forehand underhand net or clear strokes. A small backward step or pivot on the left foot may initiate action, followed by a step with the right foot. The move may also begin by a long step toward the right by the right foot. This step is followed by a shuffle step or a long step by the left foot, ending on a step by the right foot and a weight shift as the stroke is made. The player returns to center position by pushing off the right foot or by stepping up with the left foot and then backpedaling with small controlled steps.

Moving Laterally to the Left. This position readies a player for backhand drives, smashes, or drop shots from midcourt. The left foot pivots to establish the line of intended movement as the racket shoulder turns toward the net. The second step is a crossover with the right foot. If greater distance is needed a shuffle step follows with the weight on the forward right foot as the stroke is made. To return to center position the player pushes off the right foot, pivots on the left as the body opens toward the net, and falls back with small steps.

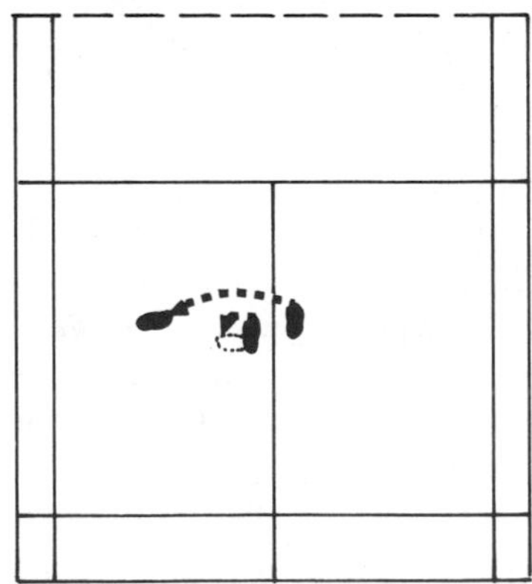

Figure 6–6 Moving laterally to the left.

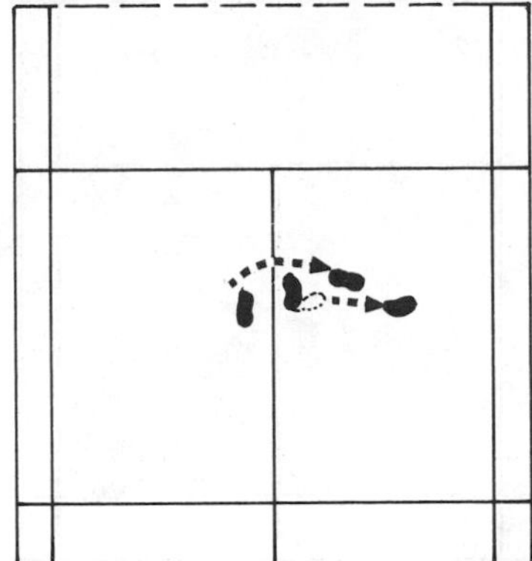

Figure 6–7 Moving laterally to the right.

Moving Laterally to the Right. This position makes possible the forehand smash, drive, or net shots. The initial step is taken with the right foot toward the right sideline as the left foot pivots. Shoulders are angled so the left shoulder is toward the center of the net, and the right shoulder is directed to the back, right corner of the court. The second step is with the left foot or a left-right-left shuffle step, the last step being made with the right foot. The left foot remains closer to the center of the court. The return to center position is initiated by a push off with the right foot followed by small shuffle steps.

Moving Directly Backward. This is for forehand clears, smashes, drives, or drop shots and is accomplished by backpedaling with small running steps. The return to ready position is a natural recovery accomplished by small walking or running steps.

Moving to Right Back Position in the Court. This movement establishes a player for forehand overhead strokes such as the clear, drive, and drop shot. The left foot pivots as a step toward the right back corner is taken by the right foot. The shoulders turn so the right shoulder points to

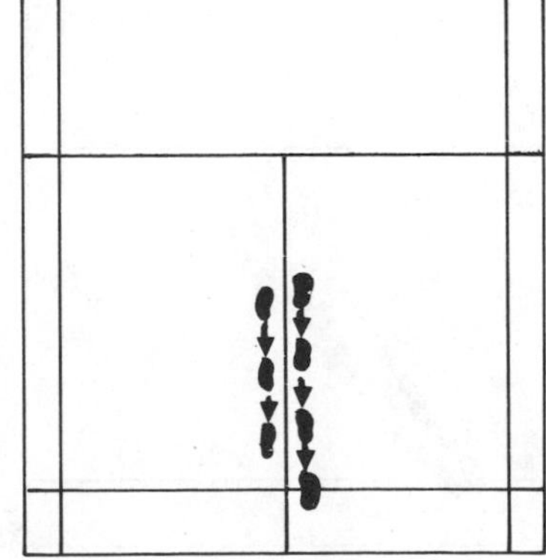

Figure 6–8 Moving directly backward.

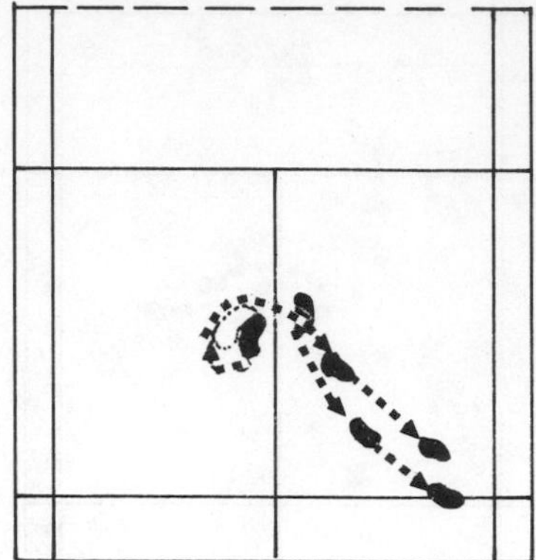

Figure 6–9 Moving to right back position in the court.

the right back corner of the court. The left foot closes toward the right and this shuffle continues until the proper position is achieved. The last step is with the right foot; however, as the stroke is executed, weight shifts to the forward left foot. Shoulders and hips turn parallel to the net as the stroke is executed. The return to ready position is accomplished by short, bouncing steps.

Moving to the Left Back Court Position. This movement positions the player for backhand drives, clears, and other overhead strokes. The movement from center position is initiated with a pivot on the right foot and a step back toward the middle of the court on the left foot. The right foot crosses over with the toe directed toward the right back corner. The shoulders and hips turn with the right shoulder pointing toward the left net post. A step left precedes the final right step. Each of these steps serves to adjust the player to the proper position for the shuttle's descent. As the stroke is executed the body weight is over the right foot, and the player's back is toward the net. Following the stroke the return to center is initiated by a push off from the right foot as the left pivots and the body

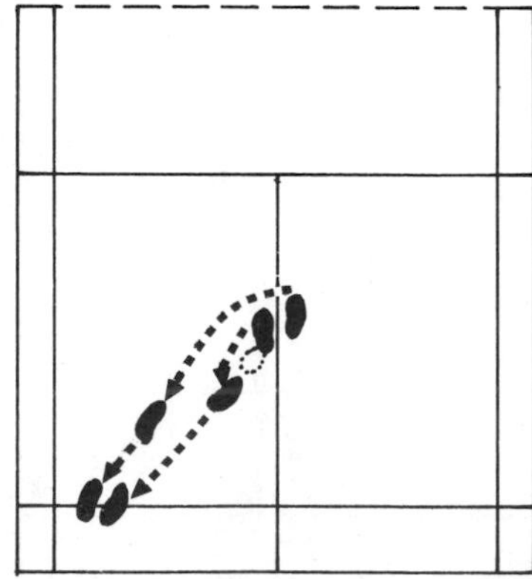

Figure 6–10 Moving to left back court position.

turns to face the net. Small shuffle steps return the player to center position.

Movement to the Back Left Court for Round-the-Head Strokes. The player will find that there are times when the round-the-head shots of smash, clear, or drop must be executed to protect the backhand corner and return the shuttle with more power than is possible on the backhand. The left foot steps back and toward the back corner followed by a right step backward. Shoulders are open to the net. The player backpedals with alternating left and right steps until the proper court position is approached. The last step backward should be a step on the right foot and a hop left so the weight is fully supported on the left foot. Toes are directed toward the left side and left net post. The left shoulder points to the deep sideline as the right shoulder and right leg move toward the net. The right foot is off the ground for balance. As the shuttle is contacted around the head, body weight is shifted to the right foot. Small steps return the player to ready position.

Serve. The serve is an underhand stroke that puts the shuttle into play. It may be executed on either the forehand or backhand. The rules of badminton state that the serve must be underhand, the shuttle must be contacted below the server's waist, and the *entire* racket head must be below the serving hand.

Service strategy and execution vary for singles and doubles play. The grip of the racket, stand, and court position vary with stroke execution. The server is positioned several feet behind the short service line and just inside the center line in her service court. The player stands at least a foot closer to the short service line in doubles, for she is responsible for all net

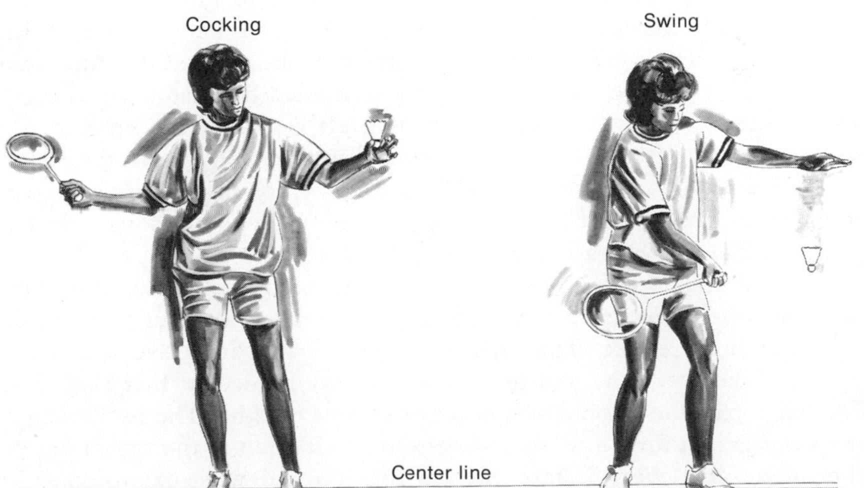

Figure 6–11 The serve. (From Johnson, M. L.: *Badminton*. Philadelphia, W. B. Saunders Co., 1974.)

play following low service. The server is in a forward stride position with the left foot forward. Feet are placed far enough apart to assure balance throughout the swing. Body weight may shift during service, but neither foot may slide, step, or otherwise advance during the serve.

A *high, deep* serve is most often used in singles play, for a well placed, high and deep serve which drops nearly perpendicular to the baseline forces an opponent to make an excellent stroke to gain the offensive. The shuttle is held at its base by the thumb and forefinger of the left hand. The left arm is extended in front of the body at shoulder level. The racket is held with a forehand grip as the arm swings back approximately to waist level. The wrist cocks so that the racket head extends upward. The shuttle is dropped, not tossed, and the wrist of the racket hand leads the racket downward and forward in the swing. The wrist extends as it contacts the shuttle ahead of the body between knee and waist level. The follow-through is in the direction of the shuttle flight, and the finish is high over the left shoulder. After contact the server straddles the center line in ready position, awaiting the opponent's return.

The *low, short, forehand* service is used most often in doubles play because of the shortened service court and the need to avoid the possibility of a smash return on a long service. The intent of a short serve is to skim the net and approach the service court in the first few inches of the court so that the receiver must hit her return up in a defensive stroke. The grip and stance for the stroke are similar to the high serve although the server is often one to two feet closer to the net on execution. The backswing is short, and the wrist remains cocked throughout the sweeping action of the stroke. The shuttle is dropped from about chest height and contacted just below the waist. The shuttle is actually guided, rather than hit. The follow-through of the racket is low and a little less than net height.

Advanced Serves. The *backhand low* service has been used by Asian players for many years but has only recently been used by American players. The right foot is forward, and a shortened backhand grip is used. The racket is below the waist and to the left center of the body as the shuttle is held in front of the body with its base directed toward the racket face. This serve is a deceptive doubles strategy, for the shuttle comes to the receiver against a background of white clothing with unknown speed; a powerful flick can be easily executed from this position.

The *flick* and *drive* serves are advanced techniques often used in doubles play when a receiver is leaning forward or when a player persistently rushes a short service. The *drive* serve is fast and deceptive and when properly executed, the shuttle has a low, flat trajectory that rises just enough to pass the opponent's racket or cause a miss-hit. The backswing is the same as that for a low, short forehand service, but as the racket enters the hitting area there is fast forearm rotation and wrist extension. The shuttle is contacted as high as is legally possible to insure the flattest trajectory.

The *flick* serve is executed with the stance and backswing of the short service, both forehand and backhand, but as the shuttle is contacted the wrist quickly extends from its cocked position to hit the shuttle *just over* the opponent's racket and deep into the doubles service court. Generally the serve should be directed wide and deep to the doubles back service line where it intersects the doubles sideline.

Overhead Strokes. *Overhead clears* may be executed on both the forehand and the backhand and may be used either as defensive or offensive techniques. A defensive clear is a high, deep shot directed to the backline and used when the hitter needs time to position or the team needs to "regroup." The offensive clear is also deep but has a lower trajectory. It is intended to pressure the opponent's return.

To execute the forehand clear the racket is held with a forehand grip, and the body is properly positioned slightly behind the flight of the descending shuttle. The weight is on the right foot which is pointing to the right sideline while the left foot is angled toward the net. While positioning for the stroke the racket arm is raised, the wrist is cocked, and the racket head moves behind the head and shoulders. As the right shoulder moves back the cocked wrist allows the racket head to point toward the floor. The swing must be timed to contact the shuttle at the highest possi-

Figure 6–12 Overhead stroke.

ble point in front of the body and thus impart maximum power. As the torso rotates, body weight shifts from the back to the forward foot. As the stroke is executed the racket face is flat to the target area; the forearm rotates, the elbow and arm extend fully, and the wrist extends on contact. The full release of the arm directs the racket head to a flat hit without imparting cutting or slicing action to the shuttle. The trajectory of the shuttle is higher than the opponent's racket. The body faces the direction of the shuttle flight, and the follow-through is up and toward the baseline, finishing downward on the player's left side. The right foot moves through to prepare to position for the next stroke.

The purposes of the *backhand clear* are the same as those of the forehand, but the shuttle is hit on the left side of the body by a right-handed player. The backhand grip is used. If a strong midcourt position is possible the body is turned to the left sideline with the right shoulder toward the net. The left foot is directed toward the sideline, and the toes of the right foot point toward the left net post. However, if the shot must be made from the rear half of the court—requiring more power—the body faces the rear boundary line with the chest parallel to the baseline. This position increases the range of movement of the racket arm.

Body weight is on the left foot, and the elbow of the racket arm is flexed as the right hand moves past the left shoulder. The right elbow is up, pointing toward the approaching shuttle. The racket head is pointing downward with the thumb of the racket hand pointing toward the floor prior to beginning forward movement into the hitting area.

The shift of body weight to the forward foot initiates the stroke. The body rotates toward the net, and the elbow leads as the arm extends upward. The wrist extends, bringing the racket head forward to meet the shuttle in front of the body. The stroke must be upward, not forward, and the stroke must be hit hard to get maximum racket head speed at contact. The forward movement of the racket hand virtually stops when the racket is extended to allow the racket head to accelerate. A slight wrist break and forearm rotation result in the follow-through.

This difficult shot requires exact timing to exert the power needed to clear the shuttle with enough height and depth for an effective shot. Backhand clears contacted deep in the court are often hit straight down the sideline, for it is difficult to clear across court without excellent timing and release of power.

Overhead drop shots are executed on both the forehand and backhand. The name of the stroke describes the shuttle's flight, for a drop shot should travel slowly and fall just over the net in the opponent's forecourt, preferably in front of the short service line. The footwork, body position, and preliminary racket position of both forehand and backhand drops are similar to those of the overhead clear. The value of this similarity is in concealing the drop shot as long as possible.

Contact with the shuttle is high and farther ahead of the body than for a clearing shot. The racket head is perpendicular to the floor or facing slightly downward as the shuttle is contacted. The forearm rotation and wrist extension are *controlled* and less dramatic than in the clear. The shuttle is "stroked" rather than "hit." Forward and downward follow-through of the racket is imperative, since stopping the racket results in a blocked shot which lacks downward trajectory. Avoid overuse of the drop shot, for if the element of surprise is lost an opponent easily has time to execute a net smash.

Forehand, Backhand, and Net Smashes. A *smash* is a point winner, for this power stroke can "put away" an opponent's high, weak, and short returns. Both the forehand and backhand smash are executed from the basic body position of the overhead clear when the opponent's return is high and in midcourt or forecourt. The shuttle is contacted as high as possible in front of the body. Some advanced players jump from the ground to get a higher contact point.

Prior to contact, the trunk and shoulders rotate forward and weight is shifted to the forward foot. The racket arm extends, the forearm begins strong rotation, and at the instant of contact with the shuttle the racket face is angled slightly downward to insure that the shuttle will travel sharply down. Wrist rotation is fast and forceful. The follow-through is down toward the floor in the direction of the shuttle flight and across the body to the left. The body is frequently off balance after completion of a powerful smash and recovery takes longer. The player should anticipate a defensive, upward return stroke.

The speed of a smash is important, but the downward angle is of greater importance. Backcourt smashes are less effective than midcourt or forecourt smashes because of the different angle and because the shuttle decelerates over the longer distance and can be more easily retrieved by the opponent.

The *backhand smash* is a difficult advanced stroke requiring accurate and precise timing. Preliminary position and action are similar to those of the overhead clear and drop. The contact point is high and forward, and the racket face is angled down. Because of its difficulty, it carries a great element of surprise for the opponents.

The *net smash* is a special technique of smashing when close to the net so that net contact is avoided and the shuttle is not driven out of the court. The shuttle is contacted rapidly and with a firm touch, for the power must be developed and imparted at the time of contact rather than from the usual powerful follow-through.

The *half paced smash,* or half smash, is a smash stroke which imparts less speed to the shuttle. It is executed much as is the powerful smash, but it is played with less effort. If the shuttle is contacted with a partially open racket face, the shuttle can be "sliced," and it will fall closer to the net at a sharp angle. Recovery to ready position is easier than following a full smash, and fatigue is less likely with the half paced smash.

Round-the-Head Strokes. These strokes can cover for a weak backhand and can retain the attack for the hitter. They are often deceptive but overuse of such strokes may result in poor court position, for more steps are taken away from the center of the court and a perceptive opponent may use this to her advantage. For a right-handed player the shuttle is hit on the left side of the body. Using a forehand grip the player positions herself behind the flight of the shuttle. The body is open with knees flexed and angled to the net. The left foot is pulled back toward the right for a high balanced position. The right shoulder rotates back, and the right elbow and wrist are flexed to direct the racket behind and to the left of the body. Weight shifts to the left foot, and the racket arm extends to meet the shuttle as high as possible over the left shoulder. The palm of the racket hand should be facing the net on contact. The right leg swings forward as the momentum of the swing carries the racket down and to the right side of the body.

On clears the racket face is directed upward as the shuttle is hit deep in the opponent's court; for drop shots the racket face is pointed to the net, either directly or angled for a crosscourt drop. On a round-the-head smash or half paced smash the racket face is directed downward on contact.

Underhand Strokes. Underhand strokes are usually made between the short service line and the net to return a drop shot or an opponent's

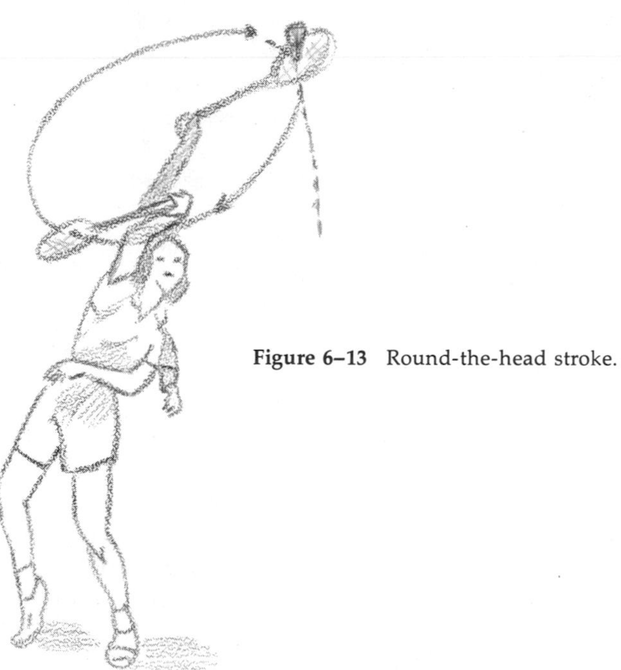

Figure 6–13 Round-the-head stroke.

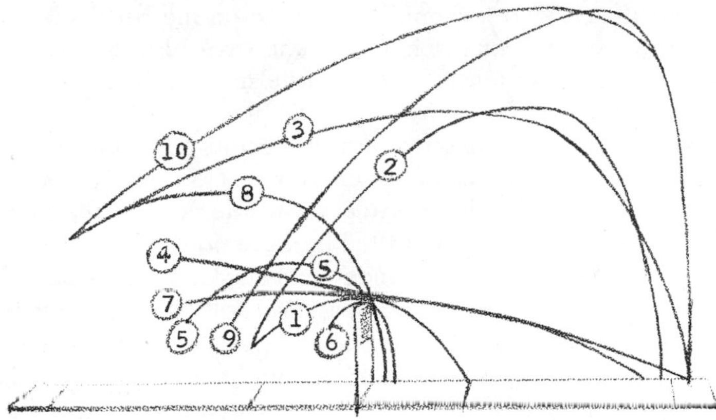

Figure 6–14 Common strokes: *(1)* short serve, *(2)* underhand clear (long serve), *(3)* overhead clear, *(4)* smash, *(5)* underhand drop, *(6)* net shot, *(7)* drive, *(8)* overhead drop shot, *(9)* long serve (underhand clear), *(10)* overhead clear.

net shot. Occasionally forehand underhand drop shots are executed from behind the short service line. A general rule for playing underhand strokes is to contact the shuttle as close to the top of the net as possible, for the lower the contact point the greater must be the upward, rather than forward, stroke.

The *underhand clear* is used to force an opponent into the back court and thus gain time to recover to center position. The *forehand clear* is similar in execution to the high, deep service. The racket is held in a forehand grip with the right foot forward; the right shoulder is turned slightly toward the net. The racket moves down and back from the ready position, and the wrist cocks so the racket head extends upward. The wrist leads the racket downward and forward under the shuttle as the wrist and forearm rotate inward; the forearm lifts the racket in a high follow-through in the intended direction of shuttle flight. The elbow remains slightly flexed throughout the swing.

To execute the *underhand backhand clear* the racket is held in a backhand grip, the right foot is forward, and the right shoulder is toward the net. The wrist is cocked, and as contact is made with the shuttle the wrist and forearm rotate as the arm lifts upward and forward. The elbow remains slightly flexed throughout the high follow-through.

Underhand drop shots are most successful when played from a position close to the net, although they may be executed from most court positions. The usual forehand grip is used on the racket side of the body, but for strokes on the backhand a modified backhand grip, with the hand turned toward the forehand, allows for wrist adaptation for the stroke. The shuttle should be contacted as high as possible. The head of the racket should be almost parallel to the floor; the wrist is cocked and remains cocked throughout the stroke. Either the left or right foot may be forward on the forehand, but the right foot should be forward on the backhand. The legs and upper arm are used for reaching, and the stroking is accomplished by the lower arm, wrist, and hand. The shuttle may be blocked or pushed with a gentle stroke so that it just clears the net.

The *hairpin net stroke* describes the trajectory of a shuttle which has dropped parallel to the net and is lifted upward close to the net so that it barely clears and falls close to the net and to the floor in the opponent's court. The stroke requires a controlled lifting action.

The *push shot* is not a "true" underhand stroke, for it is played at net level or slightly above net height. It is executed with the racket head above net level with the face angled downward. The shot is used in doubles play when the opponents are in an up-and-back position and the shuttle can be *pushed* to midcourt with moderate speed beyond the net player. Frequently the back player is forced to hit the shuttle *up* on the return.

Sidearm Strokes. The flat sidearm stroke is used on both the forehand and the backhand to send a fast, deep passing shot of low trajectory to the backcourt or crosscourt. A slower midcourt shot is used to pull opponents out of position. The forehand grip is used for shuttles on the racket side of the body. The initial step for stroke execution is on the right foot followed by a move diagonally forward by the left foot as the shoulders turn and the racket arm swings into a full backswing. The right shoulder moves back, the elbow points down, and the wrist cocks backward, bringing the racket head between the shoulder blades. As the arm swings forward body weight transfers to the left foot, the wrist uncocks and rotates inward, and the arm rotates and extends, releasing the force of the flat racket with a whiplike action.

Figure 6–15 Forehand drive.

Figure 6–16 Backhand drive and grip.

The action of the backhand stroke is similar. However, the backhand grip is used, and this grip restricts the wrist break. As the backswing begins the right foot is forward with the body weight on the left foot. The shoulders turn, and the bent elbow, pointing to the oncoming shuttle, is pulled into the backswing high so that the racket hand, with palm toward the floor, comes to the left shoulder. As the forward swing begins the weight shifts to the right foot, shoulders turn, and the elbow leads the racket. There is an outward rotation of the forearm and wrist as the racket "whips" through a flat plane to the shuttle. The follow-through is in the path of the shuttle.

PLAYING STRATEGY

Mastery of basic strokes is fundamental to competitive play, but an understanding of game tactics and the ability to utilize strategy in offensive and defensive situations are the real challenges of competition.

Several concepts are basic to singles, doubles, and mixed doubles play:

1. Offensive strokes are shots which can be directed downward, and they offer easy points; defensive strokes are hit upward and must be deceptive and accurate if they are to be point winners.
2. The angle of the opponent's return should determine a player's court position. To avoid being trapped, assume a position in the center of the angle of the return where the greatest percentage of returns will come. Be alert for the odd or low-percentage shot.
3. Generally a player may move about a foot to the side of the court to which she directed a deep baseline shot. She may move a step forward from her normal court position in anticipation of a weak return.

4. Attempt to lead your opponent into anticipation of a certain shot by establishing a pattern of down-the-line and crosscourt play, then play the unexpected shot.
5. Move your opponent up and back in an attempt to keep her off balance for her strokes.

Singles Strategy

1. A high, deep serve is basic to singles play, for it forces the receiver back in the court and gives the server more time to prepare for the return. Change pace of the serve with low or drive serves to unbalance the receiver or to take the offensive after the receiver hits up on a return of short service.
2. The serving position is three or four feet behind the short service line. From this position the server is close to the center of the court and can move easily to play the return.
3. The receiver should take a diagonal stance prior to receipt of service, since this foot position allows easy forward and backward movements. Serves are usually directed to the corners deep in the court or in front of the service court. *Most* serves are directed high and deep, and the skillful player will anticipate the direction of serve by shifting weight before actually moving.
4. The most useful shots in singles are high, deep serves, overhead clears, overhead drop shots, half smashes, underhand clears, and hairpin net returns.
5. Return high, deep service with an overhead clear. If the serve is short (approximately doubles service line) an attacking clear, drop shot, or smash may be used to gain the offensive.
6. Avoid returning a net shot with a net shot unless a quick diagonal stroke can be directed away from the opponent.
7. Direct drop shots and net strokes the greatest distance from the opponent's last stroke.
8. Avoid midcourt shots.
9. A general plan of attack is to force the opponent to return from deep backhand. To defend against the attack a player may move her center position slightly to the left or develop a strong round-the-head stroke.
10. If a player has a weak backhand it is often wise to initiate the attack to the forehand and *then* to the backhand, so that the opponent has less time to get set for defense.
11. Alternate play patterns so opponent does not know what to expect.
12. Change game pace by selection of strokes. That is, slow down with high serves, high clears, half smashes, and drop shots; increase the pace with low or drive serves, flat clears, drives, and smashes.
13. Achieve and maintain excellent physical conditioning, for the singles game is dependent upon stamina and rapid movements on the court.

Doubles Strategy

1. Doubles is a fast game that requires less individual stamina than singles but demands cleverness, strategic play, and teamwork.
2. Generally use a low short service with only an occasional driven serve.
3. The most useful shots in doubles are the low serve, driven serve, drive, half smash, smash, and net strokes.

Several systems of play are used to advantage by teams in offensive and defensive situations:

1. *Side by side.* Each player is responsible for all shots on her own half of the court, both front and back. It is an excellent defensive formation against a smash, with shots down the middle being taken by the player on her forehand side. The disadvantage of the system is that a weaker player can be harassed by the opponents or that one player can be forced to play all shots until she tires.
2. *Up and back.* This system is basically an offensive formation, for one player is always in the forecourt and the other in the backcourt. The forecourt player is positioned so that she is able to play net and cut off weak returns or block crosscourt shots. Up and back allows players to specialize in the best aspects of their game. It is a weak formation for defending against an attack to the midcourt area.
3. *Combination.* This is a system for advanced players who can rotate from up and back during offensive play to a side-by-side formation when on defense. Play begins in up-and-back formation, and when one of the players hits the shuttle upward, the net player moves back in the closer court and the back player adjusts to form the side-by-side position.

Mixed Doubles

Mixed doubles is played in the up-and-back formation with the woman playing in the front of the court covering the area from the short service line to the net. She keeps the shuttle directed downward by using net shots and half court shots. The man plays returns from the back court using fast, powerful, and deceptive strokes to force weak returns.

1. Use the low serve, frequently directed to the inside corner to narrow the angle of return. Use the flick serve occasionally to keep the receiver from rushing.
2. Return serves with drives, drop shots, or half court shots away from, or behind, the net player. Avoid using a clear.
3. To defend against a smash, the woman backpedals to defend against a crosscourt smash, and the man becomes responsible for the down-the-line smash.

CLASS ORGANIZATION

Badminton can be taught successfully to large classes if some thought is given to creative organization and planning. Early in the instructional unit a demonstration game or a film of skillful play can acquaint the students with the purposes and challenges of the game. Initially, the teacher may begin each class with a demonstration and explanation of the grips, serves, and basic strokes to the entire group. Thereafter players may be assigned to courts or improvised areas for practice and skill drills. Following an understanding of the "why" and "how" of the game, practice is imperative to develop stroke patterns and correct timing.

Ideally only two or four persons should be assigned to a court for play, but in the early stages of skill development as many as six players,

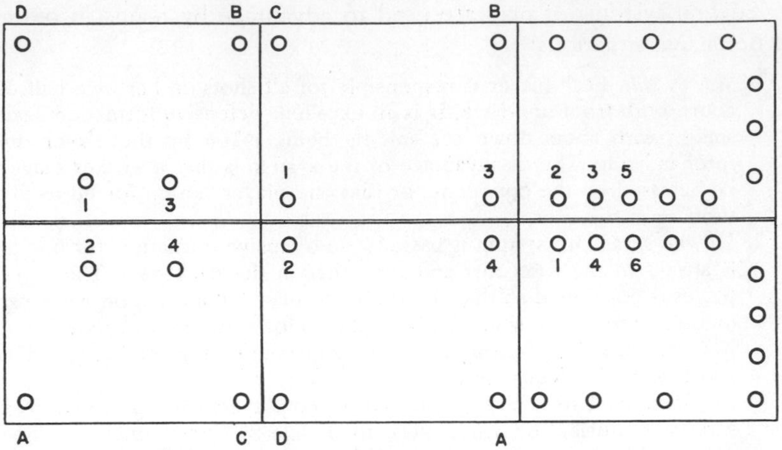

Figure 6–17 Organizational plan for a large class.
Court 1: A serves deep to B, C to D. 1 + 2, 3 + 4, net shots. Players rotate positions.
Court 2: A + B, line drives; C + B, line drives. 1 – 2, 3 – 4, net shots. Players rotate positions.
Court 3: 1 – 2, 3 – 4, 5 – 6, net shots. Rest—wall practice. Players rotate positions.

three on each side, may work as partners across the net. Court markings are not necessary for the practice of strokes early in the unit, and additional practice space can be made by stretching ropes across unused court border areas. Serving and volley drills can be conducted against wall areas.

Students can be assigned to squads, courts, and practice areas by grouping them according to skill level after the first few lessons. Players seem to benefit most by playing with others of approximately the same level of skill.

Once competitive play begins students who are not playing because of space limitations may serve as officials, raters, and evaluators for those participating.

TEACHING PROGRESSION

Any plan of teaching and skill progression is dependent upon a teacher's philosophy and successful teaching experience. Most agree that students should practice skills in a setting similar to that of a game situation and play games or participate in gamelike drills as soon as basic skills are developed. Although beginners find hitting in the overhead plane quite natural, underhand strokes are also easily developed once a proper grip is established. Underhand strokes also acquaint students with the basic pattern of the high, deep serve which should be developed early as a method of putting the shuttle in play.

In most cases the backhand stroke should be introduced following the forehand of basic strokes to prevent the tendency to hit all strokes on the forehand. Court positioning and movement patterns should be taught independently and established through footwork and skill drills. The early introduction of the forehand smash gives players a stroke which can turn a high return into a winning point. The overhead drop shot can be used effectively because most beginners do not clear deep in the court, and the drop shot can be effectively played on a return to midcourt.

The following progression quickly introduces skills needed in a singles game:

1. Underhand clear—forehand and backhand
2. High, deep serve
3. Smash—forehand
4. Overhead clear—forehand and backhand
5. Overhead drop shot—forehand and backhand
6. Short serve
7. Hairpin net stroke
8. Drive—forehand and backhand
9. Advanced net play—push and smash
10. Advanced serves—backhand low, flick, drive
11. Half paced smash—forehand and backhand
12. Backhand smash
13. Round-the-head stroke (may be introduced before backhand smash)
14. Sidearm strokes
15. Underhand drop shot

Singles games should be played early in the unit if possible, for a player develops self-reliance and is forced to move effectively on the court in order to play shots that a doubles partner might otherwise take.

Drills. Drills which progress from isolated stroke development to patterns which incorporate the stroke with footwork patterns in gamelike situations should be developed. The following drills serve as basic suggestions upon which the teacher can build.

Serving Drill. May be practiced alone or with an opponent on the opposite side of the net to collect shuttles. Player has approximately 20 shuttles. Server assumes proper court position; she serves 10 shuttles *high and deep* so that they fall in area A as noted in Figure 6–18. Serve 10 more shuttles to area B. Practice in both left- and right-hand courts.

Short Service. The server positions herself beside the center service line approximately a foot behind the short service line. Serve so that the shuttle clears the net low and lands short, first in the right and then in the left corners of the service court. Alternate courts. (See Figure 6–19.)

Footwork Drill. The player moves from center court position to right front where the singles boundary intersects the short service line. Mimetically she executes a stroke and returns to center position. She then moves to left front position, strokes, and returns to center position. (See Fig. 6–20.) The player then moves to right back position where the doubles service line intersects the singles sideline; she strokes and returns to center position. She then moves to left back position with proper foot-

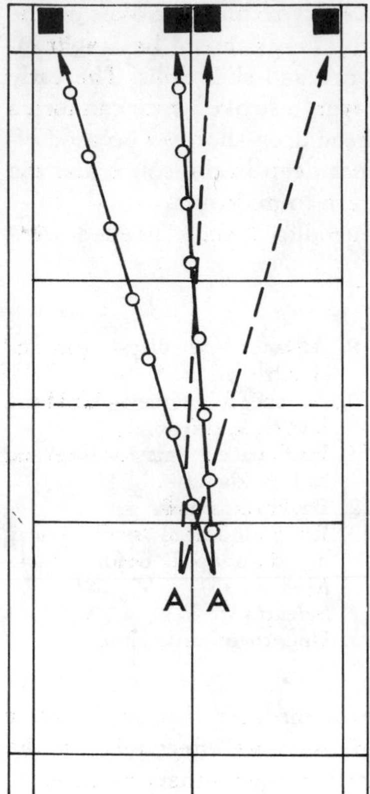

Figure 6–18 Long service drill.

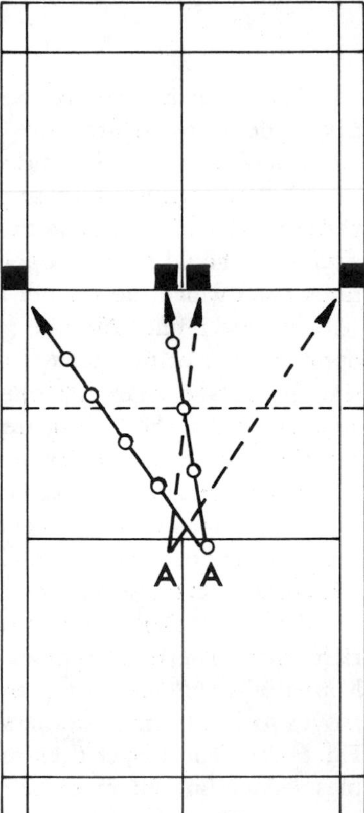

Figure 6–19 Short service drill.

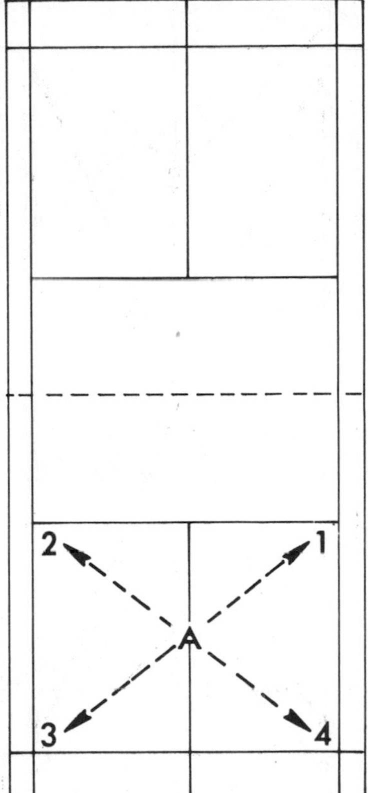

Figure 6–20 Footwork drill.

work and stroke execution. *Stress proper footwork and use of strokes appropriate to the court position.*

Overhead Clear Drill. Partners assume center position, from which they begin. (See Fig. 6–21.) One partner serves to her opponent who moves to return a clear parallel to the sideline. It is returned with a parallel clear. Repeat the procedure using crosscourt clears and clears parallel to the opposite sideline so that each player uses both forehand and backhand strokes. Each player should have the opportunity to clear from both deep corners. Return to center court position after each hit.

Smash Drill and Underhand Clear Drill. Partner B serves deep to A, who smashes parallel to the sideline at midcourt. Partner B clears high and deep, either down the line or crosscourt, and A smashes parallel to the sideline or crosscourt. Continue until both partners have cleared and smashed on both the forehand and backhand, down the line and crosscourt. (See Fig. 6–22.)

Overhead Drop and Underhand Clear Drill. Partner B serves to the backcourt, and A returns with an overhead drop shot to a front corner. B clears from the net and continues to clear to the same deep corner, and A

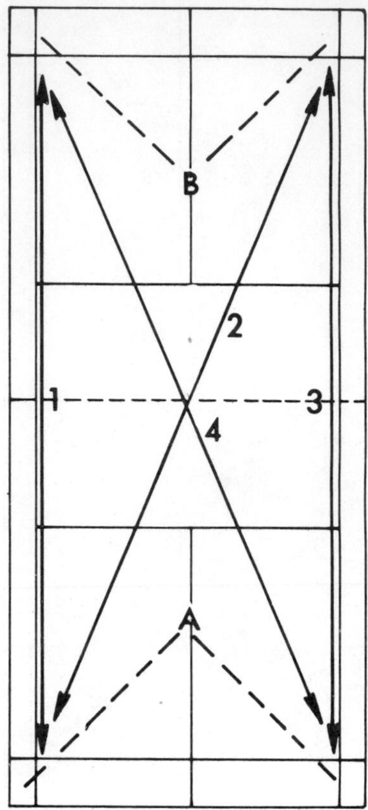

Figure 6–21 Overhead clear drill.

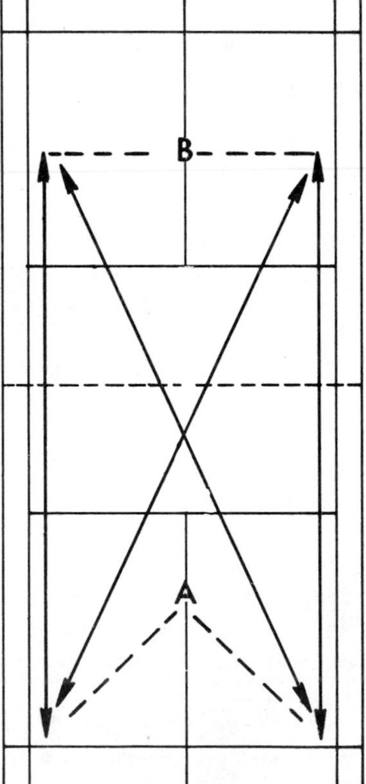

Figure 6–22 Smash and underhand clear drill.

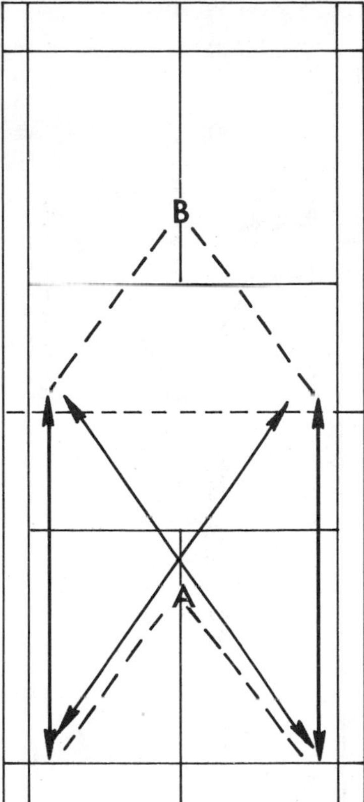

Figure 6–23 Overhead drop and underhand clear drill.

continues to drop until consistency develops. Partners then change roles. Serve to both courts; return with sideline drops and crosscourt drop shots. (See Fig. 6–23.)

Drive Drill. Two players face each other across the net and hit drives back and forth with one hitting forehand drives and the other straight backhand drives. Reverse the hitting pattern.

Players then hit crosscourt drives, forehand to forehand and backhand to backhand. Return to center position after each hit to improve footwork and endurance. Keep the shuttle low over the net. (See Fig. 6–24.)

Smash, Drop, and Underhand Clear Drill. This drill simulates a sequence of hits commonly used in singles play. A begins with a high service, suitable for a smash by B. A returns with a drop shot; B clears; A smashes and B drops, and the sequence continues until an error is made.

A sample teaching unit of ten one-hour lessons for beginners is shown below.* If instructional periods are shorter, the material can be extended over a longer period of time.

---

*For more advanced players, introduce net smash, push, round-the-head stroke, and drives.

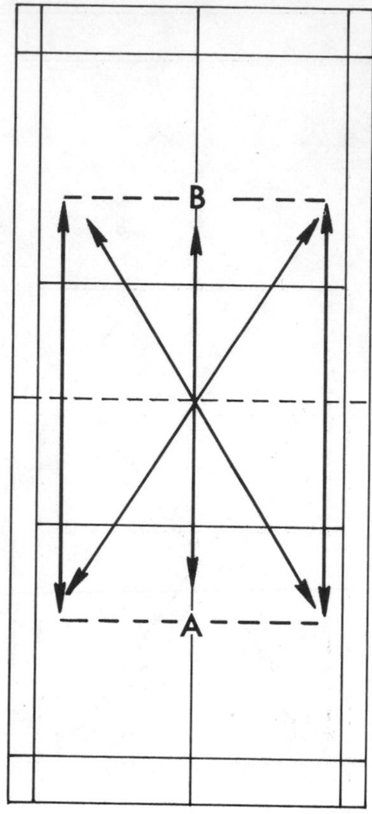

Figure 6–24 Drive drill.

Lesson I

1. History; nature of the game; prominent players
2. Equipment and its care
3. Grips—forehand and backhand
4. Hitting stance—forehand and backhand
5. Underhand stroking

Lesson II

1. Review grip and stance
2. Underhand plane—forehand and backhand clears
3. Footwork—practice footwork drill
4. Wall volley drill
5. Demonstration game or appropriate film

Lesson III

1. Review—grip, stance, clears, footwork
2. Singles serve—high and deep
3. Forehand smash
4. Practice drill—smash and clear stressing footwork and hitting stance

Lesson IV

1. Practice placement of serve
2. Explain scoring and singles rules
3. Begin overhead clears—forehand
4. Skill test of the serve

Lesson V

1. Knowledge test—rules, equipment, use of selected strokes
2. Overhead clear—review forehand and introduce backhand
3. Play singles games

Lesson VI

1. Continue singles games
2. Drop shot—forehand and backhand

Lesson VII

1. Doubles short serve
2. Footwork and strategy for doubles
3. Explain doubles rules
4. Review drop shot
5. Practice doubles play

Lesson VIII

1. Review doubles rules and court positioning
2. Net strokes—hairpin
3. Some play doubles; others take skills test on clear strokes and doubles service

Lesson IX

1. Continue skills tests
2. Begin tournament play
   a. Doubles—round robin or round robin pool play
   b. Singles—ladder tournament

Lesson X

1. Written test—rules, strategy, strokes
2. Continue tournaments

SKILL DIFFICULTIES AND THEIR CORRECTION

Grip

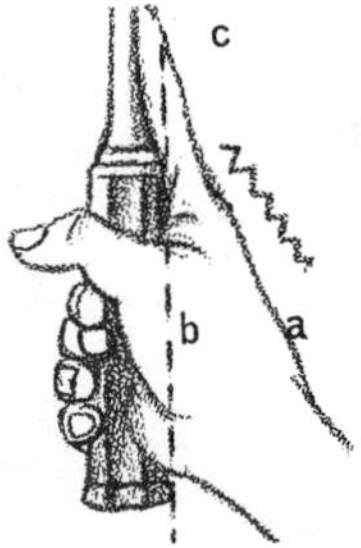

Difficulty	*Correction*
a. Choking the racket	a. Review grip; move hand down and explain the value of the longer reach
b. Holding the racket so tightly that muscles become tense, resulting in loss of power	b. Spread fingers around the handle. Hold racket with the greatest pressure exerted by thumb and first finger. Stress relaxed firmness
c. First finger extended behind the racket head, resulting in limited wrist action	c. Review grip position; some find that a piece of tape on the finger serves as a reminder to lower the finger
d. Clutching the racket with a "baseball grip" which results in limited wrist flexibility and loss of stroking power	d. Extend fingers around the handle with the racket resting at the base of the fingers
e. Failure to modify the grip for the backhand, resulting in loss of power	e. Spread fingers around the handle and extend the thumb for greater support on the backhand

Contacting the Shuttlecock

Difficulty	*Correction*
a. Missing the shuttle entirely, often caused by looking up or jumping at the stroke	a. Drill in tracking objects to the racket, such as a wool ball on a string. Have partner throw wool practice ball or shuttles at the same speed and direction until the object can be hit consistently
b. Hitting on the racket edge or throat	b. Follow the shuttle to the racket face with the eyes; remain relaxed and stroke rhythmically
c. Stroking shuttle straight up, because of stiff, inflexible arm and wrist	c. Swing freely with little regard for accuracy until the sound and "feel" assure the player she is stroking rhythmically. Follow through in the desired direction of shuttle flight

Footwork and Timing

Difficulty	*Correction*
a. Wrong foot forward and weight back, resulting in high stroke or misdirected shot	a. Concentrate on weight transfer for power and to position the player for return to center in anticipation of the next stroke
b. Allowing the shuttle to pass behind, resulting in miss-hit or poorly executed stroke	b. Stress, "always play the shuttle in front"; move quickly into position behind the shuttle to allow time to track the shuttle and transfer weight
c. Swinging too late or rushing the shot	c. As noted in b above, move to position in time to get set for the shot
d. Standing too close to the shuttle, resulting in inaccurate and rushed shots	d. Move from ready position *after* opponent strokes but move quickly and decisively so time can be taken for execution. *PRACTICE*
e. Failure to reach the opponent's return	e. Return to center *ready position* and await the next return. Move immediately following your own stroke to avoid being caught out of position

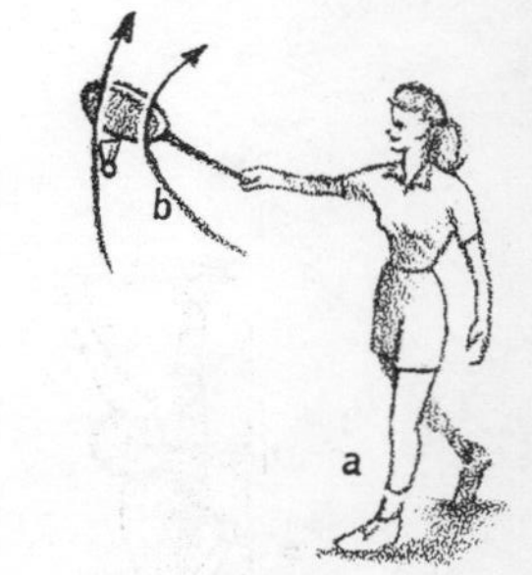

Serving

Difficulty	*Correction*
a. Missing the shuttle	a. Concentrate on dropping the shuttle before swinging the racket forward. Flex knees and watch the shuttle. Practice at a station on the wall properly marked with net height
b. Hitting the shuttle in a low trajectory into the net	b. Follow through in the direction of desired flight
c. Serving too high and shallow on a deep serve	c. Move shuttle in front of left foot
d. Serving too low or flat on a high, deep serve	d. Stress wrist and forearm flexibility. Bring racket head high on follow-through
e. Hitting too high on a low serve so that opponent can return with a smash	e. Contact the shuttle at waist level. Keep wrist cocked during swing. Lean toward net on follow-through
f. Tossing the shuttle, resulting in erratic shots	f. Concentrate on dropping the shuttle, *then* swinging the racket

Overhead Clear

Difficulty	*Correction*
a. Shot falls short and enables opponent to smash	a. Check grip to assure that power can be imparted. Be certain that contact with the shuttle is above the shoulder and forward. Use powerful body rotation, arm extension, and weight transfer for power
b. Clear has a flat trajectory	b. Contact shuttle as high as possible and follow through with an extended arm
c. Backhand clear lacks power and falls short in the court	c. Check proper grip. Swing so racket reaches shuttle when it is over the forward foot; rotate body and swing freely

Overhead Smash

Difficulty	*Correction*
a. Shuttle is driven into net	a. Contact shuttle high and drive it forward and downward with powerful wrist and forearm rotation. Follow through to the spot of intended flight
b. Shuttle slows down before crossing into opponent's court	b. Check point of execution on the court; execute smash from midcourt forward, not from backcourt
c. Smash has little power	c. Rotate the torso, shift weight, and contact with powerful wrist and forearm rotation
d. Shuttle path is a flattened arc	d. Extend arm and reach high so that contact is at the highest possible point in front of the body

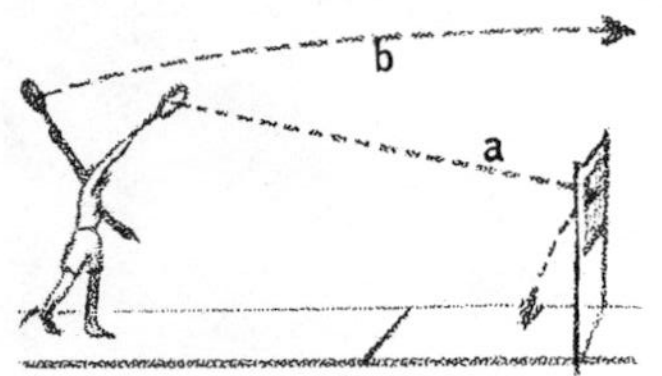

Overhead Drop Shot

Difficulty	*Correction*
a. Drop shot is identified by opponent as it is hit	a. To maintain deception make the swing appear to be a power stroke. Rotate the body strongly on the backswing
b. Shuttle travels too high and too deep into the court	b. Concentrate on the control of power with the direction of the racket head forward, rather than upward. Follow through downward
c. Shuttle falls short of the net	c. Avoid "giving" by bending the arm or collapsing the wrist. Contact the shuttle firmly and follow through

Underhand Clear

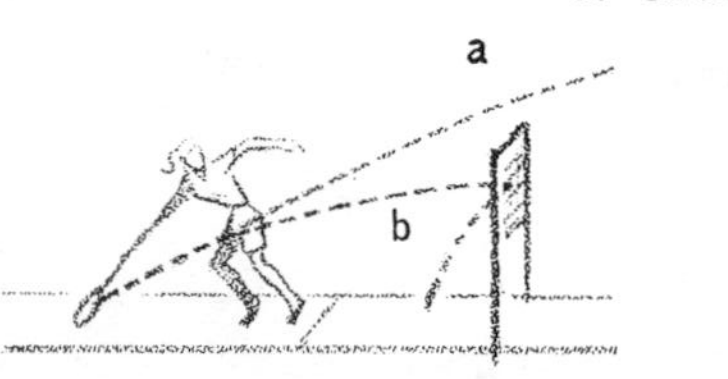

Difficulty	*Correction*
a. Shuttle travels high to midcourt	a. Check timing and contact with the shuttle. Release wrist and forearm and follow through in the direction of shuttle flight
b. Shuttle travels deep and outside court area	b. See above. Follow through *upward* as well as forward

Forehand Drive

Difficulty	*Correction*
a. Loss of power as shuttle is contacted late behind the body	a. Contact shuttle off the forward foot; rotate left side of the body to the net
b. Shuttle travels too high	b. Contact the shuttle as close to net level as possible; follow through toward the top of the net

Hairpin Net Shot

Difficulty	*Correction*
a. Shuttle goes too high and is easily returned by a net smash	a. Avoid wrist atcion. Guide shuttle over the net with a "lift' rather than a stroke. Contact the shuttle as close to the top of the net as possible
b. Shuttle does not go over the net	b. Avoid "give" of the arm or wrist which kills shuttle action. Follow through the stroke

Push Net Stroke

Difficulty	*Correction*
a. Shuttle is easily returned because of placement	a. Push shuttle *between* the two opponents
b. Shuttle travels too high or out of the court	b. Angle of racket head is toward the floor on contact
c. Shuttle is hit into the net	c. Contact shuttle above net level

Round-the-Head Stroke

Difficulty	*Correction*
a. Shuttle is driven into the net	a. Move to the shuttle quickly and contact it at its highest point
b. Ineffective midcourt shot when executing a clear. Too little power	b. Review body position, stroking action, weight transfer, and follow-through
c. Falling away from shuttle when hitting, resulting in a slow recovery to center court position	c. Transfer weight forward on the follow-through and quickly return to center position

EVALUATING THE RESULTS

Both the student and the teacher should be constantly aware of the student's progress in skill development. Class tournaments are a form of self-testing, for the proof of skill development lies in the results of competitive play. Weaknesses and strengths can be assessed systematically by testing the various strokes throughout the instructional unit. Tests for serving, clearing, and rallying can be used.

Rating Scales. Teachers frequently devise rating scales for the subjective assessment of form and effectiveness of strokes. Students can be taught to observe and use these scales; however, their evaluations should not be the basis for individual student grades. A form such as the one below might be developed using a scale of 5 (high) to 1 (low), with beginners being assessed on a limited number of skills and advanced players evaluated on a larger number of skills.

Name__________ Date__________ Class__________

Badminton game: Singles______; Doubles______

	Form/Position	Effectiveness	Comments*
Serve	________	________	
Clears	________	________	
Smash	________	________	
Net Play	________	________	
Footwork	________	________	
Drives	________	________	
Game Strategy	________	________	
Total	________	________	

Overall Rating: ______Fair ______Very Good

______Good

*Comments are helpful in individual coaching and in identifying general class weaknesses.

Knowledge Tests. Knowledge tests are frequently made by the instructor of the class to insure that the students are evaluated on course content. There are several accepted tests which have received wide use.

A beginning badminton knowledge test for college students was developed at the University of Washington. It utilizes 106 questions—31 on analysis of strokes and techniques, 41 on rules and scoring, 11 on strategy, and 23 which test knowledge of terminology.*

Neuman developed a puzzle designed to challenge the knowledge of college badminton players. It may be used as a learning alternative, a study review, or even as a test itself.†

Other standardized knowledge tests include:

Hennis, Gail: Badminton knowledge test for college women. *Research Quarterly 27,* October, 1956.

Phillips, Marjorie: Standardization of badminton knowledge test for college women. *Research Quarterly 17*:48, March, 1946.

Scott, Gladys: Achievement examination in badminton. *Research Quarterly 12*:242–250, May, 1941.

Skill Tests. Two standardized skill tests, similar in nature, are frequently used to measure general playing ability. In the Lockhart and McPherson Badminton Test* the player stands behind a starting line 6½ feet from a wall which is at least 10 feet high and 10 feet long. On signal she executes a legal service from behind the starting line to the wall, and above the one-inch line marked 5 feet above and parallel to, the floor. Thereafter she plays the shuttle against the wall as many times as possible within a 30-second time period. After the shuttle has been legally served the player may move up to a three-foot restraining line marked on the floor, but she may not cross the line. Three trials are given, and the score is the number of legal hits made on or above the net line.‡

The Miller Badminton Wall Test** is also designed as a measure of general playing ability. A one-inch line is extended across the wall 7½ feet from, and parallel to, the floor. The wall must be at least 10 feet wide and 15 feet in height. After a one-minute practice period, on the signal, "ready, go," the student legally serves the shuttle from behind the 10 foot floor line and plays it on the rebound. One point is scored for every time the shuttle hits on or above the 7½ foot wall line. If the foot or any body part goes over the line, or if the shuttle goes below the 7½ foot wall

---

*Fox, Katherine: Beginning badminton written examination. *Research Quarterly 24*: 135–146, May, 1953.

†Neuman, Bonnie: Knowledge challenger. *Selected Tennis and Badminton Articles.* Division for Girls' and Women's Sports, AAHPER, Washington, D.C., 1970.

‡Lockhart, Aileene, and McPherson, Francis A.: The development of a test of badminton playing ability. *Research Quarterly 20*:4, December, 1949.

**Miller, Frances A.: A badminton wall volley test. *Research Quarterly 22*:2, May, 1951.

line, no point is scored. However, when this occurs, the player may keep the shuttle in play. A serve may also be stopped and restarted at any time behind the 10 foot line, including when it is missed. Any stroke can be used. A "carry" or double hit counts if the shuttle is hit and goes above the 7½ foot wall line. The player may go across the line to pick up the shuttle but must be behind it to start play again. Three 30-second trials are given, and the final score consists of the sum of three trials.

Hicks* developed a battery of five badminton skills tests to measure a player's ability to execute the clear stroke, smash stroke, overhead drop shot, and her ability to move quickly and efficiently on the court. She developed a strategy test to determine a player's general ability to decide upon and execute the appropriate stroke in a competitive situation. She recommends that the clear, smash, and footwork tests be given to beginners and that overhead drop and strategy tests be administered to intermediate and advanced players.

TERMINOLOGY

ABA—American Badminton Association.

Alley—An area 1½ feet wide on each side of the court between the singles and doubles sidelines. The area is used in doubles play.

Back alley—An area 2½ feet deep between the back boundary line and the doubles back service line.

Balk—A deceptive movement by the server which is disconcerting to the opponent during service and is illegal. This fault is also referred to as a feint.

Bird—The unofficial name of the shuttlecock.

Block—A shot in which there is little stroking action. The shuttle is *met* so that it rebounds into the opponent's court.

Carry—Also called a sling or throw. An illegal stroke wherein the shuttle is held momentarily on the racket head.

Center position—Basic position in which the player stands and to which she returns in anticipation of the next stroke. It is determined by court, net, last return stroke, and opponent's position.

Clear—A stroke which causes the shuttle to travel high and deep into the opponent's back court.

Crosscourt—A stroke that moves the shuttle diagonally from one side of the court to the other.

Double hit—An illegal procedure of hitting the shuttle twice during the execution of a stroke.

Drive—A low, fast, sidearm shot hit deep in the opponent's court and skimming over the net.

Drop—A stroke—executed with deception—which has little speed and falls close to the net in the opponent's court.

Fault—Any violation of service or play which results in a point or loss of service.

First service—A term used in doubles to indicate that the first server retains her serve.

---

*Hicks, Virginia: The Construction and Evaluation of a Battery of Five Badminton Skill Tests. Unpublished doctoral dissertation. Texas Women's University, 1967. See Virginia Hicks: *The How To of Badminton from Player to Teacher.* pp. 40–50.

Flick—A deceptive stroke executed from below net level in which a shuttle is hit upward and forward by rapid wrist and forearm action.
Game—A game in all doubles games and men's singles is 15 points; women's singles games consist of 11 points.
Hairpin net shot—A shuttle stroked close to and below net level which clears the net and drops perpendicular and close to the net on the opponent's side.
IBF—International Badminton Federation; the governing body of badminton throughout the world.
Inning—A term of service, or time during which a player or side holds service.
In side—The side which is serving.
Let—A replay of the serve or point.
Love—No score; also used after setting in a tied game.
Match—Generally, the best two out of three games.
Net drop shot—A shot which barely clears the net and falls toward the opponent's forecourt.
No shot—A call used by a player to indicate she has committed a fault in stroking. The call would be used on slings, throws, and carries.
Out side—The side receiving service.
Push shot—A soft pushing action on the shuttle, rather than a stroking action, which results in a gentle hit.
Round-the-head shot—A stroke unique to badminton in which the racket is pulled overhead to the left side of the body (right-handed player) to contact the shuttle over the left shoulder for a clear, drop, smash, or half paced smash.
Second service—A term used in doubles to indicate that one server is "down" and the second now has a term of service.
Service—The serve; an opportunity to put the shuttle in play with an underhand stroke.
Setting—A method of extending the game in order to break tie games one or two points from completion. Prerogative of setting rests with the player or team first reaching the appropriate tied score. (See page 90.)
Shuttle—Common term used for shuttlecock.
Sling—A carry or throw. An illegal shot in which the shuttle is momentarily held or carried on the racket face.
Smash—A hard, fast, overhead shot that travels sharply downward into the opponent's court.
Wood shot—A shot in which the base of the shuttle strikes the racket frame or handle. Wood shots are *not* faults.

DISCUSSION QUESTIONS

1. Demonstrate and describe the high, deep service, forehand high clear, smash, hairpin net stroke, and forehand drop shot.
2. Design a teaching area for a beginning class of 42 students in a gymnasium where there are only four courts. There is ample space outside the courts and the wall space is about 25 feet from all courts. How can the space be utilized and what other activities can you have students engage in?
3. Design a rating scale for your use in observing a class of beginning students. The scale should include the basic skills and strategies you feel are needed by beginners.
4. Design an instructional module for teaching the rules of badminton—both singles and doubles—which you feel beginning players need to know.
5. Utilizing only four courts for a class of 42 students, design a doubles and singles tournament which allows for all students to participate during four class periods.
6. Devise an objective knowledge test of 25 items to be taken by your classmates. Score and evaluate the items on the test.

SELECTED AUDIOVISUAL AIDS

All-England World Championship Singles Finals. (60 min., sound, b & w.) J. Frank Devlin, RFD 2, Dolfield Road, Owings Mill, Maryland 21117. (Rental)

Badminton Fundamentals, 1950. (10 min., sound, b & w.) Coronet Instructional Films, 65 East South Water Street, Chicago, Illinois 60601. (Rental)

Beginning Badminton Series. (Instructor's Guide and Handbooks, filmstrips, 6 units, color.) The Athletic Institute, 805 Merchandise Mart, Chicago, Illinois 60654. (Purchase)

Fundamentals of Badminton. (12 min., sound, b & w.) All-American Productions and Publishers, c/o G. B. Pearson, Department of Health, Physical Education and Recreation, University of Alabama, Tuscaloosa, Alabama 35486. (Sale and rental)

Let's Play Badminton, 1947. (15½ min., sound, b & w.) General Sportcraft Company, 140 Woodbine, Bergenfield, New Jersey 07621.

Film Loops. Jim Poole, consultant. Loops include: Grip and Service, Overhead Forehand Strokes, Overhead Backhand Strokes, Underhand Net Strokes, Drives and Around-the-Head Strokes, and Footwork. Holt, Rinehart and Winston, Inc., Media Department, 383 Madison Avenue, New York, N. Y. 10017. (Purchase)

Loop Films, James Breen, consultant. Loops include: Grip and Cocking, Footwork, High Deep Serve, Low Short Serve, Drive Serve, Flick Serve, Forehand Overhead Shots, Backhand Overhead Shots, Drive Shots, Net Shots, and Around-the-Head Shots. Athletic Institute, 805 Merchandise Mart, Chicago, Illinois 60654. (Purchase)

SUGGESTED READINGS

American Alliance for Health, Physical Education and Recreation: *Ideas for Badminton Instruction.* Washington, D.C., 1967.

Badminton Association of England: *Notes for Badminton Coaches.* 81A High St. Bromley, Kent, England.

Bloss, Margaret Varner: *Badminton.* 2nd Ed. Dubuque, Iowa, William C. Brown Co., 1971.

Brown, Edward: *The Complete Book of Badminton.* Harrisburg, Pennsylvania, Stackpole Books, 1969.

Crossley, Key: *Progressive Badminton.* New Rochelle, New York, Soccer Associates, 1971.

Davidson, Kenneth R., and Gustavson, Leland R.: *Winning Badminton.* New York, The Ronald Press, 1964.

Davidson, Kenneth R., and Smith, Lenore C.: *Badminton.* Available from Shirley Bailey, 24 Westwood Terrace, Millville, New Jersey 08332, 1971.

Davis, Pat: *Badminton Coach: A Manual for Coaches, Teachers and Players.* New Rochelle, New York, Soccer Associates, 1972.

Hicks, Virginia: *The How To of Badminton from Player to Teacher.* V. Hicks, 1804 Hicks Lane, Denton, Texas 76201, 1973.

Johnson, M. L.: *Badminton.* Philadelphia, W. B. Saunders Co., 1974.

National Association for Girls and Women in Sport. *Tennis-Badminton-Squash Guide.* Current Ed. AAHPER, Washington, D.C. 20036.

Pelton, Barry: *Badminton.* Englewood Cliffs, New Jersey, Prentice-Hall Inc., 1971.

Poole, James: *Badminton.* Pacific Palisades, California, Goodyear Publishing Co., 1969.

Rogers, Wynn: *Advanced Badminton.* Dubuque, Iowa, William C. Brown Co., 1970.

Rutledge, Abbie, and Friedrich, John A.: *Beginning Badminton.* Revised Ed. Belmont, California, Wadsworth Publishing Co., 1969.

Tyler, Jo Ann, ed.: *Selected Tennis-Badminton Articles.* Division for Girls' and Women's Sports, AAHPER, Washington, D.C., 1970.

PERIODICALS

The Badminton Gazette. H. A. E. Scheele, editor. 4 Madeira Avenue, Bromley, Kent, England.
Badminton U.S.A. Beatrice Massman, editor. 333 Saratoga Road, Buffalo, New York 14226.

FREE MATERIALS

Badminton and Tennis Strokes and *Guide to Better Badminton.* Ashaway Products, Inc., Ashaway, Rhode Island 02804.

CHAPTER 7

BOWLING

Bowling, the most popular indoor sport in the United States, attracts more than 50 million participants to more than 75,000 lanes each year. Bowling is rapidly becoming an international sport, with growing enthusiasm in Japan, Canada, Great Britain, and the Scandinavian countries. It is estimated that over six million men, three and a half million women, and one million young people bowl in organized leagues throughout the world.

Although artifacts of the Stone Age indicate that the true origin of bowling games lies in antiquity, there is evidence that games using balls or discs of stone propelled towards stone or wooden objects through an archway of marble were part of the cultures of ancient Egypt, Polynesia, and Rome. The English game of "skittles" played as early as the eleventh century is undoubtedly the parent of the present games of duckpins and candlepins.

The development of the modern game of tenpin bowling can be traced from a German religious ceremony. During the third and fourth centuries, most German men carried a *kegel*—a small club resembling an Indian club—for use in strengthening wrists and forearms, for recreation, and for religious ceremony. In this ceremony a man called on by the priest to prove he was leading an honorable life had to set up his kegel, called *Heide* (heathen), and knock it over with a small round stone. The monks and laymen recognized the recreational value in bowling and continued the sport long after the religious ceremony was abolished. Martin Luther, an enthusiastic bowler of the fifteenth century, pulbished a set of rules for a game of ninepins.

The ninepin game came to America with the Dutch and German settlers, and the earliest known reference to the game was made in *Rip Van Winkle* in 1818 by Washington Irving. The game became so popular that indoor lanes, the Knickerbocker Alleys, were built in New York in

1840. Bowling suffered a setback when the ninepin game was prohibited by the Connecticut, New York, and Massachusetts legislatures because of gambling and rowdiness. It remained for an ingenious hero to add a tenth pin to circumvent the law. The additional pin resulted in a triangular set and the birth of present day bowling.

The game of tenpins attracts the greatest number of bowlers, although a group of devoted enthusiasts continue to play duckpins, candlepins and fivepins. These games require a smaller ball which is carried on the palm of the hand during delivery. The Italian lawn bowling game of *bocce ball* is enjoying new interest in this country and abroad.

The American Bowling Congress was organized in 1895 and standardized rules, equipment, and alleys. In 1916, the Women's International Bowling Congress was organized and has continued to conduct national tournaments and give leadership to the sport. The American Junior Bowling Congress, founded in 1941, sponsors tournaments and helps boys and girls receive reduced rates and free instruction. In 1966, a collegiate division was formed, filling the need for competition between the junior and adult programs. National intercollegiate championships, sponsored by the Association of College Unions International (ACU-I) and AMF, Inc., are held annually. Members of these organizations enjoy a wide range of services, including rules assistance and counseling, workshops and leadership training, awards, manuals, guides, record keeping aids, kits of league supplies, publications, audiovisual aids and publicity services.

To coordinate the activities and services of the entire bowling field, the National Bowling Council was established in 1943. Its board has representation from manufacturers of bowling and duckpin equipment, the bowling congresses and the Bowling Proprietors Association of America.

The alertness of national organizations toward meeting the needs of all ages, the emphasis given the sport by television, which brings understanding and appreciation to millions, and the "new look" of bowling establishments are the primary reasons for increased public interest. The well decorated, air conditioned alley with automatic pinsetting equipment is an attractive, desirable place for the entire family's recreation. It is, indeed, in marked contrast to the first known indoor bowling lanes—in London in 1455.

THE NATURE AND PURPOSE OF THE GAME

The object of a bowler is to roll well-aimed balls down a wooden alley and knock down as many of the triangularly set tenpins at the end of the alley as possible. Ten frames constitute a game, and each frame represents a player's turn. The bowler is allowed two balls each frame. When all the pins are knocked down with the first ball, a strike is scored. If all pins are knocked down on the second ball, a spare is recorded. Bonus points are added to the running score for strikes and spares. The maximum number of pins which can be scored in a game is 300. The bowler stands in an approach area, walks or runs toward the alley, and delivers the ball from behind the foul line so that it rolls toward the pins. Competition can be individual, with from one to five persons on an alley, or it may be in units, with as many as five on each team. A handicap scoring system allows for equitable competition among all skill levels.*

SIMPLIFIED RULES AND SCORING†

A game of American tenpins is ten frames. The number of pins legally knocked down in any frame, plus the pins knocked down by the first ball following a spare delivery, or the pins knocked down by the next two deliveries following a strike ball, is the total score of a frame. The score is cumulative from frame to frame for ten frames. A perfect score is 300. The player bowls two balls for each frame, unless she delivers a strike, which upsets all ten pins with the first ball. When this occurs a second ball is not delivered in that frame. However, if a strike is delivered in the tenth frame, two more balls are delivered immediately. If a spare is made (all ten pins upset by the first and second balls) in the tenth frame, one more ball must be rolled at a new set of pins immediately to complete the game score.

When all pins are knocked down by the first ball in a frame, a strike is recorded by an (X) in a small square in the upper right corner of that frame. Eventually, the score in that frame will be the cumulative total of all pins knocked down in the preceding frames, ten pins scored for the strike plus the total number of pins knocked down by the next two balls.

The number of pins knocked down by the first ball (other than a strike) is recorded in the first square in the frame. When all the remaining pins are knocked over by the second roll, a *spare* is indicated by a diagonal line (/) in the second square of the frame. All pinfalls must be recorded. Since many of the newer score sheets have only one box in the upper right hand corner of each frame, the pinfall (other than a strike) will be recorded in the space directly to the left of the box. The player's score in the spare frame is a cumulative total of all pins knocked down in the preceding frames, the ten pins scored for the spare, and the pins knocked down on the next ball delivered.

An *error* or *blow* has been made if a player fails to bowl down all ten pins after having completed two deliveries in a given frame, provided the pins left standing after the first ball do not constitute a split. If no pins are

---

*For tournament competition refer to WIBC *Rules for Sanctioned Leagues.*

†Official rules are established by the American Bowling Congress and the Women's International Bowling Congress.

knocked down by either or both ball deliveries, this is indicated by a straight line (—) in the appropriate space or square.

If, after the first ball is delivered, the head pin is down and two or more pins are left standing with at least one pin knocked down between them, a *split* is recorded by a circle (O). If the remaining pins are knocked down by the second ball, a spare is indicated (Ø) in the score box. When pins remain standing after the second ball, only the number of pins knocked down by the two balls is scored.

If a ball is delivered to the channel before reaching the pins, a (—) is recorded in the appropriate box.

An understanding of the foul rule is basic to accurate scoring. There are many ways in which a foul may be committed, but the most common is permitting any part of the body to touch the foul line or go beyond it during or after delivery (see Figure 7–1). A foul is indicated by recording (F) in the proper space or square.

When a foul is committed, the ball rolled shall count as a turn, but any pins knocked down or displaced are respotted; and no pins are scored. For example, if a foul occurs on the first ball rolled in a frame, the pins are respotted; and should the bowler knock down all ten pins on the second ball, a *spare* is recorded. A player who deliberately fouls to benefit by the calling of a foul is not permitted to complete the game and series, and the deliberate foul is not allowed.

A game description and illustration of recording scores are helpful in mastering scoring techniques (see Figure 7–2):

Frame 1—1. All pins are knocked down by the first ball (a strike).
Frame 2—1. Six pins are knocked down, head pin remains standing on first ball.
2. Remaining pins are knocked down by second ball. A spare is recorded and the score totaled for the first frame.
Frame 3—1. Eight pins fall on the first delivery, leaving pins 7 and 9. A split is recorded, and total can be reached for second frame.
2. Second ball knocks down the remaining pins. A spare is recorded.
Frame 4—1. A strike is recorded. Total score recorded in frame 3.
Frame 5—1. Six pins are knocked down.

Figure 7–1 Two common fouls.

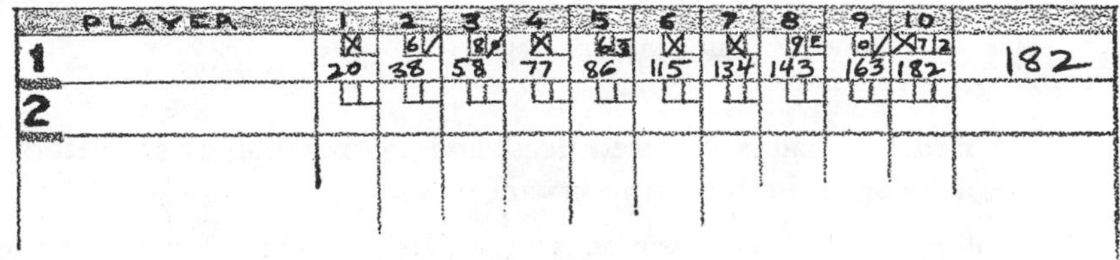

Figure 7–2 Sample score sheet.

2. Three pins are knocked down by second ball. A miss is recorded in the score box. Total score is recorded in frames 4 and 5.

Frame 6 – 1. A strike is recorded.

Frame 7 – 1. A strike is recorded.

Frame 8 – 1. Nine pins are knocked down on the first delivery. Score is totaled in frame 6.

2. The second ball hits the remaining pin, but the bowler's foot crosses the foul line. A foul is recorded in the score box, and the score is totaled.

Frame 9 – 1. The first ball runs into the channel, and no pins are knocked over.

2. The second ball knocks down all pins. A spare is scored.

Frame 10 – 1. A strike is scored. Score in frame 9 is totaled.

2. Next ball delivered knocks down 7 pins.

3. Last ball rolled knocks down 2 of the 3 remaining pins. The completed game score is recorded.

The official rules are established by the American Bowling Congress and the Women's International Bowling Congress. Basic rules include:

Legal Pinfall. Every ball a player delivers counts unless it is ruled a dead ball.

1. Pins knocked down by another pin or pins rebounding from a side partition, rear cushion, or stationary sweep bar count as pins down.
2. If it is discovered after delivery that one or more pins are not properly set, though not missing, the ball and any pinfall are counted. (It is the bowler's responsibility to determine proper pin set prior to delivery.)
3. Pins that are knocked down by a fair ball and remain lying on the alley bed or in the channels count as pins down. Pins that lean over and touch partitions or kickbacks also count. They are moved before the next ball is bowled.
4. Pins knocked down by a ball which rolls over the foul line or touches the foul line upon release are credited to the player as a legal delivery.

Illegal Pinfall. The ball counts, but the pins knocked down do not count when:

1. The ball leaves the alley before reaching the pins.
2. The ball rebounds from the rear cushion.
3. The pins contact any portion of a human pinsetter's body. Pins are replaced.
4. A standing pin falls or is knocked down by the pinsetter. It must be replaced.

5. Pins are bowled off the alley bed but rebound to standing position. These pins are counted as pins standing.
6. A foul is committed.

Dead Ball. A ball is declared dead, and any pins falling are respotted for the bowler in the following instances:

1. A ball is delivered and attention is immediately called to the fact that one or more pins were missing from the setup.
2. A pinsetter or mechanical setting device interferes or moves a pin before pins stop rolling or before the ball reaches the pins.
3. A player bowls out of turn or on the wrong lane.
4. A player is interfered with by a pinsetter, spectator, bowler, or a moving object as the ball is delivered and before delivery is complete. The bowler may either accept the pinfall or request that the pins be respotted.
5. Pins are moved or knocked down in any manner as the ball is being delivered and before the ball reaches the pins.
6. A player's ball contacts a foreign object.

Foul. A foul is committed and the ball rolled *does* count, but the pins that fall *do not* count when a part of the bowler's person touches on or beyond the foul line contacting the lane, equipment, or building during or after a delivery.

NEEDED FACILITIES AND EQUIPMENT

One of the appeals bowling has for the beginner is that it is not necessary to own a single piece of equipment to participate. An enthusiastic kegler will want to own her personal shoes, ball, and equipment bag eventually, but commercial establishments and most student unions rent shoes at a nominal fee and furnish balls.

Dress. No special uniform or costume is required. Clothing should be stylish, comfortable, and loose fitting for freedom of movement. Well fitting socks should be worn. Bowling shoes are essential for safety and skill development. For a right-handed bowler the left sole is leather, Teflon or felt to allow for sliding on the approach, and the right sole is rubber for braking this action. The sole materials are reversed for left-handed, or "wrong foot," bowlers. A leather-soled shoe or heavy sock on the sliding foot and a tennis shoe on the braking foot may substitute for regulation shoes during instructional periods in the gymnasium or corridors.

Bowling Aids. Items used by bowlers, other than balls, bag, and shoes, fall into two categories. There are (1) aids which are intended to improve scoring by helping the wrist, fingers, and palm execute their movements more effectively and (2) aids which are protective. Glove-type aids often have cushions or pads in the palm which help keep pressure off the fingers during delivery and help maintain contact with the ball. Wrist bands help maintain a straight line from elbow to knuckles. "Sure-grips" are inserts for the finger and thumb holes, and rosin is also available to help the bowler maintain a better grip. Protective aids to prevent blisters and protect calluses and open cuts are usually of nylon or cotton material and are used with a type of new skin or calodium, a sticky substance which helps the gauze adhere to the skin and thus eliminates friction from the ball. As helpful as these items may be, both physically and psychologically, nothing improves a game as much as proper practice of the basic fundamentals and techniques and planning each delivery thoughtfully.

Ball. The American Bowling Congress rules that balls may not be more than 27 inches in circumference or weigh more than 16 pounds. Balls with two, three, or more finger holes or semifingertip or fingertip grips are permissible. Most beginning women bowlers are more comfortable with a three hole ball weighing 10 to 12 pounds, while junior bowlers may select smaller balls weighing between eight and twelve pounds. Balls are manufactured of hard rubber or plastic in solid, speckled, or mottled colors. Many expert bowlers select plastic balls for their softer consistency which seems to allow them to skid farther on the hardwood before they hook.

Alley. The terms alley and lane are synonymous and include the total area where the preparation, delivery, and contact with pins take place. The area includes the approach, foul line with its electronic sensor, alley bed, channels (gutters), and pit. The ball return and rack are also part of a complete lane.

The approach is a level runway extending from the seating area and scoring table to the foul line. A minimum of 15 feet is necessary for the approach. The alley bed is 63 feet long, 41 to 42 inches wide and begins at the foul line and extends to the pit area. The alley bed is constructed of maple and pine lengths laid vertically so that the balls roll on the thickness

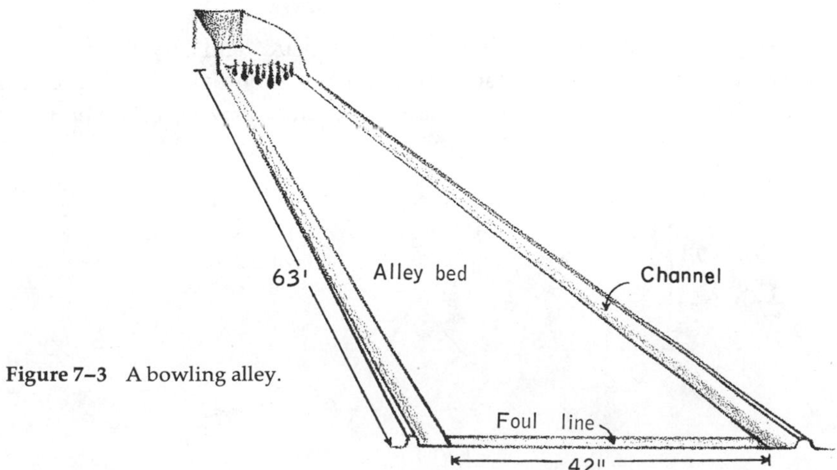

Figure 7–3 A bowling alley.

of the boards. The harder and more durable maple wood is laid at the beginning of the foul line for 12 or 15 feet, then pine, then maple again on the deck area where the pins are knocked over. Many alleys have range finders to help in selecting a point of aim in spot bowling. These darts, or dots, are usually placed where the maple and pine lengths first join on the alley bed.

On the deck, ten pin spots are marked for accuracy in setting pins. The spots are 12 inches apart, from center to center, in a triangular pattern with the apex toward the bowler. The head pin is set 3 feet from the end of the alley.

The pit, at the rear of the alley, is a depressed area into which pins are knocked and the human or automatic pinsetter works. Automatic pinsetters and ball returns are common in commercial alleys and newer college facilities.

On each side of the alley bed, there is a rounded and depressed channel or gutter 9 to 9½ inches wide. This trough carries a poorly aimed ball to the pit where it is placed manually or automatically on the ball return track either above or below the floor, and returned to the rack near the approach area.

Pins. Most official pins are made of laminated maple fitted with a plastic base and coated with plastic. Synthetic or nonwood pins have also been developed. An approved tenpin is 15 inches in height and 4¾ inches at its greatest breadth, with the weight range for plastic-coated maple core pins from 3 pounds 2 ounces to 3 pounds 10 ounces. Approved synthetic pins range from 3 pounds 4 ounces to 3 pounds 6 ounces. No pin in a set may vary more than 4 ounces from the other nine. Competition pins are white with a red stripe around the neck.

TEACHING UNITS

Suggested units for beginning, intermediate, and advanced students follow. If instructors find that two groups, rather than three, are more manageable, the intermediate and advanced units may be combined.

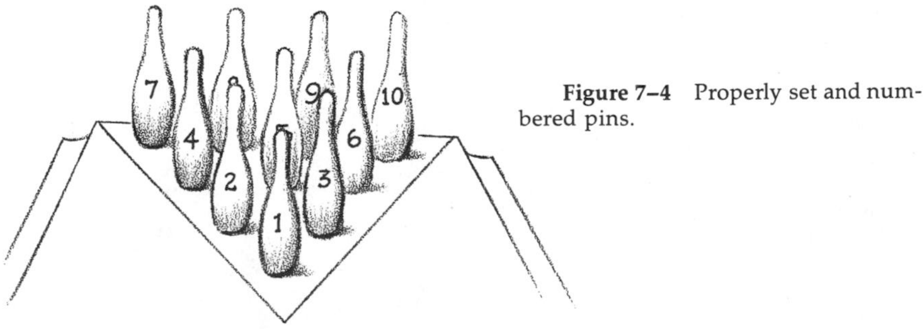

Figure 7–4 Properly set and numbered pins.

Beginners

Brief history
Orientation to alley or setting
Explanation of game
 Equipment
 Beginning safety precautions
Dress
Selection of equipment
 Shoes
 Ball
Grip
Shadow bowling, with emphasis upon the proper pushaway, steps, and delivery
Bowling games (novelty)
Fundamentals of straight ball delivery (Some instructors choose to teach the hook ball delivery from the beginning)
 Grip
 Four step approach
 Delivery
 Aiming
Scoring
Spot bowling
Cross alley bowling
Etiquette
Game bowling
Beginners' tournament
Evaluation

Intermediate Students

Review of equipment, pinsetting, scoring, etiquette, safety
Review straight ball delivery
Review spot and cross alley bowling
Spare bowling
Hook ball delivery
Game bowling (League bowling)
Evaluation

Advanced Students

General review
Game bowling
Curve ball
Explain average and handicaps
Selection of special equipment
Intensive practice on designated spare leaves
Explain "fast" and "slow" alley beds
League bowling
Elimination tournament
Evaluation

BASIC SKILLS

Ball Selection and Grip. Selecting a ball of the proper weight that permits a comfortable grip is basic to successful scoring. Ball choice is determined by an individual's strength and size and the location, size, and pitch of the finger holes. Most women use the conventional grip, rather than the semifinger or full fingertip. Many prefer using the three hole ball and have found that doing so gives them additional finger strength and ball control.

Size and pitch of the finger and thumb holes and the span of the bowler's hand determine the proper fit of a ball. The pitch of a hole is the angle at which the hole is drilled into the ball with relationship to the center of the ball. The four basic pitches used are forward, reverse, right lateral, and left lateral. The holes must be small enough to allow the thumb, middle, and ring finger to maintain contact with the edge of the hole toward the palm of the hand, yet loose enough for an easy release without scraping the fingers. Proper span for the conventional three hole grip is determined by inserting the thumb all the way into the hole drilled on the center line of the ball. Spreading the hand over the contour of the ball so the middle and ring fingers extend to the left and right of the centerline, the middle knuckles of both fingers should extend about 1/4 inch past the inside edge of the holes. If the holes are bored at the usual 3/8 inch angle, a naturally balanced grip results when the thumb is inserted its full length and the fingers inserted up to second joint. The first and little

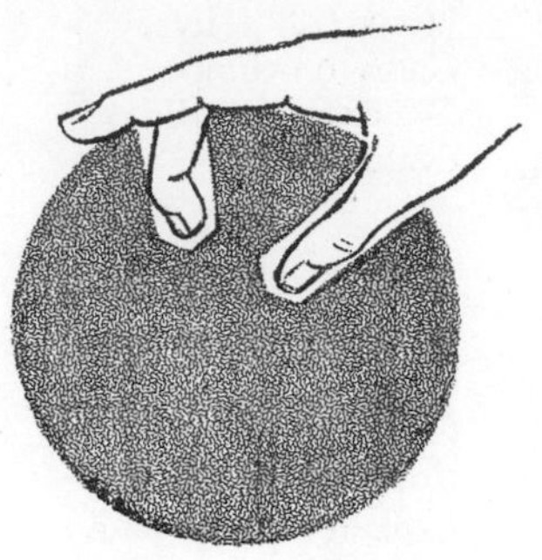

Figure 7–5 Selecting the proper ball.

fingers are straight and spread over the outside of the ball for control. A bowler can check the grip by asking: (1) Is my hand comfortable? (2) Do I have a feeling of control? and (3) Can a pencil be slipped between my hand and the ball without changing the grip? A bowler will not notice the weight of the ball as it is delivered if it fits correctly.

Stance and Approach. These two important skills are best taught as a unit because each is dependent upon the other. Stance involves grip and how and where to stand on the approach area. The bowler determines her point of origin for the four step approach by standing with her back to the alley bed, facing the end of the approach with her heels two inches from the foul line. She then takes four and one-half normal walking strides, turns around to face the pins and notes her position. The half step allows for the slide. The distance to the right or left of center will vary according to the type of ball (hook, curve, straight, or back-up) rolled and her target. Starting from a designated spot so delivery will be consistent, the bowler places her feet close together with her left foot slightly forward (right-handed bowler). The feet, hips, and shoulders are facing the pins squarely. Standing position varies among the experts: some stoop forward with ball held at the waistline, while others stand erect with the ball at chest level. In either case the upper back is straight. Beginners are encouraged to stand upright, knees flexed, weight on the heels, bending slightly forward from the hips, while holding the ball at the waistline. One hand grips, and the other hand, palm up, supports the ball weight. Each bowler should find a comfortable, relaxed position.

The approach is a series of well coordinated movements that end in the release and delivery of the ball. There are two basic methods of advancing to the foul line—the shuffle method and the heel-toe method. The feet of the bowler are not picked up off the approach area in the shuffle method. It is the preferred approach. The heel-toe advance resembles a natural walk with increasing body movement up and down as tempo increases. It is difficult to maintain a straight line approach to the foul line using the heel-toe method. Successful bowlers vary in their approaches from three to five steps, but the four step is popular as the easiest and

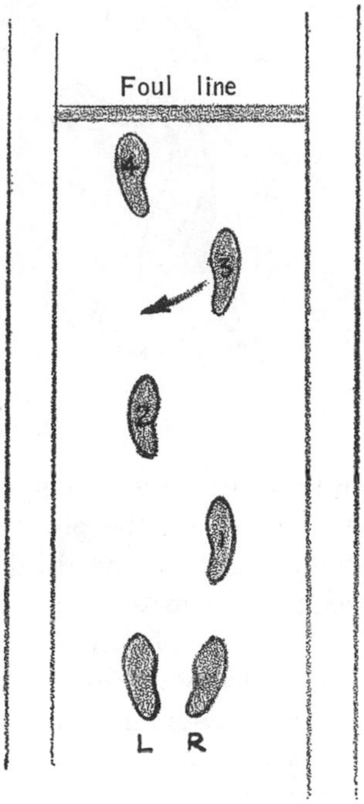

Figure 7–6 Four step approach.

most rhythmical. From a selected stance position the bowler follows a straight line to the foul line and point of ball release. The right-handed bowler moves the right foot forward in a slow, short, rhythmical step; the second step (left foot) is slightly longer and faster. Forward momentum increases as the right foot extends in a longer, faster third step leading to the fastest and longest fourth step on the left foot. Forward momentum stops as the fourth step ends in a slide. At this point, the toe of the left foot should be from two to four inches from the foul line and pointing to the target area. The right foot swings behind the body for balance and for braking action of the forward movement. The approach begins from an upright position, and as the bowler picks up momentum she increases her forward leaning position. The final steps into the slide end with the left knee bent and most of the body weight on the sliding foot. The upper body is straight and inclined forward, while the left arm is extended for balance.

Coordinated Approach. Preparation for delivery requires coordination of approach steps, arm swing, and body action. As the right-handed bowler takes her first step (right foot), the ball, held by both hands in front of the body with the left hand under the ball supporting most of the weight, and elbows close to body, is pushed forward and slightly downward. This "pushaway" extends the arm, which remains straight throughout the swing and release. While the second step is taken (left foot) the right arm swings down and straight backward in a pendulum-like motion,

Figure 7–7 Coordinated approach.

and the supporting hand leaves the ball. At completion of the second step the arm should be pointing straight down, alongside of the leg. The ball swings back on the third step. The left arm is free to swing outward to maintain balance as the body moves in a straight line toward the pins.

On the third step (right foot) the right arm and ball continue upward as the backswing carries the arm to a position parallel to the floor. This is a natural movement as the weight of the ball swings the arm to proper backswing height. The movement should not be forced. As the fourth step (left foot) begins the forward slide, the left knee bends, and the weight of the ball pulls the right arm downward and forward. The right arm and left foot move forward together and arrive at the foul line at approximately the same time. The ball passes the left leg and is released about a foot beyond the foul line. The right arm follows through toward the pins and upward to eye level. The shoulders stay parallel to the foul line, and the left foot finishes on the same board it has followed from the stance position. The right leg is extended behind the body for balance.

Delivery. The beginner should carefully develop either a straight ball or a hook ball delivery. Many instructors suggest the hook ball delivery for serious students. The back-up and curve ball deliveries, briefly described below, should not be attempted. The straight ball delivery is well suited to the occasional bowler, for it can be controlled more consistently than the hook, particularly when bowling at spares. However, the straight ball produces a lower percentage of strikes than the hook ball, which "mixes" the pins more effectively.

Straight Ball Delivery. The right-handed bowler stands in the right-hand corner of the approach area with her left foot five to ten boards from the right gutter. Throughout the coordinated approach the ball hand and arm are in line with the floorboards. As the ball is carried toward the foul line the thumb is in a 12 o'clock position, pointing toward the pins, and the fingers are under and behind the ball. As the release begins the thumb slides from the hole, and the ball rolls off the fingertips a foot beyond the foul line and six to eight boards in from the right gutter. There is no rotation of the forearm. As the ball is released the fingers impart an upward

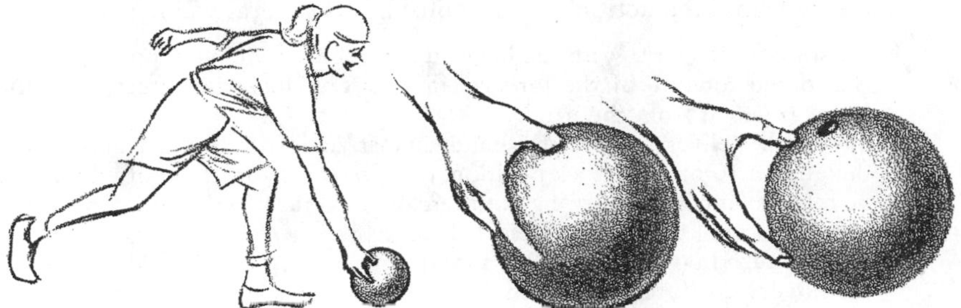

Figure 7–8 Straight ball release.

spin; then the open hand, with palm up and fingers and thumb pointing toward the pins, continues in an upward arc. There should be a feeling of pushing the ball toward the pins.

Hook Ball Delivery. The controlled hook ball has a high strike percentage because the ball hits the pins at an effective angle with a hooking action that scatters the pins. The point of origin for the bowler should be to the right of the center dot on the approach, or 10 to 15 boards from the right channel. The right shoulder should line up directly above the board where the second dot (right of center) is in line with the second arrow on the lane. This is the common strike target. The right-handed bowler turns the ball hand so that the little finger is toward the floor and the thumb is toward the body in an approximate 10 o'clock position during the swing. The "V" between thumb and forefinger points toward the 1–3 pocket. The ball is released beyond the foul line, 6 to 12 boards in from the right gutter. The thumb is released first, with the fingers following. The delayed finger release causes a right to left turn as the hand and arm follow through outward and upward toward the pins. The ball travels parallel to the right gutter toward the 3 or 6 pin, depending on the "break" of the hook. About two thirds of the way down the alley the ball angles sharply toward the pins and travels into the 1–3 pocket to the 5 pin.

Figure 7–9 Hook ball release.

Increased hooking action is accomplished in several ways:

1. Wrist hook delivery. With the hand in natural hook delivery position there is a forced rotation of the forearm in a counterclockwise direction as the ball is released from the hand.
2. Lift hook delivery. With the hand almost underneath the ball and the thumb in a 10 or 11 o'clock position, the *fingers* are forcefully lifted upward on release, imparting a strong counterclockwise turn to the ball. Once mastered, this hook allows excellent ball control.
3. Lift and turn hook delivery. With the thumb in a 10 or 11 o'clock position the fingers are forcefully lifted, with simultaneous forearm rotation. This combination delivery produces the greatest hook of the methods described.

Curve Ball Delivery. The curve is a slow, wide-sweeping ball with a counterclockwise turn which travels in an arc toward the pins. It is difficult to control because of its wide arc and the adjustment necessary to the varying slickness of alleys. It is not recommended for beginners. The width of the ball's arc determines where the bowler stands for delivery. A right-handed bowler using a small arc stands slightly to the right of the head pin. With wide-arcing balls she may move farther to the left of the approach area, possibly to the left of the head pin. The bowler's hand is placed on the ball as in a natural hook delivery, with the thumb rotated back and to the left at a 9 o'clock position. On release the thumb leaves the ball first and the *hand* and *wrist twist* from right to left to impart spin.

Back-up Ball Delivery. This delivery is not recommended, yet it is a common delivery among women and should be corrected. This reverse ball, when delivered by a right-hander, travels toward the left, then curves to the right before striking the pins. The hand is almost directly under the ball with the thumb pointing to the right of the pins (right-handed bowler). As the ball is released, a left-to-right twist causes a reverse spin.

Aiming. There are two distinct theories of aiming, and a third is gaining popularity.

Head Pin Bowling. On the first ball the bowler looks at the pins and aims for the 5 pin through the 1–3 pocket (1–2 pocket for left-handers). A straight ball delivery goes directly for the pocket, whereas a hook delivery is released so that it will break into the pocket. After the first delivery she

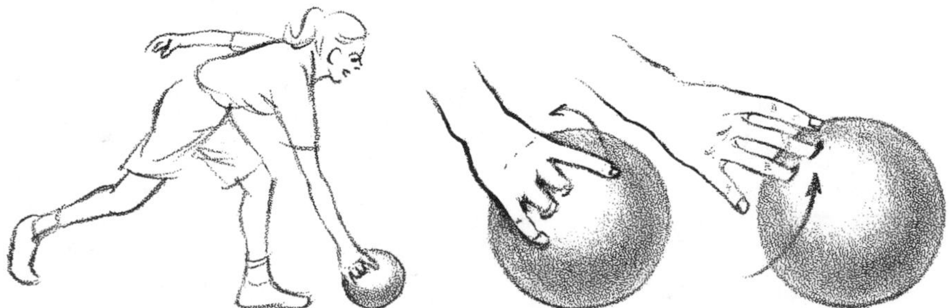

Figure 7–10 Curve ball release.

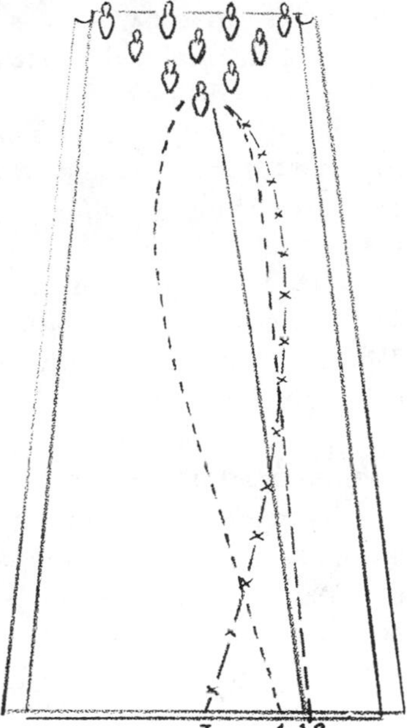

Figure 7–11 Four types of delivery: *(1)* straight ball, *(2)* hook ball, *(3)* curve ball, *(4)* back-up ball.

aims directly at the pin and area she hopes to contact. Pin bowling is less accurate than spot bowling because it is easier to hit a target 15 feet away more accurately than it is to hit a target 60 feet away.

Spot Bowling. The bowler selects one or more spots part way down the lane, between the point of release and the desired point of contact with the pins, over which she tries to roll her ball. Most modern alleys have range markers located in front of the foul line, 7 feet beyond the foul line, and 13 feet 10 inches beyond the foul line to make spot selection easier. On a straight ball delivery the bowler attempts to release the ball between the first and second delivery dots (about 7½ boards in from the

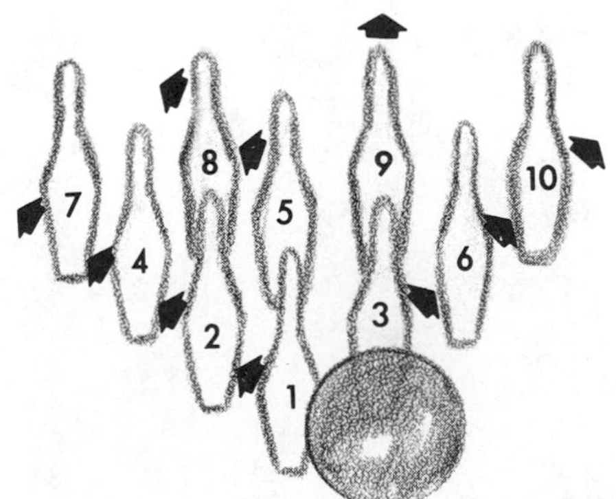

Figure 7–12 Action of the pins on a strike.

channel) so that it will cross the second alley dart (approximately 8 inches from the channel and about 14 feet down the alley).

A natural hook is released halfway between the center delivery spot and the alley edge and is aimed at the dart in line with the release spot. If the alley is not marked, the bowler judges by the number of boards, measured from the alley side. The amount a ball hooks determines the varying release positions.

Line Bowling. This is a combination of pin and spot aiming methods. The line bowler draws an imaginary line from the stance position to the 1–3 pocket. She has four check points: the starting position, the slide position, the chosen spot, and the strike pocket. At any time she can select another spot and then change the other check points. This is a precision method of aiming which requires concentration and practice.

Spare Bowling. The bowler who hopes to score well must develop individual approach positions for picking up basic spare leaves and splits. Five basic positions that help in determining the correct angle approach and position for converting many spares* follow:

1. Strike position—used for the first ball of every frame and any pin combination containing 1 and 5 pins.
2. 7 Pin position—used for 4, 4–7, or 7 pin leaves
3. 8 Pin position—used when 2–4–5–8 pins are in various combinations

*For more details, see Curtis, Joyce: Convert that spare with proper ball placement. *Bowling—Fencing—Golf.* D.G.W.S., 1971–73, pp. 17–20.

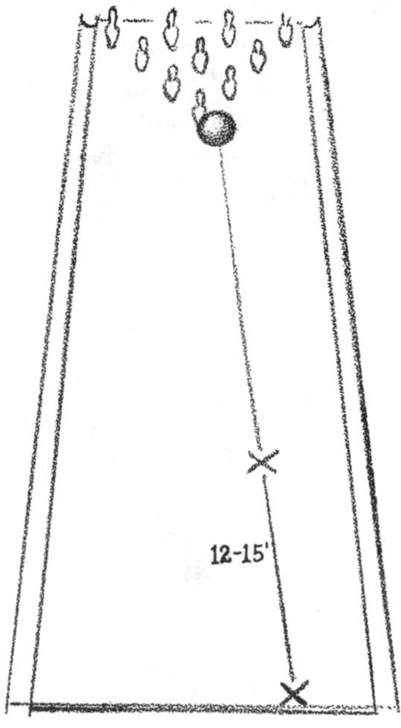

Figure 7–13 Spot bowling.

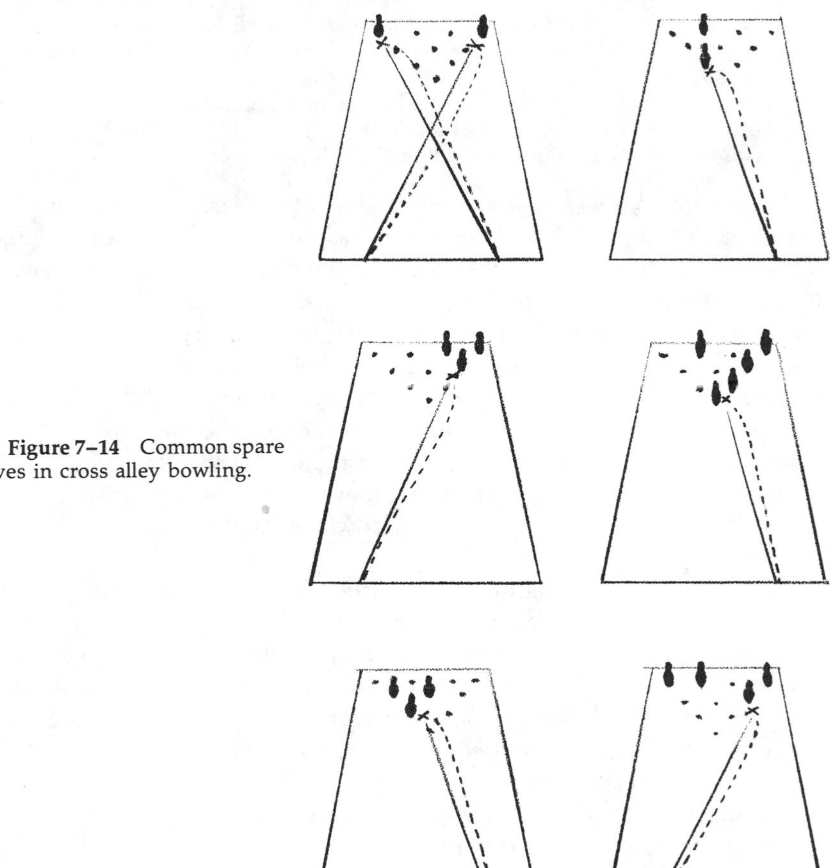

Figure 7–14 Common spare leaves in cross alley bowling.

4. 9 Pin position—used for leaves involving 3–5–6–9 pins
5. 10 Pin position—the best approach angle for conversion of 6, 6–10, and 10 pin leaves

The spare position used should usually be the one which places the ball closest to the middle of the leave. For example, 9 pin position is selected for the 3–5–6 leave.

The bowler's analysis of the split to be converted may lead to one of the three following decisions:

1. Go-between split—When the leave is two pins side by side, the attempt is to place the ball between the two adjacent pins. The diameter of the ball is approximately 9 inches, and the space between the two pins is approximately 7 inches; consequently, a well placed ball will contact the two pins easily.
2. Slide-one-over split—The spacing of the split requires that sliding pin action be considered in the conversion, as well as ball action. For example, in the 5–7 split, the 9 pin position is used. The ball contacts the 5 pin so it

slides to the 7 pin. Similarly, for 5–10 split, use 8 pin position; 4–10, 4–9, and 4–7–10 splits use 7 pin position; and for 6–7, 6–8, and 6–7–10, use 10 pin position.

3. Go-for-sure-count split—When pins are parallel and one or more pins are down between them it is not likely that a pin will slide across. It is usually wise to take sure pin count rather than to risk a conversion.

There are two widely accepted methods for spare bowling. The first, cross alley bowling, is based on the principle that as much of the alley width as possible should be between the delivery spot and the standing target. Therefore, when a pin or pins are on the right side of the alley the bowler moves to the left of her regular first ball delivery spot. Conversely, when the leave is on the left, she begins to the right of the regular delivery spot. The leave and type of delivery dictate how far the bowler moves in each direction. The second system is based on the principle that the strike ball line can be used for leaves on the left of the alley *if* the ball is released left of the strike ball release position and the point of aim adjusted. For spare leaves on the right, bowl a straight line, parallel to the alley bed, toward the spare.

Speed and pin deflection are important to spare bowling. A fast ball may cause the pins to move so that they do not fall horizontally and knock down additional pins. Yet a slower ball may itself be deflected to the right or left if it does not hit a pin head-on or have sufficient momentum to carry through. The bowler should remember that some leaves are three feet behind the head pin, and additional thought should be given to speed and type of delivery to these pins.

Game Courtesies. Developing bowling etiquette is a social skill necessary for game enjoyment. In brief:

1. Always observe the foul line.
2. Walk directly back from the foul line after delivery.
3. Be alert and ready for your turn.
4. The bowler addressing the pins has the right of way. If players on adjoining alleys address the pins simultaneously, the bowler on the right has the privilege of bowling first.
5. Avoid talking and jesting with a bowler addressing the pins.
6. Select one ball and use only that ball throughout the game.
7. Control your temper. Bowling is a game to be enjoyed. It should not defeat the bowler.
8. Do not carry refreshments into the lane area, since spilled foods and liquids can cause problems for other bowlers.

CLASS ORGANIZATION

Class organization is largely dependent upon the instructional setting. If possible, no more than five students should be assigned to each alley. Forty-five students is the maximum desirable number for a single instructor who hopes to give some individual assistance. A class period should be at least 45 minutes so a full game can be completed.

Some instructors, by choice, or when alleys are not available, teach basic skills in the gymnasium, in a corridor, or on a hard surfaced outdoor area. Plastic bowling balls and pins are used successfully on wooden floors, whereas rubber pins and balls can be used on other surfacing. A portable alley is now on the commercial market for gymnasium use. If none of this equipment is available, Indian clubs and softballs or playground balls can be used. The basic skills of stance, approach, and delivery, as well as scoring, etiquette, and strategy can be taught effectively.

TEACHING PROGRESSION

The instructional unit can be introduced in the gymnasium through selected novelty games such as duckpins, candle pins, skittles, or improvised games using Indian clubs. As soon as possible, students should be assigned to instructional groups and begin tenpin bowling. Working in their groups in the gymnasium, students learn scoring methods and techniques of stance, approach, and delivery.

Once in the alley, the instructor helps the student select shoes and a ball for permanent use. The teacher makes temporary alley assignments and explains class organization and conduct while in the lane. She then introduces basic rules of safety and courtesy and explains pinsetting, if necessary.

Suggested course outlines for beginners follow:

Lesson I

1. Acquaint students with equipment, costume, and facilities
2. Explain and demonstrate ball selection and grip
3. Assign balls and alleys
4. Teach safety precautions and courtesy skills
5. Shadow bowling

Lesson II

1. Review proper grip
2. Review guides to safety and courtesy
3. Demonstrate and explain stance and four step approach
4. Students select stance spot and practice approach without ball
5. Explain and demonstrate coordination of arm swing with steps. Stress pushaway, free pendulum-like swing, and release
6. Explain and demonstrate straight ball release (Some prefer to begin with hook ball delivery)
7. Practice straight ball delivery at pins 1, 3, and 5

Lesson III

1. Review starting spot, stance, and coordinated approach in straight ball delivery
2. Explain strike bowling, and practice delivery at the 1–3 pocket
3. Explain speed and deflection
4. Bowl at all ten pins

Lesson IV

1. Show film demonstrating straight ball and hook ball delivery and the

Lesson IV *Continued*

theory and technique of spot bowling.
2. Show film which demonstrates differences among straight ball, hook, back-up, and curve ball

Lesson V

1. Review complete approach and delivery
2. Introduce hook ball delivery (if not introduced in Lesson II)

Lesson VI

1. Explain and demonstrate scoring using terminology of strike, spare, split, and error
2. Practice session at all pins. Score complete game

Lesson VII

1. Review head pin aiming
2. Describe and demonstrate spot and cross alley bowling
3. Practice bowling at seven pin and ten pin
4. Bowl and score a complete game
5. Informal evaluation by teacher and pupils of group progress

Lesson VIII

1. Practice session—review scoring procedures
2. Informal skills test

Lesson IX

1. Regulation game bowling
2. Students record scores on official records

Lesson X

1. Bowl
2. Teacher gives individual assistance
3. Explain individual and team handicaps

Lesson XI

1. Bowl
2. Discuss spare bowling
3. Practice selected spare leaves

Lesson XII

1. Skills examination
2. Begin class tournament

Lesson XIII

1. Written test
2. Complete tournament

In additional lessons stress individual improvement in delivery, and practice at designated splits and spare leaves. As students become more advanced, stress hook ball delivery.

SKILL DIFFICULTIES AND THEIR CORRECTION

Selecting a Ball

Difficulty	*Correction*
a. Hand tires quickly from weight of the ball	a. Select a lighter ball; assure the student she will soon get used to the ball weight
b. Span between the finger holes is too wide or too narrow	b. Review techniques for selecting a well fitting ball. Teacher checks proper span by inserting a pencil between palm of the hand and ball
c. Thumb and finger holes are too tight, too loose, or incorrectly angled	c. Select a ball which does not scrape or irritate the thumb or fingers on release or tire the hand by tense gripping of closely set holes. Have the student release the ball in order to recheck before the final choice is made

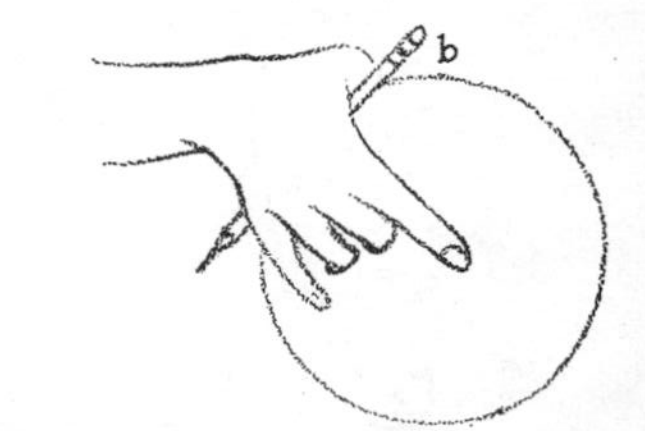

Stance

Difficulty	Correction
a. Body weight unequally distributed. Wrong foot forward on release	a. Teacher suggests a comfortable standing position with feet apart and left foot (right-handed bowler) slightly forward for greater balance base. Exaggerate the clumsiness of the wrong stance to help student see how awkward and unnatural it is
b. Tension in the knees and body	b. Take a deep breath and relax. Flex the knees and allow the body weight to settle. Remind student to "relax"
c. One shoulder turned toward pins forcing poor body alignment	c. Stress that shoulders should be squared toward pins at all times. Have one student check only this as her partner bowls
d. Variation in distance from starting spot to the foul line causing fouls, uneven approach steps, and variance in timing	d. Teacher reviews method of selecting stance position and guides the four steps to position. Teacher marks student's starting position with chalk

Four Step Approach

Difficulty

a. Completing approach too far from the foul line or over the foul line

b. Approaching in a zigzag fashion

c. Bobbing up and down during the approach

d. Approaching too fast or too slow resulting in rushed or delayed delivery

Correction

a. Student practices the approach mimetically with back to the foul line before selecting spot for stance

b. Teacher reviews the use of the left arm in maintaining balance throughout the approach. Place a chalk line on the approach area which the student straddles as she approaches the foul line

c. Teacher suggests that an imaginary bucket of water might be carried on the head without spilling during a rhythmical approach.

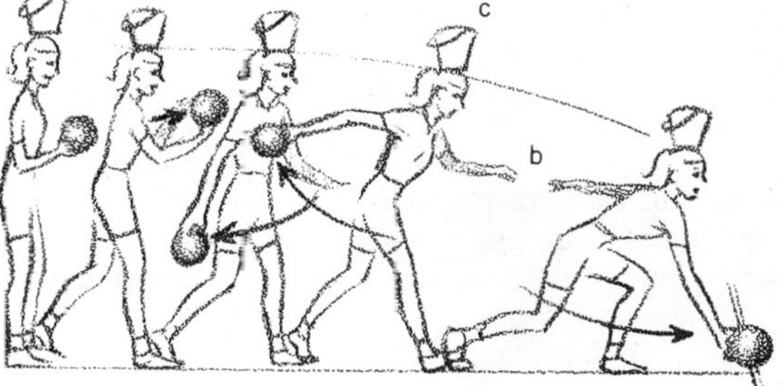

d. Suggest a rhythmical pattern for the student to repeat while practicing mimetically. For example, "Slow, fast, faster, fastest," or "Short, long, longer, longest"

Coordinated Approach

Difficulty	*Correction*
a. Failure to push the ball straight forward and down to begin the downward arc	a. Push the ball forward and down as if handing the ball to someone
b. Tension in arm and shoulder inhibiting a free swing	b. Relax and allow the ball weight to swing the arm
c. Taking too short a backswing resulting in a slow ball, improperly delivered on the alley	c. Review length and timing of approach steps and be certain there is enough time for a full arc. Bend knee deeply on third step and allow the weight of the ball to carry the arm naturally into a powerful backswing
d. Taking unnecessarily long backswing resulting in uncoordinated delivery or a ball dropped on the approach area	d. Teacher checks approach and initial forward push of the ball. Emphasizes the importance of keeping the shoulders square during the delivery. Other students watch for shoulder rotation
e. Swinging ball in an outside-to-inside or inside-to-outside arc causing the ball to curve or angle toward side of the alley	e. Concentrate on keeping the shoulders parallel to the foul line. Relax the arm and let the ball swing freely. Teacher helps the student get the feeling of a "pendulum" swing by moving her arm in correct arc

f. Bending forward from the waist causing poor balance at time of delivery	f. Teacher demonstrates how the knees bend to support the hips while the upper back remains straight. The left knee bends deeply, the right leg is bent, and the right foot helps maintain balance.

g. Dropping the shoulder of bowling arm causing ball to be delivered early and ineffectively	g. Avoid twisting shoulders and "listing" toward bowling arm

Ball Release

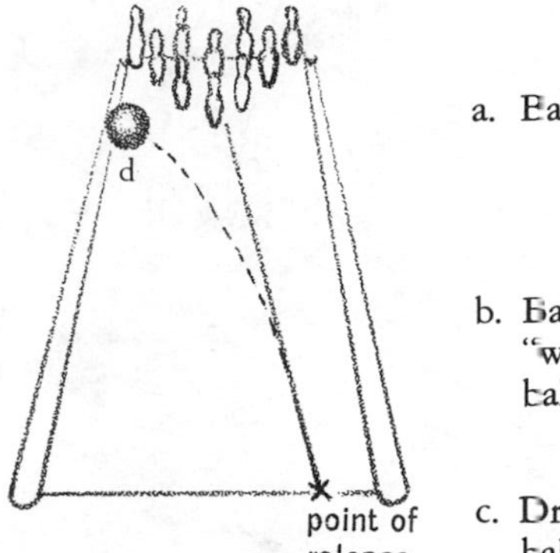

Difficulty	*Correction*
a. Ball curves too much	a. Check thumb position and wrist position. Thumb should be positioned at 10 o'clock, wrist and back of hand in a straight line
b. Ball fails to spin as it travels. Is not "working," or it results in a back-up ball	b. Check to see if wrist collapses at release. Lock wrist in with thumb in 10 o'clock position. Reach out *strongly* for the target
c. Dropping, lofting, or throwing the ball as a result of trying to control the	c. Develop rhythm of the approach. Bend the knee deeply on the third

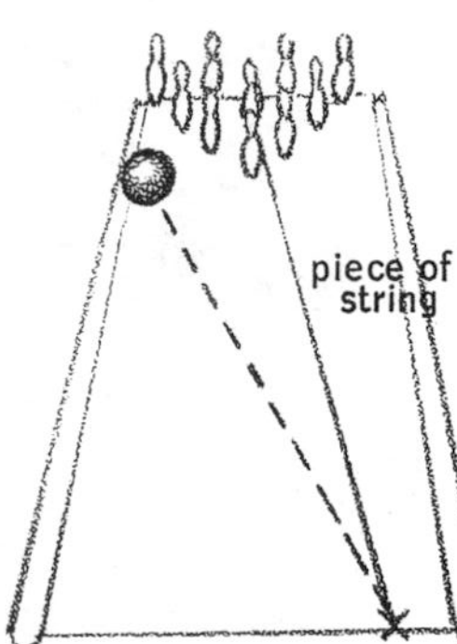

rhythm of the armswing during the approach	step and with the natural armswing forward on the fourth step, the ball moves off the fingers. Check weight of the ball to be sure it can be properly controlled
d. Ball curves as it travels down the alley	d. Check body position throughout delivery—shoulders level and parallel to foul line. Teacher emphasizes that hand is under or behind ball throughout delivery, rather than on either side. Teacher places a piece of string from point of release to number 5 pin so student can concentrate on straight delivery
e. Ball consistently rolls too far across the alley	e. Teacher stresses follow-through. The bowling arm follows the ball and then moves upward until the thumb touches the ear on bowling arm side

Straight Ball Delivery

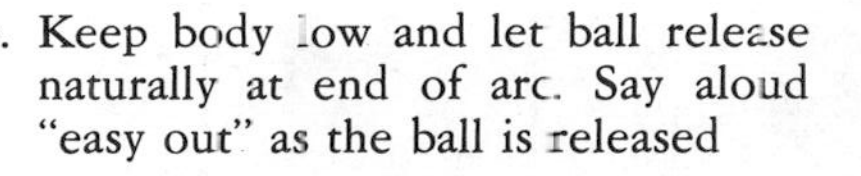

Difficulty	Correction
a. Releasing ball too early or dropping it behind the foul line	a. Be certain fingers keep contact until the ball touches the alley. Teacher reviews the arc pattern and shows how ball is released at bottom of the arc
b. Bouncing or throwing ball on alley bed	b. Keep body low and let ball release naturally at end of arc. Say aloud "easy out" as the ball is released

Hook Ball Delivery

Difficulty	*Correction*
a. Ball skids or slides as it is released	a. Teacher demonstrates hand position at time of release. Hand is at the side of ball, with fingers pointing down. Thumb is in 10 o'clock position. The "V" of the hand points toward head pin
b. Stopping swing as ball is released	b. Follow-through stressed. Show mimetically the follow-through in throwing or in hitting a golf ball
c. Ball spins erratically	c. Avoid using wrist action; wrist and back of hand form a straight line. Sufficient spin is given by fingers as they leave the ball
d. Inconsistency in degree ball hooks	d. Practice is needed to perfect delivery. Avoid twisting hand or wrist, or jerking movement at end of swing arc. Thumb leaves the ball an instant before the fingers

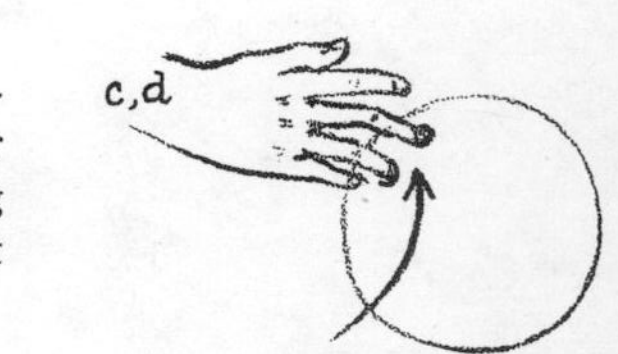

EVALUATING THE RESULTS

The evaluation program should show a fair measure of the student's skill and knowledge of rules, courtesies, safety, terminology and strategy. It may include:

1. A written examination of rules, scoring, etiquette, history, and game strategy.
2. Tournament results (ladder, double elimination, league results) and individual tournament records.
3. Observation of student's form, effectiveness, skill development, understanding of playing courtesies, and periodic rating of each of these items on a devised scale.
4. Skills tests including strike ball delivery, spare pick-up, split bowling, and spot bowling.*
5. Progress charts kept by individual students of all games bowled.

TERMINOLOGY

Alley bed—Wooden surface between foul line and pit.
Anchor—Person who bowls last in team's lineup.
Angle—A combination of the direction of the delivery and the path the ball takes toward the pins.
Approach—(1) Surface between the front of the lane and the foul line where the bowler stands to make a delivery. (2) Footwork and style used in delivery.
Arrows—Sighting targets imbedded in the lane to help a player align her starting position on the approach with the ball path to the pocket.
Baby split—A split leaving the 2–7 or the 3–10 pins after first ball is delivered.
Back-up ball—A reverse ball. When rolling, it curves toward the side of the bowler's body from which it was delivered. It curves right for a right-handed bowler.
Bed posts—A split in which only the 7 and 10 pins remain. Often called gate or goal posts.
Big four—A split in which the 4, 6, 7 and 10 pins remain.
Blow—An error. Failure to knock down pins standing (other than a split) with the second ball.
Boards—The number of boards (41 or 42) in the width of a bowling lane. The board along the channel is number 1.
Brooklyn—A crossover. A ball that hits the side of the head pin and rolls into the pocket opposite the side of the body from which the ball was delivered (1–2 pocket for a right-handed bowler).
Bucket—The 2–4–5–8 or 3–5–6–9 leave.
Chop (cherry)—Knocking down the front pin or pins of a spare leave while leaving the back pins standing.
Clean game—A game without a miss or split.
Cross alley shot—A ball that crosses the center of the alley when traveling to the pins.
Dead ball—(1) A ball which hits the pins without effectively "mixing" them. (2) A ball that does not count.
Double—Two successive strikes.
Dressing the lane—Applying oil or conditioner to a lane.

---

*See Liba, Marie, and Olson, Janice K.: "A device for evaluating spot bowling ability. *Research Quarterly*. Vol. 38, No. 2, May, 1967, pp. 193–201; Martin, Joan L.: "Bowling norms for college men and women." *Research Quarterly*. Vol. 31, March, 1960, pp. 113–116; and Phillips, Marjorie, and Summers, Dean: "Bowling norms and learning curves for college women." *Research Quarterly*. Vol. 21, Dec., 1950, pp. 337–85.

Dutch 200 (Dutchman)—A 200 score attained by alternating strikes and spares for ten frames.
Fast lane—A highly polished alley that resists the working action of the ball for hooks, curves, etc.
Foul—A rule infraction; usually touching or going beyond the foul line.
Foul line—Line separating the approach and alley bed.
Frame—One of ten large scoring squares for recording total pin count; each frame represents one-tenth of a game.
Full hit—Ball that hits the center of the target pin.
Grip—The results of several ways to drill a ball to accommodate the thumb and usually the two middle fingers.
Gutter or channel ball—A delivered ball that drops into either gutter (channel on side of alley bed) before reaching the pins.
Handicap—A bonus or score adjustment used in competition to equalize opportunity between different individuals or teams.
Head pin—Number 1 pin.
High board—An expanded or loose board in a lane which can cause the ball to veer from its course.
Hook—A delivered ball that travels in a straight line half or two thirds the length of the alley and then curves sharply away from the side of the bowler from which it was delivered. A hook veers left for a right-handed bowler.
Inning—A frame or each bowler's turn.
Kegler—A bowler.
Kick—A pin that rebounds off the sides or end of the lane.
King pin—Number 5 pin. Also refers to the headpin.
Lane—The alley or alley bed.
Leave—The pin or pins standing after delivery of the first ball.
Lift—A slight upward motion imparted to the ball as it is released.
Line—A game or ten frames.
Loft—Releasing the ball above the alley bed, thus throwing it at delivery.
Mark—To make a strike or a spare.
Mixer—A ball which hits the pocket lightly, causing pins to spin and ricochet; usually results in a strike.
Open—A frame in which the player fails to strike or spare.
Perfect game—Twelve successive strikes and a game total of 300.
Picket fence—The 1-3-6-10 or 1-2-4-7 leave.
Pit—Area behind the alley where pins fall after being hit.
Pitch—Angle at which finger holes are bored in a ball.
Pocket—The space between any two pins; usually refers to the 1-3 or 1-2 pins.
Railroad—A split. Refers to one of several kinds of splits.
Roundhouse—A wide, curving ball.
Sleeper—A pin standing behind another, such as 2-8.
Slow lane—An alley that allows curves and hooks to break easily.
Spare—Knocking down all remaining pins with the second ball in a frame.
Split—At least two pins are standing after the first ball; the head pin is down and at least one pin is down between or ahead of the remaining pins.
Spot—A mark or location on the alley to which the bowler aims.
Strike—All pins are knocked down by the first ball of a frame.
Strike out—Three successive strike balls in the tenth frame.
Tap—A perfectly delivered strike ball that leaves a pin.
Turkey—Three successive strikes during a game.
Woolworth—A split leaving pins 5 and 10.
Working ball—Ball which drives into the pocket carrying all 10 pins.

DISCUSSION QUESTIONS

1. Briefly explain the straight ball delivery, hook, and curve. Chart the path of each ball from the foul line to the pins. Which delivery is most successful? Why?
2. Score and explain a complete game including situations of a double, spare, error, split pickup, and a tenth frame strike out.

3. Explain the terms "head pin bowling," "spot bowling," and "line bowling." What are the advantages and/or disadvantages of each method of aiming?
4. Demonstrate and explain how a beginning bowler should select a ball.

SELECTED AUDIOVISUAL AIDS

American Bowls. (25 min., 16mm., sound, b & w.) Brunswick Corporation Bowling Division Film Library, Don Hill, 200 South Chester Street, Park Ridge, Illinois 60068. (Loan)

Better Bowling—How It's Done. (20 min., 16 mm., sound, color.) Ebonite Company, Division of Stowe-Woodward Company, Newton, Massachusetts 02158. (Loan)

Bowling: The Sport, The Delivery, Aiming, and Scoring. Filmstrips and recordings. The Athletic Institute, 805 Merchandise Mart, Chicago, Illinois 60654. (Purchase and rental)

Bowling. A Woman's World. (9 min., 16 mm., sound, color.) American machine and Foundry Company Bowling Products Group, Jericho Turnpike, Westbury, Long Island, New York 11590. (Loan)

Bowling Fever. (12 min., 16 mm., sound, b & w.) Brunswick Corporation Bowling Division Film Library, Don Hill, 200 South Chester Street, Park Ridge, Illinois 60068. (Loan)

Bowling Skill. (10 min., 16 mm., sound, b & w.) Teaching Film Custodians, Incorporated, 25 West 43rd Street New York 10036. (Rental)

How To's of Bowling. (25 min., 16 mm., sound, b & w.) Wheaties Sports Foundation, Title Insurance Building, Minneapolis, Minnesota 55401. (Loan)

Learn to Bowl Program for Women. (35 mm. filmstrips and disc) Brunswick Corporation Bowling Division Film Library, Don Hill, 200 South Chester Street, Park Ridge, Illinois 60068. (Loan)

Young America Bowls. (60 min., 16 mm., sound, b & w.) American Junior Bowling Congress, 1572 East Capitol Drive Milwaukee, Wisconsin 53211. (Loan)

SUGGESTED READINGS

American Bowling Congress. *Bowler's Guide.* 5301 South 76th Street, Greendale, Wisconsin 53129.

Bellisimo, Lou: *The Bowler's Manual.* 2nd Ed. Englewood Cliffs, N.J., Prentice-Hall, Inc., 1969.

Bellisimo, Lou, and Neal, Larry: *Bowling.* Prentice-Hall, Inc., Englewood Cliffs, N.J., 1971.

Bowling, Fencing Guide. National Association for Girls and Women in Sport. Washington, D.C., AAHPER, published biennially.

Casady, Donald R., and Liba, Marie: *Beginning Bowling.* Revised Ed. Belmont, Calif., Wadsworth Publishing Co., 1968.

Day, Ned: *How To Bowl Better.* New York, Arco Publishing Company, 1960.

Falcaro, Joe, and Goodman, Murray: *Bowling for All.* Revised Ed. New York, The Ronald Press, 1966.

Forslund, E. M.: *Bowling for Women.* New York, The Ronald Press, 1964.

Johnson, Don: *Inside Bowling.* Chicago, Henry Regnery Co., 1973.

Martin, Joan. *Bowling.* W. C. Brown Co. Dubuque, Iowa, 1966.

National Bowling Council: *The Guide to Teaching Bowling.* Washington, D.C., The Council, 1967.

Schunk, Carol: *Bowling.* Rev. Ed. Philadelphia, W. B. Saunders Co., 1975.

Women's International Bowling Congress: *Bowler's Manual.* 5301 South 76th Street, Greendale, Wisconsin 53129, 1974.

Women's International Bowling Congress: *WIBC Playing Rules Book.* Current Ed. 5301 South 76th Street, Greendale, Wisconsin 53129.

PERIODICALS

American Bowling Congress: *Bowling.* Greendale, Wisconsin.

Popular Bowling. Duneller, New Jersey, Joan Publishing Co.

Prep Pin Patter. 1913 West 103rd Street, Chicago, Illinois 60643.

CHAPTER 8

FENCING

The growth of fencing as a popular international sport is a tribute to the progress of civilization. From its beginnings, the skill was used as a method of war and a combative means for settling personal disputes. Through the years the weapons of fencing have reflected the purposes and types of combat of each era. The warriors of the Middle Ages used a two-handed sword for destruction and submission of their foes. The heavier weapons were eventually replaced by light rapiers with sharp points and sharp edges.

After gun powder was introduced, the sword lost its value in warfare, but the aristocracy continued to employ fencing as a method of settling personal disputes. The tragic number of injuries and deaths from combat caused nations across the world to banish the sword as a weapon. The nineteenth century saw fencing rise as a new and acceptable sport of skill and strategy rather than sheer strength and brute force. Women entered into fencing when protective equipment was developed and techniques of foil fencing were refined. Fencing is the only combative activity acceptable for women.

Fencing gains in popularity as its inherent values are recognized and the sport becomes better known. The formation of the Amateur Fencers of America in 1891 and the Intercollegiate Fencing Association in 1894 gave necessary leadership and sponsorship to competition and league formation across the United States. Fencing clubs affiliated with Amateur Fencers' League of America are active in major cities across the nation and encourage participation from both sexes and all age groups.

The introduction of electrical equipment has assured objective scoring in competition. However, the heavier equipment has de-emphasized the classic form and altered fencing tempo. The classic style which emphasized grace and precision execution has been replaced by more athletic and aggressive techniques. After hundreds of years, fencing has felt the effects of technology.

THE NATURE AND PURPOSE OF THE SPORT

Fencing is a game of attack and defense by two opponents who attempt to score touches on one another with a designated weapon. Women generally use only the foil as a weapon; however, men fence with the sabre and epée as well. The bout is conducted in a designated area—the strip—and continues until one contestant scores four valid touches or outscores her opponent within the 5-minute time limit.

The foil, lightest of all fencing weapons, is a pointed instrument theoretically capable of inflicting a puncture wound. The tip is blunted and covered in sport fencing to eliminate possible injury. Scoring touches requires precision and accuracy and the luring of the attacker to a point within striking distance of the opponent. To avoid touches the defender retreats or uses a system of blocking actions (parries) which deflect the attack.

GAME RULES AND SCORING*

The fencers stand on the strip. They salute the director, the judge, and each other. On commands from the official, they cross foils over the center line, step back, and fence. The contestants fence until the director calls

*For complete information see *Fencing Rules and Manual* of the AFLA.

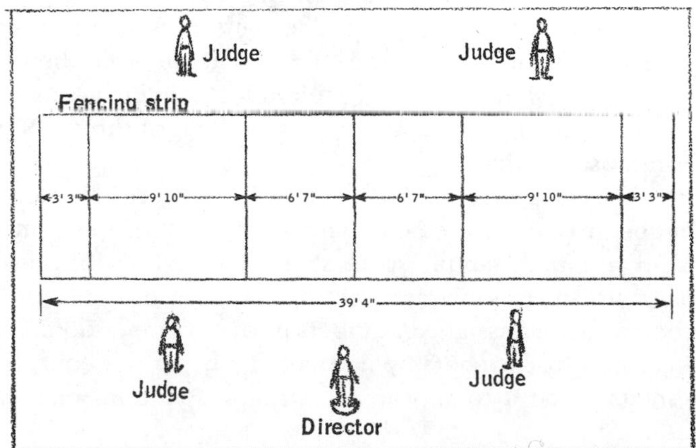

Figure 8–1 Regulation foil fencing strip (piste).

"Halt," indicating that a touch or foul has been seen.

During a bout the following rules apply:*

1. Touches are awarded on the basis of *materiality* and *priority* of the hit. Materiality is determined by evaluating the point of contact and directness of the thrust. Priority is of importance only when both fencers are hit simultaneously. The fencer whose hit results from a properly executed attack has priority.
2. Every touch, to be valid, must arrive clearly and cleanly on the target with the point.
3. A hit made directly or as a result of a parry on the body other than on the target area annuls any action that follows. The bout stops.
4. The fencer who first extends her arm with the point threatening the target gains the *right-of-way*. The defender gains the right-of-way by a parry or evasion. If a riposte follows, it must be taken without indecision or delay.
5. When simultaneous action results in simultaneous attacks and touches, the hits are annulled.
6. On a double hit (simultaneous hits with one fencer at fault) the proper touch is scored.
7. If a fencer steps off the side boundary with both feet, she is penalized by the loss of 3 feet 3 inches of ground. If she steps off the end with both feet, after a warning, she loses a touch.

Scoring. Officiating a fencing bout requires a jury consisting of a director and four judges. A scorekeeper and timekeeper assist the jury. The director stands midway between the fencers, approximately 13 feet from the strip. The judges stand on each side of each fencer. The judges to the right of the director observe touches on the fencer to the director's left. Conversely, the judges on the left observe materiality of touches on the fencer to the director's right. When only two judges are used, they are positioned to observe maximum target area. A bout conducted with electrical equipment is directed by the director. The materiality of hits is established by the electrical apparatus, but the director enforces the rules of the weapon.

The winner in a women's standard fencing bout is the person who first scores four legal touches on her opponent or outscores her opponent within the 5-minute time limit (actual time of fencing). In some bouts, usually direct elimination, a winner may be required to score eight touches with a two touch advantage. In other competitions, two out of three bouts of four touches each must be won.

Scoring of a bout is recorded by the official scorer as each touch is awarded by the director of the bout. The most common tournament is the pool (a round robin). A sample score sheet (Figure 8–2) of a five person round robin tournament illustrates scoring.

The contestants are assigned numbers prior to competition. Thereafter, the scorer calls the participants by number. To begin the bout, the scorer calls contestants 1 and 4 to appear "on strip" for an immediate bout and

*The section on techniques aids in understanding technical rules.

NAME	#	1	2	3	4	5	BOUTS WON	BOUTS LOST	TOUCHES REC'VD	TOUCHES SCORED	PLACE
Smith, S.	1		I / V	0 / V	II / V	0 / V	4	0	3	12	1
Brown, L.	2	IIII / D		IIII / D	IIII / D	IIII / D	0	4	12	5	5
Davis, J.	3	IIII / D	II / V		IIII / D	I / V	2	2	11	9	4
Fox, H.	4	IIII / D	II / V	I / V		IIII / D	2	2	11	12	3
Walker, S.	5	IIII / D	0 / V	IIII / D	II / V		2	2	10	9	2

ORDER of BOUTS

1–4	2–4
2–3	5–1
4–5	4–3
1–2	5–2
3–5	3–1

Figure 8–2 Scoring of a round robin tournament.

contestants 2 and 3 "on deck" for the next bout. As bouts are completed, each is crossed out or checked off on the Order of Bouts.

As contestants are called, a horizontal line (———) is placed in the squares corresponding to the competitors. Reading from left to right, marks above the horizontal line indicate touches the contestant received; below the line the V (victory) or D (defeat) indicates the outcome of the bout. For example, contestant number 1 (S. Smith) received two touches from number 4 (H. Fox) and number 1 won the bout. Contestant number 2 received four touches from number 3 and lost the bout. Number 2 failed to make a valid touch on number 5 during the bout. A similar recording is made on each participant in a bout.

At completion of the tournament, total scores, touches, and placement are recorded. Bouts won and lost are added across from *below* the horizontal line; touches received are added across the horizontal column corresponding to the participant's number. Touches rendered are added in the vertical column corresponding to the participant's number.

First place is awarded the fencer winning the greatest number of bouts, second place to the next greatest bout winner and so on. When a tie for first place occurs in the finals among two or more fencers, they fence each other to determine places. If ties occur for other than first place, highest placement is given the fencer with the least number of touches received. If a tie still exists, the fencer scoring the largest number of touches receives higher placement. If a tie still remains and placement must be determined, the tied contestants fence each other.*

*See *Fencing Rules and Manual* of the AFLA for complete discussion of scoring individual and team competition.

NEEDED FACILITIES AND EQUIPMENT

Schools and colleges probably will find it necessary to furnish basic materials for instruction, as fencing equipment is not usually owned by young people. Ideally, a separate fencing room in the physical education area should serve for instructional and recreational purposes. The gymnasium area should not be filled with wall targets, mirrors, or the fencer's equipment because of the possible danger to participants in other activities. Beginning fencing skill may be taught indoors or outdoors on various surfaces; however, the strip for bouting should be carefully laid out.

The ground on which combat takes place is called the field of play. The *strip*, or *piste*, is the area upon which the bout is conducted. An official strip is between 5 feet 11 inches and 6 feet 7 inches in width and 39 feet 4 inches in length and has an additional 6 feet 7 inches of level surface beyond each end. Surfacing of linoleum, rubber, cork, wood, or plastic is acceptable. The strip is divided widthwise by seven lines. At each end there is an endline, and a center line divides the strip into halves. There are two "on guard" lines, one on each side of the center line and 6 feet 7 inches from it behind which fencers begin the bout, and there is a warning line 3 feet 3 inches in front of each endline. Each of these lines is 1 inch in width (see Figure 8–1). If it is not possible to paint lines on the floor's surface because of multi-use, commercial tapes can be laid and later removed with no floor damage. The metallic piste is made of fine metallic mesh, usually brass. Such a strip neutralizes hits made on the ground by electrical weapons. If used, it must cover the entire strip and its extensions.

Mirrors, stall bars, mats, and wall targets are among the aids helpful in teaching fencing skills. Mirrors are valuable in analyzing footwork and body position and enabling each student to observe her faults and make necessary adjustments; stall bars provide a device for checking body alignment. Wall targets and dummies are invaluable for warming up and in practicing accuracy while lunging.

Foil. Women fence with French, Italian, and pistol-grip foils; however, the French foil is more popular for instructional purposes, and the Italian and pistol-grip *electric* foils are most popular, since the additional gripping surface allows greater control of the heavier electric weapon. The total weight of the foil must be less than 17.637 ounces and the length less than 43.3 inches. The foil is composed of four major parts—the *blade, guard, handle,* and *pommel.*

Blade. The blade, of fine machine steel, is quadrilateral (rectangular or square cross section) and tapers from the strong half, called the *forte*, to the weaker and more flexible half, the *foible*. The blade measures from 32 to 35 inches from guard to tip. The blunt tip must be covered with a rubber tip or wrapped with white tape.

Guard. The steel or aluminum guard is a round or oval protection of the weapon hand. The round guards are 3½ to 4 inches in diameter. The

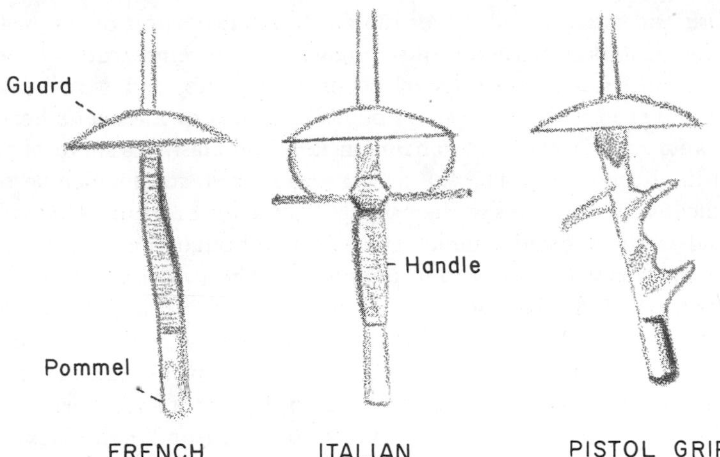

Figure 8–3 Instructional foils. French, Italian and pistol grip. (Adapted from Wyrick, Waneen. *Foil Fencing*. Philadelphia, W. B. Saunders Co., 1971.)

oval or "figure eight" guards cannot exceed 4⁵⁄₈ inches. A thumb pad or cushion is inserted between the guard and the handle to prevent friction between the metal guard and the fencer's knuckles.

Handle. The handle of the French foil is rectangular and curved to fit the contour of the hand. The wooden or plastic handle is wrapped with cord or covered by leather to aid in a secure grip. The Italian and pistol-type grips are of metal or plastic and offer more gripping surface.

Pommel. The pommel is a threaded steel knob that screws to the tang of the blade (threaded end) and secures all parts of the weapon together. The pommel acts as a balance to the weight of the blade.

Electrical Equipment. The difficulty of accurately judging hits led to the development of electrical scoring devices. These devices require the use of an electric foil with a special spring point mounted on the end of the blade. When the point is depressed by a direct hit, a relay is sent down a light wire which runs the length of the blade to the fencer's body cord. This automatically registers the hit on a scoring apparatus. Validity of the hit is determined by contact with a metallic (*lamé*) jacket worn by each fencer over the regular jacket. The jacket covers only the valid target area. If a hit is made off the target an invalid hit is registered. Hits are acknowledged by a buzzer and lights on a central machine. A red or green light indicates a valid hit and the fencer who scored it. A white light indicates an invalid hit.

Martingale. The martingale or similar strap holds the weapon near the hand so the foil will not be knocked toward fencers or spectators in case of disarmament. This is not necessary during instructional classes or when using electrical equipment which is secured to the fencer through the body cord.

Mask. A mask is as important to the sport of fencing as the foil itself. Prevention of injury and the fencer's confidence in safety make it essential.

The mask and attached bib cover the entire front portion of the head and neck. The mask is constructed of strong wire mesh reinforced with leather or cord straps, a heavy padded cloth or canvas bib, and wire headpiece (tongue) covered with cloth which bends to adjust to a fencer's head.

Jackets and Trousers. Fencing jackets and plastrons serve as protection for the upper body. The full jacket with a groin strap which passes between the legs and buckles to the back, holds the lower front of the jacket in place and is the most desirable protection, although the adjustable half-jacket is more practical for group instruction. The jacket is made of heavy white material and is padded in the front and in the upper sleeve. The shoulder seams of the jacket correspond to arm and shoulder lines. It should fully cover neck, arms, and torso and overlap the fencing breeches. Women's jackets have two inside pockets so that extra breast protection of padded material, plastic, or aluminum can be worn under the jacket. This protection is required in electrically scored competition. White trousers which fasten below the knee but are loose enough to allow freedom of movement are worn by both men and women. Skirts or shorts are satisfactory for class use, but covering the legs is desirable in recreational fencing and mandatory in competition.

Footwear. Absorbent socks which cushion the feet and absorb perspiration are essential. These white knee-length socks are tucked under the trousers. Although flat leather-soled fencing shoes are desirable on regulation strips, tennis shoes or low-heeled rubber-soled shoes are practical for classwork.

Glove. A padded, well fitting leather glove should be worn on the foil hand. The cuff must be long enough to overlap the jacket in order to prevent the blade from entering the sleeve. If students share gloves, they should wear a thin inner cotton glove to absorb perspiration.

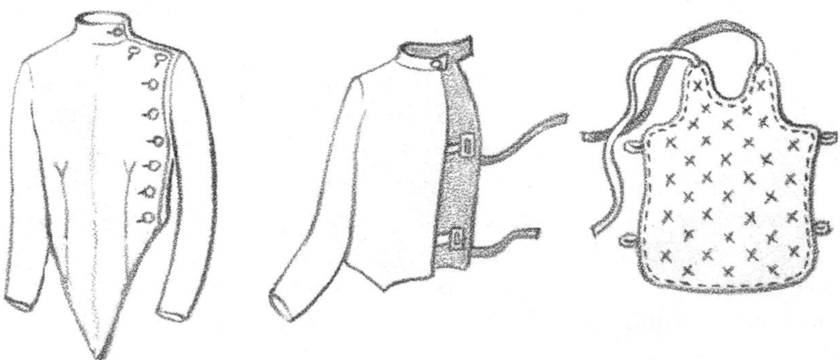

Figure 8–4 Fencing jackets.

STORAGE AND CARE OF EQUIPMENT

Multi-use of equipment requires care for cleanliness and safe condition of equipment. Students should assume some responsibility in maintenance. A few suggestions:

1. Construct a "Fencers' Caddy"* which is movable and light, yet serves as a storage area for equipment not in use. If such a device is not practical, store equipment in a central location; foils hanging so blades are not damaged, and masks, jackets, and gloves located for maximum ventilation.
2. Foil tips should be padded with rubber tips or adhesive tape. Pommels should be secured to prevent guards and blades from wobbling.
3. The blade should have a slight bend so that when a touch is scored the tip is lower than the bend in the blade. To bend or straighten the blade, rub it between the shoe sole and floor. By friction the blade is heated and becomes more pliable. Avoid using hands to straighten a blade.
4. Replace and repair protective cushions and handles before damage to fencer's hands. Thread or cord wrapped around the handle and glued at each end is satisfactory. Felt pads or padded leather serve as guards.
5. Before putting on a mask, remove excess makeup. Always check the mask for gaps or rust spots in the mesh. Wash padding and bibs frequently.
6. Store masks, jackets, and gloves in an area with maximum ventilation. Tears or rips should be repaired immediately. Wash and fluff dry jackets regularly.
7. Gloves should be aired and cleaned with disinfectant powder after use. Inner gloves should be aired and washed frequently.

TEACHING UNITS

Suggested course content for beginners and advanced students includes:

Beginners

Brief history
Care and use of equipment
Safety fundamentals
Basic skills
- Attention position
- Salute
- On guard position
- Footwork:
  - Advance
  - Retreat
  - Lunge and recovery
  - Advance-lunge

Advanced Students

Selection and care of personal equipment
Review exercises
Review safety precautions and ethics
Review fundamental skills
Advanced skills:
- Compound attacks
- Counter parries
- Cutover
- Remise
- Reprise
- Ballestra

---

*See Bernhard, Frederick and Edwards, Vernon: *How to Fence.* Dubuque, Iowa, Wm. C. Brown Company, 1956, pp. 10–11.

Warm up and conditioning exercises
Lines of attack
Simple attacks: straight thrust,
beat-attack, disengage, coupé
Simple parries: 4, 6, 7, 8
Riposte
Feint
Rules
Basic strategy
Bouting
Evaluation

Flèche
Stop thrust
Compound ripostes
Strategy
Officiating
Tournaments
Evaluation

BASIC SKILLS

Grip. The directions for the grip apply to the French foil, since it is most commonly used for instructional classes. Other foils are gripped similarly.

The handle of the foil is curved and shaped to fit the hand. Looking down on the handle, the convex portion fits in the palm of the hand, as the thumb and forefinger serve as holding digits while the remaining fingers guide the fine foil action. The index finger is placed near the cushion so that the handle rests on the second joint of the finger. The thumb is placed on top of the handle, pointing toward the blade. A pinching motion is assumed. The fleshy tips of the second, third, and fourth fingers rest lightly along the concave surface and pull the handle into the palm. The wrist is straight and the pommel rests against the middle of the wrist. In this position there is a straight line from elbow to foil tip. Precision and accuracy are dependent on the coordinated grip: the thumb and index finger directing the gross action of the blade, and the other fingers controlling the direction of the foil tip.

Attention and Salute. The attention position is taken at the beginning of the bout and after each touch. It is the beginning position for both the informal and formal salutes. The fencer faces her opponent with feet at right angles, heels together, with the forward toe directed toward the oppo-

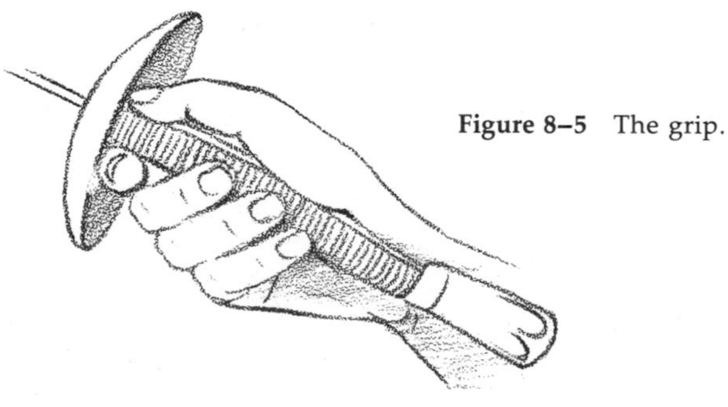

Figure 8–5 The grip.

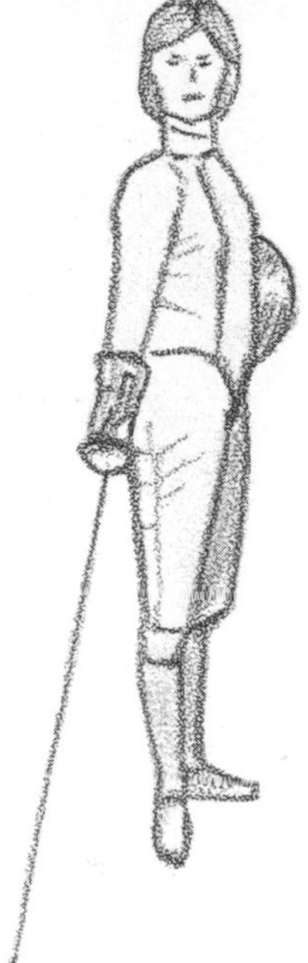

Figure 8–6 *Position of attention:* right toe pointed straight ahead, right shoulder facing opponent, foil tip held 3″ above floor, and mask tucked under left arm. (Adapted from Wyrick, Waneen: *Foil Fencing*. Philadelphia, W. B. Saunders Co., 1971.)

nent. The foil extends forward and downward with the tip about 3 inches from the floor. The mask is held under the free arm, away from the opponent.

The salute is a traditional movement of courtesy and acknowledgment between opponents and to the judges and officials. The simple salute begins from the position of attention. On the second movement the foil is raised sharply bringing the guard to the chin, the pommel is centered in the forearm, toward the fencer, and the foil tip is directed toward the ceiling. With the third count the fencer briskly extends the foil to the original low diagonal position. The formal salute moves from low diagonal position to horizontal right, to vertical, to horizontal left, return to vertical, extended toward opponent, to vertical, and to low diagonal attention position. At the completion of the salute the mask is put on, and the fencers assume the guard position.

Guard Position. The guard is the best body balanced position for offensive and defensive play. The fencer enters the guard position from an erect or attention position, knees straight and heels together at 90° angles. The forward foot points toward the opponent's foot. The body is turned so that the forward shoulder and hip are toward the opponent. The front of the body is angled in the same direction as the rear foot. The foil arm is straight and extended forward and down so that the tip of the foil is held slightly off the ground. The back arm is straight, pointing downward and slightly away from the body. The hand is straight, palm up.

Figure 8–7 The salute (in three movements).

In assuming the crouched guard position, move the forward foot approximately two foot-lengths forward. The heels remain at right angles, the knees are bent so the kneecaps are directly over the toes of each foot. The torso is erect, as if sitting on a bench, with weight over an imaginary spot between the feet, which bear equally the weight distribution. The back arm is

Figure 8–8 Guard position.

bent with the elbow at shoulder height and held in body line behind the torso. The wrist of the rear arm is relaxed, palm toward the head. The foil arm is bent and comfortably carried toward the opponent. The elbow of the foil arm is rotated toward the body line and in to a point approximately 6 to 9 inches (a hand span) from the side of the body. The foil is in a straight line with the forearm, pommel resting on the wrist as the foil tip points at opponent's eye level.

The Advance. The advance is a forward body movement used when the fencer needs to get close to her opponent for an attack. It also serves to force the opponent to retreat and to maintain a constant distance if the opponent has retreated. The advance is made from the guard position with small, even steps. Pushing off with the toe, the forward foot leads with the heel into a step of several (3 to 7) inches. The rear foot follows immediately with a step covering the same distance. The guard position is maintained, and the distance between the feet is constant. Weight is low and the torso in an erect position. The action results in a gliding motion.

The Retreat. The retreat is the reverse of the advance movement. It is a defense action which takes the fencer out of her opponent's reach, or it may be used to make the opponent advance. The rear foot moves rapidly backward followed immediately by the front foot as the toe pushes off and the heel leads to the floor. As with the advance, small, rapid steps are better than big ones. The feet do not rise far from the floor as the guard position is maintained, and weight is distributed to insure rapid movement in any direction.

Lunge and Recovery

Lunge. The lunge is an extension of the arm and body from the guard position for the purpose of delivering an attack to the opponent. The lunge

Figure 8–9 The lunge.

must be executed with split-second timing in this sequence: (1) extension of the foil arm toward opponent in line of attack (fingernails of hand up, pommel against wrist and hand slightly higher than point), arm straight and elbow and shoulder firm; (2) forcefully straighten back leg and knee as the forward foot moves toward opponent (to a position where kneecap is over instep of forward foot); (3) simultaneously with leg movements, the rear arm straightens, parallel to the leg, with the palm up to aid in balance and in preparation for recovery. The ankle of the rear foot is flexed so the foot can maintain firm floor contact.

Recovery of the Lunge. The recovery to a guard position may be accomplished backward or forward, dependent upon the opponent's movements. The backward recovery is accomplished by simultaneous movements: (1) bending rear knee as rear arm pulls to guard position, (2) pushing forcefully back with the forward toe and bringing foot to guard distance from rear foot, (3) bending foil arm to guard position. A forward recovery is accomplished by rapid flexing of the back leg to bring it to an "on guard" position. The recovery must be a smooth, rapid movement as a slow recovery presents a weak defensive position.

Advance Lunge. The advance lunge is used when fencing out of distance and the opponent cannot be reached. It is also useful on an opponent who retreats when attacked and a touch necessitates extra distance. As the rear foot contacts the floor, the foil arm is extended and is immediately followed by the lunge. Speed and determination are integral parts of the attack but the body must be controlled and balanced at all times to avoid an easy score for the opponent.

Ballestra. The ballestra is a jump lunge that has its value in speed and surprise. It is similar to, although quicker than, the advance lunge. The weight is shifted almost entirely to the rear foot, which hops forward as the forward foot, slightly raised, reaches ahead. The hop is short and *forward,* not upward. Both feet strike the floor at the same time, the rear foot landing approximately where the forward foot had been. Upon landing (in guard position) the forward toe pushes, and the rear leg thrusts the body into lunge position.

Lunge Following Forward Recovery. A lunge followed by a forward recovery and a lunge is useful when the opponent retreats just out of reach at the moment of the initial lunge. Recover from the initial lunge by bending the rear leg and bringing it forward to guard position. (It may be necessary to defend rather than continue the attack.) Immediately lunge again or advance to a better position prior to lunging.

Defenses and Attacks

The Target. The valid target area extends from the collar to a horizontal line which joins the top of the hip bones across the back and the groin line in front. The back is a valid target. The arms, from the shoulder seam outward, and the hands, legs, bib, and mask are excluded as targets.

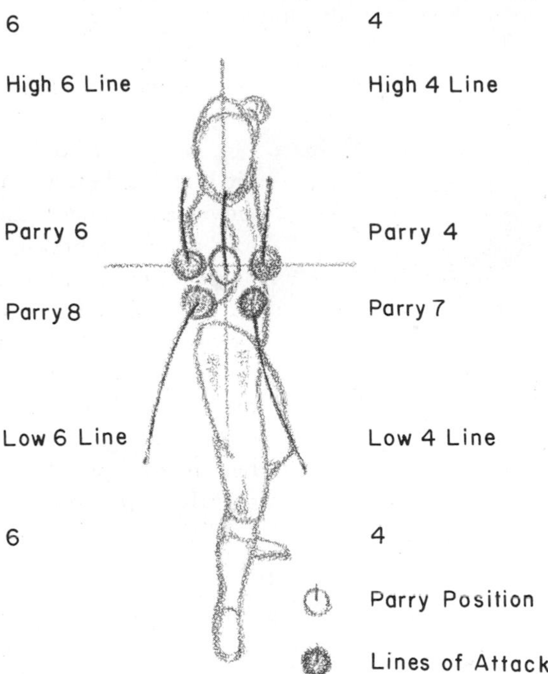

Figure 8–10 Lines of attack and parries to protect each line. (Adapted from Wyrick, Waneen: *Foil Fencing*. Philadelphia, W. B. Saunders Co., 1971.)

Lines of Attack. The target is theoretically divided into four sections, or *lines of attack*. These are determined by the relative position of the opponent's bell guard. The high line is above the foil hand; the low is below; the outside line is to the side of the foil toward the back and hip (right for right-handed fencer); the inside line is toward the front of the torso (to her left for the right-handed fencer). For clarity of discussion, the outside line is called 6 line, and the inside line is called 4 line, with the resulting four lines referred to as high 6 line, low 6, high 4 and low 4. The defensive movement of a parry is used to protect each line.

Engagement. While in guard position, opponents lightly engage their blades at foible. The tip of each foil is aimed at the target, and the hand holds the guard position to protect against a simple lunge when bouting fencers quickly learn to maintain a distance called the *fencing measure*, from which one or both can lunge with an extended arm and touch the opponent.

Parries and Guard Positions. A parry is a defensive movement that blocks or deviates the attacking blade. There are eight fundamental parries—two for each line—one with hand in supination (palm upward), and the other with hand pronated (palm down). Each may be executed as (1) an *opposition parry*, in which pressure is held against the opponent's blade until a return or riposte, and a (2) *beat parry*, which deflects the opponent's blade from the line of attack. *Direct parries* are executed by moving the foil to the

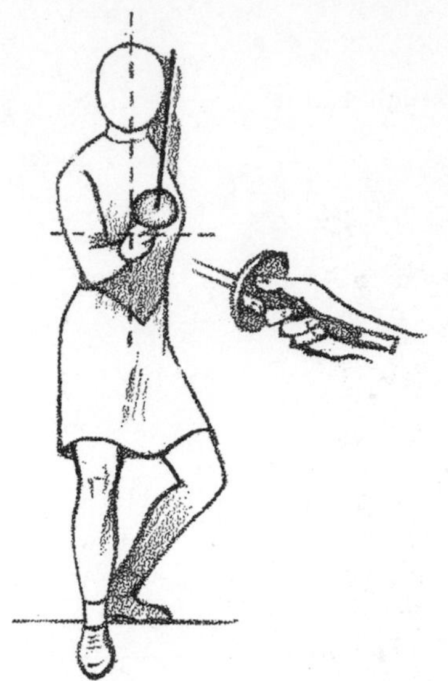

Figure 8–11 Parry of fourth.

Parry of Fourth. This defends the high inside target area. The hand moves from guard position of sixth to the left, at breast height, to the outer limits of the body to remove the threatening foil tip of the attacker. The hand is supinated, thumb up, and slightly higher than the elbow. The point of the blade remains at the opponent's eye level but moves with the bell guard slightly to the left.

left or right to defend either high or low lines. *Semicircular parries* are made when moving from low to high or high to low lines. The tip of the foil travels in an arc as the parry is executed. A *circular parry* (counter) not only deviates the opponent's blade, but sweeps it into another line of attack with a circular motion of the defender's blade. The blade is carried by using only the fingers (hand follows the blade under) and makes a small circle around the attacker's blade. It results in changing the line of engagement prior to the parry.

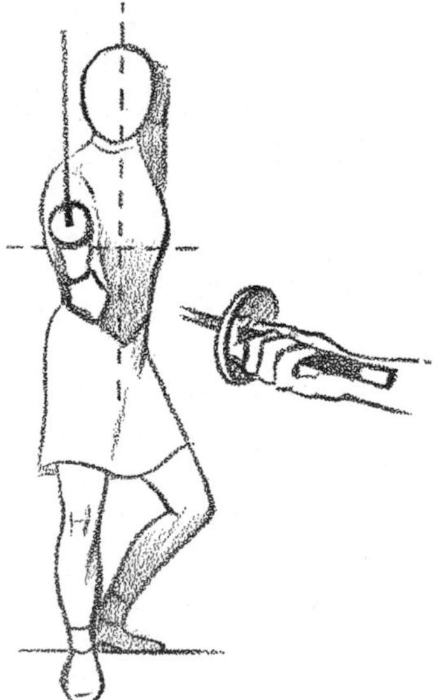

Figure 8–12 Parry of sixth.

Parry of Sixth. The hand moves from guard position of fourth to right to defend upper outside target. Fingers up, hand at breast height, point at opponent's eyes, the forearm carries the weapon from pivot point of elbow so attacking blade can be carried by the strong part of the blade to the right of the body.

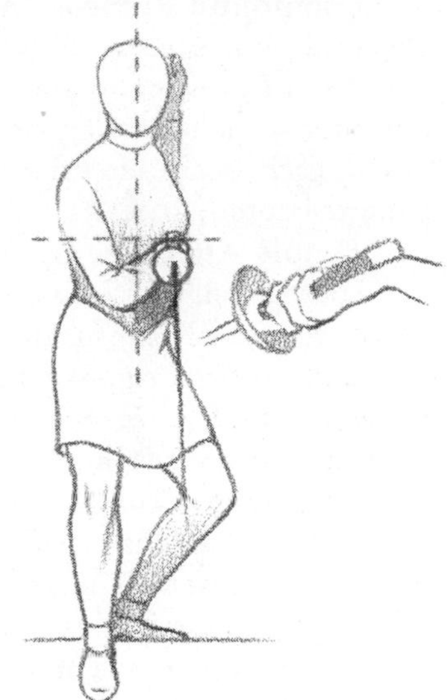

Figure 8–13 Parry of seventh.

Parry of Seventh. This defends low inside line. Foil tip moves in a clockwise semicircle toward opponent's knee level, hand to the left with palm facing upward. Foil hand does not move downward.

Parries should be looked upon as movements to guard positions and learned as movements from one guard position to another. That is, when a fencer executes a parry of sixth, she is properly moving to the guard position of sixth. They are executed in an "on guard" position with the foil arm carried in guard position. The arm does not extend and bends closer to the body *only* if the opponent is fencing closer than normal distance. Parries should deflect the blade laterally, not up and down the length of the torso.

A fencer can be competent with four sound parries—four, six, seven, and eight.

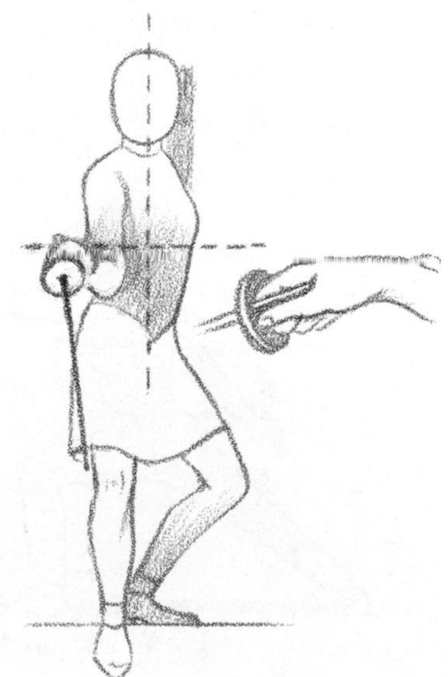

Figure 8–14 Parry of eighth.

Parry of Eighth. This defends the low outside line. The blade is moved counterclockwise, describing a C so that the foil tip points inside the opponent's knee. The foil hand does not move downward. The hand moves to the right, palm up, with the pommel directed past the body line.

Compound Parries. A compound parry is a combination of parries executed with speed and precision against a compound attack. They are designed to prevent an attacker from changing lines, and thus prevent the defender from following or lagging behind her opponent's action. Compound parries are lateral parry combinations, lateral-counter parries, or counter-lateral parries.*

Simple Attacks. Generally, an attack is considered a forward movement of the foil, with or without a lunge, toward the opponent's target. The fencer who establishes right-of-way first by extending her foil arm toward the target retains right-of-way until she hits or misses the target, or her blade is parried. A *simple* attack comprises only one fast movement such as a straight thrust, disengage, or cutover.

The Straight Thrust. This is the simplest of all attacks. It involves a quick, smooth extension of the foil arm (shoulder high and palm up) in the line of engagement. The arm extension may be followed by a lunge if distance to the opponent requires it.

The Disengage. This is a change of line of attack made by passing the blade under the opponent's blade to an opposite line of engagement. Execution begins with an extension of the arm, shoulder high, palm up. Keeping the foil close to opponent's blade, the fingers drop the tip under opponent's blade circumscribing a small semicircle or a moving "V." When changing from seventh to eighth or eighth to seventh, the disengage is made over the blade, rather than under.

The Cutover. The cutover or coupe is accomplished as the blade passes over the point of the opponent's dropped blade to change the line of engagement. It is used against an opponent's lowered blade, as an opponent

*See Wyrick, Waneen: *Foil Fencing.* Philadelphia, W. B. Saunders Co., 1971, pp. 95–98.

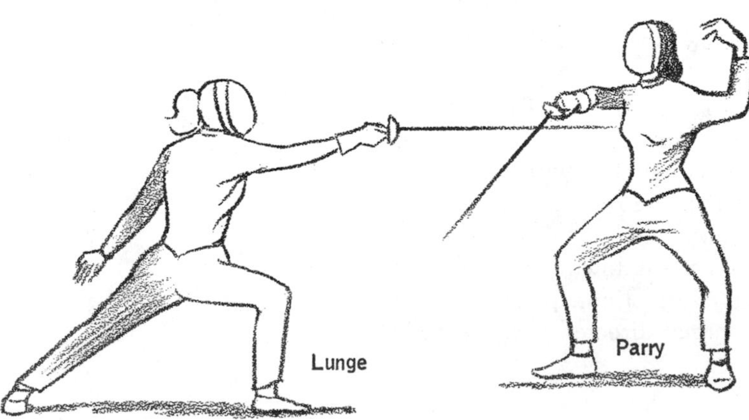

Figure 8–15 Lunge and parry.

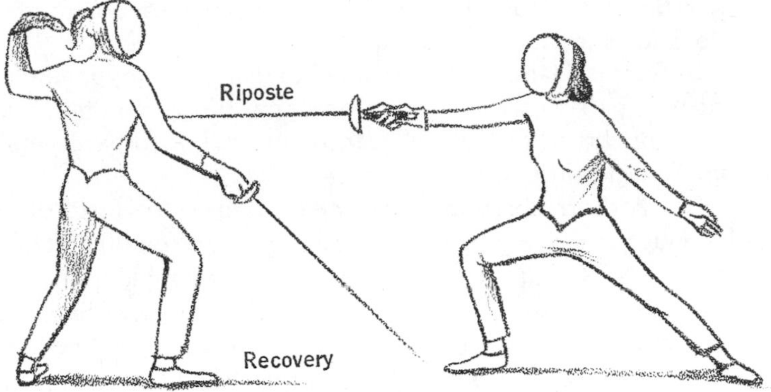

Figure 8–16 Riposte and recovery.

applies pressure with weak sections of blade against strong parts of the defender's blade, and when an opponent holds a parry too long. To execute the cutover the arm remains bent as the fingers and wrist lift the blade so the tip circumscribes a small semicircle or inverted "V" as it crosses opponent's blade. The arm is extended immediately when the foil tip clears and the lunge follows.

Beat-Attack. This is similar to a straight thrust attack, with a crisp "rap" of the opponent's blade as the foil is extended. Further discussion is noted under "Attacks Taking the Blade."

Riposte. The riposte is a return attack that follows a successful parry. The return may be a simple single thrust or an indirect or compound lunge. In any case, an immediate riposte has the right-of-way over a second attack by the original attacker. A *counter riposte* may be made following the parry of a riposte.

Compound Attacks. Compound, or composite, attacks are made in two or more movements toward the target by feints, attacks against the blade, or a combination of these. The purpose is to feint an attack into an open line and deceive the opponent's parry in that line, and then hit in the originally closed line. They include:

Double Disengage (One-Two Attack). This consists of two disengages executed in rapid succession. The first disengage, with an extended arm, is made into an open line forcing the opponent to parry. The second disengage follows immediately in the opposite direction to go on target in a newly created opening. The lunge begins with the second disengagement.

The One-Two-Three Attack. An additional disengage is added to the "one-two" attack in an attempt to make an opening and a touch.

The Double. An attack involving two disengagements in the same direction. The action consists of feinting a disengage, deceiving the counter parry, and lunging.

Attacks on the Blade. Attacks on the blade serve to create an opening in a closed line, to confuse the adversary by causing reaction to pressure on the blade, and as invitations for attack.

Feint. A feint is a false attack intended to deceive an opponent so she will close the line (parry) of attack and open a new line. A feint may take the form of a straight thrust, disengage, beat, or press, but to be deceptive it must be rapid and vigorous.

The Beat. A short, sharp movement executed so the forte of the attacker's blade raps sharply against the middle or weak (foible) part of opponent's blade. The wrist and fingers control the attacking blade and cause a sharp, slapping action. It may be firm, in an attempt to open a line, or light, in anticipation of an answering beat and thus open an opposite line for a disengage attack. From an engagement in the four line the blade moves slightly to the right as the grip of the last three fingers relaxes. Quickly the fingers pull to the hand and the blade snaps sharply. The foil must remain close to the opponent's blade as a wide preparatory or follow-through movement exposes the fencer.

The Press. Pressure is applied against the opponent's blade to remove it from the line. Without warning, it is executed similarly to the beat; however, it is a smooth, strong action. As pressure is answered, the attack may move in the same line, or the attacker may release the pressure and cutover or disengage and attack in another line.

The Glide. The glide attack, or glisé, is an advanced technique wherein the attacker moderately pressures her own blade along opponent's blade until thrust is complete.

The Pressure Glide. A difficult technique of exacting pressure downward and forward against the opponent's blade from the weakest point of the blade to the guard.

Attacks Taking the Blade. These attacks are developed to dominate the opponent's blade by removing the foil point from line by controlling the defending blade.

Opposition. Similar to the glide. However, the guard of the attacking fencer is in continuous opposition to opponent's blade. This must be a simple attack.

Bind. A method of moving an opponent's blade from high to low line or low to high line. The action is taken against a stiff extended arm by applying the strong part of the foil blade to the weak portion of the opponent's and forcing with one's own blade and forearm. For example, when making seventh bind from guard position of sixth, make a small circle over the top of the defender's blade and lower blade and forearm. This action carries the blade to seventh. A slight lateral and forward motion to the right will carry the opponent's point outside the body line. This must be a rapid action so the opponent's blade is controlled at all times.

Croise. The croise is an action similar to the bind; however, the blade crosses over and carries from high to low line on the *same* side. It is used when the opponent's blade is close to the target and a bind, which brings the blade across the body, would be dangerous.

Envelopment. This is executed against a straight arm similar to the bind. However, it is a continuous motion carrying the opponent's blade in a complete circle and returning to the original engagement.

Counter Attacks. These involve split-second timing as they are simply arm extensions toward the fencer preparing to attack.

Time Thrust. The time thrust is usually executed against a compound attack. It is made by an extension in opposition to the opponent's blade and constitutes a parry and a riposte in a single movement. It is most effective against an advancing opponent.

Stop Thrust. The stop thrust is executed with or without a lunge at the instant a careless opponent lifts her foot to advance. It should be used only when an opponent's blade moves out of line on a feint, when her blade leaves the defender's blade, or when the attacker's arm bends on advance.

Secondary Attacks. Secondary attacks follow immediately after the first, whether in the same line or another. They are effective when the opponent delays her riposte or when an opponent's riposte can be parried and immediately followed.

Redouble. This is a second attack and is executed immediately after the first is parried but is not followed by a riposte. Attack can be made from the original lunge position or from a recovery forward and reattack.

Remise (Replacement). Without withdrawing her arm after failing to hit on the first attempt, the attacker takes a second action which places the point on the target in the same line. A touch can be attempted by replacement if the riposte is delayed or the defender loses right-of-way.

Reprise. This is a second attack made after returning to guard position.

STRATEGY

The successful bout fencer is aware of her personal resources and alert to the actions of her opponent. It is important to fence your own game. Develop one or two attacks to rely and "hammer" on. Carefully develop precise skills, so that during competition full attention can be devoted to the opponent and to the ordering of skill presentation, rather than execution. Try to get opponent to fence *your way*. Several basic guides to attack and defense are helpful:

1. As the bout begins observe opponent's stance, lunge, guard position, reaction time, length of reach, and preferred attacks. Knowledge of an opponent is most important in planning bouting tactics. Much information about your opponent can be gained by watching previous bouts. Use the first minute of the bout to feel out your opponent.
2. Have a "game" plan. Use simple attacks when possible. A well planned, simple attack is preferable to compound attacks. Always lunge with an extended arm. Progress from simple to complex items by building on opponent's defensive responses to previous attacks.

3. Develop and use rapid, positive feints and false attacks for opponent's deception.
4. Recover from attacks, successful or otherwise, immediately to avoid a return.
5. Delay parries until last moment to avoid being deceived by change of line. Keep parries under control—a wide parry invites touches in an open line. There is no need to parry unless the thrust is on target. Alternate the types of parries and the times in which they are used.
6. The best time to attack is as your opponent prepares to attack. Be alert and move before the opponent's actual attack begins.
7. Keep footwork smooth and rapid. Keep feet and body as alert as the mind. Move about on the strip, keeping opponent guessing and your own body ready to move quickly and powerfully. Vary the distance at which you fence.
8. Be aggressive offensively. Pursue the opponent if she retreats continuously.
9. "Condition" your opponent by repeating an attack several times until she expects the pattern, then slightly alter the attack.

CLASS ORGANIZATION

Basic fencing skills are taught best in carefully organized and supervised class situations. The potentially hazardous nature of the sport demands more organization than some sports skills. The group should be small enough so some individual instruction can be given.

During demonstrations the group can be drawn in a semicircle close to the instructor. In a large group, the front row may kneel or sit and the back row stand. As the class begins skill practice, each individual should be assigned to a squad of at least six girls. The squads may be given names or numbers which identify them for teacher assignment to mirror or dummy practice, couple skill drill, or bouting.

The double line is an excellent formation for basic instruction, checking form, and observing general class progress. The squads form parallel lines facing each other so students are paired off. Facing an opponent, the student practices footwork, attacks, parries, and beginning bouting technique. Fencing skills should be taught as they will be used, i.e., moving and in combination with other skills. Parries and attacks are best learned together, just as they will be used. The riposte is so vital to fencing that it should be learned with simple defenses. Avoid teaching *flat-footed* responses—*move, move, move.* In order to vary opponents, have one line rotate with the leader going to the end of line at a designated time interval. Move frequently. When double line formation is used in a crowded area, the opposing line should execute a single skill, rather than individual skill practice, to avoid accidents. For example, line number 1 attacks as line number 2 retreats; line number 1 executes a disengage lunge into the fourth line as line number 2, back to the wall, parries and ripostes.

A squad serves as a unit for a round robin tournament as the students' skills develop. As two girls fence, the other members officiate and score the bout.

TEACHING PROGRESSION

A short and inspiring history of fencing helps girls and women develop the spirit and attitude for a new experience in a combative sport. At the beginning of a unit an explanation of safety precautions, demonstration, and explanation of fencing and of equipment are essential. Basic exercises are helpful in developing strength and agility and in releasing tensions often present.

Prior to class practice of a skill, the teacher should demonstrate and explain its use in a bout. Basic skills of the guard position, grip, advance, retreat, lunge and recovery should be stressed for form, agility, and effectiveness. The attention position and salute, taught early in a unit, add dignity and courtesy to informal practice. Again, stress moving and physical readiness with all attack and defense techniques.

Emphasis on the basic parries of sixth and fourth gives a fencer confidence to work against simple attacks. Addition of skills of riposte encourages agility and alertness and increases practice pleasure. Each fencer practices skills against an opponent, first on the teacher's command and later in bouting sessions. Early bouting serves to stress the importance of technique development and encourages students to return to personal skill development.

As students progress, attacks on the blade, compound attacks, and counter parries are introduced. Students should be encouraged to progress as rapidly as possible. Bouting and officiating should encourage students to participate with community fencing groups.

A sample teaching unit for beginners might include the following, although consideration should be given to those who progress at different speeds:

Lesson I

1. Brief history
2. Equipment and its care
3. Safety fundamentals
4. Explanation of the game (target, lines of attack)
5. Demonstration bout
6. Familiarization with equipment and moving in new body position

Lesson II

1. Review of previous lesson
2. Attention position
3. Grip
4. Salute
5. Guard position
6. Advance
7. Retreat

Lesson III

1. Review salute
2. Review guard position, advance, and retreat
3. Lunge
4. Drill of advance and retreat
5. Combine advance lunge, recovery and recovery forward

Lesson IV

1. Review lunge, recovery, and recovery forward
2. Guard position four
3. Combined practice of guard position four, advance, retreat, lunge, and recovery
4. Straight thrust

Lesson V

1. Review
2. Engagement
3. Demonstration and explanation of parries
4. Parry of fourth and sixth
5. Beat-thrust
6. Beat and parry four and six
7. Practice attack and parry
8. Riposte

Lesson VI

1. Discuss and explain valid target area
2. Feint
3. Review riposte
4. Beginning bouting, stress parries of fourth, sixth, and riposte

Lesson VII

1. Disengage
2. Group drill on attacks, parries, and riposte
3. Bouting strategy
4. Parries seven and eight

Lesson VIII

1. Intensive review
2. Disengage
3. Informal evaluation by teacher

Lesson IX

1. Review. Stress form in movements
2. Attack on the blade, beat
3. Drill and bouting
4. Review finer rule points
   Right-of-way
   Stopping the bout
   Acknowledgment of touch
5. Coupé

Lesson X

1. Review
2. Explain beginning techniques of officiating
3. Introduce one compound attack—beat disengage or double disengage
4. Practice bouting (stress teacher assistance)

Lesson XI

1. Review officiating
2. Begin round robin tournament using student officials

Lesson XII

1. Complete tournament

Lesson XIII

1. Written evaluation
2. Demonstration and explanation of selected advanced skills

SKILL DIFFICULTIES AND THEIR CORRECTION

Guard Position

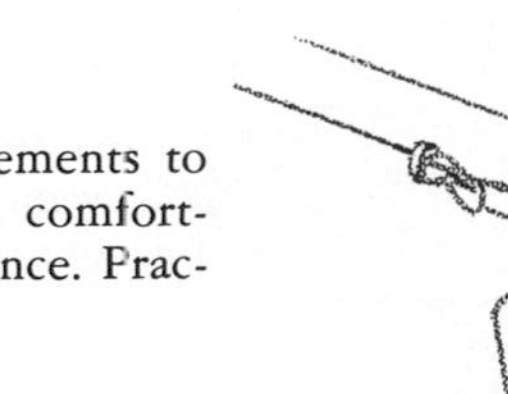

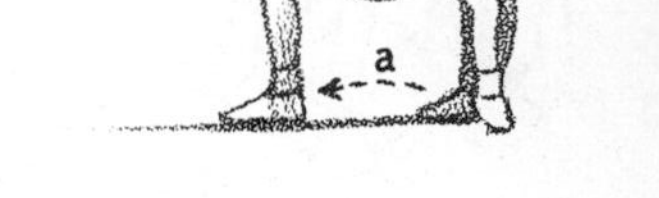

Difficulty	*Correction*
a. Feet too close or too far apart	a. Review sequence of movements to guard position stressing a comfortable step forward and balance. Practice in front of a mirror
b. Turning body toward opponent	b. Explain that shoulders are straight as in walking with rear foot. Stress value of presenting smallest target possible to opponent
c. Weight transferred to one foot	c. Have student practice lifting feet alternately and stamp feet at command
d. Body inclined forward from hips	d. Suggest student tuck hips under and practice before a mirror. Have students work in couples backing to stall bars and checking body alignment

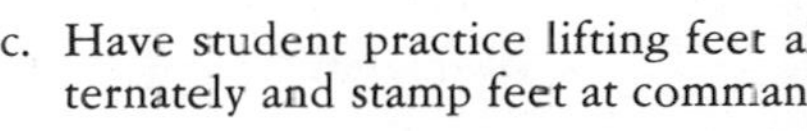

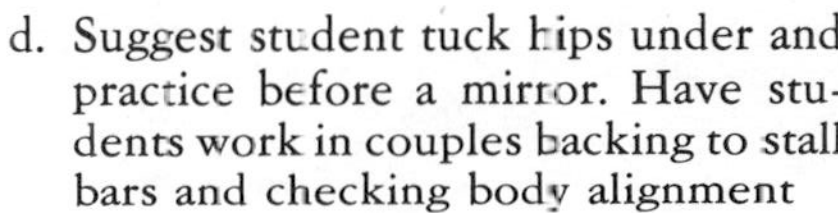

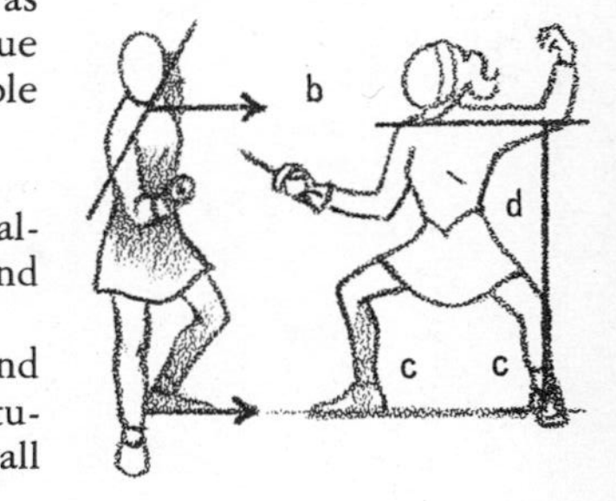

Advance and Retreat

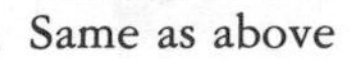

Difficulty	*Correction*
a. Body does not move forward or back in a straight line	a. Suggest student practice moving with heels on a line or particular floorboard. Emphasize that both heels stay on the line
b. Feet and heels lose their relationship and cause improper body balance	b. Same as above
c. Knees are straightened as body moves (indicated by fencer's head bobbing)	c. Have the student move slowly as the instructor counts or calls foot action emphasizing body position
d. Feet are dragged	d. Same as above
e. Feet become too close or too far apart for proper balance	e. Suggest the student stop often and check balance and foot position
f. Inability to move quickly due to overreaching and fatigue	f. Check size of steps. Work on conditioning exercise

Lunge

	Difficulty	*Correction*
a.	Body precedes arm thrust	Explain the rule of "right away" and the necessity of rapid arm extension. Teacher demonstrates proper timing and leads group by command of "thrust-lunge," "one-two," or "bing-bing"
b.	Fencer lunges too far resulting in slow recovery	Teacher demonstrates difficulty of recovery from over lunge. Review body position in the lunge
c.	Forward foot is lifted high, lunge is slow, and attack carried out of line by raised body	Teacher explains that the forward heel need not be raised more than an inch during the lunge. Student practices lunge with extended arm until body movement is smooth
d.	Failing to hit target because of under lunging	Teacher demonstrates how too short a step carries the knee past the toe. Student practices lunging at wall target to learn distance

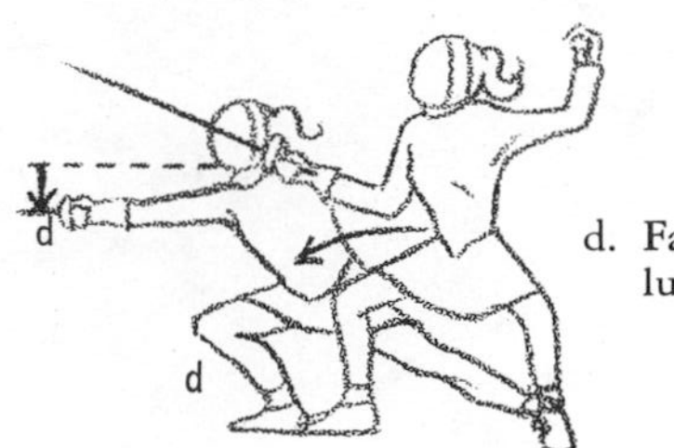

Recovery of Lunge

Difficulty	*Correction*
a. Recovery to a standing position	a. Teacher demonstrates and stresses return to a balanced guard position for coming action
b. Failure to use rear arm in recovery; slow hesitating movements	b. Suggest student recover without use of arm and then compare with properly executed recovery. Stress feeling of one movement

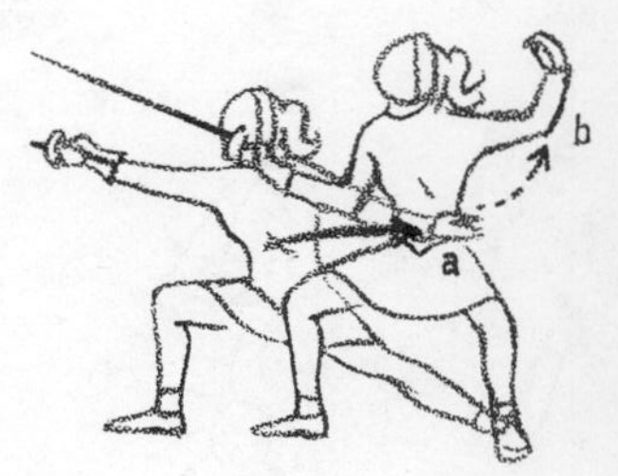

Grip

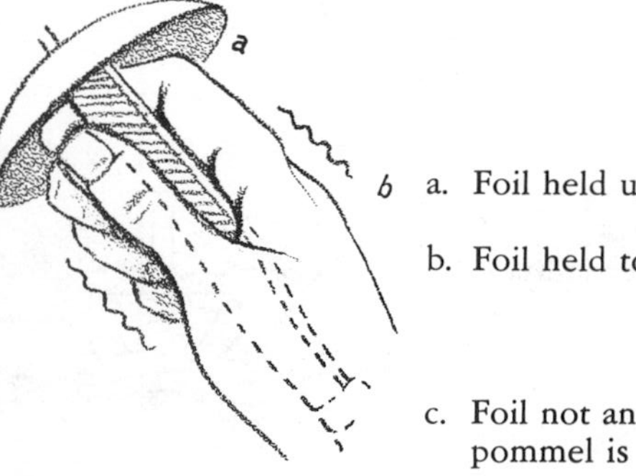

Difficulty	*Correction*
a. Foil held upsidedown or sideways	a. Demonstrate proper grip and check each student. Thumb on top of grip
b. Foil held too tightly or too loosely	b. Explain that the foil is held as if it were a baby bird. Teacher may tap blades to show how a fencer can lose control with an improper grip
c. Foil not an extension of the hand as pommel is above or below wrist	c. Relax grip. Check to be certain wrist and forearm are in a straight line

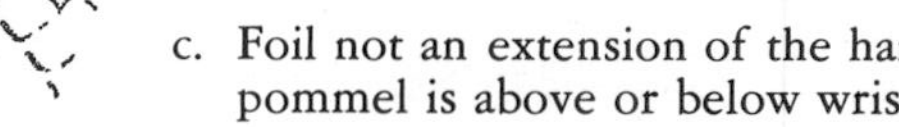

Simple Attacks

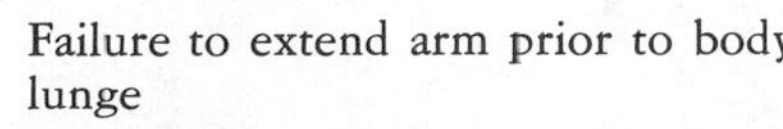

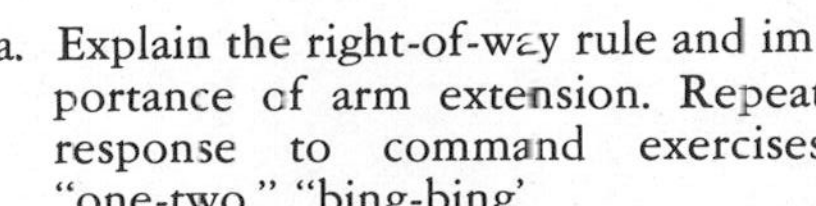

Difficulty	*Correction*
a. Failure to extend arm prior to body lunge	a. Explain the right-of-way rule and importance of arm extension. Repeat response to command exercises "one-two," "bing-bing'
b. Missing the target or being hit on a beat-attack as the blade is brought far out of line	b. Use only the last three fingers to beat. Avoid bending the wrist
c. Arm moves foil tip in disengage and cutover causing tip to move too far out of line leaving target unprotected	c. Stress importance of maintaining protection of target area—demonstrate use of fingers in moving foil tip. Student draws imaginary pictures with foil tip while keeping arm in extension and in guard position

Simple Parries

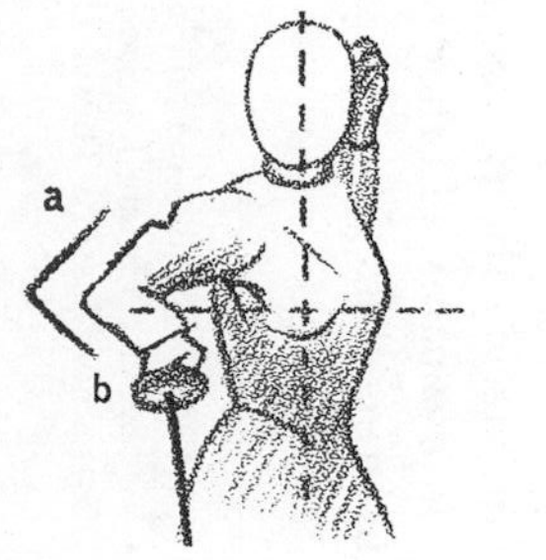

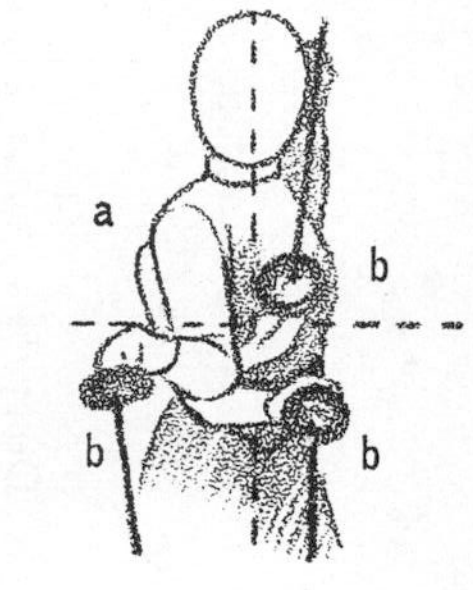

Difficulty	*Correction*
a. Parries are made by large arm movements, resulting in slow recovery and large unguarded target area	a. Practice against an opponent to get accustomed to the thrust. Keep pommel firm against the wrist
b. Extending arm or dropping hand as attack begins	b. Explain parries are made from a guard position to another guard position. Teacher gives commands "parry fourth, parry sixth, etc.," so action becomes easy before bouting begins

Riposte

Difficulty	*Correction*
a. Failure to complete a parry before beginning riposte	a. Student should practice the riposte mimetically, then at teacher's command, and against a slow lunge before bouting
b. Delaying so opponent can redouble or replace	b. Suggest student practice to command "parry-extend-lunge." Increase speed and add disengage and cutover. Instruct opponent to wait for riposte until skill is developed

EVALUATING THE RESULTS

Evaluation in fencing classes is complicated by the numerous parts contained in a single skill. An effective evaluative plan should consider the student's knowledge and understanding of rules of bouting, safety, and skills. Her ability to fence effectively should reflect her skill development. Wyrick proposed a self-testing battery to assess progress in terms of form and objective scoring.*

Rating Basic Skills. A rating scale may be developed for each skill taught. For example, the teacher may wish to evaluate separate skills of: (1) on guard; (2) footwork; (3) lunge; (4) attack accuracy; (5) bladework (lunge, disengage lunge, etc.); (6) parries; and (7) riposte.

Aside from the simple execution of the above skills, the teacher may evaluate their execution by taking into consideration the student's ability to advance, retreat, and lunge in good form with good judgment of distance and execute attacks and parries with precision and speed.

The Schutz Fencing Achievement Scales† use the lunge for speed and accuracy and the speed in footwork and lunge to measure elements important in the sport. The scales may be used successfully if the teacher remembers no attempt is made to measure general fencing ability.

Rating scales used by student officials are helpful in evaluation of general fencing ability. Tournament play in a pool may be arranged so each person evaluates all other squad members on fencing ability, strategy, and officiating ability.

---

*Wyrick, Waneen: *Foil Fencing.* Philadelphia, W. B. Saunders Co., 1971, pp. 114–119.

†Schutz, Helen J.: "Construction of an Achievement Scale in Fencing for Women." Abstract of Master's Thesis, University of Washington, Seattle, Washington.

TERMINOLOGY

Abstain—Declination of voting privilege when a judge was unable to see if a point was made.
Absence of the blade—Blades are not engaged.
Advance—Forward movement of the body toward opponent.
Attack—An initial attempt to hit an opponent by a thrust of the foil, usually followed by a lunge.
Attack on the blade—Beats, pressures, binds, and glides used to open a line of attack or deceive an opponent.
Balestra—Jump forward combined with the lunge when attacking.
Beat—Sharp rap against opponent's blade.
Bind—A method of removing an opponent's blade from high to low line. (See description p. 186.)
Call—Stamping forward foot twice to stop the bout.
Closed line—A line closed to attack due to position of foil and arm of opponent.
Compound attack—An attack consisting of two or more actions.
Compound parry—Two or more parries used in combination.
Contraction parry—A combination simple and counter parry.
Counter parry—A circular parry which carries opponent's blade to opposite line.
Counter riposte—An offensive action following the parry of a riposte.
Cutover—Disengagement made by passing over the tip of opponent's blade.
Deceive—Escaping and avoiding control of blade by opponent.
Disengage—Moving the blade from one line of engagement to an opposite line.
Engagement—Contact of two opposing blades.
Envelopment—Taking the opponent's blade and describing a circle to return to the line of engagement without losing contact.
False attack—A lunge which is intended to draw opponent's response but not intended to land on target.
Feint—An extension of foil arm as a pretense for attack.
Flèche—An attack made by running rather than lunging.
Foible—Flexible half of the blade.
Forte—Sturdy half of the blade near the guard.
Invitation—Actions that invite attack by an opponent.
Line of attack—Used to describe position of the attacking weapon.
Lunge—An extension of the arm and body from the guard position for the purpose of delivering an attack.
Measure—Distance between both fencers during the bout.
One-two—A compound attack consisting of (1) a feint and disengage and (2) a disengage. It is used to deceive a parry.
On guard—Basic balanced body position for preparatory fencing position.
Parry—Blocking an opponent's thrust by contact with foils.
Pass—Point of foil grazes target, failing to hit properly.
Phrase—A period of continuous bouting.
Pressure—Application of pressure against an opponent's blade to draw a response and open the way for an attack.
Redoublement—A second attack made when an opponent does not riposte.
Remise—A new attack initiated after first fails to hit target. The line remains unchanged and the arm remains extended in the second action.
Reprise—A new attack following a return to guard position.
Retreat—Movement to increase the distance between fencers.
Right-of-way—The right of attack gained by the fencer who first extends the foil arm, initiates an attack, or parries on an attack.
Riposte—A return or counter attack following a successful parry.
Salute—Acknowledgment to opponent and judges.
Semicircular parry—A parry from a high to low line or from low to high. The threatening blade is moved laterally.
Stop thrust—A straight thrust, with or without a lunge, made into an advancing opponent. If the hit is to be valid, it must be initiated before the final motion of the opponent's attack begins.

Thrust—An extension of the arm in a feint or an attack.
Time thrust—A counter attack made in opposition to an opponent's blade. It is usually executed against a compound attack and results in a parry and riposte simultaneously.
Touch—A valid hit on opponent's target area.

DISCUSSION QUESTIONS

1. Explain and demonstrate the difference between simple and compound attacks.
2. What safety precautions are necessary in conducting a fencing class?
3. Explain the right-of-way rule. How does a fencer secure right-of-way? Demonstrate.
4. Organize a round robin tournament for a squad of eight fencers. Explain tournament conduct, necessary officials, and the responsibilities.
5. Discuss evaluation procedures for a class of beginning fencers.

SELECTED AUDIOVISUAL AIDS

Beginning Fencing. (35 mm. foil film strips, color, with sound recordings by Maxwell Garret.) Covers offense, defense, strategy, and tactics. Related information available in *How to Improve Your Fencing* and *Fencing Instructors' Guide.* The Athletic Institute, 805 Merchandise Mart, Chicago, Illinois 60654. (Purchase and rental)

Fencing—1964 Olympics—Tokyo. (16 mm. black and white film explaining training and competitive techniques of the world's outstanding fencers.) Amateur Fencers' League of America, 33–62nd Street, West New York, New Jersey 07093. (Rental)

Foil Fundamentals. (16 mm. b & w.) Description by Professor George Santelli. Presents formal salute, on guard position, footwork, attacks, and defenses. Amateur Fencers' League of America, 33–62nd Street, West New York, New Jersey 07093. (Purchase and rental)

Instructional Foil. (16 mm., black and white film by J. Martinez Costello.) This film records a lesson progressing through foil fundamentals. Slow motion and close-ups are used; titles facilitate the recognition of attacks and parries. Costello Fencing Equipment Company, 30 East 10th Street, New York, New York 10003. (Purchase and rental)

Omnibus. (16 mm., b & w, sound.) Explains fencing to the neophyte. Amateur Fencers' League of America, 33–62nd Street, West New York, New Jersey 07093. (Purchase and rental)

Techniques of Foil Fencing. (16 mm. black and white film in which Helene Mayer, former Women's World Champion, demonstrates.) Fencing techniques in normal and slow motion close-up shots are a special feature. The University of California, Extension Film Center, 2223 Fulton Street, Berkeley, California 04720. (Purchase and rental)

SUGGESTED READINGS

Amateur Fencers' League of America: *Fencing Rules and Manual.* 33–62nd Street, West New York, New Jersey 07093.

Bowling-Fencing Guide. AAHPER, National Association for Girls and Women in Sport. 1201 16th Street, N.W., Washington, D.C. 20036.

Castello, Hugo, and James: *Fencing.* New York, The Ronald Press, 1962.

Crosnier, Roger: *Fencing with the Electric Foil.* New York, A. S. Barnes and Company, 1961.

Nadi, Aldo: *On Fencing.* New York, G. P. Putnam's Sons, 1943.

Palffy-Alpar, Julius: *Sword and Masque.* Philadelphia, F. A. Davis Co., 1967.

Sports Illustrated. *Sports Illustrated Book of Fencing.* Philadelphia, J. B. Lippincott Co., 1961.

Vince, Joseph: *Fencing.* 2nd ed. New York, The Ronald Press, 1962.

Wyrick, Waneen: *Foil Fencing.* Philadelphia, W. B. Saunders Co., 1971.

Rule Books

Amateur Fencers' League of America: *Fencing Rules and Manual.* Amateur Fencers' League of America. Contains rules for competitions and organization of competitions. Also contains administrative procedures of the AFLA and lists Olympic, Pan-American, and World Champions in fencing. AFLA, 33–62nd Street, West New York, New Jersey 07093.

American Association for Health, Physical Education, and Recreation: *Fencing-Bowling Guide.* American Association for Health, Physical Education, and Recreation. A rule book for girls' competition in fencing containing many articles about various phases of the game. Published every two years. AAHPER, 1921 16th Street, N.W., Washington, D.C. 20036.

National Collegiate Athletic Association: *The Official Fencing Guide.* National Collegiate Athletic Association. Official college and school rule book in America. Published annually with any new rules or rule changes included. Has college records and lists qualified fencing officials in the United States. College Athletic Publishing Service, 349 East Thomas Road, Phoenix, Arizona 85012.

PERIODICALS

American Fencing. Amateur Fencing League of America, 33–62nd Street, West New York, New Jersey 07093.

The Swordmaster. National Fencing Coaches Association of America, 16 North Carrol Street, Madison, Wisconsin 53703.

CHAPTER 9

GOLF

The game of golf undoubtedly grew from field hockey, the forerunner of all stick and ball games. It may actually be as old as the spirit of play when men devised games of striking stones with sticks. Many authorities believe a game similar to golf was played in Holland and the Low Countries centuries ago. Most agree that golf, as it is played today, originated in Scotland in the 14th century. Scottish Parliamentary action forbidding the game as a threat to the development of skill at archery, and thus of national defense, deterred the game only briefly until King James IV became a fan and golf was played openly.

Unlike many sports, golf has been a game played by women for centuries. Mary Queen of Scots was an enthusiastic and skilled golfer. Her attentive army cadet was the forerunner of the caddy of today. Appropriately, the most famous course in the world is the Royal and Ancient Golf Club of St. Andrews, Scotland, founded in 1754. It remains the seat of authority for all matters pertaining to the game.

Golf crossed the Atlantic to Canada and America in the latter part of the 19th century. John G. Reid introduced the game to his friends in a cow pasture in Yonkers, New York, in 1885. This Scotsman, who became known as the "Father of American Golf," was instrumental in establishing the first golf club, St. Andrews of Yonkers, in 1888. Five of the private clubs in the Eastern United States joined together to form the United States Golf Association in 1894. From its beginning, the USGA has been the ruling body for amateurs and the sponsoring body for prominent tournaments.

Early in the 20th century enthusiastic women golfers were granted playing privileges at private courses, and numerous public and college courses were built. The development of equipment for consistent and accurate play and mass manufacturing brought the price of golf into the range of millions.

In an effort to promote golf, the National Golf Foundation, United States Golf Association, the United States Ladies Professional Golf Association, and several sporting goods manufacturers offer clinics and workshops for the player, as well as for the teacher and professional. Nationally televised tournaments have done much to interest women in golf.

At present more than 10,000 courses attract 12 million participants, while driving ranges, 3 hole short courses, and instructional classes serve millions more.

THE NATURE AND PURPOSE OF THE GAME

Golf is a game of skill and accuracy that demands concentration and emotional control. It is played by both sexes from youth throughout life. A player sets her own pace, playing a fast and strenuous 18 holes or a leisurely 9 holes using a mechanical cart. Mechanized carts enable the handicapped and aged persons to participate.

Golf is also an excellent competitive sport, for the United States Golf

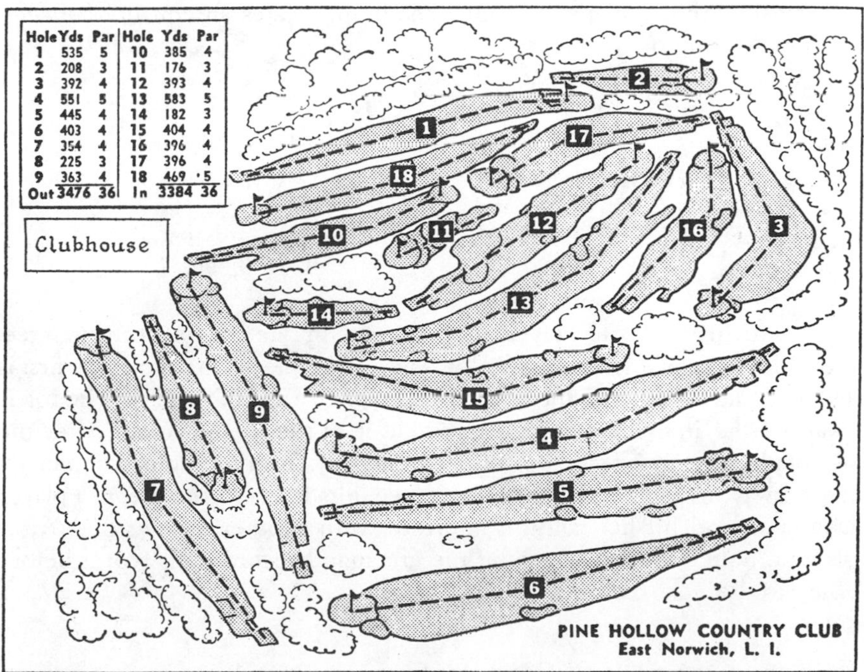

Hole	Yds	Par	Hole	Yds	Par
1	535	5	10	385	4
2	208	3	11	176	3
3	392	4	12	393	4
4	551	5	13	583	5
5	445	4	14	182	3
6	403	4	15	404	4
7	354	4	16	396	4
8	225	3	17	396	4
9	363	4	18	469	·5
Out	3476	36	In	3384	36

Figure 9–1 The layout of a typical 18 hole golf course. (Courtesy of the New York Times.)

Association has developed a system for computing handicaps that allows poor, average and skilled players to compete equitably.*

The game consists of hitting a small, hard ball with selected clubs from a teeing area across various surface areas known as fairways, hazards, and roughs to smooth patches of grass, known as greens, and into small holes, or cups, in the greens. The object of the game is to use as few strokes as possible on each hole and over the entire course.

Although golf courses are laid out in units of nine holes, most official ones have at least 18, and many have 27, 36, or 54 holes. Par golf scores are based on eighteen holes.

The 18 hole course is planned to balance play and avoid congestion. It is divided into the "front nine" (out) and "back nine" (in). An 18 hole course includes 5200 to 7200 yards of playing area, roughly equalized between the front and back nine. Each hole is assigned a par value, or an arbitrary standard of excellence, determined by length and difficulty of the hole. This value allows a certain number of strokes to get to the green and two putts on the green.

An increasing number of golf courses use the U.S.G.A. Course Rating System. The system is based on the fact that each course has peculiarities which affect its playing difficulty. Factors such as yardage, topography, prevailing winds, size of green, and hazards of each hole are considered in determining a "difficulty rating." The differential established for the course, combined with a player's individual handicap, creates an equality between players meeting on a strange course.

Course distances for par are:

Men	*Women*
Up to 250 yards, par 3	Up to 210 yards, par 3
251 to 470 yards, par 4	211 to 400 yards, par 4
471 to 600 yards, par 5	401 to 575 yards, par 5
601 yards and up, par 6	576 yards and up, par 6

Two, three, or four players may compete in one group. At the first tee, the order of teeing is decided by lot. Thereafter, the honor of playing first is awarded the winner of the preceding hole. In case of a tie, the honor is awarded the individual or side that held it at the previous tee. After the players have teed off, the person farthest away from the hole, whether on the fairway, in the rough, or on the green, hits first. On the green, a player may mark and lift her ball if it interferes with another player's line. After players "hole out" they move off the green and record their scores before going to the next teeing area.

---

*Complete information regarding the handicapping and course rating system is contained in the U.S.G.A. publication entitled "Golf Committee Manual and U.S.G.A. Golf Handicap System."

GAME RULES AND SCORING

The parent ruling body is the Royal and Ancient Golf Club of St. Andrews, Scotland. The United States Golf Association is the ruling organization for the United States and Canada. As the rules are numerous and appear difficult for the beginner it is advisable to carry the *USGA's Rules of Golf** wherever one plays. The following basic guides suggest conduct for the first rounds:

1. Be able to identify one's own ball by its markings.
2. Carry only 14 clubs. The penalty in match play is loss of one hole for each hole at which violation occurred (maximum 2 holes per round), and loss of two strokes per hole (maximum four strokes) in stroke play.
3. At the beginning of each hole the ball should be teed between the tee markers and not more than two club lengths behind the markers.
4. An intentional swing at the ball, whether a hit or a miss, counts as a stroke.
5. Loose impediments may be removed if they hinder a stroke (except in hazards); however, no growing vegetation may be removed, broken, or bent. The penalty is two strokes in stroke play and loss of a hole in match play. In a hazard, if the ball is covered by sand or leaves, some of the covering may be removed in order to see the top of the ball.
6. A ball lying near an unnatural obstacle such as a bench or hydrant may be moved no more than two club lengths, and never nearer the hole, without penalty.
7. A ball in casual water (e.g., rain water or leakage) may be dropped over the shoulder, not nearer the hole, with no penalty. On the green the ball is lifted and replaced; in a hazard it is dropped in the hazard.
8. If a ball lies against an obstacle and you term it unplayable you may (a) drop a ball no more than two club lengths from where original ball lies (not nearer the hole) and receive a one stroke penalty or (b) drop a ball anywhere behind the unplayable lie keeping that point between the player and the hole and receive a one stroke penalty.
9. A provisional ball is a second ball played when there is a possibility that the original ball is out of bounds or lost. It should be played as close to the spot of the original ball as possible.
10. If a ball goes out of bounds or is termed lost after a five minute search, a second ball must be played as near as possible to the spot from which the first ball was hit. In addition to all strokes taken, a penalty stroke is added.
11. Play the ball as it lies. A ball may be lifted on the putting green only. Although USGA does not endorse winter rules, some courses permit "preferred lies" because of the condition of the grounds.
12. When a ball rests in a hazard, the club must not be grounded in preparation for the stroke. The penalty is two strokes in stroke play and loss of hole in match play.

Scoring

Several methods of scoring are used in golf competition. Generally, competition is by stroke or match play. In *stroke play* the winner is the golfer

**The Rules of Golf.* USGA, 40 East 38th Street, New York, New York 10016.

DATE | EVENT

Hole	Yards	Bogy	Par	ELLEN	ALICE	Handicap Strokes			W+ L− HO	Hole	Yards	Bogy	Par	Ellen	Alice	Handicap Strokes			W+ L− HO
1	325	5	4	5	5	7				10	325	5	4	4	4	8			0
2	185	3	3	4	3	15				11	185	3	3	4	3	16			+
3	325	4	4	4	5	9				12	325	4	4	4	5	10			−
4	500	5	5	5	6	1				13	500	5	5	6	6	2			0
5	375	5	4	6	7	5				14	375	5	4	6	6	6			0
6	150	3	3	3	4	17				15	150	3	3	3	4	18			−
7	450	5	5	5	6	3				16	450	5	5	5	6	4			−
8	300	4	4	5	6	11				17	300	4	4	6	4	12			+
9	300	4	4	4	4	13				18	300	4	4	5	5	14			0
Out	2910	38	36	41	46					In	2910	38	36	43	43				
										Out	2910								
										Total	5820								
										HANDICAP									
										NET SCORE									

SCORER Alice Garrison

ATTEST Ellen Patterson

Figure 9–2 A completed golf score card. The out nine illustrates scoring for stroke play; the back nine illustrates scoring for match play.

using the least number of strokes over the designated course. In *match play,* or hole play, the victor is the player who wins the greatest number of holes from her opponent, regardless of the final stroke total. In match play where opponents have the same number of strokes on a hole, they have "halved" the hole and neither scores a point. Stroke play is considered more exacting since each stroke is of equal value, whereas in match play, a loss of several strokes and the loss of a hole may be recouped by a one stroke victory on a later hole.

Use of a scorecard is helpful in teaching scoring procedures, for it usually gives name and location of the course, entries for date, event, scorer's name, attestor and four players, course markings, and local rules on the back of the card. The inside scoring section indicates the number of yards for each hole, total course yardage, par for men and women, the handicap stroke ranking awarded each hole, and columns for total score for match or stroke play.

Examples of both stroke and match scoring follow:

1. Ellen and Alice play the front nine by stroke play. Ellen has a total of 41 strokes; Alice records 46. Ellen is the winner.

2. On the back nine Ellen and Alice choose match play. During the nine holes, they halved holes 10, 13, 14, and 18. Alice won holes 11 and 17; Ellen won holes 12, 15, and 16. Although both players had 43 strokes on the last nine holes, Ellen was the victor.

The Nassau system of scoring is often used in singles or doubles stroke or match play. In a single match (two competing) each match is worth three points. One point is given the winner of the first nine holes, one point for the winner of the second nine holes, and one point to the player winning the greatest number of holes of the 18. In doubles match play additional possible team points are added.

Handicapping. Golf utilizes several handicapping systems to equalize competition among players of different abilities. The USGA has detailed information for computing and establishing a handicap. Briefly, the number of handicap strokes is determined by a percentage of the difference between a player's average score on a course and the established difficulty rating of the course. For example, if the course rating is 70 and the player's score is 84, the handicap differential is 14. The total of the lowest ten handicap differentials out of the last 20 rounds is computed and applied to the U.S.G.A. differential chart to determine handicap strokes. Once a handicap is established it works as follows: player A with a handicap of 6 is competing against player B with a handicap of 8. In the match player B is allowed to subtract one stroke on each of the holes numbered 1 and 2 in the scorecard column marked handicap strokes, regardless of the sequence of the holes on the course. In stroke play, the "net" score is determined by subtracting the

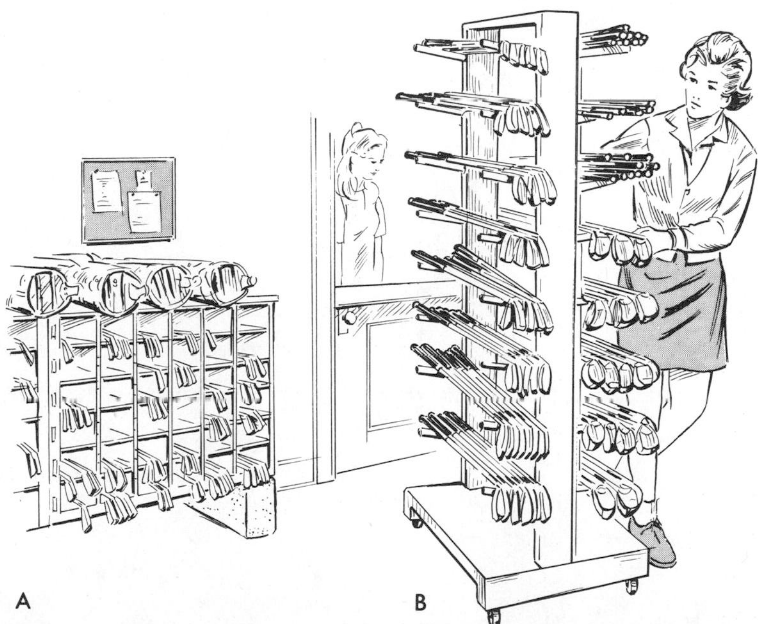

Figure 9–3 Equipment storage. *A,* Clubs should be stored in pigeon-holed racks or divided compartments (vertical or horizontal), in bags, in sets, or by clubs of like number in an assigned space. Always avoid jamming clubs together. *B,* A movable cart is recommended.

number of handicap strokes from the "gross" or actual, total of strokes for the round.

Novelty golf events and improvised tournaments often use other handicapping methods and point systems. One of the most popular methods is the Callaway system used for one-day amateur tournaments when not all players have established handicaps. The final individual score is computed (on an established table) by consideration of a player's total score and her highest single hole scores.*

NEEDED FACILITIES AND EQUIPMENT

A golf course such as the one shown in Figure 9–1 will eventually be the proving ground for all the skill and equipment of the golfer. Basic equipment includes clubs, balls, tees, and a carrying bag or rack. Other equipment may be desirable for comfort and skill improvement.

Most schools and colleges will find it necessary to furnish minimum equipment for golf instruction, for most students do not own clubs. Golf equipment for the instructional program need not be too expensive as most

*See *Competitive Golf Events.* National Golf Foundation, Room 804, Merchandise Mart, Chicago, Illinois 60654.

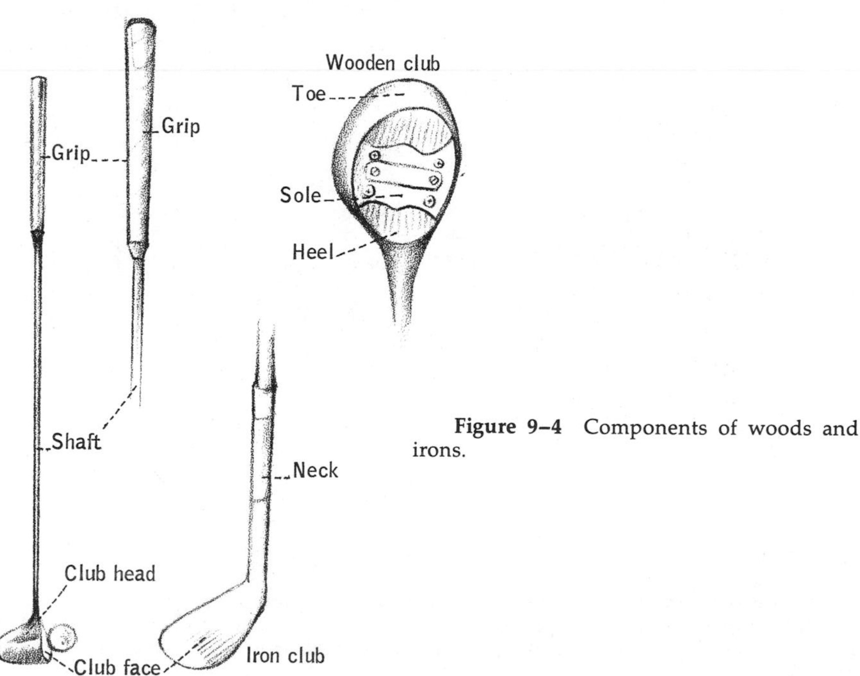

Figure 9–4 Components of woods and irons.

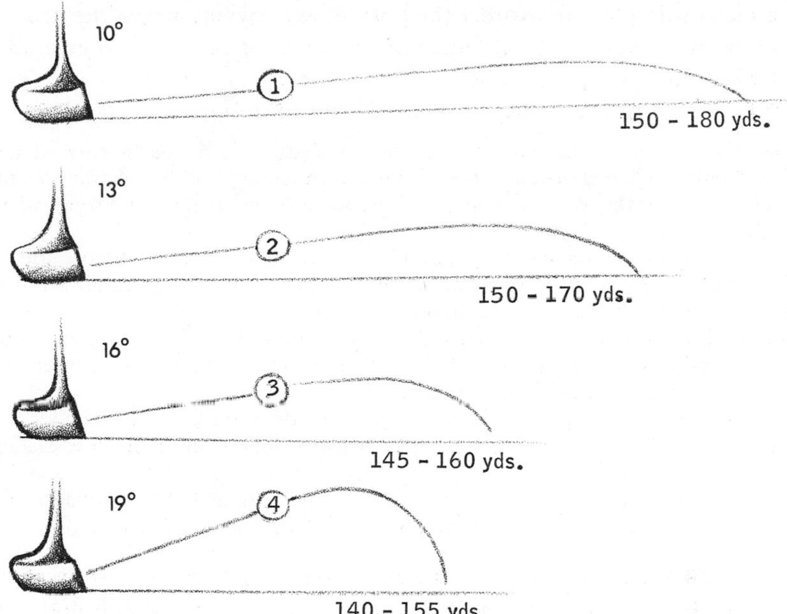

Figure 9–5 Woods. Anticipated distances for average women golfers.

club professionals and driving range operators are anxious to increase golfing interest and will sell serviceable used equipment reasonably.

Clubs. The USGA limits the golfer to the use of 14 clubs during a match. All 14 are not necessary for the beginning player, but even advanced players must be discriminating, for manufacturers now design and produce a variety of specialized woods such as 5, 6, 3½ and 4½, as well as a choice of several wedges.

Clubs are generally classified into two groups: woods and irons. The designation originally referred to the composition of the club heads; however, "woods" may have heads of plastic, magnesium, laminated wood, or persimmon wood. Essentially, iron and wood clubs have the same parts.

The main parts of the club are the grip, shaft, and clubhead. The golfer holds the club by the leather or composition covered grip at the top of the shaft. A cap at the top of the handle protects the upper portion of the grip and secures the wooden plug to strengthen the hollow shaft. The shaft is an aluminum, graphite, or tension steel tube over which the grip is placed and into which the clubhead attaches.

The clubhead is below the neck of the club where the head and shaft join. It includes the sole, or the lower part of the club that rests on the ground; the heel, or part nearest the shaft; the toe, or outer tip of the head; and the club face with its scored or grooved striking surface. Wooden clubs have a metal sole plate to protect the bottom as it swings across the ground. Iron clubs often have a metal flange on the back of the head to give additional weight and proper balance.

Wooden clubs are named and numbered to designate their use:

Number 1—Has the largest head and longest shaft with a nearly vertical face. Used only for tee shots and gives a low, flat trajectory with maximum distance to the ball. For the average woman it is 41 to 42½ inches long and weighs 13 to 14 ounces.

Number 2—Used for long shots with good lies from the fairway and from the tee. The club face has more loft, causing a ball to go higher in the air with less distance than when hit with a driver.

Number 3—Used for short tee shots and for long shots from the fairway and rough from good lies. More loft to the face and often a shorter shaft than number 1 or 2 woods which allows better control.

Number 4—Used for long shots from a poor lie or deep grass, as the smaller head and shallow face penetrate to the ball. It gives higher flight and less distance than 1, 2, or 3 woods.

Number 5—A popular club with women golfers, it has a small head and shallow face and is often used in preference to a number 1 or number 2 iron.

Iron clubs are informally grouped as long, medium, and short irons. This classification refers to both the length of the shaft and ball flight distance attained by the use of each club. The construction of the irons gives an immediate teaching cue for beginning golfers: "The larger the club number, the shorter the shaft, the more loft to the face, consequently, the higher and shorter the ball flight."

The long irons include numbers 1, 2, and 3:

Number 1—Used for long, low full shots from a good lie. The long shaft and straight face make it a difficult club for beginners. Not carried often, it is replaced by a 3, 4, or 5 wood.

Number 2—A utility club for comparatively long fairway and tee shots from a good lie.

Number 3—Used for less distance than a number 2 iron but the loft of the face allows a stroke from a relatively poor lie.

The mid-irons include numbers 4, 5, and 6:

Number 4—Used from the fairway and rough for medium distances, for occasional tee shots on short holes, and on "drag" strokes from the edge of the green.

Number 5—An excellent utility club for the beginner. As the medium length club among all, it is used from the fairway and rough for pitching a ball high to the green, for pitch and run shots to the green when a safe approach is desired, and as a tee club on short holes.

Number 6—Used from high rough for pitch shots to the green and from clean lies in a sand trap when distance is needed.

The short irons include numbers 7, 8, 9, and wedges:

Number 7—Used for short pitch shots from fairway and traps and for shots over trees and obstacles.

Number 8—Used for quick rising shots over hazards or as an approach from the fairway. Little roll follows ball descent. An excellent club when obstacles prevent a follow-through.

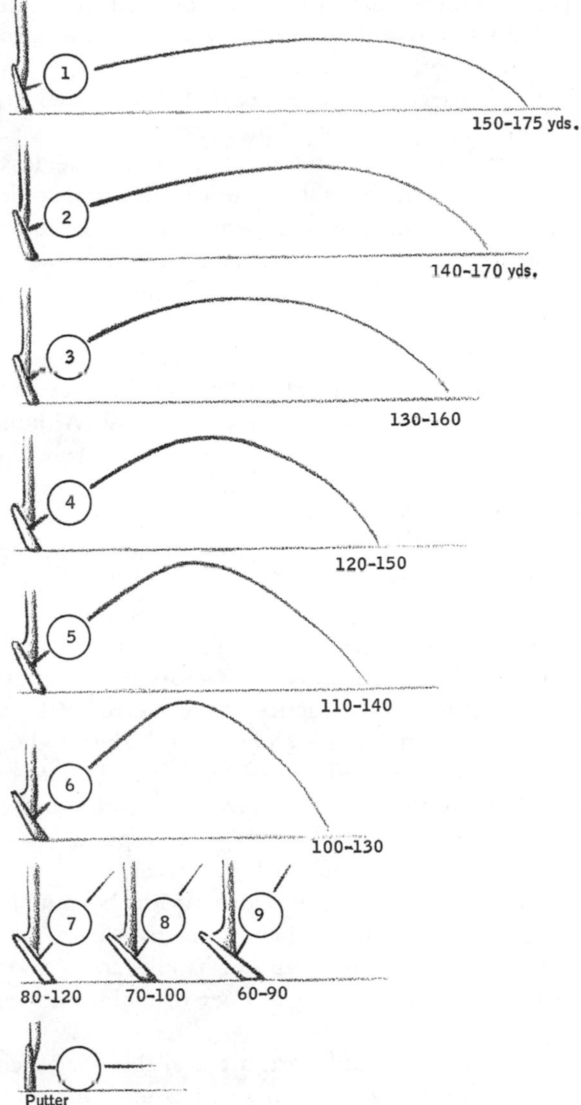

Figure 9–6 Irons. Anticipated distances for average women golfers.

Number 9—The iron with the greatest loft. Used from deep rough and short approaches to the green with little ball roll.

Wedges—Either pitching or sand wedge. The heavy, flanged clubhead has a very slanted face and is used to loft the ball from sand, high grass, and other hazards.

The *putter* is an essential club for all golfers. There are numerous designs, ranging from the traditional single blade to the weighted, large-headed putter with an offset shaft, to the mallet head. In a category of its own, this short shafted club with a straight face is used to stroke the ball over the smooth surface of the green.

Balls. Golf balls are constructed of cork, liquid, rubber, steel, or plastic centers surrounded by tightly bound rubber yarn and encased in a balata rubber cover of dimpled design and painted white. The less expensive repainted or factory-rejected balls have thick covers that decrease the chances of cutting the ball and allow inexpensive play. The more expensive balls are designed for maximum accuracy and distance. The approximate price range is from $.35 to $1.50. Personal balls should be clearly marked for rapid identification.

Large instructional groups can purchase low grade "range" balls, used ones, or manufacturers' rejects for outdoor practice. Practice balls of plastic, cotton, felt, and woolen yarn are available for indoor use. Although accurate distances cannot be measured indoors, the safe and relatively noiseless balls are superior to homemade paper or tape balls.

Tees and Tee Mats. Tees are used to elevate the ball for the first drive on each hole. Inexpensive wooden or plastic tees should be selected, since they are often broken and lost. If tee mats are used outside, rubber tees may be placed below the mat for semi-permanency.

Indoor practice mats are usually made of rubber tire strippings or coco fibers. The heavy duty rubber mats are satisfactory for tee shots; however, coco mats are better for iron club practice as they "give" with the impact of the hands and wrists and allow the clubhead to contact the ball below ground level. When using mats indoors or outdoors, the instructor should lower the mats or elevate the player's stance area so the surface simulates actual playing conditions. Strips of close pile carpeting or commercial indoor turfs can be used for indoor putting surfaces.

Bag. A light fabric "Sunday" bag is ideal for the beginning golfer with limited equipment. The more durable and attractive leather or fabric bag with shoe and ball pockets, a carry strap and handle, and a hood is a heavy burden for the woman golfer with a full set of clubs who cannot afford regular caddy service.

Golf Carts. A number of pull carts are available for purchase or rental. The lightweight pocket bag built on a cart is ideal for the golfer with limited clubs; others prefer a sturdy collapsible cart that carries a bag and rain gear and offers such accessories as a seat and score card rack. At some private clubs and public courses, caddies or power driven carts are required.

Costume. Shoes that offer comfort and help maintain balance and stability while swinging are a valuable part of a golfer's equipment. Some players find rubber-soled canvas shoes satisfactory, but many insist on spikes. Spikes can be placed on flat-soled Oxfords if an investment in golf shoes is inappropriate. Jewelry should not be worn, as rings may injure the hands, and the delicate mechanisms of wrist watches may be ruined by the stroking impact. When in doubt as to club regulations concerning dress, women should wear a skirt and a loose fitting, neat blouse or manufacturer's golf apparel, all of which are comfortable when walking and swinging a club. Shorts or slacks are acceptable on the majority of courses.

Accessories and Gadgets. There are many accessories for the woman golfer. Among the necessities are gloves, full or half, which aid in gripping and prevent calluses; an umbrella for the inevitable thundershowers; and a shade hat. Other useful items include stroke counters to aid the novice in keeping her score, ball markers for use on the green, and ball holders worn on the belt to eliminate bulging pockets.

Commercial gadgets designed to improve basic skills are numerous. Such items as a golf glove to correct improper grip, a plastic sleeve to prevent bending the elbow on the backswing, and an elastic band to keep the arms close and elbow down may have value, but should be prescribed by an instructor who analyzes the problems of your swing. These aids are not permitted in competitive play. The stroke analyzer and video tape used by competent instructors can be invaluable aids in skill development.

Indoor Equipment. In addition to balls, tees, and mats, an indoor instructional program can be more complete with putting cups, nylon nets and driving cages, targets, and sand approach areas. Nearly all of this equipment is sold commercially, yet much of it can be made inexpensively.* A movable golf cage is a valuable piece of equipment that can be used outside as well as inside and is an instructional time-saver in both settings.

Purchase and Care of Equipment

The most important items to successful golf are well fitted clubs and shoes. The golf professional at the course is the best consultant when buying these items.

A beginner should take special care in selecting clubs, for properly fitted clubs help to mold an efficient swing pattern. If poorly fitted, they may develop swing idiosyncrasies to fit the clubs, not the golfer.

Club selection is based on length and grip of shaft, flexibility of shaft, and clubhead weight and design. A beginning golfer cannot use a full set of clubs to advantage but should buy clubs from open stock, which can be added to later. A minimal basic set of matched clubs should include 1 and 3 woods, irons 3, 5, 7 and 9, and a putter.

Table 5 offers *general* suggestions for beginning golfers.

Generally, the shorter hitters use lighter shafts and more shallow wood clubfaces with lighter swingweights. As the player becomes stronger specifications change.

---

*For suggestions see Anthony E. Orlando: Make your own indoor golf area, *Journal of AAHPER,* February, 1955. Also, Jock Carter: *How to Make Athletic Equipment,* New York, The Ronald Press, 1960, pp. 239–242.

Table 5. (SEE TEXT FOR EXPLANATION)

Height of Golfer*	Shaft Length and Flex	Swingweight, Loft, Lie
5′7″ and over	42½″ driver, 38½″ or 39″ number 2 iron	Driver swingweight from C7 to C9
	Long hitters use ladies' heavy or men's light or heavy flex	Deep face driver for strong hitters; shallower face with more loft for lighter hitters
5′3″ to 5′6″	41½″ or 42″ driver, 37½″ or 38½″ number 2 iron	Driver swingweight from C3 to C6
	Medium to heavy shafts for long hitters	Medium clubface depth: 10 to 11 degree driver loft
	Light shaft for shorter hitters	
Under 5′3″	41″ driver, 36½″ or 37″ number 2 iron. All but strongest use light to medium shaft	Driver swingweight from B6 to C2 Shallow wood face; 12 degree driver loft

*Club length is determined by the length of a player's arms in relation to her body height. As there is some correlation between height and arm length, a general category of "height" is commonly used.

Care of Clubs. Clubs should be wiped dry and clean after use. Occasionally wash with mild soap and water and clean the grooves on the faces with a soft brush or a wooden tee. When thoroughly dry, wooden clubheads should be waxed (paste wax) to prevent warping and cracking. A light oil should be applied to the steel shaft. Wrappings around the clubhead and grip should be checked frequently. Often a durable glue will serve; otherwise, black linen line can be applied to the head and shaft and leather stripping to the shaft. Head covers of knit or leather protect the highly polished surface from moisture and scarring.

Little care is required to maintain irons other than drying and oiling occasionally to prevent rusting. Avoid hitting rocks or hard objects, for they nick the club, change its balance, and cause it to cut balls. Club nicks should be filed smooth when they appear on the face.

Leather grips on all clubs should be rubbed lightly with neat's-foot oil several times a year. Damaged or worn grips may be replaced at the pro shop or by the golfer with "a do-it-yourself" kit.

Golf balls should be washed before play for ease of identification. Practice balls can be "washed white" (repainted) by the golfer.

All leather equipment such as shoes and gloves should be dried slowly, away from intense heat. Gloves should be straightened and dried, out of the sun, to prevent wrinkles and cracking.

Golf carts and all metal equipment should be wiped dry after each use and oiled occasionally for better operation and to prevent rusting.

TEACHING UNITS

The suggested units for beginning and advanced students follow:

Beginners

- Nature and value of golf
- Brief history
- Care and use of equipment
- Beginning golf terminology
- Safety precautions
- Fundamental skills and swing development
  - Grip
  - Stance
  - Address
  - Pivot and shoulder action
  - Backswing
  - Top of swing
  - Wrist action
  - Downswing and follow-through
  - Exercises
- Use of number 5 iron
  - Pitch and run shot
- Pitch and pitch and run (7 iron)
  - One-quarter, one-half and three-quarter swing
- Putting
- Approach shots
- Long irons
- Wood shots
- Etiquette
- Rules
- Course play
- Evaluation
  - Written and skills tests

Advanced

- General review
- Swing
- Stances
- Pitch and run
- Pitch
- Putting and reading the green
- Approach
- Long irons
- Woods
- Tournament play
- Sidehill lie
- Uphill lie
- Downhill lie
- Sand trap play
- Intentional slice
- Intentional hook
- Advanced rules
  - Handicap procedure
- Evaluation
  - Written
  - Practical
- Suggested Activities—
  - Inclement weather
    - History of golf
    - Golf personalities
    - Purchase, care, and use of equipment
    - Indoor improvised course play
    - Films: skill development and tournament play
    - Videotape of class members
    - Golf etiquette

BASIC SKILLS

All skills are described in terms of a right-handed player. The skills and movements are applicable to left-handed players, but the terms *left* and *right* must be interchanged when developing or analyzing a skill.

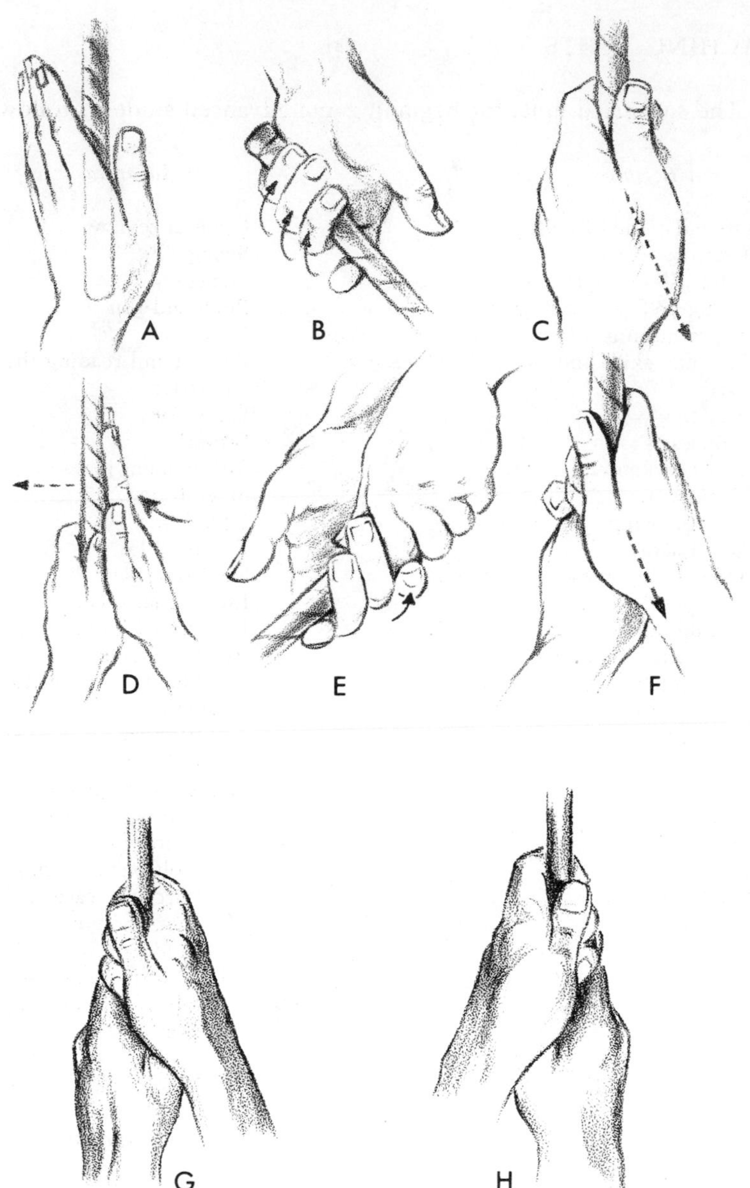

Figure 9–7 Placing the hands for proper grip. *G*, Right hander's overlapping grip. *H*, Left hander's overlapping grip.

The Grip. The positioning of the hands is of initial importance, for the hands are the only connection between the body and the ball, working through the club. A sound grip places the hands so that they return to their original position when contacting the ball. The same basic grip is used for all clubs except the putter. Three grips are commonly used by golfers: the overlap, the interlock, and the natural or "baseball." Although several championship golfers use the interlocking and natural grips, the overlapping (Vardon) technique assures more club security and greater hand coordination for most women.

To assume the overlapping grip, the clubhead rests on the ground in a square position, shaft pointing toward the golfer. The extended left hand is placed slightly over the top of the shaft (A) as the hand grips the club across the base of the fingers (B) (Figure 9–8). As the hand closes around the gripping leather the shaft lies diagonally across the hand in a combination palm and finger grip. The end of the shaft extends an inch or more beyond the hand toward the body. The grip is secured by the last three fingers with the thumb and index fingers forming a "V" line. This *solid* and *closed* line points toward the chin and right shoulder. With the left thumb slightly to the right of the shaft, the thumb and index finger exert a slight gripping pressure. Looking down the shaft, the golfer should see no more than three knuckle joints.

The right arm swings freely until the right hand reaches below the left to grip the club entirely in the fingers. The palm of the right hand is squarely facing the right side of the club shaft. In closing the right hand around the club, the left thumb fits snugly into the natural diagonal hollow of the right

Figure 9–8 Grip at the top of the backswing.

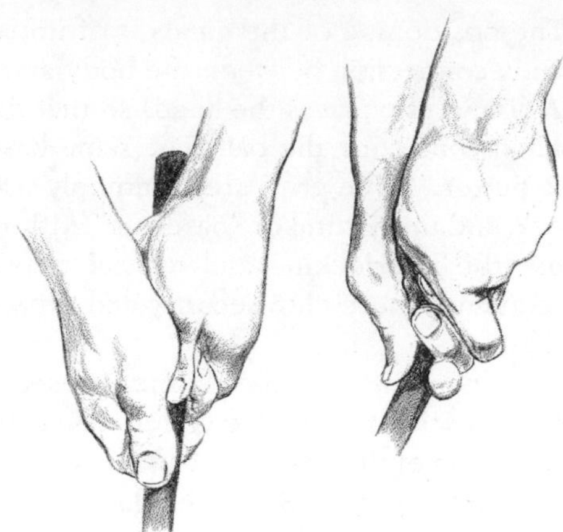

Figure 9–9 Reverse overlapping putting grip.

palm (under the butt of the right thumb). Overlap the little finger of the right by hooking it around the large knuckle of the left index finger. The next three fingers grasp the shaft as the index finger spreads to a trigger position so that there is a space between the index and second fingers. The "V" line formed by the right thumb and index finger is solid and closed and points in the same direction of chin and right shoulder. With both hands close together and working as a unit, power and control are attained.

Putting Grip. The individuality of putting begins with the grip. Many golfers use the same grip as they use for other clubs; others use a baseball, crosshand, reverse overlap, or two-hand molded grip, in which both hands and thumbs are molded together at the top of the shaft.

The reverse overlap grip is recommended for beginners, as the hands are placed on the club in a manner resembling the overlapping grip.

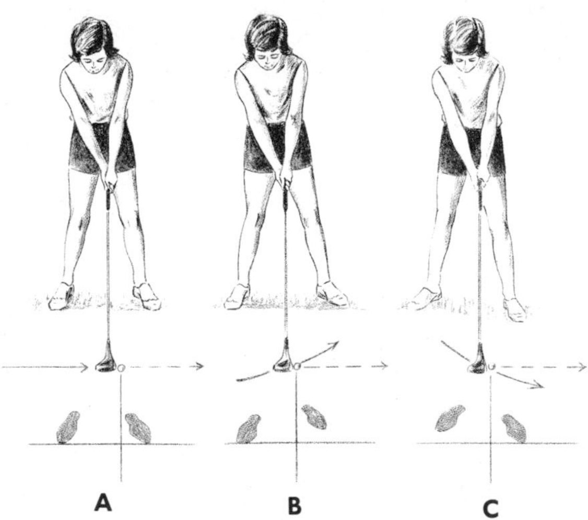

Figure 9–10 Types of stance: *A*, square stance, *B*, open stance, *C*, closed stance.

The right hand is placed a hand span from the top of the club with the thumb pointed directly down the front of the shaft toward the clubhead. The line formed by the thumb and index finger points toward the *right* shoulder. The left hand is placed above the right with the palm facing in the direction opposite that of the palm of the right hand. The back of the left hand faces the line of the putt. The thumb is down the front of the shaft. The index finger of the left hand overlaps the little finger of the right hand. The line of the thumb and index finger of the left hand should point in the direction of the *left* shoulder.

The left hand, now firmly holding the club—more in the palm than the fingers—does most of the work. The pressure of the grip in the right hand is exerted with the thumb and index finger for control. This grip permits a hinged wrist action.

Stance and Address. A firm, comfortable stance assures the balance necessary for a swing. The stance is taken in relationship to the target. The golfer views the target and then draws an *imaginary* straight line from the ball to the target. This *flight line* is parallel to the imaginary *foot line* the golfer toes in preparation for the swing. The distance between the flight and foot lines varies as the distance one stands from the ball depends on the length of the club used. In preparation for all strokes, except putting, weight is equally distributed on both feet between the balls of the feet and the heels, the toes are pointed outward, and the feet are placed comfortably apart or approximately shoulder width. The body is fairly erect with knees flexed. The body is bent slightly forward at the hips, and the back is straight. The arms extend toward the ball but do not reach so as to pull the body off balance. Sole the club directly behind the ball so the bottom is evenly placed on the turf, and the face is perpendicular or "square" to the desired line of flight.

Different stances are used to facilitate or restrict the body turn during the swing and should not affect the accuracy of club face contact of the ball. There are three general stances which a golfer assumes for a designated stroke:

Square or Parallel Stance. The feet are parallel to, and equally distant from, the imaginary line of flight of the ball. With the knees, hips, and shoulders parallel to flight line, this is a good beginning stance as it gives a feeling of balanced swing motion with an equally balanced backswing and follow-through. It is the most commonly used stance for long and medium irons.

Open Stance. The left foot is drawn back from the imaginary flight line. The body is turned slightly toward the direction of ball flight. With the right hip forward, a restricted body rotation in the backswing results, allowing the arms to stay closer to the body for a more controlled stroke. The open stance is used primarily for short irons, chipping, and pitching when less distance, power, and greater accuracy are needed. It may be used for intentional slices.

Closed Stance. The right foot is drawn back from the flight line, thus turning the body from the target and increasing backswing rotation. This stance is used for maximum power from the tee and on some fairway shots, as well as for an intentional hook shot.

Body-Ball Position. The position of the body and the club in relation to the ball greatly affect ball flight. Basically, the longer the club the fuller the swing arc. The farther one stands from the ball, the flatter the swing; the shorter the club, the closer one stands to the ball and the more upright the swing.

When the ball is contacted as near as possible to the bottom of the swing, the more perfect will be the loft for which the clubhead was designed. To get this proper position with short irons, hit *down* on the ball, which is placed an inch or two to the right of the bottom of the swing arc.

The point on the swing arc at which the ball is hit greatly affects ball spin. A forward spin, causing low ball flight and increased forward roll on the ground, results from a blow as the clubhead is traveling upward. A horizontal blow at the center of the swing arc results in a slight backspin, as the ball is hit below center. A definite backspin is caused if the clubhead hits the ball before the center of the swing arc is reached, for the club continues downward across the back of the ball.

Generally, tee shots and wood shots are made from a closed, or square, stance with the ball placed forward of center for a horizontal or upward impact of the club. The long and medium irons are most often played from a square stance off or near the center of the body. The length of the club shaft determines the golfer's relation to the ball, but the arms are easy, not forcibly reaching, and the wrists are down and firm. With shorter irons, the golfer moves closer to the ball, takes an open stance, moves feet closer together, and plays the ball in the center or right of center of the body for more loft and less roll.

Swing. The swing should be thought of as a rhythmical pattern which establishes a plane for hands, arms, and shoulders. The sequence of movement allows for weight transfer and application of force through the hands and club through the hitting area. An efficient swing is based on balance, rhythm, and a square clubhead position throughout. Although the total swing must be learned as a unit, the basic ingredients can be identified for analysis.

Assuming a proper stance with weight distributed and feet comfortably spread, exert a slight gripping pressure on the inside of the right foot and press the right thigh toward the center of the body. The body is inclined forward slightly at the waist; the right shoulder is slightly dropped so that the arm can reach properly and eventually bend on the backswing. The upper arms rest slightly against the sides of the body with the left arm fully extended but not stiff or tense. The hands are even with or slightly ahead of the ball. The shoulders and arms form an inverted triangle that is maintained throughout the swing.

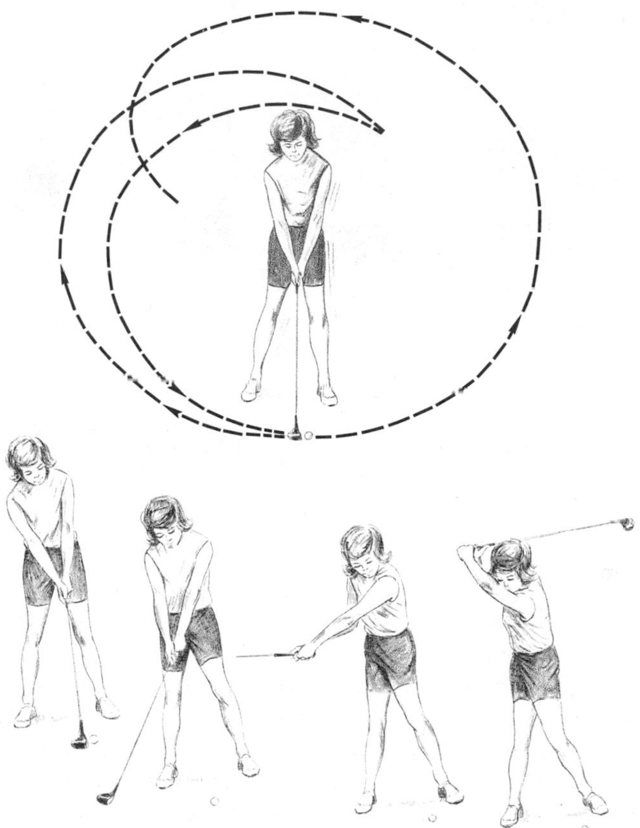

Figure 9–11 Backswing.

The *backswing* is a one-piece takeaway from the ball. The firm triangle of hands, arms, and shoulders simultaneously moves the clubhead along the extended flight line and away from the ball. The left shoulder rotates forward and down under the chin. The hips rotate around and to the right with the spine and head serving as an axis. The weight shifts across the left foot to the inside of the right foot. The left knee presses in toward the right knee. The left heel is unweighted, and in a full swing it *may* be raised about an inch from the ground. During the pivot, the arms and shoulders pull the club backward along the flight line and upward. The shoulders turn as the upper body pivots with the hips. As the arms reach approximately waist height, the wrists cock with no deliberate effort and the arms continue in an upward arc. The left arm and right leg remain firm with the right elbow bent and pointing downward. The head remains stationary.

At the top of the full swing, the body is in coiled readiness with the club shaft approximately horizontal to the ground. The shoulders are turned

Figure 9–12 Downswing and follow-through.

90 degrees; the hips 45 degrees. The palm of the right hand is under the shaft; the right elbow is pointing to the ground with the line from the right armpit to the elbow parallel to the ground.

A shift of weight back to the left foot initiates the downswing. This uncoiling begins by sliding the hips in the direction of the swing. Beginners seem to find it easier to concentrate on a vigorous push off the right foot to the left. At the same time, the left arm and hand pull the club downward. A proper shift allows the right elbow to move toward the body as the left hip leads the body and pulls the arms into the hitting area. Halfway through the downswing, the weight has returned to address position, the hips are square, but the shoulders are still turned 45 degrees. Hips continue to move forward and out of the way and the right shoulder then moves down and underneath the chin; the majority of body weight is toward the forward foot. As the arms and wrists come to the impact area the wrists uncock to strike the ball at the bottom of the swing arc with the back of the left hand leading toward the target. The golfer hits *against* a firm left side and *through* the ball.

The clubhead follows the line of intended flight until the right arm is fully extended. As weight continues to shift to the left side with the right foot pushing from the toes, the left elbow bends and the right hand takes over the club. The hips turn naturally with the turn of the arms and shoulders. At the completion of the swing the right side is fully released, the weight is on the left foot, the hands are high with the left palm under the shaft and the left elbow pointed toward the ground. The head has turned and the body is facing the target in a balanced position with the weight on the left foot.

Fractional Swings. The power of a full swing is neither necessary nor desirable for some shots and clubs. Basically, fractional swings are but segments of the full swing and are frequently used with the short irons. As the swing is shortened, the club is shortened proportionately by gripping down farther on the leather.

Quarter Swing. The hips initiate a weight shift, rather than a true rotation. The clubhead follows, going away from the ball until the arms are outside the right leg; then the wrists cock, bringing the club parallel to the ground. The downswing and follow-through carry the club to a position parallel to the ground on the left side of the body.

Half Swing. Executed by a rotation slightly deeper than that of the quarter swing, the backswing arc continues until the cap of the grip points toward the ground. The follow-through is the same length as the backswing.

Three Quarter Swing. This is executed like the full swing but less depth is taken in the ascending and descending arcs. At the top of the backswing the clubhead points to 2 o'clock; on the follow-through it points toward 10 o'clock.

Playing Wood Shots

1. Use a square or slightly closed stance with feet shoulder width apart, depending on comfort.
2. Use a full swing for maximum power.
3. When driving from the tee, play the ball off heel or toe of foot toward the target, depending on the bottom point of the swing.
4. Play fairway shots off the target foot heel or toward the center of the body.

Playing Long and Medium Iron Shots

1. Use square stance for normal flight.
2. Stand slightly closer to irons than woods so that the swing will be more upright.
3. Play long irons 2 or 3 inches to right of the left foot.
4. Play medium irons from the center of the stance.
5. Hit the ball a descending blow as if trying to bury the ball. Take turf and continue through.

Playing Short Iron Shots

1. Use square to open stance with heels 6 to 12 inches apart.
2. Play the ball from the center of the stance or slightly to the right of center.
3. The body is close to the ball; the arms close to the body.
4. Use a fractional swing for distance desired.

Chip Shot. A chip (also called pitch and run) is made when the ball is close to the green and there is a 5 yard unobstacled approach to the green. A chip should carry to the green and roll the rest of the way to the hole.

1. Use a number 4, 5, 6, or 7 iron; occasionally an 8 or 9 iron.
2. Keep the feet close together and the weight on the left foot as the ball is played in line with the left heel. There should be little body motion or weight transfer.
3. Grip club low on the handle, hands ahead of club to limit loft. The left hand controls as both wrists remain firm.

4. Use a short, rhythmical backswing. Stroke the ball crisply. The right palm faces the target throughout.
5. The follow-through is low.

Pitch Shot. The pitch carries the ball through the air in a high approach toward the green, where it stops quickly upon contact with the ground.

1. Select a wedge or 9 iron.
2. Use an open stance close to the ball with the right elbow close to the right hip.
3. Use minimum body action with a fractional swing.
4. Hit the ball several inches ahead of the bottom of the swing arc (a descending blow) to impart backspin so that it will stop when landing. The ball is hit prior to contacting the ground.
5. Follow through with clubhead pointing toward target.

Run-up Shot. The run-up is similar to the pitch and run but taken farther from the green. The ball is hit with a 6 or 7 iron and played to travel about one-half the distance to the green in the air, hit level, firm terrain, and roll onto the green and toward the cup.

Bunker Shots. The chip shot and the blast are the fundamental strokes for getting out of a sand trap. The texture of the sand and the lie of the ball determine the shot. A chip may be used when the ball is resting on top of the sand. A number 6 or 7 iron may be used in a short approach. The club, however, must not be grounded or touch the sand on the backswing.

The explosive shot is the safest when the ball is buried or must rise over a bank.

1. Select a sand wedge or number 9 iron. Open the club face slightly (angle it backward).
2. Play the ball in line with the left (forward) heel from an open stance.
3. Anchor the feet and aim an inch or two behind the ball. Take sand as a cushion to loft the ball.
4. Take a full swing; start the clubhead back at an angle outside the line of flight; swing through the ball, cutting across the direction line; and follow through completely.

Putting. Putting is the most individualized skill of golf; its success also depends largely on the player's state of mind. Although the criterion of a good putt is its effectiveness, the following techniques may help the beginner.

1. Take a square stance, with the feet 10 to 12 inches apart. Bend from the waist so that the eyes are directly over the ball. *Lock* the stance.
2. Position the ball off the instep of the left foot.
3. Keep the hands even with the ball, with the right elbow resting comfortably on the right hipbone, the left elbow barely touching the left side.
4. To execute the *wrist action putt,* the head, hips, and shoulders remain steady as hands and wrists take a short controlled backswing. To execute an *arm action putt* or *firm wrist putt,* the head and hips are steady as the arms swing from the shoulders. Elbows remain close to the sides.
5. Two methods of striking the ball are commonly used. In both, the clubhead

accelerates at the moment of impact. The *stroke putt* is a long smooth stroke with backswing and follow-through of equal distance; the *tap putt* results from a swing that crisply contacts the ball and ends in a short follow-through. This is often called a "punch putt."

6. Bring the clubhead straight back, then through the ball, following through directly toward the hole.
7. Keep the putter blade close to the green throughout the stroke.

Putts account for approximately half the strokes in a round of par golf; therefore, putting deserves concentration and practice. Line up a putt by determining the distance to the hole, the slope of the green, the grain of the grass, and ultimately the course of the ball to the hole. It is helpful to pick a spot about 6 inches along the imaginary ball course and concentrate on rolling the ball over that spot.

Playing Difficult Lies

Rough. A club is selected which will give the necessary loft to the ball. The stance is more open, the club face slightly open, and the swing upright with as full a follow-through as possible. If the ball lie is good, a 4 or 5 wood often clears heavy rough better than an iron.

Downhill Lie. On any "uneven" lie the secret is to make contact with the ball as close as possible to the exact bottom point of the swing. Normally play the ball closer to right (rear) foot with a slightly open stance. The body weight should be equally distributed or on the left foot. Select a club with more loft, to give the ball height as it leaves the ground. Avoid shifting weight abruptly or "letting up" on the swing at impact. A smooth follow-through lessens the tendency to push or slice.

Uphill Lie. Since the bottom of the swing falls farther to the left, play the ball left of center. Use a slight body pivot and a low trajectory club, as the height normally attained with a club is accentuated by the ground contour. Avoid the tendency to hook or pull by completing the body weight transfer on the follow-through.

Sidehill Lie. This stroke must be made standing above or below ball level. These shots call for planned balance and anticipation of a hook or slice.

When the ball is below the stance, use a square stance, playing the ball from the center of the body. "Sit" through the legs and aim to the left to compensate for the tendency to slice. A compact three-quarter swing is helpful.

If the ball is above the feet, it is played slightly right of center. Keep the stance slightly open and aim to the right to compensate for the hook that results from falling back on the heels.

Stroke Adjustments. Advanced golfers can take several strokes from their game by learning to direct the ball in flight.

Intentional Hook. To accomplish a deliberate curve of the ball from right to left, the golfer uses a closed stance with the ball almost opposite the right foot. Using a flat swing arc, the club contacts the ball from the inside to

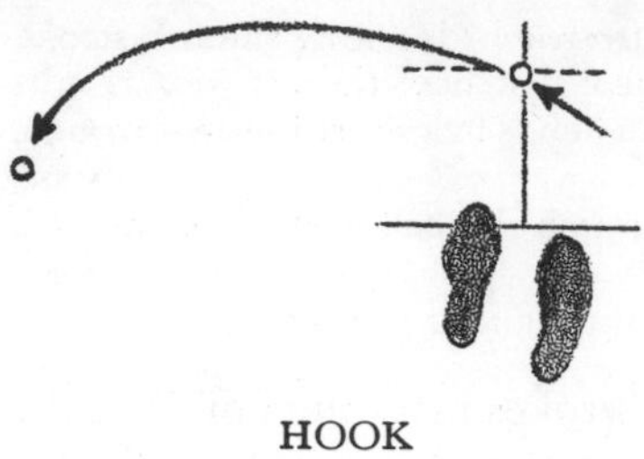

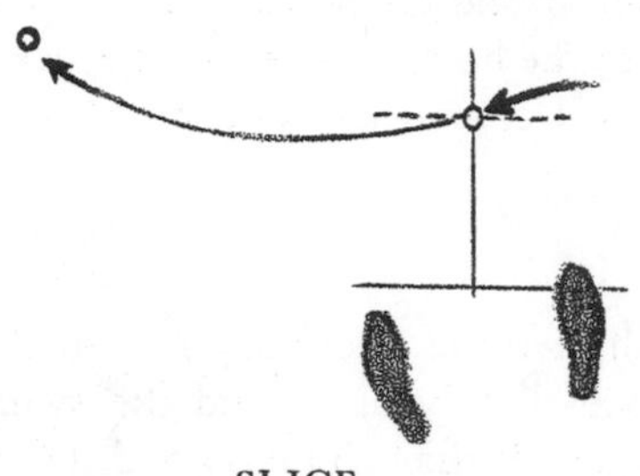

Figure 9–13 Proper stance for hook shots and slice shots.

the outside. The degree of hook can be controlled by placing the right hand beneath the shaft and the left hand on top.

Intentional Slice. A deliberate slice curves from left to right in flight because of the spin imparted to the ball. The golfer uses an open stance with the ball approximately off the center of the stance. Swing arc is almost upright with the clubhead contacting the ball from the "outside-in." For more decided slice the right hand moves to the top of the shaft and the left hand under the shaft.

High Ball. The beginning golfer should attempt to select a club with enough loft to carry the ball over obstacles or into the wind; however, advanced golfers may play the ball off the left foot and stroke the ball on the upswing with an open club face.

Low Ball. The ball is played toward the right foot and hit with a closed clubface from a flat swing arc. Hit down on the ball and take turf after ball contact. Wrists remain firm throughout the swing.

STRATEGY

A good golf *swing* is learned on the practice ground. A good golf *game* results when the skill of a sound swing is directed by knowledge and concentration. A *positive attitude* incorporating the following suggestions will add consistency and cut strokes from your game.

1. Plan each hole from tee to green. If a bad stroke forces readjustment of the plan, *dismiss* the error and replan.

2. Do not dwell on past strokes, good or bad. Play and concentrate on the situation at hand.
3. In competition be concerned with *your* play only, not that of your opponent. Compete with the arbitrary score of par rather than your opponent's score.
4. Avoid tension. Get accustomed to crowded courses and slow play. Do not let golfers behind unnecessarily rush you. Be mentally prepared to play under adverse wind and weather conditions.
5. Learn the feeling of a comfortable stance. On fairway or green if you feel uncomfortable, walk away temporarily and then establish a new stance.
6. Play safe golf for low scores. Avoid gambling on difficult shots and approaches to the green. Often a safe stroke to a good playing position saves several penalty strokes resulting from a gamble.
7. Learn your clubs and their distances. Trust your clubs. Time on the practice tee before a round renews confidence in the clubs.
8. Plan putting strategy. On wet greens stroke firmly, as putts do not break as far; play for position on the low side of the hole on sloping greens. Ball has tendency to pull up short on depressed greens, so approach more boldly. Approach less boldly on elevated greens, since ball tends to run.
9. On long putts, putt for a *certain* second putt, rather than trying to hole the ball.

ETIQUETTE

Since golf demands delicate coordination and concentration from players, a definite code of behavior is followed by experienced players. These courtesies are intended to prevent distraction and increase player safety.

The player should not:

1. Talk, move or stand close to or directly behind the ball or the hole when a player is hitting.
2. Swing clubs while a player is stroking.
3. Hit until players ahead are out of range and have taken at least their second shots.
4. Approach the green until players ahead have putted out and are off the green.
5. Stand near the cup when another is shooting.
6. Stand in line with the one putting and the cup.
7. Concede, or ask to be conceded, a putt.
8. Take a careless stroke at a short putt and expect to take another trial if the ball is missed.
9. Stand close enough to the rim of the cup to disturb turf.
10. Allow one's shadow to cross the line of a putt.
11. Place a golf bag in a sand trap, thus roughing up the sand for players following.
12. Place a golf bag on the green, where it may mar the surface.
13. Place a golf bag, cart, or flagstick on the near side of the green where it might stop the ball of a player following.
14. Record scores while standing on the green.
15. Practice putts or play them over if missed.
16. Invite players to play through when a ball is lost and then start hitting before they are out of range.

17. Take practice swings in the direction of the hole. (By taking them at right angles to the line of flight you eliminate the possibility of being questioned by opponents.)
18. Pick up a ball for identification.
19. Press down grass or weeds to get a better stroke. This is improving the lie and is against the rules.

The player should:

1. Play without undue delay.
2. Stroke from behind the markers on the tees.
3. Hold the flag for your opponent or see that the caddy does.
4. Allow the player winning the honor to tee first.
5. When a ball is lost, or players are in a slow match, invite players following to play through and allow them to get out of range before proceeding.
6. Always replace divots.
7. Elevate "dents" in the green, using the point of the tee.
8. Back out of sand traps, leveling off holes made by your club and foot tracks.
9. Admit penalty stroke.
10. Allow the player farthest away, whether on green or in field, to stroke first.
11. Call "Fore!" only if there is danger of a ball's hitting a player ahead.
12. Drop the ball over one's shoulder when taking a penalty stroke.
13. Recognize course priority: single players have no standing; two, three and four players have precedence. Any match playing a whole round is entitled to pass a match playing a shorter round.

CLASS ORGANIZATION

Class organization is largely determined by the available equipment, facilities, and instructional personnel. When necessary, instruction can be given entirely indoors in a gymnasium or large all-purpose room; however, it is desirable to have access to an indoor area, outdoor play field, a driving range and putting area, and a nine or 18 hole golf course. The golf *swing* can become a conditioned response in limited facilities, but the golf *game* can be developed only on the course.

Among the first organizational considerations are easy, safe, and rapid methods of distributing equipment. Whether indoors or out, students should be assigned responsibilities for handling, maintaining, and replacing equipment. From the beginning of the unit all should be made aware of the potential danger of a ball carelessly hit or a club swung indiscriminately.

As many as 25 or 30 students can be taught by a single instructor standing in the center of the circle of learners. When practicing in this circle formation, the swings should be directed away from the center to avoid possible injury to the instructor and students due to an accidentally thrown club or an unintentionally hit rock or dirt clod.

For certain types of instruction and demonstration, a double, triple, or multiple semicircle affords the best viewing and hearing.

When hitting plastic or sponge practice balls, time is saved in ball recovery if players face each other in parallel lines approximately 30 yards apart. Whenever regulation balls are used, players may hit from a straight line formation or a wide arching semicircle with approximately 6 to 8 feet between players. Emphasize the importance of hitting to a spot, rather than just hitting. This designated point of aim should be at an appropriate distance from and in the middle of the line to facilitate ball recovery.

If the class is large and space limited, two or three players can be assigned to one spot with players alternating hitting, assisting, and retrieving the balls.

Advanced golfers can profit from a general review of basic skills. As the class moves to an outdoor area, a threesome or foursome of those with similar skills can work together to economize on equipment and instructor's time. Selected skill practice is assigned each group with group members coaching one another, sharing observations, and retrieving balls. Whether working with the beginning or advanced player, the instructor should remember that golf is a difficult game involving many intricate skills. Too many reminders and "dos and don'ts" at one time serve only to inhibit a player's movement. Occasionally urge the student to swing freely and dispel all thoughts of specific skills; then advise her to take *one* point at a time, stress this point, and practice it thoroughly before moving to another.

When possible, all students should have a playing experience on a course. A threesome or foursome should play a minimum of three holes and preferably nine. During course play the instructor should roam the course to observe each individual and answer questions, but she should not coach if it delays the play of outside groups on the course.

TEACHING PROGRESSION

There is no single "best" progression for teaching golf. Instructors will select the methods best suited for utilization of equipment, facilities, and their style of teaching. Many teachers believe skills should progress from the grip, stance, and swing to the use of a basic club (5 iron) and then to short irons and approach shots, putting, long irons, and woods. The following suggested lessons generally follow such a plan. In any case, no matter what the progression, orthodox instruction terminates in the development of a rhythmical golf swing and an understanding and application of the game and its skill requirements.*

Lesson I

1. Explain the nature and value of golf
2. Explain and demonstrate use of equipment
3. Discuss the golf course and selected terminology
4. Allow class to hit 10 or more balls with short irons before receiving instruction

Lesson II

1. Brief discussion of the history of golf
2. Explain and demonstrate the grip
3. Explain and demonstrate stance, stressing the square stance for beginners, and line of flight
4. Explain the theory of a rhythmical swing. Allow student practice
5. Show film on the game, grip, and stance

---

*For more comprehensive suggestions see National Golf Foundation: *Golf Instructor's Guide*. 3rd ed., 1972. Merchandise Mart, Chicago, Illinois 60654.

Lesson III

1. Review grip and stance
2. Explain and demonstrate the full swing: pivot, backswing, top of swing, wrist action, downswing, follow-through
3. Demonstrate swing exercises
4. Practice hitting balls with 5 iron. For those students having difficulty, stress the pitch and run, then a fuller swing

Lesson IV

1. Review grip, stance, and swing using 5 iron
2. Introduce the short irons and their use
3. Discussion of the pitch shot and fractional swings
4. Informal evaluation period hitting to a target area

Lesson V

1. Review short irons
2. Review chip shot
3. Explain and demonstrate pitch shot
4. Informal contest using chip and pitch shots

Lesson VI

1. General review
2. Discussion of putting (lining a putt, grip, stroke)

Lesson VII

1. Practice approach shots
2. Practice putting
3. Pair students and have team contest: one member plays short approaches, the other putts. Total scores over a designated course

Lesson VIII

1. Explain and demonstrate use of long irons
2. Begin rule discussion
3. Show film on iron play

Lesson IX

1. Review long irons. Stress all components of a three-quarter to full swing
2. Group competition for accuracy and distance on long irons
3. Competition for accuracy of chip, pitch, and putting

Lesson X

1. Explain details of rules, scoring, and etiquette necessary for beginning course play
2. Explain and demonstrate wood shots using the full swing
3. Practice tee shots and fairway woods

Lesson XI

1. Intensive practice and review of clubs. Stress proper club selection
2. Individual coaching

Lesson XII

1. Introduce bunker shots
2. General discussion and analysis of the causes for topping, slicing, hooking, pushing, and pulling. Individual assistance follows

Lesson XIII

1. Intensive practice emphasizing review of short game
2. Written evaluation of knowledge, rules, and etiquette

Lesson XIV

1. Skills examination
2. Begin tournament or course play

Lessons XV to XVII

1. Continue course play
2. Introduce "difficult lies" and stroke adjustment to advanced players
3. Individual attention to skill improvement

SKILL DIFFICULTIES AND THEIR CORRECTION

Grip

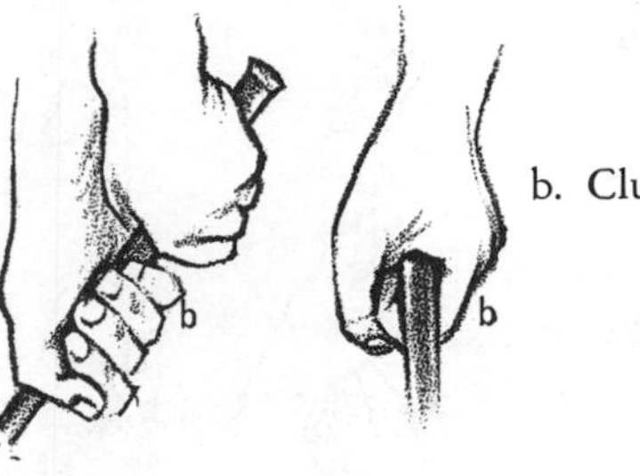

Difficulty	*Correction*
a. Gripping club so tightly the wrists and fingers become immobile	a. Teacher suggests student release grip, then places left hand on club and lifts it toward the body. Place the right hand on shaft and swing club slightly to get idea of relaxed movement. Emphasize control of the club with the left hand (right-handed player)
b. Club grasped in palm of hand	b. Teacher demonstrates how control is lost at top of backswing by moving the club. Stress the importance of feel and sensitivity in the fingers and thumbs

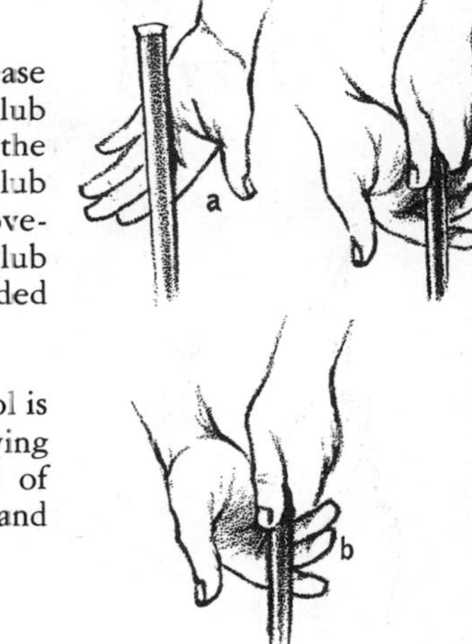

Problem	Correction
c. Improper placement of hands resulting in open or closed club face	c. Remind student that the club should rest naturally on the ground. Demonstrate what happens to the ball in flight when struck by open or closed face
d. Index finger and thumb do the gripping, resulting in a loss of control at top of swing	d. Review proper grip, stressing the left hand's firm grip with last three fingers and the right hand's thumb and first two fingers. Remind the student that the hands must work as a unit—always in firm contact with the club. Left hand controls the club back to the ball
e. Grip uncomfortable and seemingly unwieldy	e. Suggest that student's arms swing freely, comfortably grasping the club, then adjust grip

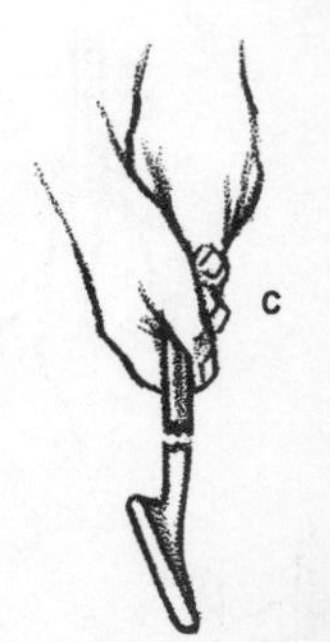

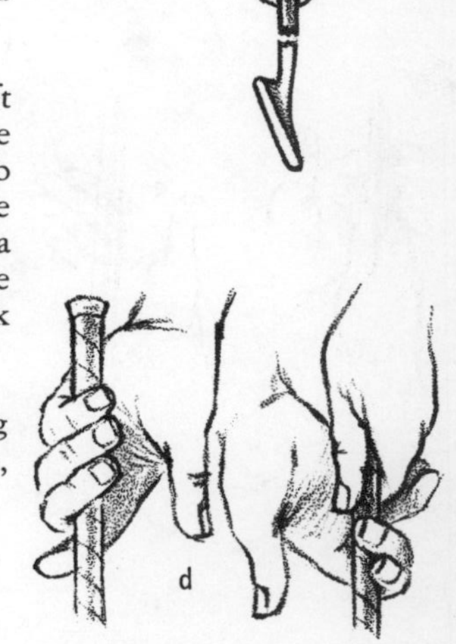

Stance and Address

Difficulty	Correction
a. Failure to align body with the imaginary flight line	a. Teacher may draw chalk line or place club across student's toes to show variance in aiming and body position
b. Using closed and open stance indiscriminately	b. Teacher explains and demonstrates reasons for limited pivot on backswing or follow-through. Asks student to explain the purpose of the two stances
c. Stiffened knees and body	c. Stress relaxation and have student practice "sitting on the ball" with easy arm position

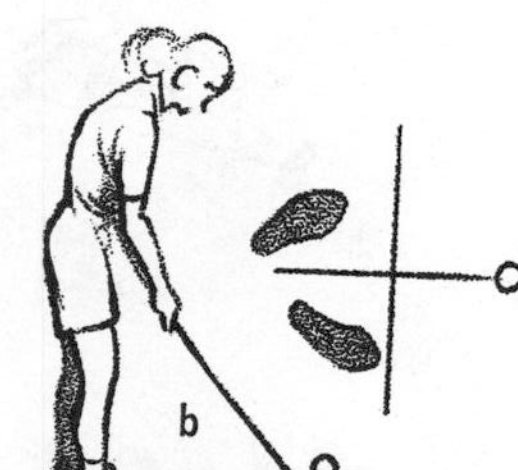

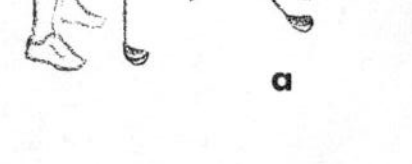

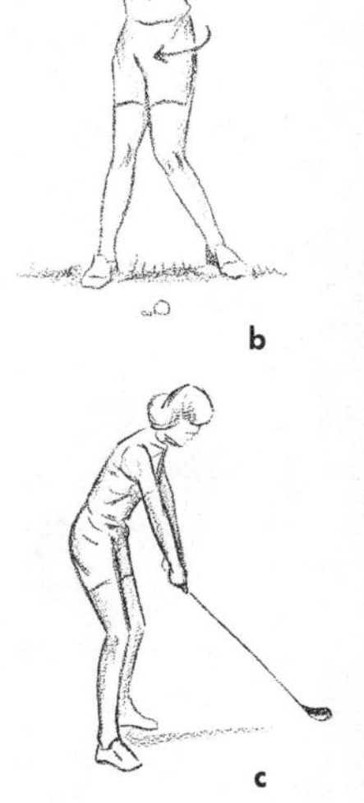

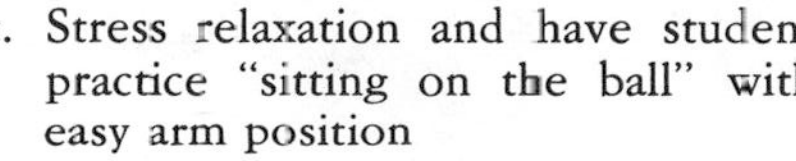

d. Standing too close or too far from the ball with weight forward on the toes	d. Explain the principles of centrifugal force, thereby showing weight must be back to balance tendency of the swing to pull the golfer off balance

Swing

Difficulty	*Correction*
a. Making a false pivot or slide, rather than a rotation on the backswing	a. Explain to student that on the backswing she could pivot in a barrel, rolling and shifting weight so the axis does not move and her hips do not touch the sides of the barrel
b. Improper shift of weight	b. Suggest that the student stand "duck footed" toeing out both feet. With club through her arms and behind her back she rolls. A proper pivot is achieved or she loses balance

c. Controlling stroke by arms, notably the right arm, in such a way that club leaves the ground abruptly, resulting in "arm golf." This may result from an immediate wrist "break" as the clubhead leaves the ball

c. Review proper sequence of the coordinated pivot: shoulders begin the action as arms and hands drag the club back along the flight line. Emphasize a low take away from the ball with firm wrists. Stress left arm domination

d. Bending the left arm on upswing and raising right elbow, or doing the reverse on follow-through

d. Teacher places a practice ball or cloth under right armpit and suggests "push the left arm." Review stance and the need for extended body tension

e. Downswing is initiated by swinging the arms, resulting in a "turn on the ball"

e. From the coiled "readiness" position, emphasize the release of the left side, followed by a pull of the shoulders and left arm, leading the clubhead to the hitting area

f. Moving or lifting the head, thus changing level of swing pattern, and "topping" ball	f. Teacher or fellow student places a club shaft on student's head so she becomes aware of her movement by club pressure. Remind her to watch the clubhead hit the ball
g. Uncocking wrists too soon, resulting in loss of power and control. This may be due to improper shift of weight when beginning the downswing	g. Stress control and relaxed, normal hand action. Review the action of the hands and wrists on downswing and follow-through. Remind the student the hands *follow* hip and shoulder action
h. Swinging too hard	h. Slow backswing and relax. Power can be imparted later

Putting

Difficulty	*Correction*
a. Tense grip and rigid arm movement	a. Relax. Teacher reminds student that putter action is like a pendulum – easy and smooth
b. Punching or jabbing the ball so control of the club is lost	b. Stress follow-through. Teacher can mark a backswing and follow-through line on the green over which the club should pass. If a punch putt is used, stress a *crisp* contact with the ball
c. Inability to line a putt	c. Suggest student think and concentrate on grass, slope, and distance. Ask her to explain the steps for lining up a putt. Emphasize the necessity of proper *distance* on a long putt and *accuracy* on short putts
d. Pulling a putt	d. Stress that the left elbow must be away from the body to prevent a putting arc. Suggest that the clubhead itself should move to the hole

FAULTY GOLF SHOTS AND THEIR REMEDIES

Slice

Slice is a ball that curves to the right (for right-handed players). A slice is the result of an "outside-in" swing with the club face in an open position at the moment of impact, thus giving the ball a clockwise spin

Causes	*Remedies*
1. An incorrect grip. Right hand may be too far under or left hand not enough on top	1. Three knuckles of left hand should be showing. Both V's should point toward right shoulder
2. Too open a stance, which cuts down pivot	2. Club face (at top of backswing) must be half closed
3. Right hand lifting the club on backswing, throwing right elbow out of position	3. Right wrist at top, under shaft. Left not under
4. Improper cocking of wrists on backswing	4. Left hand at top, fingers closed. Grip firm
5. Throwing the hands forward or away from body at start of downswing	5. Backswing. At start all in *one piece,* dominated by left side, around head as fixed point
6. Bending left arm on backswing	6. Position at top. Shaft point across line of flight, shoulders 90°, much more weight on right foot
7. Pulling the arms in at impact	7. Check sway. Head must not move
8. Lifting head too soon on downswing	8. Hitting from top, position of hands at finish will show it
9. Starting backswing on "outside"	9. Downswing. Hip slide must be first move
10. Locking left knee on follow-through	10. Hips not too far around to left on first movement
11. Overworking left arm	11. Left shoulder should not dip. Shoulders turn under head position

Push Ball

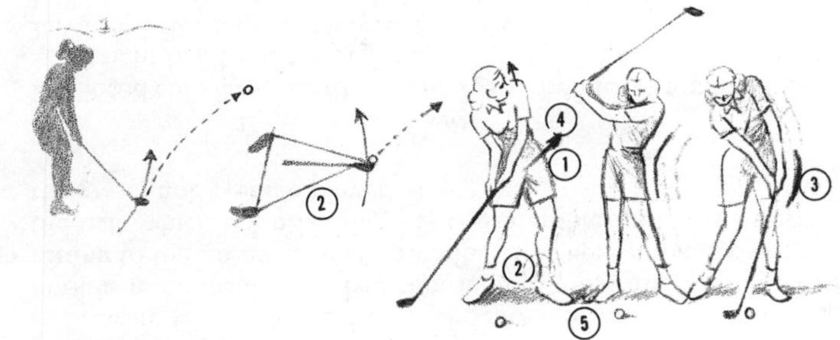

Push is a ball that travels straight to the right. A push is caused by an "inside-out" swing, with an open club face at impact

Causes

1. Improper hip shift
2. Stance too closed
3. Hands too far ahead at impact
4. Body too far ahead at impact
5. Ball played too far back
6. Flat swing

Remedies

1. Check jerking head up
2. Check sway to right on backswing
3. Check backswing, starting all in one piece
4. Check stance in relation to ball

Hook

Hook is a ball that curves to the left. A hook is caused by an "inside-out" swing with a closed face at the moment of impact. Although a hook is not considered a bad shot in golf, it has disadvantages when hitting to the green. The counterclockwise spin imparts overspin to the ball, which upon landing has considerable roll. It is an error of the good, not average player

Causes

1. Closed club face due to incorrect grip. Left hand too much on top or right hand too far under
2. Closed club due to incorrect wrist cock
3. Wrist roll to right in backswing. Start back all in one piece
4. Stance too closed
5. Exaggerated "inside-out" swinging
6. Collapse of left arm with wrist roll
7. Hands breaking at top of swing (may cause hook or slice)
8. Right hand domination

Remedies

1. Check left hand. Right hand should be well on top of club. V's point to right of chin
2. Be sure right wrist is under shaft
3. Avoid right hand control
4. Start back in one piece, hips lead

Pulled Ball

Pull is a ball that travels straight to the left. A pull is the result of an "outside-in" swing, with a closed face at moment of impact

Causes

1. Grip right hand too far over
2. Using closed stance, which limits follow-through
3. Overworking right hand. Throwing the club from the top of the swing
4. Punching at ball. Check shoulders on backswing

Remedies

1. Check right hand
2. Shift weight on the backswing to right leg. Hips pivot full 45°
3. Be sure of top position
4. Hips lead downswing. Hands and arms follow inside projected line of flight. Shoulders move under chin

EVALUATING THE RESULTS

As in all individual sports, the true evaluation of the game of golf is in the individual's ability to play a game properly with good score results. Often, it is not possible for students to play several rounds, but a fair measurement should be devised when grades and marks are given. Skill can be measured by mechanical devices, rating scales, and accuracy tests on a designated area. In addition to skill, the student's understanding of rules, etiquette, and game play should be evaluated.

Suggestions for testing include:

I. Subjective performance rating scale (observation by teacher)
   A. Proper grip
   B. Stance
   C. Address
   D. Swing execution
   E. Ability to select proper club

II. Objective skills test
   A. Putting
      1. Stance
      2. Stroke technique
      3. Ability to two-putt a green from 20 or 25 feet. (For example, using seven golf balls, the putter may score four points on each of the best five putts. The maximum score is 20; the minimum passing score is 14.)
   B. Chip Shot. (A player shoots from 30 feet from edge of green attempting to hit within 12 feet of cup with a 5 or 6 iron. Using seven balls the golfer may score four on each of best five balls, evaluated on hitting ball properly and destination of the shot. Maximum score is 20.)
   C. Pitch shot. (A player shoots 75 feet from the green. Score as the chip shot.)
   D. Five iron. (To test the player's ability to carry five out of seven balls 90 yards to the green. Score as pitch and chip.)
   E. Wood shot. (To evaluate the student's ability to hit a clean, controlled shot from the tee and fairway for distance.)

III. Written test on rules, knowledge, and etiquette

IV. Tournament results

V. Course scores and individual progress

TERMINOLOGY

Ace—Hole in one.
Addressing the ball—Placing the body and club in a position to hit the ball.
Approach shot—A shot intended to put the ball on the green.
Apron—Closely cut area adjacent to the green.
Away—Ball farthest from the hole and to be played first.
Birdie—One less than par.
Blind bogey—A phantom's score against which players may compete.
Bogey—One over par for a given hole.
Bunker—Hazard, usually artificial.
Caddie—Assistant to players; watches the ball, carries bag and clubs.
Carry—Distance the ball travels through the air.
Club—Implement used to propel the ball.
Course—Ground within playing limits.

Cup—Hole into which the ball is played.
Dead—A ball that does not roll after being hit; a ball that lies so close to the hole there is no doubt it will be sunk on the next shot.
Divot—Slice of turf cut out by club head.
Dog leg—A fairway curving to left or right.
Dormie—A term indicating that a player or team is as many holes "up" as there are holes remaining to play, and therefore cannot be beaten.
Down—Number of strokes or holes one is behind an opponent.
Driver—Wooden club number 1.
Eagle—Two under par for any hole.
Face—Striking surface of club head.
Fairway—Area between a tee and the green where the grass is cut short.
Flagstick—A staff inserted in the center of the cup that indicates the position and number of the hole.
Fore!—A warning call to those ahead when a ball is traveling toward them.
Forward press—A preliminary movement with a weight shift to the *forward* foot to prepare for a coordinated swing.
Foursome—A group of 4 persons playing together who are competing against each other or against par.
Frog hair—Area of high, yet trimmed, grass surrounding the green.
Green—Putting surface around the hole.
Grip—Part of a club that is gripped; also the method of grasping.
Halved—Tied score on a hole or complete game.
Handicap—Number of strokes conceded by a stronger to a weaker player.
Hazard—Natural or artificial obstacle other than the ordinary grass of the course.
Head—Striking portion of the club.
Heel—Part of head nearest shaft.
Hole—Cup 4½ inches in diameter into which the ball is played.
Hole out—Final stroke for a hole.
Honor—Right to play first from a tee.
Hook—A ball that curves left in flight.
Iron—Club with a steel head.
Lie—Manner and position in which a ball in play is resting; also, the angle of the club as measured from the bottom of the sole back to the shaft.
Links—The entire course.
Loft—Flight or elevation of a ball; also angle of clubface.
Match—A contest between two or more opponents or sides.
Match play—Competition based on holes won and lost.
Medal play—Competition based on total strokes per round.
Nassau—A system of scoring: one point is alloted for first nine holes, one point for second nine, and one point for 18 holes.
Neck—Angle between shaft and head of club.
Par—Standard score for a hole. Computed by length of the hole and allowing two putts.
Penalty stroke—A stroke added to score of individual or side under certain rules.
Pivot—Body turn.
Press—Effort to hit the ball unusually hard.
Provisional ball—A ball played after the ball hit originally is assumed lost or out of bounds.
Pull—A ball hit straight but to the left of intended flight line.
Push—A ball hit straight but to the right of intended flight line.
Putt—To stroke ball with putter toward hole; also the stroke.
Rough—Rough ground and long grass on either side of fairway.
Scuff—To scrape turf with the clubhead before contacting the ball.
Shaft—Handle of a club.
Slice—To hit across the ball so that it curves to right in flight.
Stance—Position of the feet.
Stymie—One ball lies on the green directly in line of another and the balls are more than 6 inches apart.
Tee—Elevation, of wood or plastic, upon which a ball may be placed for the first stroke on each hole.
Teeing ground—Designated area for starting every hole.

Top—To hit the ball above its center.
Trap—Hole with bed of sand which forms a hazard.
Up—The number of holes or strokes one is ahead of opponent.
Waggle—Preliminary movements with the clubhead, forward and back, in preparation for a swing.
Whiff—To miss the ball entirely.
Winter rules—Rules that allow player to improve the lie of the ball on the fairway.

DISCUSSION QUESTIONS

1. Discuss golf etiquette and explain its importance to the game. What consideration should you have for fellow players (a) on the tee, (b) on the fairway, and (c) on the green?
2. Demonstrate the correct grip, stance, and swing of (a) a driver used off the tee, (b) a number 2 iron used for maximum distance, (c) a number 5 iron for a 120-yard approach stroke, (d) a number 9 iron for a 40-yard pitch and run, and (e) a 25-foot putt.
3. Briefly explain the different techniques for playing a sidehill lie, an uphill lie, and a downhill lie.
4. Explain scoring methods used in golf. How would you establish a handicap at the local course?

SELECTED AUDIOVISUAL AIDS

All Star Golf, 1959-60. (b & w) Miller Brewing Company, Film Section Sales, Promotion and Publicity, 400 West State Street, Milwaukee, Wisconsin 53208. (Free loan)

Beginning Golf: The Game, Get Set to Swing, Building Control into Your Swing, Getting on the Green, Putting, Courtesy and Etiquette of Golf. (Filmstrips and recordings, 10 min. per unit, color.) The Athletic Institute, 804 Merchandise Mart, Chicago, Illinois 60654. (Rental and purchase)

Johnny Farrell Series. (16 mm., 6 units, 10 min. per unit, sound, b & w.) Ideal Pictures Inc., 58 East South Water Street, Chicago, Illinois, or 233 West 32nd Street, New York, New York 10036. (Rental)

National Golf Foundation: *Fundamental Skills of Golf.* 707 Merchandise Mart, Chicago, Illinois 60654. (6 Super 8 cartridge loops.)
(1) The Grip—The Approach Routine
(2) The Full Swing—Woods and Irons
(3) The Short Approach
(4) The Putt
(5) The Sand Shot
(6) Uneven Lies

National Golf Foundation: *Modern Golf Instruction.* (six units, 16 mm. or 8 mm., color, sound.) 707 Merchandise Mart, Chicago, Illinois 60654.
(1) Golf—A Special Kind of Joy
(2) How to Build a Golf Swing
(3) The Short Approach Shots
(4) The Special Challenge Shots
(5) Putting—Golf's End Game
(6) Courtesy on the Course

Play Better Golf: Golf Fundamentals and Golf Advanced. (16 mm., sound, b & w.) Professional Golfers' Association, Broadway and Main Street, Dunedin, Florida. (Loan through PGA member)

Rosburg, Bob: *How to Improve Your Golf.* (Recording, 33⅓ rpm.) Golf Digest, Box 550, Evanston, Illinois. (Purchase)

Shell's Wonderful World of Golf. (16 mm., 1 hour per unit, b & w and color.) Thirty-one films of matches played by experts. Shell Oil Company, 450 North Meridan Street, Indianapolis, Indiana. (Loan)

Women's World of Golf (b & w, sound.) (Series of 3.) (Rental/purchase)

SUGGESTED READINGS

Barnes, Mildred J., Fox, Margaret G., Scott, M. Gladys, and Loeffler, Pauline A.: *Sports Activities for Girls and Women.* New York, New York, Appleton-Century-Crofts, 1966.

Bowling, Maurine: *Tested Ways of Teaching Golf Classes.* Dubuque, Iowa, Wm. C. Brown Co., 1964.

Broer, Marion R.: *Efficiency of Human Movement.* Philadelphia, W. B. Saunders Co.. 1971.

Broer, Marion R., et al.: *Individual Sports for Women.* Philadelphia, W. B. Saunders Co., 1971.

Bruce, Ben, and Davies, Evelyn: *Beginning Golf.* Belmont, California, Wadsworth Publishing Company, 1968.

Cheatum, Billye Ann: *Golf.* Philadelphia, W. B. Saunders Co., 1969.

Fossom, Bruce, and Dagraedt, Mary: *Golf.* Boston, Allyn and Bacon, Inc., 1969.

Hingst, Geneive, and McKee, Mary Ellen: *The Game of Golf, Programmed Instructions of Playing Procedures.* Dubuque, Iowa, Wm. C. Brown Co., 1968.

Ideas for Golf Instruction. Washington, D.C., Lifetime Sports Education Project of the AAHPER, 1968.

Johnson, Carol and Johnstone, Ann Casey: *Golf.* Addison Wesley, Reading, Massachusetts, 1975.

Johnson, Perry, and Stolberg, Donald: *Teacher's Manual.* Englewood Cliffs, New Jersey, Prentice-Hall, Inc., 1971.

NAGWS Archery-Golf Guide. Washington, D.C., National Association for Girls and Women in Sport, AAHPER (current edition).

Nance, Virginia, L., and Davis, E. C.: *Golf.* Dubuque, Iowa, Wm. C. Brown Co., 1971.

National Golf Foundation: *Golf Coaches' Guide.* Chicago, NGF, 1975.

National Golf Foundation: *Golf Teaching Kit* (includes *Golf Instructor's Guide, Golf Lessons,* Planning and Conducting Competitive Golf Events, Easy Way to Learn Golf Rules, Visual Aids for Golf Instruction. Chicago, Current edition.

Rehling, Conrad H.: *Golf for the Physical Education Teacher and Coach.* Dubuque, Iowa, Wm. C. Brown Co., 1968.

Williams, Dave: *How to Coach and Play Championship Golf.* Englewood Cliffs, New Jersey, Prentice-Hall, Inc., 1970.

Wiren, Gary: *Golf.* Englewood Cliffs, New Jersey, Prentice-Hall, Inc., 1971.

PERIODICALS

Golf. 235 East 45th Street, New York, New York 10017.

Golfdom. 235 East 45th Street, New York, New York 10017.

Golf Digest. 88 Scribner Avenue, Norwalk, Connecticut 06856.

The Golf Journal. United States Golf Association, 40 East 38th Street, New York, New York 10016.

Golf World. Box 2000, Southern Pines, North Carolina 28387.

Journal of Health, Physical Education and Recreation, American Alliance for Health, Physical Education and Recreation, 1201 Sixteenth Street, N.W., Washington, D.C. 20036.

The Lady Golfer International. Seidal Publications, Inc., Box 1118, Scottsdale, Arizona 85252.

Par Magazine. Sports Group, Inc., 200 W. 47th Street, New York, New York 10019.

Professional Golfer. Professional Golfers' Association of America, Box 12458, Palm Beach Gardens, Florida 33403.

Tee It Up. National Junior Golfers Association, P.O. Box 27538 Station 7, Atlanta, Georgia 30327.

Woman Golfer. The Woman Golfer Publishing Corporation, 131 Lincoln Highway, Frankfort, Illinois 60423.

USGA Journal and Turf Management. United States Golf Association, 40 East 38th Street, New York, New York 10016.

CHAPTER 10

GYMNASTICS

Today gymnastics is one of our fastest growing sports for girls and women. Few other physical activities require such dedication, self-discipline, intricately refined movements, and body control. As a challenging sport it is ideal for the highly skilled as well as for those of average ability.

Man's basic drive for self-preservation makes it possible that a form of gymnastics began as a means of survival among our earliest ancestors as they learned to climb, swing, hang, jump, and twist their bodies in order to escape from their enemies, find shelter, and secure food. It is known that gymnastics was emphasized by the ancient Greeks, with whom we associate the origin of many sports, and records dating back to 2100 B.C. show that the sport was popular in China, Persia, India, and Egypt even before Greek influence. The Greeks used words meaning the naked art, athletic, disciplinary exercises, and gymnastics interchangeably. The word gymnasium, which comes from the Greek, still denotes the place wherein sports are learned, practiced, and played. In ancient Greece, gymnastic participation was required by law of every youth, and it was believed that through a variety of vigorous activities young men would become strong and courageous, develop beautifully proportioned bodies, and reach a high degree of moral integrity. Girls took only a minor part in this program, but they thrilled to it as spectators when given an opportunity to watch males vigorously competing for the prized laurel wreaths which were awarded to all winners.

In America, our earliest physical education programs were patterned after the gymnastics activities practiced in Germany, Sweden, and Denmark. German gymnastic societies (called *Turnvereins* and founded by Friedrich Jahn) and the Swedish system (resulting largely from the work of Per Henrik Ling) strongly influenced our earliest school physical education programs. Gradually, however, gymnastics was replaced in most school programs by sports and games. Today the pendulum swing is back toward a return to gymnastics. Many physical educators now believe that this is one of our finest physical activities for students of all ages. Our nationwide concern for the development of physical fitness and the touring gymnastic teams from Denmark, Russia, Japan and Sweden have given much impetus to the fast growing popularity of gymnastics.

The first AAU gymnastic competition for women was held in Philadelphia, Pennsylvania, in 1931. Since the 1960 Olympic games in Rome, the gymnastic competitive programs for women are among the most widely attended of all events. Many highly skilled women are now preparing for tryouts for membership on the United States Women's Gymnastic Team, which will compete in the next Olympic games.

THE NATURE AND PURPOSE OF THE SPORT

Gymnastics is both a science and an art. As a science it involves human movement and good body mechanics resulting from the coordinated action of the many muscles, joints, and levers of the body. As an art form, it is concerned with the beauty of human movement, the refinement of body control, and the development of free-flowing exercise patterns performed in relationship to time and space. It is perhaps the most individualized of all sports and as such develops creativity, self-reliance, and resourcefulness. The term "gymnastics" includes apparatus events, hand apparatus, free movement, stunts and tumbling, floor exercises, and modern gymnastics. Since the activities are self testing, each student progresses at her own rate of speed. Because it involves free exercises and the use of several kinds of equipment, it also provides one with an opportunity to specialize.

The major gymnastic movements are built upon basic tumbling stunts and patterns such as the head- or handstand and on the techniques of chinning, balancing, and moving gracefully over objects such as the balance beam or parallel bars. The various stunts may be done on the ground, a gymnasium floor, mat, or apparatus. Competitive activities for women include floor exercises, the vault, the balance beam, and the uneven parallel bars.

RULES AND SCORING

Events recommended for intramural and extramural competition are as follows:

1. *Individual events:* Floor exercise, uneven parallel bars, balance beam, side horse vault.
2. *All-around event:* To consist of the total points scored in the four individual events, both compulsory and optional.
3. *Special events:* Tumbling, trampoline.

This chapter is concerned only with the skills of the individual events. Prior to competition it is imperative that a student be familiar with the rules concerning each event. These are available in the *Official AAU Gymnastics Guide* and the NAGWS *Gymnastics Guide.*

Scoring. Judges award scores of 0 to 10 in tenths of a point. The only exception is in the case of the optional vaults. This exception is made because of the difficulty of the vaults.

According to the value of the optional vault, the scoring is as follows:

1. Judges award points of 0 through 10, and the scorers deduct the number of the rating below ten.
2. The judges award points of 0 through the maximum score of 10 allowed in the evaluation of the vault.

NEEDED FACILITIES AND EQUIPMENT

Desirable uniforms for girls and women are leotards and ballet-type soft-soled shoes. Although a program can be built around a minimum of improvised equipment,* if this activity is conducted as it should be, as many as possible of the following items should be available:

Well covered mats
Hand safety belts
Trampoline
Mini-tramp
Springboards
Vaulting box
Horse
Even and uneven parallel bars
Reuther board
Beat boards
Buck
Balance beam (both a low and high beam)
Stall bars
Rings

TEACHING UNITS

Relays, various kinds of self-testing stunts such as the handstand or back flip, rhythmical gymnastic exercises done on stall bars, trampolining, rope climbing, and stunts done on both the still and flying rings are recommended for inclusion in long teaching units for both beginners and advanced students in gymnastics. Any unit for beginners should aim to introduce students to many of the different kinds of basic skills needed for free exercises and apparatus work. An advanced unit should be developed around individual skill development in the use of as many different kinds of apparatus as possible.

*See the chapter, "The Purchase, Maintenance, and Construction of Equipment," in James Baley's *Gymnastics in Schools* for valuable information on how to improvise many kinds of gymnastic equipment.

Suggested units are:

Beginners

Brief history and explanation of the purposes of gymnastics
Safety procedures, squad selections, and class conduct
Lead-up activities including tumbling stunts, calisthenics, and rhythmic gymnastics
Film strip or movie on beginning gymnastics
Basic skills
  Free exercise
  Balance beam (low and elementary work on the high beam)
  Vaulting
  Trampolining and use of the mini-tramp
  Uneven parallel bars
Composition of simple routines
Evaluation of results

Advanced

Review of safety procedures and class conduct
Review of previously learned basic skills
Advanced skills in tumbling stunts, calisthenics, and rhythmic gymnastics
Free exercises
Balance beam (low and high)
Vaults
Uneven parallel bars
Movies on advanced gymnastics and gymnastic competition in the Olympic games
Individual work on selected stunts and apparatus specialization
Composition of free exercise routines
Gymnastic exhibition
Evaluation of results

SAFETY PRECAUTIONS

Concern for individual safety is of utmost importance in the instructional and competitive gymnastics program. Students are more assured learners and performers if they feel confident in their personal qualifications, safety of equipment, and instructional leadership.

All apparatus should be carefully set up with ample clearance for use of other pieces of equipment. All equipment should be checked for stability and possible hazards before use. Mats should be placed over the footings and solidly around the apparatus to lessen the danger of injury in the event of falls. Tartan floors have gained popularity for their resilience. Magnesium chalk should be used when working on apparatus for dry hands and a firm, freely moving grip.

Obviously, beginners should master the fundamental skills before being permitted to try more advanced exercises or apparatus activities; all adjustable apparatus should be lowered for the young and inexperienced performer. A capable spotter gives assurance and physical support, if needed, to a student doing a stunt or routine. When possible, a third assistant (called an observer) works with the spotter to analyze the performer's movements and aid in her improvement. The three may work as a team, changing roles to assist one another.

An instructional program should help the student develop her own warm-up program. Although this is an individual matter, dependent on her personal flexibility, strength and coordination, and the skills she is working

Table 6. Readiness Check List and Recommended Exercises for Improvement for Each Gymnast*

Quality	To Assess Present Level (Also exercises for improvement)	Self-Rating Good	Fair	Poor
Back Flexibility	1. Lie on your back. Push up into a backbend or bridge position. Move your hands in toward your feet, trying to form a deep arch.	–	–	–
	2. Lie on your stomach. Stretch arms overhead. Have another gymnast stand in a straddle position behind you and grasp your hands. Your partner pulls your arms and upper body backward, forcing a deep arch in your back.	–	–	–
Shoulder Flexibility	Lift your arms straight out to your sides. Have a partner stand behind you, grasp your hands, and gently force your arms backward. How loose do you feel in the shoulder area?	–	–	–
Toe Point	1. Point your toes as hard as you can. Have a gymnast examine the quality of arch you have developed. 2. Sit down. Stretch your legs straight out in front of you. Have a partner gently force the front part of your foot downward toward the floor.	–	–	–
Leg Spring	Jump rope. See how high and with how much resiliency your legs move.	–	–	–
Arm Strength	1. Assume the position for the wheelbarrow, i.e., walking on your hands, while someone stands behind you and holds onto your ankles. Your legs are raised and stretched behind you.	–	–	–
	2. Assume a straight arm support on the low bar of the unevens, on the horizontal bar, or on the balance beam. How long can you hold that position without your arms' giving way underneath you?	–	–	–
Leg Extension	1. Stand against a wall. Lift your leg, keeping it straight. Partner raises your leg upward, forcing it gently back toward the wall.	–	–	–
	2. Practice the splits on both sides. How far down toward the floor can your legs stretch?	–	–	–

*From Roys, Betty Maycock: *Gymnastics For Girls and Women.* Philadelphia, W. B. Saunders Co., 1969, pp. 13–14.

toward, many students prefer to warm up to music emphasizing stretches and many ballet type exercises. After a general "loosening up" she should use exercises uniquely designed for her range of flexibility for each type of apparatus or activity. For example, strength and flexibility of knees and ankles should be stressed prior to vaulting, and stretching and extension of shoulders, waist, and upper back should be stressed before working on the uneven parallel bars.

Falling properly may be an important instructional concern for use of each piece of equipment. Each student should demonstrate that she knows how to tuck, direct her landing position, and curl her body, as well as how to "brake" the rate and speed of her movements in order to gain and maintain body control. Stress the importance of keeping the head up to avoid forward motion on landing and to aid in softening the landing impact at the completion of a movement sequence.

Other safety precautions should include:

1. Never work out alone; always work with a spotter.
2. Avoid dares, clowning around and showing off at all times.
3. Do not attempt stunts beyond performance ability.
4. Keep facial muscles relaxed; avoid biting tongue, grinding teeth, or chewing gum during practices and performances.
5. Keep eyes open while performing and pull long hair away from the face. (Long hair should be well controlled when working on the trampoline to avoid catching it in the support springs.)
6. Do not wear jewelry while on the apparatus.
7. Keep fingernails reasonably short.

Each student has a personal obligation to be well conditioned before attempting any gymnastic stunt or routine. She should continually strive to maintain strength and flexibility and increase her endurance. The following readiness check list and recommended exercises may be helpful to an individual student in assessing and improving her body control, strength, and flexibility.

SUGGESTED EXERCISES

The Push-Up. Keeping a straight body, raise it from a prone position, supporting the weight on the hands, straightened arms, and toes (Figure 10–1). Add one additional push-up at each workout until 10 are reached.

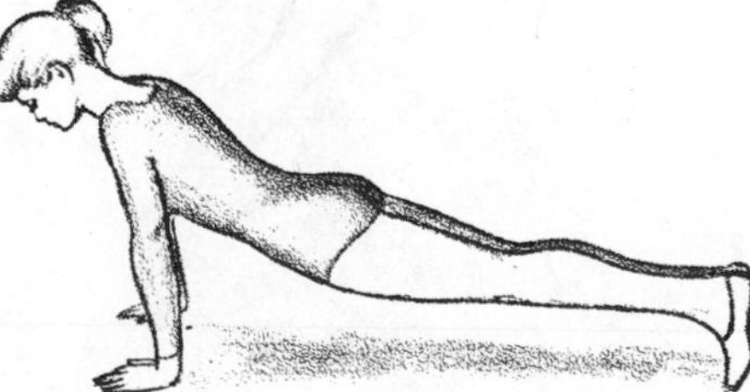

Figure 10–1 The push-up.

Figure 10–2 The pull-up.

Then strive for 15, etc.

The Pull-Up. With knuckles up, pull the body up to bring the chin over the top of the chinning bar (Figure 10–2). Repeat several times, lowering the body slowly each time by fully extending the arms. Strive to increase the number of chins each session.

Swinging. To develop hand and finger grip strength, hold the body in

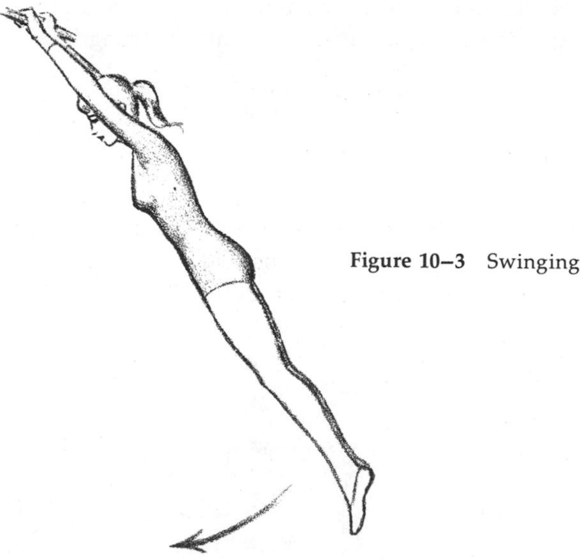

Figure 10–3 Swinging.

Figure 10–4 The front split.

a rigid position, using either the upper or under grip on the chinning bar. Swing back and forth, gaining momentum each time, then gradually decrease it (Figure 10–3).

The High Leg Stretch. Used to develop body flexibility, this exercise is done by standing with your back to the wall and lifting one leg forward and up as far as possible. Have a partner grasp your ankle and raise your leg higher. Keep weight balanced on the other leg with knee locked.

The Front Split. Used also to develop body flexibility, this stunt is done by standing with one foot far ahead of the other. Slowly move the legs farther apart. Alternate legs and repeat. Be sure to lock the rear leg tightly with the knee down. Keep the body in an erect position.

The Side Split. Also for body flexibility, this stunt is done by standing with legs spread wide apart to the sides and continuing to spread them as far apart as possible. Keep the legs and body straight, the knees locked. At the farthest point of movement, bend the upper body from the waist, keeping hands well in front of the hips to force the hips down.

BASIC SKILLS

Floor Exercises

In competitive events, floor exercises must be performed for no longer than 1½ minutes on the floor or the mat with a square area of 39⅓ feet. Ballet and tumbling movements in any combination can be used, but they must be done to music. This floor exercise routine may be made up of tumbling, dance, and acrobatics, all artistically combined with "breathers," such as poses, into an aesthetic pattern. As Loken has pointed out, "Usually, however, these exercise patterns begin with an opening sequence of tumbling, followed by the body of the routine consisting of ballet jumps, turns, spins, and balancing and agility movements, and finish with another tumbling sequence."*

All stunts used in free exercise competition should be mastered on a mat before they are tried on the floor. A spotter and an observer should assist the learner and stand where they can be of most help.

Since free exercise routines are largely built on the ability to move with grace and beauty, harmonious body movement should be the starting point in learning this activity, especially if one has not had much previous experience in dance or tumbling.

In competition a performer is given from 1 to 1½ minutes (5 seconds' leeway) to perform her routine. The varied movements and floor patterns should use the entire floor space. The music should set the pace and accent and should highlight all movements. The performer is expected to demonstrate her skill in back flexion, forward flexion and extension, arm support strength, balance holds or poses, coordination and timing in tumbling stunts, and agility in springs. Tumbling and dance should both be included in the routine, but should be carefully balanced so that neither activity is dominant. All movement changes should blend naturally together. Connectives (combinations of dance steps and poses) are used to relieve the strain of difficult movements. All should flow well together and can be made up of walks, hops, leaps, jumps, turns, slides, and other movements that can be done well and rhythmically. Directional turns, like all other movements, should lead harmoniously into the succeeding movement. Once the exercise has been created, it should be practiced over and over again until it can be done beautifully.

Ballet Movements

The Toe Stand. Stand with an erect body, rise to toes with arms extended at the sides in a relaxed, graceful position with palms down (Figure 10–5). Lower body to full standing position with arms at your side.

The Ballet Touch. Stand in a controlled, relaxed position with the right foot slightly ahead of the left. Bend and touch the forward foot with the right hand. Return to original position. Repeat, using the other foot and hand.

The Pirouette. This is a series of two or more full turns of the body on the ball of one foot while the body rotates. The head remains facing forward as long as possible, then is turned quickly around to face forward again, helping to give momentum to the turn.

The Body Sweep. With body weight held on right knee and right hand, move the left arm forward and at the same time extend the left leg. Reach for full extension of the arm and leg (Figure 10–6).

---

*Loken, Newton C. and Willoughby, Robert J.: *The Complete Book of Gymnastics.* Englewood Cliffs, New Jersey, Prentice-Hall, Inc., 1973, p. 137.

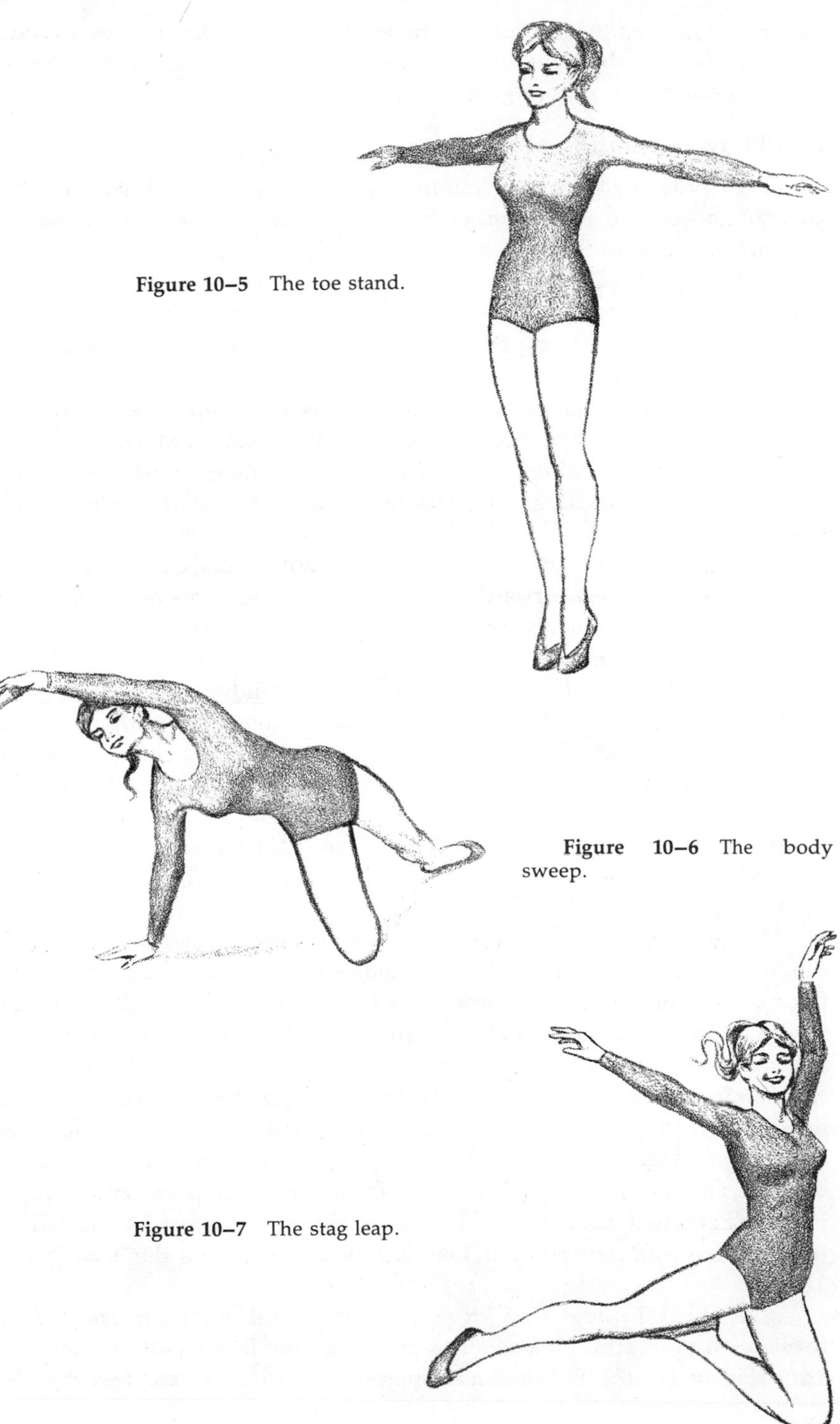

Figure 10–5 The toe stand.

Figure 10–6 The body sweep.

Figure 10–7 The stag leap.

The Stag Leap. Leap high in the air, bringing the left foot up to touch the inner thigh of the right leg above the knee. Extend the left arm upward, the right out to the side (Figure 10–7).

Flexibility and Agility Movements

The Arabesque. From a standing position, move the left leg backward and out and extend right arm, keeping the fingers relaxed. Move the left arm out to the side. Stand in a balanced position (Figure 10–8).

The Single Leg Balance. Standing balanced on the left leg, raise the other one to the side as high as you can, grasp its instep with the right hand and extend the leg, raising the opposite hand in a graceful position with palm up (Figure 10–9).

The Balance Stand. Stand on the right leg. Bend forward, keeping your trunk parallel to the floor and both arms forward. Extend the left leg backward, pointing the toes, and raise it higher than the body. Keep your head up and your back arched (Figure 10–10). This is also called a front scale.

The Needle Scale. Stand on one leg. With arms extended forward bend your body slowly forward and down until your palms rest on the floor and your forehead touches the front of the lower supporting leg. Then extend the other leg upward.

Jump to Handstand. Jump upward from a standing position. Tuck the body and land on your hands, flexing elbows slightly to cushion impact. Then fully extend and lock arms, and balance the body held in full extension. Hold for three seconds, or count 1000 and 1, 1000 and 2, 1000 and 3.

The Yogi Handstand. From a handstand position, drop the hips suddenly forward and jackknife the legs backward. Bring the head forward, keeping the back stiff. Hold for 3 seconds, or count 1000 and 1, 1000 and 2, 1000 and 3.

The Front Walkover. From a standing position, lean forward to place the hands on the floor as you do in a handstand. Bring one leg slowly off the floor and all the way over, followed by the other leg. Push with hands and return to original position. (The use of a belt or a spotter is recommended for this stunt.)

The Backover. Bend backward from the standing position until the hands touch the floor. Kick the right leg up and over, then the left one, finishing in a standing position. (A safety belt or a spotter is recommended.)

The Forward Drop. Fall forward from a standing position to land on your straightened arms; flex and hold weight on the arms. As you fall, extend one leg with toes pointed, keeping the other foot on the floor (Figure 10–12).

The Shoot Through. With your body in full extension and leaning forward on your arms, flex the hips and bring the legs rapidly through the arms (Figure 10–13). Finish in a sitting position with legs and feet together

Figure 10–8 The arabesque.

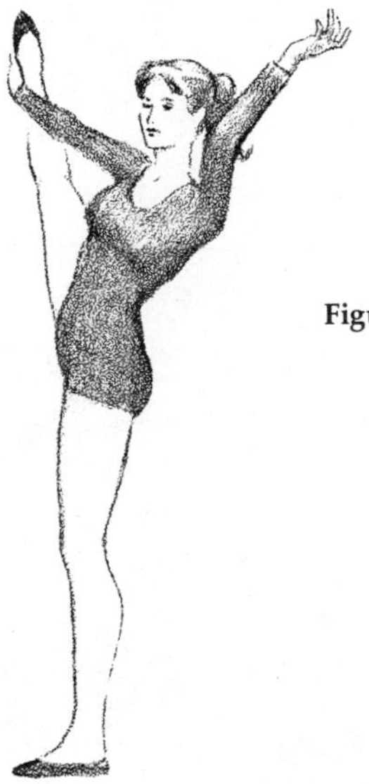

Figure 10–9 The single leg balance.

Figure 10–10 The balance stand.

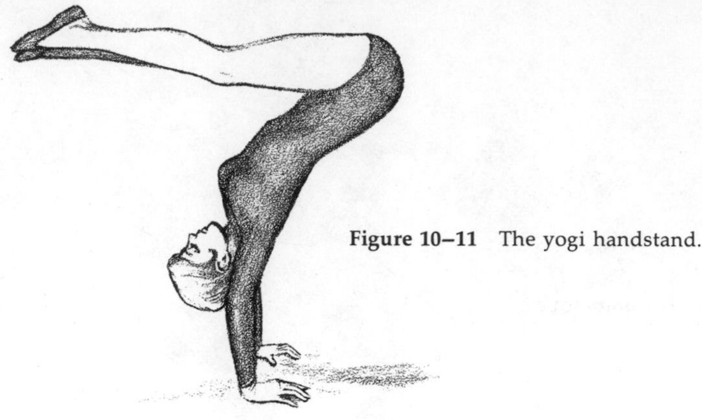

Figure 10–11 The yogi handstand.

Figure 10–12 The forward drop.

Figure 10–13 The shoot through.

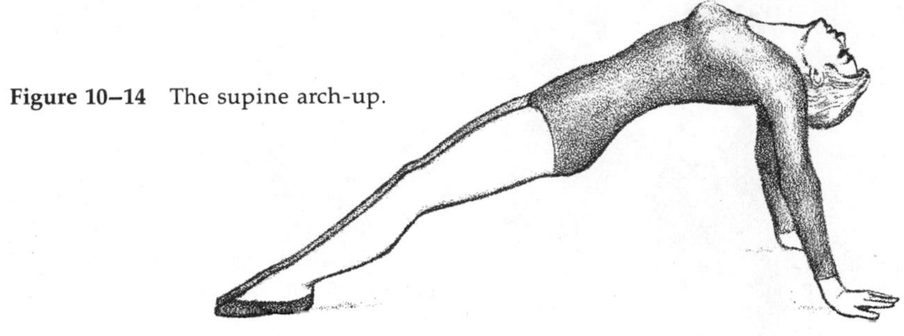
Figure 10–14 The supine arch-up.

and extended, and your body tilted backward, supported by the hands held behind shoulder line.

The Supine Arch-Up. From a supine floor position raise the body from the floor by moving the hands from near the hips to the shoulder area. Straighten the arms, arch the back, and keep both feet close together on the floor (Figure 10–14).

The Balance Beam

For competitive events the beam should be 3 15/16 inches wide, 6 1/2 inches in depth, 16 feet 4 inches long, and 3 feet 11 inches from the floor. On this board the performers must do a variety of running and balance movements, rolls, held positions, and body turns within 1 minute 20 second to 1 minute 45 second time limits. Each routine is judged by accuracy, control, and beauty of movement on the mount, on the beam itself, and on the dismount.

For safety purposes in this sport, mats should be placed under and around the beam, and the use of at least one spotter on each side of the beam is essential. For beginners the beam should be approximately 6 inches above the floor. It should be gradually raised in height as the performer gains skill and confidence. Walking and running on the beam should be the first skills mastered.

The exercises done on the beam should be dynamic and flowing and should utilize complete body movement. The arms should be held to the side with palms down and the elbows relaxed, in preparation for the mount.

Mounts

There are a variety of ways to get onto the beam. Regardless of the mount used, a spotter should be present to assist all beginners.

The Straight Arm Support Mount. From a standing position or from a series of short running steps, jump to take off with both feet, and place both hands at shoulder width on the beam. Support the straightened body with

Figure 10–15 The straight arm support mount.

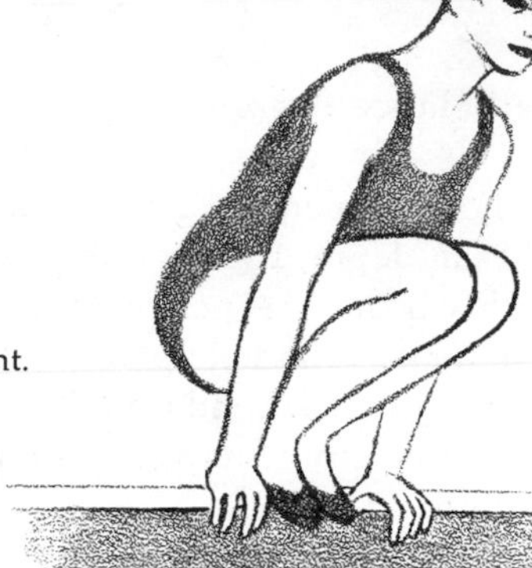

Figure 10–16 The squat mount.

Figure 10–17 The one knee mount.

Figure 10–18 The crotch seat mount.

the fronts of the thighs touching the beam. Swing the body up and onto the beam.

The Squat Mount. Jump to a straight arm support position and bring legs up between the arms. The feet are placed close together on the beam, and the body is held in balance by the toes and hands (Figure 10–16).

The One Knee Mount. Jump to a straight arm support position to land with the right knee on the beam, and point the toes (Figure 10–17). Keep supporting hands on the outside. Extend the left leg up and back. Keep head erect.

The Crotch Seat Mount. Jump to a straight arm support, and swing the extended left leg over the beam (Figure 10–18A). Turn the body one quarter turn; sit straddling the beam, legs and feet extended, and hold on with both hands behind the body (Figure 10–18B). (This mount requires skill and arm strength and should not be attempted by beginners.)

The Scissors Mount. Take off at an oblique angle from the beat board, placed almost parallel to the beam. With a scissoring movement bring the body up over the beam one leg at a time, and come to a sitting position.

Figure 10–19 The hip pullover mount.

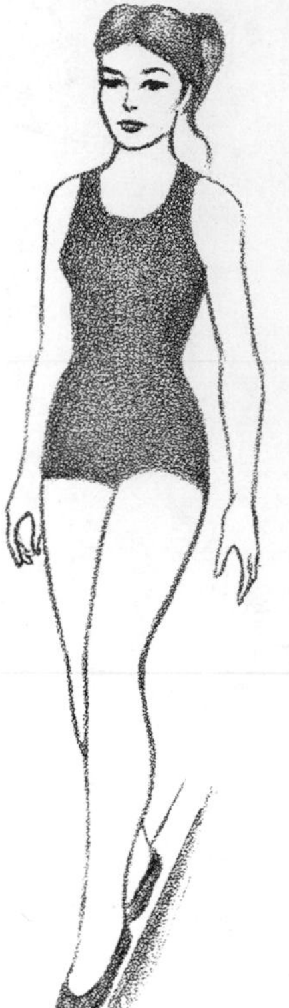

Figure 10–20 Walking the beam.

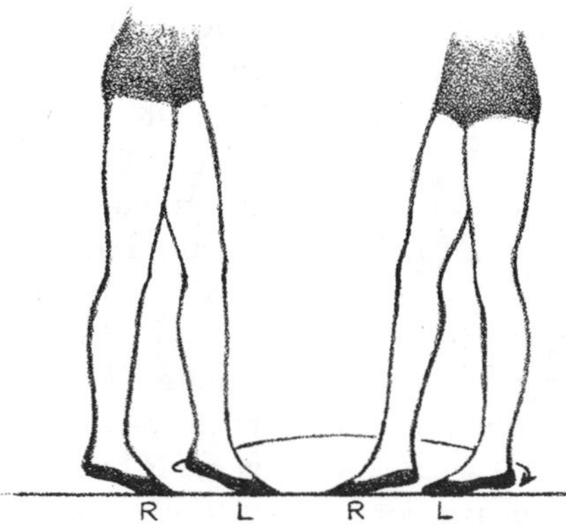

Figure 10–21 The pivot.

The Hip Pullover Mount. From a standing position, bend your knees and grasp the beam, using an undergrip. Raise first one leg, then the other (Figure 10–19). With a fast hip-circling movement bring the body under and over the beam. Straighten the body.

Poses and Movements on the Beam

All poses and movement skills done on the balance beam require courage, body control, and flexibility. Having one spotter on each side of the beam is recommended for beginners until they gain both confidence and skill. The beam should not be raised to its proper height until the students are beyond the novice stage in learning to perform the basic skills.

Walking and Running the Beam. This should be practiced until you can move with confidence and sureness. The body should be held erect with the arms hanging naturally at the sides for balance. To add polish to walking movements, make a small knee dip with each step, letting the free foot drop slightly below the beam on each step. Keep eyes focused forward and do not look down at your feet or the beam (Figure 10–20). As you gain confidence, lengthen the stride and speed of each of the movements until you can run successfully on the beam.

Figure 10–22 The pirouette turn.

Body Turns on the Beam. Although there are many ways of turning, the simplest is to pivot the body around to face a reverse position (Figure 10–21). This is done by raising oneself on the balls of both feet (held in a toe to heel position), turning the body sharply from right to left, and lowering the heels to the beam again.

To execute a pirouette, or half turn done on one foot, hold the arms overhead with fingers pointed and relaxed, and rotate the body around on the supporting right foot (Figure 10–22). On completing the turn, bring the left foot to the beam and use your arms to achieve complete body balance.

Jumps on the Beam. Jumps can be made from a run or dip position. Place your right foot ahead of the left. Jump into the air by swinging your arms upward, and reverse the position of your feet, bringing left one forward (Figure 10–23).

The Switch Step. From a standing position in which one foot is slightly in front of the other, hold your arms behind and above your head, bend your knees slightly, and then spring from the beam by straightening your legs and pushing up with your feet. Switch the position of your feet while in the air, and as they contact the beam bend your knees and make a circle with your arms. Return to a standing position. Be sure to gain good

Figure 10–23 Jumping on the beam.

Figure 10–24 The one leg squat.

Figure 10–25 The knee scale.

Figure 10–26 The straddle hold.

height on the upward spring, and lean forward slightly as you land, in order to gain better balance control.

The Front Scissors Kick. A front scissors kick can be done following several short running steps or from a running position. If from the latter, stand with the left foot slightly in front of the right and extend the arms outward at the sides. With your weight on the left foot, jump by pushing off with that foot and bringing your arms down. Then bring the right leg, locked straight, forward and sharply upward while raising your arms. Quickly swing your left leg up to make a scissors kick before coming down. Bend your knees on landing to maintain balance.

The One Leg Squat. Slowly lower your body from an erect position into a full squat, keeping your weight on the right foot, and lift your left leg parallel to the beam. Reach your arms gracefully forward to keep your balance (Figure 10–24).

The Knee Scale. Begin from a kneeling position with left knee behind the right (Figure 10–25). Tilt your body forward as you lift the back leg into the air. Straighten your arms and grasp the beam with one hand on each side, keeping your fingers together and down and your head erect.

The Straddle Hold. Sit on beam with your hands gripping the beam between your extended legs. Raise your body to balance on your straight arms (Figure 10–26).

The Forward Shoulder Roll. Begin from a kneeling position. Lower your head and one shoulder to the beam and hold on by gripping the fingers close together with each hand under the beam. Move your hips slowly up

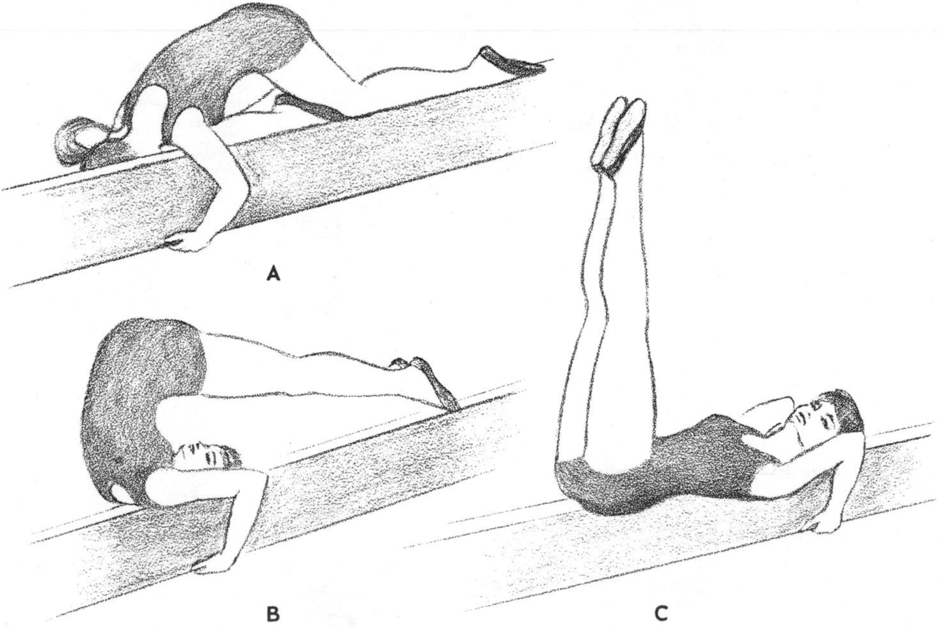

Figure 10–27 The forward shoulder roll.

and forward into a roll and finish by bringing your body into a full lying position face up. Next, bring both legs down on each side, going into a crotch seat position. The use of a spotter on each side of the beam is recommended.

The Back Shoulder Roll. Begin from a lying position with your body facing up on the beam. Lower your head to one side below the top of the beam and hold on by reaching to its underside. Slowly do a backward roll by

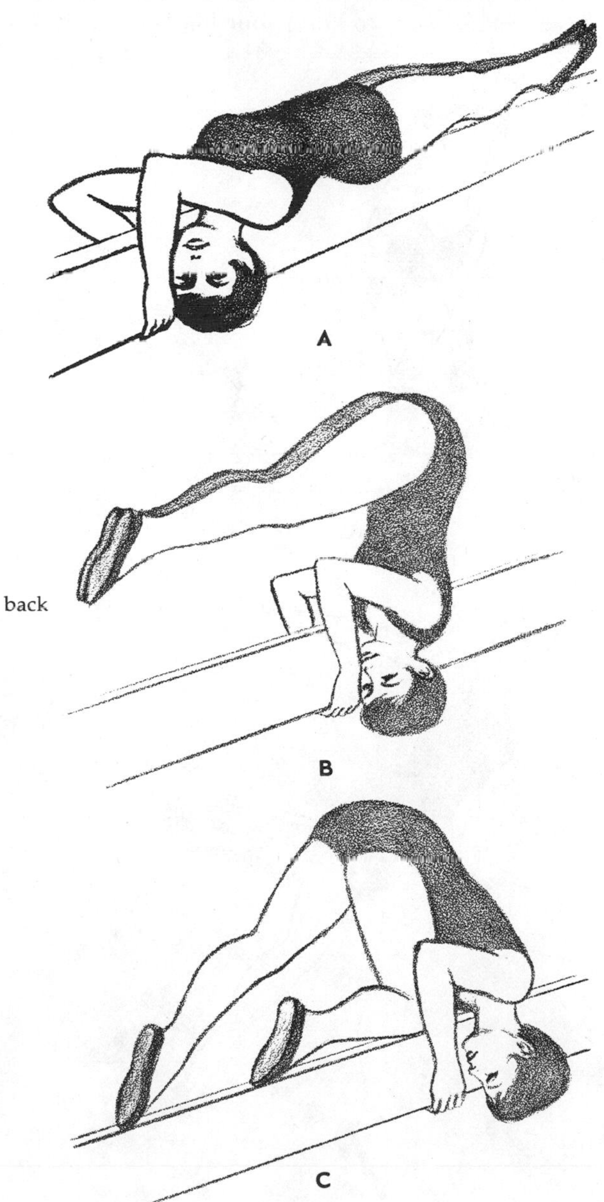

Figure 10–28 The back shoulder roll.

pulling your knees toward your chest and on over, keeping body weight supported on one shoulder. Place your right bent knee on top of the beam. Then come up into a kneeling scale. The use of two spotters is recommended for this stunt also.

Dismounts

The Jump-Off Dismount. The easiest dismount is done by leaping off the beam. Be sure to keep your movements controlled as you leap off the beam, and be sure to bend your knees to break the fall as you come down.

Figure 10–29 The side seat dismount.

The Side Seat Dismount. Seated on the beam, lean toward the right and place your right hand on the beam (Figure 10–29A). Swing the outside leg backward and lift your body up and to the side with the right hand (Figure 10–29B). Dismount and come into an erect standing position.

The Front Vault Dismount. In a front rest position, support your body on your hands and fully extended arms and feet (Figure 10–30A). Kick your legs upward, and at the same time swing your body around clear of the beam (Figure 10–30B). Dismount.

The Handstand Dismount. This may be used by students who have mastered the handstand. Hold the arms horizontally at the sides. Then go

Figure 10–30 The front vault dismount.

Figure 10–31 The handstand dismount.

into a handstand position, make a big circle outward as you come on around with your body fully extended, and dismount with feet held together.

The Vaults

In women's vaulting the pommels are removed from the horse, and the performer takes off from a beat board on one side of the horse, vaulting over the middle of the saddle so that the hands give momentary support to the body. In competition, excellence is judged by preflight push-off, vault execution, and control of body throughout and after flight.

The use of a spotter is urged until the student has progressed beyond the novice stage. Basic skills in taking off from the beat board should first be mastered.

Approach the beat board in a light run with weight on the balls of the feet. The body is straight and inclined forward and elbows are bent. A low hurdle carries the gymnast to the end of the board. The body weight lands first on the toes and then the balls of the feet. The body remains straight as it rides the quick spring upward.

The Side Vault. The most basic vault is the side or flank vault. After a few running steps, take off from the beat board from the balls of the feet. Place hands on the horse, shoulder width apart. Shift weight to the right arm. Lift the left hand from the horse, bring feet together in a horizontal position, and move the body over the horse under the left hand. Push off from the horse with the supporting hand and land with the back to the horse. As a variation, in swinging the body over, turn body downward to

Figure 10–32 The side vault.

face toward the top of the horse. Release one hand as in the side vault and land, keeping one hand resting on the horse.

The Squat Stand Vault. Take off and place the hands on the horse shoulder width apart. Bring the legs up between the arms in a squatting position. Jump forward to the mat.

The Straddle Vault. Approach, running at medium speed, spring high on the takeoff and put both hands on the horse. At the same time spread the legs far apart. Land in a standing position.

The Straddle Stand and Jump. Jump to straddle position, keeping legs outside the arms. Straighten body to full standing position. Jump with both arms and body in full extension with toes pointed to land on the mat.

The Handspring Vault. This should be done only by students who can first do the handspring. Spring from the board and come to a handstand position, keeping arms straight and locked. Tuck in your head and bring fully extended body over the horse to land on the mat.

The Giant Cartwheel. Run fast toward the horse. Leap from both feet to dive up and forward, making a quarter turn during the flight and before the hands land on the horse. The left hand should contact the horse before the body is in the handstand position. As one reaches the handstand position, the right hand should contact the horse. Then the left arm pivots sideward around the right hand to land with the right side toward the horse. The spotter should stand directly behind the performer and be prepared to grasp her wrist.

The Swan Vault. Run toward horse with speed sufficient to execute a long dive with considerable forward momentum. Push up and forward off arms with sufficient force to clear the horse, keeping the body arched and legs extended. After clearing the horse, continue to pull head backward, and arch upper back in order to cause body to pivot on its horizontal axis to

Figure 10–33 The squat stand dismount.

Figure 10–34 The straddle vault.

Figure 10–35 The straddle stand.

Figure 10–36 The handspring vault.

make landing on the feet possible. The spotter should grasp the performer's upper arms.

The Uneven Parallel Bars

The measurements for the uneven bars are as follows: the top of the high bar should be 7 feet 6 inches from the floor; the distance from the floor to the low bar should be approximately 5 feet; and the distance between the bars should be 16½ to 18 inches.

Movements on the uneven parallel bars are predominantly swinging ones. Although there are no set combinations, the best routine movement patterns are those that enable you to go from the high bar to the low one and from it back up to the high bar. Each movement should be fluidly rhythmical and continuous; static positions should be short and a required part of a combination. The three basic stages in using the bars are the mounts, the

Figure 10–37 The straight arm support.

poses and movements, and the dismounts. A beat board may be used for mounting.

The Mounts

The Straight Arm Support. Face the low bar and grasp it by placing your hands over the top with your thumbs underneath. Jump, tilt your fully extended body, and rest it on your thighs. Keep your arms straight, chest and head up, and extend legs and toes (Figure 10–37).

The Shoot Over the Low Bar. Start from behind the high bar facing the low bar. Spring up and grasp the high bar, then bring both legs up and over the low bar. Finish with your seat resting on the low bar and your hands grasping the high bar. Keep your body fully extended (Figure 10–38).

The Cross Seat Mount. Stand between the bars, grasping the low bar with your right hand. Grasp the high bar with your left hand and curl the fingers of the left hand around it on the top inner side. Jump upward to support the body largely by the left hand on the high bar and the right lower arm and hand on the low bar (Figure 10–39). Swing both legs over the low bar and come into a cross seat position, keeping legs together and toes pointed.

The Back Pullover Mount. Grasp the low bar by curling your hands and fingers around the top of it. Pull your body in toward the bar and bring legs up and around the bar, using a hip-circling movement (Figure 10–40). Finish in a straight arm support position with your body held in full extension, keeping your feet and toes pointed downward toward the mat.

Poses and Movements

The Low Bar Balance. From a straddle position on the low bar bring your right leg up onto the bar, supporting your body by grasping the bar behind you with your right hand. Take hold of the high bar with the left hand, raise your left leg, and extend the foot (Figure 10–41).

The Crotch Seat. Using a straight arm support on the inside of the low bar, raise your right leg up, over, and down to the right side of the bar and

Figure 10–38 The shoot over the low bar.

Figure 10–39 The cross seat mount.

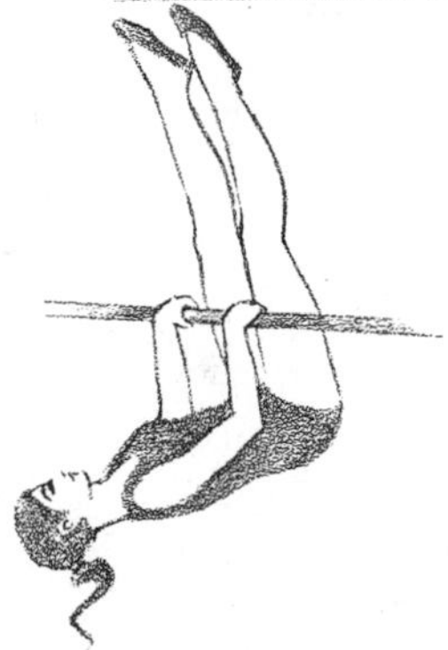

Figure 10–40 The back pullover mount.

Figure 10–41 The low bar balance.

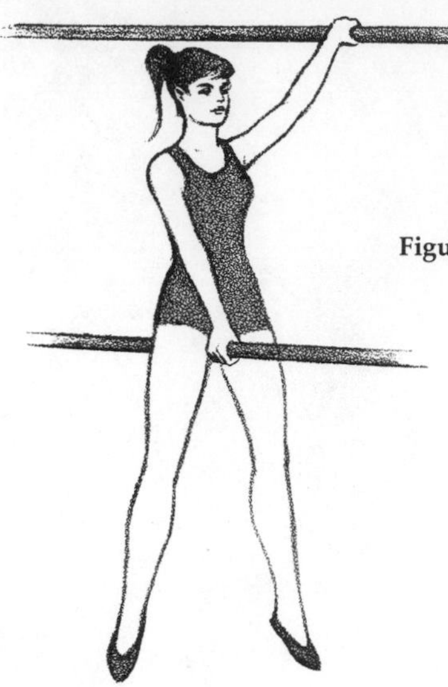

Figure 10–42 The crotch seat.

Figure 10–43 The swan.

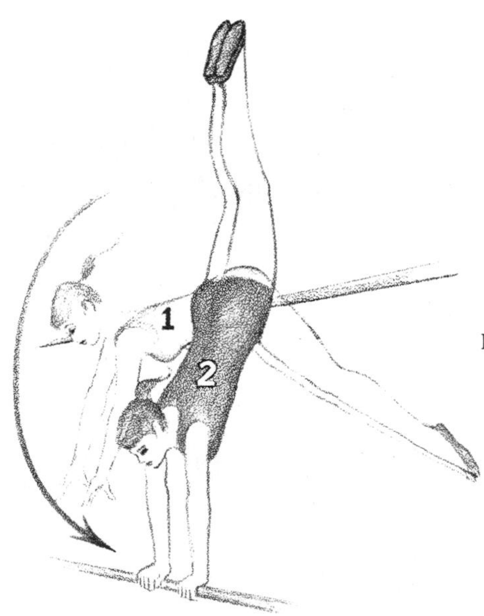

Figure 10–44 The thigh rest.

Figure 10–45 The low bar scale.

come up to a crotch seat position. Hold on to the high bar with your left hand and to the low one with your right. Keep your body in an erect sitting position (Figure 10–42).

The Swan. Moving from a straight arm support position on the high bar, balance your body on your upper thighs, raise your arms and fully extend them to the sides, and arch your back (Figure 10–43).

The Swinging Hip Circle. This is done from a hanging position on the high bar, using an overgrip, with the body fully extended and facing the low bar. Swing one leg out and up and place the foot on the low bar. Push out briskly from bar and begin a backward body swing. Wrap your legs around the low bar on the forward swing and let go of the high bar to come to a sitting position on the low bar facing out.

The Thigh Rest. From a front rest position on the high bar, move your body slowly down and grasp the low bar with both hands. Raise both legs together keeping your toes pointed and come into an arched position, supporting your body on the bars with your hands and upper thighs (Figure 10–44).

The Low Bar Scale. Hold on to the top bar with the left hand and support your body in a squat position on the right leg. Raise your body and extend your left leg behind you. Next bring your body forward, keeping your right arm extended and your hand in a relaxed position (Figure 10–45).

The Arch Back. Hang from your knees on the high bar facing the low one. Reach backward and pull your body up above the bar. Arch your body and straighten your arms on the low bar (Figure 10–46).

Figure 10–46 The arch back.

Figure 10–47 The side cross-hand balance.

The Side Cross-Hand Balance. From a front lying position on the high bar, lean forward toward the low bar, and grasp the high bar with the left hand in an overgrip position. Bring the body slowly downward and place your right hand on the low bar. Turn your body somewhat to the left and slowly move it away from the high bar. Keep your left arm bent, your right arm straight, and your body arched and in full extension with both legs together and your feet pointed (Figure 10–47).

The Dismounts

There are many dismounts that may be used. However, you should learn to do a few of them well before trying to add to these skills. Great care must be taken in dismounting, for doing so too quickly can cause jerky, uncontrolled movements and spoil the entire routine. A dismount properly done puts the finishing touch on the movements done on uneven parallel bars, giving both a last and lasting impression of a performer.

The Front Vault Dismount. This is done from a swinging position between the bars. Hold both bars in an overgrip, locking the lower arm for support. Begin by making a controlled swing between the bars; then, after a forceful backswing, push vigorously out from the high bar, and with your feet leading, lift your arched body over the low bar (Figure 10–48).

The Single Leg Side Vault Dismount. Sit in a slight sideward crotched position on the low bar with your left leg in front, knee flexed. Hold on to the bar with your left hand behind you in an undergrip position. Keep your right leg in full extension downward and grasp the high bar in an overgrip

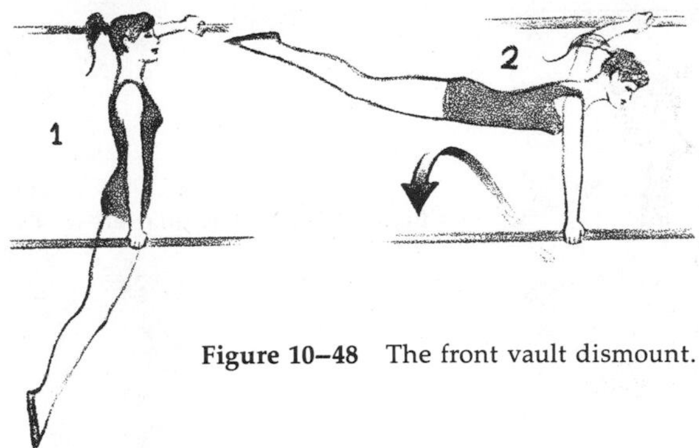

Figure 10–48 The front vault dismount.

position Next, swing your right leg up and over the right side of the bar, using your left arm to support your body. Release your grip on the high bar as you move your right leg over the bar and jump toward the mat with both feet (Figure 10–49). Keep your left hand and the left side of your body close to the bar. Stretch your right arm out to full extension to the side in order to maintain balance.

The Quarter Twist Dismount. From a straight arm support position on the low bar facing the high one, swing both feet slightly forward, then backward, and make a quarter turn (Figure 10–50), and drop to the mat in a standing position, keeping your left side near the bar and holding on to it with your left hand until you have made a controlled landing.

The Underswing Dismount from the High Bar. Stand on the low bar and grasp the high bar with both hands. Jump into a half pike and swing both legs under and up toward the high bar. Then swing under the high bar, raising both arms above your extended body before you land on the mat behind the high bar (Figure 10–51).

Figure 10–49 The single leg side dismount.

Figure 10–50 The quarter twist dismount.

Figure 10–51 The underswing dismount from the high bar.

Figure 10–52 The double leg dismount.

The Double Leg Dismount. Lean slightly forward from a straight arm support position between the bars. Swing both legs back and then over the low bar. Push off from the high bar and make a quarter turn with your body, coming over the low bar in a seat position to a standing dismount on the mat (Figure 10–52).

The Even Parallel Bars

Development of skills on the even parallel bars may be helpful in preparation for the uneven bars. If uneven bars are not available for instruction, even bar work fills a need for some students. The basic movements performed on the bars are those of tumbling combined with swinging movements. The width between the bars should be adjusted for beginners.

The Straight Arm Support. Since this is the starting position for most stunts, it should be learned first. With each hand, grasp the top of the two bars near the end. Jump upward, straighten and lock your arms, keeping your body erect with back arched and toes pointed (Figure 10–53). To travel up and back on the bars, shift your body weight from one hand to the other, just as you shift body weight from foot to foot in walking.

The Riding Seat. Swing your body forward on your hands and fully extended arms and then bring both legs sharply over one of the bars to come into a sitting position. Support your body with one hand held behind you and the other grasping the other bar. Extend your rear leg fully, and flex the forward one. Keep body erect, eyes focused ahead, and feet pointed downward. You can do a series of these side seats by swinging your legs up, back down to a straight arm support position, and back up again.

The Straddle Seat. Jump forward and support your weight on your hands and fully extended arms. Swing both legs forward between the bars.

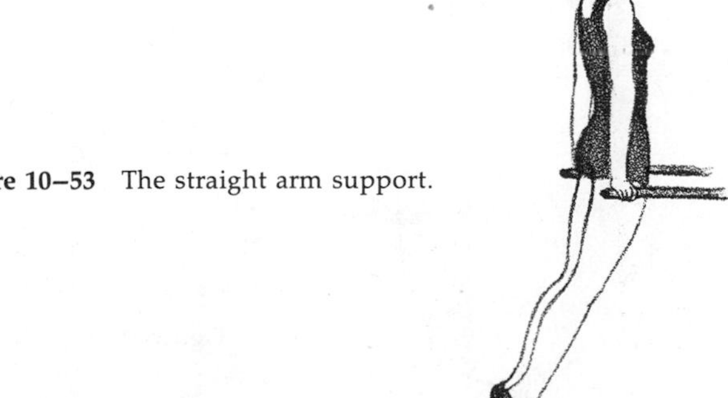

Figure 10–53 The straight arm support.

Figure 10–54 The straddle seat.

Separate them and straddle the bars, bringing your body up into an erect sitting position, holding on to the bars with each hand behind your back. Raise both arms horizontally, and fully extend both legs, keeping your feet pointed toward the mat (Figure 10–54). To travel the length of the bars, lean forward, placing your hands on the bars in front of your legs, whip your legs backward and over the bars to a straight arm support position, and then go forward into another straddle position.

The Back Roll to a Straddle Seat. Begin by standing facing out between the bars at the end, grasping the bars in an overgrip. In one continuous motion bring your legs up sharply, coming into an inverted hanging position arch your back, fully extend your body, and move your face back away from the mat. Then, by circling around the bars, go into a straddle

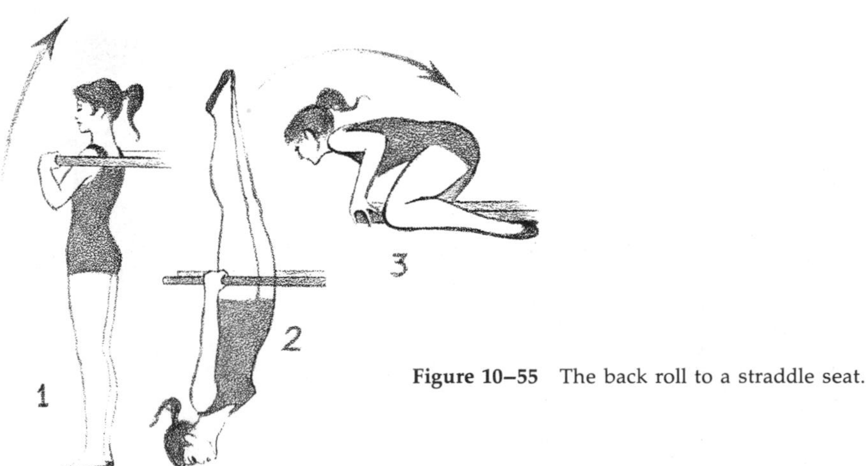

Figure 10–55 The back roll to a straddle seat.

Figure 10–56 The forward roll.

position Sit with your arms out to your sides with palms up, legs and feet fully extended.

The Forward Roll. From a straddle position, bend forward, placing both hands on the bars ahead and go into a forward roll. Come up over on the upper arms, and when your body starts to come down, place your hands close together behind your back to make a bridge to roll your body across, and end up in a straddle position (Figure 10–56). The use of a spotter for this stunt is recommended.

The Shoulder Balance. Get into a straddle seat position and place your hands on the bars in front of your body. Lean forward, placing your upper arms on the bars, and slowly lift your legs and body into shoulder balance position. Straighten your body into full extension, arch your back and point your feet upward.

The Single Leg Flank Dismount. Begin from a sitting position with your body facing sideward on the bars, the right leg over the forward bar and right hand holding on to the bar, palm facing out. Rest your fully ex-

Figure 10–57 The single leg flank dismount.

Figure 10–58 The double leg dismount.

tended left leg and foot on the rear bar and keep your left arm and hand fully extended and slightly back. Swing your left leg and arm up around and over both bars as you push on from the front bar and dismount to the mat.

The Double Leg Dismount. Swing your body back and forth several times from a straight arm support. On the forward part of the last swing, bring your body and both legs, feet together and toes pointed out, up and over the right side of the bar. Dismount to the mat.

CLASS ORGANIZATION

The class should be divided into squads of five to ten students, preferably fewer, of similar ability. Members of a gymnastic team, if available, or more highly skilled students should act as squad leaders or teaching assistants. The teacher should move freely around the teaching area to give needed assistance, increase individual motivation, and check to see that correct spotting methods are being used. When the class is ready to learn any new basic skill or stunt, it is best to have everyone except the individual or group demonstrating and the instructor seated or otherwise grouped to observe. Basic instruction is effective in groups followed by small squad practice. A student can improve only by her individual effort and practice. Individuals will progress at widely varying rates, and the more advanced students must be identified so the instructor can work with them on selected skills and pieces of equipment. The teacher must be ever alert to see that the more daring students have first mastered the basic skills that are prerequisites for any new stunt.

The apparatus used should be stationary, and squad groups should be rotated so that each group has an opportunity to learn how to use each piece. When teaching stunts and tumbling skills, it is best to arrange several mats in a circle and have students do activities and stunts across the mat, moving as a single group. After completing a stunt in one direction, the squad can turn about, and repeat the stunt in the reverse direction. With this spoke arrangement, students can easily see and hear the teacher. She, in turn, can quickly reach anyone needing special help. This is especially so when standing on the outside of any part of the spoke.

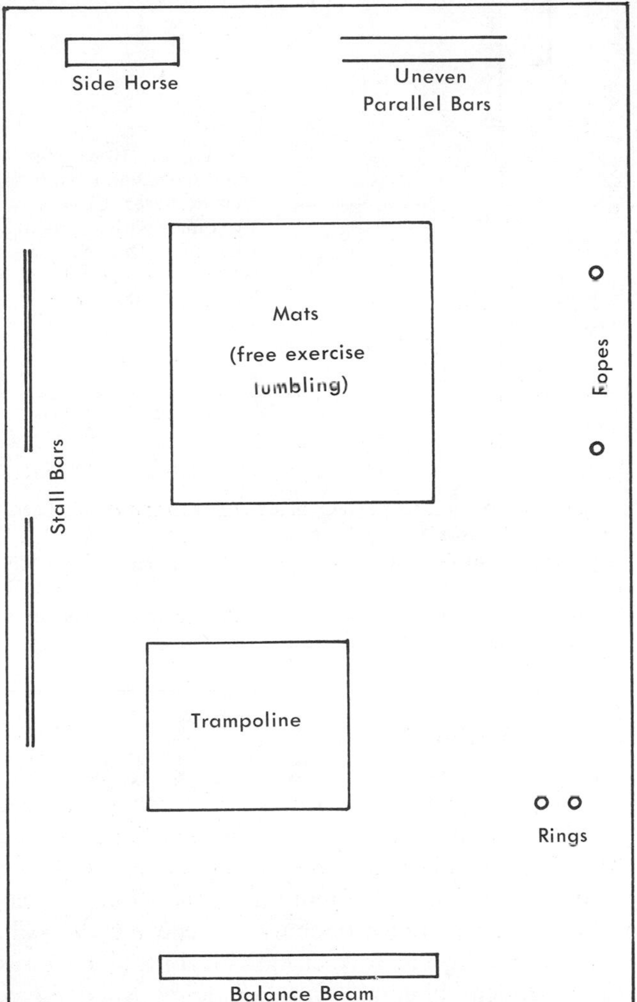

Figure 10–59 Suggested placement of equipment for teaching tumbling and gymnastic activities.

Every class should begin with warm-ups and free exercises. The use of strength developing exercises such as push-ups, sit-ups, leg raises, and back arches should be followed by having each student work on perfecting such free exercises as front and side scales, single leg circles, handstands, and backflips. Students should follow one another closely when working on all apparatus as a means of fully using all class time. For most balancing stunts, partners should be paired so that the topmost person weighs least.

Enthusiastic student participation will result when the teacher:

1. Shows and clearly tells how to do each stunt or movement and can quickly diagnose learning snags or the cause of faulty movements.

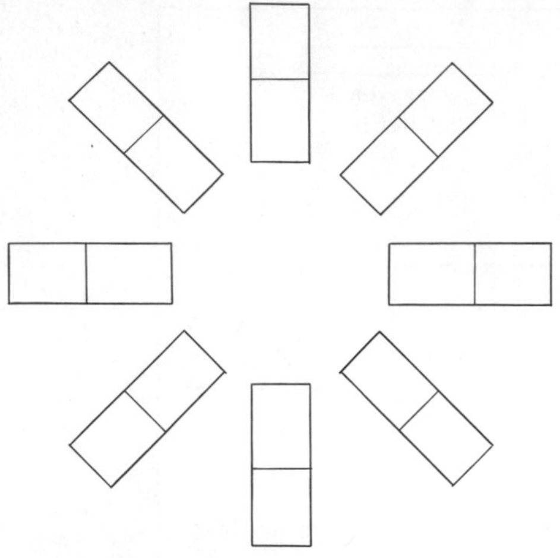

Figure 10–60 Spoke arrangement of mats for teaching stunts and free exercises. Class may be divided by squads with a student leader to use each mat. The teacher should stand where she can see the entire class and move from there to help those needing help.

2. Encourages each person to perfect basic skill fundamentals before attempting more difficult tasks.
3. Develops a competitive as well as a cooperative spirit within each individual, squad, and class.
4. Individualizes instruction so that each student gains a sense of security, accomplishment, and greater challenge.

TEACHING PROGRESSION

Unlike most sports, gymnastics is made up of many different kinds of skills which are performed on several different kinds of equipment. Progress of an individual or class in mastering floor exercise skills and stunts on each piece of apparatus is dependent on the individual's strength, coordination and perception of the proper way to execute the skill, and the teacher's ability to identify and correct individual problems—to challenge and motivate the student while assuring her safety. Adequate equipment and practice time are obviously essential. Suggested skills to be mastered in each area of gymnastics are found below:

Exercises with Rhythm Balls

Throw forward and up, with the ball in both hands, then in alternate hands
Throw under one knee, then alternate knees
Throw overhead and catch
Bounce, catch, throw straight up and catch
The bodywave
Swing, throw, and catch
Forward, backward, and sideward bending with swings and ball throws
Throw the ball with 180 degree turn
Forward diagonal step with armswings and throws

The Balance Beam

Mounts and dismounts
Running, skipping, turning on the beam
Forward roll
Backward roll
Headstand
Shoulderstand
Catwalk forward
English handbalance
Front, knee, needle, and side scales
Split
The back shoulder roll

Mat Work and Tumbling

Elementary forward and backward rolls
Headstands
Handstands
Cartwheels
Headsprings
Handsprings

Rebound Tumbling

Straight bounce
The tuck
The jackknife
Jump and turn
Knee drop
Seat bounce
Backdrop
Hand-knee drop
Front drop
Front to back to feet drop
Swivel hips
Back flip to seat
Front flip

Free Exercise

Toe stand
Ballet positions
Pirouette
The body sweep
The stag leap
Arabesque
Single leg balance
The balance stand
Needle scale
Jump to handstand
Yogi handstand
Front walkover
The backover
Forward drop
The shoot through

The Even Parallel Bars

Straight arm support
The riding seat
The straddle seat
The backward roll to a straddle seat
The forward roll
The shoulder balance
Single leg flank dismount
Double leg dismount

The Vaults

Squat vault
The side vault
Squat stand dismount
Straddle vault
Straddle stand and jump
Handspring vault

The Uneven Parallel Bars

Straight arm support
The shoot over the low bar
The cross seat mount
The back pullover mount

Poses and Movements

The low bar balance
The crotch seat
The swan
The swinging hip circle
The thigh rest
The low bar scale
The arch back
The side cross hand balance

The Dismounts

The front vault dismount
The single leg side vault dismount
The quarter twist dismount
The underswing dismount from the high bar
The double leg dismount

The following lesson plans are both detailed and comprehensive. They are ambitious for all but the most skillful student. The teacher will find that students improve at different speeds and develop specialized interests during the instructional unit. The progression is designed to cover basic tumbling, free exercise, balance beam, vaulting, and uneven parallel bars. Depending on the skill of the students, each lesson may have content for several class meetings.

Lesson I

1. Brief history of gymnastics
2. The purpose and value of gymnastics
3. Safety procedures
4. Explain and demonstrate the use and care of equipment
5. Show film strip on beginning women's gymnastics
6. Have students write down any questions they have concerning film strip and bring to next lesson

Lesson II

1. Review previous lesson, giving special emphasis to safety procedures
2. Question and answer session about film strip previously shown
3. Demonstrate and have class do selected warm-up exercises
   - Arching
   - Backward leg raise
   - Push-ups
   - Sit-ups
   - The bridge
   - Headstands
   - Cartwheels
4. Demonstrate and have class learn on mats the front and side scales and single leg circles

Lesson III

1. Warm-up exercises
2. Divide class up into squads of 5–10 or less, according to similar ability
3. Arrange mats in a spoke, one squad to each
4. Explain, demonstrate, and have class perform forward roll, backward roll, and several rolls in succession
5. Move from squad to squad, giving individual help where needed

Lesson IV

1. Warm-up exercises
2. Repeat previously learned stunts on mats
3. Learn handstands
4. Balance beam
   - Walk from one end of balance beam to other, jump off
   - Walk on tiptoe from one end of beam to other, jump off
   - Walk backward on beam
   - Walk backward on beam on tiptoe
   - Jump and turn
   - Practice a variety of mounts and dismounts

Lesson V

1. Warm-up exercises
2. Balance beam
   - Repeat previous lesson
   - Skip
   - Take small jumps forward
3. Springboard training
   - Springboard with mat
   - Short slow run, last step about a yard from springboard (depending on speed and size of performer) make low jump, straight up in air, land feet on mat, knees slightly bent

Lesson VI

1. Warm-up exercises
2. Mat work
   - Handstand
   - Cartwheel
   - Backflip
3. Balance beam
   - Walk to middle of beam, swing one leg forward, standing foot on tiptoe, turn 180 degrees and walk backward to other end of beam. Walk to middle of beam, stand on right foot, arms extended forward, shoulder high, raise left leg backwards from hip to front scale position. Repeat, using right leg. Walk to end of beam, jump down to the side and come to resting position, hand resting on beam
4. Review springboard training
5. Vaults
   - Squat vault
   - Side vault

Lesson VII

1. Warm-up exercises
2. Mat work

Lesson VII *Continued*

Practice handstand
Cartwheel
3. Free exercise
Toe stand
Arabesque
Balance stand
Single leg balance
4. Repeat balance beam skills
5. Vaulting
Review flank vault (side)
Squat stand vault

Lesson VIII

1. Warm-up exercise
2. Mat work
Practice tumbling stunts learned
3. Free exercise
Practice ballet movements of previous lesson
Demonstrate and have class do the forward drop
4. Balance beam
Jump up on one foot to squat position at end of beam. Place hands so far forward there is room for the foot behind. Other leg hanging down relaxed. Stretch to standing. Walk, run, or move forward in short jumps. Sit down in squat position and rise again
5. Continue vault progression

Lesson IX

1. Warm-up exercise
2. Free exercise
Have students combine previously learned tumbling and ballet stunts into a simple routine
3. Balance beam
Repeat previous lesson
Practice sitting down on the beam and rising to standing position
Lying on back, do backward roll
Free exercises

Lesson X

1. Review previous skills learned
2. Allow students to work on favorite stunts
3. Introduce other vaults to more advanced students

Lesson XI

1. Review selected skills
2. Uneven parallel bars
Various mounts and dismounts
Straight arm support
Shoot through over the low bar
Front vault dismount
3. Free exercise practice

Lesson XII

1. Review of previous lesson
2. Uneven parallel bars
Back pullover mount
Low bar balance
Crotch seat
Front vault dismount

Lesson XIII

1. Review and practice of selected skills

Lesson XIV

1. Warm-up with skill practice
2. Uneven parallel bars
Swan
Low bar scale
Arch back

Lesson XV

1. Practice previously taught skills
2. Uneven parallel bars
Thigh rest
Swinging hip circle
Side cross hand balance

Lesson XVI

1. Review of all previously taught skills
2. Performance skill test

TERMINOLOGY

Aerial—Body rotation around a horizontal axis in midair wherein, for a brief moment, body weight is supported by neither arms nor legs.
Approach—The movement of the performer toward the apparatus to be used.
Arabesque—A body position in which one leg supports the weight and the other is raised in alignment with the trunk; arm position varies.
Beat board—A small springboard from which the performer jumps to mount a piece of apparatus.
Combined grasps—Holding on to the apparatus with one hand curled toward the performer and the other away.
Cross support—Supporting the body weight by the hands in the parallel bars by placing one hand on each bar.
Crowhop—A false or double takeoff.
Flank—A movement in which one side of the body is toward the apparatus.
Landing—Jumping from the equipment to the mat or floor and bending the knees, hips, and ankles to absorb the force of the body coming down onto the mat.
Near side of the apparatus—The side approached by the performer for the takeoff or at the beginning of a stunt.
Ordinary grasp—Holding on to the apparatus with the palms facing each other or the backs of the hands toward you.
Overspin—To overrotate the body or any of its parts.
Pike—A body position in which the legs are straight and the trunk is at right angles to them.
Recovery—Regaining body control after a break from a point of contact such as the floor, beam, or bar.
Reverse grasp—Holding on to the apparatus with backs of the hands facing each other or the palms turned toward the performer.
Scale—An arabesque in which the trunk is parallel to the floor; weight may be supported by either one foot or one knee.
Spotter—A person who helps a performer do a routine safely.
Straddle seat—Used on the even parallel bars. The legs straddle the bars and one is placed on each bar either in front of or behind the body.
Takeoff—A preliminary spring done on one or both feet.
Tuck—A position in which hips and knees are bent and knees are pulled toward the chest.
Turn-out—The angle of rotation of the leg in the hip joint.
Twist—A spiral movement along and around an axis of the body.

DISCUSSION QUESTIONS

1. Devise a teaching unit of ten lessons in the use of the uneven parallel bars.
2. Plan and organize a one hour gymnastic show for the public.
3. Read and summarize an article found in the current NAGWS *Gymnastic Guide.*
4. Demonstrate and correct faulty movement patterns likely to be seen when teaching vaulting to students.
5. Devise a ten lesson unit for beginners in the use of the balance beam.

SELECTED AUDIOVISUAL AIDS

Gymnastics for Girls and Women. (4 slide film units.) The Athletic Institute, 805 Merchandise Mart, Chicago, Illinois 60654.
NCAA Gymnastic Meet Films. NCAA, 209 Fairfax Building, Kansas City 5, Missouri. (Rental)
Skills and Techniques of Advanced Gymnastics. Nissen Corporation, 930 27th Avenue, Cedar Rapids, Iowa.
See NAGWS *Guide* for recent films and records.

SUGGESTED READINGS

Amateur Athletic Union of the United States: Official Guide. New York City Amateur Athletic Union, (Current edition).
Baley, James: *Gymnastics in the Schools.* Boston, Allyn and Bacon, 1965.
Cochrane, Tuovi Sappinen: *International Gymnastics for Girls and Women.* Addison-Wesley, Reading, Massachusetts, 1969.
Cooper, Phyllis: *Feminine Gymnastics.* Minneapolis, Burgess Publishing Co., 1968.
Drury, Blanche J., and Schmid, Andrea B.: *Introduction to Women's Gymnastics.* Palo Alto, California, National Press Books, 1973.
Drury, Blanche J., and Schmid, Andrea B.: *Gymnastics for Women* 3rd ed. Palo Alto, California, National Press Books, 1970.
Frederick, A. Bruce: *Women's Gymnastics.* Dubuque, Iowa, Wm. C. Brown Co. 1966.
Gymnastics Guide. Current ed. AAHPER, NAGWS, 1201 16th Street, N.W., Washington, D.C., 20036.
Loken, Newton C., and Willoughby, Robert J.: *The Complete Book of Gymnastics,* 2nd ed. Englewood Cliffs, New Jersey, Prentice-Hall, 1973.
New Gymnastic Skill Charts for Girls: Side Horse Vaulting, Uneven Parallel Bars, Balance Beam, Free Exercises—Balancing and Beginning Tumbling, Free Exercises—Acrobatics and Intermediate Tumbling (one dollar each). Nissen Corporation, 930 27th Avenue, Cedar Rapids, Iowa.
Norman, Randi: *Gymnastics for Girls and Women.* Dubuque, Iowa, Wm. C. Brown Co., 1965.
Roys, Betty Maycock: *Gymnastics for Girls and Women.* Philadelphia, W. B. Saunders Co., 1969.

SUGGESTED RECORDS FOR FLOOR EXERCISES

Hector Records HLP3090: "Music for Competitive Free Exercises." Gene Cipriano, Piano, Dick Zuber, Director.
Hector Records HLP4006: "Artistic Gymnastics." (Floor exercises, novice and intermediate) Evelyn Novy, Piano, Mildred Prchal, Director.
Orion Records, Inc. LLP112: "Gymnasts—Music for You." Dorothy Fuchs, Piano, Louise Engstrom, Coordinator.

PERIODICALS

Amateur Athletic Union Gymnastic Yearbook. 233 Broadway, New York, New York.
The Gymnast. P.O. Box 110, Santa Monica, California 90406.
The Journal of Health, Physical Education, Recreation. 1201 16th Street, N.W., Washington, D.C. 20036.
Mademoiselle Gymnast. Sundby Publications, P. O. Box 777, Santa Monica, California 90406.
The Modern Gymnast. Sundby Publications, P. O. Box 777, Santa Monica, California 90406.

CHAPTER **11**

SWIMMING, DIVING, AND SYNCHRONIZED SWIMMING

When and how man first learned to swim is a mystery. Perhaps he swam in search of food, to survive a pursuer, to fulfill a religious rite, or by accident when he fell into water. Pictures on the walls of caves in the Libyan Desert indicate man's ability to swim as early as 9000 B.C. Throughout history there is mention of "bathing" for hygienic, military, or pleasurable purposes, and there is written evidence that swimming instruction was given to select groups in Egypt around 2160 B.C.

The art and skill of swimming as it is practiced today may be traced to Nicolaus Wynman, a German professor of languages, who wrote the *Art of Swimming* in 1538. His description of the breaststroke served as a basis for technique until the desire for speed resulted in adaptations of the sidestroke, side overarm, and trudgen.

It is believed the ancient Indians of the Western Hemisphere were capable swimmers, and some experts attribute the overarm stroke to their technique. Swimming was vigorously pursued in early America, and a swimming school flourished in Boston by 1827.

Great progress has been made in stroke development in the last 100 years. The Australian crawl, American crawl, inverted breaststroke, back crawl, breastroke, butterfly, and a refinement of the trudgen have expanded the interest, skill, and recreational value of this sport. Development of scientific equipment and underwater skills has revealed an underwater world for study and pleasure.

Diving combines the skills of tumbling and swimming into a form of aerial acrobatics. A newcomer to the sports field, the first diving competition was in England in 1905, and today has developed into a skillful and exciting activity for millions.

The development of synchronized swimming has refined a sports skill into an aesthetic art form. The origin of the term synchronized swimming is credited to Norman Ross, who used it when announcing a water show prepared by Katherine Curtis for the 1933 Chicago World's Fair. Prior to this time Germany's floating formations, England's group swimming, and Canada's "ornamental swimming" were largely floating formations with minimal swimming or sculling.

The growth in popularity of synchronized swimming is primarily the result of interest and development of the Women's National Aquatic Forum, the Association of Synchronized Swimming for College Women, and the International Academy of Aquatic Art. The Amateur Athletic Union has sponsored competitive events and has been instrumental in co-operation with Fédération Internationale de Natation Amateur, in encouraging synchronized exhibitions at the Olympic games and the Pan-American games.

Swimming events are especially thrilling to see in the Olympic games, and it is interesting to note that many who win gold medals are young Americans of both sexes.

THE NATURE AND PURPOSE OF SWIMMING, DIVING, AND SYNCHRONIZED SWIMMING

Swimming serves us today as it has for centuries—survival, food, and pleasure. As a healthful and beneficial form of exercise, it attracts more participants of all ages than any other form of sport. Swimming skills are basic to all aquatic activities, from fishing, canoeing, boating, water skiing, synchronized swimming, to skin and scuba* diving and surfing. The age-old struggle for self-preservation and survival is a strong motivating factor in our space age.

Regardless of one's motive in swimming, the principles basic to a co-ordinated stroke are the same. The body, on its front, side, or back, is propelled through water by movements of the arms and legs. Skill development is complicated by the different body position from normal active position and by the human being's inability to breathe under water. Effective stroke development is dependent upon learning to inhale on top of the surface and exhale below the water's surface.

*Scuba is an abbreviation for "self-contained underwater breathing apparatus."

Diving serves to get the swimmer into the water in the most efficient way. Fancy diving is primarily a spectacular and skillful sport.

Synchronized swimming is both a sport and an art form of rhythmical water activity that is performed in a definite pattern and synchronized with a prescribed accompaniment.

Synchronization implies movements of individual swimmers synchronized with vocal, percussive, instrumental or other accompaniment. When more than one swimmer participates, her movements are synchronized with those of other swimmers—either in unison or in a planned order. Basic swimming strokes, modified strokes, and water stunts are the basic techniques the swimmer uses in conjunction with accompaniment.

SIMPLIFIED RULES AND SCORING*

Swimming competition is conducted in dual, triangular, and group meets in which a contestant can participate in no more than three individual events, one team event in dual or triangular competition, and a larger designated number of individual and team events in group and championship meets. Individual events include freestyle, backstroke, breaststroke, and butterfly competition and individual medleys. Team events include medley relays and freestyle relays.

General Rules for competitive racing follow:

1. No swimmer may swim more than one distance of a relay.
2. A contestant begins from the starting marks (in the water on backstroke) at the official's signal. Two false starts disqualify a swimmer or a relay team.
3. Swimmers must keep a straight course to avoid contact with others.
4. Swimmers must execute the stroke properly and make legal touches on the turns and at the finish.
5. As a relay team member a swimmer must not leave her mark before the incoming swimmer touches the end of the pool.

If a swimmer fails to comply with these rules she is disqualified, and her team is disqualified if disqualification occurs in a team relay event.

Form swimming has been dropped as a competitive event, due to time involved and the subjectiveness of judging the events.

The general rules for diving are as follows:

1. A written record of the required and voluntary dives and of the manner of takeoff selected must be presented before the meet begins. Only dives mentioned in the approved table or agreed upon by the officials may be executed.

---

*For complete rules and scoring of swimming and diving see NAGWS *Aquatics Guide* and AAU *Official Swimming, Water Polo and Diving Rules.* For synchronized rules and scoring see AAU *Official Synchronized Swimming Rules.*

2. A diver has one attempt to execute each dive unless the referee rules that the circumstances warrant another attempt.
3. Dives are executed and judged on (1) starting position, approach, and takeoff (all springboard dives with forward takeoff may be performed either standing or running at the option of the diver), (2) height, (3) position in the air, and (4) entry.

Scoring. Places in a swimming meet are determined by the point total of each team. Places in *racing events* are decided by the fastest times. Places in each event are scored on an assigned value for team relays or individual events. These values vary with the type of meet, i.e., dual, triangular, or group. A system for awarding points for tied events is also covered in NAGWS *Guide* and AAU *Official Rules.*

Diving competition is based on the execution of compulsory and voluntary dives, each one being evaluated by three to five judges on a half point scale of 0 to 10. The winner is the contestant earning the greatest point total. When determining a team total, points are awarded for diving as well as for other individual events in a meet.

At the present time most competition in synchronized swimming is conducted under AAU rules. Awards are presented to solo, duet, and team entries. The productions are limited in time (usually 5 minutes) and include required and optional stunts of specified difficulty. Individuals are required to participate in stunt competition (three compulsory and three optional), and their scores are added to the routine score. AAU publishes a stunt difficulty rating scale.

In solo, duet, and team competition judging is based on *execution* and *style.* Execution includes the performance of strokes, stunts, and figures from the standpoint of perfection. Style includes (1) synchronization—with others and with the accompaniment; (2) construction—structure of the routine, interpretation, fluidity, and pool utilization; (3) variety, difficulty, and originality—diversity and creativity in the routine. The techniques of grading are similar to those used in diving. Three or more judges score first on execution and then on style, using a half-point scale from 0 to 10.

NEEDED FACILITIES AND EQUIPMENT

The Swimming Area. Although swimming can be pleasurable in many bodies of water, a sound instructional program should be conducted in a well controlled, sanitary swimming area. Instructors training competitive swimmers and divers should work in 75 foot or meter areas with one meter and three meter diving boards at least 16 feet long and 20 inches wide in a minimum of 12 feet of water. The most common teaching area is a pool, although lake and river fronts serve many camps. An increasing number of schools, recreation departments, and YWCAs are including regulation pools in their building plans. Elementary school children are also being increasingly served by school, private, and commercial pools.

For synchronized work the swimming area should be at least 60 feet by 20 feet, with water at least 9 feet deep in half of the area. This depth is necessary to allow for proper descent in executing stunts. Clear water and a light pool bottom and sides with sufficient overhead light are necessary for viewing by participants, spectators, and judges.

Teaching Accessories. Many instructors prefer to teach without any artificial aids; others like the feeling of security and isolated practice offered by swimming jackets, kickboards, leg floats, shoe fins, and hand paddles. All swimming areas should have minimum equipment for the safety of swimmers. The area dictates the use of ring buoys, bamboo poles, shallow water markers, canoes, boats, and other equipment.

Phonograph equipment, amplifiers, underwater speakers, and adequate lighting are necessary for synchronized routines and desirable for general instructional periods. Properly selected music is helpful in developing relaxation, coordination and stroke rhythm.

Costume. Women should wear full suits which do not interfere with body movements. Competitive swimmers seem to prefer the one-piece nylon or durene speed suits. Caps, although infrequently worn by recreational swimmers, not only protect the swimmer's hair and prevent annoyance, but preserve the natural hair oil and keep hair out of the pool and filtration system. Bobby pins and clips should be removed to prevent loss, falling to pool bottom, and eventual rusting on bottom.

The synchronized swimmer should have a nose clip. This simple clip squeezes the nostrils together and prevents water from entering the nose and sinuses as one executes stunts.

Costumes are important for colorful productions. Their nature is dictated by the composition and the funds available.

Slides or clogs may be used when walking to and from the swimming area.

Regulations Concerning Pool Use. Students and teachers should establish basic safety and sanitation rules for every swimming area. The following is a sample list of rules:

1. Soap shower without suit before swimming.
2. Remove all jewelry and accessories.
3. Expectorate only in designated receptacles.
4. Chewing gum and candy are prohibited.
5. Street clothes and shoes are prohibited in pool area.
6. Running and "horseplay" are not allowed on pool deck and in the pool only with instructor's permission.
7. Persons with ear and eye infections, cuts and abrasions, and athlete's foot are not permitted in pool.

TEACHING UNITS

Suggested topics for a swimming unit include:

Beginners

Value and purpose of swimming
Safety procedures and class conduct
Relaxation and breath control
Jellyfish and turtle floats
Prone and back floats and recovery
Prone and back glides
Prone and back kick glides
Human stroke (optional)
Finning
Sculling
Changing body positions
Elementary backstroke
Rhythmic breathing
Crawl stroke
- Flutter kick
- Overarm stroke
- Breathing

Jump into water
Sidestroke
- Scissors kick
- Arm stroke
- Breathing

Elementary surface dives
Elementary land dives
Treading water
Side overarm stroke
Trudgen
Simple water stunts and games
Evaluation

Intermediate and Advanced

Review safety procedures
Review fundamental swimming and diving
- Trudgen crawl

Back crawl
Breaststroke
- Kick
- Arms
- Breathing

Inverted breaststroke
Diving
Lifesaving skills
Racing starts and turns
Butterfly stroke
Underwater swimming
Advanced stunts, routines and water games
Officiating meets
Evaluation

BASIC SKILLS

No matter the age of a beginning swimmer, there are certain steps of skill development to be mastered.

Water Adjustment and Beginning Skills. The beginner wades into waist deep water, splashing her wrists, body, and arms to lessen the shock and becomes accustomed to the new environment. She should dunk to chin depth, jumping up and down cautiously. Standing with feet apart for balance, she should inhale, hold breath for five or six counts, and exhale. She should then move to shoulder depth, bend forward to submerge her face, and repeat breath holding. Lengthening the time of breath holding, the exercise should be repeated until the beginner shows confidence and has the ability to submerge her entire head. She should then open her eyes under water and count toes, fingers, or objects on the pool floor.

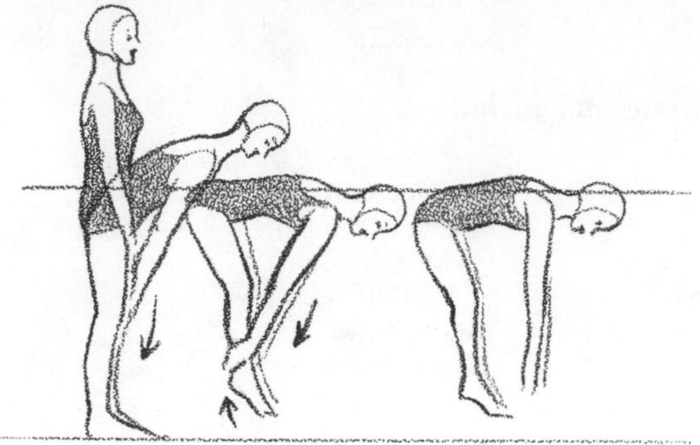

Figure 11–1 Jellyfish float.

Jellyfish Float. In waist deep water bend from the hips, submerge face, and slowly reach for the ankles. As feet rise from the bottom, grasp ankles, hold for three counts, and slowly release. Extend the legs and recover to standing position.

Turtle Float. Begin as in jellyfish float, raising knees to chest, arms encircling knees. Allow the water to move the body, then extend legs and recover.

Prone Float. Assume a turtle float and go to full extension, gently pushing arms forward and legs back. Hold the float ten counts and recover by bringing knees to chest and extending legs toward bottom. The head rises and arms press downward and back as the body becomes vertical.

Prone Glide. Place one foot against side of pool, bend forward at hips, take a breath, and put face in the water. Gently push against the side of the pool and glide forward. Recover to standing position.

Back Float. Submerge with shoulders below the surface, in waist deep water. Raise arms to the sides, palms up. With partner supporting the back of the head with one hand, push off gently. Lift the hips and extend arms, palms up. The head is back and ears are in the water.

A partner aids in recovery until the beginner can return to standing position by dropping the chin forward and bringing the knees toward the

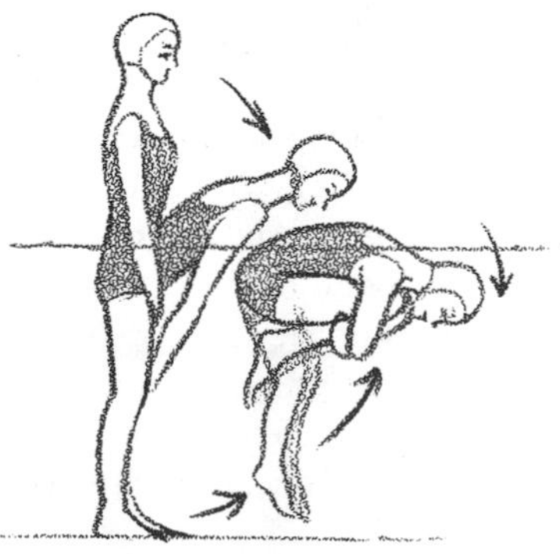

Figure 11–2 Turtle float.

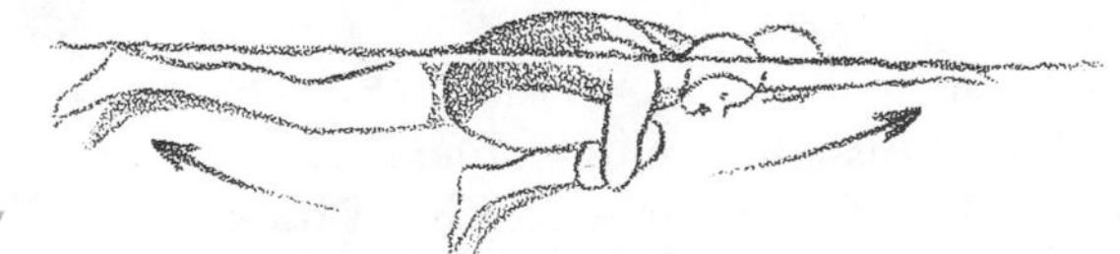

Figure 11–3 Prone float.

chest as the hands move through the water toward the feet and apply pressure toward the surface of the water.

Back Glide. Hold the pool bracket with both hands, facing wall. With head back, ears in the water, draw both feet against the side. (In shallow water push from the bottom.) Remove hands from the side and firmly straighten the legs, pushing away. Hands should be close to the side for balance, and the legs close together. Recover as in a back float.

Kick Glide in Prone Position. With the body in a prone position, the legs move up and down alternately from the hips in a thrashing action with loose knees and relaxed ankles. Emphasis should be on the "up kick."

Kick Glide in Back Position. From a back glide flatten the back, tuck the chin, and look toward the toes. A flutter kick from the hips, with relaxed knees and emphasis on the up kick, moves the body forward.

Arm Movements on the Back

Finning. To combine arm movements with back glide and kick, start with the arms straight and hands at the side. Elbows bend as hands simultaneously move up the body approximately one foot. With fingers pointing away and heel of hand near hips, the hands thrust out and down with a wrist flip to original position.

Winging. In a back glide, hands and arms work together. Begin with arms straight and hands at side. Hands move up, and then elbows bend and follow the line of the body until fingertips are at waist level. Arms extend to side (45 degree angle) and pull to original position. When combined with a resting phase, this is an excellent lead-up for elementary backstroke.

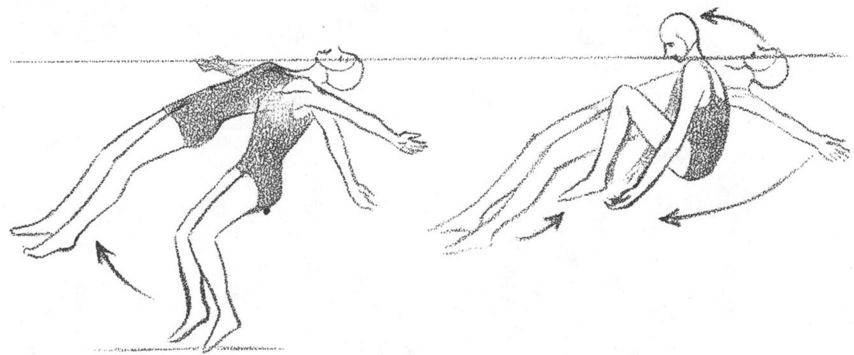

Figure 11–4 Back float.

Sculling. From a back glide, palms near the legs, paired arm action begins by turning hands (rotating wrists) so thumbs are down and back of hands toward legs. Press the hands out and slightly down for about eight inches. Turn thumbs up, and move each hand back to the legs with palms facing body. Keep wrists flexible and arms firm.

Arm Stroke in Prone Position. Take a prone glide position, face in water, arms extended. Pull the left arm below the surface and through the water by directing pressure backward underneath the body. As the pull is being made the elbow bends, and the shoulder relaxes so the left hand touches the midline of the abdomen. As the left hand extends toward the chin and moves underwater toward its beginning position, the cupped right hand and arm begin a similar pattern.

Combined Elementary Movement

The Back. Combine simple flutter kick with finning, winging, or sculling while breathing naturally through the mouth.

The Front. Combined leg and arm movements result in the human stroke or dog paddle. The head is held above the surface with hips below the surface and back arched. The arms reach and pull alternately, recovering below the surface (see "Arm Stroke in Prone Position"). The kick is the elementary flutter with a pronounced knee bend. As the left arm pulls, the right leg bends downward and kicks. Legs alternate with two beats for each arm cycle. Later, three leg beats to a single arm stroke can be developed in preparation for the crawl.

There will be greater stroke efficiency when the face is in the water and raised only for inhalation. Develop a pattern of inhaling from the side and exhaling in the water. If the right side is the most comfortable, turn the head to the right, lifting it slightly for a breath as the right hand pulls through and the left arm recovers. As the right arm begins recovery the face turns into the water and exhalation begins.

Changing Body Positions and Directions. Confidence and control are gained by the beginner who can move on the front and back and change positions easily.

Turning from Front to Back. From an extended glide position with both arms overhead, bring the right arm down and across the body and roll left as the head turns left.

Turning from Back to Front. Head and shoulders remain low and

Figure 11–5 Human stroke.

horizontal with arms at side. As right arm and right leg reach across the body, both arms extend to an overhead prone position.

Turning Right, Left, or Around. Stop swimming action and allow the body to drop to a near vertical position. Extend hands and pull in the direction of desired change. Return to front or back position and resume stroke.

Treading Water. This is a support skill which has value for personal safety. Combine a scissors, frog, or breaststroke kick with a sculling or finning hand and arm action. Treading is done in a vertical position and requires individualized adaptations.

STROKE SKILLS

Elementary Backstroke. This resting stroke enables one to cover long distances without undue exertion. Since it is easily mastered by beginners, it should be taught after the horizontal float. The body is on the back with head up, chin slightly tucked, and ears in the water. The legs are extended and straight with arms at the sides, palms downward.

Arms. The hands begin the stroke as they move up along the side, thumbs close to the body, elbows bent, and shoulders back. As the fingers reach toward the armpits, the wrists rotate, and the fingers lead the arms upward and outward to a "V" position. The arms pull firmly back to the starting position in the power phase and then rest as the body glides through the water.

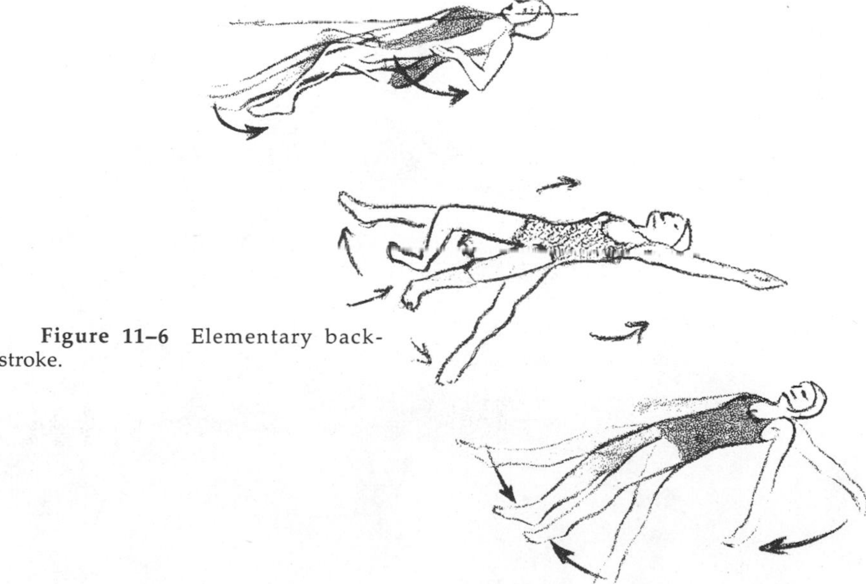

Figure 11–6 Elementary backstroke.

Legs. In the back glide position, the legs are fully extended and are held together. The knees bend, and heels are drawn toward the body with soles of feet toward the bottom of the pool. When the heels are in a position directly beneath the knees, the feet are flexed and turned so toes are pointing to the sides. The feet move to a position wider than the knees (knees will separate slightly during this phase), and the feet and lower leg move outward. The power phase is a sweeping outward and backward as the lower leg and foot are pushing back against the water. The power phase ends when the legs are back in glide position, and toes are pointed.

Breathing. Breathing is regular, with inhalation during the recovery and exhalation as the body moves.

Coordination. The stroke is done underneath the surface of the water to a smooth flowing count of four—(1) up——(2) out——(3) together——(4) glide—1, 2, 3, 4. The body coordination on each of the counts is: (1) arms and legs are drawn up on the first phase of the recovery action; (2) arms and legs are spread outward; (3) arms and legs are in the power phase simultaneously; (4) glide.

Crawl Stroke. The crawl is an efficient and graceful speed stroke using the flutter kick and overhand arm action with rhythmical breathing.

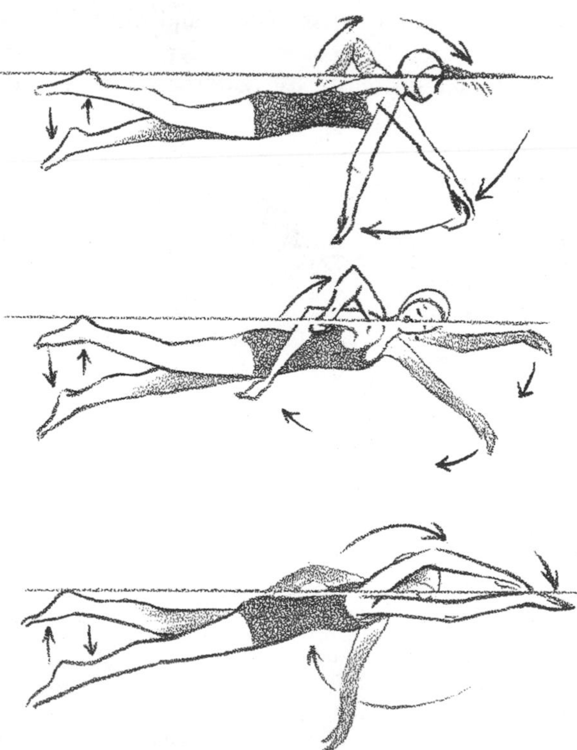

Figure 11–7 Crawl stroke.

The body is in an extended prone position with the face submerged so that the surface of the water is just below the hairline. The chin is slightly up and away from the neck.

Arms. With both arms extended forward, the left arm "catches" the water and pulls firmly through it, applying pressure backward underneath body and toward feet. As the arm pulls through the water, the elbow becomes bent with full flexion at a point directly beneath the shoulder. The arm continues to push beyond the perpendicular, and as the hand pushes away from the trunk the elbow is lifted out of the water and the left hand is swung forward in a relaxed manner. The forearm is relaxed and forward as the fingers enter the water directly in front of the shoulder and begin a new pull with the cupped hand.

The right arm begins identical action as the left begins its recovery forward. The hands enter the water at a natural arm's length.

Legs. The kick begins with slightly "pigeon-toed" leg extension with emphasis upon the up kick. Right leg bends slightly at the knee as it drops downward from the hip. As the right leg snaps back to extended position, the left leg drops. The action is primarily from the hips with relaxed knee and ankle action. Legs pass close together as they penetrate 12 to 16 inches into the water and rise almost to the surface.

Breathing. Turn the head to inhale as the arm opposite the breathing side is set and forward for support. A quick "bite of air" is taken, the head turns back into the water, and exhalation begins. It continues as the head turns for a breath when the "breathing arm" pulls by the shoulder and the support arm is forward.

Coordination. The complete rhythmical stroke is a coordinated movement of six* evenly measured leg beats to a complete cycle of both arms with a breathing ratio of one inhalation and exhalation.

Sidestroke. A sidestroke is a restful, powerful stroke that is a necessity in executing lifesaving skills. Its mastery makes the overarm, side, and trudgen strokes relatively easy. The sidestroke should be learned on both sides with conventional and inverted kicks. The following description is for the right side.

Ready position is reclining on the right side with the body straight, feet together, and legs extended. The left arm is resting on the side of the thigh of the left leg, right arm is extended in the water, palm down. The head is supported comfortably by the water and right shoulder.

Arms. The right arm begins a diagonally backward pull with pressure going toward the feet. The right elbow comes in near the body, and the hand with palm down leads back to the original starting position (right arm extended forward overhead). The left arm, elbow bent, glides across in

---

*Some competitive swimmers use an eight beat kick; some a four beat synchronized cycle with a breath every two or three strokes.

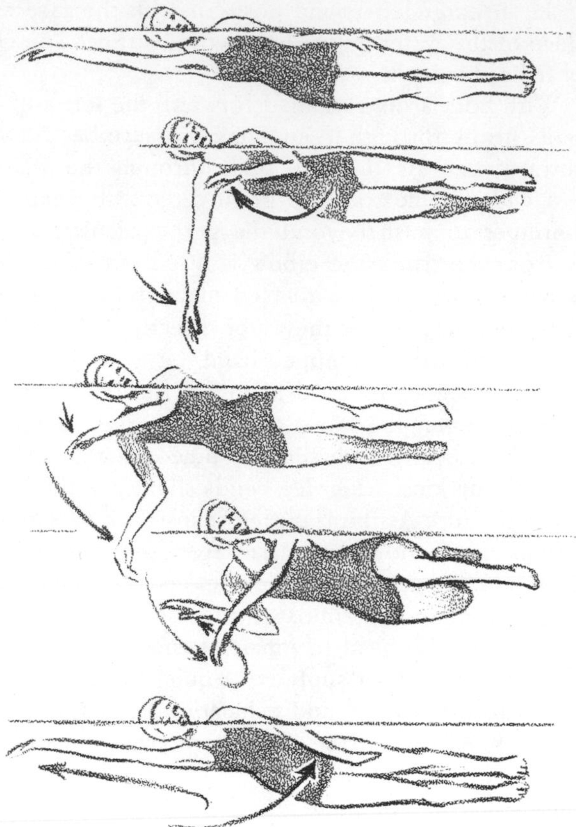

Figure 11–8 Sidestroke.

front of the body toward the right armpit. The left arm catches water and presses toward the feet ending in the original starting position. As the right arm begins its power phase the left arm is beginning its recovery phase. The hands meet approximately in front of the chest, and as the right arm is recovering, the left arm is in its power phase.

Legs. The legs execute a scissors kick. From an extended position the knees flex drawing the heels backward in line with the back. Legs remain close together. The toes lead in a lateral leg extension as the top (left) leg reaches to the front of the body and lower leg behind. Top foot flexes and lower foot remains extended. The legs, still flexed, begin driving backward and together with sole of the top foot and instep of lower foot pressing the water, then meeting, stopping, and remaining extended during the glide.

In the inverted scissors kick the top leg goes to the back of the body and the bottom leg moves forward. It serves as a change of pace and an excellent lifesaving skill for carrying a victim.

Figure 11–9 Side overarm stroke.

Breathing. Breathing is natural, as the head is out of the water. Most swimmers prefer to inhale during the power phase and exhale during the glide.

Coordination. The lower arm pull diagonally backward is the initial movement. Immediately, the top arm begins moving forward, and the legs bend. As the lower arm completes a power phase and the top arm prepares for power delivery, the legs separate and drive as the arms return to starting position.

Ride the glide.

Single Overarm or Side Overarm. The side overarm is a comparatively simple stroke following mastery of the sidestroke. The basic timing is the same in both strokes except for the recovery by the top arm above the surface.

Arms. From the sidestroke position the lower arm begins a pull to shoulder level. As it starts upward the top arm, elbow relaxed, recovers over the water and the fingers enter slightly in front of and above the forehead. Stroke continues as in sidestroke.

Legs. Scissors kick.

Breathing. Same as with sidestroke.

Coordination. The coordination stroke is similar to the sidestroke.

Trudgen. An excellent stroke for distance as it is fast, steady, and not as tiring as the crawl to the average swimmer.

Arms. Overhand (crawl) stroke.

Legs. Single scissors kick.

Breathing. Similar to crawl stroke on selected side.

Coordination. Beginning from a prone glide position, face down, the left arm begins a pull. Legs trail motionless. As the left arm begins recovery the right arm pulls and the legs draw to a modified scissors position. With the left arm forward for support, the body rolls slightly right,

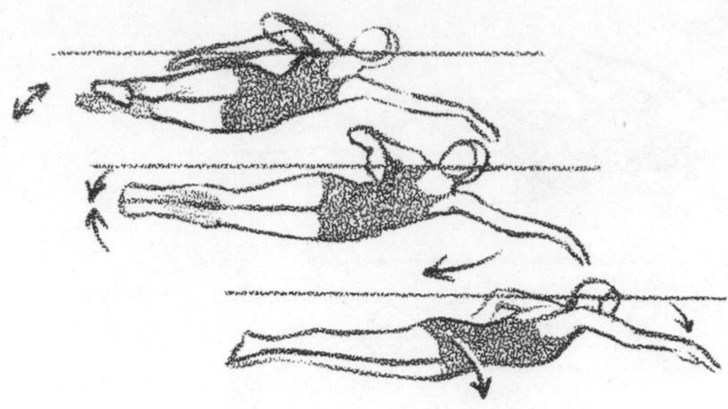

Figure 11–10 Trudgen.

mouth clears the water for inhalation and re-enters the water as the right arm recovers and the scissors kick is delivered. The body has rolled back onto the face, and exhalation continues as arm cycle is completed.

Trudgen Crawl. An efficient stroke using hand over hand arm strokes and scissors and flutter kicks. While executing a trudgen, simply add three or four flutter kicks between scissors kicks instead of allowing legs to trail. When learned from a crawl, roll to the breathing side and add a scissors kick as inhalation occurs.

Back Crawl. This is the fastest stroke executed on the back. In most respects it is a graceful and rhythmical inverted American crawl.

Arms. The arm pull should be a relatively shallow pull with a bent or

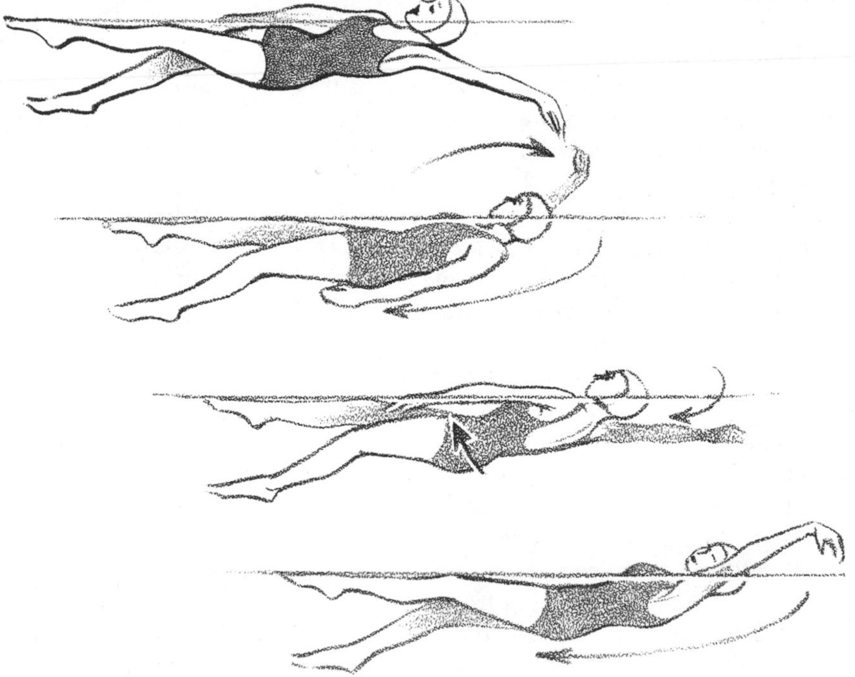

Figure 11–11 Back crawl.

straight arm recovery. The shallow pull, straight recovery is described below. On the back with chin tucked, hips slightly dropped, and eyes focused where toes will kick the surface, extend both arms to a "V" position overhead. The right arm pulls directly toward the right side with palm leading a cupped hand traveling two or three inches below the surface. As the recovery begins, the hand rotates so the palm is away from the body as the little finger leads a straight arm upward and slightly sideward. Wrists are relaxed as the fingers reach toward the water to begin a new cycle. The left arm works alternately and begins its power phase as the right arm recovers.

Legs. The inverted flutter kick is used. With legs extended, one knee bends and the foot drops 12 to 16 inches toward the bottom. A hip lift forces the leg upward, toes extended so instep presses against the water. The toes break the water as the knee remains below. As one leg begins upward pressure the other drops in an alternating action. Six or eight "pigeon-toed" kicks are done with each arm cycle.

Breathing. Since the head is out of the water, inhalation time is optional.

Coordination. As one arm begins a pull, the opposite leg begins a kick lift. A rhythm of six to eight beats is set for each completed arm cycle.

Breaststroke. The breaststroke was the first competitive stroke and has been refined more than any other single stroke. It is basic to the fast and powerful butterfly. The orthodox breaststroke is a smooth, graceful movement done from a prone position. The body is in extension with arms beyond the head several inches below the water with thumbs together and palms down. Legs are straight and together.

Arms. Arm action begins as palms turn outward, thumbs down, and pull begins diagonally backward until arms approach shoulder level. Elbows bend and are kept high, and the hands lead inward toward the chest with elbows coming close to the sides. As the fingers meet beneath the chin, palms down, arms extend forward to starting position.

Legs. Leg action begins from extension, knees draw toward the body, dropping slightly and separating easily. Feet flex outward and reach away from the body. The power and drive is accomplished by a whipping sweep out and backward with ankles and feet extended for riding the glide.

Breathing. As the arms press back against the water on the first movement, there is a natural lift to the upper body that allows for a quick bite of air before submerging the face.

Coordination. Coordination and timing are often difficult. When a four count pattern is used, the following occur:

Count 1: Arms begin press; head rises for breath.
Count 2: Arms move toward chest as legs draw toward body; face submerges.
Count 3: Arms slide forward, and legs whip outward and backward.
Count 4: Glide in extended position.

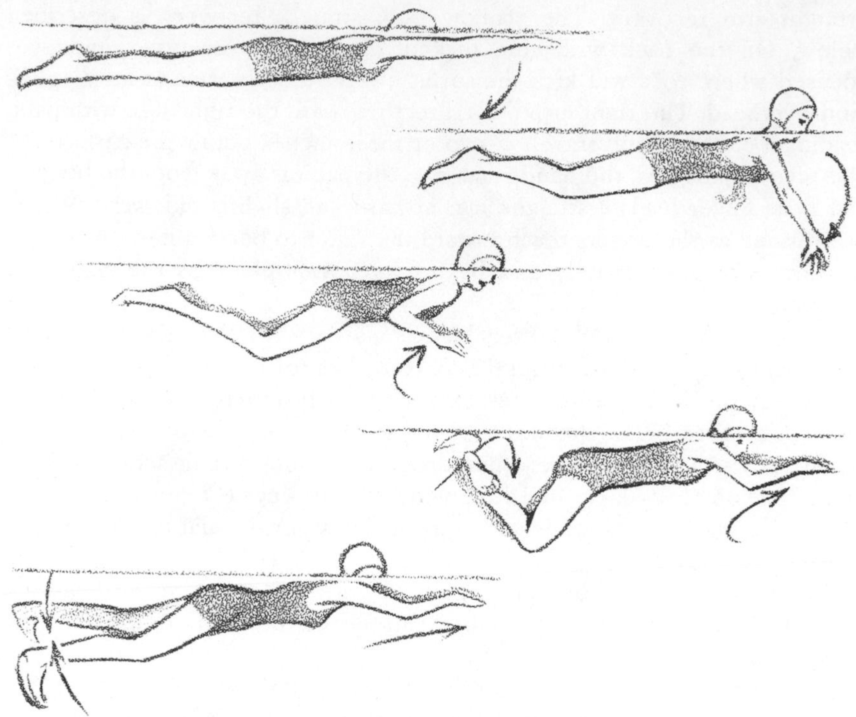

Figure 11–12 Breaststroke.

Inverted Breaststroke. This is a resting stroke similar to the elementary backstroke. The body is flat on the back with legs straight and arms extended beyond the head, thumbs touching.

Arms. Slightly cupped palms turn away from each other and pull out, down, and in to the sides. With arms still several inches below the water the elbows bend outward allowing the palms-down hands to follow the body toward the armpits where the hands turn over and fingers lead past the shoulders and under the head to initial position.

Legs. Knees bend and separate slightly as heels drop toward the bottom. Toes point sideward and back. The legs extend and whip out and together.

Breathing. Inhale as arms pull toward the body and exhale as legs kick and arms recover.

Coordination. Arms come to the sides before legs prepare for the kick. As the arms recover along the body, the legs recover and drive together. The arms then extend to glide position.

Butterfly Stroke. For this stroke both arms must be brought forward simultaneously over the water and brought backward simultaneously and symmetrically. All movements of the legs and feet must be executed

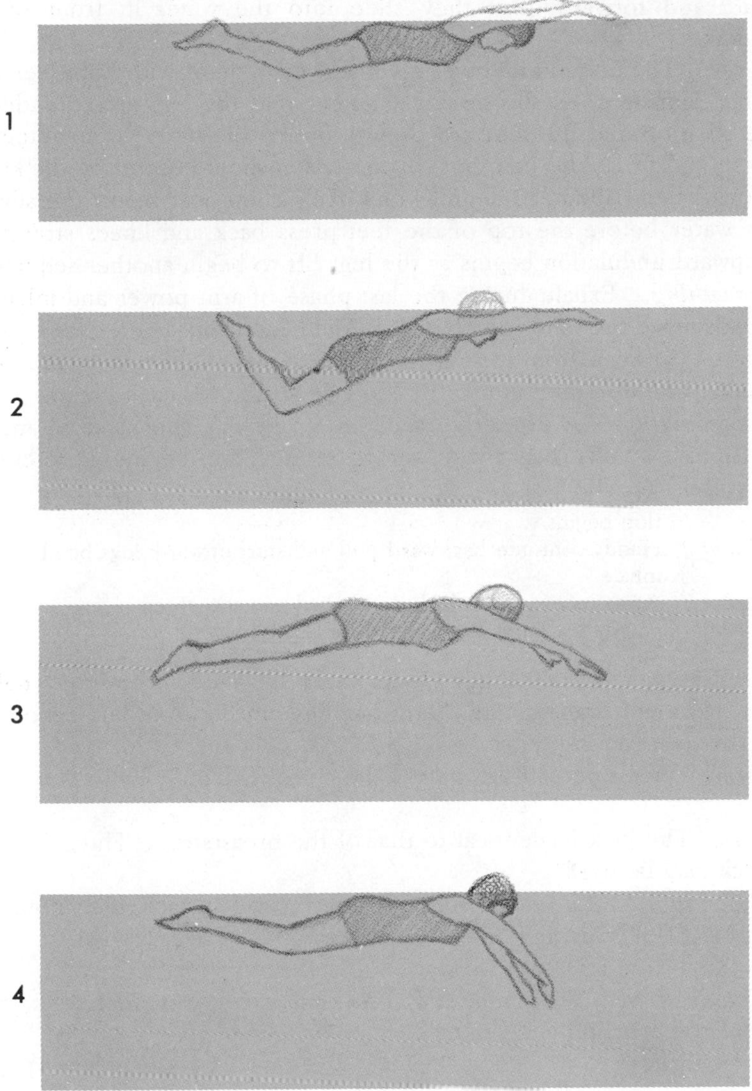

Figure 11–13 Butterfly stroke.

simultaneously. Simultaneous up and down movements of the legs and feet in the vertical phase (dolphin kick) are permitted.

Arms. Arms are extended upward from the shoulders and underwater several inches apart. Palms are cupped and face is downward. Simultaneous arm movement is down and outside the body to shoulder level, where the palms turn and press backward toward the thighs. Arms lift out of the water, upper arm first, with relaxed elbows. The hands circle outward and forward until they slide into the water in front of the shoulders.

Legs. The dolphin involves a vertical movement with both legs held together, similar to the flutter kick, except that the legs are extended in prone position and the feet are drawn toward the body by bending the knees. Hips and ankles flex, but concentration should center on the knees. The knees bend about 30 degrees and heels come just below the surface of the water before the top of the feet press back and knees straighten. The upward undulation begins as the legs lift to begin another sequence.

Breathing. Exhale during the last phase of arm power and inhale as the hands leave the water on recovery. The head is pushed forward, rather than lifted, to keep from raising the torso out of the water. Competitive swimmers often prefer a two or three cycle stroke for each breath.

Coordination. A properly executed stroke has two kicks to an arm cycle. In four counts (begin with arms extended, legs beginning to bend):

Count 1. Arms pull downward; legs push downward and straighten; exhalation begins.
Count 2. Hands continue backward pull and start upward; legs bend upward; inhale.
Count 3. Arms recover; legs kick downward and straighten.
Count 4. Hands placed in the water; legs bend upward.

Underwater Swimming. Underwater skills are increasingly necessary for skin and scuba diving. Many strokes can be used, but a modified breaststroke seems superior.

Arms. Arms pull all the way to the sides with little or no downward pressure.

Legs. The kick is identical to that of the breaststroke. Flutter or scissors kick may be used.

Breathing. Take several deep breaths at the surface, then a normal breath before submerging. Hold the breath as long as there is no tension in the chest, then release it slowly.

Coordination. The timing may be identical with breaststroke or with simultaneous arm and leg action.

DIVING SKILLS

Diving is an exciting skill which should develop with swimming. Before actually diving from the deck or float, students should learn to jump into water of various depths. While in the water, a beginner should push off in a prone glide and direct the body below the surface by dropping the head and arms. By turning the head and hands upward the body rises to the surface. Next, standing in waist deep water with arms overhead, thumbs locked together, the swimmer takes a breath, bends forward at the hips, and pushes up and forward into the water.

Surface Dives. Generally, surface dives are easily learned, since the swimmer is in the water and does not need additional courage for a ledge or board entry. Considerable skill must be developed in the use of hands, arms, and head.

To begin a head-first surface dive with a tuck, the body is in prone position on the surface. Take a deep breath and duck head sharply. As the arms pull back toward the shoulders the body is drawn into a flexed position with knees and hips bent. The arms continue a pull through to the thighs. Immediately the hips and knees straighten above the surface. The weight of the legs above helps the body glide toward the bottom as palms turn toward the head and scoop downward.

The head-first surface dive with a pike is similar to the previous dive except that there is no bend in the knees. As the dive begins, the body bends into a jackknife position. The hips straighten and the legs are extended. The feet are together and the toes are pointed to complete the dive.

The foot-first surface dive begins with the body in a vertical position, arms at sides, palms in. Palms turn toward the bottom and, with a kick, force the upper body out of the water. As the body sinks, the legs come together, the toes point, and the arms turn, palms away, and begin pressure upward against the water as the head goes below the surface. In a completed dive, the body and extended arms are submerged.

Elementary Diving. Diving from the pool deck should follow surface dives. The following progression leads to a standing dive:

Sitting Dive. Sit on pool or float edge with feet braced against the side. Place extended arms overhead, upper arms by ears, thumbs locked

Figure 11–14 Diving progression: *(1)* sitting dive, *(2)* kneeling dive, *(3)* standing one-leg dive, *(4)* standing semi-crouch dive, *(5)* standing stationary dive.

together, palms down. Bend between spread knees, take a breath through the mouth and as the body falls forward gently push with the legs. Bring legs together and straighten and extend toes.

Kneeling Dive. Place one knee close to the edge of the pool and the toes of the other foot over the edge. With arms above head, roll forward toward the water.The head remains down and between the arms, and the eyes are fixed on the entering spot. Alternate knees.

Standing One-Leg Dive. Stand on one leg with toes over the edge, and bend the other leg behind the body for balance. Arms over head and head down, the upper body bends forward and the balance leg lifts, aiming the body downward. Roll into the water bringing the stationary leg up to meet the other.

Standing Semicrouch Dive. Stand on both legs with toes over the edge. Knees are easily bent, arms extended. Bend forward at the hips and push up and into the water.

Standing Stationary Dive. Stand erect with toes over pool edge, legs together and arms at sides. Raise arms forward to shoulder height, bending knees. Lift the heels and push up and slightly out. Drop the head and shoulders between the arms before entering the water. After this is mastered begin in an erect position and swing arms upward as the legs push. Extend legs and toes.

Springboard Diving. Instruction should begin on the 1 meter board. Many teachers like students to progress through a series of jump dives prior to "headers." Foot-first practice should precede each new dive. Beginning dives are done from a standing position at the takeoff end of the board and later with an approach and hurdle.

The Front Jump. Standing several inches from the takeoff end, jump up and down and push (riding the spring) with balls of the feet as the arms reach forward and upward. To keep the body from falling forward, press the head and shoulders back against the arm pull. At first let the arms stay extended overhead for the feeling of lift; later, bring arms down along the sides of the body before entering the water.

Standing Front Header. Preparation for the takeoff is the same as the foot-first entry. Allow the body to follow arms upward then turn over and enter the water with legs together and extended and toes pointed.

Running Front Dive. All running dives have an approach which includes the stance, walk, hurdle, and takeoff. A beginner determines where to begin her approach by placing her heels on the takeoff end of the board and mimetically taking desired steps and a hurdle. Once the spot is determined, begin each dive there unless the approach pattern is changed.

Stance. Stand erect with chest and chin up and eyes focused on the end of the board and the desired height of the dive. Arms are firmly by the sides, palms in, feet together and parallel.

Walk and Run. A minimum of three steps must be taken in the approach and many divers prefer four. The steps are natural, increasing in

Figure 11–15 Running dive.

momentum. The arms move slightly forward with the first step, slightly backward on the second step, and then forward with the third step. The eyes look straight ahead, and the head is up.

Hurdle. As the leg and knee lift for the hurdle, the arms move strongly forward and upward pulling the diver off the board. Both feet then come down together on the end of the board, and the arms move downward toward the hips to add weight to bend the board. As the board rebounds, the legs and ankles straighten, the arms lift upward, and the chin and chest rise. The eyes are on an object at the end of the pool.

Action Position in the Air. The diver leaves the board in an upward and slightly outward direction with arms reaching overhead, legs straight and toes extended. The back arches very slightly.

Entry. The point of entry is in front of the board, directly beneath the body and descending downward toward the pool bottom. In a header, the fingertips touch the water first; the body follows in a straight line at right angles to the water surface. On a foot-first entry the body is erect and extended with arms at the sides.

Fancy Dives

There are five groups of dives as categorized by the AAU and NAGWS: forward, back, reverse, inward, and twist. The handstand group is not given official competitive status. Selected dives from the five groups will be described.

Forward Group

Swan Dive. In competitive events the running front and swan are considered the same. The difference is in the arm movements. As the diver leaves the board her hands are lifted from the hips and spread straight from the shoulders with a slight backward angle. At the peak of the dive the body rotates, and the head slowly drops between the arms as they close for entry.

Front Jackknife. The diver climbs with hands extended. At the end of the reach, the arms reach down as legs and toes are pressed forward with hips higher than the head. Hands contact the feet, and the body remains piked for an instant before the legs lift slowly for a vertical entry with head between the arms.

Forward Somersault. This may be done in a tuck, pike, or layout position. In a tuck the knees are close to the body, in pike position the body is bent at the hips with legs straight, and in the layout the body remains straight and in the same plane throughout the dive.

Figure 11–16 Swan dive.

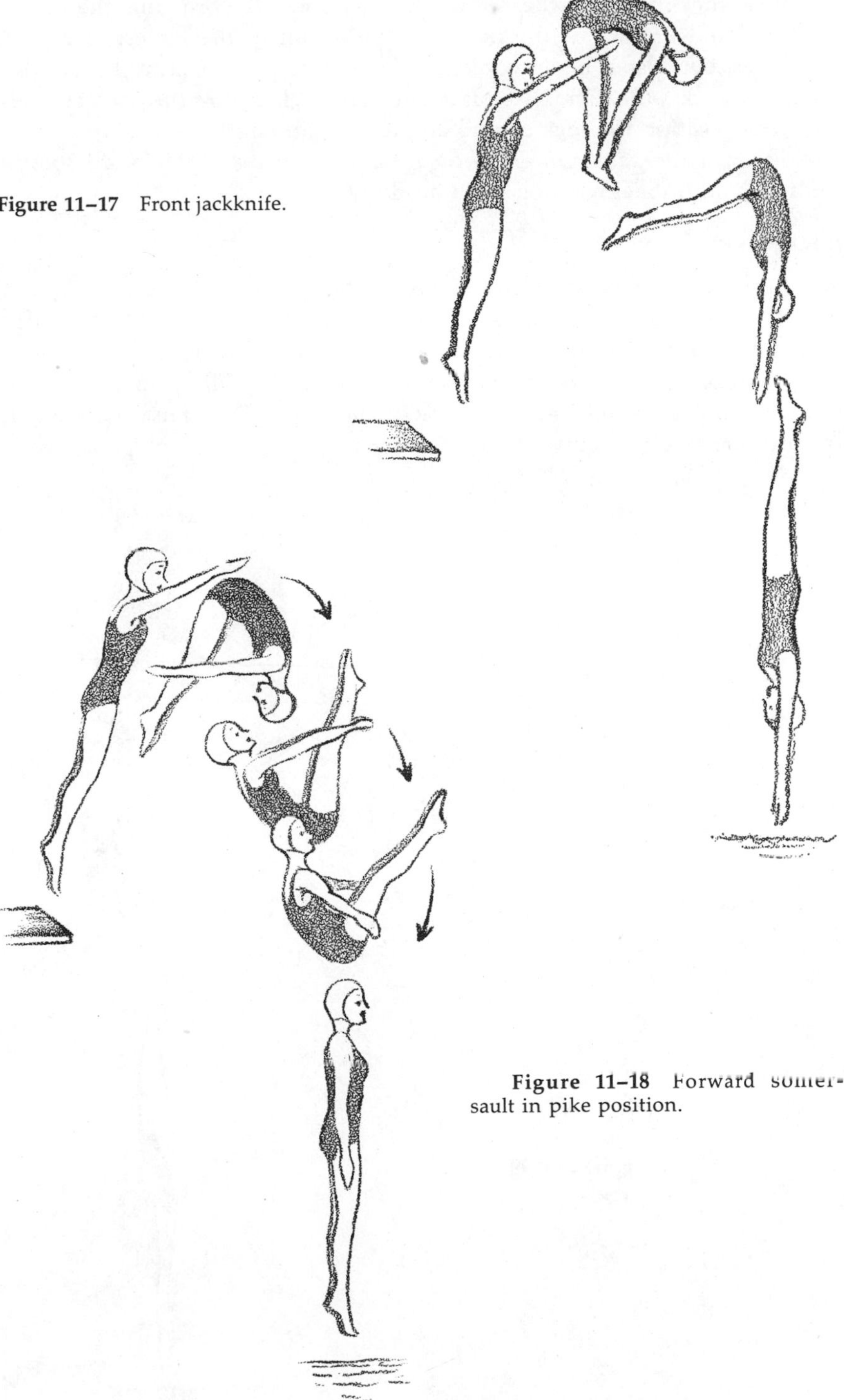

Figure 11–17 Front jackknife.

Figure 11–18 Forward somersault in pike position.

In a tuck or pike the somersault is made by bringing the heels backward and upward as the head and chest pull to the knees. In a tuck the knees bend and heels come to the buttocks with arms below the knees. In a pike, the hands are placed at shin level. Before the body reaches a vertical position the legs extend and feet begin entry.

Forward One and One-Half Somersault. This is like forward somersault with additional rotation for a head entry.

Back Group

Back Dive. This is a standing rather than a running dive. Standing at the end of the board, eyes focused on the back wall, raise arms to shoulder height in front of the body. Toes and balls of the feet carry body weight as heels are extended over the end of the board. To lift from the board, lower arms to side and lower heels simultaneously. Then raise the arms in front of the face and upward above the head.

Figure 11–19 Back dive.

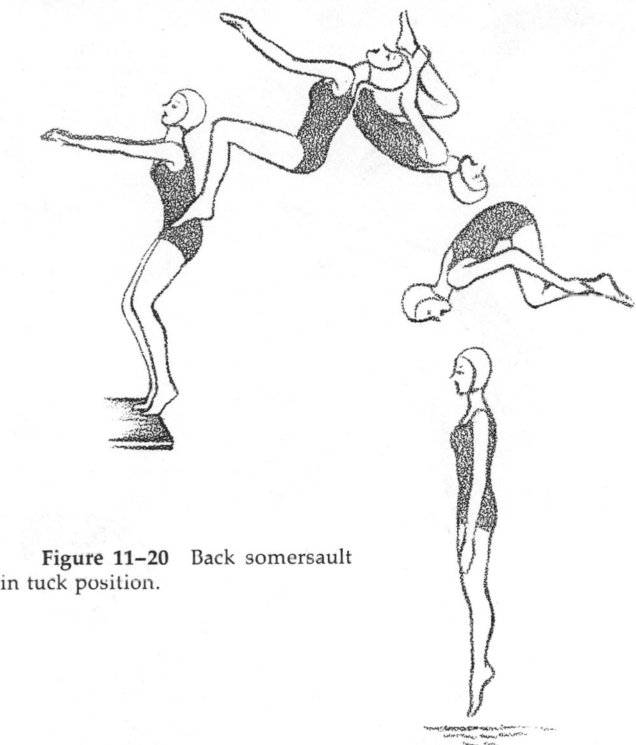

Figure 11–20 Back somersault in tuck position.

The diver leaves the board straight upward with arms extended. At the height of upward momentum, the head stretches backward, the back arches, and the eyes focus on the water. For a swan, the arms move out at shoulder level and come together as they pass the end of the board on descent.

Back Somersault. The back somersault can be done in pike or tuck position. From takeoff position, rise and lift the arms forcibly. Immediately lift the knees to the chest in a tuck or bend at the hips for a pike. Pull the head backward and continue backward motion until the body falls in line for a vertical descent. Straighten legs and point toes downward as arms straighten by the thighs.

Reverse Group

Half Gainer (Islander). The half gainer is a beautiful dive that requires excellent hurdle and takeoff control. Simply, it is a backward dive from a forward takeoff. At the end of the lift with arms in spread position, the head, arms, and shoulders pull backward and the chest, hips, and legs are lifted in stretched position. As the body reaches a horizontal position the legs remain lifted and relatively stationary as arms, shoulders, and head

Figure 11–21 Half gainer.

Figure 11–22 Back jackknife.

continue rotation downward. The arms are brought close to the head at board level and lead a vertical entry.

Inward Group

Back Jackknife. Begin as if a back dive. Lift from the board, forcing hips upward, and bring hands down to touch the instep in pike position. Raise hips and legs and lower the head between the arms for head-first entry.

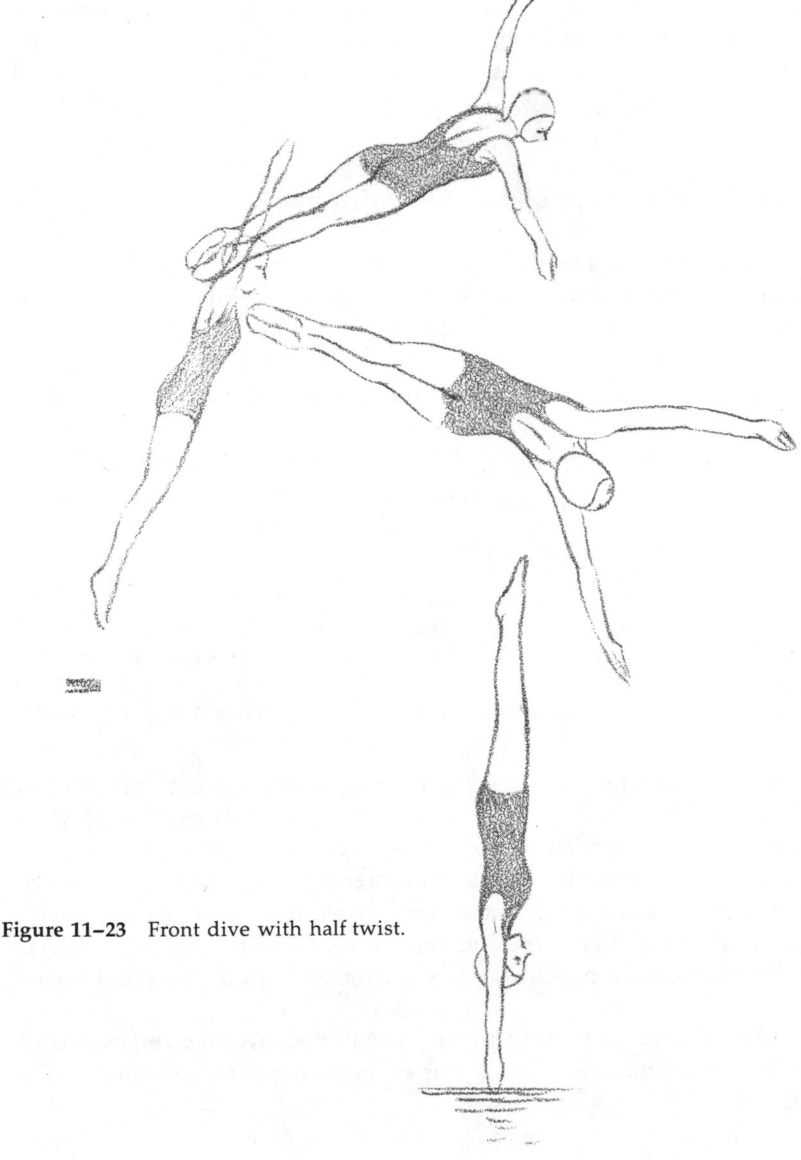

Figure 11–23 Front dive with half twist.

Twist Group

Half Twist. Takeoff as in a front header with arms reaching up and out from the shoulders. At the peak of the reach, if the twist is made to the right, lower the right shoulder and direct the right arm toward a spot of entry in the water. The head turns, and the eyes focus on the lowered right arm. Entry into the water is straight with back toward the board.

Full Twist. Rise from the board in a swan position. If twisting to the right, thrust the left arm across the hip and downward. Raise the right arm above the head as legs bear upward during rise and descent. A half twist is completed while rising and continues as the head turns forcibly to the right and the left arm extends by the head with the right arm upon entry. In a piked dive with a twist, the twist must not start until there is a marked pike.

SYNCHRONIZED SWIMMING SKILLS

Swimming strokes and techniques termed "stunts" are the basic skills of synchronized work. Five strokes, often modified, provide the methods of moving from place to place in a manner in keeping with the atmosphere of the composition. A swimmer should develop strong standard strokes of crawl, backstroke, elementary backstroke, sidestroke, and breaststroke. The inverted breaststroke may also be helpful.

Basic Stroke Modification. All strokes must be adapted so that:

1. The face is above the water to observe other swimmers and hear the accompaniment if there are no underwater speakers.
2. The arms are carried higher for effect.
3. The legs kick deeper. They are lowered by raising the head and arms in order to prevent a splash of the kick at water level.
4. Only the head and arms are visible above the water. The arm action is frequently seen and must be timed, directed, and positioned in keeping with that of others.
5. Breathing can be timed and conditioned for the stroke and in preparation for a stunt.

Stroke Variations. By varying the stroke the pattern may become more interesting and more in keeping with the accompaniment. Such variations include accenting parts of the recovery (e.g., extending the top arm in the sidestroke and holding it above the water before entry), changing arm actions above the water (e.g., in the front crawl, recovering forward, withdrawing the arm, and finally entering the water), on a change in the action of the stroke itself (e.g., a two-arm overwater recovery in the inverted breaststroke).

Combined and Hybrid Strokes. Combined stroking refers to complete strokes performed in a series. For example, a front crawl, followed by a backstroke, and then a breaststroke.

Figure 11–24 A floating formation.

Hybrid strokes combine parts of two or more standard or modified strokes to set a pattern, rhythm or effect. For example, begin with a backstroke left, turn to a sidestroke left, turn to a backstroke right, and roll to a sidestroke right.

Duo Skills. Once the modified standard strokes and selected combined and hybrid forms are learned, swimmers begin working in pairs to accompaniment. They may be attached or unattached. Unattached pairs swim in vertical, horizontal, or staggered lines. *Tandem* swimmers are directly behind one another doing identical or complementary actions. They may be attached at the neck, under the arms or at the waist.

Floating Formations. Swimmers maintain these so-called "floating" formations by sculling or other hand motions. Groups of from two to 16 or more swimmers make a colorful presentation, whether in a stationary pattern or one moved by other swimmers.

Fundamental Positions Basic to Stunt Execution. These positions are defined, for they represent basic starting positions for stunt execution.

Layout Position (Supine Position). Contract the abdominal muscles so that the small of the back is as flat as possible. Keep the back of the head in a straight line with the spine. Toe tips, ankle bones, hip bone, shoulders, and ears are in a straight line. Hands begin in a flat sculling position.

Vertical Body Position. The body alignment is the same as in layout position except that the body is vertical in the water. This position is used for stunts that involve a lift or descent from the pool in a straight line.

Back Layout Position. This position is similar to the layout position. The head is lifted slightly forward, chin in, shoulders back and relaxed. Thighs and feet are close to the surface of the water.

Front Layout Position (Prone). Lying on the face, contract the abdominal muscles. The body is slightly arched, head above the surface, and heels at the surface. Arms and hands are under the body near the sides, in basic sculling position.

Pike Position. The body bends sharply at the hips. The legs are extended and the toes pointed sharply. To tighten the pike the head moves close to the knees, and the hands close to the ankles.

Tuck Position. The knees bend as the thighs pull into the chest. Toes are extended and the heels press against the buttocks. The head is positioned close to the knees and the back is rounded.

Sculling. This movement is basic to skill development in synchronized swimming. It is estimated that there are nine types of sculling, all using either a flexion or hyperextension of the wrists and a small outward push and inward pull of the hands beneath the surface.

To control the body in a floating formation or in a back layout position in preparation for a stunt, the arms are close to the body, and the hands are near the surface with fingers and wrists level during the *flat scull.*

The *standard scull* moves the body toward the head when in a layout position (supine). The arms are at the sides with elbows close to the body; hands are at the hips. Paired arm action begins so that palms turn down and out and press outward through arm action. The thumbs turn up, then the palms are whipped toward the feet and back to starting position.

Sculling feet-first with the *arms at the sides* is accomplished by turning the palms out and pulling against the water in a small semicircle away from the feet and toward the head. The wrists relax to complete the circle and return to original position.

When sculling with the *arms and hands overhead* so that the body moves *toward the feet*, the palms are turned away from the body, and pressure is applied outward and downward. The hands move no more than the width of the shoulders. The palms face each other and the thumbs touch on the recovery. This is often called *propeller sculling.*

For *reverse sculling* the hands are lifted behind the head with the same hand position described for sculling feet-first. At the beginning of the outward pull, the backs of the wrists touch. At the end of the inward movement the fingertips are facing. The body moves toward the head.

To scull so that the body moves *sideward*, one arm pulls in the desired direction as the other pushes.

To *circle* around the head or feet, one hand pulls or pushes near the pivotal point to maintain position as the other pulls or pushes with larger sweeping sculling motion.

Surface Dives. A review of surface dive execution, particularly the foot-first entry, will be helpful at this point.

Simple Stunts. A stunt may be performed above, on, or below the water level. There is difference of opinion concerning the difficulty of learning and executing these stunts. The following progression is suggested:

Tub. Begin from a back layout position with a flat scull. The knees are drawn to the chest so that the hips sink and the swimmer is sitting in the water. The toes are extended and the lower legs remain near the surface. The sculling motion of the hands turns the body in a circle.

Back Tuck Somersault. Begin from a back layout position. Draw the knees to the chest; legs remain together and toes are pointed as the hips sink. The body drops backward as the arms press down, back, up, and forward in a circle. The body remains tucked until the somersault is completed and legs then straighten to starting position.

Front Tuck Somersault. Begin from a front layout position. The knees are bent and pulled toward the chest as the head is dropped forward toward the bottom of the pool. Palms turn out, and arms press outward, backward, and upward and then downward and forward. After a complete turn the body returns to starting position.

A somersault in a *pike* position is executed in a similar way, but the body is bent only at the hips. Legs remain together, knees extended and toes pointed.

Corkscrew. Begin in a front layout position with one arm at the surface extended in front of the head and the other arm at the side. The body rolls around the extended arm by turning the head and body in the direction of the turn and away from the extended arm. The side arm sculls for additional pull.

Porpoise. This is similar to a surface dive in a pike position. From a front layout the trunk bends at the hips as the head moves forward and downward. The arms (positioned at side or forward) scoop sideward and downward. As the hips are brought over the head the back straightens and the legs are brought up perpendicular to the water surface. The hands sweep forward to maintain this position. The hands then pull the body below the water in this vertical position. Once under the water the recovery begins by lifting the head, arching the back, and pulling in the direction of the surface.

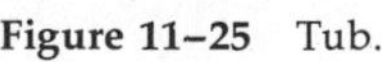

Figure 11–25 Tub.

Flying Porpoise. The figure begins with a vertical foot-first surface dive to the bottom of the pool. Flexed knees and ankles push the body to the surface. When the upper half of the body is above the water, the body assumes a pike position to execute a porpoise. Once started, there is no break in the movements.

Side and back porpoises, after the body "flies" from the water, are variations.

Dolphin. Begin in a back layout position. The shoulders and upper back arch as the arms extend and execute a scooping movement outward and upward to pull the body gracefully downward. The body describes a large circle as the arms continue the pulling action (down, around, and up) to return the extended body to original position.

Flying Dolphin. From a vertical foot-first surface dive the body lifts halfway out of the water. Execute a dolphin from the top of the lift.

Shark. Begin with the body in a side layout position. The body arches and the top arm extends overhead in a continuing arc. (The top arm position may vary for effect.) The lower hand and arm execute a shallow arm pull and with small scooping movements pull the arched body, with locked knees and extended toes, in a wide circle.

Marlin. Begin on the back with arms extended from the shoulders, palms up. To turn left, the right knee bends to the chest and the left arm moves above the head. The body rolls left as the right arm lowers to the thigh to assist the roll. When on the chest, keep head up and again extend arms from the shoulders. Continue rolling in the same direction by pushing downward with the right arm. The arms are at shoulder level at the end of the roll. Return leg to extended position. The stunt may be executed with both legs straight; but in either case, at completion of the roll, the feet remain on the pivotal spot and the body has moved horizontally 90 degrees.

Ballet Legs. To execute a single ballet leg the body is in layout position. The hands execute a flat scull. One leg remains extended at the surface as one knee bends toward the chest and then rises to a vertical position with knee and toe firmly extended. The leg bends back to the chest

Figure 11–26 Dolphin.

Figure 11–27 Ballet leg.

and is extended to starting position. Legs should be alternated to develop equal skill.

A *double ballet leg* is accomplished by simultaneous (paired) leg movements. With the additional body weight over the hips, sculling becomes more vigorous.

Catalina. Begin from a back layout position. Assume a right ballet leg position. Drop the head and turn under the left arm, maintaining the ballet leg as the body reaches a vertical position, with head down. Arch the body and raise the left leg from the surface to meet the right leg. Submerge and recover.

Submarine. Begin from a back layout position. One leg extends vertically as the hands move back and forcefully press toward the surface and

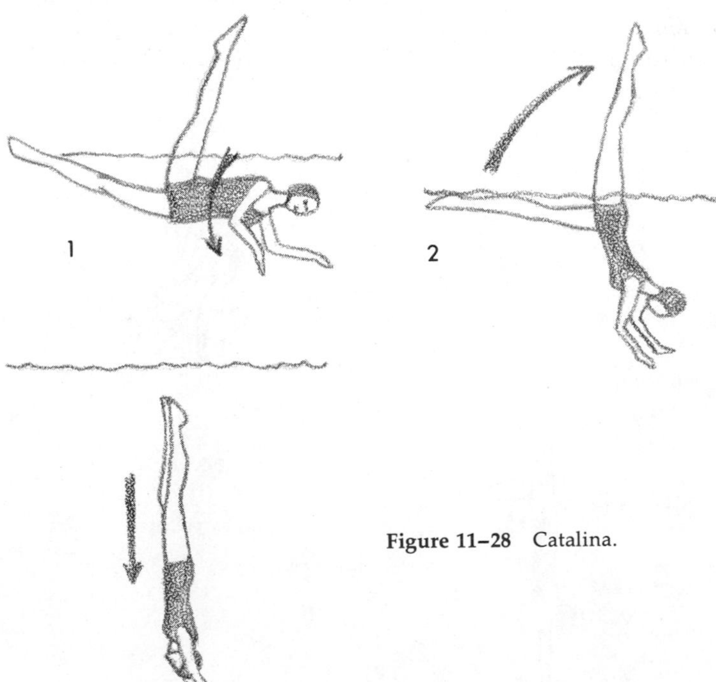

Figure 11–28 Catalina.

Figure 11–29 Submarine.

sideward to pull the body directly down. A portion of the leg may remain above the water or it may submerge completely. Rise to the surface by pressing downward with the palms of the hands.

Oyster. From a back layout position the arms swing down and then up over the head as the hips flex and the body pikes sharply. The hands are near the ankles as the hips lead to a submerged position.

Kip. In a back layout position the knees are drawn sharply to the chin. From this tucked position roll backward by pulling the head down and under the hips while pressing down with the hands. Once the torso is vertical in the water, legs and head extend. Completely submerge, vertically, and recover as in a dolphin.

Variations include a split or scissors with extended legs before submerging.

Somer-Sub. From an extended prone position, begin a pike somersault. When the legs are parallel to water surface the back is toward the bottom of the pool and the face is toward the surface. Extend one leg in a vertical position and the other forward and parallel to the water surface.

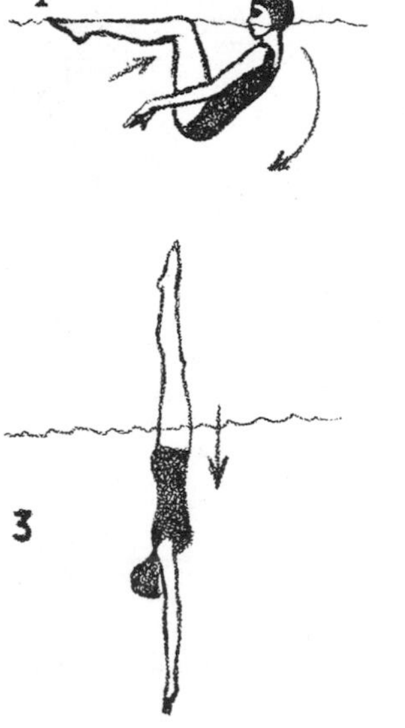

Figure 11–30 Kip.

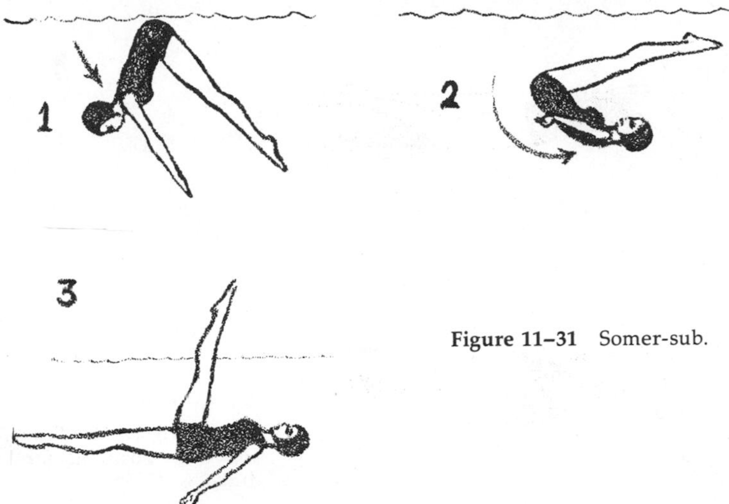

Figure 11–31 Somer-sub.

Rise to the surface with the vertical leg leading. Once on the surface, bend the knee of the vertical leg, draw it to the chest, and then lower it to join the extended leg.

Choreography. The key to success in composing a routine is *simplicity.* Select a theme that expresses a central idea, and then select music or other accompaniment to support this theme. Break the accompaniment into basic phrases so that the swimmer can understand the rhythm and expression of the action. Select stunts in keeping with the performers' abilities. As the central routine is developing, plan strong entrances and exits to reinforce the theme. Next, combine action into phrases in keeping with the accompaniment, and plan for the transition from one formation to another.

Much of the initial work involved with timing and phrasing is best accomplished by land rehearsals. Stunts should be perfected independently and added to the routine later. Costuming and lighting must be planned early and should be kept simple so that they do not detract from the theme and total performance.

CLASS ORGANIZATION

Class conduct is dependent upon the varying skill levels, facilities, and equipment available. Swimming, diving, and synchronized skills are best learned by the whole-part-whole method of presentation. The teacher demonstrates and explains the whole movement, breaks it into component parts for mastery, and then develops the coordinated skill.

Following a progression of land drills and shallow water drills prior to deep water drills, the arms, the legs, and breathing skills are developed.

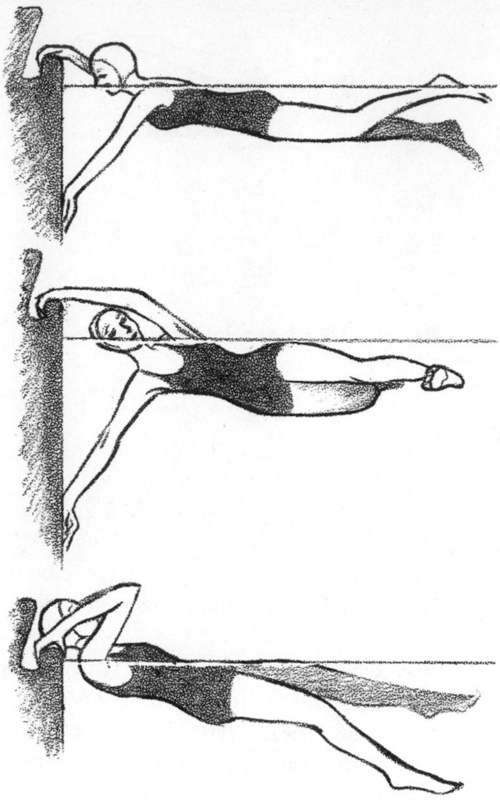

Figure 11–32 Prone, side, and back positions for bracket drills.

Land drills may be done standing, lying on the deck, or partially on the deck leaning into the pool. In shallow water, arm drills can be done in both stationary and moving positions. Leg strokes are practiced in bracket drills at the side of the pool.

In both shallow and deep water, practice formations are helpful in ob-

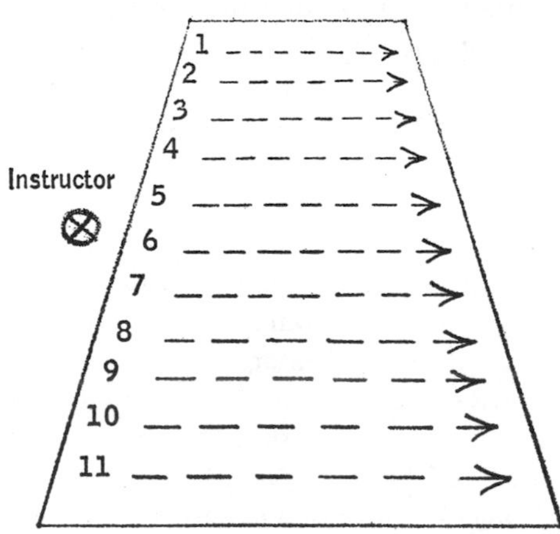

Figure 11–33 Wave formation.

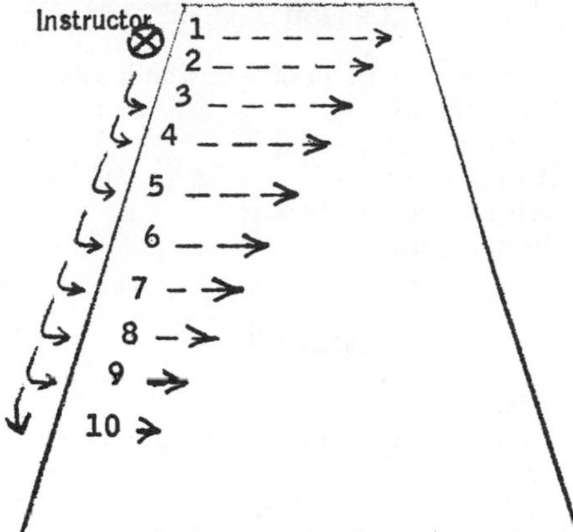

Figure 11–34 Stagger formation.

serving class progress. When mass practice is desirable in a large group, have the class form one, two, or three squads and use a wave formation.

If teachers want to observe each swimmer for a few strokes, a stagger formation should be used.

Distance swimming is accomplished by dividing the pool into lines, or courses, with swimmers staggering their starts to avoid collisions.

TEACHING PROGRESSION

The following plans are suggested for beginning swimmers. Progression will vary considerably, and the teacher should prepare for increasing variance within a class. It is common for some students to be in the early stages of the lesson progression after several weeks.

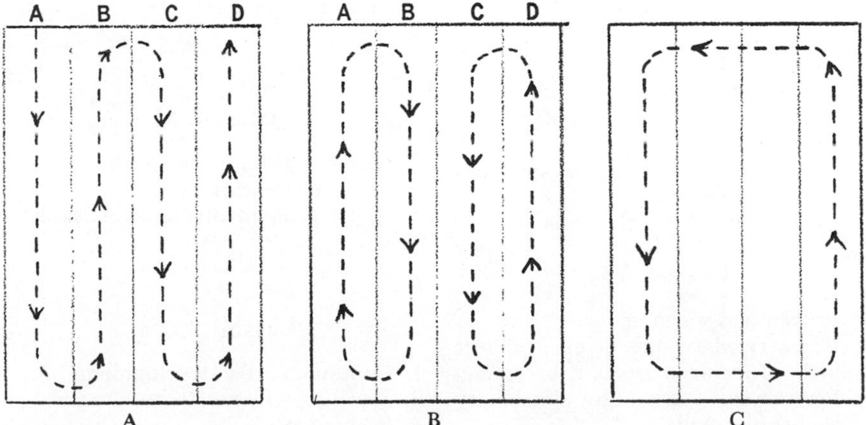

Figure 11–35 Three practice courses: *(A)* long course, *(B)* short course, *(C)* circle course.

Lesson I

1. Explanation of pool rules and class progression
2. Nature of swimming
3. Brief history
4. Adjustment to the water
5. Simple game

Lesson II

1. Warm up
2. Practice relaxation and breath control
3. Jellyfish and turtle floats
4. Prone float, prone glide, and recovery
5. Back float, back glide, and recovery

Lesson III

1. Warm up
2. Kick glides
3. Elementary arm movements
4. Simple tag game
5. Changing body positions

Lesson IV

1. Review and warm up
2. Introduce the human stroke (optional)
3. Jump into shallow water
4. Simple game

Lesson V

1. Review and warm up
2. Finning and sculling
3. Practice elementary backstroke—land and water drills
4. Practice turns and strokes on front to back. Reverse

Lesson VI

1. Review and warm up
2. Begin crawl by practicing a. flutter kick, b. overarm stroke, c. breathing
3. Play a water game using elementary backstroke skills

Lesson VII

1. Review all parts of the crawl
2. Coordinate the crawl
3. Begin elementary diving, perhaps introducing a surface dive
4. Play water game requiring surface dives

Lesson VIII

1. Review and practice coordinated crawl
2. Practice elementary backstroke
3. Continue diving progression

Lesson IX

1. Review and warm up
2. Begin sidestroke, stressing the scissors kick
3. Elementary land dives—sitting and kneeling
4. Free practice

Lesson X

1. Review and warm up
2. Drill arms for the sidestroke
3. Coordinate arms and legs in the sidestroke
4. Continue diving

Lesson XI

1. Distance swim in the crawl
2. Practice sidestroke
3. Water game involving diving skills

Lesson XII

1. Continue stroke development
2. Treading water
3. Evaluation

SKILL DIFFICULTIES AND THEIR CORRECTION

Basic Water Adjustment

Difficulty

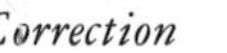

Correction

Difficulty	*Correction*
a. Tension caused by fear	a. Teacher stresses fun and security in the water. Play games and encourage the student with any progress
b. Inability to float	b. Encourage the student to relax. Have a partner help her into a comfortable float. Demonstrate the buoyancy of the body
c. Inability to recover from floats	c. Demonstrate slowly and place hands on student to assist in developing timing

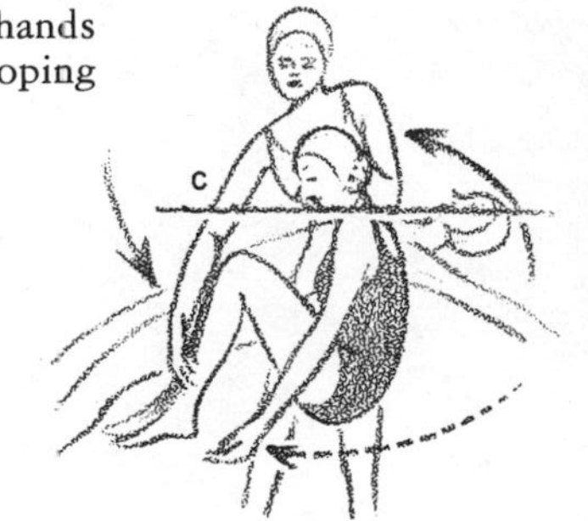

c. Inability to recover from floats

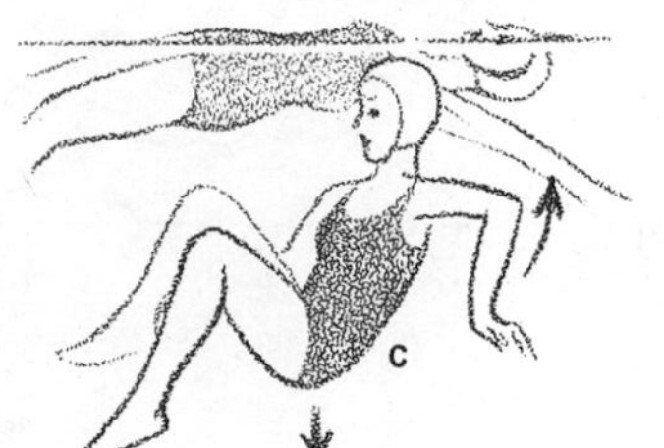

Elementary Backstroke

Difficulty	*Correction*
a. Legs sink or break water	a. Keep the head back and avoid bending at the waist. Suggest the stroke be practiced slowly
b. Arms move upward rather than by side on recovery	b. Explain principles of water resistance
c. Failure to glide	c. Explain and demonstrate the value of the glide in moving the body and as a resting phase

Crawl Stroke

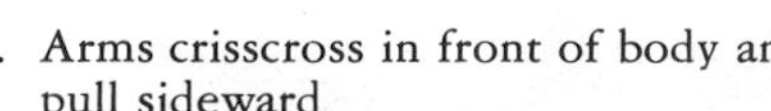

Difficulty	*Correction*
a. Arms crisscross in front of body and pull sideward	a. Teacher may demonstrate the loss of power in the stroke. Tie strings to suit inside the shoulder line so arms cannot cross unnoticed

	Fault	Correction	
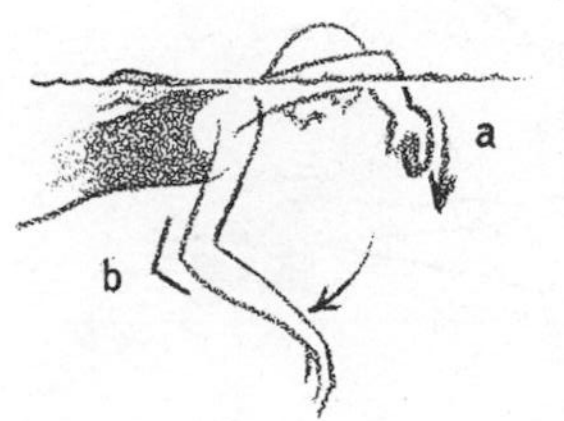	b. Pull is too shallow and done with a bent arm	b. Reach forward and pull back. As the arm comes through the water bend it and pull underneath the body	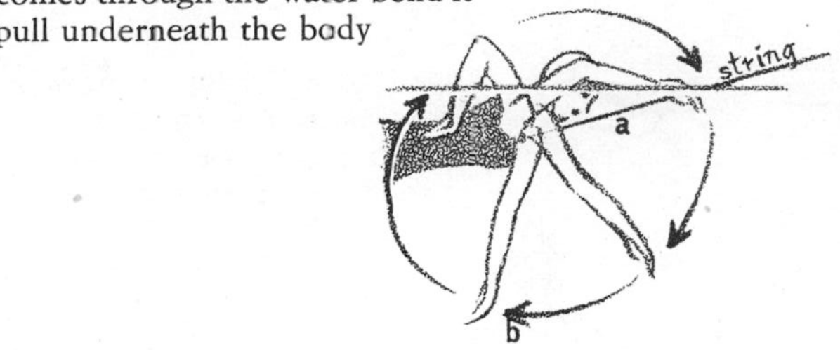
	c. Arms overpull	c. Demonstrate how an overpull makes recovery difficult. Review pattern of the arm stroke	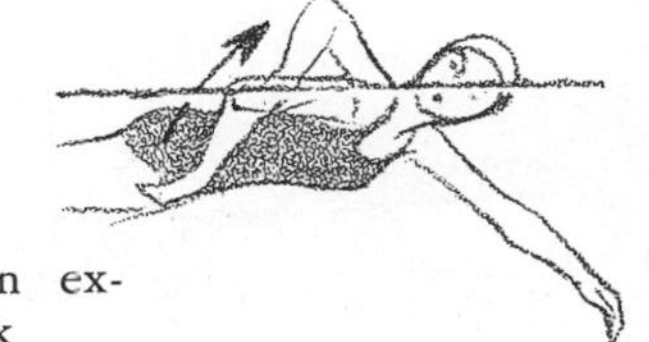
	d. Knees bend too much, lifting feet out of the water	d. Stress relaxed knees, but an extended position with a hip kick	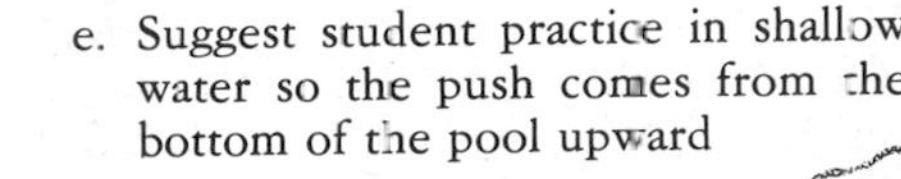
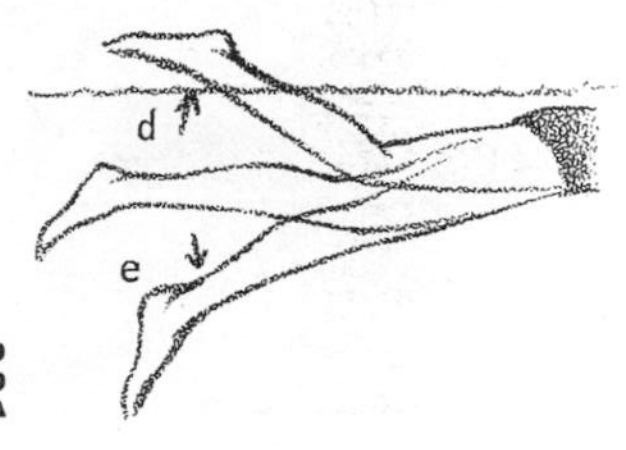	e. Pressing down with legs so body is stationary or moves backward	e. Suggest student practice in shallow water so the push comes from the bottom of the pool upward	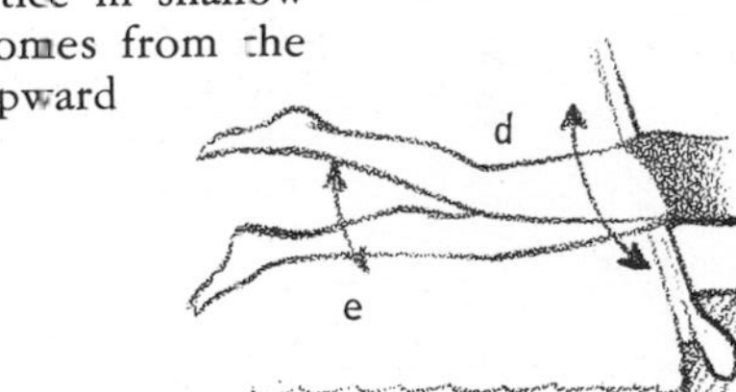

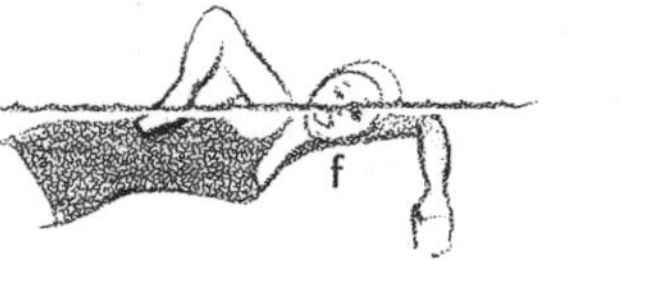

f. Inability to breathe properly

f. Teacher should review rhythmical breathing and have student practice without moving arms or legs. Stress a small "bite of air" through the mouth and exhalation through mouth and nose under water. Have student time her breathing with the stroke of one arm and rotate her head and breathe only when that arm pulls by the shoulder. At all other times the face is kept in the water and exhalation is through the mouth or mouth and nose

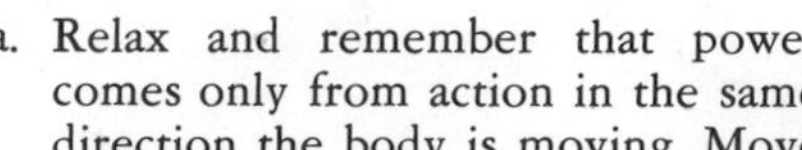

Sidestroke

Difficulty	*Correction*
a. Forcing the legs apart and recovering the knees toward the chest	a. Relax and remember that power comes only from action in the same direction the body is moving. Move heels toward the hips

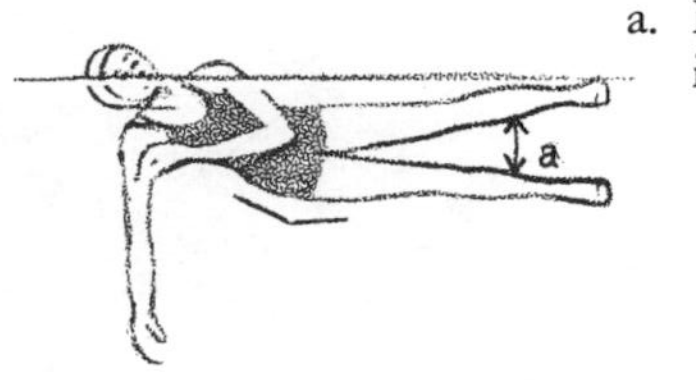

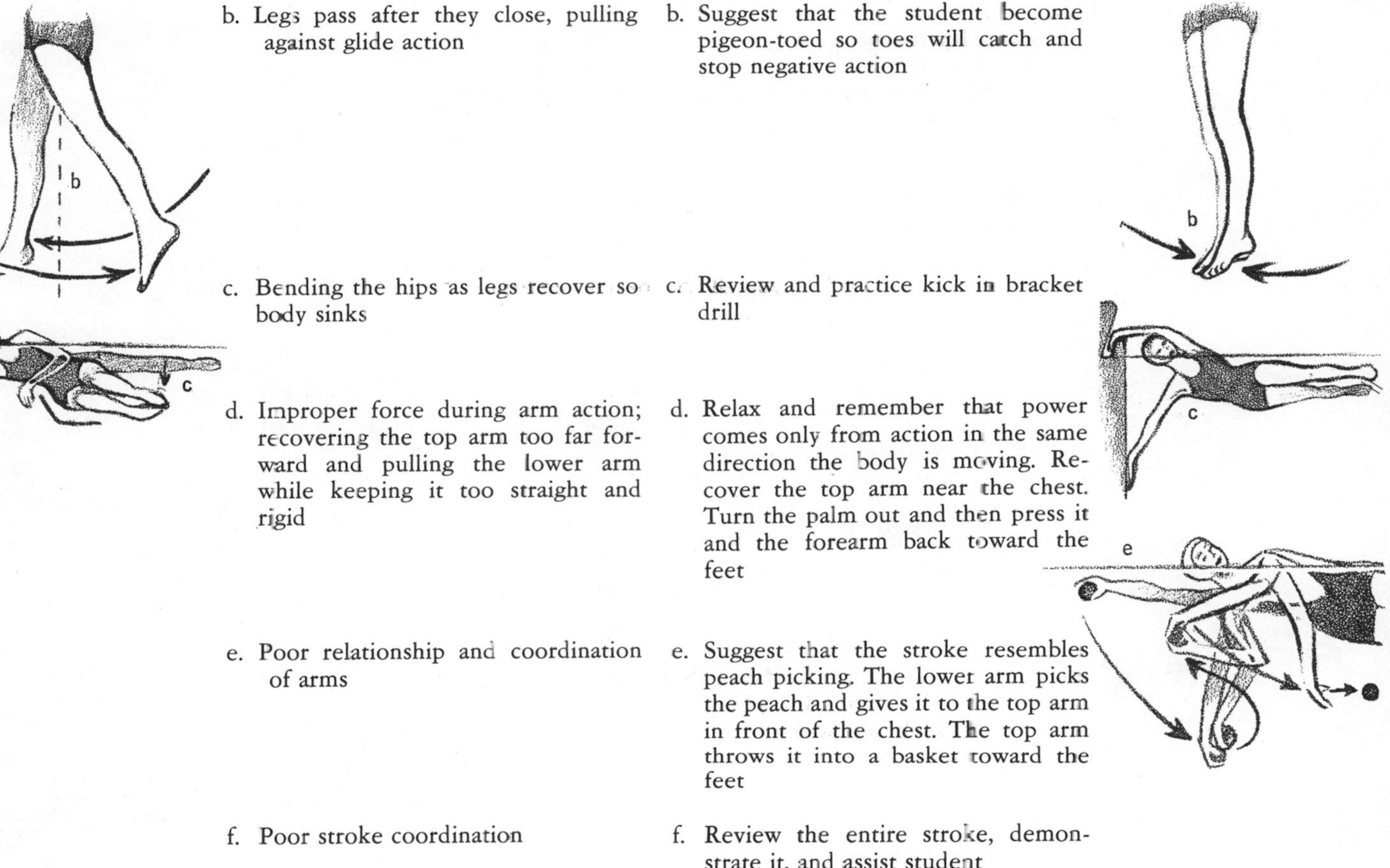

Fault	Correction
b. Legs pass after they close, pulling against glide action	b. Suggest that the student become pigeon-toed so toes will catch and stop negative action
c. Bending the hips as legs recover so body sinks	c. Review and practice kick in bracket drill
d. Improper force during arm action; recovering the top arm too far forward and pulling the lower arm while keeping it too straight and rigid	d. Relax and remember that power comes only from action in the same direction the body is moving. Recover the top arm near the chest. Turn the palm out and then press it and the forearm back toward the feet
e. Poor relationship and coordination of arms	e. Suggest that the stroke resembles peach picking. The lower arm picks the peach and gives it to the top arm in front of the chest. The top arm throws it into a basket toward the feet
f. Poor stroke coordination	f. Review the entire stroke, demonstrate it, and assist student

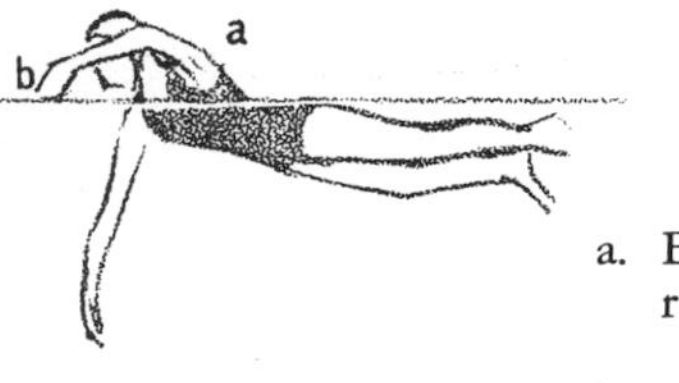

Side Overarm Stroke

Difficulty	*Correction*
a. Body lunges out of the water as arm recovers over water	a. Stress a relaxed recovery with arm low over water
b. Body rolls on face	b. Avoid overreaching

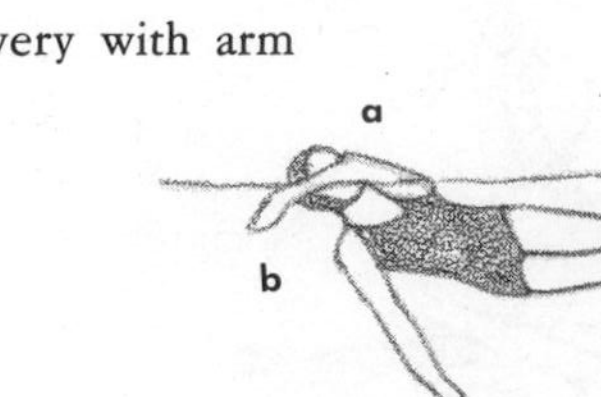

Trudgen and Trudgen Crawl

Difficulty	*Correction*
a. Incorrect coordination	a. Review crawl coordination and demonstrate the insertion of the scissors kick
b. Failure to maintain an "uneven" rhythm	b. Remind student that the scissors kick causes a natural uneven rhythm and a slow recovery for arm on breathing side

Back Crawl

Difficulty	*Correction*
a. Legs are rigid and cause body thrashing	a. Relax. Teacher may suggest that the kick is like riding a very small bicycle. The student should have flexible ankles and "rubber" knees

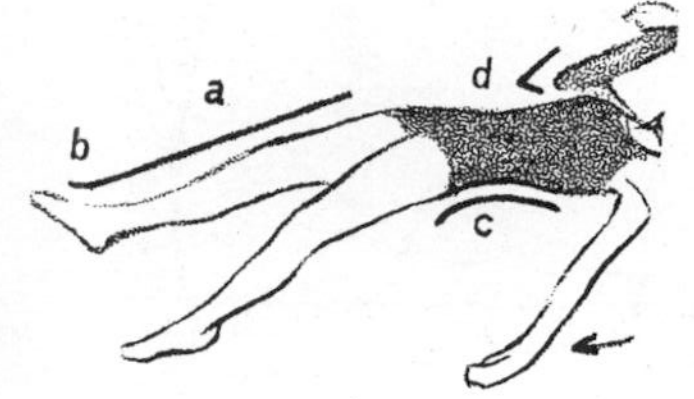

b. Ankles are rigid	b. Develop floppy ankles by pretending there is mud on the instep and the swimmer is trying to kick it off
c. Body is too flat in the water and head too far back or too high	c. Drop hips slightly, tuck chin and look toward the feet. Focus toward the feet and keep the head at surface level
d. Elbows drag through the water on recovery	d. Emphasize the backpull of this error and suggest a lift up and back
e. Completing one arm cycle before the other arm starts	e. Suggest land drills practicing alternating action
f. Hands recovering too far over head causing loss of power pull and stiff body	f. Remind the student that the power comes from the backward pull from shoulders to side. Arms should form a "V" as they enter the water

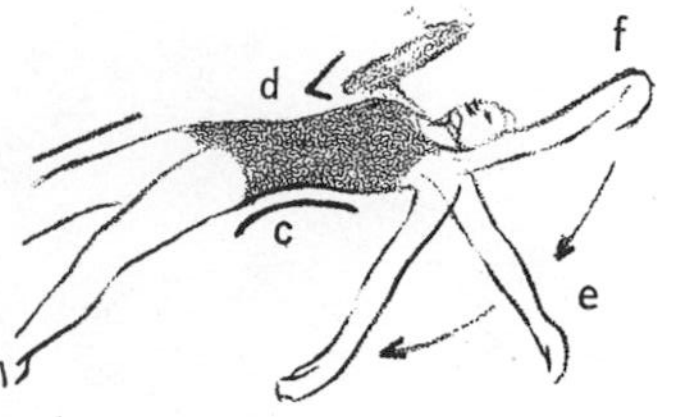

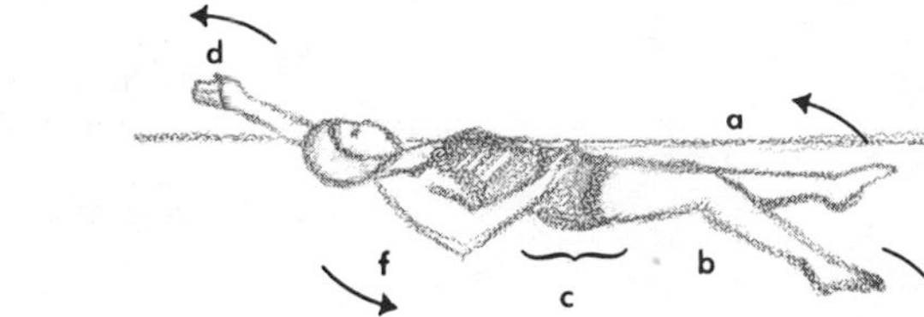

Breaststroke

Difficulty	*Correction*
a. Overpulling arms causing a bobbing motion through the water	a. Review arm stroke stressing an even, relaxed movement
b. Using incorrect kick, generally the scissors	b. Suggest the student practice on pool bracket with body parallel to pool side. Leg movements are paired and identical. Practice with kickboard
c. Failure to glide	c. To prevent the arm pull too soon, student may lock her thumbs during arm recovery and hold for the glide
d. Inability to coordinate, usually due to simultaneous arm and leg action	d. Review complete stroke

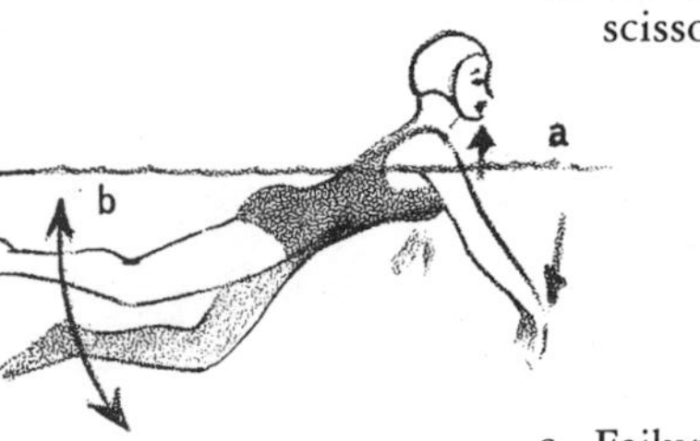

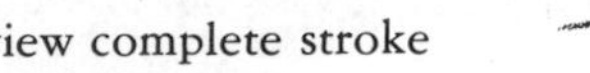

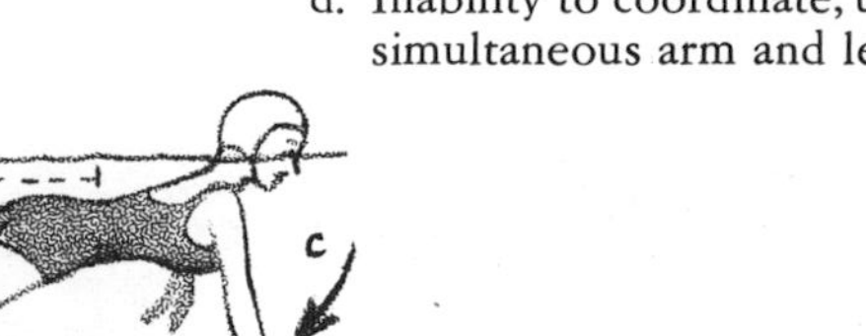

Inverted Breaststroke

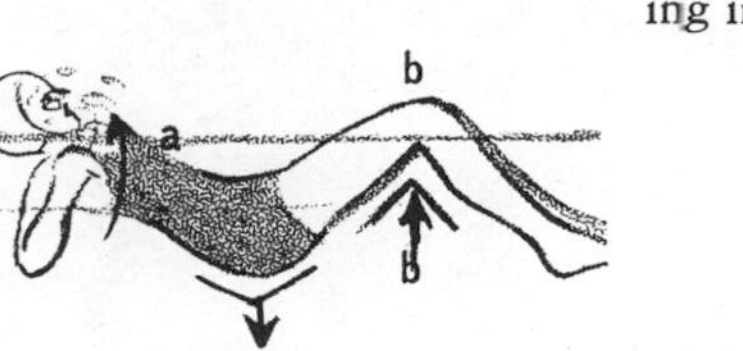

Difficulty	*Correction*
a. Throwing water onto face and upper body as arms recover	a. Arms should recover below the head with slight force
b. Bending knees out of water resulting in body sinking	b. Review breaststroke kick

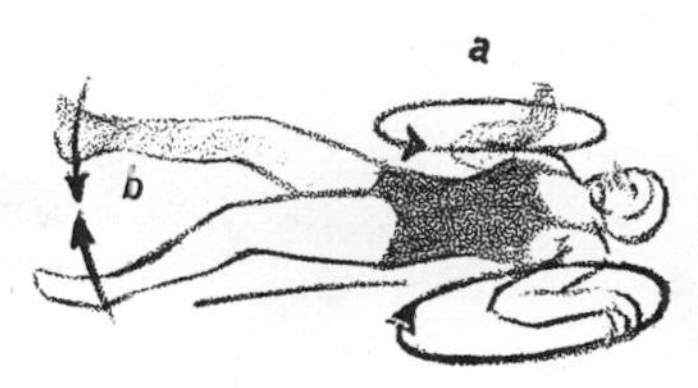

Butterfly Stroke

Difficulty	*Correction*
a. Failure to keep elbows firm on arm pull, thus destroying leverage	a. Pull with firm elbows and arms
b. Arms trail through water on recovery	b. Straighten arms and keep head low in water as arms rotate forward

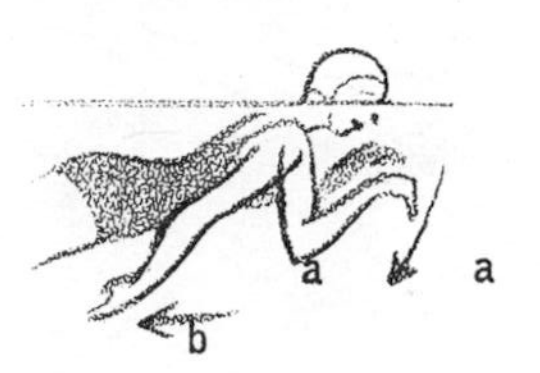

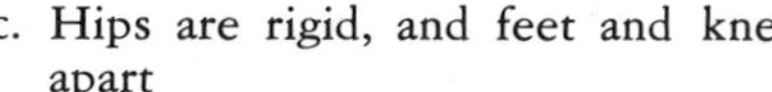

c. Hips are rigid, and feet and knees apart

c. Relax hips and ankles and allow the body to undulate. Practice kick with arms at the sides

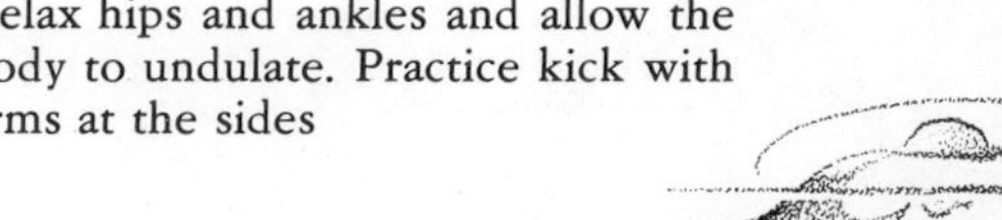

d. Improper timing for inhalation

d. Review arm-breathing coordination

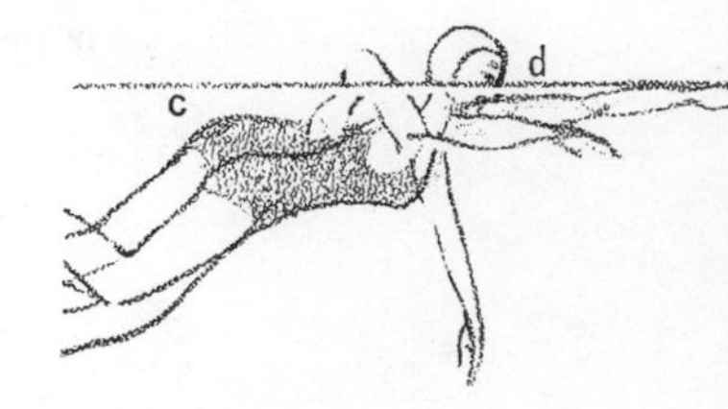

e. Only one leg kick for complete arm cycle

e. Teacher reviews stroke rhythm

f. Gliding

f. The student should work toward a continuous arm pull and leg action

Elementary Diving

Difficulty	*Correction*
a. Legs overthrow the head	a. Student should avoid dropping the head too soon or pulling the arms down with excessive force
b. Landing flat or too far out	b. Teacher should remind student "as the head and arms go—so goes the body." Duck head between the arms and push *up* rather than *out*
c. Knees collapse upon entry	c. Stress body extension with legs firm and ankles extended. Point toes

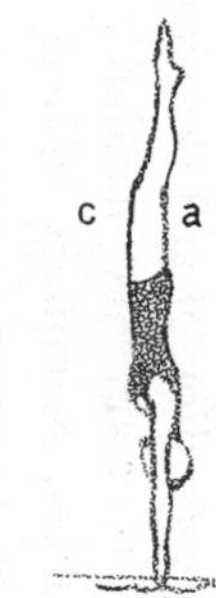

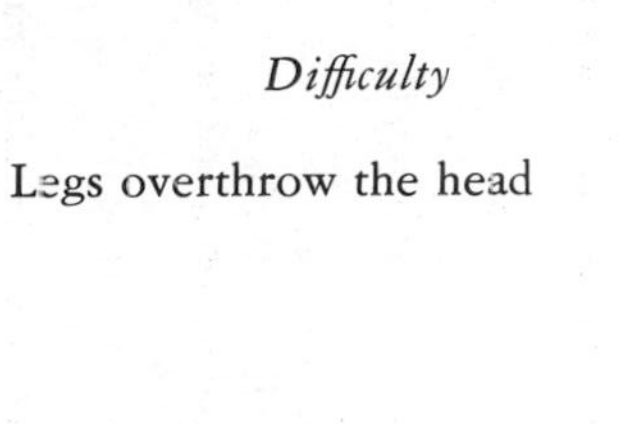

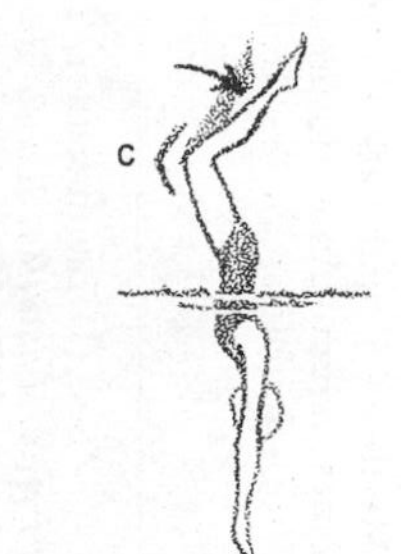

EVALUATING THE RESULTS

Every swimmer should be tested on her understanding of and skill in swimming and diving. The American Red Cross has established standards for beginners, intermediates, swimmers, and advanced swimmers. Individual skill tests have been established and are available to serve as measuring devices for skill attainment.*

Tests should be used sparingly. It is helpful to evaluate the skills of an individual when instruction begins and at least once more at the end of the instructional unit. An instructor finds it helpful to set skill goals upon which to rate students and to equate improvement based upon the goals of the class.

Measuring speed and distance is relatively simple. The former should be a concern for advanced and competitive swimmers.

Proper execution of dives and water stunts is more difficult to evaluate. It is advisable to explain the checkpoints very carefully. Discussion of dives, stunts, and officiating techniques helps students understand points upon which they are evaluated.

If grades are given they should be based upon written and oral tests and individual skill and achievement.

TERMINOLOGY

Swimming and Diving

Aquatics—Water activities of all kinds: swimming, diving, skiing, surfing, skin and scuba diving, water games, synchronized swimming, boating, and sailing.
Beat—A phase of the flutter kick, a thrust of the leg. "Six beat kick" refers to six thrusting movements of the legs to one complete cycle of both arms.
Bobbing—Process of raising the head from beneath the surface and then submerging again in a rhythmical pattern.
Buoyancy—Property and tendency of the body that makes floating possible.
Catch—Applying pressure to the water with the hand just before the power phase.
Coordination—Proper movements controlled accurately as to direction, force, and timing to produce efficient action.
Cycle—Complete movement of both arms and legs in executing a total stroke.
Dive—A descent into the water.
Entry—The movement of the entire body or a part of the body (usually arms) into the water.
Extension—To reach or stretch out a selected part or the entire body.
Flexion—Bending of the body at a joint.
Float—To sustain the body position with little or no movement.
Layout—Body, arms, and legs fully stretched out at the water surface.
Medley—A combination of strokes or distances in individual or relay events.
Natatorium—An enclosure containing a pool.
Pull—Initial part of the stroke used to move the body through the water.

---

*See (1) Baumgartner, Ted A. and Jackson, Andrew S.: *Measurement for Evaluation in Physical Education, Review and Resource Manual.* Boston, Houghton-Mifflin, 1975, pp. 166–171, and (2) Safrit, Margaret J.: *Evaluation in Physical Education.* Englewood Cliffs, New Jersey, Prentice-Hall, Inc., 1973, p. 281.

Recovery—The phase of arm or leg action which is without propelling force. It follows the power phase.
Scuba—Self-contained underwater breathing apparatus.
Stroke—A complete pattern of arm and leg movements which propels the body through the water.
Surfing—*Body* surfing uses the waves to carry the extended body to the shore. *Board* surfing consists of riding the waves on a board in a sitting, kneeling, or standing position.
Thrust—Movement of the legs to move the body through the water.
Turn—A reversal of direction at the end of the pool or course.

Synchronized Swimming

An extensive glossary is not appropriate, since basic terms are defined in the body of the chapter. Several terms deserve emphasis, and a few musical terms warrant definition.

Accent—In music, the beat of a measure that is regularly emphasized.
Aquatic art—The integration of swimming stunts, strokes, and floating figures with other art forms such as music and dance in order to create compositions.
Combined strokes—Two or more complete strokes performed in a series.
Hybrid strokes—Combination of two or more parts of standard strokes to set a pattern, rhythm, or effect.
Measure—A unit of music that divides the basic rhythm at regular intervals.
Modified strokes—An adaptation of standard strokes for synchronized use.
Phrase—In music, usually a grouping of four measures. There is a natural break in the rhythm at the end of a phrase.
Rhythm—Musically, the pattern the notes make, including the accents, rests, and time spacing. Also, a sense of understanding the relationship of the underlying musical beat with a movement.
Sculling—Use of the hands in propelling the body through the water.
Section—A portion of a musical selection composed of a group of phrases.
Synchronized swimming—Coordination of movements of a swimmer to musical accompaniment; when there are two or more swimmers, their movements must be coordinated with each other.

DISCUSSION QUESTIONS

1. Define the power and recovery phases of a stroke. Describe any stroke and define the specific phases.
2. What is meant by the term aquatics? Elaborate on the activities included. What should be included in a school aquatic program?
3. Describe the body position for a front running dive during approach, takeoff, and entry into the water.
4. What are the differences between combined strokes and hybrid strokes?
5. Which stunts begin from a back position and go immediately to a tuck?

SELECTED AUDIOVISUAL AIDS

Swimming and Diving

All Events Film on Women's Swimming, 1973. (8 mm., 16 mm., or super-8, silent, b & w.) Sports Market Publications. P.O. Box 1293, Los Altos, California 94022. (Purchase)

Diving Skills Learned on the Trampoline, 1964. (16 mm., 14 min., b & w.) Hubert Billingsley, 1504 Matlock Road, Bloomington, Indiana 47405.
Fundamentals of Diving. Norman Sper, 1943 North Cherokee, Hollywood, California.
Matt Mann and His Swimming Techniques. Coronet Productions, Glenview, Illinois.
Springboard Diving. Bell and Howell, Inc., 1801–1815 Larchmont Avenue, Chicago, Illinois.
Springboard Diving, 1953. (12 min., 16 mm., sound, b & w.) University of California Film Services Department, University Extension, Visual Department, 2272 Union Street, Berkeley, California 94704. (Purchase and rental)
Springboard Techniques. Mike Peppe, Coronet Industrial Films, 65 East South Water Street, Chicago, Illinois.
Swimming: Dolphin, Butterfly, Breaststroke, 1955. (16 mm., b & w, sound.) State University of Iowa, Bureau of Audiovisual Instruction, Iowa City, Iowa.
Swimming and Diving Today, 1974. (17 min., 16 mm., sound, color.) Official Sports Films, 400 Leslie Street, Elgin, Illinois 60120.
Swimming and Diving by the Rules. Official Sports Films, 400 Leslie Street, Elgin, Illinois 60120.
Swimming, Elementary, Advanced and Fundamentals of Diving. Fred Cady, Division of Audiovisual Education, Los Angeles County Schools, 808 North Spring Street, Los Angeles, California.
Teaching Johnny to Swim, 1973. (15 min., 16 mm., sound, color.) American Red Cross, 18th and E Streets, N.W., Washington, D.C. 20006. (Purchase and free rental)
The Science of Swimming. (Four strokes—crawl, backstroke, breaststroke, and butterfly) (12 min., 16 mm., or super-8, sound, b & w.) Councilman Co., Inc., R.R. #12, Box 200, Bloomington, Indiana 47401.
Women's Diving, 1973. (8 min. 16 mm. or super-8, silent, b & w.) Sports Market Publications, P.O. Box 1293, Los Altos, California 94022. (Purchase)

Synchronized Swimming

Champions on Film—Synchronized Swimming, 1956. (2 sets, 16 mm. loops, b & w.) Champions on Film, 1643 South State Street, Ann Arbor, Michigan. (Purchase)
Fundamentals of Creative Swimming, 1961. (24 min., 16 mm., sound, b & w and color.) Colburn Film Distributors, Inc., Box 470, 668 North Western Avenue, Lake Forest, Illinois.
Synchronized Swimming, 1974. (loop, 3½ min./film, 16 mm. or super-8, silent, color.) Set of 12. Champions of Film, 745 State Circle, Ann Arbor, Michigan 48104. (Purchase)
This is Synchronized Swimming, 1958. (3 reels, 16 mm., color, sound.) Jole and Company, 1027 Camino Ricardo, San Jose 25, California.

SUGGESTED READINGS

Armbruster, David A., Sr., and Morehouse, Lawrence E.: *Swimming and Diving.* 6th Ed. St. Louis, Missouri, The C. V. Mosby Co., 1973.
Barone, Marian: Beginning Diving. Mayfield, Palo Alto, California, 1973.
Council for National Cooperation in Aquatics: *The New Science of Skin and Scuba Diving.*
Counsilman, James: *The Science of Swimming.* Englewood Cliffs, New Jersey, Prentice-Hall, Inc., 1968.
Clotworthy, Robert: *Diving.* Camden, New Jersey, Thomas Nelson and Sons, 1962.
Coryell, Helen (Ed.): *Progressive Synchronized Swimming Program.* New York, Association Press, 1974.
Council for National Cooperation in Aquatics: *Water Fun For Everyone.* 291 Broadway, New York, Associated Press, 1965.

Fairbanks, Anne Ross: *Teaching Springboard Diving.* Englewood Cliffs, New Jersey, Prentice-Hall, Inc., 1963.
Goss, Gertrude: *Swimming Analyzed.* 200 West Foster Street, Melrose, Massachusetts 02176.
Gundling, Beulah, and Seller, Peg: *Aquatic Art.* 403 Iowa Theater Building, Cedar Rapids, Iowa, 1957.
Hobden, F. W.: *Springboard Diving.* London, William Clowes & Sons, Ltd.
Jones, Frances L. and Lindeman, Joyce I.: *The Components of Synchronized Swimming.* Prentice-Hall, Inc., Englewood Cliffs, New Jersey, 1975.
Midtlyng, Joanna: *Swimming.* Philadelphia, W. B. Saunders Co., 1974.
Moriarty, Phillip: *Diving.* New York, The Ronald Press, 1959.
NAGWS: *Aquatic Guide.* AAHPER, Washington, D.C., Current edition.
Peppe, Mike, and Phinizy, Coles: *Sports Illustrated Book of Diving.* Philadelphia, J. B. Lippincott Co., 1971.
Rackham, George: *Synchronized Swimming.* London, Faber & Faber, 1972.
Spears, Betty: *Beginning Synchronized Swimming.* 2nd Ed. Minneapolis, Minnesota, Burgess Publishing Co., 1958.
Talbot, Don: *Swimming To Win.* New York, Hawthorn Books, 1969.
Torney, John A., and Clayton, Robert: *Aquatic Instruction, Coaching and Management.* Minneapolis, Minnesota, Burgess Publishing Co., 1970.

PERIODICALS AND AQUATIC GUIDES

A.A.U. Official Synchronized Swimming Handbook. A.A.U. House, 231 West 58th Street, New York, 10019.
Advanced Aquatic Skill in Synchronized Swimming. C.N.C.A., 1201 16th Street, N. W., Washington, D.C. 20036.
Amateur Athletic Handbook. 233 Broadway, New York, 10007.
American Red Cross (1968): Swimming and Water Safety Textbook. Order from local Red Cross.
Aquatic Games, Pageants and Stunts. Beach and Pool Magazine. 425 4th Ave., New York.
Aquatics Guide. NAGWS, AAHPER, 1201 16th Street, N.W., Washington, D.C. 20036. Published every two years.
Junior Swimmer—Swimming World. A monthly for competitive swimmers and divers. 12618 Killion Street, North Hollywood, California 91607.
Manual of Canadian Synchronized Swimming. Peg Seller, 19 Bayview Avenue, Lakeside, Montreal, P.Q., Canada. Useful for familiarity with Canadian rules.
Surf Guide. Box 1278, Santa Monica, California.
Surfing. Peterson Publishing Co., 8490 Sunset Boulevard, Los Angeles, California 90069.
Swimming Pool Weekly and *Swimming Pool Age.* Hoffman Publications, Inc., 3000 N.E. 30th Place, P.O. Box 11299, Ft. Lauderdale, Florida 33306.
Swimming Technique. 12618 Killion Street, North Hollywood, California 91607. (Quarterly)
Swimming Times. A monthly magazine. Published in England. Distributed by Sport Shelf, Box 634, New Rochelle, New York.
Swimming World and Junior Swimmer. 12618 Killion Street, North Hollywood, California 91607. (Monthly)
Synchro-Info. 11902 Red Hill Avenue, Santa Ana, California 92705.
The Aquatic Artist. Official publication of the International Academy of Aquatic Art. Write: Henry Gundling, 403 Iowa Theater Building, Cedar Rapids, Iowa. Price: $5 a year, individual membership; $15 a year, club membership. (Monthly)
The Water Skier. American Water Ski Association, 7th Street and Avenue G., S. W., Winter Haven, Florida.

Women's National Aquatic Forum Report. Muriel Sloan, Lathrop Hall, University of Wisconsin, Madison, Wisconsin.

CHARTS

Three Water Ballet Charts. F. Coleville, G. Goss, 200 West Foster Street, Melrose, Massachusetts 02176.

Aquatics—Technique Charts. AAHPER, 1201 16th Street N. W., Washington, D.C.

CHAPTER 12

TENNIS

Although the French are often credited with originating tennis, actually it evolved from a game played by the ancient Greeks and Romans which is similar to modern handball. The English popularized an Irish version of the sport, and played it on a court bounded at the sides by two parallel nets staked down at the center, so that each was shaped like an hourglass. At first a hard leather, hair-stuffed ball was batted between partners back and forth across a rope by their bare hands; several years later by a gloved fist, then with a glove protected by leather thongs wrapped around it. Later, a parchment tambourine was used to swat a linen ball, then a crude short-handled paddle was devised, and finally a racket and ball similar to those of today were used. It is believed that the word "tennis" comes from *tenez,* the second person plural form of the French verb *tenir* ("to hold").

Early scoring was complicated with 15 "chases" given for one point from which arose the 15, 30, 40 game method of scoring. "Love," or nothing, which is symbolized by a zero or egg-shaped O, comes from the French word for egg *(l'oeuf),* which is very similar in sound to the English word "love."

King Louis X of France is responsible for tennis's being called "The Sport of Kings." He jealously guarded the game for members of his court and banned the game for the masses when he found them playing it. In spite of the ban, the game became an activity for the "masses as well as the classes" and spread rapidly into England. It was during this period that a mesh net replaced the rope, and a crude racket replaced the tambourine.

The popularity of tennis swept out from England into the world. Major Walter C. Wingfield, a British army officer, did much to give the game impetus at home and in the colonies. Mary Outerbridge, an American visitor in Bermuda, was intrigued with the sport and returned to the United States in 1874, well supplied with rackets and balls. Although delayed several hours by customs officers while they debated whether or not to permit her to bring such strange gadgets into the country, she not only succeeded in doing so, but with her brother successfully introduced the game to Americans. Because of their efforts and following among enthusiastic fans, the official governing body of this sport, the United States Lawn Tennis Association, was founded in 1881. By 1900 the Davis Cup Matches for international competition among men were established, followed shortly afterward by the Wightman Cup Matches for women in the United States and England.

Interest in learning how to play tennis among students on all educational levels and among the general public of all ages is now at an all-time high. As a spectator sport it also ranks high in popularity. Billie Jean King, Chris Evert, Margaret Court, and Rosemary Casals are but a few of the players who will be remembered as pioneers in the development of both amateur and professional status for women players. Intercollegiate tennis competition among women is rapidly growing, and many of these young women have high hopes of becoming professional players.

THE NATURE AND PURPOSE OF THE GAME

Tennis is a game played with racket and ball on an indoor or outdoor court by two or four players. In both singles and doubles play the object of the game is to score points while preventing opponents from scoring. Points are scored by serving and ball placement, which cause opponents to miss the ball, drive it into the net, or drive it out of the court area. The skill of the game lies in mastering serving techniques, offensive and defensive strokes, footwork, and game strategy. In competition a player strives to win points, games, sets, and ultimately, the match.

The singles game is played on a 27 by 78 foot court. The area is divided by a net strung tautly across the court, parallel to the baselines. The top of the net is 3 feet 6 inches at each net post, tapering to 3 feet in the center of the court. Each half of the court is divided into a back- and forecourt. The forecourt is further divided into the right and left serving or receiving areas. The doubles court is $4\frac{1}{2}$ feet wider on each side. In a doubles game the additional "alley" area becomes valid playing space only *after* the service.

Play begins as the server delivers the ball from behind the baseline, to the right of the center of the court, and within an imaginary extension of court sidelines. Serving from the right, she serves to her opponent's right court. Play between opponents continues until the winner of the point is determined. The server then moves to the left of center and behind the baseline to serve and begin play for the second point. Serving positions are alternated until the game winner is determined.

GAME RULES AND SCORING

The point progress of a game is 15, 30, 40 and game. When the score is tied 40–40, the score is called deuce. The tie is broken and the game won by the winning of two consecutive additional points. If the server wins the first point after deuce it is called *advantage server.* If the receiver wins the first point it is called *advantage receiver.* Players speak of it as "ad in" and "ad out." When a player has no score, it is referred to as "love." The server's score is called first during a game, whether officiated by tournament officials or by the players themselves. For example, the server's score would be love–30 if she has lost the first two game points, or 40–30 if she gains the next three. Singles and doubles are scored in the same way. The VASSS* is an alternate scoring system. It is used in many professional and team tennis matches, for the simple system is easily understood by spectators. It employs a 9 point tie break to eliminate the lengthy "marathon" set.

A set is won by the player or team who first wins six games, provided they have at least a two game lead over the opponents. A set can be won at 6–0, 6–1, 6–2, 6–3, and 6–4. It cannot be won at 6–5 but may terminate at 7–5.

In 1970 the Executive Committee of the United States Lawn Tennis Association approved a "sudden death" tie breaking procedure. The procedure has gained wide acceptance in recreational and tournament play. There are two authorized methods which may be used after the score of 6–all is reached: 5 out of 9 points and 7 out of 12 points. The decision regarding the selection of method is left to individual players or the tournament committee. The 5 out of 9 point method is described, since it is most often used by women players. *In singles play* (5 out of 9 points): The player (A) whose turn it is to serve the next game after 6–all shall serve the first two points of the tie break. Point 1 is served from the right court, point 2 from the left court. The opponent (B) shall then serve points 3 and 4 from the right and left courts, respectively. The players then change sides of the court and the first server (A) serves points 5 and 6; the second server (B) then serves points 7 and 8. If either player wins five points, the set is terminated. If the score is tied 4–all, the second server (B) serves point 9 from the right *or* left court at the option of the receiver. The set shall be recorded as 7–6 games, and the last player to serve in the tie break situation shall be the first server in the next set. *In doubles play* the tie break procedure is the same as that described for the singles game, provided that each player serves from the same end of the court that she has served from during that particular set. A *match* is made up of the win-

*See NAGWS. *Tennis-Badminton-Squash Guide.* June 1974–1976, pp. 89–91.

ner of two out of three sets for women and for mixed doubles. Men's competition requires the best three out of five sets.

General Rules

Service. Each server serves a complete game. The first serve of the game must be from the right half of the court behind the baseline. The server has two chances to send the ball over the net diagonally into her opponent's service court. If the first ball is good, a second is not used. The next serve is made from the left, and so on until the game is completed. A double service fault (such as hitting the first ball into the net and the second out of bounds) causes a loss of point. The ball must land in the opponent's service court before it can be hit by the receiver, who must wait until it bounces before returning it. After the service the ball may be hit before it bounces, throughout the game.

The serve is a fault if the server (1) does not take the proper position before serving, (2) commits a foot fault, (3) misses the ball if attempting to strike it or hits it slightly with the racket,* (4) fails to hit the ball into the correct service court, (5) hits any permanent structure with the served ball other than the net, strap, or band, or (6) hits her partner or anything she wears or carries with the served ball.

The penalty for any one of the above is a single fault, and it is a double fault and loss of point if such an error happens on both serves.

Foot Fault. It is a foot fault on the serve for the server (1) to change her position by walking or running or (2) to step on or over the back line as the ball is hit.

The Let. The ball is considered to be a "let" when (1) a served ball touches the net, strap, or band, and is otherwise good; (2) because of circumstances beyond a player's control of interference, she is unable to play the ball; or (3) the ball is delivered before the receiver is ready.

Loss of Point. The player loses a point if (1) she does not return the ball to her opponent's court on the volley or first bounce after service, (2) she or anything she carries or wears touches the net on any play, (3) she reaches over the net to play a ball unless it has bounced back over the net because of a spin or a strong wind, (4) she throws her racket at the ball, (5) she hits the ball more than once, (6) she misses the ball or hits it out of bounds or into the net, or (7) she plays a served ball before it bounces.

Good Returns. A ball is considered good (1) if it lands in the court or on any line, (2) if it touches a net post or the net and falls into the proper court, (3) if a player reaches outside the net posts to play a ball and returns

*The server may toss and catch the ball on an attempted serve without penalty if her racket does not touch it.

it successfully, and (4) if the player's racket on the follow-through goes over the net but does not touch it.

Changing Sides. Players should change courts at the end of odd-numbered games, i.e., after the first, third, fifth, etc., so that each side will compete under the same sun, wind, court, and spectator conditions. If the total number of games played in the set is an even number, however, courts should not be changed until the end of the first game of the next set.

Doubles Rules

Service. The players on one side take turns serving. The order of serving should be determined before the beginning of each set. One of the alternating serving pair should serve games 1, 3, 5, 7, and so on, while those of the opposite side should alternate serving the even-numbered games. The order of serving must be consistent throughout the set, but may change at the beginning of a new set. During the serve, the server's partner may stand anywhere on her half of the court. When one serves out of turn, the proper server must serve as soon as the error is discovered, but all points already earned should be counted. If a complete game is played before the error is known, the game counts, and the service order should remain as altered.

Receiving. Before each set begins, the couple receiving in the first game should determine which one will receive first; that player should continue to receive first in all odd-numbered games of the set. The opponents should also decide which one will receive first in the second game; such a person should receive first in all even-numbered games.

When a player receives out of turn, she should stay in that position until the game then being played is over. The partners should then return to their original receiving order.

GAME COURTESIES

1. Play to win every game, but do not make excuses or show poor sportsmanship should you lose.
2. Do not return the first ball on the serve if it is a fault.
3. When both you and your opponent are in doubt of the score or about a line decision, play the point over.
4. Do not serve until your opponent is ready.
5. Always have two balls in your hand before you start to serve.
6. As a spectator, do not applaud until a point has been made, and never walk behind or on a court wherein a game is in progress. Do not applaud a fault.
7. Do not have temper tantrums or show that you are upset about your own mistakes or an umpire's decision.

8. Win graciously.
9. Be courteous to the others playing on adjoining courts.
10. Be sure to shake hands after a match in tournament play.
11. Play honestly whether or not an umpire is present.

NEEDED FACILITIES AND EQUIPMENT

Court. The outdoor court has a surface of grass, clay, concrete, crushed stone, asphalt, or other composition material. Indoor play is on a wooden floor, canvas covering, or on synthetic surfaces. Markings on concrete and asphalt courts should be painted in white or bright yellow. Dry or wet lime is usually used to mark grass or clay courts, although cotton and plastic tapes stapled securely in the ground are favored in some sections of the country, especially for camp use.

Net. The net may be made of steel or other metal, and of hemp or cotton cord twine. Although tarred nets are more expensive, they are almost a must for outdoor use and should be strung on a weather-resistant cable. The official net height is 3 feet 6 inches at the net posts and 3 feet at the court center. The net is held down at the center by a strap not more than 2 inches wide. The band covering the cord or metal cable should not be more than 2½ inches in depth at each side. The net for singles should be 33 feet long—42 feet for doubles—and it should touch the ground along its entire length and come flush to the net posts at all points.

Costume. The recommended costume for this sport is a tennis dress, shorts and blouse, and a warm-up suit in appropriate weather. Tennis clothing in pastel colors or white clothing with colored trim is becoming accepted and more widely worn. Tennis socks and comfortable, smooth soled sneakers or tennis shoes are imperative.

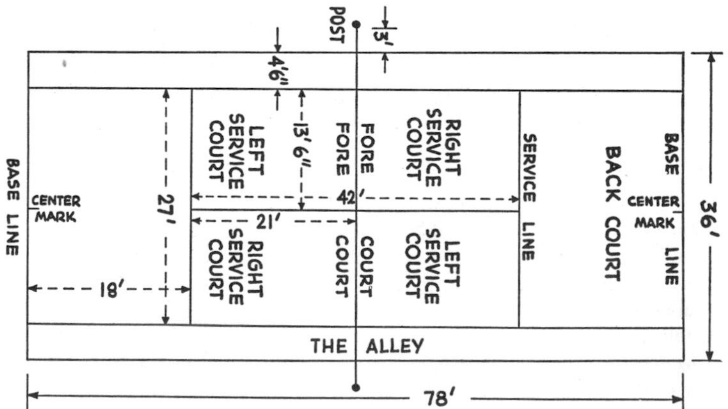

Figure 12–1 Official tennis court.

Other necessary personal equipment includes balls and a racket with a head cover. Racket frames are made of wood, steel, aluminum, plastic, or fiber glass, and are strung with steel, aluminum, plastic, silk, nylon, or gut. A maximum of 18 main strings crossed by 20 evenly spaced, lateral strings is standard and meets the specifications of the United States Lawn Tennis Association. Quality rackets have handles made of basswood or Malacca and covered with fine leather. Others have "leather" grips made of rubber, plastic, or imitation leather. The racket for women should weigh between 12 and 13½ ounces with a grip of 4⅜ to 4⅝ inches. For girls between 9 and 12 years of age, the racket should weigh 11 to 13 ounces with a grip of 4 to 4½ inches. Above all, the racket should not seem too heavy when swung vigorously back and forth for several minutes, and the grip should be small enough so that the hand fits comfortably around the handle.

Good balls are a must for all players, regardless of skill. Balls are manufactured under specifications of the United States Lawn Tennis Association, which requires that balls have a uniform outer surface, be more than 2½ inches and less than 2⅝ inches in diameter, and weigh more than 2 ounces but less than 2¹⁄₁₆ ounces. Those meeting such specifications are packed and sealed in air-tight containers bearing the approval of USLTA. "Seconds" are not always marked, although some companies indicate that they are slightly defective by stamping out the letters USLTA. These cheaper balls are usually available at sporting goods shops upon request and are suggested for the use of the beginner or a school with a limited budget.

Instructors with more than adequate funds might well purchase an electric ball machine which "feeds" balls at various heights and angles across the net to players. This device can reduce teaching time by speeding stroke skill mastery.

Helen Driver, along with many other noted tennis instructors, believes that a backboard is the best opponent a player can have because it usually returns the ball.* The best backboards are made of heavy beaverboard or pressboard in regulation half tennis court size and are painted green with a white line 3½ feet above the ground. They should be located at one end of each court. A line 39 feet from the backboard and parallel to it should be painted on the area to indicate a court baseline. Additional lines, 12 and 25 feet away, enable students to station themselves quickly for short and long rallying distances.

A stroke developer, which is simply a ball suspended on a string, is available from the Tom Stowe Enterprises, Berkeley, California. This device can be used in indoor locations as well as on the sides and back of

---

*See Helen Driver: *Tennis For Teachers.* Enlarged Edition. Printed and distributed by the author, 803 Moygara Road, Frost Woods, Madison, Wisconsin 53704.

outdoor courts. Footprint mats should be used with it. Although these can be obtained commercially, they can easily be hand painted on court and practice areas in two different colors to designate the foot patterns during the forehand and backhand strokes.

Backboards, stroke developers, electric ball machines, foot patterns, tetherball sets, and rebound nets are all ideal for teaching large classes effectively. By careful planning and ingenuity a skilled teacher can keep everyone actively learning in a class of 20 to 35 students, although ideally the group should be smaller.

All wall space within the gymnasium should be fully utilized for backboard practice. The net line should be clearly marked on the wall, as well as a line 10 feet above it to indicate the area above which all balls (with the exception of the lob) should not land if they are to be considered within bounds. A line indicating the baseline of the court should also be drawn on the floor 39 feet in front of each wall area being used for ball practice. Other lines, 12 and 25 feet away, should be drawn to show the short and long rallying distances best for practicing drives.

If a ball-throwing machine is used for instructional purposes, the students should be taught to develop accuracy by hitting to specific target areas across the net.

A strength developer may be made by taking a used bicycle inner tube, tying a knot at each end, and cutting the valve off. Have a player stand with tube under her right foot, and wrap it around her body, passing it in front of her right knee, around her left hip, and across her back. Then have her grasp the opposite end of the tube with her right hand and begin to shadow practice the forehand swing. For the backhand stroke she

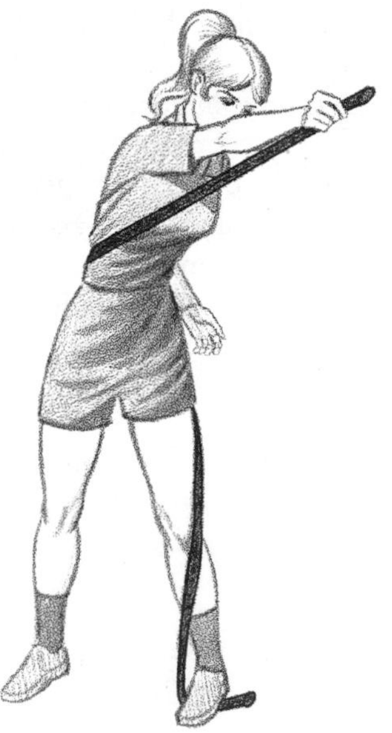

Figure 12–2 A strength developer.

should stand on the tube end with her left foot and wrap the tube around her right hip and across her back.

The use of colored tennis balls can help students visually track the ball during play and easily identify their own balls. These can also be used effectively by different squads when each is given a distinguishing color.

The use of jump ropes to develop agility, unstrung or partially strung rackets to teach students to use the center of the racket, used bicycle tires to develop accuracy, and temporary painted lines to teach court marking add variety to teaching methods and can produce more effective and more rapid student learning.

CARE AND REPAIR OF EQUIPMENT

Balls

1. Brush dirt from balls before putting them back into the can.
2. Dry balls thoroughly before using them again.
3. Store at normal room temperature and avoid extremes of heat or cold.
4. Consult local suppliers for information regarding repressurizing balls.

Net

1. Take twine nets indoors nightly and fold (do not roll) them.
2. Repair broken threads, using the fisherman's knot.
3. Slacken rope cables when nets are not in use.
4. Dip cord nets in creosote before storing.
5. Clean the steel cable with an oily rag and remove rust with emery cloth or heavy steel wool dipped in kerosene.
6. Wipe metal nets with an oily rag at least once a month.
7. Replace canvas bindings with bindings purchased either from sporting goods suppliers or direct from the manufacturer.

Rackets

Wood

1. Wipe the racket with a dry cloth before putting it in a waterproof cover.
2. Put it squarely in a press and tighten the four screws evenly.
3. Alternate methods of hanging the racket in a storage room of even temperature. The temperature should not exceed 75 degrees and the humidity should not exceed 60 per cent.
4. At the end of the season, apply a thin coat of shellac over the strings and a thin coat of wax over the entire frame.
5. Have broken strings repaired at a local sporting goods shop or by the manufacturer.

Metal

1. Occasionally wipe the racket with a good cleanser which has a wax base to prevent rusting.

2. Although broken shafts and heads can be welded in local machine shops inexpensively, this can often be done better by the manufacturer.

Fiber Glass and Plastic

1. Wipe off carefully before storing.
2. A press or cover is not necessary for these rackets.
3. Return to the manufacturer for restringing or other repairs.

TEACHING UNITS

Beginners

Brief discussion of history and game purpose
Selection and care of equipment
Fundamentals
- Grip
- Footwork
- Forehand
- Backhand
- Serve
- Volley

Rules and scoring
Strategy for singles and doubles
Round robin tournament
Evaluation

Advanced

Review of entire unit for beginners
Advanced skills
- Smash
- Lob
- Half volley
- Chop
- Varied serves

Advanced strategy for singles and doubles
Individual skill development
Elimination and ladder tournament
Evaluation

Rainy Day Materials

Films and filmstrips
Chalk talks on game strategy for singles and doubles
Care and repair of equipment
Discussion and illustrated talk on tennis champions

BASIC SKILLS

Footwork. The ability to get around the court quickly, moving forward or back, to either side, as well as to shift body weight and position, is the prerequisite to successful play. The knees should be kept relaxed and slightly bent with body weight carried forward. Players should be taught to shift their weight to the forward foot (usually the one opposite the hand holding the racket) and to *move into* each stroke with full power, as well as to move quickly around the court in order to play the ball *in front of the body.*

Jump rope drills are ideal for teaching students to push off from the balls of the feet as they start each movement, as well as for general warm-up purposes. Suggested patterns include:

1. Skip in place 25 times on both feet, 10 hopping from the left foot, 10 from the right.

2. Skip 10 times forward, 10 backward, 10 to the left, 10 to the right.
3. Skip in place on both feet facing forward, turn to the left and hop twice, return to place, hop twice to the right, return to place.
4. Move forward with fast running steps, skip backward, round in a circle, to both sides, changing directions suddenly upon command.
5. Repeat all four patterns mimetically swinging a racket, then with an actual racket.

The Grip. Three standard grips are the Eastern, Western and the Continental, a modification of the other two. Although there are certain values to be found in all three, the one most commonly and most successfully used is the Eastern, for it permits easy, free ball stroking. The Continental grip is described in the discussion of the service grip.

The Eastern Grip. Shake hands with a racket held perpendicular to the ground, holding the first two fingers directly behind and well around the handle, with the heel of the hand at the end and the index finger spread slightly apart, thumb extended.

The Serve. An effective serve results from a combination of proper stance, ball toss, swing, and transfer of weight. The arm movement is similar to the overhand softball throw. The student stands sideways to the baseline with feet spread comfortably apart, weight equally distributed, toes of left foot pointing toward right net post (right-handed server), and the forward shoulder pointed in the direction the ball is to go. The racket is held in the *Continental grip* (similar to the Eastern backhand with the racket shifted from one-sixteenth to one-eighth of a turn toward the forehand grip). With this grip all three serves (flat, slice, and twist) may be hit. The difference lies in where the ball is tossed and contacted as well as

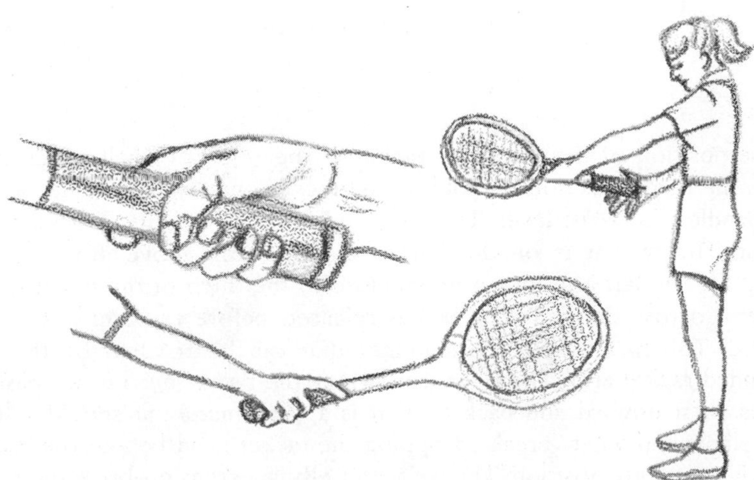

Figure 12–3 The grip.

Figure 12–4 The serve.

in the position of the hand and racket at the instant of ball contact. Assume the ready position by holding the racket out toward the net so that the handle is at waist level. The left hand holds both balls and the racket throat. The weight is on the left foot. Both arms move down and up together. The left arm moves down close to the thigh of the left leg, then upward to toss the ball. The ball is released before the arm is fully extended. The ball is lifted to a height that can be reached by the fully extended racket arm. The right arm swings the racket head down past the knees, then upward and back until it is approximately at shoulder level. The elbow and wrist "break" dropping the racket head behind the back in a back-scratching position. The wrist and elbow extension bring the racket up to hit the ball. At this point the body, arm, and racket are fully extended. After contacting the ball the follow-through is out (not down) in the direction of the ball flight and ending with the racket's swinging past the left leg.

The amount of spin put on the ball is determined by the angle of the racket at the moment of contact. Determination is largely a matter of individual experimentation and discovery. Although spin or twist serves are often difficult to learn and to teach, they have many advantages to the player who masters them. Those desiring to play competitive tennis will find it necessary to develop several serves.

In the flat serve, the same footwork, ball toss, and arm motion patterns are used. This serve is best for those beginners who are experiencing difficulty with the coordination of the serve. Progression steps in teaching the serve include:

1. Toss drills:
   a. Toss ball to get proper height and position.
   b. Toss and catch ball with tossing hand, palm facing upward.
2. Hitting drills:
   a. With racket in back-scratching position, toss and hit ball.
   b. While standing inside baseline, toss and hit ball using complete swing.

The Forehand Drive. This stroke is most frequently used in game play and is usually the one most easily mastered by the beginner. Stand sideways to the net, feet in a forward-back position, and hold the racket in the Eastern forehand grip. The backswing may be straight, in a flat plane, or more circular. The racket is moved back until it is pointing to the back fence and at the approximate height of the approaching ball. The following discussion is for the right-handed player; left-handed players need only reverse the terms "left" and "right." On the backswing, pivot on the right

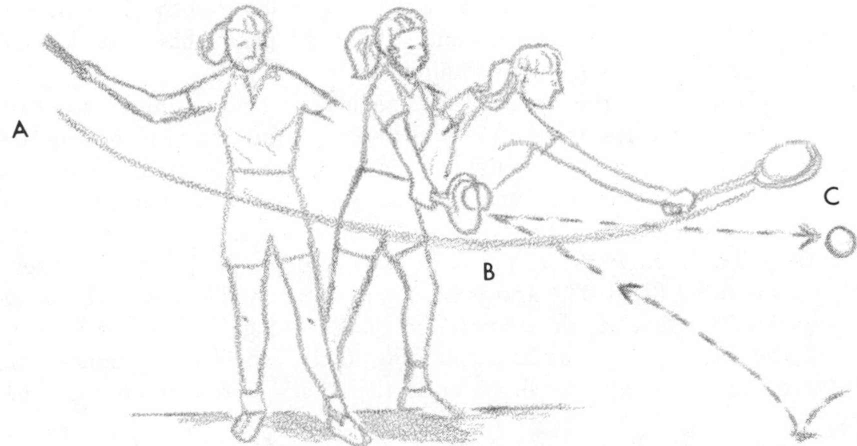

Figure 12–5 The forehand drive.

foot to get the left side of the body to the net. The right upper arm and elbow should stay fairly close to the right side of the body; the elbow is slightly bent. The left arm is free to be used for balance. In execution of the *forward swing,* the weight shifts with a step into the ball with the left foot. The left knee remains bent, the body pivots and hips and shoulders rotate as the arm swings the racket forward. The wrist of the racket arm remains firm, and the arm is extended from the body with the elbow slightly bent. The racket face should remain square to the ball as long as possible.

During the follow-through, continue the forward swing *through* the ball in the direction of intended ball flight. The racket head remains perpendicular to the court. The right hand will be about shoulder height at the end of the swing, and the racket head will be held higher than the player's head.

The left hand and arm are used in balancing the body during the swing. The left hand also assists in holding the throat of the racket before the swing, helps the right arm bring the racket back, and then may reach out to grasp the racket on the follow-through.

The Backhand Drive. While it is similar to the forehand drive, the backhand drive is often more difficult for right-handed players to master, whereas many left-handed players will develop a backhand superior to their forehand. Hold the racket in the Eastern grip, move it one quarter turn forward, and extend the thumb behind the handle for additional support. The body is standing facing sidewards, feet in a forward and back stride with knees relaxed. The racket head is held perpendicular to the ground with the hand placed on the grip so that the palm is on the top plane. The knuckle of the index finger should be on the center of the top plate. The fingers wrap around the grip with the thumb diagonally across the back or wrapped all the way around to rest next to the second finger.

The *backswing* begins with a pivot on the left foot so that the right side of the body is facing the net. The left hand pulls the racket back to a position just past the left hip. The right arm bends slightly. This movement pulls the right shoulder around so that the player has to look over the right shoulder to see the oncoming ball.

The initiation of the *forward swing* begins as weight is shifted forward and a step is taken toward the net with the right foot, prior to hitting the ball. The ball is contacted at waist level in front of the body. The hips and shoulders turn to start the racket swing. As the hand and racket move away from the hip, the arm straightens and is brought around the body. On the *follow-through,* the racket head goes through the ball in the direction of intended flight. The arm is held away from the body with the hand about shoulder level at the completion of the swing. The racket head is high. The left arm remains back, pointing to the fence while maintaining balance and stabilizing the shoulder so that the side remains toward the net.

Students who have great difficulty learning the forehand and back-

Figure 12–6 The backhand drive.

hand strokes can often be helped by the use of a portable stroke developer, a device in which a ball is suspended from an iron pipe.* An ingenious instructor can improvise a similar gadget using adhesive tape, a fishing pole, and a wire hook.† Similar equipment is excellent for assisting those having problems hitting the ball or getting the feel of a full, powerful, but relaxed swing.

Progression steps in teaching ground strokes include:

1. Footwork drills.
   a. Players shuffle to the right and left, stress keeping weight on balls of feet.
   b. Players shuffle backward and forward.
   c. Players move from side to side using a crossover step.
2. Hand and ball drills.
   a. Self-drop and catch at waist level in front of the body with hitting hand.
   b. Self-drop and hit to partner six feet away.
   c. Partner drop and catch with hitting hand.
   d. Partner tosses underhand; attempt to hit ball back and forth to each other.

---

*See Jane Williamson: Improved Tennis Aids, *Official Tennis-Badminton Guide.* AAHPER, DGWS, 1952–1954.

†See Mary K. Browne: *Streamline Tennis.* New York, American Sports Publishing Company, 1940.

3. Racket and ball drills (use choked up racket).
   a. Self-drop and hit against wall, fence, or backboard.
   b. Self-drop and hit to partner 20 feet away.
   c. Partner tosses underhand; return hit by partner.
4. Full racket swing with proper grip. Follow preceding and succeeding steps.
   a. Self-drop and hit over net.
   b. Partner drop and hit over net.
   c. Rally against wall.
   d. Rally on court with partner.

The Volley. Any ball which is hit in the air before it bounces is a volley. A volley may be hit either forehand or backhand, and the stroke is used primarily at the net and in the forecourt. It is an essential offensive tool. The Continental grip is best if there is no time to change to the Eastern forehand or backhand grip. In the ready position the player faces the net, racket held in front of the body with racket head higher than the wrist. On the forehand, the left shoulder is turned toward the net, the racket head is kept higher than the wrist, and the ball is contacted in front of the left shoulder with a *punching,* rather than a stroking, motion. On the backhand, the right shoulder is turned toward the net, the racket head is kept higher than the wrist, and the ball is contacted in front of the right shoulder with a punching motion. There is no backswing in either the forehand or backhand volley. It is well to remember not to swing at the ball—move the racket forward to punch. Shoulders and hips do not turn as much as they do when executing groundstrokes.

Progression steps in teaching the volley include:

1. With partner, toss ball and catch it in front of body with the hand.
2. With partner, toss and punch ball with the hand.
3. Partner stands at service line and tosses ball to hitter, who punches ball with racket.
4. Partner stands inside baseline and hits ball to hitter, who punches ball with racket.

Figure 12–7 The volley.

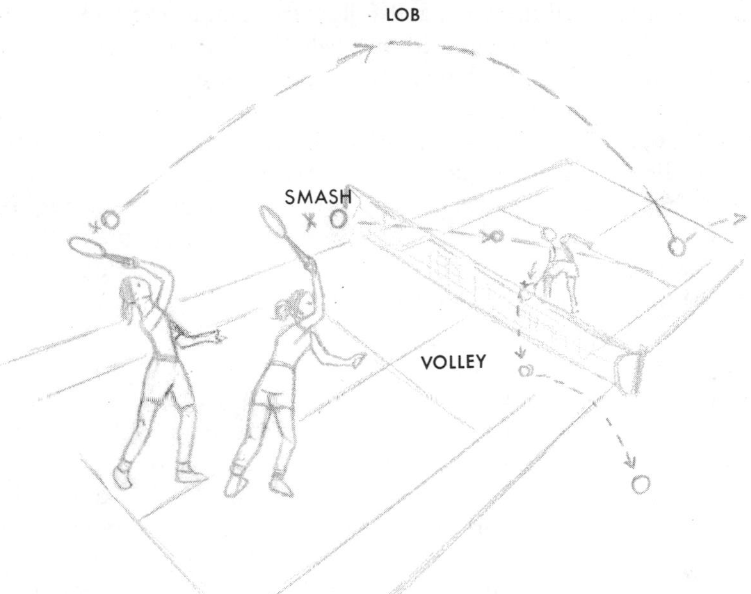

Figure 12–8 Types of strokes.

The Half-Volley. This is not a true volley, but a groundstroke in which the ball is hit immediately after it has bounced and is rising. The player turns sideways, shortens and controls the swing, bends the knees, and lowers the racket behind the ball. When executing the stroke, the grip and wrist remain firm. *Stay down with this stroke.*

The Smash. Similar to the serve, this stroke can be a forceful attack shot of great speed. It is executed using the same grip, footwork, and timing as the serve and is most effective when used on a high, weak return at the net or in midcourt. The player watches and waits, after positioning herself, until the ball drops toward the court.

The racket is carried past the head and is dropped behind the back to the back-scratching position. The player positions her side toward the net as if she were serving. The swing is up and forward so the ball can be contacted in front of the body with a fully extended arm. The left arm may be used to "point the ball" as it drops toward the body. Step in the direction of the shot and follow through.

The Lob. The purpose of the lob is to move the opponent around the court or to send the ball over her head when she has moved to the net. A lob may be offensive or defensive, depending upon the height of the ball. It is a defensive time-gainer and should be placed strategically on the court. It is played on the forehand or backhand side with a swing that resembles the groundstroke. Shorten and slow down the backswing, lift the ball with a forward upswing, and follow through as the racket, with its face tilted back, makes contact with the ball. This often effective but delicate stroke can send a high, flatly hit ball into an unguarded area and thus often become a point winner.

The Chop. The chop stroke is more defensive than offensive and is used to break up a strong drive or service. For both forehand and backhand chops the racket is held in a grip halfway between the Eastern forehand and the backhand. A short backswing precedes a descending blow on the back of the ball with an open racket face. The downward and forward follow-through completes the action, which results in a ball that bounces short and low in the opponent's court.

The Drop. The drop shot resembles a groundstroke until the ball is hit, and it serves as a change of pace or deceptive stroke intended to place the ball just over the net and catch the opponent deep in the back court. Use a grip similar to that used for the chop stroke. As the racket swings forward, open the face in order to hit *under* the ball and give it backspin. At contact, relax wrist and grip to slow down the ball. The body faces the net more squarely than for a drive, and a short backswing leads the racket to the ball. The racket strokes the ball *lightly* so that it barely clears the net in the intended direction. The follow-through should be very short.

GAME STRATEGY

The attacking style is usually played at the net with the defensive players moving back to baseline positions. Many players "beat themselves" through their own errors. This may be avoided by carefully analyzing all mistakes made and not repeating them. Consistent, steady play is more fruitful than taking unwise chances or trying to "kill" as many shots as possible. Beginners especially should learn (1) to hit the ball *away* from their opponents, (2) to *anticipate* where the returned ball will land on the court and *be ready* to receive it, and (3) to *outsmart their opponents* by placing returned shots to their weaknesses. Other aspects of general strategy include:

1. Return to the center line at fore or back court position after each stroke.
2. Conserve strength by letting impossible shots go past and going after those you can get.
3. Take your time and get into proper position before hitting the ball, and *play it in front of your forward foot.*
4. It is not how *hard* you hit the ball, but *where* you hit it.
5. Always win your own serve and vary its speed and placement.
6. A deep cross-court shot is usually much more effective than a baseline drive.
7. Disguise your intended return as long as possible.
8. Play every point one at a time, for it is this point-by-point concentration coupled with skillful ball placement that makes a winner.

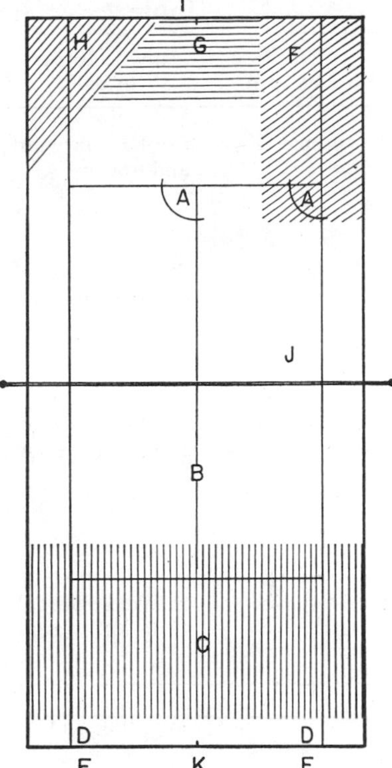

Figure 12–9 Strategic court positions and placements. *A,* Placement of serve to weakness (opponent's backhand). *B,* Center net position when ball has been played to center of opponent's court. *C,* Avoid standing in shaded zone; play in front of or behind it. *D,* Position in receiving a slow serve. *E,* Position in receiving a fast serve. *F, G, H,* Where to place the lob. *I,* Position in serving to right service court. *J,* Partner's net position when I is serving to right service court. *K,* Back court on guard position. (From Fait et al.: *A Manual of Physical Education Activities,* 2nd ed. Philadelphia, W. B. Saunders Company, 1961.)

9. Hit the ball *away* from your opponent, trying to make her move around the court, from back to front to baseline.
10. Direct most serves to your opponent's backhand, if this is her weakest stroke (this is often not true of left-handed players). Remember that the flat serve is most successfully placed when it lands in the backhand corner of the forehand court and also that the American twist serve is placed best when it lands in the backhand corner of the backhand court.
11. Vary the pace, spin, depth, and direction of your strokes in order to keep your opponent guessing and on the defensive. Master the art of anticipating what your opponent is going to do.

DOUBLES STRATEGY

Teamwork is necessary for success in doubles. Although advanced players prefer to play side by side, beginners should be taught the up and back method, the side by side, and a fast shift to either one. Since the most advantageous court spot is at the net, this position should be gained and held as long as possible. Other suggestions include:

1. Keep the ball in the opponents' back court as much as possible.

Table 7. Analytical Chart of Spins

Kind of Spin	How to Impart to Ball	Action of Ball on Bounce	How to Play
1. Topspin	Stroke forward and upward	Ball rotates away from striker in flight; as ball hits court it will dive down	1. Impart the opposite spin (underspin) 2. Half volley
2. Underspin	Stroke forward and downward	Ball rotates toward striker in flight; as it hits court it will "bite" and bounce higher than normal	1. Impart the opposite spin (topspin) 2. Drop shot 3. Half volley
3. Sidespin to left	Stroke across ball from right to left	Ball rotates about its oblique axis from right to left in flight; as ball hits court it will hop to the right on opponent's court	Aim ball to side of court from which opponent's racket started in its stroking
4. Sidespin to right	Stroke across ball from left to right	Ball rotates left to right and hops left on opponent's court	Same as above, only aim left of opponent

2. Make the opponents hit the ball up to you on their returns by placing it at their feet.
3. Until an open spot appears, play the ball so that it lands along the baseline. When an open spot appears, shoot quickly for it.
4. The server should come to the net after most serves if both partners are especially good net players.
5. Smash, volley, and lob as often as possible and keep the ball back into the far court.
6. Keep your opponent guessing and on the move by playing to her weaknesses and using a variety of shots.
7. Make your opponent hit the ball up so you can hit it down on the return.
8. Keep attacking and moving in.
9. When all four players are at the net, drive the ball hard to the closest player; when both players are equal distances from the net, hit the ball so that it lands low down the center of the court or is hit to the weaker opponent.
10. Remember that in doubles most points are won from the net position.

Key phrases to use to teach strategy are (1) play through your *strengths* to your opponent's *weaknesses,* (2) anticipate your opponent, (3) keep your opponent moving, (4) change the pace, and (5) always change a losing game.

CLASS ORGANIZATION

Although every teaching situation differs in time length, class size, available facilities, and other factors, there are certain essentials to keep in mind when teaching the tennis unit. These are as follows:

1. Follow a clearly given demonstration (explained as briefly as possible) with student activity as soon as possible. Explain by using key phrases and terms and remember that students learn largely by *doing*, not by watching or listening.
2. Give enough time for students to experiment and explore stroke movements until they get the "feel" of what they are doing and *why* they are doing it.
3. Use a variety of teaching methods, remembering that some people are quickly motivated by their own movement experimentation, while others may be motivated by watching a demonstration of a skillfully played game.
4. Grouping is of utmost importance in the successful teaching of tennis. Even in a class of beginners, there will be marked skill-learning differences. A simple wall-test is suggested for quick homogeneous class grouping. Have each player stand behind a line 20 feet away from the backboard or wall and try to hit the ball continuously for as long as possible. The player should be allowed to use any hitting method she wishes. After noting the differences in stroking ability, divide the class into matched skill groups of not more than six students. Since some persons will learn more quickly than others, move individuals up to a more advanced group as they progress in skill. At the same time keep providing new learning challenges for the highest group. Such changing of groups can be a great learning motivator.
5. Students should be encouraged to practice on their own after class hours in order to perfect their skill. Playing with a more advanced player, hitting the ball against the backboard, and joining a school tennis club are all highly recommended. Round robin and ladder tournaments held after school will help increase student interest. Such things as a tennis bulletin board and the attending of local matches help students become tennis enthusiasts. A school-sponsored tennis play day will also help to create interest in the sport.

Careful planning coupled with good teaching is necessary if each class is to be an educational experience in which all students gain skill and learn new things. Driver, Le Fevre, Gould, and Murphy have splendid and specific suggestions for organizing classes for each tennis lesson.* Although their methods must be tailored to fit each instructor's unique situation, they will serve as excellent patterns. Regardless of which of the many techniques given below for grouping students is used, class members should develop their own rotation system so that each student receives the same amount of time in each assigned role, such as ball tosser, hitter, coach, or retriever (see Fig. 12–10).

---

*See the list of suggested readings for exact titles and publishing sources.

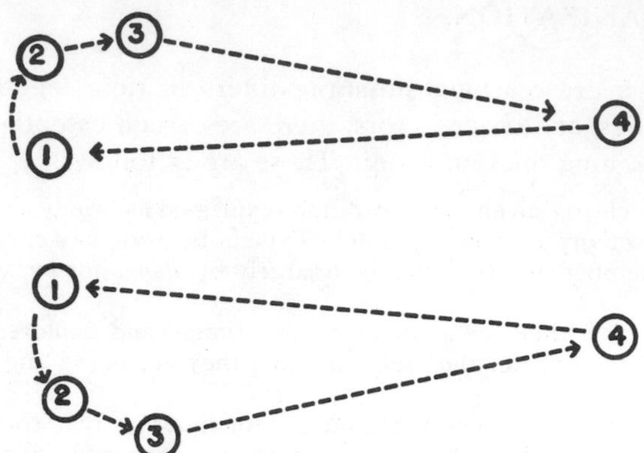

Figure 12–10 Player 1 strokes the ball, 2 drops the ball so that it bounces waist high for 1, 3 analyzes the form and makes suggestions for improvement, and 4 retrieves the ball. (From Vannier and Fait, *Teaching Physical Education in Secondary Schools.* 2nd ed. Philadelphia, W. B. Saunders Company, 1964.)

Suggested formations for teaching the forehand and backhand drives are as follows:

1. Face the class, which is in a single or staggered line so that all can see and hear well. Explain briefly how the strokes are done, demonstrate them, and have the class repeat them mimetically, without a ball or racket. Have them copy movements as you, with back turned to the group, perform each stroke. Repeat, using the racket.
2. Have one group of four demonstrate stroking backhand and forehand shots while the rest watch.
3. Have the class work in partners hitting the ball back and forth.
4. Have partners count one each time the ball is hit successfully across the net by a player and count two as it is returned, etc. Have each couple begin again if the ball is missed. Play until one group reaches 10 points first, then 15, then 25.
5. Have groups of four work in assigned roles (see Fig. 12–11). Have the one who is coach award one point each on a checksheet to the hitter when she uses the correct grip, stance, footwork, backswing, and follow-through for the forehand and backhand.
6. After players have learned placement fairly well, award one point for each time they succeed in making the opponent move around the court in order to get the ball, and one point for the hitter who succeeds in returning each well placed ball.
7. Award three points for a ball correctly returned cross court, two points for one in the back court, and one point for a ball correctly returned at mid-court.

Suggested group formations for teaching the serve are as follows:

1. Teacher demonstration and brief explanation followed first by mimetic movements done to counts, and then by using the ball and racket.
2. Use the following pattern: A serves to B who then serves to A, C to D,

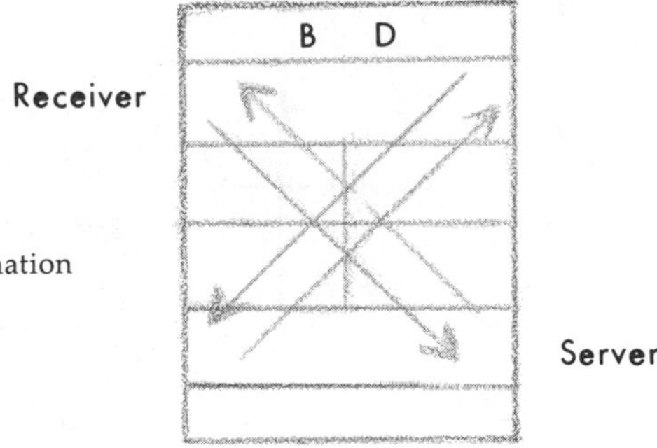

Figure 12–11 Suggested group formation for teaching the serve.

followed by D to C (see Fig. 12–11). (Additional students can be assigned to coach each server, then to become the server and her partner, her coach.)

Suggested group formations for teaching the smash and lob are as follows:

1. Have students work in couples. A throws the ball to B first near the net, and then at midcourt for the smash. Partners change roles.
2. Repeat formation for practicing the lob. A throws to B for a midcourt, then backcourt lob, first on forehand side, then backhand. Partners change roles.
3. Have students lob back and forth to each other using their rackets each time instead of throwing the ball.

Suggested group formations for teaching the volley are as follows:

1. Have students in couples with two, four, or six on a court. Those at baseline drive to their partners who volley ball back. Partners change roles.
2. Arrange six players as illustrated below (Fig. 12–12). F drives the ball to A, B, or C, and the one who receives it volleys back to anyone on the baseline. Play continues until all are eliminated for missing the ball or using the wrong stroke. Players change roles.

Suggested group formations for working at a backboard include the following:

1. Have players stand 20 feet from the board,* feet together, and strike the ball from a bounce, hitting each rebounded ball by stepping into the shot, using either forehand or backhand stroke.
2. Place two, four, or six players in a file. The first in each line rallies against the board, then the second, and so forth. The one hitting the ball above the tennis net line the greatest number of consecutive hits for a given time period wins.
3. Have players work in partners. Two, four, six, or eight can be in each line.

*A line, the exact tennis net height, should be drawn on the board. A target area, and a ten foot line from the floor to show where the ball should not land should also be drawn. Players should always aim at the target and play the ball between the two lines.

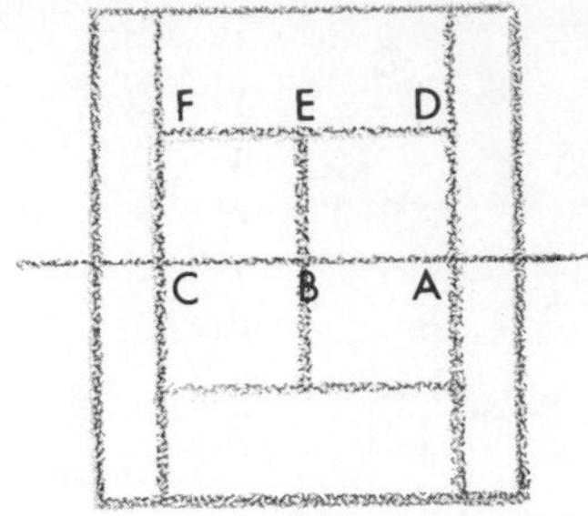

Figure 12–12 Suggested group formation for teaching the volley. A, B, C—hitters; D, E, F—tossers.

The first two, working together, keep the ball in play alternating shots, trying to do so longer than any other couple.

4. Same couple formation. First two in each line compete to see which one can outrally the other. One point is scored for each person doing so, and all compete to win for their line or team.
5. Players working singly hit first one forehand stroke, then one backhand, two of each, three, four, etc.
6. Practice serves from behind a line 39 feet from the target. Score one point for each correctly placed ball which lands in a target area above the net line and below the ten foot top line. Have each person serve 10 balls.
7. From behind a line 25 feet from the target, have each student rally the ball 20 times against the wall without missing.
8. Have each student practice 25 backhand and forehand strokes, alternating each shot.

TEACHING PROGRESSION

Although some instructors favor starting a tennis unit with the volley, the majority of experts claim that most students will learn other strokes more readily after they have mastered grip, footwork, timing, and the rhythmic feel of the forehand. Regardless of how the class is started, throughout the unit each student should receive as much individual coaching from the teacher as possible, and the player should be encouraged to develop her own style of playing as long as it is done in good form. Little time should be spent in the initial lesson discussing the history of the sport or explaining how a stroke is done, game strategy, or rules. Rather, the group should begin practicing and experimenting with the basic movements of each stroke after they have been demonstrated by the teacher. The forehand and backhand drives can be taught in a single lesson, especially to skilled students. The serve, usually more difficult to master, should be taught early in the unit, too, so that by the third lesson the group can start playing a game. Rules can be more easily learned as the class progresses and can be taught in conjunction with strokes to which they apply. Usually a rainy day is the best time to catch up on scoring rules or game strategy, and these can best be taught through films or filmstrips, followed by a class discussion.

Since the use of backboard practice for at least 15 minutes at a time is far superior to working with a poorly skilled partner, each player should be assigned a backboard practice time, whether it be during the class or after school hours. Students should be encouraged to *think through their mistakes* and to analyze for themselves when they fail to hit the ball correctly or send it out of bounds. The teacher, through the repetition of key statements such as "stroke the ball" or "hit in the *sweet part* of your racket," can help each person grasp their meaning more quickly. Since many girls need to develop back and shoulder girdle strength, a certain portion of each class period should be spent doing specific exercises which will do this. Emphasis should be placed in each lesson upon mastering good form and the rhythmic movement of the body, for accurate ball placement and speed depend upon these two factors.

Since the whole-part-whole method of teaching is most productive in helping students learn quickly, early in the unit the class should watch a demonstration game of both singles and doubles played by experts. Likewise, when teaching each stroke, the teacher should demonstrate the correct way of doing it. This should be followed by pupil experimentation before the class begins to work on single aspects of a stroke, such as proper ball toss in learning the serve or the basic footwork of the forehand. Above all, each class member should have a pleasurable learning experience each period and should go away from the lesson with a feeling of having accomplished something of real value as the result of her investment of time, energy, and much hard work. The instructor should stress positive actions such as "do this" instead of "don't do that." With encouragement, a motivated drive to learn to play tennis correctly and skillfully will spur student effort until this desired goal is obtained.

A suggested unit consisting of ten lessons for beginners and intermediates follows. Skills of lob, volley, smash, and chop may not be appropriate for all groups.

Lesson I

1. Warm-up exercises
2. Brief discussion of the history and basic idea of a tennis game
3. The three grips (Eastern, Western, Continental)
4. Bounce ball up from the "sweet part" of the racket 50 times without moving the feet; down for the same number of times
5. Basic footwork patterns
6. The forehand stroke
7. The backhand stroke
8. Backboard practice
9. Trial practice across the net with a partner

Lesson II

1. Warm-up exercises
2. Review of previous lesson
3. Brief illustrated chalk talk on ball spins
4. Supervised backboard and court practice of forehand and backhand strokes
5. Watch a singles and doubles game demonstration and explain simplified game rules for singles and doubles as students watch the game
6. Review footwork and change of grip for the forehand and backhand.

Lesson III

1. Warm-up exercises
2. Review of previous lessons
3. The serve
4. Supervised backboard and court practice of the serve
5. Play the best two out of three games of doubles

Lesson IV

1. Warm-up exercises
2. Review of previous lessons
3. Supervised backboard and court practice of the serve, forehand, and backhand
4. Play the best three out of four games of singles

Lesson V

1. Warm-up exercises
2. Review of scoring
3. Supervised backboard and court practice
4. Volleys at the net and midcourt
5. Give a simple serve test. Judge on the basis of the number of good serves out of 10 trials.

Lesson VI

1. Warm-up exercises
2. Assign backboard practice for after class
3. Teach the lob (to those ready for new skills)
4. Practice the volley
5. Play the best two out of three doubles games

Lesson VII

1. Warm-up exercises
2. Review the lob and volley (where appropriate)
3. Play any ball placement games
4. Give intensive individual help on all strokes.
5. Play doubles games

Lesson VIII

1. Warm-up exercises
2. Review the serve, volley, forehand, and backhand strokes
3. Discuss briefly game strategy for singles
4. Start a round robin, one set tournament in singles and doubles (the rest of the games to be played during after-school hours)
5. Teach the smash

Lesson IX

1. Warm-up exercises
2. Discuss briefly game strategy for doubles
3. Play two out of three doubles games as teacher observes, giving individual coaching hints

Lesson X

1. Warm-up exercises
2. Teach the chop (only if the students have learned other strokes well)
3. Play singles or doubles
4. Review entire unit
5. Give skill test and written test on rules (may be given in ninth lesson)

Rainy Day Plans

1. Discuss history in more detail
2. Show films and filmstrips
3. Discuss the purchase and care of equipment
4. Repair or learn how rackets are repaired
5. Learn about the tennis "greats"
6. Inside wall practice

SKILL DIFFICULTIES AND THEIR CORRECTION

The Forehand and Backhand Drives

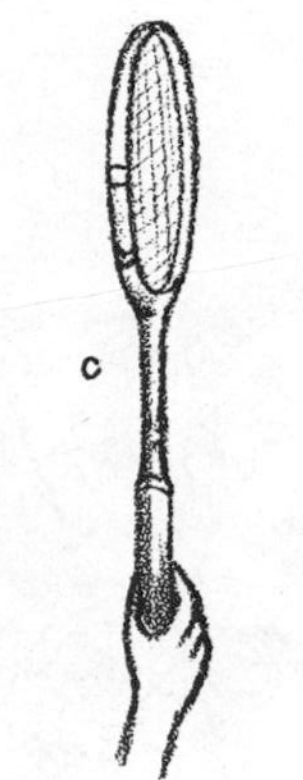

Difficulty	*Correction*
a. Forefinger extended	a. Remind student to curl all fingers around the racket
b. Too tight and tense a grip, or holding the racket too loosely	b. Say "relax" repeatedly to the student during the period. When racket is held loosely have student repeat "grip" as she begins her backswing and "stroke" as she swings forward
c. Racket face tilted back or forward too far	c. Demonstrate correct position; have student regrasp the racket several times and check the face position with her then and several times during the period. Put racket against net to show way it should be held
d. Awkward incomplete swing; swinging the racket too close to the body	d. Instructor places her hand over student's hand, and they do the stroke together until the latter gets the "feel" of the stroke

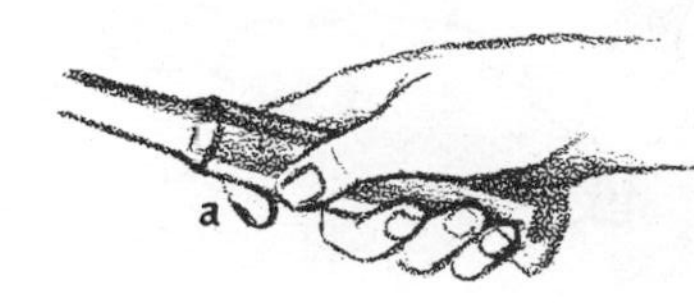

e. Body gets in the way of the backhand stroke

e. Have student stand with back to net, eyes on the ball, looking back over her shoulder with racket in backhand position. Teacher drops ball, arm-and-racket length away, and student hits the ball at the top of the bounce. Stress weight shift and hips leading the forward motion

f. Wrong foot forward

f. Demonstrate law of opposition in movement

g. Weight shifted at wrong time

g. Demonstrate weight shift. Take hold of student's hand and have her do it with you until she gets the feel of the movement (see e)

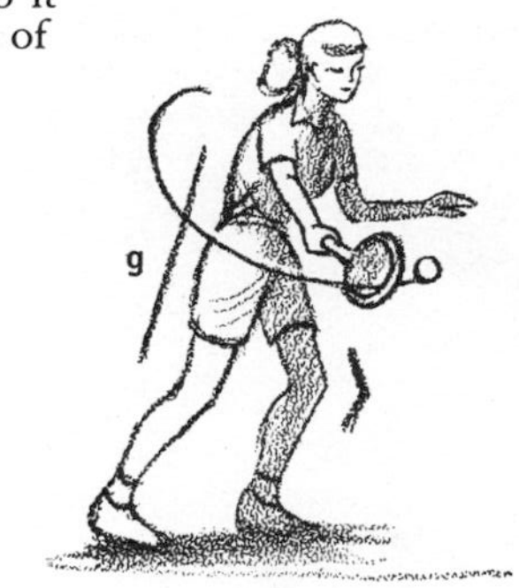

h. Unrhythmic movement, "punching" at the ball

h. Demonstrate a rhythmic stroke, have student copy it without, then with, a racket; stress a full swing each time the ball is hit

i. Swinging racket up or down instead of in a straight line in a faulty follow-through; turning the racket face too far forward or back	i. Demonstrate the 9 o'clock past 3 o'clock stroke. Check and remind student to check position of the racket face
j. Wrist and racket head dropping during the stroke	j. Demonstrate correct form for stroking and have student copy the movement. Suggest student do "towel wringing" exercises to develop wrist strength
k. Incorrect wrist action	k. Keep wrist in a more locked, restricted position

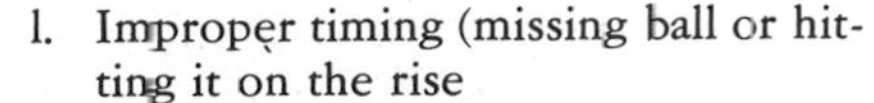

l. Improper timing (missing ball or hitting it on the rise

l. Start backswing sooner. Start forward swing before the ball bounces in front of the body. Remind student to *get set,* wait, and then stroke as ball descends

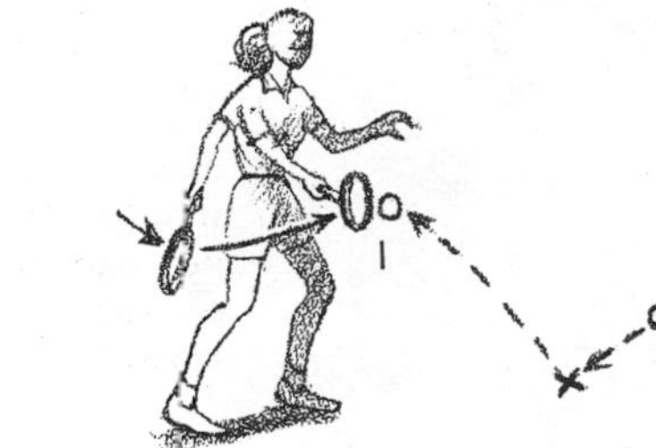

m. Dropping the ball too near body, or too close, or at side of body

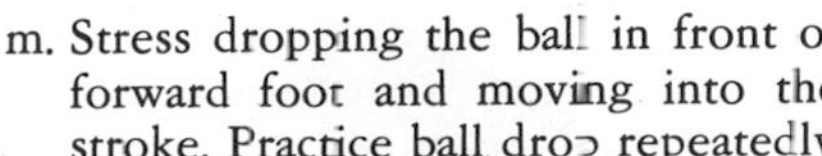

m. Stress dropping the ball in front of forward foot and moving into the stroke. Practice ball drop repeatedly

The Serve

Difficulty	*Correction*
a. Incorrect grip 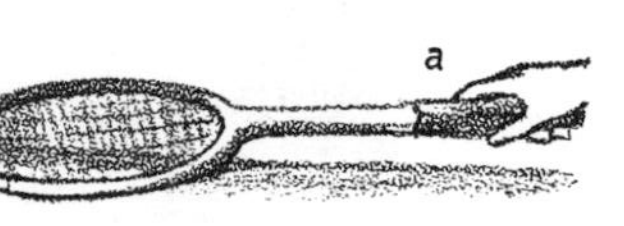	a. Check grip and have student do it correctly for you several times 
b. Incorrect wrist action	b. Stress flexible wrist. Demonstrate the similarity to the overhand softball throw. Have student copy movement with and without the racket. Stress "throw the racket at the ball"
c. Ball toss too far in front or behind, too far left or right, too low or too high 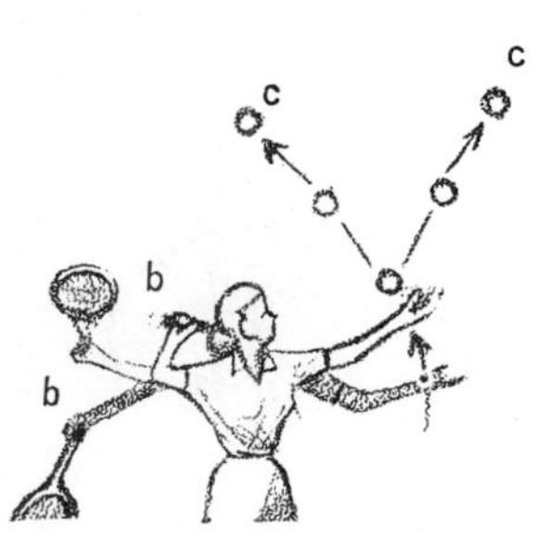	c. Practice correct ball "lift" stressing correct height in relationship to body position; have student toss and catch several balls correctly without using the racket; stress a "lift" with entire arm, *not* a wrist toss 

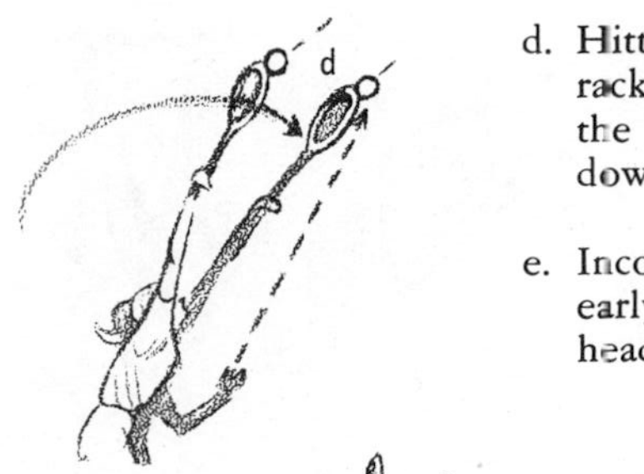

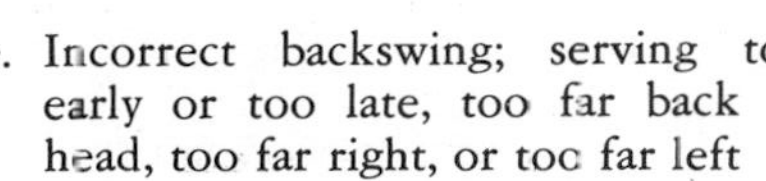

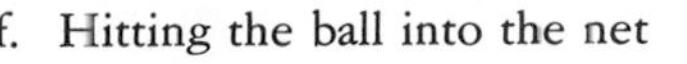

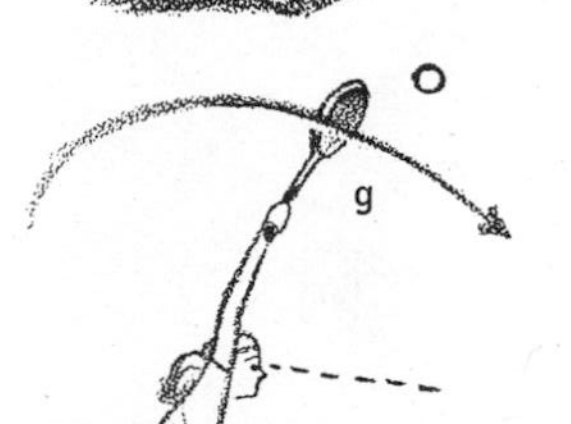

Fault	Correction
d. Hitting the ball with the wood of the racket; failure to connect ball with the racket; pulling racket and arm down on follow-through	d. Stress hitting the ball on the "sweet part"; observe and correct timing of ball toss and swing; stress high toss and hitting with extended arm
e. Incorrect backswing; serving too early or too late, too far back of head, too far right, or too far left	e. Teach by demonstrating whole serve; work on individual part of the serve; reemphasize correct timing of swing to the ball toss
f. Hitting the ball into the net	f. Toss ball higher up and out in front of body; hit it above the head instead of at eye level to get it over the net. Stress correct rhythm of coordinating toss and arm swing
g. Missing the ball entirely	g. Stress "watch the ball." Have student repeat ball bounce drills; work individually with the player against the backboard.

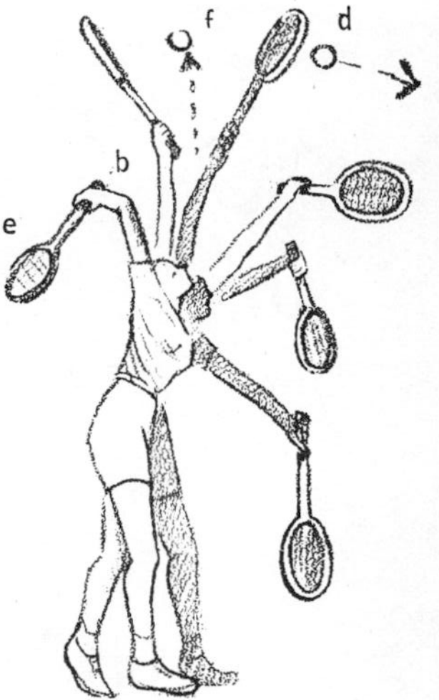

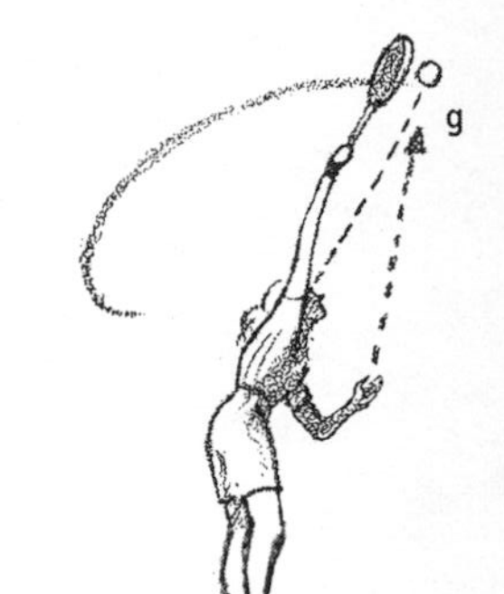

The Volley

Difficulty	*Correction*
a. Player too tense	a. Stress a relaxed, easy body position with knees slightly bent
b. Standing too near or too far from the net	b. Show again the correct court position which will be the middle of the service court
c. Dropping the head of the racket	c. Have student do the stroke in slow motion several times and point out each time this error is made. Stress keeping the racket head above the wrist. If ball comes low, bend the knees. Be sure student knows what this mistake causes the ball to do
d. Wobbly wrist action	d. Tighten grip slightly before stroking the ball
e. Missing the ball entirely	e. Stress "watch the ball" until it becomes automatic to do so

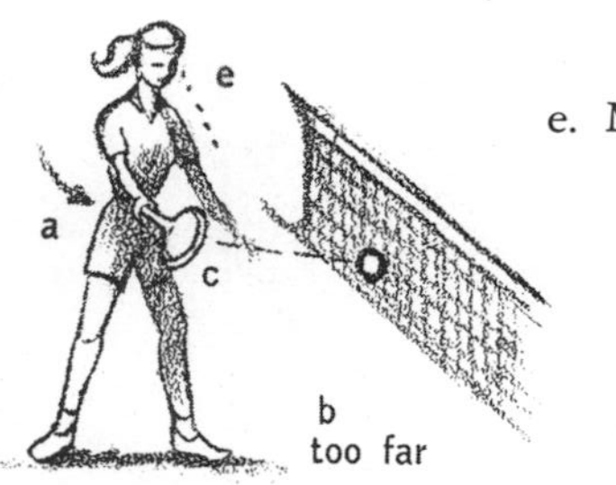

The Lob

Difficulty	*Correction*
a. Not hitting the ball high enough into the air; hitting it too much like a line drive	a. Open racket face more. Stress stroking the ball up; show what the opponent can do to an incorrectly played lob
b. Inability to fool opponent whether a lob, forehand, or backhand drive is to be used	b. Discuss and demonstrate the defensive and offensive lob; demonstrate and stress modifying the stroke at the last minute so as not to give the opponent enough time to be prepared for it

The Smash

Difficulty	*Correction*
a. Missing the ball entirely, or failing to hit it squarely	a. Stress relaxation and watching the ball at all times. Do not rush stroke. Watch ball. Keep ball in front of body. Reach *up* to hit ball with arm at full extension
b. Hitting the ball into the net	b. Correct hitting the ball too low and too far out from the body. Review serving form

EVALUATING THE RESULTS

Experts are generally agreed that a player's skill can be evaluated by means of (1) a form rating scale, (2) tournament standing, (3) recording of rallying accuracy against a backboard, and (4) checking one's ability to place the ball accurately into certain court areas. But as Driver states:

> Unfortunately there is no proof that a player's *form* rating, or her *rallying* ability, or her *placing* ability correlate satisfactorily with her playing ability. Moreover, when we look at the records of nationally ranked tennis stars, we find tournament results are not always reliable. A player, eliminated one week in a tournament by an inferior opponent, may win the next week over a player ranked far above herself.
>
> Tennis tests, however invalid and unreliable, are worthwhile for two reasons: (1) they measure ability to rally, place the ball, use correct form, and show the amount of improvement the student has made, and (2) they are an incentive for practice, for they establish tangible goals.*

A Form Rating Scale. Since the mastery of good form is imperative if one wishes to become a skilled tennis player, the instructor should use a form rating scale for each student at least twice during a unit, observing and rating her during game play as well as at practice against a backboard. Such a rating scale might well include the items shown in Figure 12–13.

*See Helen Driver: *Tennis for Teachers.* Enlarged edition. 803 Moygara Road, Frost Woods, Madison, Wisconsin 53704.

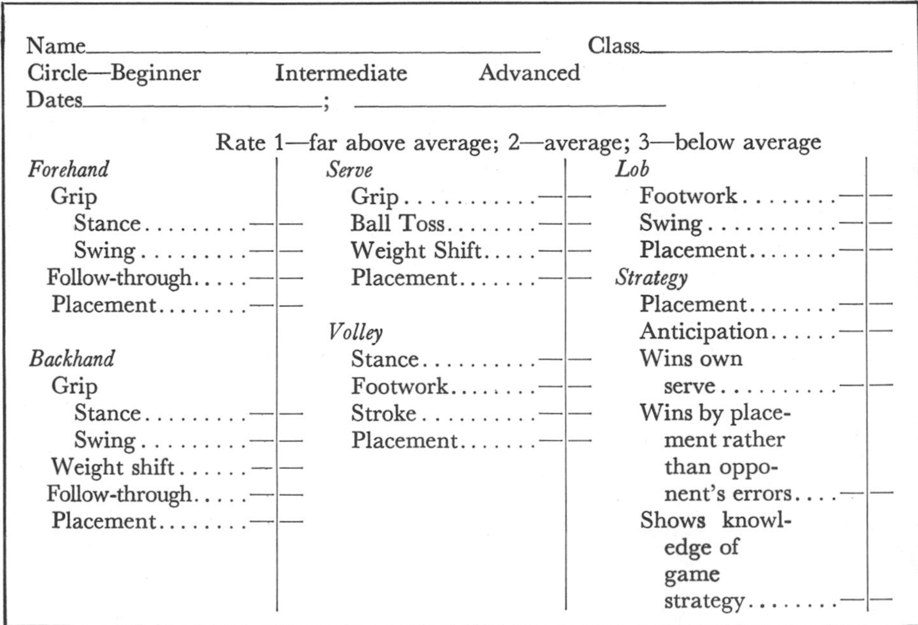

Name____________________ Class____________
Circle—Beginner Intermediate Advanced
Dates____________; ____________

Rate 1—far above average; 2—average; 3—below average

Forehand	*Serve*	*Lob*
Grip	Grip . . . . — —	Footwork . . . . — —
Stance . . . . — —	Ball Toss . . . . — —	Swing . . . . — —
Swing . . . . — —	Weight Shift . . . . . — —	Placement . . . . — —
Follow-through . . . . . — —	Placement . . . . — —	*Strategy*
Placement . . . . — —		Placement . . . . — —
	Volley	Anticipation . . . . . . — —
Backhand	Stance . . . . — —	Wins own serve . . . . — —
Grip	Footwork . . . . — —	
Stance . . . . — —	Stroke . . . . — —	Wins by placement rather than opponent's errors . . . . — —
Swing . . . . — —	Placement . . . . — —	
Weight shift . . . . . . — —		
Follow-through . . . . . — —		
Placement . . . . — —		Shows knowledge of game strategy . . . . — —

Figure 12–13 A scale for rating form in tennis.

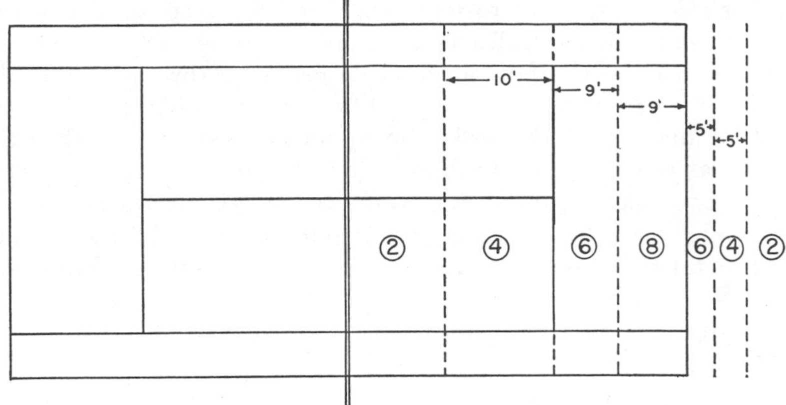

Figure 12–14 Court markings for the Broer-Miller Tennis Test. (From Mathews: *Measurement in Physical Education.* 4th Ed. Philadelphia, W. B. Saunders Co., 1973.)

Accuracy Test. The Broer-Miller Tennis Test is recommended for discovering the strengths and weaknesses in the forehand and backhand strokes and placement ability. For this test a rope is stretched 4 feet above the net top and the court is marked off in areas for scoring as shown in Figure 12–14. In order to score the value shown, the ball must go between the rope and net top and land in the area or on a boundary line of that area. Those which go over and land in another area score only one-half of the value for that area. A trial is counted if the ball is missed, but let balls may be taken over. Each player has 14 balls for forehand tries and 14 for the backhand. A curved scale for rating all in the group can be made, and the test, although time-consuming to give, does motivate players to work harder on both their strokes and their placement skill.

The Tennis Drive Skill Test. The purpose of this test is to evaluate the subject's performance in hitting tennis drives from an oncoming ball in what is as nearly like a game situation as possible. The test determines the degree of accuracy the player has in stroking the ball properly so that it is hit low across the net and deep in the backcourt.†

Tournament Standing. A ladder, round robin, or double elimination tournament is suggested for obtaining a more accurate knowledge of a player's ability to compete. Because these tournaments are time-consuming, some may have to be played outside regular class time.

Rallying Against a Backboard. Hewitt's Revision of the Dyer Backboard Test is recommended for the purpose of rallying against a backboard. A line 3 inches wide and 3 feet from the floor is drawn on a back-

---

†For directions for giving this test consult the June 1972–June 1974 DGWS *Tennis-Badminton-Squash Guide,* pp. 39–42.

board or smooth wall area to represent a net. A restraining line is drawn 20 feet from the wall base. Each student, tested one at a time, has two balls in one hand, access to a box of extra balls placed nearby, and a racket. The object of the test is to hit the ball with any type of stroke so it will strike above the net line on the wall as many times as possible in 30 seconds. The ball is put in play by a hit from a single bounce. All balls hit while the player is over the restraining line do not count. If control over any ball is lost, another one may be put in play. A point is counted for each ball hit above the three-foot line. The average of three trials is the student's score.*

TERMINOLOGY

Ace—A skillfully placed serve which the receiver cannot return or touch with her racket.
Backspin—Reverse ball spin done by hitting down under the ball.
Break a serve—Winning a game served by the opponent.
Chop stroke—A sharp hack-like stroke which causes the ball to backspin and bounce low.
Double fault—Failure on both service attempts.
Fault—A served ball which goes out of bounds or into the wrong service court.
Foot fault—Moving the feet or stepping on or over the baseline while serving.
Half-volley—Hitting the ball when it begins to bounce up from the court.
Hold—The server wins the game she serves.
Let—(1) A serve which hits the top of the net but is otherwise good. (2) A point played over because of interference.
Lob—Upward ball flight which sends the ball over the opponent's head.
Opening—A defensive error which gives the opponent a good chance to gain a point.
Rushing—Coming up to the net after hitting an approach shot.
Slice—A ball that is caused to underspin by being hit at an angle 45 degrees to the ground.
Smash—Hitting the ball down with great force.
Volley—Playing the ball before it bounces.
Wide—A shot that lands beyond the sideline.

DISCUSSION QUESTIONS

1. Devise a tennis unit of eight lessons for beginners, intermediates, and advanced players. Give the objectives, course content, techniques to stress, and means of evaluating each one.
2. Plan the organization for a four hour tennis clinic for teachers. If possible, present the clinic to a group of teachers in your community. Evaluate what you have learned from this experience.
3. Observe a set of singles and doubles. Score one point each time each player uses good game strategy. Discuss your findings with them.
4. Read and summarize any chapter in any book from the reading list found below. Give a brief report in class on what you learned from this experience.
5. Demonstrate the correct footwork for the serve, forehand drive, backhand drive, volley, and lob.
6. Write a short, one page paper on any one of the world's tennis greats. Give the reasons why this person became a champion.

---

*For suggestions of tennis tests of forehand placement, backhand placement, service placement, service speed, and rallying ability see Ted A. Baumgartner and Andrew S. Jackson: *Measurement for Evaluation in Physical Education: Review and Resource Manual.* Boston, Houghton Mifflin, 1975.

SELECTED AUDIOVISUAL AIDS

Anyone for Tennis. (color.) United States Lawn Tennis Association, Education and Research Center, 71 University Place, Princeton, New Jersey 08540.

Beginning Tennis. All-American Productions, P. O. Box 801, Riverside, California 92502.

Beginning Tennis Series. (6 slide films, 35 mm., sound, color.) Athletic Institute, 705 Merchandise Mart, Chicago, 60654. (Purchase and rental)

Championship Tennis. (20 min., color.) Tennis Associates, 13170 Lorene Court, Mt. View, California 94040.

Don Budge Instructional Films: Tennis for Beginners, Tennis for Everybody, Slow Motion Long Films for Tennis Instruction, United States Lawn Tennis Association, Education and Research Center, 71 University Place, Princeton, New Jersey 08540. (Purchase and rental)

Elementary Fundamentals. (b & w, color.) All-American Productions, P. O. Box 91, Greeley, Colorado 80632.

Elementary Tennis. (15 min., color.) Dennis Van der Meer, World Tennis, Box 3, Gracie Station, New York 10028.

Fundamentals of Tennis. (b & w.) University of Arizona, Tucson, Arizona 85721.

Great Moments in the History of Tennis. American Safety Razor Co., Phillip Morris, Inc., 100 Park Avenue, New York, New York 10017.

The How To's of Tennis. Wheaties Sports Federation, Title Insurance Bldg., Minneapolis, Minnesota 55401.

Intermediate and Advanced Fundamentals. (b & w, color.) All-American Productions, P. O. Box 801, Riverside, California 92502.

Intermediate and Advanced Tennis. (b & w.) T. N. Rogers Productions, 6641 Clearsprings Road, Santa Susana, California 93063.

Tennis Class Organization. (16 mm., 25 min., sound, color) T. N. Rogers Productions, 6641 Clearsprings Road, Santa Susana, California 93063. (Rental)

Tennis Class Organization. (25 min., color.) United States Lawn Tennis Association, Education and Research Center, 71 University Place, Princeton, New Jersey 08540.

Tennis for Beginners. (b & w, color.) United States Lawn Tennis Association, Education and Research Center, 71 University Place, Princeton, New Jersey 08540.

Tennis for Everybody. (b & w, color.) Allegro Film Productions, 201 West 52nd Street, New York, New York 10019.

Tennis Fundamentals. (color.) Tennis Films International, Inc., 137 Newbury Street, Boston, Mass. 02116.

Tennis—A Game of a Lifetime. (19 min., b & w.) United States Lawn Tennis Association, Education and Research Center, 71 University Place, Princeton, New Jersey 08540.

Tennis—Sport of a Lifetime. Part One: Class Organization. (30 min., color.) Youth Tennis Foundation of Southern California, 609 West Cahuenga Boulevard, Los Angeles, California 90028.

Tennis Singles Strategy. (11 min., 16 mm., sound, color.) *Doubles Strategy.* (11 min., 16 mm., sound, color.) All-American Productions, P.O. Box 801, Riverside, California 92502.

Tennis Techniques. (16 mm., 12 min., sound, color.) T. N. Rogers Productions, 6641 Clearsprings Road, Santa Susana, California 93063. (Purchase)

The Way to Wimbledon. (20 min., b & w, color.) British Information Services, 45 Rockefeller Plaza, New York, New York 10020.

SUGGESTED READINGS

American Association for Health, Physical Education and Recreation: *Ideas for Tennis Instruction, Lifetime Sports Education Project.* Revised Ed. Washington, D.C., 1967.

Barnaby, John: *Racket Work: The Key to Tennis.* Boston, Allyn and Bacon, 1969.

Broer, Marion: *Individual Sports for Women.* 5th Ed. Philadelphia, W. B. Saunders Co., 1971.

Everett, Peter, and Skillman, Virginia: *Beginning Tennis.* Rev. Ed. Belmont, California, Wadsworth Publishing Co., 1968.

Gould, Dick: *Tennis, Anyone?* Palo Alto, California, National Press Books, 1971.

Johnson, Joan, and Xanthos, Paul: *Tennis.* Dubuque, Iowa, Wm. C. Brown Co., 1967.

Gensemer, Robert: *Tennis.* 2nd Ed. Philadelphia, W. B. Saunders Co., 1975.

Laver, Rod: *How to Play Championship Tennis.* New York, The Macmillan Co., 1965.
Murphy, William, and Murphy, Chester: *Tennis for Beginners.* New York, Ronald Press, 1958.
Murphy William, and Murphy, Chester: *Tennis for the Player, Teacher and Coach.* Philadelphia, W. B. Saunders Co., 1975.
Pearce, Wayne, and Pearce, Janice: *Tennis.* Englewood Cliffs, New Jersey, Prentice-Hall, Inc., 1971.
Pelton, Barry: *Tennis.* Pacific Palisades, California, Goodyear Publishing Co., 1969.
Sports Illustrated Editors: *Sports Illustrated Book of Tennis.* New York, J. B. Lippincott Co., 1961.
Talbert, William and Olds, Bruce S.: *Stroke Production in the Game of Tennis.* Philadelphia, J. B. Lippincott Co., 1971.
Talbert, William, and Olds, Bruce S.: *The Game of Doubles in Tennis.* Philadelphia, J. B. Lippincott Co., 1968.
Telmanis, Gundars: *Advanced Tennis for Coaches, Teachers and Players.* Philadelphia, Lea and Febiger, 1975.
Tennis and Badminton Guide. AAHPER, DGWS, Washington, D.C.
Trengrove, Alan (ed.): *Tennis the Professional Way.* New York, Simon and Schuster, 1964.
Unit on Tennis: The Serve, Return Service, Forehand Drive, Net Attack, Doubles, Practice and Training for Match Play. United States Lawn Tennis Association, 120 Broadway, New York, New York.
USLTA-AAHPER: *Tennis Group Instruction.* Washington, D.C., American Association for Health, Physical Education and Recreation, 1963.
Vannier, Maryhelen, and Fait, Hollis: Teaching Physical Education in Secondary Schools. 4th Ed. Philadelphia, W. B. Saunders Co., 1975.
Xanthos, Paul J: *Tennis, A Pictorial Guide for Teachers.* Woodland Hills, California, Pierce College, 1963.

SUGGESTED TEACHING AIDS

Tennis Kit: How to Organize and Conduct a Tennis Clinic, How to Improve Your Tennis, Tennis Instructor's Guide, Rules of Lawn Tennis, Your Guide to Good Courtmanship, Tennis Lessons for Young Players. A Tennis Program for Elementary and Secondary Schools. United States Lawn Tennis Association, Education and Research Center, 71 University Place, Princeton, New Jersey 08540.
Tennis Practice Set. (sandbag, ball on an elastic cord). Moody Company, Milford, Connecticut.
Whiffle Plastic Tennis Balls. Cosom Corporation, 6030 Wayzata Boulevard, Minneapolis, Minnesota.
Fleece Puff Balls. Tennis Fleece Company, 111 South Green Street, East Stroudsburg, Pennsylvania.
Short Rackets (23", 22" length). Swing Tip Company, 112 Parkview Terrace, Newark, New Hampshire.
Pick-Up Ball Basket. Ball Hopper, 1328 Woodland Drive, Deerfield, Illinois.
Stroke Developers on Electric Cords. (Available from most athletic supply companies.)
Tennis Group Instruction. AAHPER, 6 posters.
Tennis Technique Charts. NAGWS-AAHPER, 12 charts.

PERIODICALS

American Lawn Tennis. South Carolina Avenue, Clinton, South Carolina.
Lawn Tennis Magazine. Lowlands, Wenhasten, Halesworth, Suffolk, England.
Sports Illustrated. 541 North Fairbanks Court, Chicago, Illinois 60611.
Tennis Features. P.O. Box 5, Ravinia Station, Highland Park, Illinois 60035.
Tennis U.S.A. Box 2248, South Hackensack, New Jersey 07606.
Tennis West. Box 5048, Santa Monica, California 90405.
Tennis World. 116a High Street, Bechenham, Kent, England.
World Tennis Magazine. Box 3, Gracie Station, New York 10028.

CHAPTER 13

TRACK AND FIELD

Track and field includes activities as old as basic human movement. The competitive events of today undoubtedly grew from the first men who gained pleasure in running, leaping over streams and fallen trees, and throwing rocks and spears. These survival skills turned to sport as man became less dependent on them for existence.

During the Golden Age of Greece, the pattern for modern track and field events developed. In the Olympic Festival of 776 B.C. men participated in broad jumping and discus and javelin throwing in much the same form as in the Olympic games of today. Although women were barred as competitors and spectators at the Olympiad, they engaged in a special festival, the Herea, in which they competed in foot races in specified age groups.

Competitive track was not popular until brief enthusiasm for it grew in England in the middle of the nineteenth century. The real emphasis came with the opening of the modern Olympic games in 1896. At this time, women were not included as participants in track and field events, and it was not until after World War I that international interest was aroused for competition between women. Lacking permission to compete in the Olympics, five countries sent 111 athletes to an international track and field meet for women in 1921. With this added pressure, the governing body of the Olympics reconsidered allowing women to enter, and in 1928 six events were open to them in track and field competition. Expansion of interest and participation continued, and in the 1964 Tokyo Olympic games women participated in 12 events, including the challenging pentathlon.

American men have long been enthusiastic competitors and have dominated track and field events. American women, however, have only competed in track and field events in the Olympic games since 1928. Since that time women have been excellent performers in the 100 meter dash, 800 meter run, 400 meter relay, the running high jump, the discus throw, the 200 meter dash, the javelin throw, the shot put, 80 meter hurdles, and the long jump.

NATURE AND PURPOSE OF THE SPORT

Track and field events are divided into the three major groups: running, jumping, and throwing. Many forms of competition use a combination of these skills. The track events include dashes, runs, relays and hurdles. Girls and women participate in events modified and designed for their age and ability levels. Field events are the running high jump, long jumps, shot put, discus throw, basketball and softball throw, and javelin throw. Performance is individual, but a group may combine and participate in selected team events with or against a given group or against various record holders in a number of events from the past. Track competition recognizes individual skill as well as team score. The variety of events assures everyone an activity in which she can develop speed, skill, agility, and endurance.

SUMMARY OF RULES AND SCORING*

Dash, Relay and Hurdle Events

1. At the start, runners may not touch on or over the starting line before the gun is fired. Two false starts disqualify a runner.
2. Each runner must stay in her own lane during the entire race on a straightaway track.
3. She finishes the race when any part of her *torso* has reached the finish line.
4. When hurdling, the individual must pass over the hurdle. She is disqualified if any part of her body passes to the side. Knocking down hurdles does not disqualify the runner.
5. Relays are run by four different girls running their prescribed distance.
6. In pursuit relays, the baton must be passed in the 22 yard zone. If the baton is dropped, it must be picked up by the same runner and then passed.
7. The events are timed from the pistol flash to the moment the finish line is crossed.

All the jumping events allow three time trials and the running jumps permit unlimited approaches. (The seven best competitors have three additional trials.) In competitive meets, a competitor is allowed two minutes from the time her name is called to commence her approach.

---

*See NAGWS *Track and Field Guide* for detailed rules, changes in rules, and recommended events for all age groups.

Running Long Jump

1. Using as long a run as she desires, the runner uses only one foot to leave the takeoff board.
2. The scratch line is the edge of the takeoff board nearest the jumping pit. If the jumper touches the ground in front, the jump is a foul.

Standing Long Jump

1. The jumper may curl her toes over the end of the board. Part of both feet must remain in contact with the takeoff board until the jump is made.
2. If the jumper touches the ground in front of the scratch line with any part of her body, the jump is a foul and not measured.
3. As in the running long jump, measurement of the jump is made at right angles from the scratch line to the nearest break in the sand made by any part of the body of the jumper.

Running High Jump

1. The jumper may take an unlimited approach, but she may use only one foot on take-off.
2. Three trials at each height are allowed. Three successive failures at one height disqualify the jumper.
3. Displacing the bar, passing under it, crossing the line of the bar extended, or leaving the ground are trials.
4. The measurement is taken from the ground to the lowest part of the upper side of the bar. The last jump cleared is recorded as the jumper's best effort.

In all throwing events, the competitor has three throws. (The seven best competitors have three more throws.)

Shot Put and Discus

1. No part of the person may touch the stop-board, circle, or ground outside the circle before the distance has been marked.
2. Valid puts must fall within the sector lines.
3. The put must be made with one hand on a line with, and in front of, the shoulder.
4. Both shot and discus throwers leave the ring from the rear after the throw is marked.
5. The discus may be thrown with or without a body turn.
6. Valid discus throws must fall within a 60 degree sector extending from the center of the circle.
7. Measurement of the throws is made from the nearest mark of the object to the inside circumference of the circle (on a line from the mark to the center of the circle).

Javelin Throw

1. The javelin must be thrown over the shoulder or upper part of the throwing arm from a standing position or a run, but only one hand (little finger nearest to the point) may grip during the approach and throw.
2. The throw must be made behind the scratch line arc of a circle drawn with a radius of 26 feet 3 inches. The runway is 13 feet 1½ inches wide, terminating at the arc.
3. A valid throw must fall within the sector formed by extending the radii through the ends of the arc for 295 feet.
4. Touching on or over the arc or runway lines is a foul but counts as a trial.
5. The point of the javelin must hit the ground first, but the javelin does not have to stick in the ground.
6. Measurement is taken at the inner edge of the circumference of the arc (made on a line from the nearest mark made by javelin point to the center of the arc circle).

Ball Throws

1. The throws may be made with or without a run.
2. Throws are made from behind a scratch line 10 feet long and 2 inches wide.
3. Stepping on or over the line before the throw has been marked is a foul.
4. The delivery must be made with one hand.
5. Measurement is taken from the nearest mark to the inside edge of the center of the scratch line.

Scoring. Many persons are responsible for an efficient meet. The judges and timekeepers are directly responsible for determining the correct times and winners of the running events and distances for the field events. A point award system is suggested, which will make it possible to recognize any number of place-standings in the competition.*

If there is a tie for any place, unless specifically covered in the rules, as for the running high jump, the sum of the points of the places involved is equally divided among the tied competitors. Team scores are the total of individual and relay event points.

NEEDED FACILITIES AND EQUIPMENT

One of the advantages of track and field in the instructional program is the small amount of equipment necessary for large groups. The facilities should be laid out in one central area so a single teacher can supervise all the activities. No dangers are hidden in the events, but the usual safety precautions are necessary when throwing events are practiced while students are working on other field events and on the track.

Track Area. The track is an oval, usually 1/4 mile in length with curves having a radius of 80 to 110 feet. The outdoor track has a hard, level subsurface covered with cinders, tartan, or composition materials.

*See NAGWS *Track and Field Guide.*

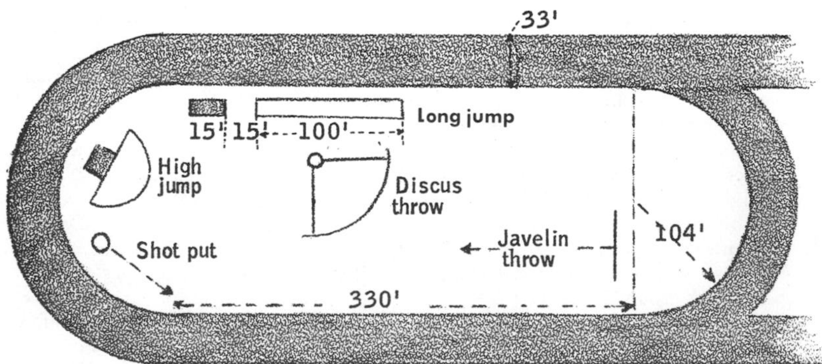

Figure 13–1 Athletic field and quarter mile track.

It must be smooth and properly graded for drainage. The indoor track is wood, clay, or dirt. In both cases one side is known as the straightaway and is measured for dash events. It should be a minimum of 22 feet wide to allow for six lanes of 42-inch hurdles. The curves and back side should be 18 feet, allowing a minimum of 3 feet for each of six lanes.

Field Area. Field events are generally held inside the running track. When properly placed and conducted, there are no safety hazards. The following markings are necessary:

1. Shot put—a circle 7 feet in diameter with a white stop board 4 feet long, 4½ inches wide, and 4 inches high.
2. Discus—a circle 8 feet, 2½ inches in diameter (made of wood, steel, or iron, painted white, and sunk on the ground).
3. Softball and basketball throw—a line 10 feet long and 2 inches wide.
4. Javelin throw—two parallel lines 13 feet 1½ inches apart, leading to a scratch line are drawn from a point so that the radius is 26 feet 3 inches. The arc is wood or metal 2¾ inches in width, painted white, and sunk flush with the ground. The radii extend for 295 feet to form the sector lines.
5. Long jumping events—a pit at least 15 feet in length by 9 feet in width filled with sawdust or sawdust and sand to aid drainage. A takeoff board must be 4 feet long, 8 inches wide, 4 inches high, and sunk flush with the ground. It is painted white.
6. High jump—a pit at least 16 feet 4 inches in length and 13 feet 1½ inches in width and built up no more than 28 nor less than 12 inches above the ground. Standards and a crossbar 13 feet 1½ inches long complete basic equipment. The crossbar may be made of wood, metal, fiber glass, bamboo, or other resilient material.

Equipment. For competition the following are essentials: pistol, cartridges, whistle, steel measuring tapes, stop watches, wool yarn, marking sticks, rakes, and shovels.

Equipment for specific events includes: starting blocks, batons, hurdles two feet six inches high and 2 feet nine inches high; beat board or raised takeoff board; high jump standards and bar; shots—6 pounds for elementary girls, 8 pounds for high school girls and 4 kilograms (8 lb. 13 oz.) for women of college age; discus measuring between 7³⁄₃₂ and 7⁵⁄₃₂ inches in diameter and weighing 2 pounds 3¼ ounces; javelin of metal or solid wood with a metal point weighing no less than 1 pound 5.2 ounces and measuring no less than 7 feet 2½ inches; official softballs and basket balls.

Costume. Students and instructors should be governed in their selection by safety, comfort, and attractiveness. Shirts of knitted material that cling to the body yet allow freedom, are more comfortable than those made of materials that whip in the wind. Shorts should fit the leg snugly and comfortably. Elastic in the undergarment or outer shorts is desirable. Tennis shoes and sneakers are satisfactory for class work and may be used in competitive meets, provided all persons wear similar type shoes. Spikes are unquestionably valuable and may be used for competition. Thin white socks or pushers (half-socks) may be worn with track and field shoes. A warm-up suit should be worn before and after all events.

TEACHING UNITS

The unit for beginners should aim to introduce a student to many events of track and field. The advanced unit is developed around specialized techniques and individual skill development in selected events. A suggested unit for beginning and advanced students includes:

Beginners

Purpose and value of track and field
Brief history of track and field and women in track
Warm-up and conditioning activities
Fundamental techniques of running
  Dashes
  Middle distance runs
  Long distance runs
Techniques of throwing
Techniques of jumping
Explanation of events
Specific skills
  Starts
  Competitive running
  Relays and baton passing
  Hurdling
  Softball throw
  Basketball throw
  Discus
  Shot put
  Javelin (high school and college)
  Running and standing long jump
  Running high jump
Intraclass meet
Evaluation

Advanced

Intensive review of all skills
Advanced techniques and competitive strategy
Specializing in two or three events; train and compete
Competitive meets
Officiating
Evaluation

BASIC SKILLS

Warm-up and Conditioning Activities. Warm-up activities should be designed to increase flexibility of all parts of the body. An organized program of conditioning should increase strength and endurance in all events. Jogging is an excellent way to begin. Jog high on the toes, feet straight, at a tempo slightly faster than a walk. Swing arms freely and increase jogging pace. Light calisthenic exercises that stretch and relax the muscles are beneficial in preparing the body for increased movement and preventing strains and pulls. Bicycling, leg stretches, reaches, and torso bends should be included in the warm-up. The 5 to 10 minute period should terminate in a series of one or more wind sprints. Begin on a 40 or 50 yard course in a jog, and increase speed until full effort is being given at the end of the course. Walk or jog back to the starting point and repeat the run. Sprints are usually run in series of three.

Those who are interested primarily in class or recreational track events should always have a warm-up period before starting specific events, whether this be throwing the discus or high jumping. For those who wish to take up this sport seriously, a good conditioning program should include preseason, early season, and competitive conditioning. Each of these should also include warm-up stretching, endurance, and flexibility exercises, individual as well as group exercises needed for each type of event, and distance and speed running. Students should also be taught warm-downs to do after they have performed, in order to bring the body back to its normal heart rate and temperature more quickly.

Cross-country running is an ideal conditioner as well as a developer of endurance, desirable body weight, and strength. Fartlek, or "speed play" for running at variable speeds and distances (from a 50 yard dash to jogging a given number of miles, for example) is also recommended. Interval training, in which the student runs at continuously changing paces at fixed times over fixed distances, (a fast 220 yard run in 35 seconds is followed by a two mile jog) is recommended. Repetitious running (doing 300 yards at 53 seconds four times, coupled with reducing rest intervals between runs) is also highly recommended. However, since running (wind sprints) is by far a more strenuous conditioner than cross-country running, Fartlek, and interval running, it should be used only after the student has developed a reasonable level of conditioning.

Resistance exercises or weight training can be used for general development or to develop strength in specific muscle groups, such as arms or legs. Handweights and free exercises are suggested also, since they constitute a new experience for many girls, who often enjoy doing them to music.

Running Events

Some skills are basic to all or part of every dash, run, or relay.

The Start. The runner begins from starting blocks or holes dug for the feet to aid in drive and speed at the takeoff. There are three general starting positions—the bunched start, the medium, or medium elongated, position, and the elongated start. In the bunched start the toe of the rear foot is opposite the front heel. In the more common medium start the knee of the rear leg is slightly ahead of the toes of the forward foot (this position is sometimes described as the knee of the rear leg opposite the instep of the front foot). In the elongated position the knee of the rear leg is opposite the back of the heel of the forward foot. Experience has shown that a slightly modified medium start is the one women use most often.

Block position is determined in the following manner: the front block is placed as close to the starting line as is comfortable for the runner. This is generally about 2 hand spans from the line, allowing for minor adjust-

Figure 13–2 The start.

ments. The back block is placed according to the type of start to be used by the runner. The runner sets her foot in the front block and adjusts the rear block prior to the start. Minor adjustments may be made if the feet seem too close or too far apart. At the official's signal "take your mark" the runner backs into the blocks and places the stronger leg (usually the left) in the front block with her toe on the ground and ball of the foot pushing. The rear foot touches the block and the knee drops to the ground. The hands are shoulder width apart. The thumb and index finger are placed parallel to the starting line as the other fingers extend to the ground, forming a firm, triangular base beneath the shoulders and extended arms. Body weight is on the thumb and fingers, the rear knee, and the foot of the forward left leg. The eyes look down the track 8 to 10 yards.

Three common starting commands are, "Take your mark," "Set," and "Go." (The last may be given by a voice, a whistle, or a gun.) On the signal "set" the hips are raised a bit higher than the head. Weight moves forward, and the back knee is raised approximately 4 inches from the ground. Weight is carried primarily on the hands and forward foot. If using a bunched start with feet close together, the hips rise more than in the other starts. The hips are at least level with the back. The position is held for approximately 2 seconds before the gun is fired.

The gunshot is the signal for both legs to drive. The back leg immediately leaves the block as the knee comes forward with foot low to the ground. The front leg pushes forcefully against the block, and arms and hands begin a powerful thrust as the body pulls out at a 45 degree angle (see Fig. 13–3). The arm, in opposition to the leg moving forward (right arm as left leg moves out), reaches forward forcefully as if trying to grasp something.

As the body is thrust forward, not upward, the back foot lands about 18 to 20 inches in front of the starting line. Succeeding strides should be

Figure 13–3

about 3/4 of an inch longer than the one before until full stride is reached. The arms work in opposition—the left one swings upward as the right foot swings through. Shoulders move forward and slightly up as the head and chest rise with the first strides until the runner is at proper sprinting angle in six or seven steps.

The *standing start* is used by the second, third, and fourth runners in a relay and in distance runs. For races in which all runners use a standing start, the starter uses only the command "Set" before firing the gun. The runner leans slightly forward with feet comfortably spread, arms in opposition to legs. The initial push is from the forward leg as the back leg steps out; arms continue coordinated opposition movements.

Sprinting. The concept of sprinting applies to 50 yard, 75 yard, 100 yard, 220 yard, and 440 yard dashes. A common misconception is that a short choppy stride is more effective than a longer stride for sprinting. A sprinter should try to reach her full stride as quickly as possible and hold it throughout the race. At full stride the body is angled about 20 or 25 degrees to benefit from the pushing power of the kick. On each stride the rear leg just completing the drive is brought forward with the heel under the hip as the knee is lifted fairly high in front to take advantage of the back leg drive. Weight lands on the ball of the foot, knee straightens, and pressure is

Figure 13–4 The standing start.

applied through the foot as heels almost touch the ground. The arms, held close to the sides with elbows bent at right angles, swing directly front and back.

Breathing should be as normal as possible. Take a breath on "go" and at least two or three while running if natural breathing is too tiring.

Regular running form should be continued until the torso crosses the finish line; then the runner gradually diminishes her speed. It is not advisable to jump, lunge, throw the head back, or raise the arms to throw the chest out when crossing the finish line.

Middle and Long Distance Running. In middle distance races, such as the 880 yard or 1500 meter, a runner finds that when trying to run full power she may suffer muscle fatigue. She must learn to "float" or coast for part of the distance. She applies full power for the first third, floats for the middle third, and reapplies power to finish.

In 1 mile or 1500 meter, 2 mile or 3000 meter, 1½, 2, and 2½ mile cross country races (or 4000 and 10,000 meter runs on track and marathons where sanctioned), when a given speed must be maintained over the distance, the knee lift is not as great. The runner is more erect, takes shorter strides and uses more of her foot.

It is important to help students discipline themselves through a training program so that they can become excellent middle and long distance runners. Running on grass as well as on the track is suggested for workouts early in season, and periodically throughout it, in order to prevent boredom. All runners should be constantly encouraged to improve their performance daily, but care must be taken not to push them to a point of physiologic fatigue and emotional staleness. Each should be encouraged to follow a planned, progressively more challenging practice schedule in order to progress from one proficiency level to a higher one.

Relays. Relay races are of two types—pursuit and shuttle. In both types each member of a team of four girls runs a specified distance, each then being relieved by another at some designated point.

All the techniques of starting and sprinting apply in the short distance relays. A shuttle relay involves a team traveling over and back across the same ground touching right shoulder, hand, or passing a baton for the exchange. In the more popular pursuit relay an awaiting runner is followed by her teammate and contact is made as both run to continue the course in the same direction. Generally, the most advantageous placement of runners is to begin with the second fastest, then the slowest, and the next slowest third. The fastest runner is the last, or *anchor.*

In pursuit relays the baton is passed in a nonvisual or blind exchange, or a visual or sight exchange. The visual exchange is the safest but also the slowest method. The condition of the incoming runner determines the type of pass. If she has come only a short distance and is not too tired to control the placement of the baton, a blind exchange is made. Use a sight exchange if the runner is obviously too fatigued to control the baton. This is the most popular pass for beginners.

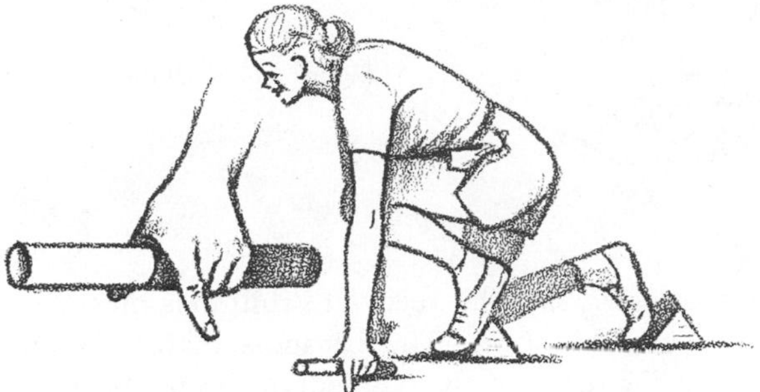

Figure 13–5 Starting with the baton.

The first runner starts from a crouched position with the baton grasped back of center by the three last fingers of the left hand. The thumb and index finger are arched behind the starting line.

The baton transfer must be completed within a 22 yard zone or the team suffers disqualification.

In pursuit relays up through 880 yards or 800 meters, the runner who will receive the baton may begin running eleven yards outside the passing zone, but the baton must be passed only in the 22 yard zone. When the oncoming runner reaches a predetermined mark, the waiting runner begins to sprint. The passer must have sufficient reserve speed to overtake the runner and place the baton. *Blind exchanges* with the right hand are as follows:

Basket Pass. The receiving runner places fingertips on hips, elbow out at the side. The baton is placed in the open palm by a downward motion. This pass loses an arm's distance in the exchange and is dangerous for beginners, as the elbow often blocks the opening or the thumb blocks the baton placement.

Figure 13–6 Inverted basket pass.

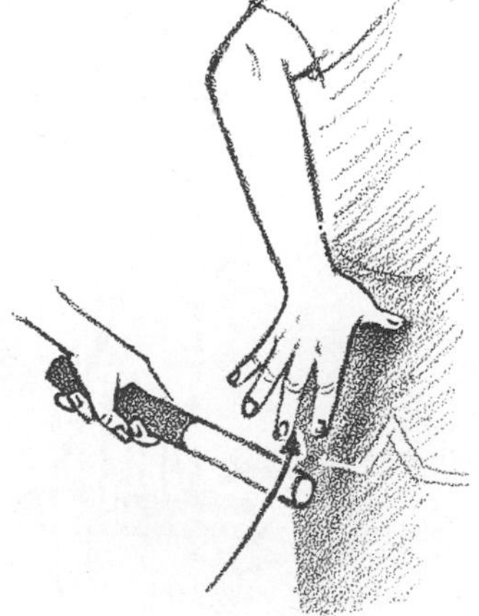

Figure 13–7 Underarm extension palm-up pass.

Inverted Basket Pass. The receiver's thumb is on the hip, palm open, fingers spread out and down. The baton is placed in the palm by an upward swing. It has some of the dangers of the basket pass.

Underarm Extension Palm-up Pass. The arm of the receiver is extended to the rear in an underarm fashion with palm up. The baton is placed by a downward motion.

Underarm Extension Palm-backward Pass. The arm and hand extend to the rear with thumb and fingers spread so that the palm is toward the oncoming runner. The baton is placed in the "V" of thumb and forefinger on upward swing. This is a safe pass, once the receiver learns to keep her arm from wavering when receiving. It is often called the "natural" pass and is probably the most commonly used today.

Visual exchanges with the receiver watching the approaching runner are as follows:

Overarm Extension Palm-up Pass. Arm of the receiver is palm up reaching back as the runner places the baton with a downward swing.

Overarm Extension Palm Outward. The receiving thumb and fingers are extended with palm out to receive the baton passed perpendicular to the ground.

Underarm Extension Palm-backward Pass. Executed like the blind underarm extension, this pass is excellent for beginners because the movements are simple and familiar.

The baton must be actually passed, not thrown or dropped. If it is dropped, it must be picked up by the same runner and then passed. After grasping the baton securely, the runner transfers it to her left hand if she is

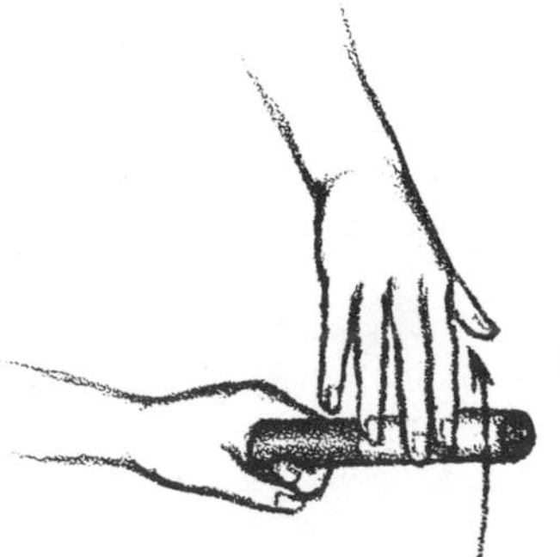

Figure 13–8 Underarm extension palm-backward pass.

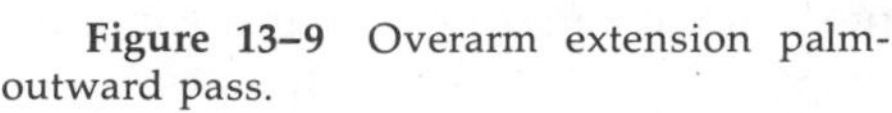
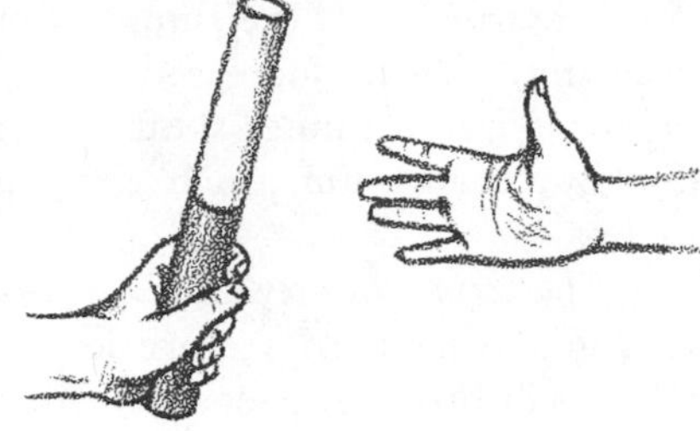

Figure 13–9 Overarm extension palm-outward pass.

to pass to another runner. After the pass has been completed, the runner finishing her "leg" should jog straight ahead. She then leaves the track as soon as possible.

Baton passing is more difficult in shuttle relays, and beginners should use a hand or shoulder touch in preference to a baton. When using a baton, the right hand of the receiver should be raised above the shoulder, palm upward and forward. The incoming runner slaps the baton across the palm of the receiver between the thumb and forefinger.

Cross-country Running. Increasingly, women are becoming interested in and are participating in this sport of distance running in open areas. Long a favorite of many male athletes, it is not an official competitive event for women at the present time. Jogging enthusiasts, sprinters, and other runners who become bored with running around the same track, will welcome the opportunity which this sport brings for working out on various kinds of turf, whether they be flat, rugged, grassy, or sandy terrain, or wooded and open areas.

Figure 13–10 Overarm extension palm-up pass.

The training of the runner should be progressive, since the miles covered are gradually increased. A distance of one half mile is suggested for beginners. Each runner should set and work toward reaching an advanced goal by a certain time, such as striving to run five miles within three months or less.

The cross-country course for competitive events should be varied terrain in the form of a cloverleaf and have a smooth-surfaced finish line which will provide spectators and officials with a good view of all racing finalists.

Hurdling. The techniques of the start, sprint, and finish as previously described also apply to hurdles. Hurdling is divided into the phases of start, approach, hurdle stride, and sprint between hurdles.

Start. The start is the same as that described for dashes, except that some runners find it necessary to reverse the position of the feet so that the forward foot at the start is the takeoff foot in clearing the hurdles. Usually the foot that is back at the start is the one that leads over the hurdle.

Approach. A runner defines her stronger leg as the takeoff leg. The first hurdle is 39 feet 4½ inches, 42 feet 7¾ inches, 52 feet 6 inches, or 147 feet 7½ inches from the starting line, depending on the distance of the event. The runner counts her strides to the takeoff point in front of the hurdle. If she uses seven strides, her takeoff leg is placed on the rear starting block; if eight strides, the takeoff leg is on the front block with the lead leg behind. Timing and consistent starts are important. If adjustments must be made they should be at the block rather than at the hurdle. Watch the hurdle bar rather than predetermined marks on the track.

In hurdle events, the hurdle height is 2 feet 6 inches or 2 feet 9 inches, with 26 feet 3 inches, 27 feet 10½ inches, 62 feet 4 inches, or 114 feet 10 inches between hurdles.

Hurdle Stride. When the takeoff leg is 5 or 6 feet from the hurdle, the lead leg is brought straight forward with a high knee lift. The toe is

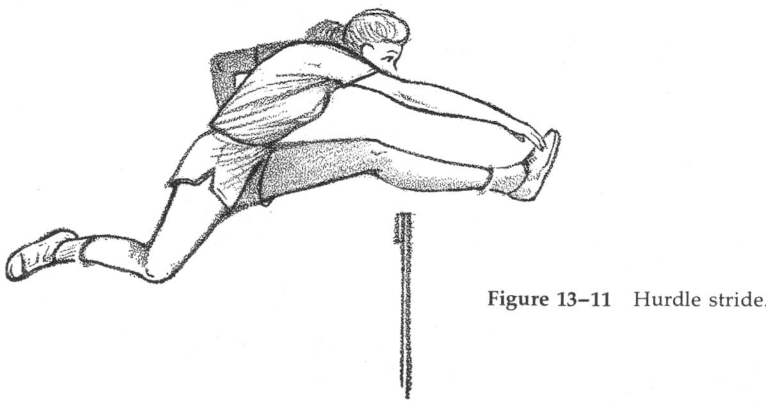

Figure 13–11 Hurdle stride.

pointing upward with slight flexion in the lead leg. The body leans forward with shoulders kept square. The lead arm swings in opposition to the lead leg and extends with the body thrust.

Correct hurdling form duplicates, as nearly as possible, basic movements of sprinting action. The take-off leg should push the center of gravity forward and upward for the body to clear the barrier. The leg extends fully so the hurdler "runs over" rather than jumps up and down. The head of the skillful hurdler remains at the same level—that is, does not bob—when she is sprinting or hurdling. As the leg rises to a position parallel to the ground, the knee rotates so that the toes are pointing away from the body with the knee and ankle flexed. The knee is higher than the toes, and the toes are higher than the ankle.

Sprint. The lead leg comes to the track on the ball of the foot with toes pointing straight ahead and close to the barrier so that a sprint push can begin. The ball of the foot is beneath or behind the body to insure a balanced landing. Assume a sprint position and stride toward the next hurdle. The distance between hurdles is measured so that an odd number of strides is taken and the takeoff and lead legs are the same for each barrier.

It is suggested that the hurdling barriers be low for beginners, preferably 1½ feet high and that the proper techniques for clearing these barriers be mastered before each student is allowed to run a full course of gradually raised barrier heights, reaching the full height of 2½ or 2¾ feet.

Field Events

Field events include all jumping and throwing skills.

Running High Jump. The jump is preceded by a running approach, which develops momentum to get across the bar. To determine the spot to begin the approach, go to the front of the bar and turn the takeoff side to the bar. A girl who kicks a ball with the right foot usually uses the left as the takeoff foot. Extend the left arm and step away from the bar so that the knuckles of the left hand are touching the bar. This is the takeoff spot. Turn and angle off at approximately 45 degrees, taking a seven stride run. From this mark, turn around and begin on your right foot angling to the bar for a seven step approach. This is the left foot takeoff used by most girls.

The Jump. The western roll, straddle roll and back (Fosbury) flop have replaced the "scissors" form of clearing the bar in a sitting position with legs scissoring.

Take-off. As the jumper approaches the bar with a relaxed, springy stride, her left shoulder is toward the bar. From the longer final stride and a wide takeoff base, she leans slightly backward to achieve a vertical take-off. With the eyes above the center of the cross-bar she kicks the right leg forward and upward moving the body directly over the left foot. Upward

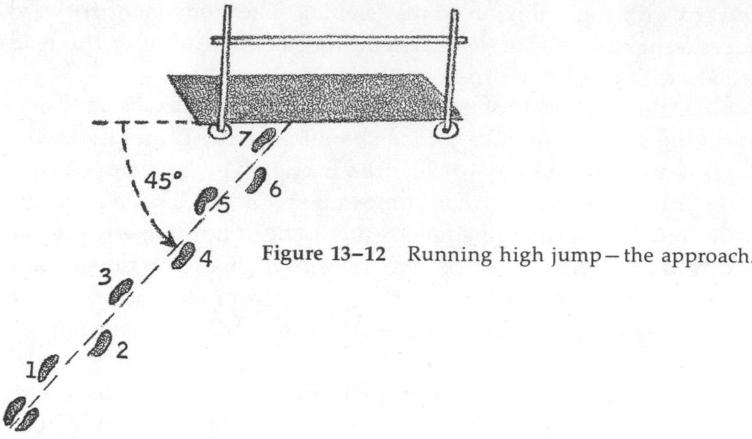

Figure 13–12 Running high jump – the approach.

drive is helped by forcefully lifting both arms, with emphasis on the left to correspond with right leg swing-up. The takeoff foot pushes off the toes when the kick-up leg is between the waist and the chest.

Western Roll. The takeoff leg (left) tucks by the side of the right leg with toes almost touching behind the right knee as they pass over the bar. Crossing the bar, the body is on its side, thighs close together. The action of thrusting the left arm and head downward raises the left hip an inch or more over the bar. Once over the bar, the left leg touches the ground first with the hands following quickly. As the body turns after passing over the bar, the right leg is extended behind.

Figure 13–13 The western roll.

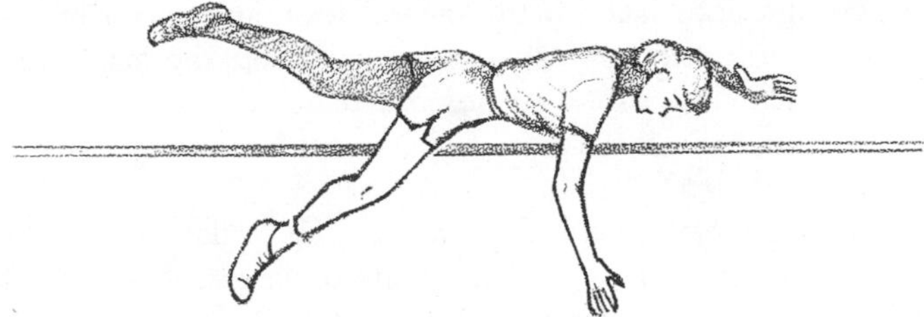

Figure 13–14 The straddle roll.

Straddle Roll. The straddle roll is considered easier by many jumpers and more effective for height. With a similar approach and takeoff, the right (lead) leg swings up, and as the left foot leaves the ground the layout begins. The toe of the left leg turns out, and the knee twists out and up. The body is facing down as it passes the bar with right arm and head clearing the bar first. The left arm and shoulder are up and back from the bar until the body is over the bar. The head turns to the left to aid in the roll as the body clears the bar. The body will roll so that the landing is on the jumper's back and seat. If the roll is not full, the landing is on the right leg and both hands, followed by a roll to the right shoulder. This should be considered when learning or jumping at low heights.

Long Jump (Running). The total jump includes an approach, takeoff, flight, and landing.

Approach. For the *approach* the runner finds her starting position by standing on the takeoff board with both feet and stepping out with the foot opposite the desired takeoff foot. Run 16 to 20 full strides (approximately 85 to 110 feet) while someone counts the third or fourth, seventh or ninth, and sixteenth to twentieth strides. Selection of checkpoints depends upon the runner's choice, but mark the last stride as the starting point. Use these checkpoints to standardize the stride and determine speed and takeoff

Figure 13–15 The running long jump.

position. Begin the approach on the takeoff foot, and sprint forward. The run should provide optimum, not maximum, speed the last three strides before takeoff. The last three strides are used for gathering force and power for the jump; the last stride is shortened before hitting the takeoff board with the heel first.

Takeoff. The *takeoff* begins from a heel first or flat-footed position on the board. The leg straightens, and the body rocks over the foot as the toe and ankle aid the drive of the takeoff leg. The first movements after the takeoff are concerned with gaining maximum height in the jump. The eyes should look above the horizon.

Flight. There are two basic methods of flight—the *tuck jump* and the *hitch kick.* The tuck jump is an easier technique for beginners, but some feel there is more power in the more difficult hitch kick. In executing the hitch kick the lead leg is forward; it then straightens and swings down and back as the takeoff leg kicks forward and upward. The original lead leg kicks forward, and the legs are extended and brought together for landing. The arms work in opposition to leg action and are thrust forward vigorously on landing.

The takeoff is the same for the tuck (also called sailing jump, or float). The lead leg swings upward, and the takeoff leg kicks forward as both knees come toward the body. The body appears to be sitting in the air with legs extended.

Landing. In preparation for landing, the legs and heels are extended. At the moment the heels touch the ground, the lowest point of the buttocks is but a fraction above the level of the extended heels. As the heels contact, the head and shoulders thrust forward and downward, and the chin is pulled between the knees. The arms are thrust forward simultaneously, and the knees bend quickly and fully allowing the body to fall forward.

Standing Long Jump. The jumper stands with both feet on the takeoff board. With toes over the edge, the body rocks forward and back. The takeoff is made by simultaneous drive and spring from both legs as the arms swing upward lifting the body. At the height of the jump the arms are forward, the heels are near hip height, and the upper part of the body is leaning forward. Legs swing forward as the arms remain extended to assure a forward or sideward fall.

Throwing Events

Basketball Throw. In addition to being an independent field event, this throw is used to lead up to the discus throw. A running approach may be used prior to delivery. (For specific techniques refer to running approaches in the section on the javelin.) The hurler stands with feet apart and left shoulder toward the throwing line. The official ball is held by the right hand and supported by the wrist and fingers. As the body bends to the right over a bent right knee, the left leg and arm extend. Hips lead through, and weight transfers to the forward left foot before the right arm whips through in a sidearm delivery with a wrist and finger snap. A reverse follows.

Softball Throw. The softball throw is generally preceded by a run ending in a hop-step. (Refer to running approaches for the javelin throw.) The preferred overarm throw begins by facing the throwing line with the left foot slightly in front. Both hands grasp the ball at chest or chin level. The hands pass over the head as the left leg lifts. The body leans backward, rotating slightly to the right. The right knee flexes as the bent right arm comes back to a position parallel to the ground. The left arm is up for balance. The body braces against a firm left leg and the right arm follows with a whiplike motion and a flick of the wrist and fingers. This throw is often used to lead up to the javelin throw.

Shot Put. The shot put is classified as a throwing event, but beginners should remember that it actually involves a pushing or thrusting action rather than a throwing action. The following description is for a right-handed delivery. Grip the shot near the base of comfortably spread fingers with the hand behind the shot. The shot *must not* rest in the palm of the hand. As control and strength of the hand increase the shot is held by the first three fingers with the thumb and little finger curled under and around the sides. The shot is tucked against the neck, close to the jawbone and slightly in front of the shoulder. The hand is behind and under the shot, and the right elbow is bent, pointing sideward and away from the body.

Stand at the back of the ring with the left shoulder pointed in the direction of the put and the left arm extended forward and upward for balance. The body is facing backward and supported by a bent right leg. The feet are comfortably spread with both feet angled toward the rear of the

Figure 13–16 The shot put.

circle. The left leg lifts and may swing forward and kick backward (to front of ring) several times in anticipation of forward momentum. As the left leg kicks backward close to the ground for the last time, a quick gliding hop of the right leg is immediately followed by a pivot of the right foot; and as the right leg, still bearing the body weight, straightens, the hips and trunk rotate toward the left.

The weight is transferred to the left foot as the torso and hips push through and the shot is brought forward. The shot must not advance in front of the body before the hips rotate. The push-off is made from the right toes, but the foot stays in contact with the ground until the shot is released. (The body push comes from both legs and the hips, *not* the shoulders.)

As the body faces front, the right arm extends firmly and smoothly and pushes upward and forward at approximately a 45 degree angle. The shot is released with a wrist snap and finger push. At the moment of release the weight is over the left foot, and the left arm remains at shoulder level.

After the shot is released the right foot replaces the left in the follow-through, and the left arm pulls back to aid in the reverse. This reverse action helps stop forward momentum so the putter does not step on or over the toe board or circle.

Discus. The right-handed thrower places the discus on the palm of the right hand and hooks the end joint of the first three fingers over the rim. The thumb and little fingers are spread across the back, covering the discus with as much of the hand as possible. To aid in support, the back edge of the discus rests against the wrist.

Beginners should master the *standing throw* before attempting a turn. Place the left side of the body toward the direction of the throw, and spread feet comfortably. Several preliminary swings are executed to gain rhythm and momentum prior to the release. In preparation, the right arm, slightly flexed, is in front of the body, and the right hand is holding the

Figure 13–17 The discus throw.

discus with support by the palm of the left hand. The right arm extends and swings backward at waist level as far as possible. The discus is no longer supported by the left hand but remains in the fingers of the right hand through the force and momentum of the swing. The left arm is bent and in front of the body at chest level. As the backswing begins, the knees are bent and relaxed, the weight shifts to the right foot, and the hips and shoulders rotate to the right.

The return forward movement of the body is initiated by the right foot, leg thrust, and hip rotation. The arm and discus follow the rotation of the trunk and the shift of weight to the left foot.

After a limited number of purposeful preliminary swings the discus is released at approximately a 40 degree angle by a vigorous armswing and snap of the forearm, wrist, and fingers. The discus leaves the index finger last so that a clockwise spin is imparted.

At the moment of release the body weight is over the left leg, and the head and chest are raised. The throwing arm continues upward and across the body at eye level and ends in a "salute" position by the head. In a vigorous throw the hurler may be carried into a half turn so that her right foot ends where the left was at the start.

Throw with a Turn. To gain more power the throw is preceded by a turn. The turn must be smooth and rapid throughout the gliding action. Both knees are flexed and the body is slightly bent as it faces the rear of the circle. Both feet point to the rear of the circle with the right slightly forward of the left in a stride stance position. The turn begins as the arm swings back from the last preliminary swing. The weight shifts to the left foot, and the body pivots over and around the left foot. The right foot, without breaking momentum, steps in front of the left in continuing the turn. The hurler has now completed a full turn and is again facing the back of the circle. From this point, with body weight on the right leg, the hips initiate action, and the turn continues with the throwing arm trailing as the left leg steps through. The arm follows the body turn, and action terminates in the release as described above. The right leg steps forward and extends in a reverse to stop the forward momentum of the thrower.

Javelin Throw. The techniques of the javelin throw are similar to an overarm ball throw and should be familiar movements to the beginning javelin thrower. The throw may be taken with or without a run, but the beginner should practice it from a standstill before coordinating all movements for a running delivery.

Grip. The most common grip used by women is the *American grip.* It is quite natural and somewhat similar to the tennis handshake with the arm extended. The thumb and index finger grasp the rear edge of the 5⁷⁄₈ inch cord binding near the middle of the shaft, and the other three fingers close around the binding. The javelin rests across the palm diagonally from between the thumb and index finger to the base of the palm. The grip is relaxed and the wrist flexible.

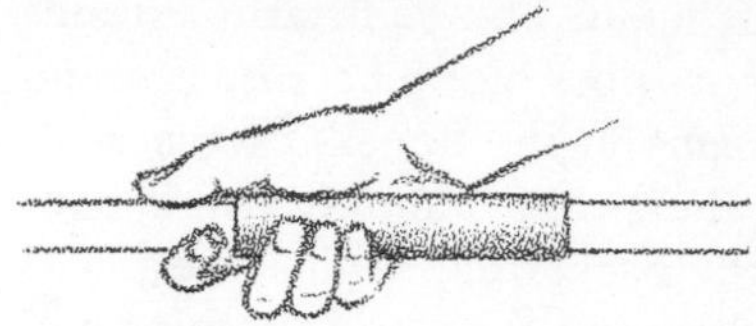

Figure 13–18 The American grip.

Carry. The carry is an important phase in the preparation for delivery. The most natural and frequently used carry is the *Finnish carry.* In executing this carry the elbow is bent and pointing downward, and the hand is over the shoulder and carried about eye level. The palm is up, and the tip of the javelin is pointing slightly downward toward the front as the arm moves smoothly and easily with the run.

In the *over the shoulder carry* the elbow is bent and pointing forward to the throwing line, and the point of the javelin is raised upward.

Approach Run. The purpose of the approach run in any throwing event is to develop momentum and thereby gain speed and force for the throw. To measure the distance and establish a pattern for the run, measure the distance of the run as if preparing for the running broad jump. Begin at the throwing line and run approximately 90 feet, marking two check points—one at the beginning of the run and one about 30 feet from the throwing line. The second check point should be six strides from the throwing line where the cross-step prior to the throw begins.

The run begins from a standing position in which both feet are together. The runner steps out on her left foot and starts running slowly. She accelerates until she hits the second check point with her left foot (at this point she should be running at optimum speed). She then begins the preparation for the throw and reverse by one of the following methods:

Finnish cross-step. This technique of preparing for the throw is considered superior to the two other techniques that follow. Most throwers prefer this technique, but some find the hop-step more satisfactory and less difficult.

The cross-step begins after the left foot hits the check point. (1) The right foot strikes the ground with toes pointing straight ahead in the direction of the throw. The body begins to lean backward, and the throwing arm begins to straighten backward. The shoulders remain parallel to the throwing line. (2) The left foot steps forward and slightly into the path of the right foot with toes pointing toward the throwing line. The body turns slightly, placing the left side toward the line, as

Figure 13–19 Javelin carries.

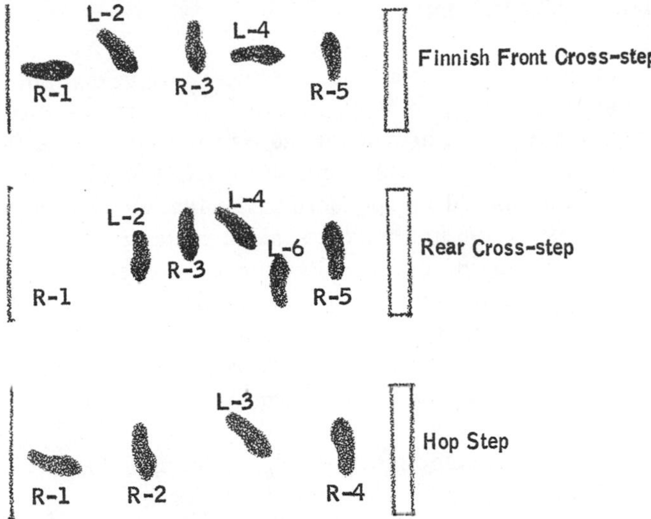

Figure 13–20 Approach runs.

the right arm extends farther back. The tip of the javelin remains at eye level. (3) The right foot and leg cross the left with the body turned slightly and the left shoulder angled toward the direction of delivery. (4) The left foot steps forward with the toes angled slightly to the right and toward the delivery line. As the left foot is moving into this step, the body whips into the throw, and the arm moves forcefully overhead to release the javelin at approximately a 45 degree angle. (5) The throw is completed and the right foot steps left to reverse the forward action and prevent fouling.

In practicing the cross-step, the rhythm of the steps is important. Diagrammed it is: 1. . .2–3. . .4. . .5.

Rear cross-step. After the left foot reaches the check point, the right foot moves forward, the left foot moves into the path, turning left side toward line. The right foot moves up and *behind* the left, and the left foot moves forward and to the right. After the throw the right foot reverses.

Hop-step. After the left foot hits the check point, the right one moves forward, going right. On the second count the right foot hops with foot parallel to the line. On count three the left foot moves forward, and the throw and reverse follow.

The Throw. As mentioned previously, the throw is similar to an overarm ball throw for distance. The throw begins as the body is pushed upward and forward by leg thrust and torso and hip action. The extended arm bends slightly as it moves upward and forward. The head is up, eyes are focused on the line of flight, and the left arm is extended for balance. The javelin rests on the palm. The forward thrust is given by the arm, shoulder, and body until the instant of the whiplike release when the wrist snaps forcefully. "The height of the javelin throw is more dependent upon the backward angle of the trunk than it is upon getting the point high."*

*See Phebe M. Scott, and Virginia R. Crafts: *Track and Field for Girls and Women.* New York, Appleton-Century-Crofts, 1964, p. 149.

CLASS ORGANIZATION

One teacher can instruct a large class with proper equipment and facilities. She should determine what activities are appropriate for each age level. Ideally, by the end of high school all girls should have participated in each track and field activity suggested by NAGWS. Intramural and interscholastic events should be sponsored. The teacher gives a general introduction and instruction in the basic skills of running events. General instruction is also given in jumping and throwing events. Using student assistants, the class can be divided into squads for practice, and the instructor can roam and assist each squad in techniques of running, jumping, and throwing events. In this way she makes the best use of her facilities.

Heats should be lined up for the fastest use of the track where lanes are limited.

To prevent boredom and fatigue in the early instructional periods, the squads should have a rotation plan that allows for a new event to be undertaken as soon as the one being studied is mastered to a satisfactory degree. As the students progress, keep time trials and distance records to encourage individual improvement.

Class members should be introduced to conditioning and warm-up exercises and be encouraged to loosen up by themselves before the instructor begins. Some teachers prefer that class leaders conduct warm-ups at the beginning of each lesson.

Many basic skills can be taught indoors during inclement weather. Starting, baton passing, throwing form, hurdling, running, and even the hitch kick while swinging on a rope can be practiced. Relays, selected films, and officiating techniques are part of the indoor program.

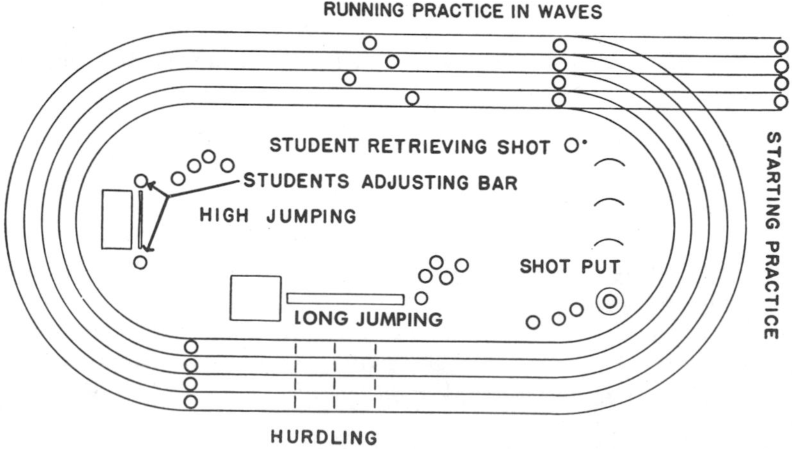

Figure 13–21 Class organization for teaching track and field events.

TEACHING PROGRESSION

As previously mentioned, teaching progression is largely dependent on the teacher's choice of presentation and the available facilities. If progression is from one activity to another after basic skill development, begin with known skills and move to the more complex. The progression within the events is:

Running Events	Jumping Events	Throwing Events
Dash	Standing long jump	Softball
Runs	Running long jump	Basketball
Relays	Running high jump	Discus
Hurdles		Shot put
		Javelin

A teaching unit of 15 lessons for beginners might include:

Lesson I

1. Explanation of the nature and value of track and field
2. Brief history of track and field and women in track
3. Techniques and use of warm-up exercises
4. The crouch start
5. Sprints

Lesson II

1. Warm up
2. Review start
3. Practice sprinting
4. Explain and demonstrate techniques of throwing softball and baseball

Lesson III

1. Warm up
2. Review throws
3. Practice basketball throws
4. Demonstrate and teach the standing long jump. Practice

Lesson IV

1. Warm up
2. Practice 50 yard dash
3. Introduce and practice running long jump.

Lesson V

1. Warm up
2. Practice baton passing and relays
3. Introduce and practice the high jump

Lesson VI

1. Warm up
2. Review high jump
3. Begin use of the rotation plan with stations for starts, middle distance runs, throws, long jump, high jump, and baton passing

Lesson VII

1. Warm up
2. General review
3. Use squad rotation plan as described above

Lesson VIII

1. Warm up
2. Introduce and practice discus throw
3. Introduce and practice shot put

Lesson IX

1. Warm up
2. Review discus and shot put
3. Teach techniques of the hurdle. Practice

Lesson X

1. Warm up
2. Introduce the javelin throw. Practice
3. Squad rotation to long distance runs, discus throw, shot put, hurdles, and javelin

Lessons XI and XII

1. Warm up
2. Individual practice and skill improvement using the rotation plan
3. Rules and officiating

Lessons XIII and XIV

1. Conduct official class meet. Record time and distance of each event for each student
2. Utilize students for meet officials whenever possible

Lesson XV

1. Written examination
2. Student-teacher evaluation of the unit

SKILL DIFFICULTIES AND THEIR CORRECTION

Starts

1.a b

Difficulty	*Correction*
a. Spreading feet too far in blocks resulting in loss of power and push. Feet too close together with hips high resulting in runner's exerting force upward and body's reaching an upright position too soon	a. Review technique of setting distance in blocks. Try several distances and have teacher check speed and position leaving blocks
b. Shoulders low and head down	b. Be sure the elbows are firm and the arms are directly below the shoulders. Chin should be up and eyes should look slightly down the track. Back and head form a straight line parallel to the ground
c. Rising too quickly when leaving the blocks or leaning too far forward during the dash. (This is often the result of throwing both arms back when leaving the blocks or moving the arms in too wide a forward and backward arc)	c. As the rear foot steps out, the opposing arm reaches out and forward. Keep arm action in opposition and the moving action limited between the hip and shoulder. Concentrate on stepping out at a 45 degree angle rising slowly to 70 degrees after five or six strides

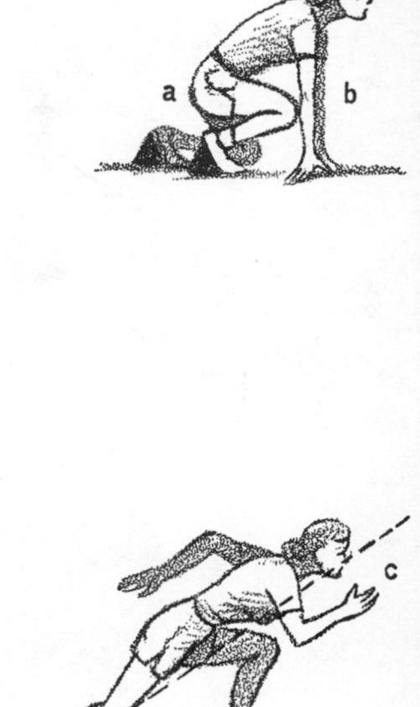

Running Form

Difficulty	*Correction*
a. Swinging arms across the midline of the body causing shoulder and body sway and a "curvy" run. Fists clenched tightly or fingers firmly extended resulting in tension	a. Imagine the arms are clock pendulums and can move only up and back. Avoid forcing movement. Keep the angle at the elbow about 90 degrees and allow the arms to move close to the sides with relaxed (not floppy) hands
b. High rear knee lift resulting in loss of time in stride, standing up too straight, or leaning backward on forward knee lift	b. Concentrate on hitting with the ball of the foot and "pawing" the ground
c. Tension displayed by reduced rhythm, exaggerated arm movement, and swaying head	c. Allow hands to hang loose and mouth to open with jaw sagging to encourage relaxation
d. Slowing before crossing the finish line or lunging as one approaches the line	d. Encourage the runner to run "through" rather than "to" the finish line without changing form. Continue speed for 5 yards beyond the finish line then slow gradually

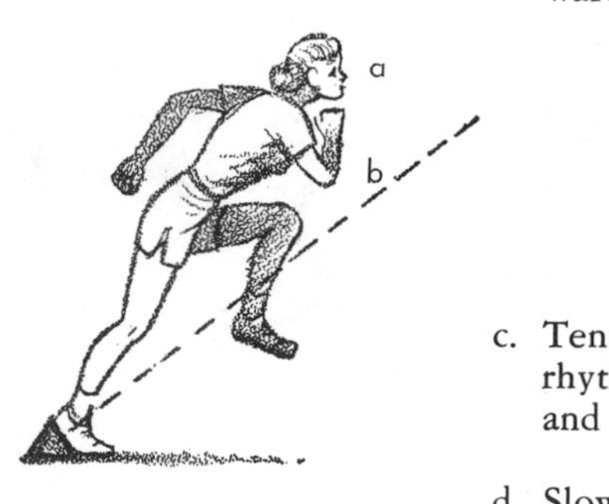

2. a

Relays

Difficulty	*Correction*
a. Dropping the baton on the pass	a. Practice solves this problem. As the baton touches the receiver's hand, the passer exerts pressure and the receiver firmly grasps it. Try visual exchange if working with a young or inexperienced group
b. Failing to pass the baton in the 22 yard zone resulting in disqualification	b. Check the mark that the incoming runner crosses to signal takeoff for receiver. If receiver runs out of zone before getting baton, delay takeoff 11 yards from the passing zone. If the incoming runner overruns the receiver, move the receiver's start closer to the zone

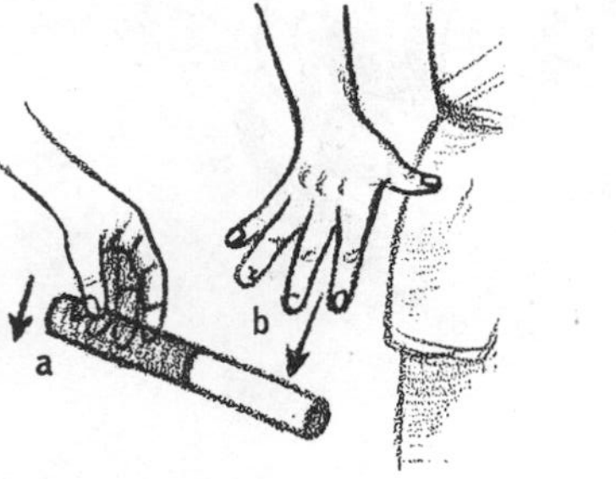

Hurdles

Difficulty	*Correction*
a. Jumping up and down, thereby losing forward momentum and running stride	a. Start flight over the hurdle sooner. Emphasize that hurdling is not jumping, but *running* over the barrier by extending takeoff leg and pushing forward. The faster the run the farther from the hurdle the runner's takeoff leg will be
b. Failure to use arms for balance and pulling power when crossing the hurdle	b. As the lead leg is lifted by knee lift, the shoulders are square to the front. The arm, working in opposition, moves forward and down as if trying to grasp a bar to help pull the body over. This reach helps keep the body straight on takeoff and landing and helps maintain balance on landing. Forcing the jaw forward also aids in driving over the hurdle

Difficulty	Correction
c. Trailing leg drags over barrier	c. As the body runs over the barrier, the knee and toe of the trailing leg are pointed toward the side and pulled close to the body with toe parallel to the ground
d. Loss of stride between hurdles	d. The landing leg snaps down close to the barrier for a push as soon as the foot clears the hurdle. Be sure trailing leg is placed in front, not to the side of the leading leg to maintain balance and stride distance

Running and Standing Long Jump

Difficulty	*Correction*
a. Using the toe on takeoff	a. Practice a heel-to-toe roll from the board with emphasis on an upward lift of the body

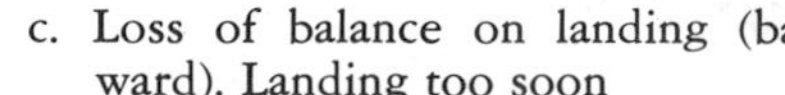

b. Jumping forward rather than *up.* Failure to get desired height	b. Stress vigorous use of arms at take-off. Hold chest high. The takeoff leg is fully extended and the opposite knee drawn up in line with the waist
c. Loss of balance on landing (backward). Landing too soon	c. Approach landing in extended sitting position with feet up. Thrust arms forward *when the heels touch the pit.* Pull downward and forward with head and shoulders to raise hips forward

High Jump

Difficulty	*Correction*
a. Jumping into rather than over the bar. (May result from taking off too far from the bar or leaning into the bar with the shoulder). Incorrect takeoff leg	a. Remeasure approach and narrow angle. Lift shoulder upward and raise arms. Stress that the lift of the non-jumping leg is parallel to the bar, not toward it
b. Leg or toe dragging bar	b. In western roll stress hips high so legs are easily raised. In straddle roll stress knees and toes up and out

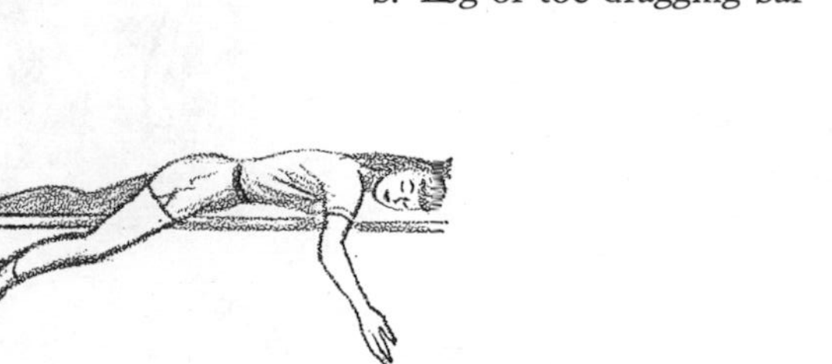

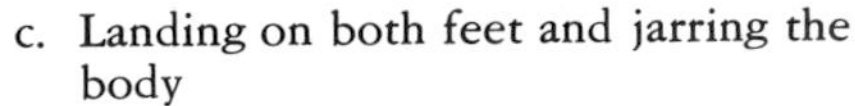

c. Landing on both feet and jarring the body	c. Land on one foot (usually jumping foot) and both hands in western roll. The body is rolling in the straddle roll and landing should be on back or side. Stress natural motion; do not try to stop rolling momentum

Shot Put

Difficulty	*Correction*
a. Holding shot too far in palm of hand resulting in loss of power and control	a. Shot is held by the first three fingers with the thumb and little finger curled under and around the sides
b. Failure to utilize the entire body in preparing for the put	b. Be comfortable and balanced before starting preparations. As a balance check, lift forward leg and extend the left arm

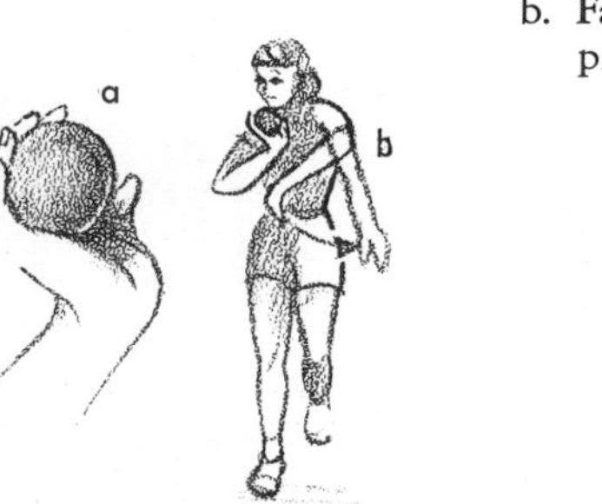

c. Hesitating between steps resulting in loss of power.	c. Develop a smooth delivery Practice form mimetically
d. Failure to use entire body for power	d. Review the principles of any throwing action. As the put begins, the body is braced, the hips and body weight move through ahead of the arm
e. Throwing the shot with arm action similar to a softball throw	e. The shot is tucked around the neck and the push is from this point, not from on or behind the shoulder
f. Stepping over the circle on follow-through	f. Review and practice the reverse *following* the delivery

Discus Throw (See common errors of shot put for those applicable)

Difficulty	*Correction*
a. Placing the finger too far over the rim resulting in a rough throw and lack of control	a. Review grip and place hand so the palm is behind center of the discus weight and only one joint of the fingers is over the edge
b. Inability to develop rhythm of preliminary swings	b. Lead student with a verbal pattern such as the following: "one"—starting position "and"—arm swings back, "two"—arm comes forward, "and"—arm swings back again, "step"—student steps forward on left foot, "throw"—discus released, "step"—student steps forward on right foot to reverse momentum
c. Discus flies to left of hurler due to simultaneous body and arm turn	c. The body turns and the discus and arm trail the body action. This results in a whiplike action and release off the index finger in a clockwise rotation

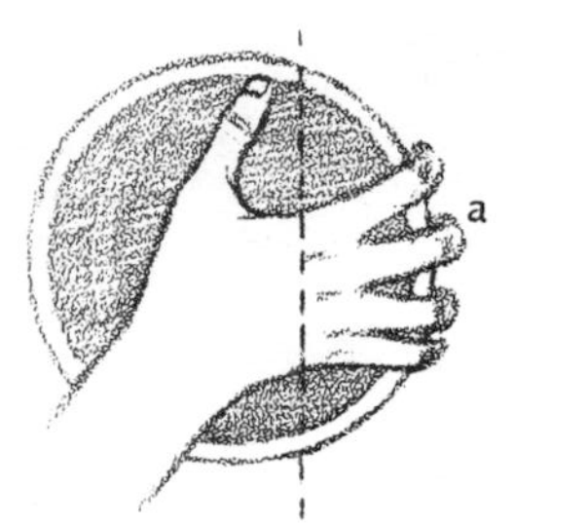

Javelin Throw (In addition to approach problems mentioned previously)

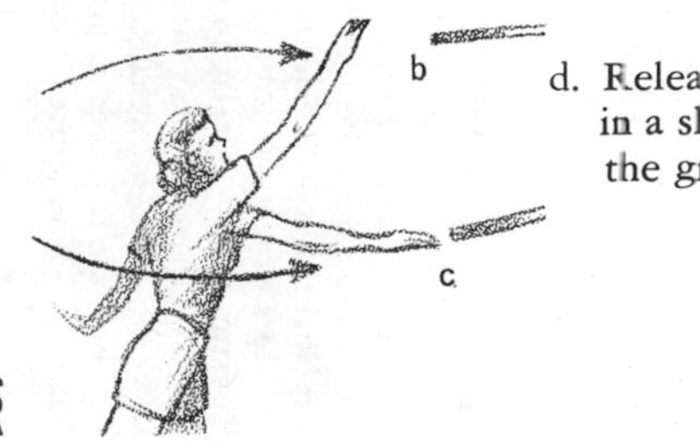

Difficulty	*Correction*
a. Loss of power of delivery. Inability to get desired height in the throw	a. The trunk extends backward before the body weight moves through. The arm action is delayed until trunk and shoulders have moved through. (The arm trails the hip and shoulder action)
b. Release goes to the left (usually due to sidearm swing)	b. The arm comes over the shoulder to release the javelin at an angle of approximately 45 degrees with the ground
c. Javelin lands with back end first	c. Release later and check angle of delivery
d. Releasing javelin too late, resulting in a short powerful throw arriving at the ground with unexpended power	d. The release should be practiced from the run. It is upward and forward on the count before the reverse

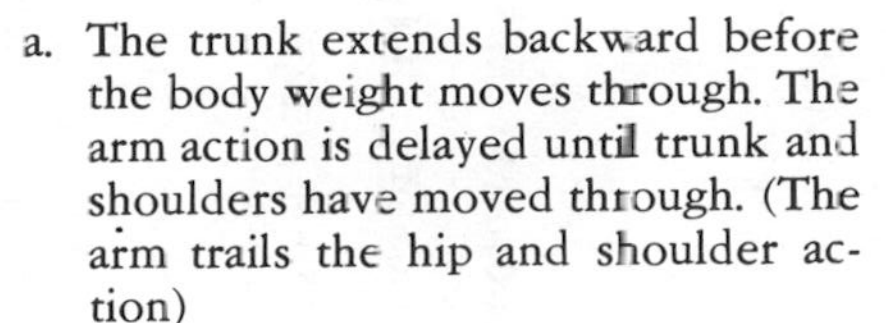

EVALUATING THE RESULTS

There is little need for additional evaluative instruments if periodic records are taken on every student. The real purpose of evaluating—self-improvement—is served as the student sees her skill progress. The results of the meet at the end of the unit are further indications of a student's growth. Student understanding and ability in conducting a meet should be included in evaluation when grades are given.

TERMINOLOGY

Anchor—Final, or fourth, runner in a relay.
Barrier—A hurdle.
Baton—A tubelike object made of wood, metal, plastic, or cardboard which is passed from one runner to the next in a relay.
Beat board—An elevated takeoff board used for the standing broad jump. It is generally used indoors.
Blind pass—A relay exchange accomplished without looking back at the passer.
Break—Making a movement from a set position before the gun sounds.
Break in the pit—Mark made in the pit by the jumper.
Checkpoint—A visual mark used by a competitor to insure accuracy in stride.
Course—The path of the runner.
Curb—Inside border of the track.
Dash—A short distance race run at top speed the entire distance.
Dead heat—A race in which two or more runners cross the finish line at the same moment. It results in a tie.
Exchange zone—An area the width of one lane and 22 yards long in which the baton must be passed in a relay race.
False start—The forward movement of any part of the competitor's body after the command "Set" and prior to the firing of the gun.
Finish yarn (or tape)—A cord stretched across the track above the finish line to aid the judges in determining the first runner across the line.
Foul throw—A throw counted as a trial but not measured, because of some violation of the field event rule.
Heat—A preliminary round of a race. The winners of heats participate in the semifinals or finals of the race.
Inside lane—The lane on the inside or curb of the track. Often referred to as the pole position.
Jog—Easy, slow, short-stride running action.
Kick—Increased speed and power exerted at the end of a race.
Lane—The path marked on the track for a race which defines where the runner must stay during the race or for a portion of the race.
Lap—One complete circle of the track.
Lead-off runner—The first runner on a relay team.
Medley relay—A relay in which runners run different distances.
Pace—The rate of speed at which the runner selects to run after considering the distance and her available energy.
Pit—Area where the jumper lands. It is usually filled with sand, sawdust, or foam rubber.
Preliminaries—A series of heats in running events and trials in field events which eliminate less expert participants.
Pursuit relay—A relay in which all runners run in the same direction.
Recall—Bringing the runners back after a false start.
Reverse—The interchange of feet after release in a throwing event. Also called recovery because it serves to maintain balance.
Runway—The approach to the scratch line or takeoff board in field events.

Scratch line—The line which may not be crossed on takeoff in the standing long jump or when executing the basketball or softball throws.
Sector lines—The boundary line within which the discus, shot, and javelin must land to be a fair throw.
Shuttle relay—Relay run with half of each team at opposite ends. Alternate runners travel back and forth over the same course.
Staggered start—The placement of runners in a step-like position at the start of a race to be run around a curve so that all competitors will run an equal distance.
Straightaway—Straight area of track between curves.
Takeoff board—Board set flush in the ground for the long jump.
Takeoff foot—The foot that leaves the ground last and drives the jumper.
Toe board—Curved piece of wood used as a foul line for the shot put.
Trailing leg—Takeoff leg or the rear leg in hurdling.
Trial—An attempt in a field event.
Wind sprint—An all-out effort of speed and power over a short prescribed course (usually 50 yards) followed by a brief rest before repeating the sprint.

DISCUSSION QUESTIONS

1. What are the values of warm-ups for both track and field events according to your knowledge of physiology?
2. Explain the difference between the straddle roll and the western roll. Which do you think is more efficient for the skillful jumper? Why?
3. Analyze the throwing events. What are some movements common to each of these events? From the standpoint of body mechanics, can you explain why these movements are necessary for efficiency?
4. Teach a beginner to throw the javelin and the shot put. Write a short paper on what you learned about teaching from this experience.
5. Conduct a track and field sports day for a group of senior students interested in becoming physical education majors when they enter college. Evaluate the results of this event.

SELECTED AUDIOVISUAL AIDS

Fundamentals of Track and Field for Girls. (3 parts, 16 mm., color, sound.) Aims Instructional Media Services, Inc. P. O. Box 1010, Hollywood, California 90028. (Rental, purchase)
Girls' Track Clinic. (16 mm., color, sound, 14 min.) U.S. Olympic Headquarters, 57 Park Avenue, New York, New York 10016. (Rental)
Track and Field for Girls and Women. (3 reels, 16 mm., color, sound.) Teaching Aids Service, Inc., 31 Union Square West, New York, New York. (Purchase or rental)
Track and Field Today. (16 mm., color, b&w, sound, 28 min.) Contact State High School Association or Official Sports Films, Inc., P.O. Box 98, Elgin, Illinois 60120. (Purchase, rental)
Women's Track and Field. (Super 8 mm. cartridge, color.) Instructional films and teacher's guide. Athletic Institute, 805 Merchandise Mart, Chicago, Illinois 60654. (Purchase)

SUGGESTED READINGS

Amateur Athletic Union: *The AAU Official Track and Field Handbook and Rules.* AAU House, 231 West 58th Street, New York, New York 10019.
American Alliance for Health, Physical Education and Recreation: *What Research Tells the Coach About Distance Running.* Washington, D.C. AAHPER, 1968.
Bresnahan, George T. et al.: *Track and Field Athletics.* 7th ed. St. Louis, The C. V. Mosby Co., 1969.

Doherty, J. Kenneth: *Modern Track and Field.* 2nd ed. Englewood Cliffs, New Jersey, Prentice Hall, Inc., 1963.
Foreman, Kenneth E. and Husted, Virginia: *Track and Field Techniques for Girls and Women.* 2nd ed. Dubuque, Iowa, Wm. C. Brown Co., 1971.
Jackson, Nell C.: *Track and Field for Girls and Women.* Minneapolis, Burgess Publishing Co., 1968.
National Association for Girls and Women in Sport: *Track and Field Guide.* AAHPER, Washington, D.C., Current edition.
Parker, Virginia, and Kennedy, Robert: *Track and Field For Girls and Women.* Philadelphia, W. B. Saunders Co., 1969.
Proceedings of the First and Second National Institutes on Girls' Sports. American Association for Health, Physical Education, and Recreation. 1201 16th Street, N.W., Washington, D.C.
Wakefield, Frances, Harkins, Dorothy, and Cooper, John: *Track and Field Fundamentals for Girls and Women.* St. Louis, The C. V. Mosby Co., 3rd ed. 1973.

PERIODICALS

Amateur Athlete. 156 Broad Street, Lynn, Massachusetts.
The Sportswomen. P.O. Box 2611, Culver City, California 90230.
Track Technique. P.O. Box 296, Los Altos, California (quarterly).
Women's Track and Field World. P.O. Box 371, Claremont, California 91711 (monthly).

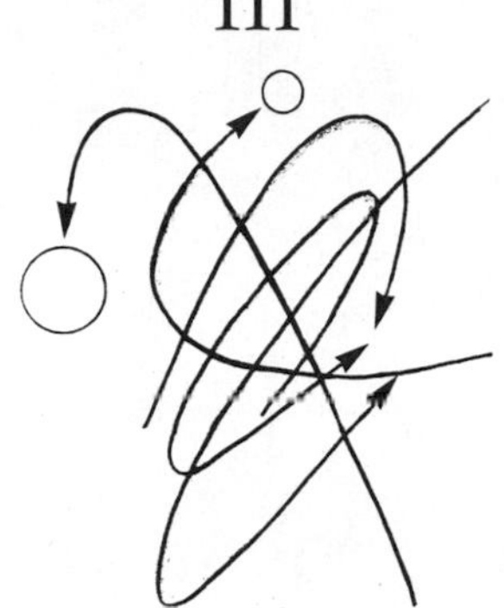

PART III

TEAM SPORTS

CHAPTER 14

BASKETBALL

Basketball is truly the "all-American game." Created by Dr. James Naismith to fulfill a class assignment at the YMCA Training School, at Springfield, Massachusetts, basketball has grown into the most popular participating and spectator team sport in the country. The game as originally played was a simple, 13 rule indoor winter sport that served the same team purposes as football during the fall and baseball in the spring. Originally, a large number of men composed two teams and were allowed to bat, pass, and throw in an attempt to get the ball into peach basket goals nailed to each end of the gymnasium balcony.

Although women were not in Dr. Naismith's original plans, they quickly saw the value of the game. A short two weeks after the game was introduced, a group of women teachers asked to play. The game spread rapidly, but misinterpretations and misunderstanding of the rules led to confusion across the nation. A rule misinterpretation by Miss Clara Baer in 1893 at Newcomb College in New Orleans ultimately developed the three division court game. The first rules committee met in 1899 and accepted the three court game. The first basketball guide for women was edited by Senda Berenson and eliminated snatching and batting of the ball, limited the dribble to three floor contacts, and ruled a foul for holding the ball more than 3 seconds. It was in 1936 that the two division game with three forwards in one half of the court and three guards in the other was recognized by the basketball rules committee. This basic pattern remained for a quarter of a century, followed by the six player game which allowed two roving players to move the full length of the court.

During the past ten years, women's basketball has undergone major transitions which have culminated in the acceptance of the five player game by the joint NAGWS-AAU Basketball Rules Committee. The transition to the more physically demanding and strategically challenging game has created more opportunity for general skill development among all players. Although a limited number of high school athletic associations continue to play six player rules, the National Federation of State High School Associations (NFSHSA) has adopted the five player game, and it is only a matter of time before high school, collegiate, and international players use five player rules.

Since 1905 there has been an active and permanent basketball comittee that revises rules. The joint NAGWS-AAU Women's Basketball Rules Committee continues to experiment with rules which provide for player safety and meaningful competition for all groups it serves.

THE NATURE AND PURPOSE OF THE GAME

Basketball is played by two teams of five players each on a rectangular court no larger than 94 by 50 feet. The court is divided into two equal areas so that each team has a front court, where its own basket is located, and a back court, which has the basket it defends (the opponents' basket). Each team tries to get the ball and move it by passing, throwing, batting, bouncing, rolling, or handing it to a player who may shoot it into her basket and score a goal. The team not in possession of the ball tries to keep the opposing team from scoring as it tries to intercept, tie, or otherwise gain the ball and eventually make a scoring effort. The score of a team is the total of its field goals and free throws.

GAME RULES AND SCORING

The current official *Basketball Guide,* published by the National Association for Girls and Women in Sport of the American Alliance for Health, Physical Education, and Recreation or the *Basketball Rulebook,* published by the National Federation of State High School Associations, should be consulted for complete rules. The following summary is based upon the rules recommended by the Joint NAGWS-AAU Women's Basketball Rules Committee.

Playing Time. Playing time for collegiate and independent teams consists of two 20-minute halves with a 15-minute intermission between halves. High school age teams play four quarters of eight minutes each, with two-minute intermissions between the first and second quarters and the third and fourth quarters, and a 10-minute intermission at the half. Playing time may be reduced for younger age groups or inexperienced players.

If the score is tied at the end of the regulation playing time, the game continues, without a change of baskets, for *one or more extra periods.* Each extra period is preceded by a two-minute intermission. The extra period is five minutes in length in games played with 20-minute halves; the period is three minutes in length in games played in 8-minute quarters. Each period is started by a jump ball in the center circle. The game is terminated if either team is ahead at the end of the extra period.

During the game, a *time-out* is taken for the following situations:

1. A coach requests a team time-out from an official when her team is in possession of the ball; a coach requests it from an official or the scorer when the ball is dead.
2. A player on the court requests a team time-out from an official when her team is in possession of the ball *or* at any time when the ball is dead until a player on the team putting the ball in play has positioned herself out of bounds with the ball. Five one-minute periods are allowed for each team during regular playing time with an additional one allowed for each overtime period.
3. Fouls.
4. Violations.
5. Jump balls.
6. Substitutions (maximum of 30 seconds for each team).
7. Injuries and loss of contact lens. (May be charged to the team or to officials at the discretion of the officials.)
8. Suspension of play or at any time at the discretion of an official.

Time-in begins:

1. When the ball is tapped by either player on a jump ball.
2. When the ball touches a player on the court from a throw-in from out of bounds.
3. When a player on the court touches a missed free throw that has touched the ring of the basket.

Conduct of the Game. Play begins with a jump ball in the center circle between any two opposing players. The same procedure is followed at the beginning of each half (or quarter) and in each extra period. The captain of the visiting team has the choice of basket. If both teams are "home," the winner of the coin toss has the choice of baskets. Teams exchange goals at the end of the first half. Each of the two opposing players participating in the jump has one foot near the center line of the circle. Each must stay in the half of the restraining circle farther from her own basket during the jump. The other four members of each team position themselves so that they can attempt to gain offensive control of the ball, yet maintain defensive position in the event the ball goes to the opposing team. All players, other than the jumpers, must stay outside the circle until the ball is tapped. They may alternate positions around the outside of the circle but must then hold that initial position until the ball is tapped.

The official tosses the ball upward between the two opponents to a height greater than either can reach when jumping. After reaching its highest point the ball drops between the jumpers, and one or both players tap the ball with one or both hands. Neither player may tap it more than twice. If the ball falls to the floor without being tapped the toss must be repeated.

When a team gains possession of the ball, a try for goal must be made within 30 seconds. If the ball goes out of bounds during this period, a new 30-second period begins as play resumes. The touching of the ball by an opponent, without gaining control of the ball, does not start a new 30-second period. Failure to try for goal in the allotted time results in a violation for the offending team.

Whenever a field goal is scored, the ball is put in play by a member of the opposing team at any point behind the endline where the goal was scored.

During play, as a player attempts to gain possession of the ball and score, she may:

1. Throw, bat, bounce, hand, or roll the ball to another player, or she may shoot for a goal.
2. Catch, retain, or throw the ball with one or both hands.
3. Take or tap the ball from an opponent. (The hand is considered to be part of the ball when in contact with the ball.)
4. Advance the ball by means of a dribble or an air dribble, taking any number of steps between the release and the recovery of the ball.
5. Hold the ball for five seconds in bounds if closely guarded, 10 seconds on a free throw, and five seconds out of bounds. (Following a goal, the first player to possess the ball out of bounds may pass to a teammate who is behind the endline; the five-second limit for returning the ball to play begins with the first out-of-bounds player.)
6. Touch the ball to the floor while retaining possession of it. This shall not be considered part of a dribble.
7. Use two steps after receiving the ball in the air, on the run, or on the completion of a dribble.
8. Catch the ball while both feet are off the floor, land on both feet simultaneously, and take a second step on either foot.
9. Use either foot as a pivot foot after catching the ball while standing still.
10. Use either foot as a pivot foot after coming to a stop on the first step.
11. Use the first foot to strike the floor as the pivot foot on a two-step stop when catching the ball in the air, or at the end of a run, dribble, or air dribble.
12. Lift the pivot foot when releasing the ball for a pass or try for goal. The ball must leave the hands before the pivot foot again touches the floor.
13. Lift the pivot foot from the floor only after the ball has been released on a dribble.
14. Jump while holding the ball, providing it is released before she lands from the jump.
15. Continue to play a ball which happens to touch an official on the playing court.

During play, tie balls, violations, fouls, and out-of-bounds balls occur.

A *tie ball* is called when two or more players of opposing teams have one or both hands firmly on the ball in such a way that neither player can gain possession without undue roughness. A blocked shot which results in brief suspension of the ball between the hands of opposing players also results in a tie ball. In judging tie balls the hands are considered part of the ball when they are in contact with the ball.

A *violation* is a rule infringement which results in the ball's being put in play from out of bounds—at the side or at the endline—by a member of the opposing team. The following chart summarizes the most common violations and the resulting actions.

Violation

1. Jump ball
   a. Failure of jumper to position one foot near center line
   b. Stepping on line or in opponent's half of circle
   c. Tapping ball before it reaches highest point
   d. Tapping ball more than twice
   e. Catching ball
   f. Playing ball before it has been played by a nonjumper or before it touches floor, basket, or backboard
   g. Failure of players to hold position around circle until ball is tapped
   h. Players on circle extending arms or legs in front of or behind adjacent player positioned within three feet of circle

2. Three-second lane violation
   a. A player without the ball remains for more than 3 seconds in the free throw lane while her team is in possession of the ball. (A player receiving the ball in the lane within the 3 seconds has an additional 3 seconds to shoot or leave the lane)
   b. Stepping off the court to avoid a three-second lane violation

3. Ball handling violations
   a. Kicking ball intentionally
   b. Striking ball with fist
   c. Dribbling illegally as a result of palming or fumbling ball
   d. Air dribbling illegally or combining dribble and air dribble
   e. Holding ball more than five seconds out of bounds or more than 10 seconds on a free throw
   f. Traveling with ball

4. Thirty-second violation
   a. A team in possession of the ball does not attempt a goal within 30 seconds

5. Out-of-bounds violations
   a. Causing ball to go out of bounds
   b. Placing ball or foot against wall when playing on a small court
   c. Touching boundary with body or ball when in possession of the ball
   d. Carrying ball into court from out-of-bounds play
   e. Leaving court without ball and returning at a more advantageous position; returning to court in a more advantageous position following a throw-in
   f. Touching ball when in bounds after having put it in play from out of bounds before it is contacted by another player
   g. Holding ball more than five seconds out of bounds before passing it into the court
   h. Moving from spot designated by official for throw-in
   i. Contacting boundary line or reaching beyond it while guarding a player making a throw-in
   j. Failure to stay 3 feet from boundary line where ball is being thrown in where out-of-bounds space is limited

6. Field-goal violations
   a. Throwing for basket when put-

ting ball in play from out of bounds

b. Goaltending—interfering with ball or basket when ball is on a downward path toward basket, when ball is on the rim or passing through the basket

7. Free-throw violations by shooter
   a. Failure to shoot within 10 seconds
   b. Failure to cause ball to enter basket or touch rim on goal attempt
   c. Touching floor on or beyond line or restraining circle while taking free throw

8. Free-throw violations by players other than shooter
   a. Entering restricted area (circle, line, or floor beyond) before ball touches rim, backboard, or enters basket
   b. Entering or leaving lane space after ball is given to shooter
   c. Player entering another player's space or extending arms into adjacent space
   d. Player disconcerting the player taking the free throw

9. Double violations by members of opposing teams

Ball Awarded to Opponent

1. a. to h. Out of bounds at sideline opposite circle where violation occurred

   b. and g. Official sounds whistle only if ball is gained by team whose member committed violation

2. a. and b. At sideline opposite point where violation occurred

3. a. to f. Out of bounds opposite the spot closest to point of violation

4. a. Out of bounds opposite the spot closest to point of violation

5. a to j. Out of bounds at the spot where violation occurred

   i. and j. Official holds whistle to assure that penalty would not be to advantage of the team committing the violation

6. a. Goal does not count if made, and ball is awarded out of bounds at sidelines at spot of violation. If goal is missed, ball continues in play

   b. If violation by defensive player, goal counts whether made or missed; if violation by offensive player, goal does not count and ball is awarded to opponent out of bounds at sideline nearest point of violation

7. a. and b. Out of bounds at sideline opposite free-throw line

   c. If goal is made it does not count, and ball is awarded to opponent out of bounds at sideline opposite free-throw line

8. a. to d. If violation is committed by defensive player, goal counts if made, and ball is put in play from out of bounds at the endline by opponent of player taking free throw. If goal is missed, free-throw is repeated

If violation is committed by an offensive player, goal, if made, does not count and whether made or missed, the ball is awarded an opponent out of bounds at the sideline opposite the free-throw line

If violations by players of both teams occur, the goal, if made, does not count, and whether made or missed, play begins with a jump ball between the two involved players in the nearest restraining circle

On multiple free throws, if violation is committed on any free throw before the last, ball is put in play following last free throw as if no violation had occurred

9. Jump ball in nearest restraining circle between players involved

Fouls are rule infringements that result in a penalty for the fouling individual or team. Theoretically, basketball is a noncontact game; however, some contact is implied as players move in efforts to gain possession of the ball and prevent opponents from scoring. Personal contact is not penalized unless roughness results. Fouls are classified as follows:

1. *Personal foul* involves contact with an opponent while the ball is in play.
2. *Common foul* is an unintentional and nonflagrant personal foul committed against a player *not* trying for a field goal. It is not a part of a double foul or a multiple foul.
3. *Double foul* is called when two opponents foul simultaneously.
4. *Multiple fouls* occur when one player fouls two or more opponents or when two or more players simultaneously foul an opponent.
5. *Offensive foul* is a common foul committed by a player while she or a teammate is in control of the ball.
6. *Technical foul* is a noncontact foul committed by a player or nonparticipant or a contact foul committed by a player when the ball is dead.
7. *Flagrant foul* involves a violent unsportsmanlike act. It may or may not be intentional; it may be personal or technical, but it always results in disqualification for the person fouling.
8. *Intentional foul* can be a personal or technical foul which is premeditated.
9. *Unsportsmanlike conduct foul* is a technical foul resulting from unethical conduct.

Personal fouls include:

1. *Blocking*—personal contact which impedes the progress of an opponent with or without the ball. It results from illegal screening, from an opponent's entering the path of a moving player without giving the player adequate opportunity to stop or change direction, and from extending the body over the vertical plane of an opponent.
2. *Charging*—movement—by a player in possession of the ball—of either the ball or her body into an opponent whose position is legal or whose path of movement is already established. Forward momentum of a player following a pass or goal shot resulting in contact of an opponent is also charging.
3. *Hacking*—striking wrist or forearm of an opponent in an attempt to tie the ball, stop a pass, or block a shot.
4. *Holding*—use of the hands or arms to inhibit movement of an opponent or from continual contact which is disadvantageous to the opponent.
5. *Pushing.*
6. *Tripping.*

Technical fouls are noncontact and may be committed by player or nonplayer. They also include contact fouls by players when the ball is dead. Technical fouls by players include:

1. Disrespectfully addressing an official.
2. Using gestures or language deemed offensive.
3. Obstructing vision of an opponent by waving hands near the eyes; baiting an opponent.
4. Delaying the game by preventing the ball from being put into play promptly.
5. Failing to raise hand, or raising it in indignation, when charged with a foul.
6. Changing playing number without informing scorer and referee.
7. Substituting illegally.
8. Participating in the game after disqualification.
9. Wearing a number identical to one worn by a teammate.
10. Attempting a free throw to which she is knowingly not entitled.
11. Persistently disconcerting a player taking a free throw or interfering with the flight of the ball to the basket.

Technical fouls by teams, coach, substitute, or spectators include:

1. Failure to supply scorers with team roster 10 minutes before start of game.
2. Failure to indicate starting players three minutes before game begins.
3. Taking more than allotted number of time-outs.
4. Addressing opponents or officials in disrespectful manner.
5. Inciting undesirable crowd reactions.
6. Attempting to influence or intimidate officials' decisions by rising from the bench or gesturing.
7. Entering the court without official's approval to attend to an injured player.
8. Leaving her place to follow action on the court when the ball is in play.
9. Displaying any other unethical behavior.

Awarding Penalty for Fouls. Personal fouls are charged to the individual offender, and a player must leave the game when she commits five fouls or a single flagrant disqualifying foul. Fouls charged to an individual and fouls charged to a team are both penalized by awarding a free throw, ball possession, or both to the opponent.

Clarification of the bonus rule is basic to understanding the administration of free throws following fouls. Briefly, no free throws are awarded for common fouls until a team has committed its fifth personal foul in games played in quarters and its seventh personal foul in games played in halves. On the fifth and seventh personal foul in each half and thereafter, the offended player receives one bonus free throw if the first free throw was successful. Free throws are never taken for offensive fouls and always taken if a foul is committed against a person who is in the act of shooting or if the foul is flagrant or intentional. Technical fouls and some personal fouls also result in the offended team's receiving the ball out of bounds after the free throws.

The following summary is helpful in understanding when the offended player or team is awarded free throws:

1. One free throw for:
   a. A foul against a field goal shooter whose attempt was successful.

   b. Each foul which is part of a multiple foul. A multiple foul against a player in the act of shooting whose shot was unsuccessful results in three free throws.
   c. A technical foul charged to an opponent. Any player on the offended team may take the shot. The ball is awarded to the offended team at midcourt following the shot.
2. Two free throws for:
   a. A foul against a player in the act of shooting who failed to score.
   b. Intentional foul.
   c. Flagrant foul. Player fouling is disqualified, and following the free throws the ball is awarded to the offended team at midcourt.
3. No free throws for:
   a. Each common foul before the bonus rule is in effect. Ball awarded to opponent at nearest point out of bounds.
   b. Double foul. Jump ball between any two opponents in center circle resumes play.
   c. Offensive foul. Ball awarded to opponent at nearest point out of bounds.
4. Bonus free throw for:
   a. Each common foul, other than offensive fouls, beginning with the opponent's seventh personal foul in games played in halves and fifth personal foul in games played in quarters, providing that the first attempt was successful.

On *double technical fouls,* free throws are awarded each team and a jump ball in center circle resumes play.

Players and Substitutes. Each team consists of five players. There may be any number of substitutes who may reenter the game any number of times unless disqualified. Substitutes request a time-out for substitution from the scorer. The substitute must then be recognized by an official before entering the game (except during intermissions). A team must have at least five players to start the game. When the team has no eligible substitutes and one or two players are injured or disqualified, the team may continue to play with three players. If the team loses three or more players by injury or disqualification, the game is defaulted.

Scoring. The score of a team is the total of its field goals and free throws. Each field goal counts two points, and each free throw counts one point. The team with the larger score at the end of the official playing time is declared the winner. If the score is tied at the end of the playing time the game continues for one or more extra periods. The game is terminated when one of the teams is ahead at the end of any extra period.

When a game is discontinued the score is recorded as 0 to 0. A defaulted game score remains unchanged if the defaulting team had the lesser score. If the defaulting team was leading, the score is recorded as 2 to 0.*

---

*Methods of scoring a game are explained in the NAGWS *Basketball Guide,* current edition.

NEEDED FACILITIES AND EQUIPMENT

The Court. Basketball is played inside and outside with leather and rubber balls in many informal settings; however, an official game is played on a rectangular court at least 74 feet long and 42 feet wide and no larger than 94 feet by 50 feet. The desirable measurements are 50 by 84 for high school age and 50 by 90 for college and independent teams. There should be at least 22 feet of overhead clearance. The outer boundary lines and center dividing line across the court width are two inches wide. Contrasting colored floor areas may be used instead of the two-inch boundary lines. The center circle and free-throw lanes may also be painted in colors contrasting with the other playing area. Where possible, the boundaries should be 10 feet from any outside obstruction. The center restraining circle is marked in the center of the court and drawn with a radius of six feet, measured to the outside of the line, which is two inches wide.

A free-throw lane (12 feet wide) measured to the outside of each lane boundary and the semicircle with the free-throw line as a diameter, shall be marked at each end of the court. The free-throw line (two inches wide) is marked from a spot 15 feet from the center of the face of the backboard and extends six feet in either direction, parallel to the endline. A free-throw circle with a six foot radius is drawn from the center of the free-throw line. Lines two inches wide from the free-throw line to the endline enclose the 12 foot wide free-throw lane. The lane space marks, two inches wide and eight inches long, are perpendicular to each of the lane lines and are located 11, 14, and 17 feet from the endline. A neutral zone mark, 12 inches wide and eight inches long, begins seven feet from the endline on each of the lane lines. (See Fig. 14–1.)

Backboards. Rectangular or fan-shaped backboards are made of plate glass, wood, metal, or other flat rigid material. The white or transparent boards with white markings hang four feet inside the regulation court and are parallel to the endline. The transparent rectangular backboard is most often used in collegiate competition; the fan-shaped backboard is most frequently used in high school play. The orange metal basket rings are attached to the center of the backboard with the ring 10 feet above the floor. White cord nets are attached to the basket rings to check the ball momentarily as it passes through the ring.

Ball. The leather, rubber, or synthetic covered round ball is tan or an orange shade, between 29½ and 30¼ inches in circumference, weighs between 20 and 22 ounces, and bounces between 49 and 54 inches when inflated to manufacturers' specifications and dropped from a height of six feet.

Costume. The official gymnasium attire is satisfactory for most game situations within the school. Attractive shorts and shirts which allow freedom are desirable for intramural and recreational play. Footwear is an

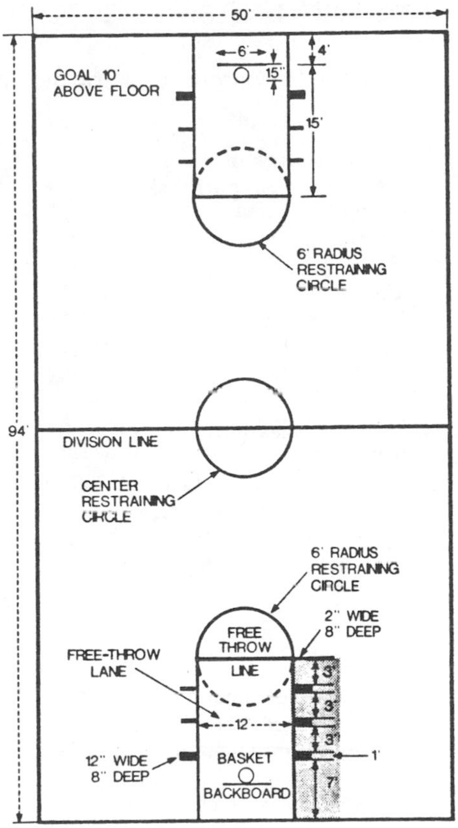

Figure 14–1 Diagram of basketball court showing permanent lines. On short courts, when the backboard is placed against the wall, there shall be an endline, the inner edge of which is 2 inches out from the wall. On narrow courts, when the playing court is the full width of the floor, there shall be a sideline, the inner edge of which is 2 inches out from the wall. (From NAGWS *Basketball Guide*. Washington, D.C., AAHPER. Current edition.)

important safety consideration. Each player should wear one or two pairs of socks that cushion the feet and prevent blisters. Basketball shoes (leather or canvas) designed for court wear are generally preferred over the tennis type shoe for competitive play.

Competing teams should wear uniforms of contrasting colors. A solid-colored number, contrasting with the color of the uniform, must be worn by each player and substitute. The numbers on the back of the uniform must be six inches high, and front numerals must be four inches high. Each numeral must be at least 3/4 inch wide. The single digits "1" and "2" should not be used, nor should any digit over "5." Combinations of two digits from "0" to "5" should be used. If pinnies are worn to distinguish teams, they should have designated numerals of official size.

TEACHING UNITS

Suggested content units for beginning and advanced students follow:

Beginners

History and nature of the game

Fundamental body control skills
- Stance
- Starting
- Running
- Change of direction
- Two-step stop
- Pivot
- Feinting

Fundamental ball control skills
- Catching
- Chest pass (all passes to stationary and moving receiver)
- Overhead passes
- Underhand pass
- Dribbling

Basic shooting skills
- Lay-up shot
- One-hand set shot
- Two-hand set shot
- Foul shooting techniques

Individual defensive techniques
- Defense positioning when guarding a player without the ball
- Defense positioning when guarding a player with the ball
- Player-to-player defense tactics

Individual offensive techniques
- Pass and cut
- Screens
- Out-of-bounds situation play
- Jump ball situation
- Basic weave pattern

Team defensive strategy
- Basic zone defense (1–3–1 or 2–1–2)
- Switching player-to-player

Evaluation
- Skills tests
- Playing ability
- Written tests on rules and strategy

Advanced

Complete review

Individual ball control skills
- Hook pass
- Jump pass
- Dribble with nondominant hand
- Change hands during dribble
- Rebounding—offensive and defensive
- Bounce passes
- Feints and fakes

Advanced shooting skills
- Jump shot
- Hook shot
- Crossover lay-up
- Tip-in

Individual defensive skills
- Guarding post players
- Defensing screen plays
- Blocking out
- Defensive rebounding

Offensive strategy and tactics
- Fast break
- Offensive patterns:
- Deliberate offense
- Offense against the zone
- Jump ball situations
- Out-of-bounds situations

Defensive strategy and tactics
- Defense against fast break
- Basic zone defenses (2–1–2; 1–3–1; 3–2; 1–2–2)
- Zone pressure defense
- Systems of player-to-player defense

Officiating techniques

Evaluation
- Skills tests
- Written tests
- Player performance charts
- Officiating test

BASIC SKILLS

The successful basketball player must learn to control her body, to maneuver on the court with and without the ball, to develop techniques for gaining and maintaining possession of the ball, and to be effective as a shooter from the court and from the free-throw line. A discussion of individual basketball skills can be organized into: (1) fundamental movement and body control skills and (2) individual offensive and defensive skills. Discussion of individual skills combined with one or more teammates is included under the strategy section.

Fundamental Movement and Body Control Skills

Footwork, body balance, and body control are fundamental to both offensive and defensive play.

Stance. In anticipation of receiving a ball or in preparation for moving from one position to another on the court, the player positions herself with her feet about shoulder width apart in a stride stance with one foot slightly ahead of the other. The knees are flexed to lower the center of gravity as the body bends slightly forward at the waist. Weight is distributed on the balls of both feet. The head and chin are up, the shoulders are slightly forward, and the elbows are flexed and away from the body.

Starting. From the stance position the trailing leg drives as the knees flex for greater force. As a result, the body is lowered and the shoulder and head lean in the direction the player wishes to move.

Running. Short, choppy strides are used for acceleration and longer strides are used to maintain momentum. The body leans slightly forward as the feet remain close to the ground for mobility. The arm action is natural and relaxed with hands ever ready to receive or intercept a ball. A shuffling action, as a result of toe-to-heel braking action, is used to reduce speed or maintain slow speed when anticipating a change of direction.

When changing direction while running, shorten the stride in one direction, lower the body weight, and push with one foot as a full stride is taken in the new direction. For example, if a player wishes to cut left, she plants her right foot, pushes firmly, lowers the left shoulder, turns her body left, and takes a stride with the left foot.

Stopping. There are basically two methods of stopping running momentum while in possession of the ball, and both methods are used without the ball, as well. These methods are the *two-step stop* (stride stop) and the *jump stop.* To execute either stop the hips are low, knees flexed, back straight, and trunk of the body inclined slightly forward. The head remains over the center of the body for balance.

The *two-step stop* can be described as a half skip followed by a sudden stop. The player lands on one foot, followed by the other, resulting in a forward-backward stride position. The body weight is lowered for balance. The *rear foot* becomes the pivot foot. This stop is more desirable than the jump stop when an offensive player is in the scoring area for it leaves the player in a balanced stance suitable for passing, shooting, or dribbling. Players should be able to use either foot as the pivot, for many coaches feel that the right foot should be the pivot foot when the player is on the right side of the court and the left foot should be the pivot foot when the player is on the left side of the court. Other coaches feel that greater balance and body control are achieved when a right-handed player uses the left foot as the pivot foot and the left-handed player uses the right foot as the pivot foot regardless of the side of the court the player is on.

In executing the *jump stop,* the entire surfaces of both feet contact the floor simultaneously in a side-stride position. Either foot may be used as the pivot foot. This stop is often necessary for an offensive player when a defensive player forces a dribbler or a pass receiver to the sideline or endline. The stop is frequently used prior to execution of a jump shot.

Jumping. Development of leg power and body balance are necessary for high, controlled jumps. The techniques are specific to the situation, such as rebounding, tip-in, jump ball, or jump shot. The situation may call for a jump from one or both feet or from a stride stop. Leg force is exerted with a push from the toes and balls of the feet over flexed knees as the body "stretches out" high off the floor. The landing is in a balanced position on the balls of the feet as the knees flex to absorb the landing shock.

Evading and Maneuvering Techniques. There are many skills involving body control which are important in both offensive and defensive situations.

Pivots or *turns* are used by a player, with or without the ball, who wishes to change or reverse body direction to elude an opponent. Throughout the pivot, the pivot foot or feet must remain in contact with the floor. When catching a ball while standing still, following a one-step stop or on a jump stop, either foot or both feet may be used as pivot feet. Following a two-step stop or a foot fake, the pivot must be made on the pivot foot only.

A *simple pivot turn* may be made by pivoting on the balls of both feet simultaneously without lifting either foot. This turn is used frequently to turn in the direction of a pass. Following a two-step stop the pivot is made on the ball of the rear foot as the forward foot steps in the direction of the pass.

The *reverse turn* is frequently used by both offensive and defensive players who desire to change directions rapidly to a reverse direction. It is used when the player is in a forward stride position. Weight is over the rear foot as it pivots and the forward foot (at the stop) steps in the opposite direction. The knees are bent and the body low as the shoulder on the turning side is lowered. The turn may be executed as a $^{3}/_{4}$ or half turn.

For a half turn the body moves as if commanded, "to the rear march" in the direction of the rear foot and away from the forward foot.

Inside and outside pivots are used following a jump stop when a player is forced to a line and must turn quickly to the court to pass. For an inside turn the player pivots on the foot nearer midcourt as she swings the outside foot backward until her body is opposite her original position. The ball should be protected by keeping the elbows close to the body during the turn.

In executing the outside turn the foot nearer the line serves as the pivot foot. The turn is frequently used by pivot players who receive the ball with their backs to the basket and then turn for a shot.

Feinting. *Feints* or *fakes* are movements of the body or ball which are used to deceive an opponent and draw her out of position. Usually, the movement is contrary to the intended final movement of the feinting player. Although fakes are usually considered offensive techniques, they should be developed and used by defensive players as well. Offensively, feints are used when a player without the ball is trying to elude the defense in order to receive a pass or when she has possession of the ball and is trying to free herself for a shot or a better court position. Defensively, a player uses body fakes in an attempt to deceive or conceal her intended movement from her offensive adversary.

Feints include:

1. *Ball fake*—accomplished by moving the ball in one direction and shooting, passing, bouncing, or dribbling in another. Keep elbows in so that the ball is protected within the lines of the body.
2. *Foot fake*—placing one foot in one direction and then moving the body or ball in another.
3. *Eye feint*—looking one way and passing another.
4. *Head fake* or *Shoulder fake*—the head, shoulder, or upper part of the body makes a movement in one direction and then the player suddenly turns and dribbles, passes, or shoots in another.
5. *Arm fake*—thrusting the arm upward or sideward to raise the opponent's defense and then passing below the defensive player's arms.

In execution, feints may employ skills of pivoting as well as body, eye, and ball movements. They should be executed quickly and crisply while maintaining the center of gravity over the base of the body so that time is not wasted in bringing the body weight back before completion of the intended movement. It is wise to turn the head and eyes in the direction of the fake.

Several feints are of particular value on offense when the offensive player is trying to draw the opponent close so that she can drive around her. The most obvious is to fake a shot, draw the opponent in, and then drive around her.

The offensive player uses the *jab step* to get an opponent off balance. She executes one or more short steps in one or several directions before a return to starting position and a drive. The jab begins from a side stride position. Only one foot may be used in these foot feints.

The *crossover step* is most easily executed from a side stride position (which can be assured after a two-step stop by drawing the forward foot back). For example, the offensive player fakes a drive to the right with the right foot as the weight is carried over the left flexed leg. Quickly, the right foot crosses over to the left side as the right shoulder turns between the ball and the opponent. As the drive moves to the left, the ball is dribbled with the left hand.

It is wise for the offensive player anticipating a fake to focus on the defender's feet. She can note weight shift and determine the direction in which she is best able to move. A defensive player is more vulnerable when a drive is made in the direction of her front foot, particularly if it is weight bearing.

Individual Defensive Skills

Defensive skills deserve as much attention as the offensive skills of ball handling and shooting, for it is only through effective individual and team defense that a team gains possession of the ball. The body control and movement skills mentioned previously are fundamental to the various guarding positions and to rebounding.

Basic Defensive Stance. The defensive player is responsible for preventing an opponent from receiving the ball; however, if a pass is received she is then responsible for keeping her from penetrating the defense and scoring. In essence, this implies that an individual defensive player must learn to guard a player with or without the ball and to guard a dribbler whether using player-to-player or zone defensive tactics. Once fundamentals of the basic player-to-player defense are mastered, players learn to press and apply their individual skills in a variety of zone defensive patterns.

A primary concern is the *basic defensive stance when guarding a player with the ball.* The feet of the defensive player are approximately shoulder width apart in a forward-backward stride position. One foot is approximately 6 to 10 inches ahead of the other. The knees and hips are flexed to lower the body to a low boxer's crouch. The trunk is held relatively erect. Inclining too far forward throws the center of gravity forward and results in slower directional movements. The entire surfaces of both feet contact the floor, but the weight is carried on the *balls of both feet.* Even distribution of weight over both feet is desirable, but when weight shifts it is better to weight the rear foot, *never* the forward foot, to assure that the defensive player can move backward and sideward. The defensive player moves in short, sliding steps, avoiding crossing the feet. Since it is easier and quicker to move backward in the direction of the rear foot, this rear foot represents the defensive player's strong side. The forward foot, left or right, represents the weak side. The defensive player must learn to place either foot forward in order to take advantage of her court position and the position of other defensive players. The *inside foot* is the one nearer the midline of the court, and the *outside foot* is nearer the sideline.

Most coaches prefer to force offensive players to the middle of the court where it is more congested and where there are more defensive players to assist. Therefore, they suggest that the outside foot should be to the rear so that the defensive player is in better position to defend against the drive to the outside. A few coaches prefer players to position with the inside foot back and the outside foot forward to force the dribbler to the sideline where shooting angles are poorer.

The arms of the defensive player in a basic stance are flexed, and the hands—palms up—and fingers are almost fully extended. The arms and hands remain low to keep the center of gravity low, thus facilitating more rapid movement.

A player with the ball has the options of passing, dribbling, and shooting. Basic guarding position is designed to protect against the pass and the dribble. When guarding a player with the ball the defensive player focuses her eyes on the opponent's waistline or hips, since movement in this area telegraphs the direction of player movement. The defensive player always faces the ball when her opponent has possession, and she positions herself on the ball side of the offensive player. That is, she is closer to the ball than to the opposing player. The defensive player should keep one hand, palm up, by the ball and the other at the side, about waist level. If the left foot is forward, the left arm is forward toward the ball. When a defensive player is attempting to harass the offensive player or steal the ball, her hand should be used in an upward motion to avoid fouling. The defensive player is approximately an arm's distance from the opponent. If the offensive player is very quick, the defense plays a little farther away; she plays slightly closer to a good shooter and much closer to a medium or low post player.

In *defending against the dribbler* the defensive player extends her lead arm (the one in the direction she is moving) toward the sideline and the other arm toward the ball and player. She makes jabbing motions toward the ball with the palm of the hand up as she tries to overplay the dribbler to the sideline and force her to the center of the court. If the offensive player is fast, it may be necessary for the defensive player to play her slightly loosely while still controlling her. If an opponent stops after dribbling and keeps the ball, the defensive player moves in and attempts to tie the ball.

As an opponent prepares to shoot, the defensive player moves in. With weight controlled backward, she places one hand over the ball in an attempt to prevent the offensive player from raising the ball for a shot. If the offensive player gets the ball up, the defense tries to jab the ball upward. If this fails, the defensive player jumps vertically, *not forward,* when the offensive player leaves her feet to shoot. The defensive player blocks right-handed shots with the right hand and left-handed ones with her left hand. The defensive player turns slightly in the air to avoid fouling and lands facing the basket in preparation for a rebound.

When a defensive player is *guarding a player without the ball* she positions herself so she can see both the ball and the person she is guarding without moving her head. As the ball is passed the defensive player adjusts so she can keep the ball and her opponent in view. The body is positioned so that the offensive player cannot make cuts into the lane or to the basket. A defensive player must be ready to assist a teammate and to defend against a dribbler who is free or a cutter who has evaded her guard.

Guarding post players requires techniques to prevent the pivot player from receiving a pass as well as preventing effective shots. A pivot player's position within 15 feet of the basket makes her a dangerous scorer once in possession of the ball.

A *high post player* usually stands with her back to the basket. The defensive player should be on the ball side of the player, one foot beside the post player's foot, the other to the rear of the pivot player. Her forward arm is extended, and the other is back. The defensive player slides behind the post player as the ball is passed to the other side. Since the high post usually passes to cutters and is not in the best scoring position, she may be more loosely guarded once in possession of the ball.

When guarding the *medium post player* the defensive player moves more to the front of the pivot with the front arm extended to prevent her from receiving a pass. In this position the defensive player is vulnerable to the high lob pass and other defensive players must be ready to defend in this situation. If the pivot receives the ball, the defensive player should overplay and attempt to force her to the sideline.

The *low post* must be prevented from receiving the ball because of her potential threat as a scorer. The defender may play with her body three-quarters in front of the pivot player, or she may move in front and face either the player or the ball with her arms extended. As the ball is passed to the other side of the court the defensive player moves in front, on the ball side, of the pivot. If the offensive player receives a pass the defensive player tries to force her to her weakest shooting side.

On *screen plays* the options of the defense are: (1) step closer to the offensive player and squeeze around the screen; (2) go behind the screen by stepping back from the offensive player and going between a teammate and her offensive player; and (3) switch defensive responsibilities with a teammate.

Rebounding skills must be developed by both offensive and defensive players for game statistics indicate that control of the backboard is a major factor in winning. Height is an obvious advantage, but the smaller player can compensate by blocking out her opponent and properly timing her jump.

Defensively, the guard has the initial advantage of inside position. The defensive player first blocks her opponent from moving to the basket. She turns so her shoulder is perpendicular to the forward, observes her movements, and pivots in front of her with a large stride to present a wider obstruction. When the shot is up she watches the ball, the force of the shot, and the angle of rebound. The player jumps slightly forward from a wide stride position, bending at the waist to prevent an opponent from reaching over her shoulder. Her arms are extended upward to catch the ball with both hands. The player lands with the ball held firmly and drawn to the body. The elbows are away from the body to protect the ball. Legs are spread in a balanced position as she lands.

Offensive rebounding enables a team to get "easy scores." An offensive player must get around her defense to an inside position unless she has a great height advantage. Getting inside is best accomplished by a player who anticipates a shot by her teammate and who gets a step on her defensive opponent. A shooter may step inside following a quickly executed fake. Once the ball is controlled it may be tipped back to the basket or passed out to a teammate.

Individual Offensive Skills

Offensive skills include all body control skills, ball handling techniques, and shooting techniques as well as the skills of gaining possession of free balls, jump balls, and rebounds. In order for an offense to be effective, its passes must be accurate, properly timed and paced, and effectively caught. Careless passes and fumbled catches can destroy a team's offensive attempts.

Catching. The type of catch used depends upon the position of the ball, the position of opposing players, and the anticipated move to follow. In preparation, the arms are relaxed, the elbows are away from the body, and the hands are at waist level. The fingers are relaxed and spread upward or downward depending on the height of the ball. With the receiver facing the oncoming ball, she moves forward to meet the ball with arms extended, elbows in, and hands extended. The receiver should watch the ball until it is in her hands to avoid fumbling. As the ball reaches the fingertips it is cushioned into the fingers as the arms pull back slightly to "give" to ball momentum. The ball is caught by the pads on the tips of the fingers and the thumbs. Whenever possible the ball should be caught with both hands. If one hand is used when the player is closely guarded or catching a lob pass, the other hand should secure the ball quickly.

If a pass is not made immediately the ball should be securely held at chest level, ever ready for the pass, dribble, or shot opportunity.

Passing. Passing is the essence of basketball; it makes basketball a *team* game. There are numerous ways of passing; the type used by a player

Figure 14–2 Catching.

depends upon the position of the body and hands of the passer and intended receiver.

Chest Pass. The two-hand chest pass is most widely used because it can be caught at chest height and lead to a speedy and accurate shot or return pass. The body may be almost erect or crouched with the ball at chest level close to the body. Both hands hold the ball with fingers spread from the rear to the side, and pointing slightly upward. Thumbs are behind the ball with palms near, but not touching. Elbows are flexed and close to the body. The arms push forward from the shoulders as the elbows extend, and the wrists snap as the ball is released in a straight line. As the ball leaves the hands, the thumbs give a simultaneous push and the palms turn toward the line of ball flight. The hands rotate forward and outward on the follow-through as thumbs point downward and fingers extend in the direction of the pass. If it is not a deceptive pass, body weight should be transferred to the forward foot to give additional power.

Two-hand Underhand Pass. This pass can be used as a "feed" pass or hand-off to a player breaking for the basket. It is more effective as a short

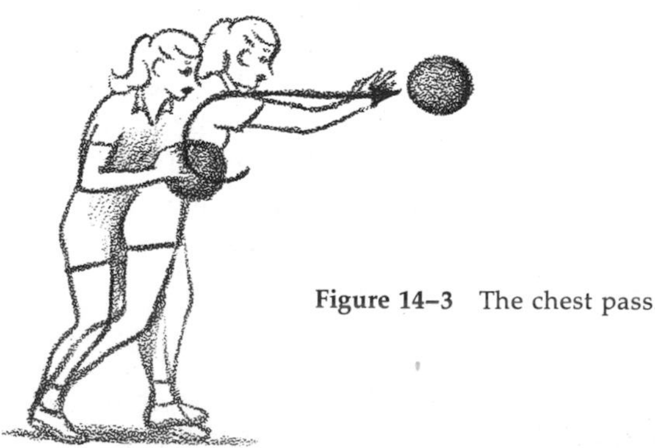

Figure 14–3 The chest pass.

pass, since a long two-handed underhand pass is slow because of the necessary extended backswing.

The pass may be made off the front of the body or from either hip. In any case, the cupped hands grasp the ball with fingers behind and on the side pointing downward; thumbs are on top pointing toward the line of flight. When passed off the front of the body by a pivot player with her back to the basket, the elbows are flexed and point away from the body more than in the chest pass. Feet are in side stride position as the player steps in the direction of the pass (left foot moves if pass is left) so that the leg can serve as a screen. The arms extend forward as the elbows straighten, and wrists snap upward as the ball is released at waist height. The arms follow through low with thumbs pointing up and fingers toward the path of the ball.

When the ball is passed off either hip, body position varies slightly. To pass from the right hip the body is in forward stride position with the left foot forward. The hands draw the ball to the right hip so the right elbow is bent, pointing outward from the body, and the left elbow is across the body with the back of the left hand resting on the hip. The ball moves forward with an arm extension and wrist snap as the body weight transfers to the forward left foot. The release and follow-through are the same as when the pass is executed from the middle of the body.

Two-hand Shoulder Pass. The two-hand shoulder, or sidearm, pass is useful as a short quick throw at the completion of a pivot, or as a deceptive pass when the ball moves one direction and the body another. The pass may be made from either shoulder. The ball is held in both hands so the fingers and thumbs point upward and back and cover the sides and rear of the ball. When passing from the right shoulder across the body to the left, the elbows are flexed so the right arm is close to the side and the left is across the front of the body. Feet are in forward or stride position with the body rotated to the right from the hips and waist. The arms extend and wrists snap in a rapid movement as the weight shifts to the left leg. The body follows the ball as the arms and the hands extend and rotate as in the chest pass.

Two-hand Overhead Pass. This pass is used frequently to feed the post player or by the post player to feed cutters. It is also used by a tall player who wants to release the ball quickly after catching a high pass. The ball is raised above and slightly behind the head, with the fingers at side and rear and thumbs beneath the ball. The elbows are slightly bent and the wrists flexed. The body inclines forward and weight shifts forward as the arms extend and wrists and fingers snap to add thrust to arm and shoulder power. The ball is released at a point in front of the body about head level as the hands follow the ball to eye level and turn, palms down and thumbs toward one another. If the player is in a side stride position, the force is imparted by arm extension and rotation of the hands so the palms face outward at completion of the throw.

Figure 14–4 The two-hand underhand pass from the right.

Figure 14–5 The two-hand shoulder pass.

Figure 14–6 Two-hand overhead pass.

Figure 14–7 One-hand underhand pass.

Figure 14–8 One-hand overhand pass.

One-hand Underhand Pass. The underhand pass is effective from both sides of the body as a short, low pass that can be used to pass the ball under the arms of a defensive player with her hands held high. The pass resembles the underarm softball pitch. In executing a pass from the right side, the left foot is forward, and the body is comfortably crouched. The right hand is spread over the back of the ball, and the right wrist and lower arm support the ball. The right elbow bends and leads the arm and ball past the hip as the left hand is placed on the ball as a guide. As the right arm starts forward the left hand moves away. The arm swings by the body and parallel to it; the arm extends and weight transfers to the forward foot. The ball is released at waist height as the fingertips, hand (palm up). and arm follow the ball flight.

One-hand Overhand Pass. The pass is much like an overarm softball throw and is effective as a well controlled long or medium distance pass. To execute the pass the feet are comfortably spread and body weight equally distributed. The right hand is spread behind the ball so that it is supported by the fingers and thumb. The ball is brought behind the right ear and over the right shoulder by bending the elbow back and away from the body. The left hand comes across the body to serve as a steadying guide as the trunk rotates to the right. The left shoulder points in the direction of the intended pass. As the body weight shifts to the left foot, the left hand leaves the ball. The right arm brings the ball forward passing close to the ear. The right elbow extends, and the wrist extends as the fingers thrust forward and pass under the ball causing a slight reverse spin. The throwing hand and arm follow through in the direction of the ball and end with palm down and fingers extended forward.

Bounce Passes. One- and two-hand bounce passes are used for short passes in the scoring area, or any other place on the court when an opponent who has her arms up is between the passer and receiver. They are often used on out-of-bounds plays.

For the one-hand bounce pass the preliminary movements are similar to the shoulder pass, except that the ball is brought between the shoulder and waist on the right side of the body. When throwing with the right hand, the left hand may balance the ball as the right hand is behind and toward the top with fingers extending upward. The right elbow is flexed and close to the side. The ball is pushed to the floor so that it bounces and rises to a level at which the receiver can get it easily. The arm follows through toward the floor with palms down. If a waist level rebound is desired, the ball should bounce three or four feet from the receiver. If a lower rebound is necessary, the ball should bounce farther from the receiver.

The two-hand bounce is executed much like the two-hand chest pass, except the action begins about waist height and the force is exerted downward rather than forward. The fingers are spread to the sides with the thumbs behind the ball. The elbows are close to the sides as the ball is pushed with a firm arm extension out toward a point on the floor. The arms rotate outward as the wrists and fingers thrust the ball away at waist level. At certain times a spin is valuable with the bounce pass. On a long pass or when the ball must rebound close to the receiver with considerable momentum, top spin can be added by cocking the wrists back and then uncocking them vigorously on the release. The ball leaves the small fingers first and the index fingers last as the thumbs roll over the top of the ball at release. The hands follow through so that the fingers point toward the floor.

Backspin is used on short, relatively fast passes where a rebound up and away from the receiver is desired. The ball is released by a vigorous cocking action of the wrists toward the passer's body. The fingers release the ball after pulling upward and backward and the thumbs complete the action by pushing the ball down and forward. As the ball leaves the hands of the passer it is spinning toward her; the palms of the hands follow through facing the spot where the ball strikes the floor.

Side spins are applied when it is necessary for the ball to bounce right or left on the rebound. To spin the ball so it bounces to the receiver's right side, bring the left hand to the right (under the ball) while pulling the right hand forcefully to the left (on top of the ball). At the moment of release, the ball is spinning in a counterclockwise direction. As the ball hits the floor it "jumps" to the passer's left. A reverse hand action results in a clockwise spin and a bounce to the left of the receiver.

Tip Pass. This advanced pass is also called the volley pass and is an effective way of clearing the ball from under the basket or controlling a rebound or pass without really gaining possession of the ball. As the ball comes toward the receiver, she pushes the ball toward a teammate by using one or both hands. The hands and fingers are firm and extended, elbows flexed. The wrists are flexed as the hands meet the ball. The arms extend and the wrists extend, giving direction to the ball. The palms and firm arms follow through in the direction of the pass.

Hook Pass. The hook pass is an advanced technique used when a

Figure 14–9 The hook pass.

player is closely guarded and a pass in front of the body is not possible. It is often used effectively to return a ball to an inside court position when the player is held along the sidelines. For a right-hand hook pass, the body is in forward stride position, left foot forward. Initially the ball is held firmly by both hands at waist level. The body turns so the left shoulder is toward the receiver as the left hand moves toward the left side, leaving the right hand (fingers spread and pointing upward) and right forearm supporting the ball. When a passer is standing or jumping upward, her right arm, fully

Figure 14–10 The jump pass.

extended, is raised sideward so it crosses the right shoulder and passes overhead, where the ball is released by a forceful wrist and finger snap. The left arm remains extended for balance while the right hand pulls under the ball as it rolls off the fingertips. The hand (palm down) and fingers follow the path of the ball as far as possible. If this hook pass is executed with a jump, the last step is with the left foot, and the right knee is raised high to gain elevation.

Jump Pass. This advanced pass technique is executed from an extended jump position while the body is in the air. Following receipt of a pass, dribble, or rebound, the jump may be made from a stationary position in which the player is standing on both feet or by stepping forward and jumping from one leg with the other following. The ball is held in position for either a two-hand overhead or one-hand push pass. If taking off from both legs simultaneously, the knees bend deeply and both legs thrust the body directly up from the floor. If the jump follows a bounce or dribble, one leg thrusts upward forcefully and the other immediately comes alongside. As the player leaves the floor, the ball is brought in front of the body and raised high and directly overhead for a two-hand overhead pass or high overhead and slightly toward the shoulder side for the one-hand push pass. To avoid contact with an opponent, the jump must be directly upward rather than forward. The player must jump as high as possible, for the greater the height the less opportunity for interception or blocking of the pass by an opponent. At the height of the jump, when the passer is motionless for a brief instant before returning to the floor, she releases the ball in the direction of the intended receiver.

Dribble. This is the skill of imparting impetus to the ball one or more times causing it to rebound from the floor while controlling and maintaining possession of it. Players should remember that accurate passing is a faster way of moving the ball and that the dribble is used to get somewhere with the ball (as in a fast break situation), to allow time to establish and execute an offensive pattern, and to avoid losing possession of the ball. The hand is cupped and fingers are spread as the first impetus to the floor is given by one or both hands, but thereafter contact must be made with only one hand until the ball is passed or the dribbler touches the ball with both hands to complete the dribble. As the ball rebounds from the floor the pads of the fingers and thumb meet the ball, ride the ball upward for an instant and then impart force downward with shoulder, arm, and hand action. The dribbler bends her knees and inclines forward from the hips. Her head is up and her eyes are forward, watching players rather than the ball. Greater speed and distance result from a high dribble, but a low dribble results in better ball control.

Players should develop the ability to dribble with both hands, as well as the skill of changing hands during a dribble series. When driving right a player should use her right hand and when moving left, she should use the left hand, as she places the ball farther from the opponent and uses her

Figure 14–11 Preparing for a jump ball.

body as protection for the ball. The free arm is carried high to keep the opponent farther from the ball and for more effective screening.

Jumping for Jump Ball. The player crouches in a forward stride position with both feet on the floor. A player must choose to place either shoulder toward her opponent and reach with the arm and hand closer to her opponent. The weight is forward on the toes, and the body weight is down through flexed hips and knees. The first push-off comes from the rear foot (right when players have left shoulders together); the final push-off comes from an extension of ankles, knees, and hips. Simultaneously, the contact arm swings forward and upward with the tapping hand extended, fingers cupped, wrist flexed. The tap is timed so that the ball is touched and directed to a teammate or open area at the height of the jump.

Shooting. Shooting incorporates all the skills of stance, body balance, arm, hand, and finger control, and follow-through. The type of shot a player makes depends upon her position on the court. Figure 14–12 gives an indication of when a player should use a rim shot or a bank or angle shot off the backboard.

Two-hand Set (Chest) Shot. This set shot is used from relatively long distances when the offensive player is not too closely threatened by a defender. The feet may be in forward or side stride position. The body is relaxed in a semi-crouch, weight equally distributed, and eyes focused on or slightly over the rim, where the shooter will generally aim. The ball is in front of the body at chest level (lower for a very long shot) and is grasped by the fingers behind and to the sides. Fingers point upwards and thumbs toward each other. The relaxed shoulders help keep the elbows comfortably close to the body. The force of the shot begins as the knees flex and the wrists "cock" allowing the ball to drop *down* toward the shooter. As the arms extend the ball upward in front of the chest, the body extends upward and forward, and the wrists straighten as the fingers direct the ball in an upward arc. The palms of the hands follow through to face the basket, and the fingers maintain extension as the shooter moves forward for a possible rebound.

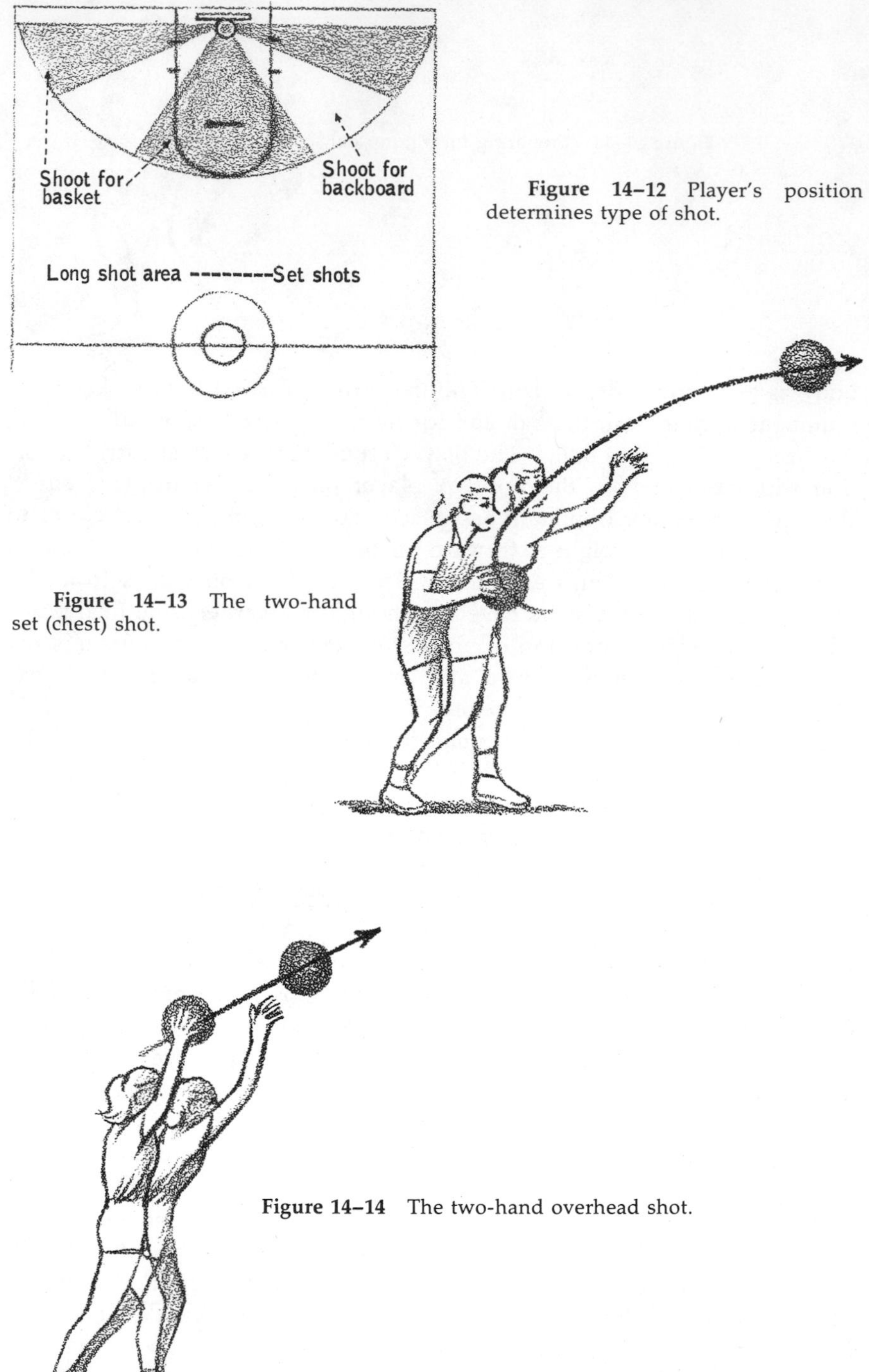

Figure 14–12 Player's position determines type of shot.

Figure 14–13 The two-hand set (chest) shot.

Figure 14–14 The two-hand overhead shot.

Figure 14–15 The one-hand set (push) shot.

Two-hand Overhead Shot. This is used effectively by tall players for a short or medium distance set shot. Proper execution requires strong arm and finger action. The body is erect, head up, and eyes on the target. The knees flex slightly as the ball is raised above the forehead by easily bent elbows and held by the thumbs behind and underneath, with the fingers pointing outward on the sides and rear half of the ball. The arms and knees extend as the body weight shifts to the toes. The shot can be executed with or without a jump. The wrists extend and the fingers and thumbs drive the ball toward the basket.

One-hand Set (Push) Shot. This shot can be used effectively when the shooter is closely guarded in a set position, or as a moving shot following pass receipt, bounce, or dribble. If the shot is executed while the player is moving, the left foot is the take-off foot when shooting with the right hand. When used as a set shot, the player's right foot is forward. The arm movement is similar to the lay-up shot. The knees bend slightly in preparation and extend as the ball is released. As the body rises away from the defender, the right arm extends upward and forward. The ball is released well above the shoulder with hand and finger extension at the height of body extension or of the jump.

Lay-up Shot. Often called an angle or under-the-basket shot, it is made from a position close to the basket, from the front or either side. An angle shot from the side is banked off the backboard. Players should develop lay-ups from both sides. Shooting from the right of the basket should be done with the right arm from a left-foot takeoff; the opposite should be done in shooting from the left. A lay-up from the right may be analyzed as follows: A player moving in from the right cuts for the basket, receives the ball, and may bounce, dribble, or move directly to the shot.

Figure 14–16 The lay-up shot.

The ball is carried with the left hand to the front and underneath and the right hand on top and slightly behind. Both hands carry the ball to shoulder or head height as the left foot pushes off. The higher the ball is carried the more easily it can be *placed.* The right knee rises to lift the body, the guiding hand leaves the ball as the right arm and wrist straighten and direct the ball to the backboard. The ball is laid against the backboard at a point to the right of the basket and slightly higher than the rim. The palm of the right hand follows in the direction of the backboard as the fingertips "guide" the ball. The player turns as she lands from the jump so she partially faces the court, ready to play for a rebound.

When shooting from the left side the ball is caught as a step is made with the left foot. The shot is made off the right foot from the left hand.

When playing a lay-up shot from the front of the basket, use either hand to lay the ball over the rim. When executing an *underhand lay-up,* the player carries the ball toward the basket with the hand, palm up, under the ball.

Crossover Lay-up. The crossover lay-up is used when the offensive player is deep along the baseline and goes under the goal before releasing the ball. She shoots the ball backward over her head, imparting spin to bank it from the backboard. She may also use the hook shot motion with her body turning as she releases the ball.

Hook Shot. This shot is executed from both the right and left sides when the shooter is facing away from the basket and is closely guarded from the rear, or when the shooter is moving away from the basket. Initially the ball is held by both hands at chest level. To shoot with the right hand the player slides the left foot sideward or forward (quarter turn) as the left shoulder turns toward the basket. Simultaneously, the ball, now held by the fingers and supported by the heel of the right hand, is brought upward in an overhead arc and toward and above the left shoulder by the fully extended right arm. The left hand is high to protect the shot and the player's right leg crosses the front of her body. The right knee is high for elevation. The fingertips and wrists guide the arcing ball over the rim (if shot is from the front) or to the backboard. The arm follows through overhead and toward the basket as the body turns in rebounding position.

Jump Shot. The jump shot is the most effective way to rise above an opponent to execute a shot. This shot has done more to change the style and pace of play than any other single development. The shot is most effective from within 15 feet of the basket and enables a player to shoot very quickly following movement. The shot is "executed much like a one-hand shot except the player jumps high in the air and does not release the ball until she has reached her maximum jump height. The take-off is from both feet, the jump is straight up or slightly backward if the forward momentum has been fast (fade-away shot). The ball is carried upward into shooting position during the jump. There is a brief instant of relaxation at

Figure 14–17 The hook shot.

the height of the jump before the ball is released. A fade-away shot is most effective against a defensive player who guards very closely."

Tip-in. The tip-in is an advanced offensive skill that is most often used on a rebound and is occasionally used to control a misdirected goal shot by a teammate. The player jumps to meet the ball with fingers spread wide just before the height of her full jump is reached. She controls the ball momentarily and then shoots or pushes it to the basket at the top of her jump *before* returning to the floor. The shot is the result of pressure by the tips of the fingers, a slight wrist flip, and arm extension rather than a batting or slapping action. This skill requires excellent timing and a strong and agile hand.

Foul Shooting. Several types of shots are successfully used in the attempt for a free throw. It is generally agreed that a player is more successful using her *best* personal shot. This will frequently be a one-hand shoulder shot and occasionally a two-hand chest or overhead shot. Whatever the shooting technique, the player taking a free throw stands directly in front of the basket with toes behind and near the foul line.

Occasionally, players find the two-hand underhand loop shot the easiest and most accurate free throw. To execute an underhand loop shot, the feet are spread and toe out from the body to insure balance. A side stride offers the best balanced position. The fingers are spread over the sides of the ball pointing downward, and the thumbs are on top and forward. The arms hang comfortably down as the eyes focus on the forward rim of the basket. The body remains erect as it sinks with a knee bend and the heels rise from the floor.

The force of the throw begins as the body straightens naturally and the arms and hands extend upward and forward toward the basket. The hands release the ball at the closest point to the basket without applying a

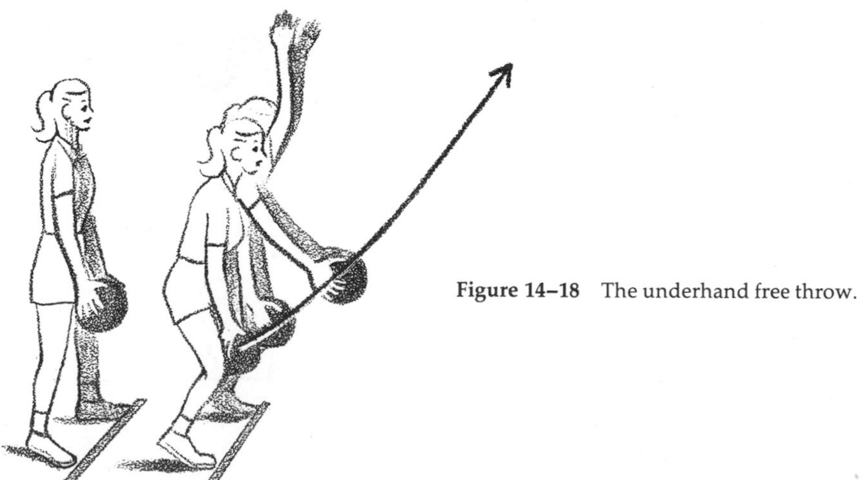

Figure 14–18 The underhand free throw.

deliberate spin. At the completion of the shot the weight is forward and the body is balanced and erect. The arms and hands are outstretched to the basket.

GAME STRATEGY

Basketball is a game of offensive and defensive tactics with the ultimate team objective of scoring goals and preventing opponents from scoring. The team in possession of the ball is the offensive team. The system of play used by both the offensive and defensive teams is dependent on the style of play and the skill of the opponents. "Strategy is simply determination of how one chooses to play in varying situations. Several general guides direct offensive and defensive play.

"1. Play the opponent's style of game only if it is also your team's best game.... Invariably, a team will do its best when playing the style of game to which it is accustomed. A competitive game is not the place to change well-rehearsed patterns.

"2. Make your opponents play your style of game. Try to set the patterns of play by forcing tempo and style. Players and coaches often become confused when their normal pattern is blocked.

"3. Be prepared for any eventuality. . . . The best preparation for meeting the unknown is ball control, rebound strength and fundamental defense skills with consistent shooting.

OFFENSIVE STRATEGY

"Offensive styles and options are limitless but there are certain essentials found in all successful offenses, regardless of the patterns. The ability to shoot, to pass, to dribble, to drive and to execute basic screens is essential. When incorporated into a team offense they afford: (1) movement of the ball; (2) movement of players; (3) obtaining the good shot; (4) obtaining the second shot; (5) maintaining floor balance, and (6) maintaining one-on-one situations.

"It is obvious that the offense must move the ball if the defense is to be penetrated, whether it is a player-to-player, zone or combination defense. The team that passes the ball slowly allows the defense time to shift, sag or otherwise move to counteract the offense. The team that keeps the ball moving keeps the defense off balance.

"Sound offensive patterns allow for movement of players in conjunction with movement of the ball. Constant movement, fakes and cuts are necessary. When players pose no offensive threat, the defense can use sinking or double teaming strategy and congest potentially vulnerable areas.

"The offense must work for the good percentage shot, one that the shooter has the ability to make and one that the rebounders are positioned to recover if missed.

"Good offensive play will keep players in open positions to eliminate congestion in and near the basket and prevent one defensive player from guarding two offensive players.

"Fast Break. The fast break is the strategy by which an offensive team beats the defense to the basket for a score. Its execution develops in three phases: (1) ball possession; (2) clearing pass and (3) player movement.

"1. Ball possession. A fast break is initiated only after clear possession of the ball. The best opportunity occurs from defensive rebounding but may result from ball interception, loose ball recovery or out-of-bounds play.

"2. Clearing action. After possession the fast break is initiated by a controlled clearing pass or a dribble. Dribble *only* to secure possession, to allow better timing or spacing or to make a defensive player commit herself to cover the dribbler and open breaking lanes for teammates. The outlet pass should be quick and sharp. Occasionally rapid relay passes are useful in initiating the break.

"3. Player movement. Players without the ball quickly react and move to the outlet area. This is the secret of the controlled fast break. Players spread as wide as necessary to fill the three lanes. Players running down court must be ahead of opponents or they must change pace to let the defensive opponent pass them so that the ball can be handled behind. One defensive player through gives 3 on 1; two defensive players through gives 3 on 2; three through, 3 on 3. If more defensive players pass, the break should be abandoned and a deliberate attack set. Do not let the break become helter-skelter. *It must be held up and possession of the ball retained when good scoring opportunity or control is not certain.*

"The two basic types of fast break are the three lane and the crisscross. The simplest is the three lane pattern in which a player with the ball breaks down the center with cutters in the outside lanes breaking toward the goal.

"When utilizing crisscross patterns, players cut across lanes hoping to deceive defensive players; however, the purpose of getting the ball to the center lane player with outside lane players cutting into the scoring area remains unchanged. If pattern play is disrupted, players should capitalize on free-lance options.

"Deliberate Offense. Most scoring efforts involve only two or three players in execution. Realizing this, offensive patterns involving two or three persons form the basis of all offense. These fundamentals prepare the offense to attack a variety of defenses, including player-to-player, switching player-to-player, combination defense, varying zone defenses and pressure defenses.

"In working against player-to-player the problem the offense faces is simply getting around one or perhaps two players to get a shot. Screen, dribble and cut against the player-to-player defense. The simple offenses noted include both two and three player patterns. (See Fig. 14–19.)

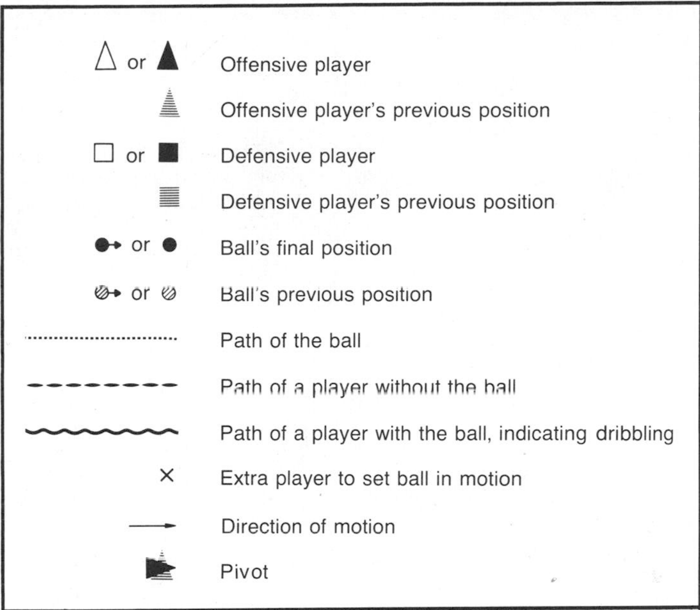

Figure 14–19 This chart explains the symbols which appear in the diagrams in this chapter. (From Poindexter, Hally B. W. and Mushier, Carole L.: *Coaching Competitive Team Sports for Girls and Women*. Philadelphia, W. B. Saunders Co., 1973.)

"A *screen* is set when an offensive player positions herself between another offensive player with the ball and her guard. The screen allows the offensive player to make an unguarded shot or drive toward the goal behind the protection of the screening player. The player with the ball, going off the screen, has the responsibility to make the screen effective. She fakes her defensive player and cuts as close to the screen as possible so the defense cannot get through (Fig. 14–20). To complete the pick and roll pattern the screener turns toward the cut using a back pivot with a long step. She then moves toward the basket looking for a pass if the defense switches. If she receives a pass and is stopped by a deep defensive player she may pass to an unguarded pivot (Fig. 14–21).

"Screens can also be set away from the ball to free an offensive player on the side opposite the ball. The offensive player then fakes her guard toward the baseline, cuts around the screen and receives a pass as she goes toward the boards. A pivot player can also break from the post position and set a screen for a forward. If the screen and roll pattern is stopped by an ineffective screen, the offensive player with the ball moves out and another screen is set.

"*Give and Go Pattern.* An offensive player passes to a teammate, then runs a path designed to look like a screen. At just the right moment she

Figure 14–20 Basic screen play. (From Poindexter, Hally B. W., and Mushier, Carole L.: *Coaching Competitive Team Sports for Girls and Women.* Philadelphia, W. B. Saunders Co., 1973.)

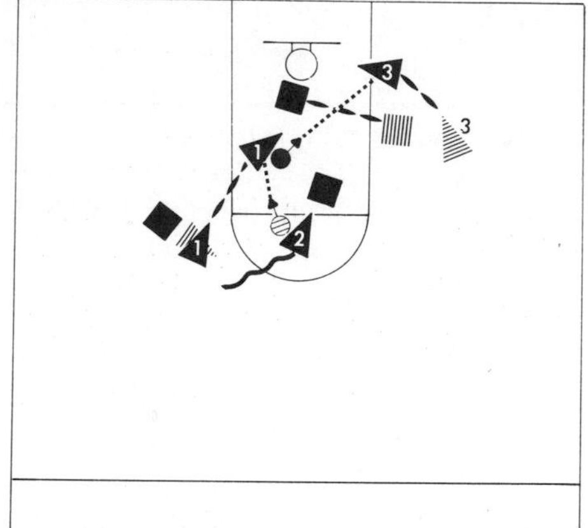

Figure 14–21 Screen and roll. (From Poindexter, Hally B. W. and Mushier, Carole L.: *Coaching Competitive Team Sports for Girls and Women.* Philadelphia, W. B. Saunders Co., 1973.)

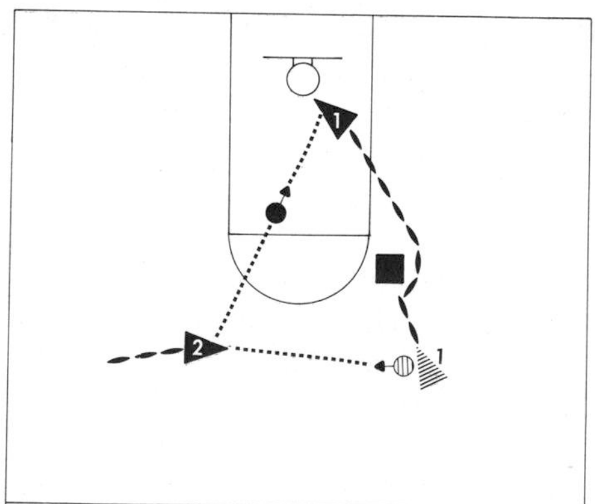

Figure 14–22 Give and go pattern. (From Poindexter, Hally B. W. and Mushier, Carole L.: *Coaching Competitive Team Sports for Girls and Women.* Philadelphia, W. B. Saunders Co., 1973.)

plants her lead foot and cuts toward the basket. She extends her lead hand as a target and catches the ball near the basket (Fig. 14–22).

"*Go-behind.* An offensive player passes to a teammate, follows the pass and runs to the outside of the teammate. She brushes her guard on the teammate and drives for a return pass.

"*Cat and Mouse.* This pattern is run in the same manner as the go-behind but the cutter stops in back of her teammate for a return pass. She may shoot over the screen if there is no pressure, or drive to the opposite side if the defense attempts to move past the screen.

"*Screen and Step Back.* It is run like other screens but the screener steps back for a return pass when the guard sags to stop the cutter.

"*Split the Post.* This is a simplified pattern with several options. The pivot player moves to a high post position and the two closest offensive players form the three player pattern. The ball is passed to the post by a forward who immediately fakes away from the intended cut and then scissors around the post attempting to screen her guard on the post player. The pivot may pass the ball back to the cutter if her guard was screened. The cut of the first forward is followed by a fake and a cut by a second forward who moves around the other side of the post. If her guard is held by the screen she may receive the pass. If the pivot player's guard switches on either cutter, the pivot player may shoot or drive for goal. If none of these options develops, a pass may be cleared to a player whose guard has sagged to defend against a cutter (Fig. 14–23).

"The literature is replete with offensive plays that can be run from patterns of three-two; two-three; one-three-one; single pivot post; double pivot post and figure eight."* An offense must find its own best plays and system.

---

*From Poindexter, Hally B. W. and Mushier, Carole L.: *Coaching Competitive Team Sports for Girls and Women.* Philadelphia, W. B. Saunders Co., 1973.

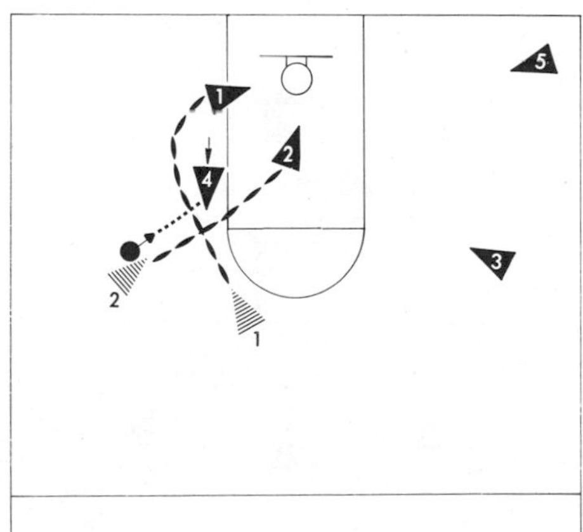

Figure 14–23 Split the post offensive pattern. (From Poindexter, Hally B. W., and Mushier, Carole L.: *Coaching Competitive Team Sports for Girls and Women.* Philadelphia, W. B. Saunders Co., 1973.)

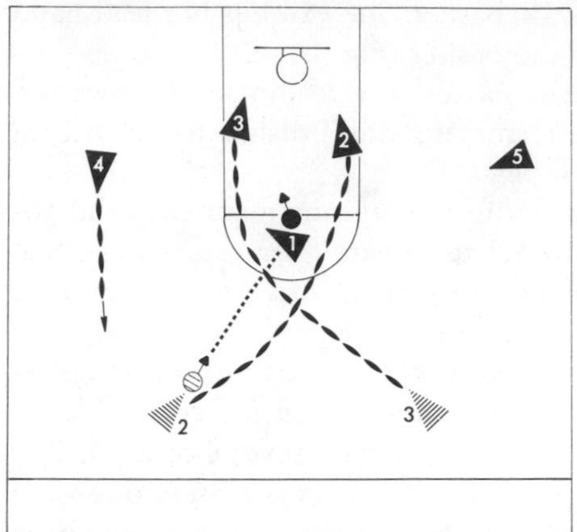

Figure 14–24 Single pivot post offense. (From Poindexter, Hally B. W. and Mushier, Carole L.: *Coaching Competitive Team Sports for Girls and Women.* Philadelphia, W. B. Saunders Co., 1973.)

"*Single Pivot Post Offense.* This pattern is built around the basic concept of the split the post pattern previously described. The idea is to get the ball to the pivot player and have the passer cut in for a return pass and shot. Player #4 takes #2's position in case of an interception (Fig. 14–24).

"*Double Pivot Post Offense.* This is a variation of the single pivot. The two tallest girls are on either side of the lane. The closer they are to the basket the greater their threat as shooters. Their main functions in the double pivot pattern are as ball handlers and screeners. The real advantage of this type of offense is the excellent rebounding position gained. Figure 14–25 illustrates a basic pattern. Player #1 passes to #5 who moves in the key by the screen set by #4.

"*Weave Offense.* The figure eight pattern is an excellent offense to combat player-to-player defense but ineffective against a zone. Ball handling skills and timing of the break are essential if the weave is to accomplish the major purpose of keeping the opponents moving until a

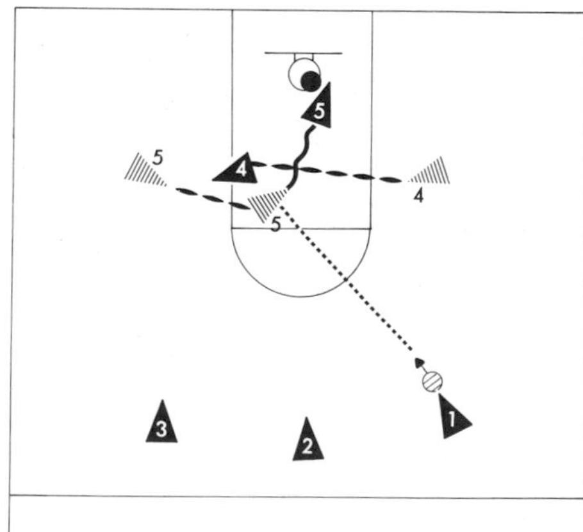

Figure 14–25 Double pivot post offense; basic pattern. (From Poindexter, Hally B. W. and Mushier, Carole L.: *Coaching Competitive Team Sports for Girls and Women.* Philadelphia, W. B. Saunders Co., 1973.)

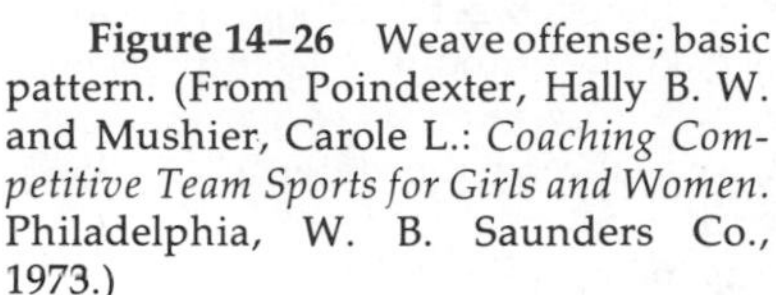

Figure 14–26 Weave offense; basic pattern. (From Poindexter, Hally B. W. and Mushier, Carole L.: *Coaching Competitive Team Sports for Girls and Women.* Philadelphia, W. B. Saunders Co., 1973.)

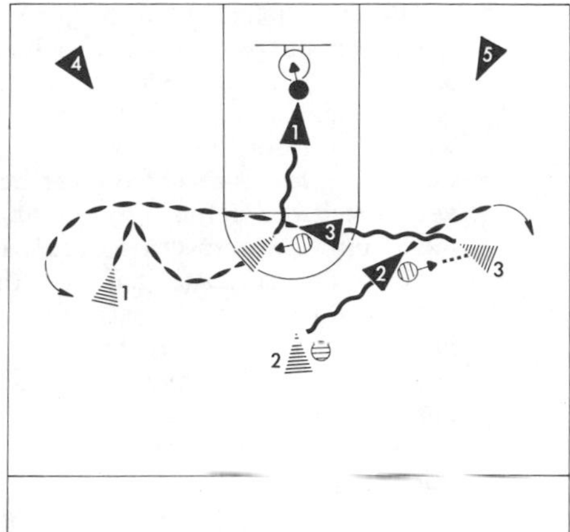

screen can be set and a player freed to break for a lay-up. The basic pattern begins with three players in front, two in the corners and the ball in the middle so it can be run left or right (Fig. 14–26). The simplest option finds one of the three players running the weave to cut for the goal.

"The weave can be run on the side of the court with only three players.

"*One-Three-One.* This offense has gained popularity for it can be used against player-to-player and zone defenses. The pattern enables the tall player to stay close to the basket in good rebounding position; spreads the defense so the offense can drive and it tends to keep defensive rebounders in poor position. The offensive spread, relying heavily on out-court screens and jump shots, eliminates some of the effectiveness of the zone. . . ."* To those who believe it is possible to screen and drive against the zone, the 1-3-1 presents the basic pattern.

"Offense Against a Zone Defense. The purpose of the zone is to concentrate defense players close to the basket to reduce the easy shots. Dribbling, driving around a guard and passing to teammates cutting around screens are not as effective against zone patterns. Consider the following in combating a zone defense:

"1. A team should use an offensive pattern not too different from its basic offense to conserve learning time and to maintain the same tempo and style of play.

"2. Effective outside shooting is the best weapon against the zone for it forces the defense to spread or switch to player-to-player.

"3. Fast break as often as possible before the defense is set.

"4. Quick, sharp and accurate passes are vital to combating a zone. When the zone is set the success of the offense lies in its ability to move the ball faster than the defensive players can shift.

---

*From Poindexter, Hally B. W. and Mushier, Carole L.: *Coaching Competitive Team Sports for Girls and Women.* Philadelphia, W. B. Saunders Co., 1973.

"5. Quick shots, particularly the jump shot, must be used. Most offensive systems attempt to move a player into an open spot for quick pass reception and a shot. Once inside the zone the player must get the shot away quickly. At the same time, a player must know *when* to take the quick shot and when to wait for the sure shot or for teammates to get in rebound position.
"6. Offensive players away from the ball (weak side) should constantly maneuver to split the defense by moving between two defensive players. They move into open spaces to receive a pass, spread the defense and keep pressure off teammates handling the ball.
"7. Overloading a zone is basically aligning players so that the offense outnumbers the defense. Attempt to get an alignment of three on two or four on three and then move the ball quickly until a player is momentarily unguarded and can get a shot. If the defense moves players into the overloaded area, an offensive player on the weak side should be open briefly.

"Offense Against Pressure Defenses. A team can expect to meet various styles of zone and player-to-player pressure defenses—full court, three quarter court and half court. To combat *player-to-player* presses the following points warrant review:

"1. The greatest weapon against the full court press is to start the attack as soon as possible and not allow the defense to get organized.
"2. Keep the offense spread and move passes and players toward the sidelines to keep out of congested areas.
"3. Work the ball to the offensive court as quickly as possible by using short passes, screens and drives around the defense.
"4. Remain calm and make certain the passes and ball handling are good.
"5. Never take one's own guard to the ball as it gives the defensive player an opportunity to double team the ball handler.
"6. Players must keep moving to meet the offensive passes and to prevent a defensive player from intercepting a pass.
"7. Dribble only if a pass is not possible.
"8. Protect the ball when it is possessed. Avoid pivoting toward a guard.

"To combat a *zone press:*

"1. Quick passes will prevent the defense from setting up correctly. The ball must get to the offensive court before the defense is set; once in the offensive court the opposing team must go to its regular zone or player-to-player pattern.
"2. If the zone is set, be deliberate, for most zones do not play the ball handler closely but stay back to intercept the dribbler or the low pass.
"3. A good long pass can break the press but a poor pass may lose the ball.
"4. The middle of the court is the weak area in the zone suggesting that one offensive player should cut across the center line at center circle or up center of the court. This may pull the zone in to this player and leave another player open.

"Special Offensive Situations. Each team should have several rehearsed plays for bringing the ball in bounds, for jump balls and for free throw situations.

"Out of Bounds Play. During a game a team will have situations which allow them to bring the ball in bounds from both sidelines and from

the endline by the opponent's goal. A standard pattern for an inexperienced team in all situations is to use two receivers who drive toward the basket as the ball handler signals and then cut back sharply toward the ball to free themselves to receive the ball.

"*Jump Ball Situations.* The key to control of the tip is the height of the jump and the timing and touch in contacting the ball. In *center jump situations* where one team has the advantage, the center may tap the ball to an aggressive player in the offensive court who takes possession and moves the ball quickly.

"If there is not a clear jump advantage, the ball may be tapped between two players who rotate in an attempt to cut in front of a defensive player. The direction of the rotation, clockwise or counterclockwise, should be signaled by the jumper. Tip toward the offensive basket so more time is available to adjust if opponents gain possession.

"If it appears the tip will go to the opponents, one player goes deep to forestall a fast break while the other defensive players rotate toward the defensive area in an attempt to steal the tap.

"When jumping in the *offensive circle,* if control is certain, the ball is tipped to the pivot or one of the two side players. Both side players move toward the pivot on the tap. If the pivot player receives the ball, she may have a shot or she can pass to either side player who has pulled out.

"If the control of the tip is uncertain in the offensive circle, a center jump alignment can be used. If the opponents have a clear advantage, it is advisable to defense a fast break.

"When jumping in the *defensive circle* it is safer to have a good defensive alignment with two players back and the others ready to move to the offensive players as the ball is tapped. If the advantage is clearly with the defensive team a diagonal (diamond) pattern may be used with four players equally spaced around the circle.

"*Foul Line Play.* The defending players have a clear rebounding advantage because they occupy close positions in both lanes. In addition, a fast break team has a psychological advantage controlling the defensive boards, for the conservative offense pulls away to defend against the break.

"The offensive team places its tallest players near the backboard. They attempt to tip the ball back for an easy score. Failing a tip-in, the rebounding player taps or passes the ball to a teammate.

DEFENSIVE STRATEGY

"The basic defensive systems are player-to-player and zone patterns. There are numerous combination systems.

"Player-to-Player Defense. Player-to-player defense should be a basic pattern to all teams. In strict player-to-player play each defensive player is responsible for play on a single opponent. The defense closest to the player with the ball pressures the attack in hopes of forcing a bad pass, dribble or inaccurate shot. The defensive players away from the ball *sag* to intercept the ball or a loose player evading her defensive player.

"*Switching Player-to-Player.* This is designed to stop the screening offense. When a defensive player is screened, the closest defensive player calls a switch if the defensive player cannot slide through the screen (between the offensive screen and her defensive teammate). The defensive player calling the switch then guards the offensive player of the screened defense. The player screened switches to the offensive player left by the switching defense.

"*Player-to-Player Pressing Defense.* This pattern pits the skill of each defensive player against her opponent. Each defensive player moves to her opponent as soon as the offensive team gets the ball (loose ball, rebound, throw-in, etc.). On a throw-in the player guarding the out of bounds player overplays to one side, forcing the throw-in to the other side. The offense is vulnerable on the throw-in. Players away from the ball play loosely in an attempt to cut off passing lanes or force players to the ball so they can double team the player with the ball. The defense tries to force the offense to pass to the congested middle of the court. Defensive players harass the dribbler and force her to pickup or go to the sideline for a trap.

"Zone Defense. The zone defense is designed to concentrate five defensive players relatively close to the basket to limit the sure shots by the offense. The zone gives up occasional outside points. It focuses on the ball and identifies specific areas to be covered. In execution it involves player-to-player techniques with principles of zone responsibility. Effectiveness depends upon teamwork but zone patterns are easily learned by players with sound individual defensive techniques. The advantages of the zone when compared to player-to-player are:

"1. It limits driving, cutting and screening patterns of the offense.
"2. The number of fouls committed is usually fewer.
"3. It affords good defensive rebounding positions.
"4. It lends itself to initiating a fast break offense.
"5. It forces the offense to rely on outside shooting by keeping the defense massed between the ball and the basket.
"6. It is effective in changing the tempo of the game and is less tiring to individuals when alternated with player-to-player patterns.

"Each zone pattern has particular strengths and weaknesses in rebounding position, defending the pivot player, guarding shooting areas and setting for the fast break. The selection of zone patterns depends upon defensive personnel and the opposition one expects to meet. The following examples illustrate basic formations and the zone shift in relation to ball movement.

"The 2-1-2 zone defense is designed to protect against strong post offense (Fig. 14–27). As the ball moves to the corner player E near the ball assumes responsibility. Player C moves to protect against a pass to the post

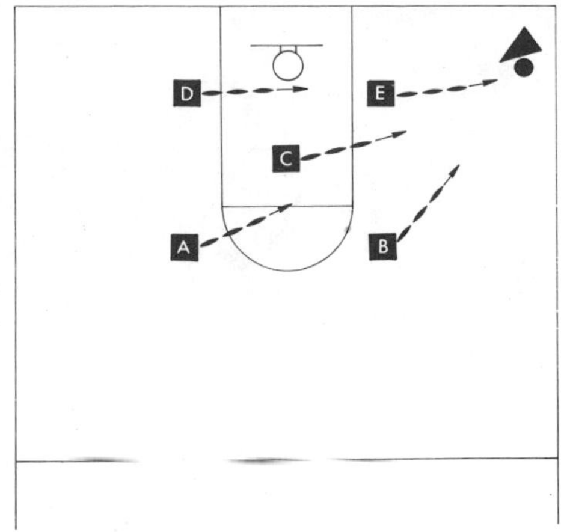

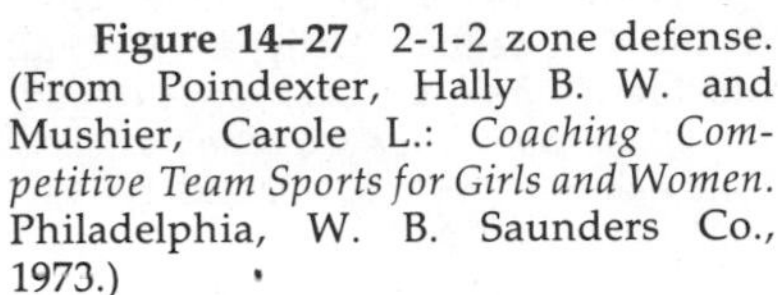
Figure 14–27 2-1-2 zone defense. (From Poindexter, Hally B. W. and Mushier, Carole L.: *Coaching Competitive Team Sports for Girls and Women.* Philadelphia, W. B. Saunders Co., 1973.)

player or a cutting player. Player A moves toward the free throw line to prevent a pass to a high post or cutting player.

"Three large players are placed under the basket and two smaller players move as chasers in the 2-3 zone defense pattern (Fig. 14–28).

"In the 3-2 zone the personnel are reversed from 2-3 pattern with the strength at the top of the key (Fig. 14–29). Movement keeps players out of the dangerous shooting area.

"The diamond defense, 1-3-1 zone, is popular because of its adaptability and versatility in running the fast break. It is used to stop the big pivot player as there are three players between the ball and the basket at all times. This zone allows defensive players pursuing the player with the ball to take more chances as two players are behind to cover mistakes. The zone is weak in the corners so player E must be quick in covering corners. Player A has a major responsibility in moving play to one side of the floor

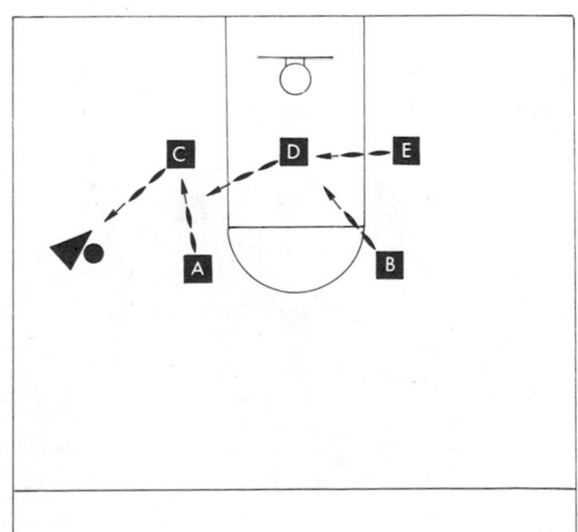

Figure 14–28 2-3 zone defense. (From Poindexter, Hally B. W. and Mushier, Carole L.: *Coaching Competitive Team Sports for Girls and Women.* Philadelphia, W. B. Saunders Co., 1973.)

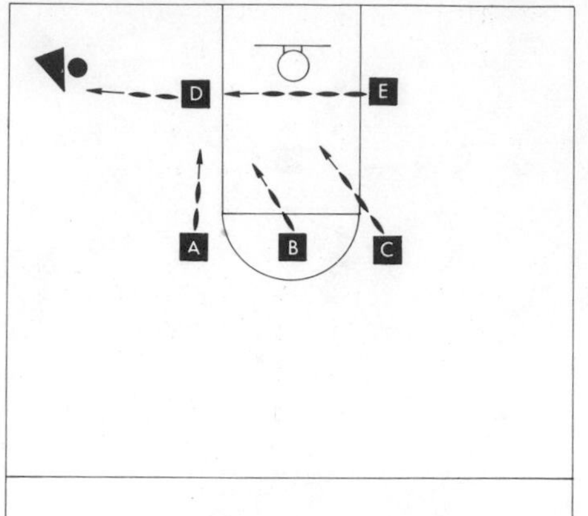

Figure 14–29 3-2 zone defense. (From Poindexter, Hally B. W. and Mushier, Carole L.: *Coaching Competitive Team Sports for Girls and Women.* Philadelphia, W. B. Saunders Co., 1973.)

by herding the offensive player with the ball. This prevents E from being out of position if she can anticipate play on one side of the floor. Player C should be the best rebounder; she must be agile, as she has a large area and distance to cover in directing the defense (Fig. 14–30).

"The 1-2-2 zone defense is called a box and one pattern (Fig. 14–31). As the ball is moved the player closest to the ball becomes the point and the other players then form a box behind her. The box re-forms each time the point changes.

"**Zone Pressure Defenses.** The press is designed to defense the back court in an attempt to steal the ball or prevent a pass. The offense is allowed to bring the ball in uncontested. Executing a *1-3-1 press* the double team concept is followed with the point and wing on the side with the ball. The middle player 3 protects against the pass down the sideline with the wing and deep player overplaying the area where the pass might go. The deep player overplays on the ball side of the court. . . .

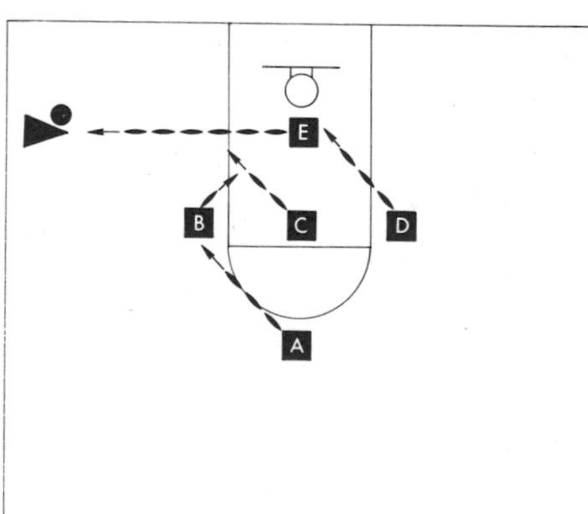

Figure 14–30 1-3-1 (diamond) zone defense. (From Poindexter, Hally B. W. and Mushier, Carole L.: *Coaching Competitive Team Sports for Girls and Women.* Philadelphia, W. B. Saunders Co., 1973.)

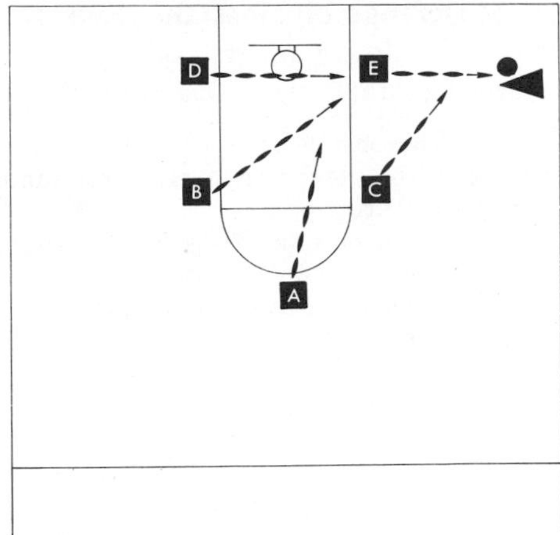

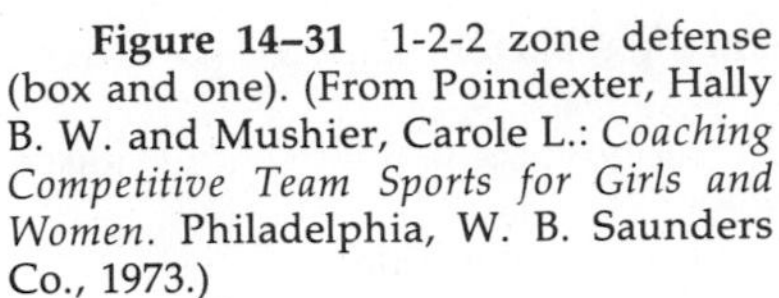
Figure 14–31 1-2-2 zone defense (box and one). (From Poindexter, Hally B. W. and Mushier, Carole L.: *Coaching Competitive Team Sports for Girls and Women*. Philadelphia, W. B. Saunders Co., 1973.)

"The 2-2-1 zone press allows the ball to be brought inbounds only in front of the first two defensive players. The front line defensive player on the ball side of the court forces play toward the center. The other front defensive player moves to the middle to stop a return pass to the inbounding player or to intercept passes to cutting players. The second line defensive player on the side of the court with the ball protects against a pass along the sideline. The other second line player moves to the center to intercept cross court passes. The safety player moves along the ball side of the court to protect against or to intercept the long pass (Fig. 14–32).

"If the offensive team gets through the press, the defense must quickly shift to its forecourt defense pattern.

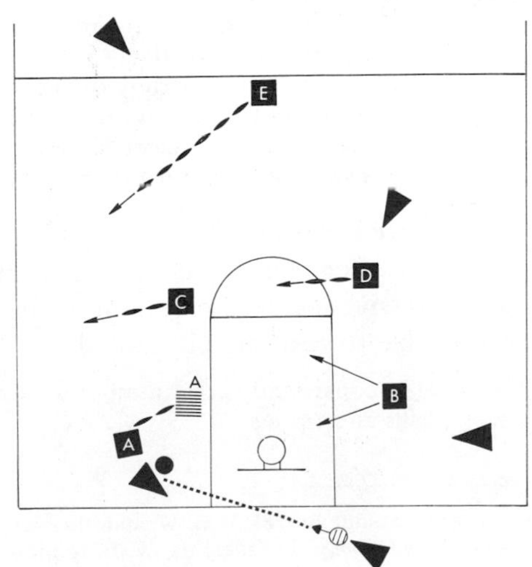

Figure 14–32 2-2-1 zone press. (From Poindexter, Hally B. W. and Mushier, Carole L.: *Coaching Competitive Team Sports for Girls and Women*. Philadelphia, W. B. Saunders Co., 1973.)

"**Defense Against the Fast Break.** Principles of the fast break should be clearly understood from the explanation of offensive tactics. The following guides serve as a defensive summary.

"1. The best defense is strong rebounding.
"2. If the other team gets the rebound, harass the player with the ball to deter a clearing pass.
"3. If a team spot passes, be alert to interceptions at these points. A few unsuccessful passes will force a play change.
"4. If a single player is defending, she should stay in the middle of the lane and feint as offensive players approach. Eventually she must move to the ball to slow play even though she leaves an opponent open. Only the player with the ball can score.
"5. With two defense players it is wise to drop back in tandem position beneath the goal. The front defensive player, A, attempts to stop the ball; the deep defense, B, moves from the middle of the lane to defend against the player receiving the pass. Player A drops to the middle of the lane to stop a cross court pass. . . ."*

DUTIES AND SPECIFIC SKILLS OF PLAYERS

All players have both offensive and defensive responsibilities and must display skills and aggressiveness necessary for each of these roles. The specific tasks of forwards, center, and guards suggest additional skill development for players in these positions.

Forward Position

1. Speed and endurance are necessary, particularly when playing the fast break type of offense.
2. Alertness to scoring opportunities and ability to move to take advantage of these opportunities.
3. Alertness to defensive opportunities to make opponents commit errors.
4. Skill in deception, both offensively and defensively.
5. Ability to follow shots for rebound opportunities.
6. Ability to jump effectively in jump ball situation and for rebounds.
7. Skill in shooting a variety of shots; skill from corner position.
8. Quick reaction and movement to receive a pass or overtake an opponent.
9. Excellent passing in close situations and under pressure.
10. Consistent shooting at the free-throw line.

Center Position

The center must be an excellent forward and additionally have height and aggressiveness to direct jump balls, rebound at both ends of the court, and be able to take the physical abuse required of her position. She must:

1. Be a consistently good jumper with good control of the finger tips on jump balls and tip-ins.

---

*From Poindexter, Hally B. W. and Mushier, Carole L.: *Coaching Competitive Team Sports for Girls and Women.* Philadelphia, W. B. Saunders Co., 1973.

2. As a post player be able to shoot in a confined space. Must have a good hook shot and a good jump shot.
3. Be an aggressive rebounder.
4. Be an accurate passer under pressure.

Guard Position

Height is an obvious advantage, but an aggressive, controlled player can more than compensate for her lack of height. She must:

1. Be agile, deceptive, and able to shift.
2. Have excellent timing on jumps, attempts to tie the ball, and when feinting.
3. Be a master of defensive strategy, both individual and team.
4. Serve as the playmaker of the team. Be able to spot and pass to an open player.
5. Read fakes with a great degree of accuracy.
6. Be a good outside shooter.
7. Display aggressiveness and tenacity in gaining and maintaining possession of the ball.

CLASS ORGANIZATION

Class organization should allow maximum participation and instruction in skills of offensive and defensive play. Drills should be conducted so all available floor space and baskets are utilized at all times. Ten or 12 players can usually participate in each drill. If stations are set up, squads can rotate during the drill sessions and larger numbers can be handled. One on one, two on two, and three on three drill and game situations can be used to improve ball handling skills and defensive tactics if space, outdoor, or indoor, is adequate. Half-court play is advisable when classes are large and the players are not conditioned to a full court; however, official full-court games should be important in the unit. Officiating and observing should be planned and evaluated as part of the unit.

Basic skills may best be learned in simple drills, as illustrated in Drill 1, below; however as skills increase the drills should approximate the game situation as closely as possible in speed, pressure, and challenge. Drill 6, "Lay-up drill," is an example of a situation geared for developing a soft lay-up shot under pressure play. The following drill formations are helpful in developing specific skills:*

---

*See Poindexter, Hally, B. W. and Mushier, Carole L.: *Coaching Competitive Team Sports for Girls and Women,* Philadelphia, W. B. Saunders Co., 1973, pages 60 to 69, for detailed information and examples of skill and situational drills.

1. *Catching and passing drill.* Player 1 in each line runs forward to meet, pass, and return the ball to A. Players should be encouraged to meet the ball on the move. The ball should be received without crossing the center line. Passes should be delivered from the catching position. Player A is changed after the complete squad has practiced.

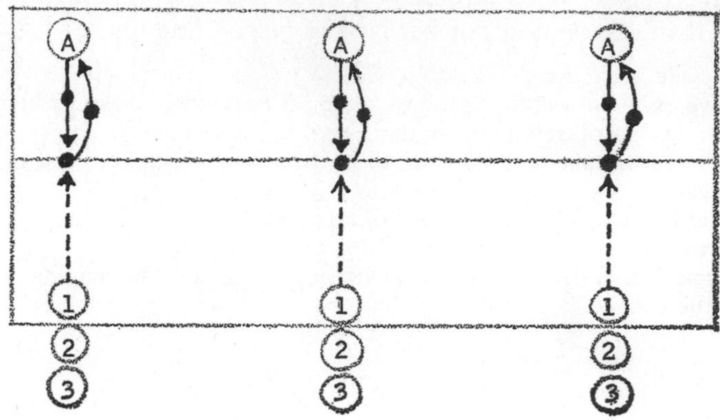

2. *Dribble screening-shooting.* Player 1 dribbles to the left of a defensive player trailed by teammate 2. Player 1 screens as 2 shoots.

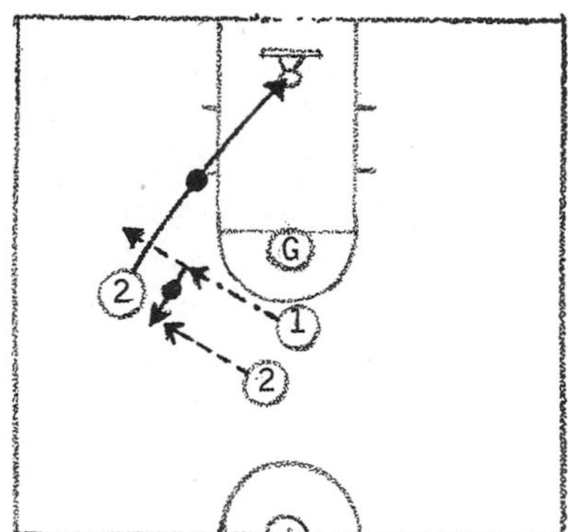

"3. *Figure eight passing, breaking.* Three columns are formed at one end of the floor. Player #2 passes to #3 who crosses to the other side of the court. Player #2 goes behind #3 after passing the ball; #3 then passes to #1 crossing to the other side of the court. The player who passes the ball goes behind the player to whom she passed.... Players should avoid pinching toward the middle; use the entire width of the court. Play continues to the end of the court. Variations include shooting at the end of the court and moving the ball against defensive players.

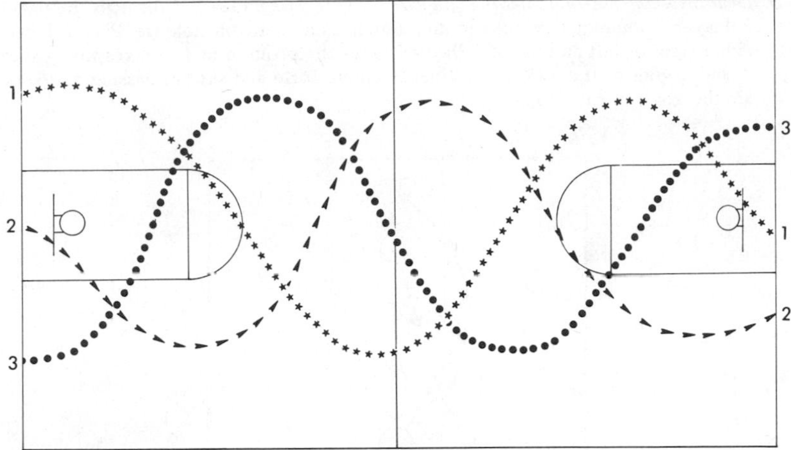

From Poindexter, Hally B. W. and Mushier, Carole L.: *Coaching Competitive Team Sports for Girls and Women*, Philadelphia, W. B. Saunders Co., 1973.

"4. *Star drill.* The drill requires the player to *meet the pass, pass quickly* and *accurately* and *move to a new position.* The drill is continuous.

a. Four players form a square standing ten feet apart with a fifth player in the middle (Fig. 14–33).
b. Middle player has the ball; she passes to any player and then takes her place.
c. Receiver passes to either player on her right or left and takes her place.
d. Second receiver passes across the square to the opposite corner player and takes her place.
e. The third receiver passes to the player on her right or left and takes her place.
f. The drill continues with the ball moving across (corner to corner), to the side, across, side, etc. For variation differ the passes, add pivot or fake before the pass."*

---

*From Poindexter, Hally B. W. and Mushier, Carole L.: *Coaching Competitive Team Sports for Girls and Women.* Philadelphia, W. B. Saunders Co., 1973.

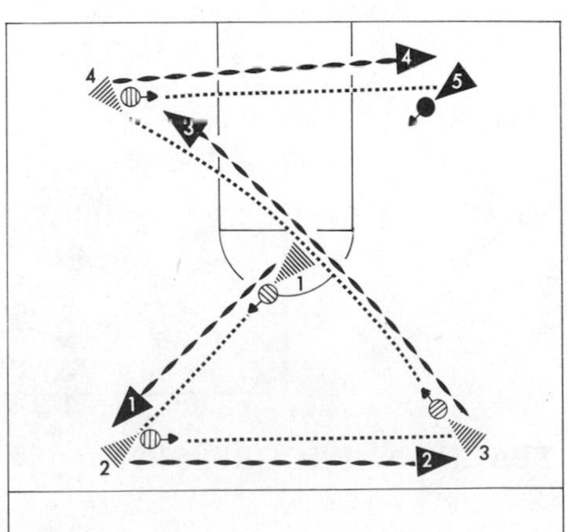

Figure 14–33 Star drill (one variation). (From Poindexter, Hally B. W. and Mushier, Carole L.: *Coaching Competitive Team Sports for Girls and Women.* Philadelphia, W. B. Saunders Co., 1973.)

5. *Drill involving passing, catching, guarding, and shooting.* Player 1 receives the pass from 2. Player 2 immediately runs in and simulates a guard on defense. Player 1 dribbles either right or left and shoots. Player 2 takes the position of 1; 3 takes the position of 2; and 1 goes to the end of the line. Accurate form and skill in passing and shooting are the goals of the drill.

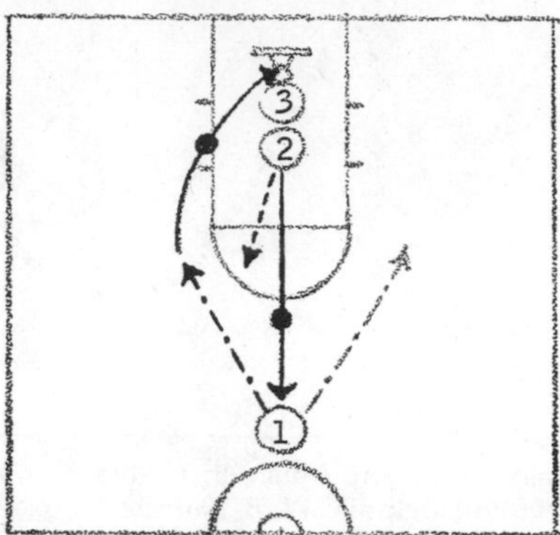

6. *Lay-up drill.* In line 1 are the shooters, line 2 the chasers (opponents), and line 3 the rebounder-passers. With beginners and when the drill is first introduced, the shooters should be given a two-step lead over the chasers. As soon as the rebounder-passer secures the ball, the shooter should break toward the basket at top speed. The pass must be accurate, as the chaser is not far behind. This drill is also used for shooting from the left. The player shooting with the right hand from the left side will be hard pressed by the chaser. This will show the players why the use of both hands for shooting is necessary. As the skill of the players increases, the chaser is moved to a position level with the shooter. Now it is imperative that top speed be used and the pass be accurate. A possible addition to the drill is another line of chasers as opponents for the rebounder-passers. In any case, players should rotate from one line to another.

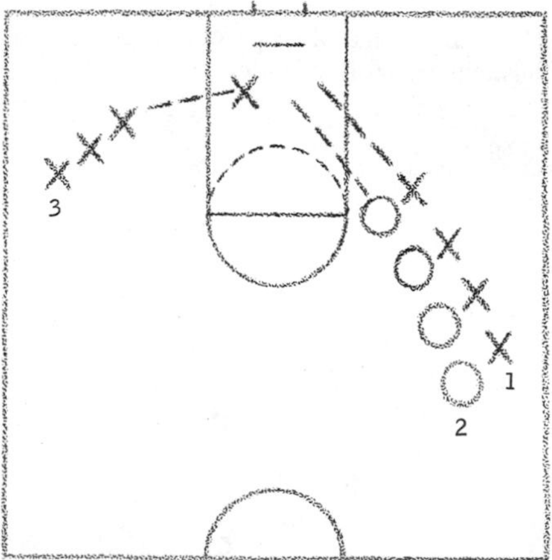

TEACHING PROGRESSION

It is obvious that teaching content and progression will vary, depending on the maturity, skill level, and experience of the students. Every teacher has her own ideas about the concepts and skills of play she deems most important to the game of basketball. The following content units are simply recommendations and reminders of skill and knowledge which might be included in a beginners' class unit on basketball. The emphasis placed on each area will vary as the teacher evaluates the strengths and weaknesses of members of her class.

A teaching unit for beginners or young intermediates might be planned as follows:

Lesson I

1. Nature, purpose, and value of basketball
2. Fundamental body control skills; stance, running, changing direction
3. Catching
4. Chest pass—to stationary and moving players

Lesson II

1. Brief history of basketball
2. Review
3. Two-step stop
4. Overhead passes
5. Lay-up shot (dominant hand)
6. Pass, catch, lay-up drill

Lesson III

1. Review; discuss basic rules of play
2. Pivot
3. One-hand shot
4. Basic defensive technique for guarding player with ball
5. Drill: pivot, pass, shoot

Lesson IV

1. Dribble
2. Pass and cut offensive technique
3. Underhand pass
4. Player-to-player defensive pattern
5. Two-on-two or three-on-three situational play

Lesson V

1. Feints
2. Defensive tactics for pass and cut
3. Defensive skills for guarding a player without the ball
4. Jump ball tactics and strategy
5. Situational drills

Lesson VI

1. Screens
2. Defense against screens
3. Review pass and cut, and shooting
4. Official half game with students observing officiating techniques

Lesson VII

1. Switching player-to-player defensive tactics
2. Offensive drills stressing fast breaks and lay-up shots
3. Game

Lesson VIII

1. Free-throw techniques and practice
2. Rebounding—offensive and defensive
3. Game situation using player-to-player and switching defense
4. Stress offensive tactics in game

Lesson IX

1. Introduce 1-3-1 zone defense
2. Offensive tactics against the zone
3. Out-of-bounds play

Lessons X, XI, and XII

1. Skills tests
2. Written evaluation of knowledge of rules and strategy
3. Incidence charts based upon game play

SKILL DIFFICULTIES AND THEIR CORRECTION

Individual Defensive Skills

Difficulty	*Correction*
a. Player is eluded by offensive player with the ball	a. Check to be sure that body weight is on the rear foot so that weight shifting can be made easily. If overplaying the opponent, step back slightly
b. Slow to respond to opponent's movement	b. Be alert! Body weight must be balanced
c. Offensive player drives as defensive player steps sideward rather than backward	c. Since the offensive player begins an instant before the defense, the defensive player must make the first move backward and then sideward to stop the drive
d. Offensive player passes the ball by defensive player	d. Watch the ball carefully and keep one hand on or near the ball and the other positioned to stop the drive or dribble
e. Defensive player fouls	e. Watch the ball and player carefully and strike at the ball with the hand, palm up, in an upward motion
f. Defensive player jumps when her opponent fakes a shot and opponent drives around her	f. Be alert to feints and jump only when the offensive player commits herself

Difficulty	Correction
g. Defensive player attempts an interception when guarding a pivot player and fouls or loses her defensive position	g. Defensive player should not leave her position unless the interception is assured
h. Defensive player makes no effort to break a screen, and the offense has a protected shot	h. Although other defensive players may help by switching defensive responsibilities, the defensive player must step closer to the offensive player and squeeze around the screen or step back and go behind the screen

Rebounding

Difficulty	*Correction*
a. Player fails to block opponent	a. *Watch opponent,* anticipate her move and step in front with a wide stride
b. Player has ball tied after rebounding	b. Keep back to opponent and pull the ball—protected by extended elbows—to the body
c. Failure to achieve height in jump or jumping too late or too early	c. Watch the ball and judge its speed and trajectory after contacting the rim or board. Swing the arms vigorously to gain elevation

Catching

Difficulty	*Correction*
a. Player "fumbles" the catch	a. Watch the ball until it is in the hand
b. Ball hits hands or fingers and bounces free	b. Arms relax and reach for the ball. Fingers and thumbs are relaxed, and fingers point downward or upward—*never* toward the ball. "Give" with hands and arms toward the body
c. Ball is intercepted by opponent as intended receiver stands and waits	c. Cut or step toward the ball to meet it before an opponent intercepts

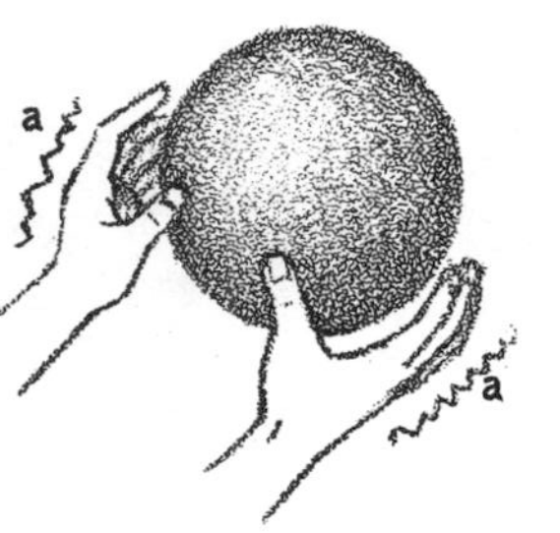

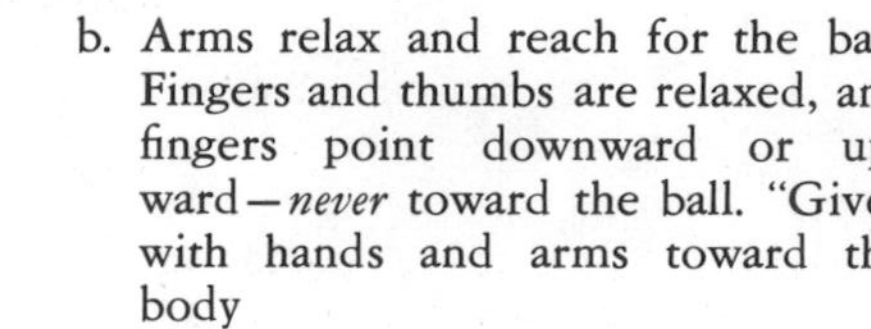

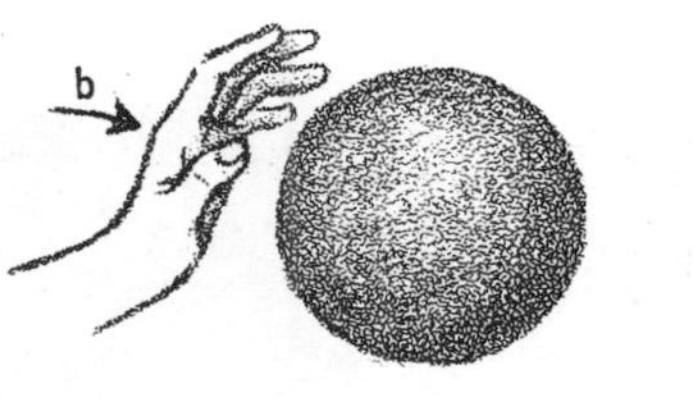

d. Ball gets by a player who is attempting to catch on the side of the body	d. Move so the body is in line with the ball. This protects the ball from an opponent to the rear of the body

Passing

Difficulty	*Correction*
a. *Errors committed on all passes*	
1. Ball is pushed with palm of the hand, resulting in loss of control and force	1. Control the ball's path and momentum with fingers and wrists

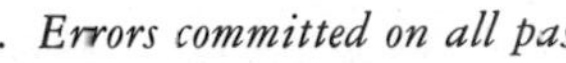

2. Pass is slow and looping, allowing opponent time to intercept due to poor arm extension

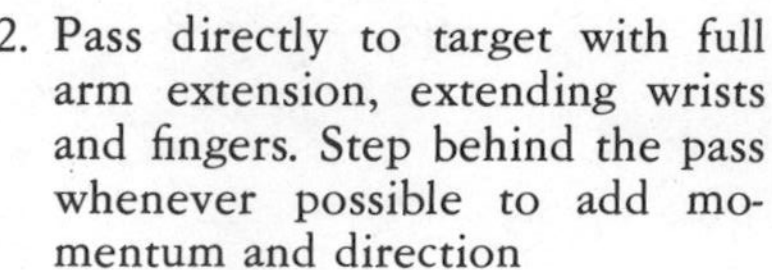

2. Pass directly to target with full arm extension, extending wrists and fingers. Step behind the pass whenever possible to add momentum and direction

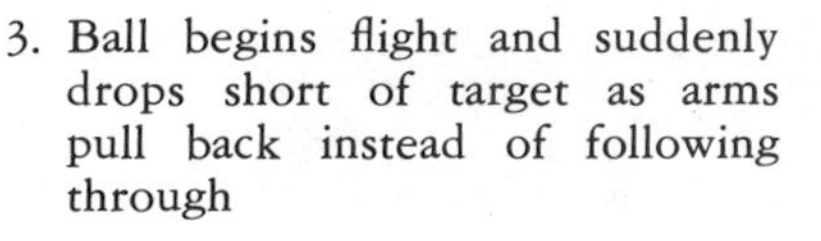

3. Ball begins flight and suddenly drops short of target as arms pull back instead of following through

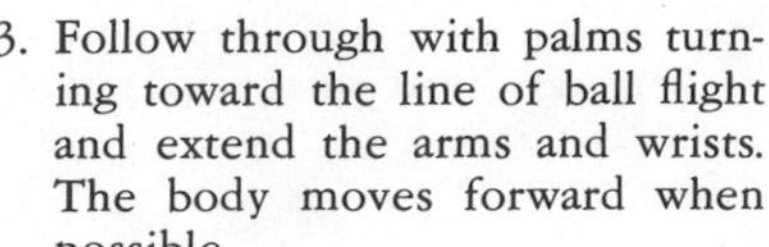

3. Follow through with palms turning toward the line of ball flight and extend the arms and wrists. The body moves forward when possible

b. *Chest pass*

1. Loss of power and direction as hands push from the sides with elbows away from the body

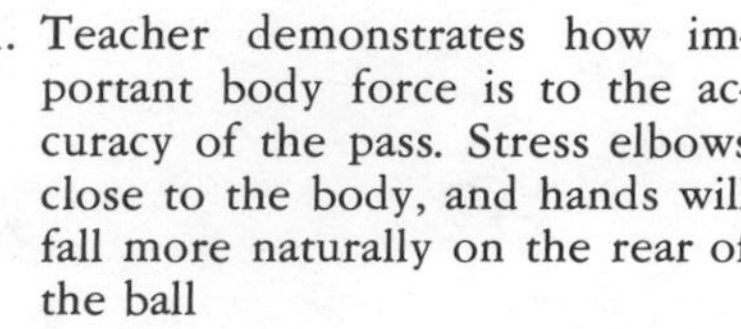

1. Teacher demonstrates how important body force is to the accuracy of the pass. Stress elbows close to the body, and hands will fall more naturally on the rear of the ball

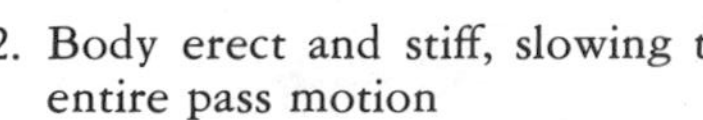

2. Body erect and stiff, slowing the entire pass motion

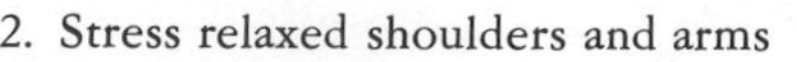

2. Stress relaxed shoulders and arms

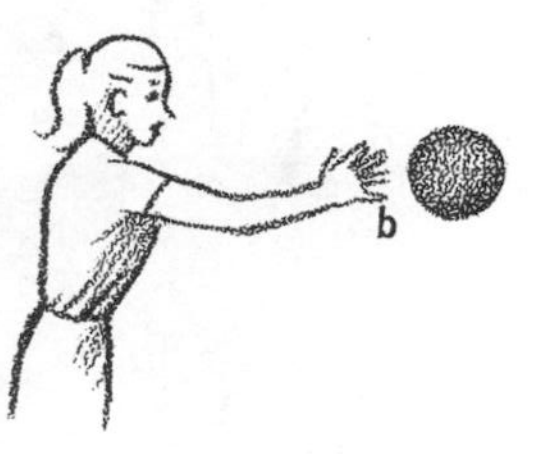

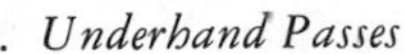

c. *Underhand Passes*

1. Ball loops high due to delayed release

1. On two-hand pass, release ball about waist level with a wrist snap *in the direction* of ball flight. On side passes be certain the passing elbow is away from the body. On one-hand pass step forward to flatten the swing arc, and let the ball roll off straightened fingers at waist level. The teacher may mark a wall target for student to throw toward in practicing the release

2. Ball is fumbled or lost as a player attempts to tie it

2. Keep both hands on the ball until the release. Use the underhand passes cautiously when opponent is guarding closely

d. *Shoulder Passes*

1. Ball is fumbled or tied as the beginning passer brings the ball back on one hand

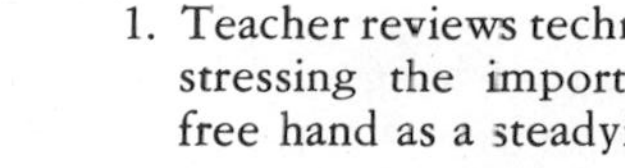

1. Teacher reviews technique of pass, stressing the importance of the free hand as a steadying guide

e. *Two-Hand Overhead Pass*

1. Pass is overused, causing slow game, and encourages charging when guarded closely 2. Pass loops high as ball drops behind the passer's head before delivered	1 and 2. Use the pass sparingly and quickly when a high pass is received. Practice passing to a teammate, avoiding the drop behind the head. Step forward to flatten the flight even more

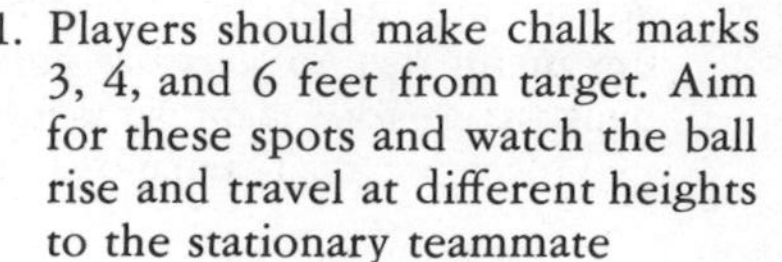

f. *Bounce Pass*

1. Players bounce the ball too close or too far from teammate so she has trouble gaining possession	1. Players should make chalk marks 3, 4, and 6 feet from target. Aim for these spots and watch the ball rise and travel at different heights to the stationary teammate

2. Ball is brought high over the shoulder and thrown straight down, resulting in a high bounding vertical pass easily intercepted	2. Keep the ball close to the shoulder. (See 1 above.) Follow through with the arm in the direction of the ball flight to the floor.

g. *Goal Shooting*

Many errors of shooting due to loss of power, direction, and momentum are caused by poor hand and wrist action, follow-through, and body position as described in passing difficulty and correction. (See the preceding section.) Errors common to all shots are:	
1. Failure to arch the ball due to stiff wrists, a palm push, or loss of power by elbows extended to the side	1. Teacher should review common principles in chest and shoulder shots. Elbows are in toward body, fingers and wrists release the ball upward as the arm(s) and hand(s) follow through. (See 2, p. 486)

2. Releasing the ball and lunging with the body result in a hard rebounding ball	2. Stress the importance of a medium arch. Demonstrate and explain that a low, flat arch cannot enter the basket from above, and a very high arch is difficult to control and slow, allowing the opponents time to get set for a rebound
3. Failure to spot and deliver to selected lay-up spot	3. Suggest that student stand by the basket, select a spot and an angle and *watch* the spot and ball as she delivers. Repeat several times, then trot and run in—"always get as close to the spot as possible by running and jumping and keep watching the spot until delivery"
4. Taking off from the right foot for a lay-up (right-handed), resulting in improper balance and awkward landing	4. Teacher reviews mechanics of opposition movement. Demonstrate how the body turns toward the court so the shooter is ready to rebound
5. Shooting too soon or too late in the jump shot, resulting in loss of height advantage and power	5. Review jump without ball until student "feels" point at which ball should be released
6. Batting or ineffectively pushing a tip-in	6. Review timing and basic progression. Practice against a wall

EVALUATING THE RESULTS

Evaluation should be used to assess the level of a student's knowledge of rules and strategy, her individual skill, and ability on specific skills and as a team member. Evaluation techniques serve as feedback information to students in assessing their own progress and to teachers and coaches in determining their effectiveness.

Most skills tests are designed to measure isolated, specific skill performance, rather than total playing ability. The AAHPER Basketball Skills Test (1966)* is widely accepted in high schools and colleges. It consists of nine different tests with norms available for girls and women. The test items include: front shot, side shot, foul shot, under basket shot, speed pass, jump and reach, overarm pass for accuracy, push pass for accuracy, and the dribble.

Leilich,† in an attempt to determine achievement levels for women physical education major students, studied all basketball skill tests available and identified three tests which measured factors underlying basketball skill. The test items are: bounce and shoot, half-minute shooting, and push pass.‡

Ideally, teachers should construct their own knowledge tests, for only they are aware of the emphasis directed toward terminology, strategy, and rules as well as their own approaches to technique development.

Assessment of playing ability involves charting and statistical analysis of game results. Coaches of competitive teams will train managers and other students to use charts to record the statistics of game play. Free throws attempted and made, field goals made, and individual and team fouls are commonly recorded in the scorebook. A more meaningful assessment of a player's profile during the game is gained by a *shot chart,* noting where shots are taken, whether they are made or missed, and the type of shot attempted, a *rebound chart,* to discover which players rebound offensively and defensively in a game situation, and a *turnover chart,* to identify those players who help the team gain possession of the ball and those players who lose possession of the ball.**

*AAHPER: *Basketball Skills Test Manual for Girls.* Washington, D.C. AAHPER. Also see Johnson, Barry L. and Nelson, Jack K.: *Practical Measurements of Evaluation in Physical Education.* 2nd Ed. Minneapolis, Burgess Publishing Co., 1974.

†Leilich, Avis: *The Primary Components of Selected Basketball Tests for College Women.* Doctoral Dissertation, Indiana University, 1952. Leilich identified four basic factors in the tests: basketball motor ability, speed, ball handling involving passing accuracy and speed, and ball handling involving accuracy in goal shooting.

‡Miller, Wilma K, Chairperson: Achievement levels in basketball skills for physical education majors. *Research Quarterly.* 25:4, December, 1954.

**For suggestions on charting and statistical analysis see Poindexter, Hally B. W. and Mushier, Carole L.: *Coaching Competitive Team Sports for Girls and Women.* Philadelphia, W. B. Saunders Co., 1973, pp. 98–100, and Barnes, Mildred J.: *Women's Basketball.* Boston, Allyn and Bacon, 1972, pp. 311–317.

TERMINOLOGY

Air dribble—A play in which a player taps or throws the ball in the air and gains possession of it again before it touches the floor or is touched by another player.

Assist—Credit given a player whose pass to a teammate creates a shooting opportunity which results in a field goal.

Back court—The half of the court which contains the opponents' basket.

Ball control—A style of offensive play in which a team moves the ball cautiously and deliberately in an attempt to work for a high percentage shot.

Block—Personal contact that impedes the progress of an opponent with or without the ball.

Blocked shot—A successful effort by a defending player to stop an attempt for goal by stopping the ball in flight after it leaves the shooter's hands or by placing one or both hands on the ball while it is still held by the shooter.

Bonus rule—A shot awarded for each common foul (except offensive) beginning with opponents' seventh personal foul in each half of the game played in halves or the fifth personal foul in each half played in quarters.

Bonus shot—An additional free throw that is awarded when the first free throw was successful with the bonus rule in effect.

Buttonhook—An offensive maneuver by a player without the ball in which she cuts away from the ball and then reverses and turns back toward the ball.

Clear out—A movement by an offensive player to vacate an area to make room for a teammate.

Closely guarded—Guarding within three feet of the player with the ball.

Cut—An offensive maneuver in which a player moves to a clear space to get free to receive a pass or to clear a space for a teammate.

Defense—The tactics by which a team attempts to prevent opponents from scoring.

Defensive players—Players whose team does not possess the ball.

Defensive team—The team not in possession of the ball.

Double team—Tactics by which two defensive players guard one opponent in an attempt to tie the ball or force a bad pass. Frequently utilized when employing a zone press.

Dribble—The skill of imparting impetus to the ball one or more times, causing it to rebound from the floor while controlling it and maintaining possession of it. The first impetus may be given with one or both hands, but thereafter, contact must be made with only one hand until the ball is passed or the dribbler touches the ball with both hands to complete the dribble.

Drive—A sudden move by an offensive player to an opening or to the basket by dribbling the ball.

Fast break—A maneuver in which the offensive team moves the ball from its own back court rapidly down court in an attempt to gain more offensive players than defensive players in the front court so that a shot can be made before the defense organizes.

Feint—A fake or a pretense of moving the body or ball in an effort to deceive the opponent.

Foul—A rule infraction by a team or individual for which one or more free throws (or ball possession if bonus rule is not in effect) may be given the opponent. Free throws are not awarded on offensive fouls or double fouls.

Free throw—An unguarded shot taken from behind the free-throw line. It is awarded to a player as the result of an opponent's foul.

Front court—The half of the court that contains the goal for which a team is shooting.

Fronting—A defensive maneuver in which the player stands between the ball and her opponent in an effort to prevent the offensive player from receiving a pass.

Give and go—An offensive strategy in which a player passes to a teammate and immediately cuts for the basket in anticipation of a return pass.

Goal tending—Interference, by either an offensive or defensive player, with the ball or basket when the ball is on a downward flight to the basket, on the rim, or en route through the basket.

Held ball—A ball held more than five seconds by a player who is closely guarded.

High post—A pivot player who plays about 15 or more feet from the basket. Serves primarily as a passer to cutting players.

Jump ball—A method of putting the ball in play by tossing it between two opponents in one of the three restraining circles. Jumpers attempt to tap the ball to their respective teammates.

Low post—An offensive player who positions herself about eight or nine feet from the basket outside the free-throw lane and moves through the lane as opportunities arise for receiving passes and scoring.

Offense—The tactics a team uses in attempts to score.

Offensive players—Players whose team is in possession of the ball and who are attempting to score.

Offensive team—The team in possession of the ball.

Overloading a zone—An offensive tactic which positions two players in a zone covered by one defensive player.

Percentage shot—A shot near the goal and from an advantageous position which has a good chance for success.

Perimeter—The area outside and away from the basket beyond the defending players.

Pick—A screen by which a player with the ball drives around her stationary teammate in an attempt to lose her guard.

Pivot guard—The defensive player guarding the pivot player.

Pivot player—An offensive player who moves close to the basket, often through the free-throw lane, to shoot or pass to cutting players.

Player-to-player defense—A defensive pattern in which each defensive player is assigned a specific opponent to guard.

Post—Another name for pivot.

Press—An aggressive, pressure defensive tactic intended to force the opponent to make errors. A team can execute a press using player-to-player or zone defenses in full, three-quarters, or half court.

Screen—An offensive technique designed to prevent an opponent from reaching a desired court position by delaying her progress or forcing her to alter her path of movement.

Strong side—The side of the offensive pattern which has three or more offensive players.

Turnover—Loss of ball possession without an attempted shot.

Violation—An infraction of the rules which results in a throw-in from out of bounds by the opposing team. When both teams have simultaneous violations, play is resumed by a jump ball.

Weak side—The side of the offensive alignment which has two or fewer offensive players.

Wing—A player's position, indicating a place on the court 10 to 12 feet on each side of the free-throw line.

Zone defense—A defensive method in which players are responsible for a particular court area, rather than a specific player. Players move in relation to the position of the ball.

DISCUSSION QUESTIONS

1. Why is so much emphasis placed on the mastery of the jump shot for advanced players? Describe the mechanics of the jump shot.
2. Compare the advantages and disadvantages of player-to-player and zone defensive patterns.
3. You have been hired to coach a high school basketball team. The school has never had a team, but the girls have had instruction throughout their high school years. Plan the first five practice sessions for forty girls.
4. Do you agree or disagree with the statement below? Why? "Under present rules and technique of play in basketball, the dribble is a relatively unimportant skill."
5. Describe the techniques of, and teaching progression for, the lay-up shot.
6. Demonstrate and describe the defensive positioning and movements when guarding an offensive player without the ball.

SELECTED AUDIOVISUAL AIDS

Women

Women's Five-Player Basketball, 1973. (Super 8, 8-loop series, silent, color.) The Athletic Institute, 705 Merchandise Mart, Chicago, Illinois 60654. (Purchase)

Men

Basketball. (Super 8, 9-loop series, silent, color.) The Athletic Institute, 705 Merchandise Mart, Chicago, Illinois 60654. (Purchase)

Basketball Conditioning Drills, 1968. (16 mm., 14 min., sound, b & w.) Coronet Instructional Films, 65 E. South Water St., Chicago, Illinois 60601. (Purchase and rental)

Bill Russell's "Red Check" Basketball Films. (16 mm., sound color, 3 units of 4 films each, 5 min. per film.) Scholastic Coach Athletic Services, 50 West 44th Street, New York, New York 10036. (Purchase and Rental)

Individual Defensive Skills. (16 mm., 9 min., 35 sec., sound, color.) Sunkist Growers, P.O. 2706, Terminal Avenue, Los Angeles, California 90054. (Purchase)

The Basketball Series, 1967. (Super 8, 14-loop series, silent color) McGraw-Hill Films, 1221 Avenue of the Americas, New York, New York 10020. (Purchase)

SUGGESTED READINGS

Barnes, Mildred J.: *Women's Basketball.* Boston, Allyn and Bacon, 1972.

Bell, Mary M.: *Women's Basketball.* 2nd Ed. Dubuque, Iowa, William C. Brown Co., 1973.

Cousey, Bob, and Power, Frank, Jr.: *Basketball Concepts and Techniques.* Boston, Allyn and Bacon, 1970.

Ebert, Frances H., and Cheatum, Billye Ann: *Basketball:Five Player.* Philadelphia, W. B. Saunders Co., 1972.

Miller, Kenneth D., and Horky, Rita: *Modern Basketball for Women.* Columbus, Ohio, Charles E. Merrill Publishing Co., 1970.

National Association for Girls and Women in Sport. *Basketball Guide.* Washington, D. C. AAHPER. Current edition.

National Federation of State High School Associations. *Basketball Rule Book.* 400 Leslie Street, Box 98, Elgin, Illinois 60120. Current edition.

Neal, Patsy: *Basketball Techniques for Women.* New York, The Ronald Press, 1966.

Stutts, Ann: Women's Basketball. 2nd Ed. Pacific Palisades, California, Goodyear Publishing Company, 1973.

Turnbull, Anne C.: *Basketball for Women.* Reading, Massachusetts, Addison-Wesley Publishing Company, 1973.

Wooden, John R.: *Practical Modern Basketball.* New York, The Ronald Press, 1966.

CHAPTER 15

FIELD HOCKEY

Hockey is one of our oldest team games. Early Greek art and Egyptian hieroglyphics show figures playing the sport with sticks similar to those used today. The word "hockey" comes from the French word *hoquet,* but the game has been played for many years as "hurley" in Ireland, "shinty" in Scotland, and "bandy" in Wales. As an international sport for men, field hockey has achieved Olympic games status. Although there are a limited number of men's clubs in the United States, girls and women participate widely in field hockey as a fall sport in schools, colleges, and local associations.

Field hockey was brought to the United States from England in 1901 and introduced to college women at Vassar, Bryn Mawr, Smith, Wellesley and Mount Holyoke by Constance Applebee. The sport spread from the East to the Middle Atlantic and Midwestern states and later to the West Coast. A growing number of southern schools and colleges are introducing field hockey. In 1922, the United States Field Hockey Association was organized and USFHA remains the organization responsible for the rules and development of the sport. In 1967, the USFHA adopted the rules of the International Federation of Women's Field Hockey Associations and joined over thirty other nations who have accepted these rules.

Modified hockey is played in elementary schools, and the official game is taught and played competitively in secondary schools and colleges. Over fifty local associations offer "club" competitions for adult women. Each year, teams of college and association players compete in sectional tournaments which culminate in a National Tournament conducted by the USFHA. The outstanding players are selected for the first and reserve teams, and they represent the United States on tours, in international competition, at clinics, and as hosts for international touring teams.

NATURE, PURPOSE AND SCORING OF THE GAME

Hockey is a vigorous field sport in which two teams of 11 players each try to score goals by using a wooden stick to direct a hard ball. Players move the ball by dribbling and passing.

Scoring. For a goal to count, at least one member of the attacking team must contact the ball within the defenders' striking circle. Goals count one point and are scored only if the whole ball passes over the goal line into the goal cage.

Players. A hockey team is composed of five forwards (a center forward, two inners, and two wings), three halfbacks, two fullbacks and a goalkeeper. "Right" or "left" precedes the position names of inners, wings and fullbacks. Halfbacks are called "right," "left," or "center." Every player must carry a stick during the game and use it to move the ball (except the goalkeeper who does not have to *use* the stick although she holds it). The ball may be stopped with the stick or the hand, but the goalkeeper is the only player who may advance the ball with her body, legs, or hands.

The Game. An official game is played in two 35 minute halves with a five minute interval between halves, as players change ends of the field. Halves may be shortened for young or inexperienced players by agreement of the team coaches or captains or by officials in a tournament situation. The game may be suspended by an umpire for injury, game interference, or any reason deemed appropriate. The ball is put into play with a center bully at the beginning of each half and after a goal has been scored. At the end of playing time, the team with the larger score is declared winner.

SUMMARY OF GAME RULES*

As play progresses after the center bully, out-of-bounds balls, fouls, and specific situations occur. The following summary attempts to clarify how the ball is put in play, legal and illegal acts, and penalties for fouls and violations.

Out of Bounds

If a ball goes:	*The ball is put in play by:*†
1. Over the sideline off stick of player or players on same team	1. Roll-in for opponents
2. Over sideline off sticks of two opponents simultaneously	2. Bully on 5 yard line
3. Over sideline off body of player	3. Free hit for opponents
4. Over endline off stick of attack	4. Free hit by defending team 16 yards from the goal line opposite the spot where ball crossed goal line

*For complete rules, see *The Code of Rules for the Game of Hockey for Women.* The Women's International Hockey Rules Board; and NAGWS *Field Hockey-Lacrosse Guide.* Current edition. AAHPER, Washington, D.C.

†See p. 494, "Play for Specific Situations," for explanation of skill execution.

5. Over endline off sticks of two opponents simultaneously	5. Twenty-five yard line bully
6. Over endline unintentionally off stick of defense behind 25 yard line	6. Corner
7. Over endline intentionally off stick of defense	7. Penalty corner
8. Over endline unintentionally off stick of defense beyond 25 yard line	8. Free hit by defending team 16 yards from the goal line opposite the spot where ball crossed goal linc
9. Over endline off body of defense	9. Penalty corner
10. Over endline off body of attack	10. Free hit for opponents

Fouls

1. *Sticks:* Raising any part of the stick above shoulder level while playing the ball.
2. *Dangerous hitting:* Undercutting the ball so that it goes into the air in a manner dangerous to an opponent, or hitting the ball directly into an opponent.
3. *Advancing:* Permitting the ball to rebound off any part of the player's body in any direction that gives an advantage to that player or her team. The ball may be stopped with an open hand or caught, but it must be dropped directly to the ground. An exception is made in the case of the goalkeeper, who may kick the ball or let it rebound from her hand as long as she does not place or throw it. The goalkeeper loses these privileges when outside the circle or participating in a penalty bully.
4. *Wrong side of stick:* Playing the ball with the rounded side of the stick.
5. *Hitting the ball between own feet.*
6. *Hitting or interfering with opponent's stick.*
7. *Personal contact:* Tripping, pushing, shoving, or striking opponent.
8. *Obstruction:* Putting any part of the body between an opponent and the ball, preventing her from playing the ball, or running between an opponent and the ball so as to break her stride.
9. *Playing without a stick in hand.*
10. *Offside:* Being ahead of the ball in opponent's half of the field when fewer than three of the opposing team are between you and the goal and the ball is struck or rolled in by a member of your team. An individual cannot be offside when in possession of the ball.

Penalties for Fouls

For fouls outside the striking circle:	*The penalty is:*
1. By members of one team	1. Free hit for opponents on spot where foul occurred*
2. By members of opposing teams simultaneously	2. Bully on spot
3. By player taking a corner hit	3. Free hit for opponents anywhere in circle

*A penalty corner may be awarded if the umpire rules the defender *inside her own 25 yard area deliberately fouled.*

For fouls inside striking circle:	*The penalty is:*
1. By attacking team	1. Free hit for opponents from any spot within circle
2. By defending team	2. Penalty corner, except for deliberate or repeated fouling or when a sure goal was stopped by fouling, in which case a penalty bully is awarded
3. By members of opposing teams simultaneously	3. Bully on the spot. An umpire may warn or suspend a player from the game

Specific Situations and Penalties for Incorrect Execution

1. *Roll-In.* Roll-in for opponents if (1) the ball is bounced or spun, (2) the ball does not touch ground within 3 feet of where it went out, and (3) any part of the roller's body or stick crosses sideline before roll. The roll-in is repeated if any players are in the alley before roll or the ball does not enter field of play.
2. *Bully.* A bully is repeated if (1) one of the players is not standing squarely, (2) one of the players moves her feet before the completion of the bully, (3) the bully is incomplete, or (4) any other player is closer than 5 yards.
3. *Penalty Bully.* The bully is repeated if (1) there is interference by any other player, (2) the bully is incomplete, (3) defense sends the ball over the endline which is within the circle, not between goal posts, (4) both sticks simultaneously send the ball over endline not between goal posts, or (5) ball lodges in clothing of a player. The bully is over and play is restarted with a 25 yard line center bully if (1) the attack sends the ball over the endline not between goal posts, (2) the defense sends ball out of the circle into the field of play or (3) the attack fouls. A penalty goal is scored if: (1) the attack or defense sends the ball over goal line between goal posts or (2) the defense fouls.
4. *Corners and penalty corners.* These are repeated if (1) players are not lined up correctly, (2) the defense crosses the endline before ball is hit, (3) a player swings and misses but does not make sticks, or (4) the defending forwards cross the 25 yard line before the ball is out of the circle or before the ball is touched by another player. There is a free hit for the defense if (1) a player taking a hit fouls, (2) she plays the ball before someone else has touched it, or there is (3) any other breach of corner or penalty corner rule by the attackers.
5. *Free hit.* A free hit is repeated if (1) a player swings and misses but does not make sticks, (2) another player is within five yards, or (3) the hit is not taken on the spot where the foul was committed. A free hit for opponents occurs outside the circles if (1) a player fouls, (2) the ball is not motionless, (3) the ball is lofted above knee height, (4) the player taking a hit plays it again before it has been touched by another player. An improper free hit inside the circle results in a penalty corner.
6. *Accidents and interference.* The umpire may stop the game for not more than 5

minutes in case of injury to a player. She may also stop the game to take care of any other matter which may be interfering with the progress of the game. Play shall be restarted with a bully on the spot, unless a foul was involved in the injury or interference, in which case the appropriate penalty will be administered.

7. *Substitution.* A substitute may replace an injured player; the injured player may not return to the game. Only *two* substitutes are allowed during a match unless modified rules permit substitutes at half time.

NEEDED FACILITIES AND EQUIPMENT

The following items represent a minimum list of necessary equipment and facilities which should be available. They are discussed in more detail below.

1. A well marked, turfed, and smooth field.
2. A stick for each player.
3. At least one ball for every 8 to 10 players.
4. Shin guards for each person.
5. Two pairs of goalie pads and kickers.
6. Distinguishing team pinnies.
7. Whistles, official rule guide, and score book.
8. First aid kit.

Field. The field is a level, turf-covered rectangle 100 yards long and 60 yards wide. Three-inch white lines mark the sidelines, goal lines, center line, and 25 yard lines. The two lines each 25 yards from a goal line and parallel to it, are marked by dotted lines across the width of the field. Parallel to the sidelines and five yards in are the dotted five yard lines. They run the length of the field on both sides. Lines not exceeding twelve inches in length are placed on each five yard line, parallel to and 16 yards from the goal line. Corner marks are placed on the sidelines five yards from the goal line. The five yard line serves as the marker on the goal line. Penalty corner hit lines are five yards and 10 yards on either side of the goal posts. Four foot flagposts are placed on each corner of the field and one yard outside the field at each end of the center line.

At each end of the field is a striking circle. The circle is actually composed of two quarter circles, measured 16 yards from the corresponding goal post and joined in front of the goal by a four yard line parallel to the goal line.

Goals. The goal is four yards wide and seven feet high and placed in the center of the goal line. The fronts of the two inch wide goal posts touch the outside edge of the goal line. The rectangular box is 4 to 6 feet deep

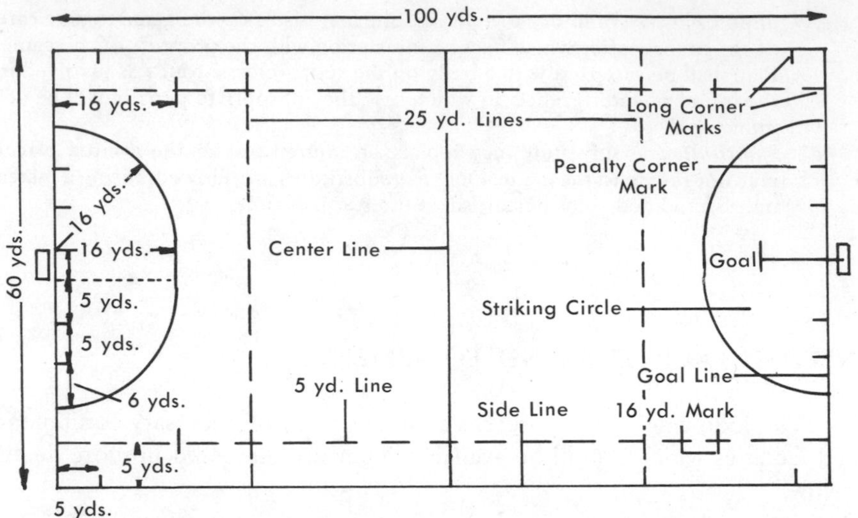

Figure 15–1 Hockey field as specified by USFHA.

with all parts other than the goal mouth covered with netting. The front of the goal facing the field of play is painted white.

Stick. The hockey stick has two major parts—a shaftlike handle, and a curved head. The left side of the head is the flat hitting surface; the right side is rounded. Only the flat side may be used to contact the ball. There are no left-handed hockey sticks; right-handed and left-handed players use the same stick and grip.

Hockey sticks vary in weight, height, and hand grip and should be selected to fit the individual player. A stick must be of a size that can be passed through a 2 inch ring. As in all sports equipment, hockey sticks vary in quality. The head is made of ash or mulberry, and the grain of the wood

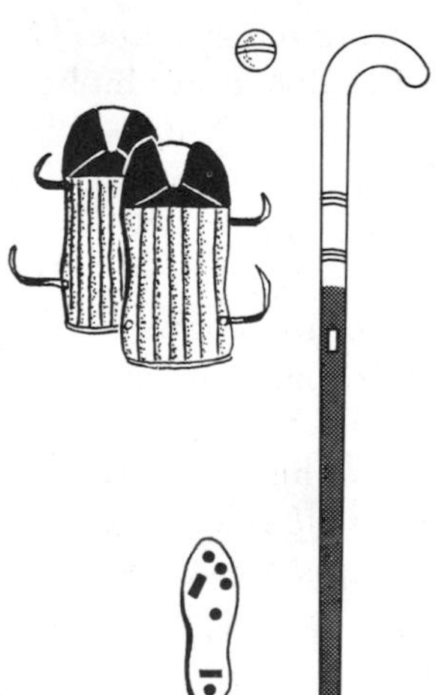

Figure 15–2 Field hockey equipment.

should follow the curve of the blade. The handle, or shaft, is cane with rubber or cork insertions bound with string and encased in a rubber grip.

Selection of a stick depends on the player's height, arm length, playing position, and preference. To determine the length of stick needed, stand erect, hold the stick with both hands at the top of the shaft as if preparing for a drive. The blade should just clear the ground. Weight and size of blade should also be considered. The usual stick length is 35 to 37 inches; weight 18 to 19 ounces, although sticks to 23 ounces are allowed. The short-toed stick is currently preferred. Forward line players may prefer lighter sticks with thinner blades, backfield players may choose sticks with heavier heads.

Balls. Official hockey balls are made of cork and string, covered with white leather or leather painted white. White plastic balls are often used for practice, since they do not absorb moisture and are easily wiped clean. They are usually "livelier" than leather. Composition balls are also available for outdoor practice and pudding balls for indoor practice. The ball must weigh between $5\frac{1}{2}$ and $5\frac{3}{4}$ ounces. The circumference is not less than $8\frac{13}{16}$ nor more than $9\frac{1}{4}$ inches

Costume. The player's gymnasium costume is satisfactory for instructional purposes but for school or club games the traditional tunic or the more popular kilt and blouse are recommended. Pinnies of distinguishing colors and position letters are helpful to beginning players. Warm-up suits provide warmth on cold fall days. Freedom of motion and appropriateness are the chief determining factors.

Shin guards should be worn by beginners and should be available to all players. They afford protection to the instep, ankle, and shin and reduce fear of injury. They are made of durable canvas, ribbed with cane, and fitted with adjustable leather straps. They are buckled on the outside of the leg.

Shoes. Shoes should afford protection and maneuverability on the field. Although a tennis-type shoe can be worn, canvas or leather shoes with rubber, plastic, or leather cleats reduce the possibility of slipping. Socks are essential.

Goalkeeper's Equipment. The goalkeeper wears white leg pads and heavy shoes. The leg pads are much larger than shin guards, extending from the thigh over the instep. They should be buckled to the outside of the player's legs. If pads extend only to the ankles, kickers should be worn. Cleated, square-toed, padded shoes protect the goalkeeper when kicking the ball. Squares of sponge rubber inserted over the instep increase protection for the foot.

CARE OF EQUIPMENT

Many players will want their own equipment and should care for it to insure long life.

Stick. During the season the stick should be carefully wiped and stored in an upright position. If splinters appear, they should be sanded immediately. After each season all dirt is removed and rough places sanded smooth. A dry ash stick is treated with linseed oil, excess removed, and wax applied for protection against moisture. A mulberry stick is treated with oil only. Varnished sticks may only require cleaning if the surface is not marred. If worn, the rubber grips will need to be replaced and the decorative stringing holding the grip in place will need to be retied. Sticks should be stored in a cool, dry place.

Ball. Match balls probably will need repainting after each match. Practice balls, depending on amount of use, should be repainted two or three times during the season. A ball rack makes painting easier and holds freshly painted balls. Plastic covered balls can be washed very easily and should not be painted.

Shin Guards. Straps and rubber pieces should be kept in repair. Buckling shin guards in pairs after use is a time saver.

Goalkeeping Equipment. Goal pads should be brushed, straps checked and buckled in pairs and then stored in a dry, well ventilated place. Soiled pads and kickers should be scrubbed with a brush and soap and water, dried and white shoe polish applied.

Goalkeeper's shoes collect mud and often require scraping. Neat's foot oil is used to protect the leather.

TEACHING UNITS

Hockey teaching units may be built around the following suggested topics. Three units are suggested to assure progression to the more difficult skills.

Beginners

Brief history
Nature and purpose of the game
Safety measures
Grip and carry
Footwork
Dribble
Passing
Quick pass
    Drive (straight, left, right)
Fielding
Tackles (straight)
Goalkeeping
Roll-in
Bully
Rules
Basic game strategy
    Basic defensive plays of marking and covering
    Basic offensive positioning
Evaluation
Intramural play

Intermediates

Review basic skills
Push pass
Left tackles (two hand and left hand lunge)
Circular tackle
Advanced fielding skills
Dodges
Situational strategy
    Interchanging
Pointers for corner play
Pointers for penalty corner
Beginning officiating
Evaluation
Intramural and extramural play

Advanced

Perfect skills at top speed
Scoop
Jab
Flick
Use of reverse stick

Advanced strategy
Officiating
Interscholastic or intercollegiate competition
Evaluation

Rainy Day Suggestions

Indoor practice and gymnasium hockey
Films and filmstrips of game and rules
Chalk talk and discussion of rules and strategy of individual and team play
Care and repair of equipment

BASIC SKILLS

Development of hockey skills is extremely important for enjoyment of the game. For clarity, an explanation of skills is divided into three main categories: (1) controlling and advancing the ball, (2) fielding and tackling, and (3) play for specific situations. Within each category the skills are presented so that there is a progression from less complex to more exacting skills. Basic to all skills is footwork.

Footwork. Agility, speed, and control of one's body while handling the stick is necessary for putting the body in the best position for playing the ball. As a situation in play changes and different strokes are needed, the player must "get her feet around" so that they are always in proper relationship to the ball. As skill develops, players learn to hit off either foot while maintaining balance and forward direction. A beginning player will do well to develop small, sure steps, particularly when running at top speed, in order to be ready for quick changes in direction. The eyes must be on the ball, glancing up only to see the position of other players, and the feet ready to move. Poor footwork results in inaccurate strokes and fouls.

CONTROLLING AND ADVANCING THE BALL

Holding the Stick. Place the head of the stick on the ground, toe pointing forward and the top of the handle against the front of the leg. Place the left hand at the top of the stick and grip easily. Raise the stick to a vertical position, toe pointing upward. The right hand is placed six to eight inches below the left, fingers curled around the handle. A "V" formed by the thumb and index finger of each hand is in line with the toe of the stick. Lower the stick to a perpendicular position, so that the head is slightly to the right and in front of the right foot and the flat hitting surface is facing forward. The left forearm is straight and in line with the stick, and hands and wrists are relaxed. This is the basic grip position. The left hand seldom changes this position, but the right hand moves for various strokes.

Figure 15–3 Carrying the stick.

Carrying the Stick. The stick is carried in a comfortable position for running and in such a way that it may quickly be used for play. Beginners should be encouraged to carry the stick with two hands, maintaining a dribble grip, with the toe of the stick comfortably close to the ground.

When quite a distance from the ball, more advanced players may find it easier to run with the stick parallel to the ground with toe facing up. The elbows are easy and flexed. The left hand is at the top of the handle, and the right is 6 to 8 inches down, holding the stick in front of the body and parallel to the ground. The stick should swing easily with the running motion. Other advanced players may prefer a one-hand grip in anticipation of the immediate play of the ball. The stick is held by the left hand at the top, and the blade of the stick is carried close to the ground, facing in the direction of the oncoming ball.

Dribble. The dribble is a series of short taps on the ball that enables a player to advance the ball while running. Players use a "close" dribble when near opponents or expecting to pass or shoot momentarily. A "loose" dribble allows additional speed when the field is clear and there is no threat of an interception or tackle. Avoid dribbling when it is possible to pass.

The left hand is at the top of the handle with the back of the hand facing forward. The right hand is placed 3 to 4 inches down the stick with palm forward. Advanced players tend to move the right hand closer to the left. The stick is gripped firmly with thumbs circling. The arms are away from the body and firmly extended. The left forearm is in the same plane as the stick, and the left elbow points diagonally forward. The player should have the feeling of reaching for the ball with the stick nearly perpendicular and slightly to the right of the right foot. The body faces forward. The left

Figure 15–4 The dribble.

shoulder should be slightly ahead of the right in good upright running position. A free wrist motion is used to execute short successive taps. The action is one of reaching and tapping with the left hand with additional control of the stick by the right hand.

In a controlled dribble the ball is never more than a stride away from the stick. The loose dribble in the clear field allows the player to hit the ball harder and farther ahead of the stick. This series of "passes to oneself" must be well timed and used sparingly to avoid interception.

Quick Pass. This rapid pass is frequently called a "chop" drive, for it is a fast stroke with a minimum of backstroke and follow-through. It is an excellent first pass for beginners, for it is executed with the hands in a dribble grip position. After fielding the ball, or from a dribble, the stick moves away from the ball only a short distance and in a line directly opposite the intended direction of the hit. The wrists cock (right more pronounced than left) and the right hand *may* be raised higher than the left but not above

Figure 15–5 The "chop" drive.

waist level. The right hand controls the stick and pushes the head to the ball. On contact, the wrists extend firmly and both arms extend in a short, definite follow-through. The head is kept low over the ball to avoid lofting.

The ball is hit to the right of the right foot for a *straight pass,* to the right and opposite the rear foot for a *hit right,* and in front of the body nearer the left foot for a *hit left.* The upper body must rotate accordingly, so that the stick comes on a direct path to and through the ball on every pass.

Drive. Drives are powerful strokes used for passing, clearing, shooting, defense hits, free hits, and corner hits. The body is in an upright position whether standing or running (avoid crouching), and the hands are close together near the top of the stick. The shoulders pivot and the arms swing easily back. The left arm is firm, slightly flexed, and close to the body; the right elbow bends close to the body and points toward the back of the player. The right wrist cocks, and the left remains firm to limit the backswing and the possibility of "sticks." At the moment of impact the head is over the ball and the right hand hits through the ball as the wrist uncocks. Keep the stick on the ball as long as possible. The left hand guides the stick into a low follow-through in line with the intended path of the ball, wrists remain firm to prevent swinging the stick above the shoulders. The force of a moderate or long drive is applied by shoulders, arms, wrists, and weight transfer.

Straight Drive. A stationary straight drive is used for free hits, defense hits, and corner hits. Lead with either foot. The feet should be $1\frac{1}{2}$ to 2 feet apart and the body turned sideways to the direction of the intended hit. The ball should be slightly nearer the forward foot, about 18 inches from the toe.

The straight drive must also be perfected when running at full speed. For example, on a straight drive for goal when force is needed, the left shoulder pivots to position the body so the left side is pointed toward the path the ball will take. The ball is in front of the forward foot and slightly to the right of the body to assure the force of body weight will go into the ball. On all drives, remember to *place your feet in relation to the ball,* rather than placing the ball in relation to the feet. Be certain to follow through rather than pull back on the stroke.

Drive to the Left. The ball is played in front of the body and feet, slightly nearer the left foot. The stick swings back in a straight line from the ball as weight shifts to the right foot. As the pendulum arc swings forward, the body weight shifts, arms and firm wrist's extend, and the extended arms carry the stick in a low follow-through in the direction of the drive.

Drive to the Right. The ball is to the right of the body and farther behind the feet than in the straight drive position. With a strong twist of the shoulders to the right, both arms swing into the backswing as the left shoulder moves toward the direction of the pass. The wrists cock sharply and then uncock firmly as the ball is hit. The arms follow through in the direction of the hit as the body continues in a forward path.

Figure 15–6 *A*, The drive; *B*, the drive to the right.

In addition to the extra power gained by extending the lever arm by placing the hands close together, some players seem to achieve extra power with a quick side step around the ball while executing the backswing, so that the left side of the body is moving in the direction of the pass.

Push Pass. The push pass is used for short, accurate passes or for a scoring attempt when there is no time to execute a backswing and a drive. After fielding or from a dribble, the stick remains in contact with the ball.

Figure 15–7 The push pass.

The right hand moves down the stick, slightly farther than for dribble position. Immediately before power is applied, the blade is directly behind the ball and the top of the stick slightly ahead of the blade. The left shoulder leads as the player takes a long, lunging step, transferring weight to the forward foot. As both arms move, they sweep the stick along the ground so that the stick remains perpendicular as long as possible. With the arms extended to the limit of their reach, the right hand pushes sharply foward simultaneously with a slight pull back with the left. The follow-through continues in the direction of the pass. On passes of some distance, the player finishes low and the stick is *almost* parallel to the ground with left forearm and stick in a straight line, the right arm extended, and the toe of the stick facing up.

Flick. Accurate and hard to intercept, the flick is used in passing to a marked teammate and in shooting at close range. It is a difficult shot to intercept, for it travels off the ground and the stroke itself disguises the path of the ball. The grip and body position are similar to those of the push pass. The body is in a semicrouched position, and weight is distributed between the toe of the rear foot and the entire forward foot. The ball is positioned to the right and ahead of the forward foot with the face of the stick in contact with the right side of the ball. There is no backswing in preparation for the stroke.

With simultaneous movements the stick face moves behind the ball as the left hand pulls the stick handle to the body and the right hand pushes the blade under the ball. Wrists snap and the body pushes forward force-

Figure 15–8 The flick.

fully from the back foot. Short flicks can be executed from the semi-crouched positions, but longer, more forceful flicks are accomplished by a lunging step with additional body extension. As the ball is raised from the ground, the left wrist twists to the right, the right wrist to the left, resulting in the "flicking" action. The blade turns slightly toward the ground at the completion of the stroke. Emphasis is placed on a low body position and a low follow-through.

Scoop. The scoop is used for short passes, an occasional goal shot,

Figure 15–9 The scoop.

and to evade an opponent's tackle. It is executed from a dribble grip with the ball in front of the player.

The stick is extended, flat side up, in front of the body at approximately a 40 degree angle. There is no deception as the player places the blade behind and under the ball, scoops up, and shoves the stick forward by pulling upward and forward with the right hand while using the left hand to stabilize the movement of the right. The stroke must be smooth and gentle to avoid scooping under the ball. The stick is about knee high at the completion of the stroke, and the body weight is over the forward foot. When avoiding a tackle, the most effective scoop is to the dribbler's left over the attacker's stick side.

Fielding and Tackling

Fielding is the skill of gaining control of the ball so that it may be dribbled or passed or a goal shot executed. The stick is held with the left hand at the top and the wrist over the top end of the stick. The left elbow is bent up and out and the forearm is in line with the stick. The right hand, palm facing forward, is spread in dribble position. The body is inclined forward, weight over the forward foot and head over the stick. Closely watching the approaching ball, point the toe of the stick toward the ball to line up its path of travel. Prior to contact, the stick is lowered to a perpendicular position, left shoulder forward, and the blade grazes the ground as the flat surface moves directly behind the oncoming ball in an easy, gathering motion. The left hand remains firm while the right is relaxed enough to give with the stick on contact. Allow the hands and handle to move ahead of the ball. The faster the speed of the approaching ball, the greater the forward reach of the left hand. The force of the oncoming ball determines the amount of give necessary to avoid rebound and loss of control. If the ball is bouncing, follow it carefully with the eyes while maintaining an easy grip and relaxed arms to field it off the ground if necessary.

Passes come at varying angles and speeds and from all possible directions. Only playing experience affords the opportunity to judge speed and angles and to establish one's own timing and techniques of fielding.

To field a ball approaching from behind and on the right side, the feet remain positioned toward the goal being attacked, the player turns her head to watch the ball and twists her shoulders far enough to the right so her stick can meet the ball at right angles. She reaches for the ball, making certain it does not get too close to her feet, and "gathers it in." She must not wait for the ball; she must go to meet it.

A ball coming from the left at sufficient speed should pass in front of the player before it is fielded. It is met by the blade, close to the ground and at right angles to the path of the ball. The ball is in position for immediate dribbling or driving. A ball approaching slowly from the left, or left and

Figure 15–10 Fielding the ball.

behind the player may be met in several ways. Beginners often find more success in moving to the ball, circling it and positioning the feet, *prior* to fielding. More advanced players may twist the upper part of the body, reach for, and field the ball simultaneously with "getting the feet around."

Stopping the Ball. The ball may be *stopped* with the stick or hand. When using the hand, catch the ball or stop it with an open hand so that it rebounds or is dropped as nearly perpendicular as possible. A slight forward motion of a falling ball due to a player's forward momentum is not considered a foul. A foul will be called if it rebounds to the player's advantage or if the player made an effort to place the ball with her hand.

Stopping a ball "dead" with the stick is similar to fielding. On the rare occasions when a ball should be stopped still, allow more give with the stick, so the ball can be trapped in the angle formed by the ground and the stick.

Tackles. Tackles are used when a player wants to get possession of the ball from an opponent or force her to rush a pass. An approach may be made from the front or from the right or left side of an opponent. Tackles should be made when the ball is off the opponent's stick.

Straight Tackle. The tackle is made on an opponent approaching directly from the front. With the stick held as if the ball were to be fielded and hands about 6 to 8 inches apart, move forward to meet the opponent with the stick close to the ground. Face the opponent and keep slightly to her stick side. Keep eyes on the ball and opponent's stick while maintaining controlled balance, and be ready to move in any direction. At the moment the ball is farthest from the opponent's stick, take a stride forward, extending the top of the stick slightly. Trap the ball with a firm stick and solid body position. Hold this position momentarily to gain control before dribbling or passing. The opponent should overrun the ball.

Figure 15–11 Straight tackle.

Two Handed Left Tackle. The two handed left tackle is a basic tackle used by all players when an opponent is on the left of the tackler running in the same direction. The tackler chases her until she is parallel or close enough to reach the ball *with both hands on the stick.* The tackler reaches

Figure 15–12 Two-hand left tackle.

Figure 15–13 Left-hand lunge.

forward and to her left and places the stick just ahead of the ball so that it strikes the blade and interrupts the progress of the dribbler. The tackler immediately pivots, getting her feet around, and controls the ball. More skillful players develop the ability to reach the ball with the toe of the stick, pull it from in front of the dribbler and simultaneously pivot and control the ball.

Left-Hand Lunge. The tackler is on the opponent's stick side running in the same direction. While running with the opponent, the stick is in carrying position. To attempt a lunge, the tackler must be close enough to reach the ball with one stride and a long reach. (If she is able to get closer she should use a safer two-hand tackle.) The tackler pulls the stick to her right side, keeping it low, and at the moment her opponent taps the ball, the tackler reaches left with both hands (until right hand can reach no farther) and then firmly extends the left arm and lunges with weight on the left leg. The stick head is "thrown" down just in front of the ball so that it traps the ball on the stick. The tackler quickly turns to her left (as opponent overruns the play), places her right hand on the stick, and gains possession of the ball. Hitting the stick of an opponent is a foul and players should avoid slashing or chopping at the ball or opponent's stick.

Circular Tackle. This is used by a tackler approaching an opponent who is on her right. Both players are running in the same direction or the tackler is coming diagonally from the left of the dribbler. With stick held in dribble position the tackler must move a stride or two ahead of her opponent so her stick is even with the ball when it is off the dribbler's stick. The stick is close to the ground, the left shoulder and arm lead; the right shoulder is back. The hips move around, following the shoulders. As the ball is moved with short, quick taps in a small circle, the tackler's feet move in a larger circle to the left of the ball. The body leans and turns toward the ball. Right shoulders of the players pass as the dribbler's momentum carries her beyond the ball. As the tackler circles in front she must avoid touching her opponent or in any way obstructing her movement. She must time her tackle to contact the ball when it is off her opponent's stick.

Figure 15–14 The circular tackle.

The Jab. The jab is a one-hand spoil stroke used when maximum reach is needed. *Either hand* may be at the top of the stick and the jab is made from either side of the opponent. To avoid obstruction, it is wise to hold the stick in the left hand (right shoulder back) on the opponent's non-stick side. Skillful players achieve their greatest reach using the right hand if the dribbler is on their right and using the left hand if the opponent is on the left.

In preparation for the stroke, grasp the end of the stick with one hand, wrist on top. Lay the blade of the stick back, and as an attempt is made at the ball, bend the body forward and take a long stride. Extend the stick arm close to the ground as far as possible. The edge, heel, or toe of the flat side of the stick jabs at the ball when it is off the opponent's stick. This "last resort" stroke must be timed perfectly or several jabs may be needed to contact the ball and the danger of fouling increases. The jab must be followed by another play immediately to gain control of the ball.

Dodges. These techniques are used by the player with the ball to evade a tackler. Remembering that the intent of a tackler is to take the ball, slow the dribbler, or force a hasty and inaccurate pass, the dribbler has the option of passing or dodging. A dodge should not be attempted if a well controlled pass to a teammate is possible. A pass may be the first option when challenged by a fast opponent with an effective circular tackle and a left hand lunge.

Basically, a dodge is a well controlled pass to oneself. The elements of surprise and speed are important for effectiveness. A dribbler who slows down prior to execution of the dodge falls prey to the tackler. As an opponent approaches for a straight tackle, the dribbler accelerates from her normal speed prior to execution of a dodge. With experience, a player will learn to fake one dodge and execute another.

Right Dodge. At the moment the tackler begins to tackle, the ball is passed to the tackler's non-stick side with a short diagonal pass so that it rolls by her left toe and behind her. The dodger runs past the stick side of her opponent, controls the ball, and continues play. Often called "push right, run left," this dodge must be perfectly timed so that the opponent is out of ball reach but not so far from the play that she has time to change directions.

Left Dodge. The ball is kept in normal dribbling position in front of the right foot. The dribbler increases her speed just before she expects to be tackled, and, as execution of the tackle begins, the dribbler quickly pulls the ball about 6 inches directly to her left as her feet move left with small, quick steps. (Move the ball only far enough to avoid the tackler's reach.) Immediately she continues her dribble forward with increased acceleration. This dodge is often referred to as an "L" because of the pattern of the ball path.

Figure 15–15 Left dodge.

Reverse Stick Dodge. Although not frequently used, the reverse stick dodge can be most effective when a player is about to be tackled with a left-hand lunge. As the opponent begins her lunge, the dribbler reverses her stick by wrist and lower arm roll and immediately pulls the ball directly to her right. She then either continues to dribble or passes.

Scoop. As in the scoop stroke, the ball is lifted and pushed forward. The ball must be slightly forward, so that the blade of the stick can be laid back. When the tackling player extends her stick for the ball, the dodger scoops over the opponent's stick and continues dribbling.

Triangular Pass. This is an effective dodge as well as a fundamental play. The dribbler passes diagonally to her left or right to a teammate as the tackler approaches. The initial dribbler runs past the tackler's stick side, passes her, and receives a return pass from her teammate.

Play for Specific Situations

The Bully. The players taking the bully stand facing each other and opposite sidelines. The player's own goal line is on her right. The players' feet are apart, knees bent, and weight forward. Their heads are over the ball. The left hand is near the top of the handle, the right hand well down the handle for strength. The right hand *may* be turned slightly to the right, fingers pointing upward, to deceive opponents as to the stroke that will follow the bully. Each player taps the heel of the stick on the ground and then taps her opponent's stick with the flat hitting surface. Do this three times. Sticks are tapped on the ground on either side of the ball and they tap each other above the ball. After the third tap of the sticks either player may

Figure 15–16 The bully.

play the ball attempting to direct it to a teammate. Players bullying may not move their feet until the bully is completed. All other players must be at least 5 yards away until the bully is completed.

Offensive plays should be planned following the bully. The following suggestions initiate an offense after hitting sticks for the third time:

1. Pull the ball toward the center of the body while moving the feet back with the pull. The ball is passed left. (Be careful not to obstruct with the right shoulder on the pass to left inner.)
2. Reverse the stick; draw the ball backward and diagonally to the right. A short backswing precedes a hit to the right.
3. Reverse the toe of the stick and tap the ball back to a defensive player backing up the bully.
4. When both players' sticks are firmly pressed against the ball, a firm upward and forward movement of the stick lifts the ball over the the opponent's stick. The pass following must be quick.

Penalty Bully. This bully is taken 5 yards in from the center of the goal by the defensive player who fouled and any selected member of the attacking team. All other players, including the goalkeeper when she is not participating in the bully, must stand beyond the 25 yard line and stay out of play until the bully is completed. If the goalkeeper is bullying, she may not remove her pads or use her kicking or rebound privileges. The defensive player must have precise movements and should attempt to keep contact with the ball until she can clear it from the circle. Two effective bullies are the pull and pass left and the lift over. (See above.)

Corner. Two formations of corners are awarded to give an advantage to the attacking team.

The corner is often called the long corner. It is awarded an attack player on a spot 5 yards from the corner of the field on the side or goal line. The ball is played on the side of the goal where the ball went out.

Penalty Corner. A "short" corner is awarded an attack player at a spot 10 yards from the goal post on the goal line.

Corner Formation. The wing usually takes the hit. On a long corner, play must be on the sideline or goal line on the side of the goal where the ball went out. On a penalty corner the attacking team selects the side of the goal for the hit. The attacking forwards must be at least 5 yards from the ball and outside the circle until the hit. The four forwards line up with feet and sticks near the outside of the circle poised to move. Halfbacks back up the forwards. (See Figure 15–17.)

Six defensive players must stand with feet and sticks behind their own goal line and at least 5 yards from the ball until the hit. Usually these players are the goalkeeper, two backs, and three halfbacks. The forwards of the defending team must remain beyond the 25 yard line until the ball is touched by a player other than the wing taking the corner, or until the ball has come out of the striking circle.

The wing attempts to hit a firm ball, with no bounce, to a forward, who

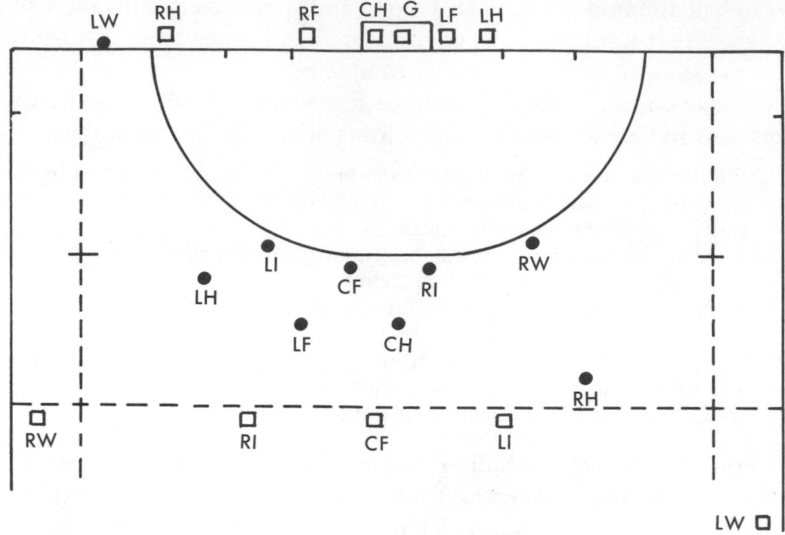

Figure 15–17 Lineup for corner.

controls the ball and makes a quick goal shot. The ball may be deflected or passed, but a goal *must not* be attempted until the ball has been controlled on the ground by an attack player or has touched the stick or person of a defender.

Free Hit. The ball is played by the defensive player in whose area it lies. In the circle, it is usually taken by a back at the circle edge. All other players must be 5 yards away.

The ball must be motionless and may be hit with any legal stroke as long as it does not rise above the knees if it goes into the circle. It may not be played again by the hitter until touched by another player. A free hit should be taken quickly to gain advantage before the defense is set.

Roll-In. This technique is used to put the ball in play after it has gone out of bounds over the sideline, unless put out by two opposing players simultaneously. It is usually taken by a wing halfback. The ball is rolled by the player outside the field to a teammate on the field. All other players must be on the field of play and inside the 5 yard line bounding the inside of the alley. The player making the roll-in must have feet and stick outside the field and her stick in one hand. The left halfback should roll the ball with her right hand; the right halfback with her left hand.

The player crouches in a forward stride position, getting low to the ground, and uses an underhand swing. She must roll the ball, *not* bounce or throw, so that it touches the ground within 1 yard of the point where it left the field. She immediately reenters the field but may not play the ball until it is touched by another player. Positioning and strategy vary with the position of the ball in the defensive or attacking area. The roll-in may be long and forward to a wing, diagonally forward to an inner, or parallel or back to a defensive player.

Figure 15–18 The roll-in.

GAME STRATEGY*

There are no rules of thumb governing strategy, for there is great variation based on general team ability and individual playing skill. A few proven principles are helpful in building a skillful team.

1. Encourage speed, alertness, and creative play on the field.
2. Forwards must create spaces by pulling away from the ball to deceive the defense.
3. Defensive players must constantly observe their forwards and move and position accordingly.
4. When the defense moves with a forward, the ball is hit or rolled to a space; if the defense does not move, the ball is hit or rolled to the forward's stick.
5. Forwards must move on roll-ins and free hits to create a target or space and outwit the defense.
6. Vary style of play by change of speed and strategy, particularly if the team is not functioning well.

Offensive Tactics. There are several options for positioning on the center bully. Figure 15–19 shows a variation with left fullback up on one team and right fullback up on the other. This depends upon team strengths and play options. As the bully is completed the forward line of both teams moves forward and the defense moves to back up forwards and to mark opposing forwards. All forwards not participating in the bully move into opponents' field to receive the ball from teammates or to intercept from opponents. Forwards play in a line, staying 10 to 12 yards apart, with the dribbler slightly ahead. A pass usually should be ahead of the intended receiver and perfectly timed for her to pick up and dribble forward.

The wings should try to move the ball upfield down the alley to keep

---

*For more detailed strategy, see Hally B. W. Poindexter and Carole L. Mushier: *Coaching Competitive Team Sports for Girls and Women.* Philadelphia, W. B. Saunders Co., 1973.

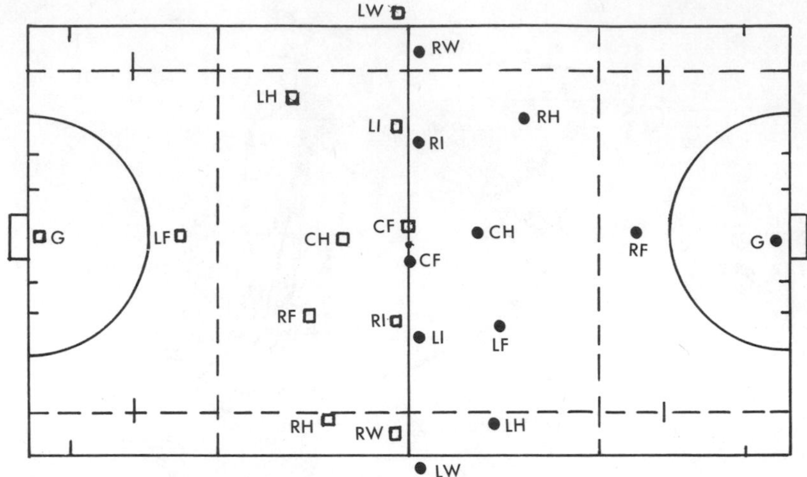

Figure 15–19 Line-up for center bully.

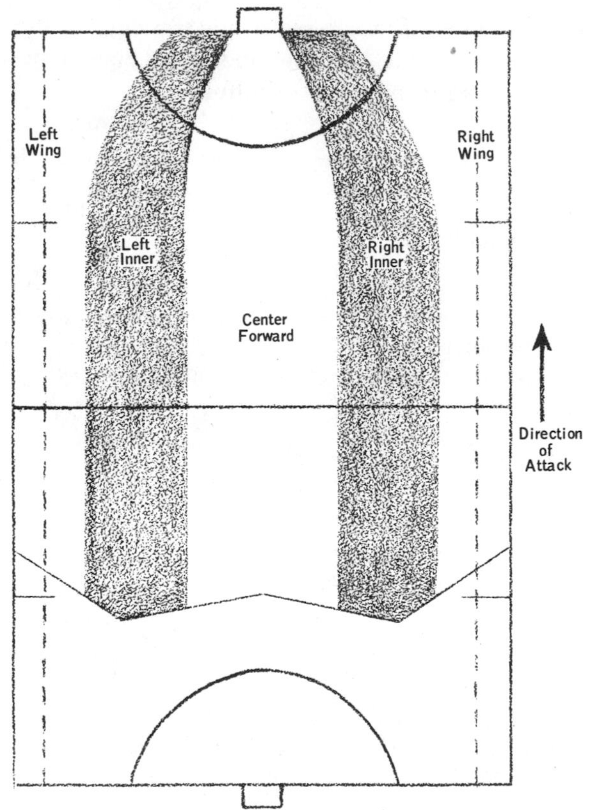

Figure 15–20 Areas for forwards.

the defense spread and to move rapidly. As the wing moves near the 25 yard line she tries to center to an inner or center for a goal shot. The halfbacks follow and back up the forward line, and one fullback follows on offense while one remains to cover in a defensive position.

The forwards converge slightly as they near the circle. At the circle a strong hit should be made for the goal. The inner and center forward should then rush the center of the goal, and the wings should position themselves near the edge of the circle to pick up the goalkeeper's clears to the side.

Wings do not have the opportunity to shoot as frequently as other forwards, but they occasionally make shots from the edge of the circle.

Corners. Corners and penalty corners occur frequently in a game and afford a scoring opportunity for the attack. Player positioning is the same for both, the difference being that the corners are taken five yards from the corner of the field and the penalty corner is taken not less than ten yards from the goal post. (See Rules, p. 492.) As Figure 16–17 indicates, a wing usually takes the hit which is directed to a forward on the edge of the circle. The hit should travel smoothly and accurately so that the forward need *not* move to the ball. She can then await it, quickly control it, and immediately shoot for goal. At least two other forwards should rush the goal at the instant the shot for goal is made. Statistics indicate that the majority of goals are scored on the second or third shots by rushing forwards.

Defensive Tactics. At the initial bully, players may take positions indicated in Figure 15–19. One team has the left fullback up, opposing the opponents' right inner and protecting the non-stick side of the center halfback. The right fullback is in covering position. In beginning play, most bullies won by the offense move to the left of the defending team. With more experienced players and more skillful bullies, play may require either fullback to be up.

Initially the forwards tackle back in an attempt to regain the ball. If the ball passes to the opponents, each defensive player becomes responsible for the area and player she marks.

An aggressive forward line pulls back into its own half of the field in a "W" formation to await a clear from the defense. The center forward is on approximately the 30 yard line in center field, the inners are on their respective sides of the field at about the 25 yard line, and the wings are close to the 50 yard line in either alley (Figure 15–20).

Marking. Each back is responsible for marking her opposing forward. Marking implies that the defensive player is between her opponent and the goal and within a stick's reach of her opponent, positioned to intercept her passes or tackle. The right halfback should mark the left wing; the right fullback, the left inner; the center halfback, the center forward; the left fullback, the right inner; and the left halfback, the right wing.

Interchanging. On the bully, the center halfback should be about 5 yards away in order to intercept an opponent's pass or gain control of the

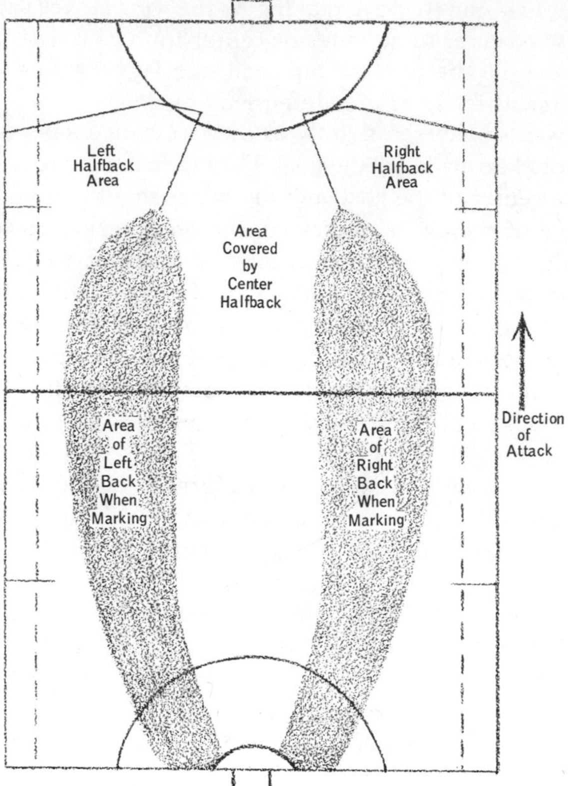

Figure 15–21 Areas for defense.

ball. Although a beginner should learn to play her own position well, advanced players should master the techniques of interchanging and covering, i.e., the defensive players change positions either as safety players or as hastily shifted defensive blocks to catch an unguarded, rapidly advancing player with the ball. This tactic is used largely when the forwards have moved down to, or behind, the 25 yard line as the remaining defensive players cover to stop the advance.

Covering. To facilitate the interception of long passes and to cover their half of the field more adequately, fullbacks, and occasionally wing halfbacks, may play in a deeper defense position. Center halfbacks rarely get involved, for their first responsibility is staying with the opposing center forward. For example, if the ball is controlled by an opposing right wing who is being tackled by the left halfback, the left fullback is marking the right inner. The right fullback covers in a deeper position, closer to the center of the field. Should the ball be passed to the right side of the field, the right fullback moves up and the left fullback shifts back to a covering position closer to her own goal and near the center of the field. Fullbacks may move from side to side with the play if this can be done without the defense's getting behind the play. The halfback on the side away from the ball moves in to cover. She plays in line with the opposing inner and deeper than the halfback on the same side of the field as the ball.

Intercepting. Timing is vitally important in gaining possession of a ball being dribbled or passed to others. Team members must quickly move into position to receive the pass or change the direction of the ball going up- or downfield. In order to be adept at such interception, players must watch the ball closely at all times and be ready to move quickly into free space through which a pass might be attempted.

A good defense has all opposing forwards near the ball well marked, with one player in strong covering position. As the attack nears the circle, all forwards are closely marked with no covering player. Inside the circle defensive players must avoid blocking the goalkeeper's view when a shot is made.

DUTIES AND SPECIFIC SKILLS OF PLAYERS

Attack. All forward players should be fast and agile runners skilled in the dribble, drive, pass, dodge, tackle, and goal shooting.

The center forward should be:

1. An exacting shooter with a variety of shots
2. Capable of receiving passes from left and right
3. Able to direct play with accurate passes and drives to left or right
4. Excellent at the bully
5. Fearless at rushing the goalkeeper
6. Capable of dodges to both sides
7. Able to move in small spaces
8. Capable of creating spaces
9. Capable of immediate acceleration

The inners should be:

1. Excellent shooters
2. Good at dodges on both sides
3. Capable of creating spaces
4. Able to accelerate
5. Agile and difficult to mark
6. Fearless in rushing the goalkeeper
7. Aggressive and capable of tackling back
8. Able to execute quick hits

The *left inner* must master the ability to field from the right and pass to the right while running at full speed.

The wings should be:

1. Capable of good running speed
2. Able to accelerate rapidly
3. Able to execute an accurate, hard, and smooth corner hit

4. Excellent at centering the ball
5. Accurate at passing and shooting from the edge of the circle
6. Capable of dodges

The *left wing* must be able to receive passes from the right and be able to drive and pass right while running.

In fulfilling the real job of scoring points as often as possible, the following tips may be helpful to forwards:

1. Move up the field in a line spaced across the field so one defense player is required for each attack.
2. Pass the ball when possible so that the defense has less opportunity to "get set."
3. Wings do their hardest work between the two 25 yard lines. Use the wings to keep the defense spread out and set up other forwards for goal shooting.
4. Be alert to the occasional opportunity to take the ball through the defense alone. This serves to vary the attack as well as to score when other forwards are left behind.
5. It is often a good practice to keep the ball until the opponent is drawn in to tackle. A pass made too soon is easily intercepted.
6. Avoid following your pass. Pull away to create space and draw your defensive opponent.
7. When the ball is taken, be alert to "tackle back" if it does not interfere with your own defense. If the ball is recovered, pass it ahead quickly to a teammate and regain your place in the attack. A quick pass gains time and lessens the chance of being tackled back.
8. In the circle, know where the ball is in relation to the goal. Never assume a shot is going into the goal; be ready to rush a shot for goal.

Defense. A good rule for beginning defensive players is for each one to accept responsibility for the same area of the field as that of the forward she marks (see Figure 15–21). Additional responsibilities are learned later.

Halfbacks are both offensive and defensive players. They should be capable of:

1. Backing up forwards and occasionally shooting for goal
2. Fast, steady and versatile play. This requires endurance and conditioning
3. Excellent passes and drives from a run or from a free hit.
4. A variety of tackles
5. Anticipation necessary for interceptions

The *center halfback* marks center forward and should be capable of distributing play left and right.

Right halfback should be skilled in:

1. Roll-in (with left hand)
2. Covering as well as marking
3. Left-hand lunge

Left halfback should be skilled in:

1. Roll-in (right hand)
2. Covering as well as marking
3. Circular tackle

The fullbacks work as a pair, each aware of the other's position. Each should be:

1. Steady and capable of changing quickly from defensive to offensive play
2. Excellent at well timed tackles
3. Skilled at accurate, hard drives
4. Capable of coordinating play with other fullback and marking and covering equally well
5. Able to back up the bully
6. Able to pass or drive quickly following a tackle or interception

The *left fullback* must be skilled in executing the circular tackle.

In preventing goals and feeding the offense, the following suggestions may prove helpful:

1. Understand the abilities and functions of other defensive players.
2. Mark your opponent and don't interfere with others by trying to do too much.
3. After gaining possession of the ball, try to get rid of it quickly and accurately. It is rarely wise to dribble the ball other than to control it.
4. Stay about a yard from the opponent you are marking, slightly on the ball side, nearer the goal than the attacker. Try to intercept instead of waiting to tackle.
5. If passed by the opposing forward, first try to overtake her and tackle. If another back has moved to tackle, cross over to the side of the field left unprotected. It is usually advisable to interchange only when the goal is threatened or when a defensive player is hopelessly behind her opponent.

Goalkeeping. Aside from sound stickwork, goalkeeping requires skills quite different from those of other positions. The goalkeeper's privileges in the circle require that she learn to stop the ball with an open hand (the ball may be advanced but may not be thrown) and with legs and feet. She must be effective and accurate in clearing the ball with her feet. She must be skilled at bullies while dressed in pads and kickers.

Awaiting an attack, she stands in an imaginary semicircle that runs from goal post to goal post and extends a yard in front of the goal line. Standing at an angle that gives the best protection from the oncoming attack (Figure 15–22), she faces the field with feet together, weight on balls of feet, and knees bent, ready to shift position quickly with sidestepping movements. The stick is held in the right hand, part way down the handle, and on the ground. It is used only in an emergency. Avoiding jumping into the ball, she waits in direct line with the path of the ball, and as the ball strikes her legs she "gives" on impact so that it stops close. She quickly clears it with the inside of the toe to a back or a side halfback waiting to relay it upfield. She must be equally adept at using both feet.

When a hard shot is so directed that a two-leg stop is impossible, she must stop the ball with the inside of one foot while maintaining balance to prevent falling and an obstruction.

Although it is safer to stop the ball before clearing, often there is not enough time. Avoid high kicks toward rushing forwards.

Figure 15–22 Goalkeeper's positions for varied attacks.

The goalkeeper should come out of her position cautiously and only (1) when she can reach the ball before an opponent, or (2) to meet a lone forward if the goalkeeper is the only defensive player in the striking circle. She should not come out when two forwards are free in the circle.

If a shot is going to miss the goal, she should hold her position and allow the ball to cross the end line.

Above all, the goalkeeper must be aware that it is the back's job to prevent shooting, but it is *her* duty to stop a shot once it is made.

TEACHING PROGRESSION

A suggested field hockey unit of ten lessons for beginning players meeting for 50 minute periods might follow this pattern:

Lesson I

1. Brief history and nature and purpose of the game
2. Grip and carry, footwork, and dribble
3. Quick hit
4. Fielding

Lesson II

1. Review; stress fielding
2. Passing (review quick hit)
3. Game situation (stress positioning)

Lesson III

1. Review of skills
2. Straight tackle
3. Right and left dodge
4. Positioning and tactics
5. Brief game

Lesson IV

1. Review skills
2. Right and left drives
3. Drill on passing, dodging, dribbling, and tackling
4. Bully
5. Roll-in
6. Basic offensive play situations

Lesson V

1. Review
2. Left-hand lunge
3. Left or right dodge
4. Shooting
5. Basic defensive strategy
6. Half field game

Lesson VI

1. Right tackles
2. Coached game (interrupted for explanation and practice of bully, free hits, roll-ins, and corners)

Lesson VII

1. Chalk board discussion of defensive play (stress marking and covering)
2. Goalkeeping
3. Play

Lesson VIII

1. Push pass
2. Offensive positioning and play
3. Game stressing offensive tactics

Lesson IX

1. Situational drills—free hit, corners, bullies
2. Written evaluation (if appropriate)
   or
3. Officiating techniques

Lesson X

1. Tournament or regulation game
2. Evaluation of the unit by students

CLASS ORGANIZATION

Since students learn active skills by doing, the class meetings should be active ones whether students are beginners or highly skilled competitive players. Developing hockey skill is dependent on the development of (1) techniques of footwork and ball control and (2) tactics, including observation, anticipation, and teamwork. Whether the class is small, just enough for six player hockey, or very large, the principles of participation and organization are the same.

Students warm up prior to each class using the skills of the game. Skill reviews should be conducted during most classes with drill stations established so a student may move to all stations or select those most helpful to her individual development.

As skills must eventually be used while running, the basic individual skills of footwork and stickwork should be taught while moving. Begin the basic skills of dribbling, passing, and shooting and fielding while walking, and then increase speed as quickly as possible. Whether on the field or in the gymnasium, stickwork drills, relays, and novelty games make the learning of basic techniques easier, faster, and more enjoyable. (When playing indoors, the stick head is encased in a sock, and special indoor balls are used.) Although the teacher or coach will develop her own drills, a few examples may be helpful initially.*

1. In dribbling, run and tap the ball with the left hand only to emphasize the importance of its strength. As speed increases, place the right hand in dribble position on the stick, and while running, hit the ball a given number of times in a limited distance to develop a close dribble and avoid the bad habit of a hit-and-run dribble.
2. Four or five players dribble in a clockwise direction in a large circle. On signal, they turn to the center of the circle and continue in the opposite direction. On signal, they turn again to the right and continue in a clockwise direction.
3. Dribble and weave around classmates or Indian clubs placed about 10 yards apart. Make a complete circle around the last object and either shoot for goal or dribble back to original position.

Receiving the ball from front, right, left, right and behind, and left and behind the player should be taught early in skill development. Players may work in pairs initially, alternating rolling to each other from various positions. The drill serves to teach the roll-in when throwing position with the stick behind the line is emphasized. Progressing, the players should hit the ball to one another from a walk and then a run from all five positions.

As soon as possible the skills of dribbling, hitting, and receiving the ball should be combined in drills and game situations.

Shooting for goal should be a part of every practice. This should be done whenever possible with a goalkeeper in position. Initially the ball is stationary at the edge of the circle as a player approaches from about 10 yards. Progressing, the player dribbles the ball to a point just inside the circle and shoots; soon she is able to receive a pass, dribble, dodge, and shoot.

A simple drill, diagramed in Figure 15–23, emphasizes passing, shooting, and tackling techniques. Both the O's and the three X's move as a unit. If the O's retain possession of the ball, they are to shoot for a goal when in the striking circle. The X's are to do so if they gain control of the ball and can successfully dribble it downfield, passing it back and forth, to a point within the striking circle.

---

*For further suggestions see articles by Kathleen Laurie, Agneta M. Powell, and Eileen Taylor in *Selected Field Hockey and Lacrosse Articles,* AAHPER, DGWS, 1963.

For suggestions for individual conditioning and skill development see Jackie Westervelt: You, Your Stick, and a Stopwatch. *Field Hockey-Lacrosse Guide.* 1972-74, DGWS.

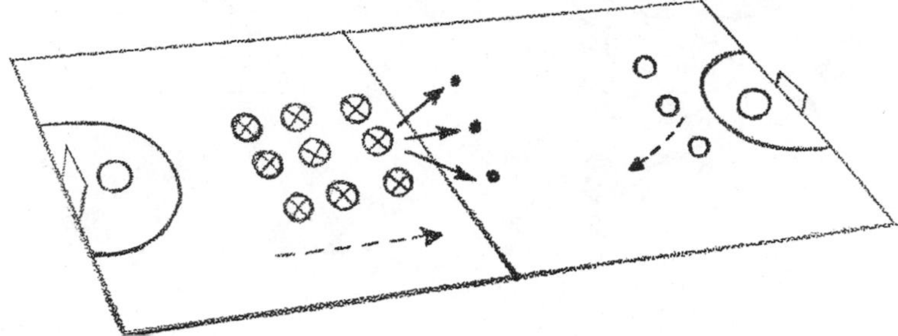

Figure 15–23 Drill formation for passing and tackling.

Early in the unit the class should either watch a game played by experts or see one on a film in order to gain a basic understanding of game play.* After viewing the film, a special effort should be made to learn field positions and the individual's responsibility to each position. Chalk board talks are helpful in demonstrating tackling, intercepting, marking, and covering after the tactics have actually been seen.

When beginning the first game, line up the two teams close together, and then position the forwards of one team on their side of the line facing the opposing forwards. Spread the defensive players on each team. Explain the role of the defensive players in marking the forwards and intercepting. Begin with a bully by opposing wings or inners (avoid center bullies until players realize it is poor team play to bunch in the center). Stop the game every time the players get in a muddle, and stress positioning and have each player check on her own position. Coaching "position" to beginners, rather than individual play, tends to strengthen team play in tackling, intercepting, marking, and covering. Strategy and game tactics of bullies, roll-ins, free hits, corners, and penalty corners are logically taught as they arise in a game situation. Players should be asked to study strategy of team and individual position play. Play as many games as class time permits, for nothing develops game skills like actual game situations.

Those not playing in the game should be practicing skills on the sidelines or observing and coaching position play. Skill and knowledge tests, although time consuming, do serve as a means of motivating students, and they also help the teacher to evaluate both the student's learning progress and her own teaching ability.

*A film of the USA-England Wembley Match (90 minutes, 1962) is available from USFHA Film Service. It is an excellent film for viewing skilled play.

SKILL DIFFICULTIES AND THEIR CORRECTION

Carrying the Stick

Difficulty	*Correction*
a. Beginners carrying stick with only one hand and with blade pointed up	a. Suggest use of both hands. The stick should be carried across the body, hands spaced, blade pointing toward and close to the ground

Dribble

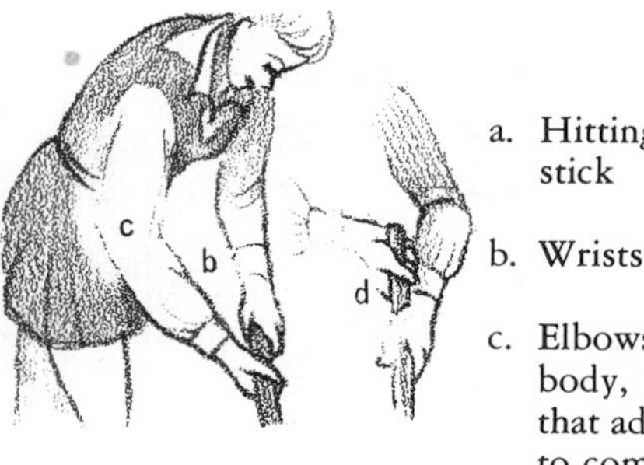
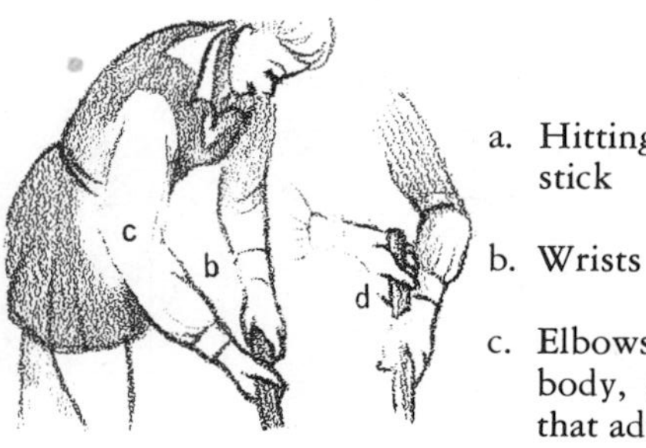

Difficulty	*Correction*
a. Hitting the ball too far ahead of the stick	a. Stress tapping the ball so it is never more than a stride from the stick
b. Wrists too stiff	b. Keep wrists flexible
c. Elbows stiff and kept too close to the body, resulting in inconsistent hits that advance too far or cause the ball to come too close to the feet	c. The left elbow should lead and be held more away from the body than the right. Practice dribbling with left hand only

Difficulty	Correction
d. Stick held incorrectly and with right hand too far down the stick, resulting in an abnormal crouched position	d. The left hand should be at the top of the handle with the right slightly below it; the stick should be held ahead and slightly to the right of the player with the top and blade inclined forward
e. Playing the ball too far on the right side of the body so a sideways run results	e. Review and stress body-ball relationship when dribbling.

Quick Hit

Difficulty	*Correction*
a. Raising stick too high on backswing	a. Limit shoulder rotation and stress natural cocking of the wrists
b. Failure to uncock and forcefully straighten right wrist, thus losing power and direction	b. Demonstrate ball flight with (1) cocked wrist, (2) flexible wrists, and (3) firm, extended wrist
c. Failure to follow through *or* follow through upward rather than forward	c. Explain mechanical principles of the low, short follow-through for a fast, well directed hit. Explain the short "chopping action" of the complete stroke

Drive

Difficulty	*Correction*
a. Stick is raised too high above the shoulder	a. Emphasize a short backswing and a low follow-through
b. Right hand not close to the left one	b. Review drive grip. Keep hands together at the top of the stick
c. Inability to rotate the shoulders for an effective drive to the right	c. The right foot should be forward and the ball just back of the heel for easier rotation

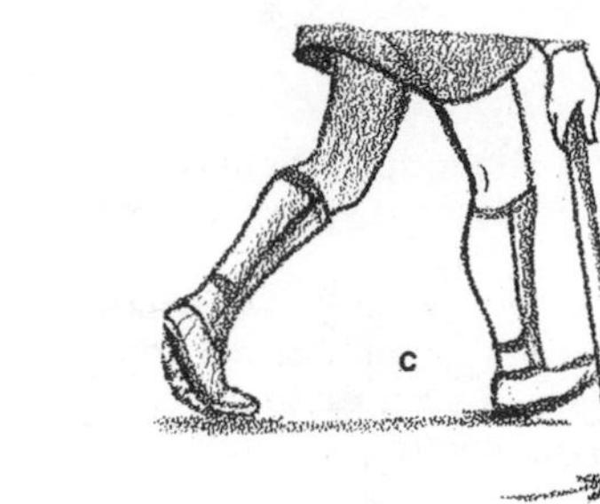

Push Pass

Difficulty	*Correction*
a. Inflexible wrists; hands together	a. Stress pliable wrists for force and direction; keep hands apart
b. Backswing, wrong foot forward, and poorly timed shift of body weight	b. Since there is *no* backswing, body weight must be shifted accurately as one steps into the shot. The pass to the right should be outside of the right foot with body twisted right and toes pointed straight ahead
c. Both hands not working together properly; one pushing too much	c. Push forward with the right hand, stabilize with the left, and *step* into the stroke in the direction of the pass

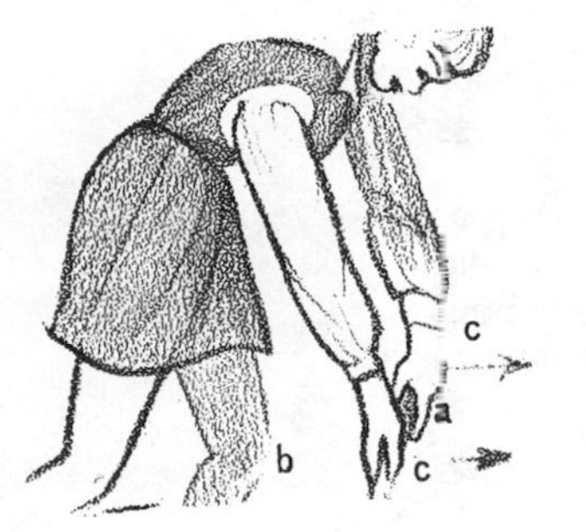

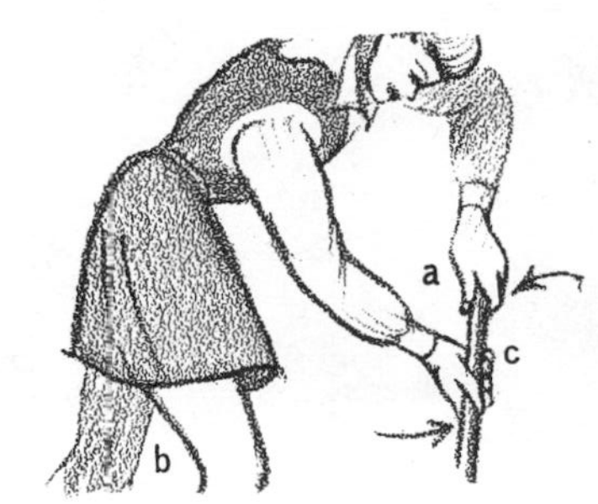

Scoop

Difficulty	*Correction*
a. Handle held against the body; right hand not down the handle far enough and all fingers, rather than hand, holding the handle	a. Hold stick well in front at sharp angle to the ground with hitting surface upward; move right hand down with thumb on top and palm of right hand up
b. Stick blade up too much; too much wrist action, resulting in the ball being raised too high.	b. Raise the ball only slightly off the ground with a *controlled* right hand. Practice slowly with a stationary ball
c. Weight not moved forward	c. Shift weight forward and make a short follow-through with the stick in the direction of the scoop
d. Pushing the stick forward too far so that the ball rolls back over the stick	d. *Place* the stick behind and under the ball before beginning scooping action

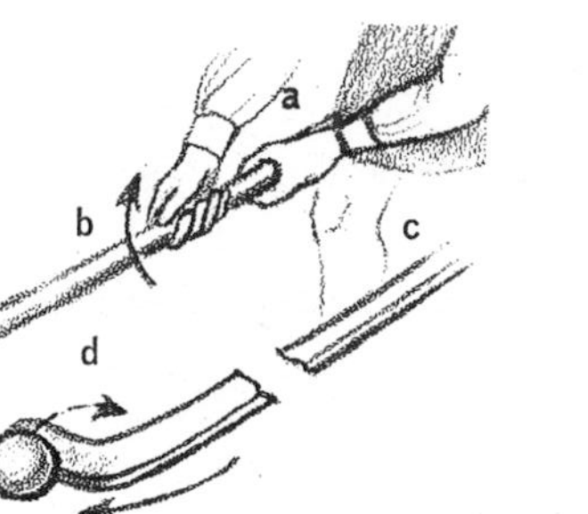

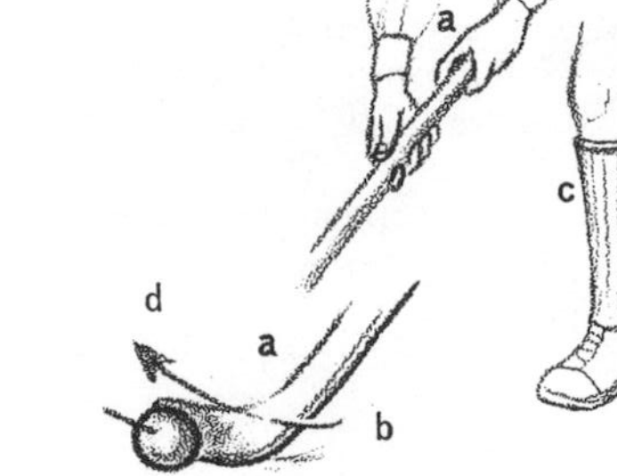

Flick

Difficulty	*Correction*
a. Wrists too stiff, resulting in inability to loft the ball	a. Emphasize initial push of the ball followed by forceful wrist action. Review skill description
b. The ball back or at the side of player's foot	b. The ball should be slightly ahead and outside the right foot
c. Incorrect hand positions on the stick	c. The back of the left hand and palm of the right should face in the direction of the stroke
d. Inability to get an effective "flicking" action or	d. Once the movement begins, stress continuous action
e. Exaggerated lofting of the ball	e. Emphasize wrist action and "drive" of the body into a low follow-through

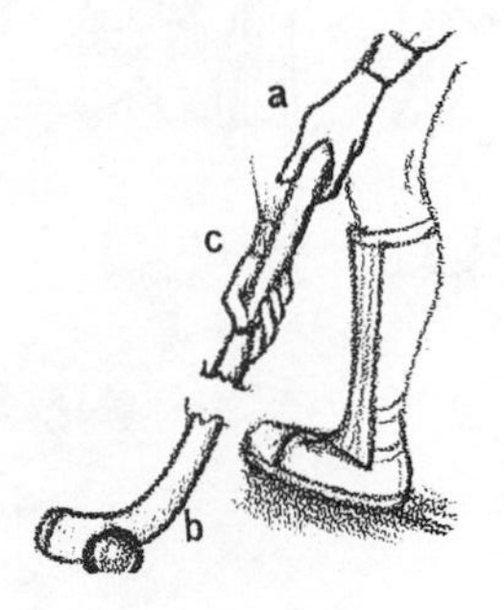

Fielding the Ball

Difficulty	*Correction*
a. Not giving with the stick enough as the ball is contacted	a. Give with the stick more in order to absorb the ball impact; get the feeling of "gathering" the ball and keeping it near the stick
b. Missing the ball by holding the stick incorrectly; taking the eyes off the ball	b. Separate hands 6 to 8 inches, pull left hand back, and point the toe of the stick toward the ball. Watch the ball closely, lowering the stick to a perpendicular position. The blade grazes the ground, and the flat surface gathers in the ball
c. Failure to meet the ball and failure to get the feet directed for a dribble or pass	c. Stress moving to meet the ball and positioning the feet *in the direction* the player will go. Practice fielding balls approaching from all possible angles

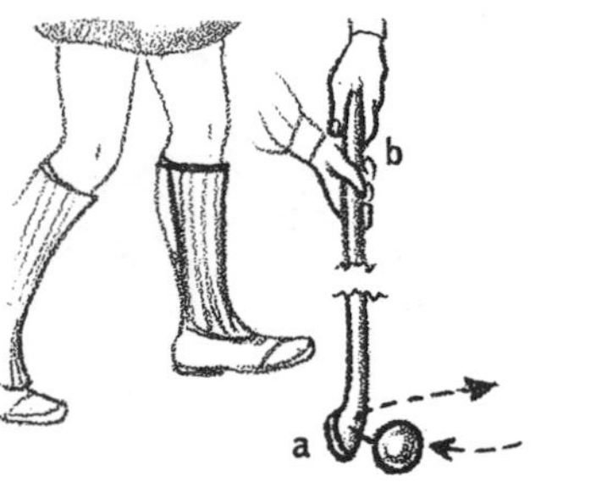

Straight Tackle

Difficulty	*Correction*
a. Tackler in wrong position	a. Tackler should be slightly to the stick side and facing her opponent
b. Hands held too close together on the stick	b. Keep hands apart for strength
c. Wrong stick position with stick too near player's body	c. The stick should be held approximately at right angles to the ground with the handle slightly farther from the player than the head. The left arm should be extended, and left shoulder leads
d. Slashing at opponent's stick rather than the ball. Tackling when the ball is on the opponent's stick	d. Stress control, timing and positioning, and the danger of mistimed tackles

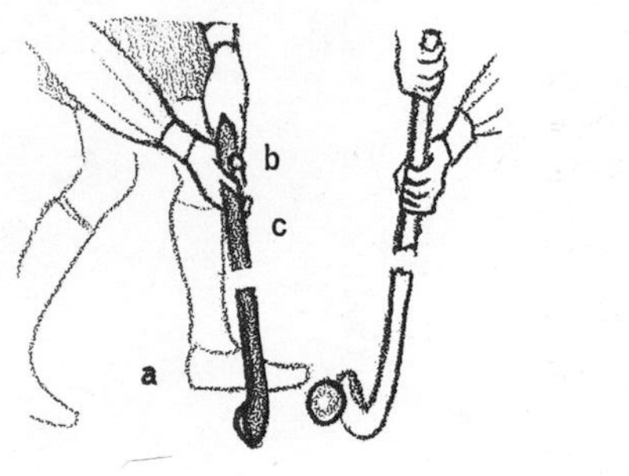

Left-Hand Lunge

Difficulty	*Correction*
a. Tackler on the wrong side	a. The tackler should be on the opponent's right
b. Path of the stick directly toward ground	b. Stick path should be diagonally toward the ground. The left hand throws the stick down to the left and in front of the opponent's ball
c. Tackler not reaching enough or using whole body; arms and body are held too rigidly	c. Tackle from slightly behind, bending and reaching far forward with the whole body
d. Making "sticks" before the downswing	d. Keep the arc of the stick low and straighten the elbows slightly
e. Improper timing (going for the ball too late or too soon); slashing at opponent's stick	e. The stick should contact the ball just after it leaves the opponent's stick on the dribble. Emphasis is on placing the stick in front of the ball rather than on hitting *at* the ball

Circular Tackle

Difficulty	*Correction*
a. Being too close to the opponent and obstructing on the tackle	a. Begin tackle only when you are even with or ahead of the opponent. Get feet ahead before tackling, and lead with the left shoulder
b. Starting the tackle too soon	b. Begin just as the ball leaves the opponent's stick
c. Losing control of the ball after getting it away from the opponent	c. Finish the tackle by continuing the circular movement and dribbling or passing

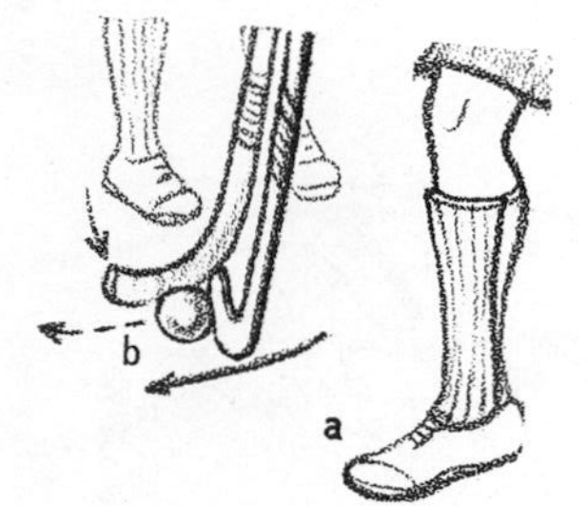

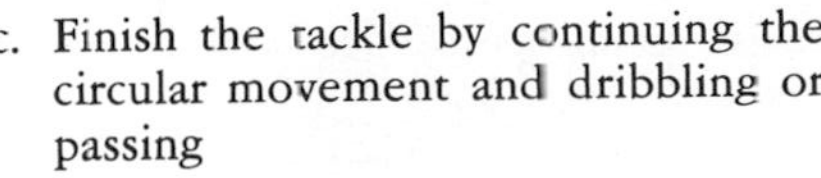

Jab

Difficulty	*Correction*
a. Flat of the blade is thrown downward so the back of the stick jabs toward the ball	a. The hitting surface should be upward as it is extended toward the ball
b. Hitting the ball in an extended stroke	b. Jab at the ball with a quick, sharp movement

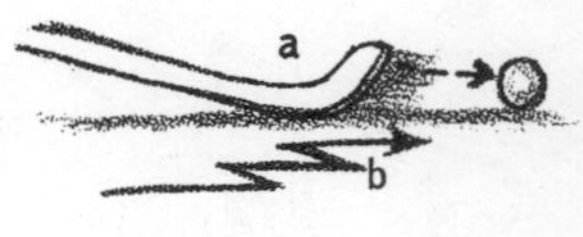

Bully

Difficulty	*Correction*
a. Body held too rigidly upward	a. Head should be over the ball
b. Raising the stick too far off the ground	b. Since speed is vital, raise stick just over the ball

c. Holding the stick with hands too close together	c. Experiment to find hand position that gives greatest control over pressure of an opposing stick
d. Failure to direct the ball to a teammate	d. Plan ahead and have a well rehearsed plan

Roll-in

Difficulty	*Correction*
a. Rolling the ball in directly to the marked player	a. Roll the ball in front of the player so it can be quickly picked up and dribbled forward
b. Stick held improperly so that part of it is over the line	b. Hold the stick in outside hand. Roll with inside hand
c. Letting the opponents know which direction the ball will be rolled by telltale body position	c. Practice and perfect looking and facing one way and rolling-in in another

EVALUATING THE RESULTS

The use of incidence charts during game play, rating scales to evaluate individual performances, progress charts, tests on specific skills, tournament standing or results, and knowledge tests on rules, strategy, and other aspects of the game are all recommended as means of evaluating players. The AAHPER Field Hockey Skills Tests, made available in 1966, offer varied tests of individual skills. Test norms are also available for girls in grades 5 through 12. The tests are intended to measure the execution of fundamental skills. They were not designed to be predictive of total playing ability. They should be regarded as practice tests intended to be used by players as a means of improving fundamental game skills.

Kelly and Brown have developed an 88 item objective test designed particularly for major students.* Strait has developed a timed test that utilizes skills of dribbling, dodging, and passing. Limited space and simple equipment are needed to administer the test.† Perhaps the best skill test for college women is that devised by Schmithals and French.‡ This test is us-

*A sample copy of this test may be obtained from Dr. Ellen Kelly, Illinois State University, Normal, Illinois.

†Jane Strait: New field hockey skills test. *Field Hockey-Lacrosse Guide,* AAHPER, DGWS, 1962–64, pp. 41–44.

‡Margaret Schmithals and Esther French: Achievement tests in field hockey for college women. *Research Quarterly. 11,* pp. 84–92, December, 1940.

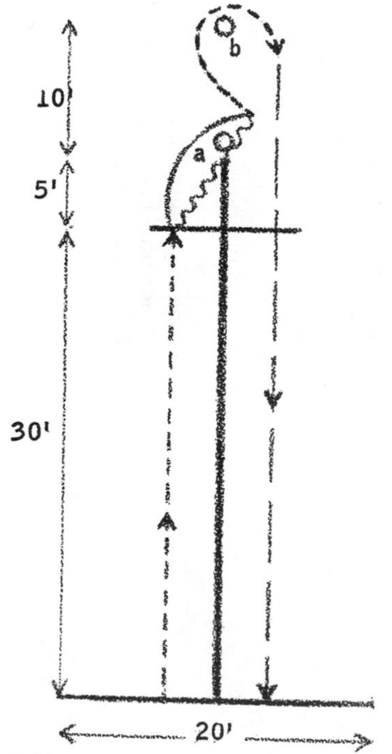

Figure 15–24 Field markings for the ball control skill test.

able also for high school girls. The battery of three tests is designed to measure (1) dribble, dodge, circular tackle, and drive; (2) goal shooting; and (3) fielding and drive. For the ball control test the field is marked as shown in Figure 15–24.

On a signal, each player dribbles forward to the left of the foul line until she reaches the restraining line where she shoots the ball to the right of the first obstacle and runs around to the left of it to recover the ball. She then dribbles around the second obstacle, turns to the right to recover the ball, and drives it back over the starting line. Six trials are given, and their average is the final test score. If the ball or player crosses over the foul line before coming to the restraining line, or if at the first obstacle the ball is not sent from the left side of the foul line, the trial does not count.

TERMINOLOGY

Advancing—A foul resulting from moving the ball to one's advantage with any part of the body.

Attack—Forward line players.

Backing up—Staying close behind a teammate who has the ball or who is tackling an opponent.

Bully—The technique used to start or restart play when both teams are to have an equal opportunity to get the ball. Two players face each other squarely. Each touches first the ground, then opponent's stick (with her stick) three times. Following this, each tries to play the ball.

Corner—A hit awarded an attacker on a spot 5 yards from the corner of the field on the side or goal line when a member of the defending team causes the ball to go out of bounds over the goal line but not between the goal posts.

Covering—A defensive strategy by one or more players who place themselves to cover spaces so they may intercept a pass or tackle a free opponent.

Dangerous hitting—Undercutting the ball (playing a ball so that it rises dangerously) or hitting the ball directly into another player even though it remains on the ground.

Defense—Players positioned as halfbacks, fullbacks, and goalkeeper.

Dodge—A technique used by a player with the ball to evade an opponent and still retain possession of the ball.

Drawing on opponent—Forcing one's opponent to mark closely or to attempt a tackle so that space will be left clear for a pass to one's teammate.

Dribble—A series of short strokes with the stick that are used to maintain possession of the ball and move it while running.

Drive—A forceful stroke used to advance the ball medium to long distances.

Fielding—Stopping the ball with hand or stick. Receiving a pass and controlling it close to the stick so that it may be played immediately.

Flick—A stroke in which the ball is pushed with a strong twist of the wrists, putting spin and loft on the ball.

Free hit—An uncontested hit awarded when the opposing team fouls or sends the ball out of bounds except in situations of corner hit, penalty corner, penalty bully or roll-in.

Interception—Taking possession of the ball as it is passed from one opponent to another.

Interchange—A temporary exchange of positions between teammates to assume duties of a teammate left behind or out of position.

Marking—A defensive technique of keeping oneself in position in relation to a specific opponent so that one can either intercept the ball intended for her or tackle her once she has it.

Obstruction—A foul resulting when a player goes between an opponent and the ball with any part of her body and hinders the opponent in playing the ball.

Offside—An infringement that occurs when a player is nearer the opponent's goal line than the ball when it is hit or rolled, while fewer than three opponents are between the player and the goal. It occurs *only* in opponent's half of the field and is penalized only if the team gains advantage.

Penalty bully—Awarded on a spot 5 yards in front of the center of the goal line to a member of the attacking team and the offending defensive player who has violated a rule when a goal would have been scored or who has willfully and repeatedly fouled in the circle.

Penalty corner—Awarded the attacking team at a spot at least 10 yards from the goal post on the goal line when the defense commits a foul in the striking circle or intentionally sends the ball out of bounds over the end line.

Reverse stick—Use of the stick so that its toe points down.

Roll-in—Technique used to put the ball back into play after it has gone out of bounds over the sideline.

Sticks—A foul caused by raising the stick above shoulder level when playing the ball.

Tackle—An attempt to take possession of the ball when it is in the possession of an opponent.

Tackle-back—Trying to regain the ball from one who has successfully tackled you.

DISCUSSION QUESTIONS

1. Describe and demonstrate three types of tackles. When would you use each one in a game?
2. Draw a suggested team play for a corner, and explain the rules applying to corners.
3. Explain (a) backing up, (b) marking, (c) interchanging, (d) obstruction, and (e) covering.
4. Where is the best place for a goalie to stand for a shot coming (1) to her *non-stick* side, (2) to her stick side, and (3) directly in front of the cage?

SELECTED AUDIOVISUAL AIDS*

Field Hockey. Filmstrips compiled by Marjorie Pollard. (25 frames, 35 mm.) SportShelf, 10 Overbrook Terrace, New York, New York, 10033. (Rental)

Field Hockey Loop Films. (12 films on techniques) Consultants: Grace Robertson and Betty Shellenberger. Athletic Institute, 705 Merchandise Mart, Chicago, Illinois, 60654. (Purchase)

Hockey Basic Strokes 1956. (18 min., silent, b & w.) Marjorie Pollard Publications Ltd., The Deanery, Bampton, Oxford, England.

SUGGESTED READINGS

Barnes, Mildred J.: *Field Hockey: The Coach and Player,* Boston, Allyn & Bacon, Inc., 1969.

Delano, Ann Lee: *Field Hockey.* Dubuque, Iowa, W. C. Brown Co., 1966.

Field Hockey-Lacrosse Guide, AAHPER, NAGWS, 1201 Sixteenth Street, N. W., Washington, D.C. 20036.

Hausserman, Caroline: *Hockey for Beginners.* Boston, Allyn & Bacon, Inc., 1970.

Poindexter, Hally Beth and Mushier, Carole L.: *Coaching Competitive Team Sports for Girls and Women.* Philadelphia, W. B. Saunders Co., 1973.

Mackey, Helen: *Field Hockey: An International Team Sport.* Englewood Cliffs, New Jersey, Prentice-Hall, Inc., 1963.

Meyer, Margaret H. and Schwarz, Marguerite M.: *Team Sports for Girls and Women.* Philadelphia, W. B. Saunders Co., 1965.

Richey, Betty (ed.): *Selected Field Hockey and Lacrosse Articles.* Washington, D.C. 20036, AAHPER, DGWS, 1963.

---

*Additional films, loop films, and printed materials are available from USFHA. See the current NAGWS *Field Hockey-Lacrosse Guide* for listing.

PERIODICALS

The Eagle. Official publication of the United States Field Hockey Association. Circulation Manager: Betty Shellenberger, 107 School House Lane, Philadelphia, Pennsylvania 19144.

Hockey Field. Official Publication of All England Women's Hockey Association. Available from Gertrude Hooper, 242 Highland Street, Milton, Massachusetts 02186.

CHAPTER 16

LACROSSE

Lacrosse was played on the North American continent long before white men were permanent residents, for the American Indian played the game *baggataway* as a method of conditioning for war and a ritual to gain favor with the Great Spirit. Some historians believe that the Indian game was a development from *knattleikr,* a game brought to the northeast coast of the continent by Norsemen years before.

Baggataway, a rough and dangerous game, drew entire tribes into competition on areas with no boundaries, where goals were often several miles apart. The Indians used a light, strong stick with a hoop or hook at one end. Some competitors carried one in each hand. A net of rawhide strips hung from the end to carry the wooden or deerskin-covered ball. The stick also served to beat off opponents in the heated battle of gaining possession of the ball.

In 1705 Pierre de Charlevoix witnessed baggataway in Quebec and renamed the game *la crosse* for "the stick," which resembled a bishop's crozier. Canadians developed rules and safer techniques of play, and lacrosse became the national game of that country in 1867. Introduced in England about 1865, it spread to all parts of the British Commonwealth and was introduced in the United States by Canadian enthusiasts.

The American women's game came directly from England rather than from the American men's game. The All England Ladies Lacrosse Association modified rules, eliminated the rough element, and sent players and coaches to introduce the game in the United States. By 1931 lacrosse was played in isolated spots in the northeast section of the country. This resulted in the formation of the United States Women's Lacrosse Association. This group, like the British association, maintains the game's amateur status, governs all affairs and rules, and provides help through its membership. The popularity of the sport has grown with annual national tournaments, clinics, and the exchange of British and American touring teams approximately every three years.

Lacrosse has not had the rapid growth it deserves as a team activity. It remains largely confined to the eastern sector of the United States but is developing in areas as it becomes known and overcomes the prejudice against the rougher men's game. The rules are determined and controlled by the USWLA in conjunction with NAGWS. Rules are published by NAGWS every two years.*

NATURE, PURPOSE, AND SCORING OF THE GAME

Lacrosse is a field sport played by two opposing teams of 12 members each. It is an extremely fast aerial game in which each team member advances the ball with her crosse by carrying it or passing it. She must move rapidly to a position to pass to a teammate or to score a goal by shooting into the goal net.

Lacrosse allows an individual freedom of movement and initiative during play that is uncommon in field games. Few rules govern the field and boundaries, and only limited rules are established to assure game control and player safety. Before play begins, field boundaries are established by the team captains, coaches, and umpire. The goals must be placed at least 90 yards apart and no farther than 110 yards. The minimum width should be 50 yards. An official game has two periods of 25 minutes each (unless shortened by mutual agreement) with no time-outs other than those called by an umpire. A 10 minute rest may be taken between halves.

At the beginning of both periods and after each goal, play begins with a center draw by opposing center players. The small hard-rubber ball is advanced by the use of the crosse in running, passing, catching, picking up, or shooting. Each team attempts to defend its goal and score against its opponents. At the end of playing time, the team with the larger score is declared the winner.

Players. Each team of 12 members has six attacking players and six defensive players. The attacking players are the center, right attack wing, left attack wing, third home, second home, and first home. Their primary duty is to get the ball into a position for a goal shot as quickly as possible. The defensive players—the two defense wings, third man, cover point, point, and goalkeeper—mark closely and attempt to gain possession of the ball by interception or crosse-checking. Once in possession, they move the

*NAGWS: *Field Hockey-Lacrosse Guide.* Washington, D.C., AAHPER. Published every two years.

ball to their own attack players. Distribution of players is not compulsory, and all players actually have both offensive and defensive responsibilities.

Scoring. The team scoring the greatest number of points is declared winner. A goal counts one point and is recorded when the entire ball crosses over the goal line and under the 6 foot crossbar from in front. A legal goal must be propelled by the crosse of an attacking player outside the crease or the crosse or body of a defending player. Tied games are recorded as a draw.

SUMMARY OF GAME RULES

The rules of lacrosse are simple and few, and are designed to protect the player and control the game. A field umpire and two goal umpires conduct the game with the assistance of a timekeeper and a scorekeeper.

The simplified rules below control play:*

1. *Center draw.* The draw is used to begin play at each half and after each goal. Opponents stand with one foot toeing the center line. The ball is placed between the backs of the crosses of opposing centers and on command of the umpire, "Ready . . . draw," the centers move the crosses upward and outward in an attempt to direct the ball to one of their attack players. No other player shall be closer than ten yards until the ball is up and away.
2. *Stand.* Whenever play is suspended by an official's whistle, all players must stand and hold their positions until directed by an official or play resumes.
3. *Out of bounds.* When the ball passes out of the established boundaries, the umpire stops play and awards the ball to the player who was nearest to it as it went out. If two players on opposing teams were equally close to the ball as it crossed the boundary, the two players stand 5 yards in and at least 1 yard apart, with the defense player nearer her own goal, to receive a throw-in from the umpire. Play from an out-of-bounds situation must be at least 10 yards from the goal line.
4. *Ball lodged in clothing or equipment.* A ball lodged in the goal netting or in the pads or clothing of the goalkeeper within the crease is removed, placed in the crosse, and played. If lodged in the clothing of another player, it is removed and the umpire will award a throw with her nearest opponent. When a ball is lodged in the crosse, the crosse is struck to the ground to displace it. If this fails, the umpire awards a throw where the player caught the ball.
5. *Fouls.* Two types of fouls are recognized: field fouls and crease fouls. In the field of play a player may not:
   a. Swing recklessly or check roughly.
   b. Reach over her opponent's shoulder to tackle.
   c. Hold down or check the crosse of an opponent who is not in possession of the ball.
   d. Hold down an opponent's crosse in the air or on the ground when opponent is in possession of the ball.

*For complete rules, see the current *Field Hockey-Lacrosse Guide* published by NAGWS.

e. Detain an opponent by contact with her crosse or her body.
f. Deliberately charge, shoulder, or back into an opponent.
g. Trip, push, or shove an opponent with body or crosse.
h. Guard her crosse with a raised elbow or with one hand off the crosse.
i. Intentionally touch the ball with her hands except to remove it when lodged in goal netting or clothing.
j. Throw her crosse.
k. Kick the ball intentionally.
l. Dangerously flip the ball into an opponent.
m. Move from her position when the umpire blows her whistle (except for goals) until play resumes or she is directed by the umpire.
n. Play the ball or impede an opponent unless she is holding her crosse.
o. Shoot for goal in an uncontrolled or dangerous manner.
p. Position herself with others to form a barricade to obstruct the goal.

In and around the *crease* a player must not:

a. When attacking, have any part of her body or crosse over the crease during or after the pass or shot.
b. Check the goalkeeper within the goal crease.
c. When inside the crease, hold the ball in her crosse; it must be passed at once.
d. Draw the ball back into the crease unless both feet are in the crease.
e. When in possession of the ball outside the crease, step back into or run across the crease until the ball is passed.
f. When defending, step into the crease if another defending player is in the crease.

The *penalty* for field and crease fouls is a free position. Players "stand." The umpire indicates where the player taking the free position stands. All players must be at least 5 yards from the player with the ball. On signal "play" the player with the ball may run, pass, or shoot. No free position by an attacking player may be taken within 10 yards of the goal line (measured from the line in any direction). When a foul prevents an almost certain goal, the umpire orders any defensive player, including the goalkeeper, from between the free position and goal.

When two opponents foul simultaneously, the umpire awards the throw.

Substitutes. Substitutes may enter to take the place of an injured player at any time. If a player temporarily leaves the game and no substitute enters, she may return to play when able. (In high school and college games, substitutions may be made at the umpire's discretion.)

Scoring. The winning team is the one that scores the greatest number of points. A goal counts 1 point and is recorded when the entire ball crosses the goal line from the front and stays beneath the 6 foot crossbar. A legal goal must be propelled by the crosse of an attacking player, or by the crosse or body of a defending player. Tied games are recorded as such.

NEEDED FACILITIES AND EQUIPMENT

One of the advantages of lacrosse is that the field area does not require extensive maintenance or marking, and equipment is limited and modestly priced. With proper care, equipment lasts many years.

Field Area. The field is the approximate size of a hockey or football field. A smooth surface, although desirable, is not as necessary as it is in hockey or soccer for true ball roll.

The field has no definite boundary markings, but within the established area are two goals between 90 and 110 yards apart. Minimum field width is 50 yards. Each goal consists of two posts that are 6 feet high, 6 feet apart, and joined by a crossbar 6 feet from the ground. The goal line is drawn from post to post and, with the 2 inch by 2 inch wooden or pipe frame, forms a square with inside measurements of 6 feet. The posts and crossbar are painted white. Netting of not more than 1½ inch mesh is attached to the posts and bar and pegged to the ground 6 feet behind the center of the goal line.

The *goal crease* is formed by drawing a circle with a radius of 8½ feet from the center of the goal line.

A center circle with a radius of 10 yards is drawn in the center of the field. A line 4 yards in length and 2 yards on each side extending from the center of the circle is drawn parallel to the goal lines.

Ball. The ball used in women's lacrosse is made of sponge rubber. The hard rubber ball may be any color, but white is most commonly used. It

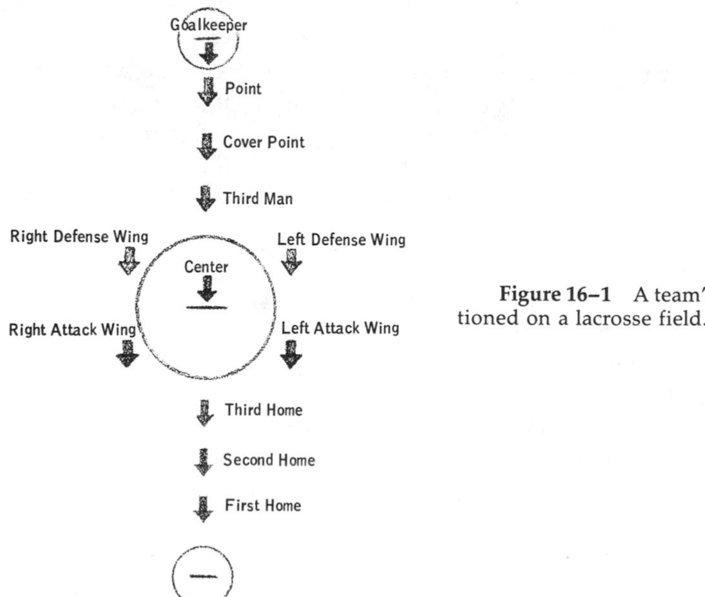

Figure 16–1 A team's 12 players positioned on a lacrosse field.

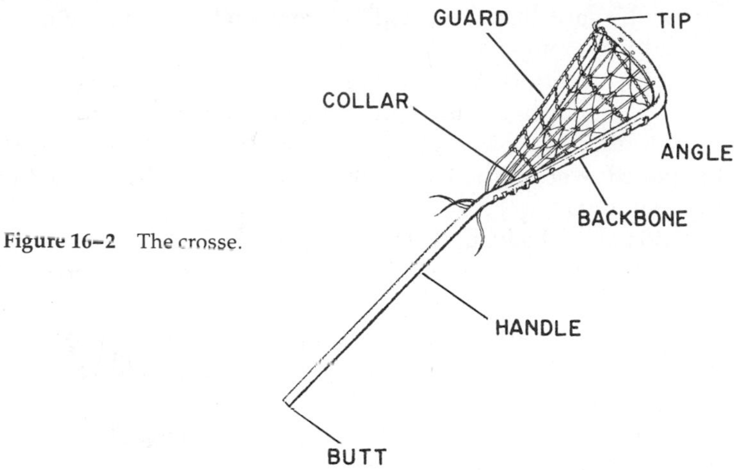

Figure 16–2 The crosse.

weighs no less than $4^{1}/_{2}$ ounces and no more than $5^{1}/_{4}$ ounces and is between $7^{3}/_{4}$ and 8 inches in circumference.

Crosse. The crosse is made of a wood or synthetic frame with a net-like section of leather and gut on the end for carrying and controlling the ball. It may not be more than four feet in length nor more than nine inches at its widest part. It must not weigh more than 20 ounces. The frame must extend down the right hand side of the bridge; left-handed crosses are illegal. A string must be brought through a hole at the side of the tip of the turn to prevent the possibility that the point of the stick will catch an opponent's crosse. The leather thongs (lengthwise strings) must be woven to within 2 inches of their termination and tightened sufficiently to prevent a ball from catching in the meshes or resting in a pocket formed by loose lengthwise strings. No metal of any kind is allowed upon the crosse.

Selection and Care of the Crosse. Special care should be taken in learning the important parts and desirable features in stick selection.

Butt and Grip. End of the handle where one hand is placed. It should be small enough and belled to fit the fingers of the hand.

Handle. Usually 25 to 27 inches. Select the length by holding the stick with the right hand at the collar; the end of the handle should touch the armpit.

Collar. Point of attachment for the thongs of the gut wall and lengthwise strings. The top of the stick. When held at the collar by two fingers, the head and handle should balance, or there should be only slightly more weight in the head tipping toward the backbone.

Backbone. Wooden or synthetic wall of the face, about $2^{1}/_{2}$ inches wide.

Angle. Curved section between backbone and tip. It should be slightly more than a 90 degree angle. As this is the weakest part of the crosse, be sure that the wood is strong and that the grain runs smoothly around the angle.

Tip. Bent portion and end of wood nearest the guard.

Guard. A heavy mesh of gut approximately 2½ to 3 inches in width. This strong upright runs opposite the backbone. Be certain that the guard is not pulled over on the face of the stick by too tight a bridge or lead string position.

Bridge. Thick gut that is placed several inches above the collar and attached to the guard and backbone to prevent the ball from lodging in the crosse.

Thongs. Leather or hide thongs running lengthwise and crosswise to form the netting for controlling the ball. These should be kept taut to avoid a deep pocket.

Care of the Crosse. Proper care insures a long life. A few rules should be followed:

1. Avoid leaning on the crosse.
2. Always loosen the leading strings after playing to relieve strain on the angle.
3. Wipe the stick after playing.
4. Treat the guts and thongs with leather conditioner or white petroleum jelly and the wooden frame with linseed oil. Do not treat the guard or bridge.
5. Hang the stick by the wood across the top when not in use. Store away from heat and dampness.
6. Mend and repair the stick as soon as possible.

Costume. Freedom and safety in running, stretching, and changing directions are the criteria that determine dress. Regular gymnasium costume with socks and tennis shoes or sneakers is appropriate class and intramural attire For college or club games, kilts and blouses have gained popularity over the tunic. Hockey shoes or leather or canvas shoes with plastic, leather, or rubber cleats are helpful in acceleration and changing directions. The goalkeeper is the only player who needs additional equipment. Her equipment includes leg and thigh pads, chest protector, glove, and a face mask.

TEACHING UNITS

The following unit for beginners aims at introducing the player to the game as quickly as possible. Skill drills are important, but they are appreciated more when their ultimate game use is understood by students. Throughout the instructional units, an attempt should be made to execute stickwork *while moving* with as much speed as possible, yet encouraging accuracy The advanced unit is centered around improving attack and defense and learning to officiate.

Beginners

- Brief history
- Object and purpose of the game
- Field dimensions
- Care and use of equipment
- Demonstration and practice of skills
  - Grip of the crosse
  - Cradling
  - Picking up
  - Turning
  - Catching
  - Overarm throw
  - Dodging and body checking
  - Marking
  - Shooting
  - Center draw
  - Crosse checking
  - Goalkeeping
- Game play and simple strategy
- Explanation of basic rules
- Intramural competition
- Evaluation

Advanced

- Intensive review of purpose and basic game skills
  - Underarm and sidearm passes
  - Varied goal shots
- Intensive explanation of rules of play
- Advanced strategy
- Interscholastic or intercollegiate competition
- Officiating
- Evaluation

BASIC SKILLS

Lacrosse skills are built upon the abilities of catching, throwing, twisting, dodging, and running forward and backward. The uniqueness of the game lies in the control of the crosse.

The Grip. The stick is held by both hands, one at the top of the handle and one at the end. Normally the throwing hand is placed on top. The skills described are for a right-handed player. The beginner can assume the correct hand position by placing the stick on the ground directly in front with the butt end close to the feet. The open part of the head (the pocket, with the backbone to the right of player) is facing up. The right hand is placed at the top of the stick, the collar, so that the "V" of the thumb and forefinger is between the player's face and the stick when held vertically. The knuckles are under the stick as the hand grips firmly. The thumb and forefinger meet to form a permanent ring.

The right hand lifts the stick until the hand is about eye level. With the "V" formed by thumb and forefinger pointing directly to the crosse head, the *left hand* reaches directly forward to grasp the butt end firmly in the entire hand. The left hand is approximately at waist level. The right elbow is relaxed and, with the forearm, is outside and close to the stick. The upper hand is the guiding hand, the lower the power hand.

Cradling. Cradling is the rhythmical swing of the stick, timed to the action of the player's body, that keeps the ball under control and in the crosse. Beginners should master the vertical cradling position first, as it

Figure 16–3 Cradling to the left.

emphasizes the close position of the stick to the body and the grip and use of the bottom hand.

With the stick almost in vertical position, both hands move in the same direction to the same side of the body. When the cradling motion reaches either side of the body, the open face is away from the body. The face is toward but above the player as it passes across the body. When the stick is on the right, the wood is turned slightly toward the player; on the left, the guard is nearest, to prevent losing the ball.

To begin the cradle to the right side, the bottom arm is at waist level and parallel to the ground. This power arm swings to the right so that it remains close to the waist. The left wrist flexes so that the hand turns in to the body The right wrist flexes and rotates inward and the forearm remains in back of and close to the stick. There is a rotation (pronation) of the forearm If the stick were removed at this point, the right arm would look like the outline of a goose, with the head (hand and wrist) moving away from the body.

Both arms work together to swing the stick vertically to the left. The forearm of the lower arm swings outward from the body but remains parallel to the ground at waist level or slightly above. The entire arm pivots around the elbow that stays close (but not frozen) to the left side of the body. At the end of the swing the wrist extends backward as far as possible.

The top hand guides the stick in front of the body by rotation (supination) of the forearm and by as much flexion of the wrist as possible at the end of the swing left.

As the arms and wrists move, the action is aided by a twist of the body in the direction of the swing. As the stick swings to either side the body turns at the waist. Leg action when trotting or running is normal and should be unaffected by upper body movement.

It is generally believed that cradling action should be practiced walking, trotting, and eventually running; however, there are indications that skill is developed more rapidly when cradling is learned at a modest run. Beginners should time the cradle to the run, stepping on the left foot to cradle left and on the right foot to cradle right. Top speed is gained as skill and confidence grow. As running speed increases, the cradle becomes faster and smaller, and as skill and speed blend, the ball will swing about halfway up in the stick and the player will find it is possible to cradle with the stick pulled well across to the left or right of the body to protect it from a tackling player.

Footwork. Footwork is extremely important in lacrosse where so much speed, twisting, turning, dodging, and change of direction is necessary. A player must learn immediately to keep her weight over the balls of her feet and be ever ready to move.

One important footwork maneuver on the field and for passing that deserves special attention is a turn in the opposite direction. When cradling with right hand uppermost, the turn about to the left is quite natural, for the right foot is forward, and the crosse is on the right. The pivot and movement of the crosse to the left are forceful but natural. However, when desiring to change directions to the right, special skill is needed. The left foot must be forward and the stick must be swung left. This is followed by a pivot *on both feet* and a push off the ball of the left foot in conjunction with a strong twist and stick swing over the head to the right. Immediately the player cradles and runs in the new direction.

Picking up the Ball. When the ball is lying or rolling on the ground it must be picked up with the crosse so that passing, running, or shooting can continue. Theoretically, the game is played in the air, but actually many beginners find picking up an important skill, for many balls get free as the result of poor passes and unskilled catches. The player will find situations where the ball is stationary, rolling away from her, or rolling or bouncing straight or diagonally toward her. The grip of the crosse is the same as when cradling.

To pick up a stationary ball, the right-handed player moves the crosse to the left of the body. As the ball is approached, the feet must be arranged so that the right foot is brought up close to the ball, on the side and pointing

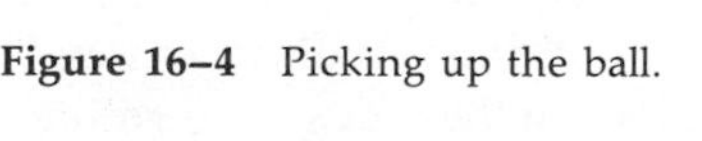

Figure 16–4 Picking up the ball.

forward. (Advanced players should learn to pick up with either foot forward.) The pick-up is done on the move, with the knees, hips, and entire body bent so that the stick can be brought close to the ground. At the moment the stick meets the ball, the hips are twisted to the left. The ball is directly alongside the right foot, and the player's head is over it. A strong bottom hand pushes the stick under the ball. As soon as the ball enters the crosse, cradling begins immediately. The action is usually left, since the body is turned slightly in that direction. The body and crosse should get upright as soon as possible. In approximately three cradles the crosse will be in a vertical position.

When picking up a ball *moving away from* a player, the same techniques of picking up a stationary ball apply, but the player must increase her running speed in order to catch up with the ball. Since it is moving away, she begins the pick-up action closer to the ball and executes the pick-up movements more strongly and sharply.

A ball *moving toward* a player should be considered an "upside down" catch. The player moves to meet the ball and positions herself behind the path of its approach. The crosse is raised to a nearly vertical position close to the left side of the body. The open face of the stick is behind the ball path as the wood across the top of the stick touches the ground. As the ball enters the stick, the hips are twisted left so that the crosse is close to the side and the feet are up to the ball. The crosse "gives" as the ball enters, and cradling action begins in the position of the catch and continues as the player returns to normal running position.

A ball rolling diagonally which is impossible to get behind must be "captured," using techniques as for a catch. The stick is turned behind the line of the oncoming ball as the body is bent low to bring the stick behind the ball. Cradling begins as the player moves on.

Catching. On all catches the player has the widest part of the face behind the ball, and cradling action begins immediately on contact. Always go to meet the ball and increase speed as it is caught. The grip on the stick remains unchanged, with the bottom hand turning the stick and the top hand guiding and positioning the face.

When catching a ball on the right (coming from the left), the stick is brought to the front of the body and the head is pointed slightly at the ball so that on contact the ball rolls into the stick. The ball should run down the stick from the widest part of the head toward the bridge. Cradling action by *both* hands begins immediately.

When catching on the left, at any height, cradle to the left and meet the ball with an open face. Continue cradling action. When a ball is approaching from straight ahead, the catcher must determine whether to open the face to the right or left.

For all catches, feel that the stick is an elongation of the arms and the *top hand* is doing the catching. The player should begin to get the feeling that she is wrapping the stick gently around the ball. The beginner should

Figure 16–5 Catching.

toss up her own ball, both to right and left sides, while walking, trotting, or running. Later she catches balls thrown from the hand or stick. When catching an extremely high or hard thrown ball, some "give" with the ball may be necessary before cradling.

Passing. Passing must be developed so that the ball travels with speed and accuracy. Two basic passes—overarm and underarm—are necessary for beginners, while advanced players often use a sidearm pass.

Overarm Pass. The stick is brought into postion by pulling the right shoulder and stick backward to the right from a left cradle position. These preparatory movements are similar to the action of an overarm throw. The preparatory cradle should be small and close to the head of the player.

With the stick on the right side, the right shoulder back, and the right (top) hand moved slightly behind the top of the stick, the bottom hand and stick end lift up and forward to point to the spot where the ball will be sent. The right arm bends slightly, the elbow drops, and the crosse head dips backward. Simultaneously, the left hand pulls forcefully to bring the hand into the right armpit as the top hand and arm thrust forward and upward. When the pass is completed, the head of the stick is pointing to the spot toward which the ball has been directed.

The length of the throw is determined by the movement of the arms;

Figure 16–6 The overarm pass.

the speed, by the thrust and stretch of the top arm. A pass to the left requires less swing back of the right shoulder; a pass to the right requires a greater twist of body and shoulder to the right.

The *sidearm pass* is similar to the overarm pass except that the path of the crosse in delivery takes the form of a forward and outward arc that is parallel to the ground. The face of the crosse is open and away from the body. The pass moves the head of the stick across the body and the butt end under the right armpit.

Underarm Pass. This is used when an overarm pass is hampered by an opponent. The ball is cradled left and the upper body turned strongly left. The lower hand lifts the butt of the stick so that the head swings toward the ground in a semicircular motion. As the body turns left, the stick is nearly parallel to the body, reaching beyond the back leg. The head of the stick, wood toward the ground, swings by the body and forward as the weight transfers and shoulders come forward. The head of the crosse finishes in front of the body, and the arms are straight. The higher the head of the stick at the finish, the higher and slower the pass.

Shooting for Goal. Effective goal-shooting is the secret to winning lacrosse, for the only way to win is to score. The majority of shots result from passing play around the goal area rather than from a play where one person runs downfield and shoots. Once basic passing skills are mastered, they can become the basis of shots. The overarm, sidearm and underarm shots can be used for effective low corner shots, waistline shots, and high

Figure 16–7 The underarm pass.

corner shots that "float" into the cage. The "around the head shot" is an advanced technique used by a shooter who has almost passed the goal. Her top hand is away from the goal, and the crosse is directed behind her head and forward.

Overarm Shot. The technique of this shot is similar to that of the overarm pass. It is used far from the goal for a bouncing shot, or closer when

Figure 16–8 "Round the head" shot. (From Poindexter, Hally B. W. and Mushier, Carole L.: *Coaching Competitive Team Sports for Girls and Women*. Philadelphia, W. B. Saunders Co., 1973.)

the player is approaching straight or diagonally. With the lever action of the lower hand and forceful guiding of the upper, the head of the stick is brought down with a strong follow-through and points in the direction of the ball's intended path.

Underarm Shot. On this shot the player is usually running with her right side angled toward the goal. As in the underarm pass, there is a big swing to the left. The ball is kept low by a minimal lift of the head of the stick on follow-through. It is an effective shot when the attack has come from behind her defense and moved across with her right side between her opponent and the goal.

Sidearm Shot. This is effective on a short play when the attack has dodged to the right of her defense. As in the sidearm pass, the left elbow is out and away from the body and the right (collar hand) arm is back with elbow close to the right side. The ball is shot as the left arm pulls toward the body and the right arm extends in the direction of delivery.

Draw. The draw is used to begin play at each half and after every goal. It is a skill which must be developed by the center. Opposing players stand with the toes of one foot on the center line. The crosses are held at hip level above and parallel to the center line with the backs of the crosses together, wood to wood, wood to ground, and angle to collar. The rule states that a player's crosse must be between the ball and the goal she is defending. Consequently, if a player holds the collar with the right hand, she faces the goal she is attacking; if the player's left hand is at the collar, her back is to the goal she is attacking. The umpire places the ball between the backs of the crosses, and on signal ("Ready . . . draw") the players lift their crosses up and out as each tries to direct the ball, in the air, to her left attack wing.

Marking. Man-to-man defense in lacrosse makes marking an important skill. A player positions herself so close to her opponent that she is *almost* touching. In this position she must be able to observe the opponent and the ball, but she remains closer to the goal she is defending than her opponent. From this balanced position she should be able to move for a possible interception or to body check.

Body Checking. The object of body checking is to impede the course of an opposing player carrying the ball and force her into a hurried and poorly executed pass or shot. No body contact is permitted. If an interception has not been possible, the player checking places herself between the attacking player and her intended goal. The "checker" is on the balls of her feet with relaxed knees and ankles so that the body weight can change quickly as the attacker moves. The defender travels in the same direction as her opponent, always facing her. Often moving backward, she follows each movement by the attack with her body and stick as she crosse checks, slows the opponent, and forces a change of course or a pass.

Crosse Checking. A player may tap an opponent's crosse in an attempt to dislodge the ball. Players making the check must have the body

Figure 16–9 The draw: *A*, the ball is placed between the backs of the crosses; *B*, the players lift their crosses up and apart so that the ball rises in the air.

Figure 16–10 Preparing to body check. (From Poindexter, Hally B. W. and Mushier, Carole L.: *Coaching Competitive Team Sports for Girls and Women.* Philadelphia, W. B. Saunders Co., 1973.)

and stick well under control to prevent dangerous play. They may not reach over an opponent's shoulder or head or in any way endanger the opponent. Both hands grip the stick firmly as the top hand exerts the force. Beginners should attempt this skill of firm, small tapping movements downward or sideward *only.* More advanced players may up-check, dislodging the ball so that it may be caught in the air.

Dodging. This is the most effective technique an attacking player can use to get around an opponent. A player must not rely on her ability to run past an opponent in a wide arc; she must be determined to run as directly as possible to her objective. A smart opponent will place herself directly in the attack's path; therefore, the attack must camouflage her actions, deceive her opponent, and pass her or risk losing possession of the ball. In essence, a successful dodge is the result of one or more feints or fakes with stick and body movements. The opponent is pulled out of position or off balance and the attack is allowed to accelerate and run past. As the attack pulls away, she protects the ball by cradling on the side away from the opponent. Once free of the threat of checking, she resumes normal cradling.

Advanced players develop a knowledge and "sense" that tells them an opponent has committed herself to "wrong footing" and a dodge may be ac-

Figure 16–11 Body checking an opponent who is attempting to dodge the body checker. (From Poindexter, Hally B. W. and Mushier, Carole L.: *Coaching Competitive Team Sports for Girls and Women.* Philadelphia, W. B. Saunders Co., 1973.)

complished. That is, on a feint by the attack to the right, the opponent pulls to her own left and weights her forward right foot. Similarly, a feint left might draw an opponent to her own right with left foot forward and weighted. A "wrong-footed" opponent can be passed by pulling to the side

Figure 16–12 Dodging.

Figure 16–13 "Wrong footing" by defense following successful feint by attack player. (From Poindexter, Hally B. W. and Mushier, Carole L.: *Coaching Competitive Team Sports for Girls and Women*. Philadelphia, W. B. Saunders Co., 1973.)

away from the feint and accelerating before she can redistribute her weight or turn and begin pursuit.

GAME STRATEGY*

The rules of lacrosse permit each player to roam anywhere on the field; consequently, it is the individual's responsibility to fulfill her duties if a team is to have an effective attack and defense.

The Attack. Attack play is a creative movement initiated by one individual and responded to by the other players. In most games, the ease of play and cooperation give the impression that the team is executing a well rehearsed play. This is not entirely true, for the game's fluidity does not allow for set formations, although basic offensive patterns can be developed. The keys to smooth operation of a game are the result of perfect stickwork, a sense of timing adapted to the speed and skill of teammates, and a total game sense in which all players work to create a space for themselves or team members in which to receive a pass away from opponents.

---

*See Hally B. W. Poindexter and Carole L. Mushier: *Coaching Competitive Team Sports for Girls and Women.* Philadelphia, W. B. Saunders Co., 1973, for more extensive discussion.

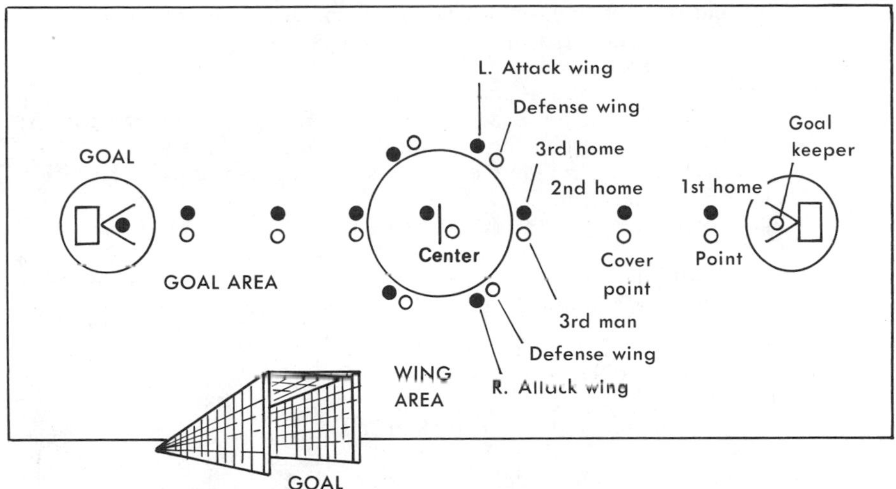

Figure 16–14 Player positioning for center draw.

A defensive player often begins the attack with a pass to an attack wing or center about even with the center circle. The third home often makes the first move to create space, thereby setting a pattern for play.

As an attacking player receives a pass she should start immediately for the goal until checked. A pass to the third home might follow, then to the second home and then to the first home for a shot. For example, the center passes to an attack wing, as she should not penetrate too deeply too often. The second home takes the next pass as the first home makes a quick dash in front of the goal to shoot as she receives the ball. The second home pulls to one side so that the first home will have space in front of the goal.

Beginners will do well to practice a triangular "play" that can be effective anywhere in the field. Player 1 passes to player 2; player 1 dodges her opponent in a path *opposite* to that of the passed ball. Player 2 passes back to player 1, who is moving rapidly for a shot.

An attack player should have the following qualifications:

1. Excellent stickwork with ability to catch, pass, pick up, dodge, and shoot at top speed.

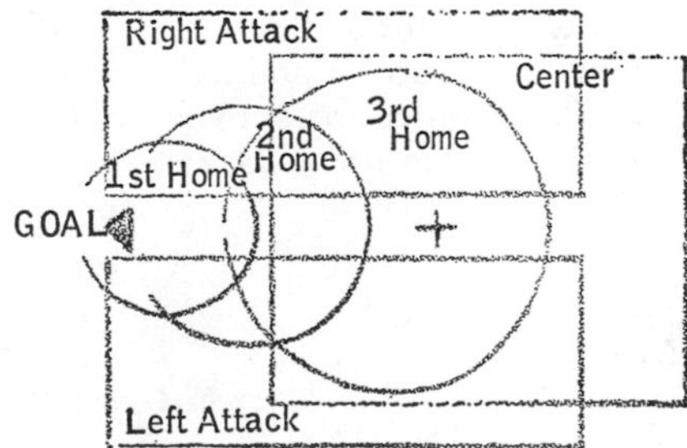

Figure 16–15 Attack players' territory.

2. Speed and sure footwork with quick, neat, and deceptive steps.
3. Alertness and ability to adapt to play of others.
4. Initiative, presence of mind, and coolness.
5. Knowledge of all positions and areas of their play.
6. Ability to draw her defense (as well as herself) from in front of the goal. At least 10 yards should be kept clear for the shooter.
7. A wide variety of skillful shots, especially a long, low, bouncing shot, which is difficult to defend against.
8. Ability to tackle back if the defense gains the ball.

The following diagrams of attacks illustrate how alert players use passing skill and field positioning to score:*

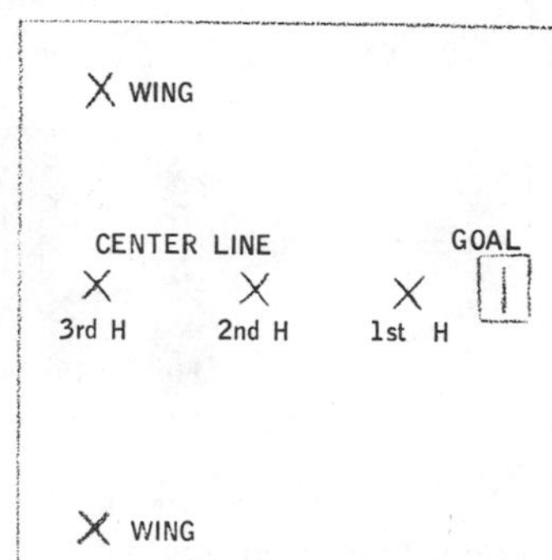

Goal is shot by 3rd H, who cuts in an arc. Play—Wing to 3rd to 2nd to 1st to 3rd. Other possibilities: 1. Wing to 3rd to 2nd to 1st and back to 2nd on "give and go" around defense. 2. Wing to 3rd to 2nd to 1st and a high pass over the defense to the opposite wing, who has run downfield and cut into a scoring position.

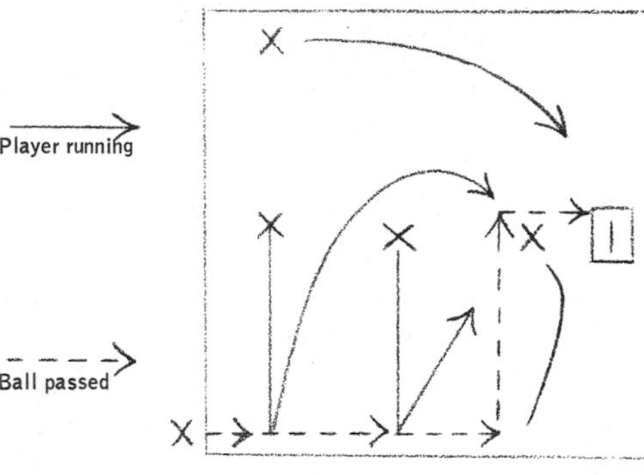

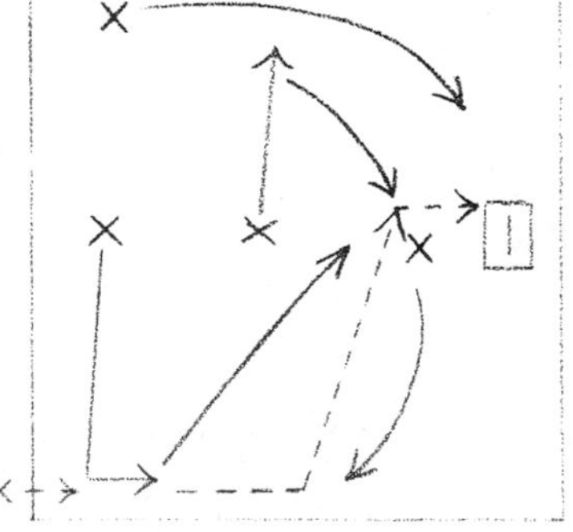

Goal scored by 2nd H, who pulls out to the opposite side of the field from the ball to draw her defense and then cuts into scoring position. Play—Wing to 3rd to 1st to 2nd. Other possibilities: 1. Wing to 3rd to 1st and back to 3rd on "give and go." 2. Wing to 3rd to 1st to opposite wing as in second possibility in previous diagram.

Official Field Hockey-Lacrosse Guide. 1946–48. National Section on Women's Athletics AAHPER, pp. 112–113.

1st H scores goal on pivot shot as she moves from the right of the goal in front of her defense. Play—Wing to 3rd to 2nd to 1st. Other possibility: Wing to 3rd to 2nd to 1st to 3rd on shovel pass.

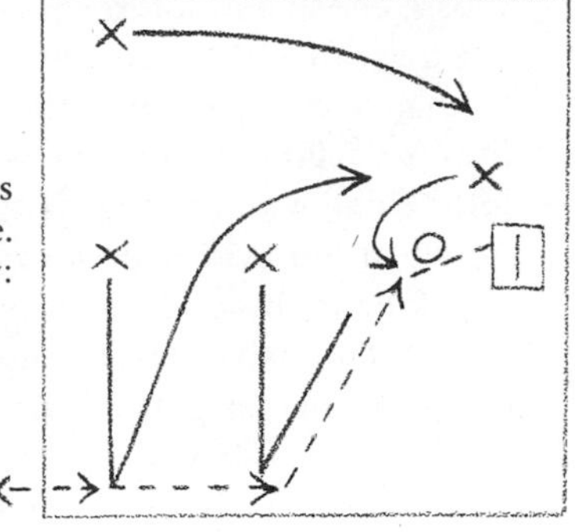

Goal scored by 1st H, who moves to opposite side of field and cuts back in front of defense. Play—Wing to 3rd to 2nd to 1st. Other possibilities: 1. Wing to 3rd to 2nd to 1st and back to 2nd. On this play, 1st blocks out defense and gives pass to 2nd who follows ball to goal. 2. Wing to 3rd to 2nd to 1st to 3rd, who cuts in arc to scoring position.

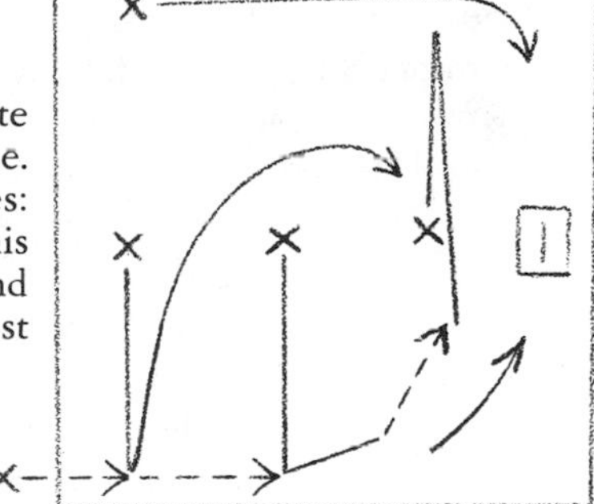

Goal by 1st H on shovel shot from left side of goal. Play—Wing to 3rd to 2nd to 1st. Other possibility: wing to 3rd to 2nd to 1st and back to 2nd or 3rd as 1st screens out defense by moving in front of her. The opposite wing could be used also.

(All these plays may be used on the other side of the field when the ball is brought up there.)

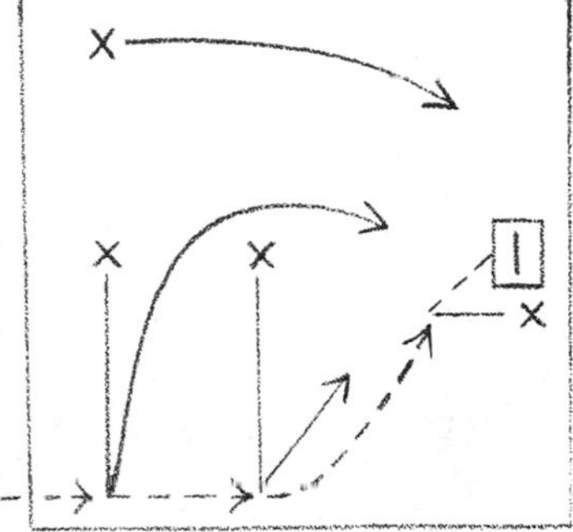

The Defense. The defensive player should have sound stickwork, excellent footwork, and the skills of marking and body and crosse checking. Along with these attributes she should have initiative and be able to anticipate the maneuvers of both the attack and the defense. The objects of defensive play are (1) to prevent opposing players from gaining or keeping possession of the ball and moving it close to the goal and (2) to gain possession of the ball for her own team's attack.

Individual defensive players mark their own opponents, body check, crosse check and intercept the ball whenever possible, pass quickly and accurately, and interchange with each other whenever necessary. Close man-to-man marking enables the defender to have an equal chance of intercepting a pass. Follow the opponent wherever she goes, making certain not to be left behind when she maneuvers and changes directions. The defender stays between the goal and the attacker and follows her crosse with a hope of checking if she dodges, passes, or shoots.

A defensive player makes decisive tackles without hesitation. The defensive player never runs up the field to meet the attack, for this makes the attack's dodge easier. She should be met on an angle so that the defensive player can body check and turn to intercept if the attack attempts a dodge.

When a defensive player intercepts a ball, she passes it if a player is free, or runs upfield until a safe pass is possible. Help fellow defending teammates by getting free for a pass when no attack is available.

Interchange is the process by which a free attacking player is intercepted. It requires cooperation, speed, and timing. The third man often makes the initial tackle if she is in good position. When this occurs, the cover point takes the third home and the nearest defense wing takes the second home. If the third man stays with the third home or is passed, the cover point takes the free attack as she approaches the goal. As the cover point tackles, the defense wing on the opposite side of the field from the free attack moves to a position in which she is able to intercept a pass to the second home or body check the second home should she receive the ball. The point marks the first home. If the point had to tackle the second home, a defense wing would come in to mark the first home.

When interchanging, each player marks closely until the last moment, and then moves definitely. The free defense must get back in the defense as soon as possible by taking the free attack player. The defensive players remain in their interchanged positions until a goal is scored or the defense clears.

DUTIES AND SPECIFIC SKILLS OF EACH PLAYER

First Home should:

1. Have ability to use neat, tight stickwork in a very small space.
2. Be the best shot of all; be skilled in handling catches and converting to shots.
3. Be deceptive in body and cradling action.
4. Tackle goalkeeper out of the crease.
5. Field balls behind the goal.
6. Be able to move quickly for short distances.

Second Home should:

1. Be able to work in small space.
2. Be an excellent shot from every angle, close and long and in small spaces.

3. Have deceptive body movements to divert the cover point.
4. Be able to replace first home, third home and attack wings.
5. Have quick acceleration and speed over moderate distances.

Third Home should:

1. Assist center and attack wings in linking defense and attack.
2. Take a position that will give her working space yet draw the third man from the oncoming player.
3. Be able to rush for goal and pass to a free attack. Move back to position to create space.
4. Be prepared to replace attack wings.
5. Be skilled at triangular pass ("give and go").

Attack Wings should:

1. Have speed and endurance.
2. Serve as links between defense and attack.
3. Always be ready to receive goalkeeper's and defense's clears.
4. Pass quickly and run rapidly toward goal.
5. Pass accurately to their homes.
6. Play out at their wing positions, cutting in when possible, but moving to create spaces.
7. Shoot well at long and close range, particularly a long, bouncing shot.

Center should:

1. Mark center closely to keep her out of shooting range.
2. As a link between defense and attack, go back to help defense bring ball to attackers.
3. Be available to shoot if there is an opening without crowding the homes.
4. Intercept and relay passes.
5. Be ready to interchange with the third home and act as an extra attack.
6. Learn to control draws—preferably to left attack wing.
7. Possess endurance and sustained speed, for she must run from goal to goal.

Defense Wings should:

1. Be exceptionally fast players with stamina.
2. Be both defense and attack players.
3. Always stay between attack wing and goal.
4. Avoid tackling opposing defense wing.
5. Be skilled in the timing and knowledge of defensive interchange.
6. Mark their opponents closely at the draw.

Third Man should:

1. Have speed, good footwork, and knowledge and ability to intercept play.
2. Be discriminating and cautious when going into attack area. Return to mark the third home quickly.
3. Interchange with the center if the center is drawn back.

Cover Point should:

1. Be the pivot of defense interchange.
2. Be excellent at body checking and close stickwork.

3. Be a steady player with skill at anticipating attacking movements.
4. Never hold the ball, but clear to an attack in good position.
5. Act decisively in defensive interchange so wing defenses will know when to come in against the second home.

Point should:

1. Be primarily responsible for closely marking the first home.
2. Be outstanding at body checking and crosse checking.
3. Be able and ready to tackle a player who is free and moving toward goal.
4. Be ready to field balls behind the goal.
5. Be able to start and stop quickly and give long passes.

Goalkeeper should:

1. Have a good, quick eye.
2. Be able to concentrate and anticipate the attack. Find out their strongest shots.
3. Place herself away from the goal line so that she covers every shot with her body or crosse, leaving the smallest possible target area.
4. Be able to catch in limited space in all positions.
5. Be able to give long, accurate passes to her attacks.
6. Avoid clearing in front of the goal.
7. Watch first home in order to intercept passes to her.
8. Never leave the crease unless she has a sure interception, or a spoiling play or has an opportunity to field a ball she is certain to reach before an opponent reaches her.

CLASS ORGANIZATION

A fairly high degree of proficiency in handling the crosse and ball is necessary before this game is enjoyable. To eliminate discouragement at their lack of skill and to minimize rough tactics, players should have some ability to cradle, catch, throw, and pick up before participating in a game. When the outdoor season is limited or more control of beginners is needed, it is desirable to begin skill development indoors.

Prior to each class, footwork drills serve as warm-ups and a constant refresher for improving speed, quick change of direction and mobility. Develop a voice or whistle command system by which players are directed to run forward, backward, or sideways to the left and right. They should be directed to change direction frequently and quickly. Some students must be taught the skills of neat, small, quick steps while maintaining body control.

All lacrosse skills should be learned while moving. Allow the player to move as fast as she can while still maintaining the ball and accomplishing the desired skill. The following drills are designed for indoor use but may be easily transferred to the field:*

---

*Excellent drill and coaching suggestions for beginners and advanced players may be found in DGWS *Selected Field Hockey and Lacrosse Articles,* 1971, *USWLA Technical Material,* and the current NAGWS *Field Hockey-Lacrosse Guide.*

Cradling. After introducing the grip and other basic techniques, ask each player to run and cradle a ball and experiment with her own technique. Soon she should be joined by a partner who will alternate observing and assisting with being assisted in *her* skill development. A circle formation is helpful in teaching players to cradle right, left, or center while maintaining a given rate of speed. Later a player cradles over a predetermined course while marked by an opponent. Gradually increase the number of attacking and defensive players working with a single ball.

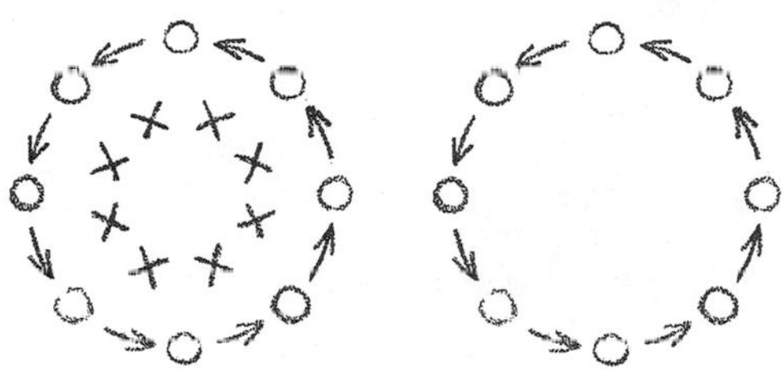

Two common cradling difficulties experienced by beginners may be corrected by the following drills: (1) if players' bottom hands drop below the waist while cradling, seat the players Indian style in a circle and teach the cradle from this position. A second group, running in a larger outside circle, can practice cradling on either side of the body. (2) If the lower elbow of the cradler swings backward without forearm rotation, resulting in a limited cradle and the flinging of the ball out of the crosse, have players stand with their backs against the wall and cradle to the left and right. The knuckles of both hands should touch the wall at the same time.

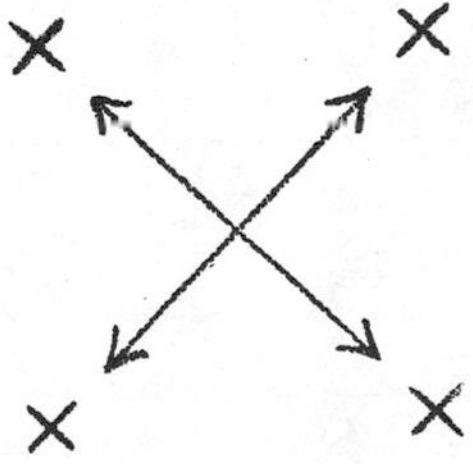

Picking Up and Cradling. (1) Place a ball on the floor about 6 feet ahead of teams of equal number. Each member runs forward, picks up the ball, cradles, turns at the end of the gymnasium, and replaces the ball. (2)

Roll the ball away from self, repeating the same formation. (3) Teammate rolls the ball to a player who picks it up, cradles, and returns.

Tossing and Catching. (1) Players run and cradle, tossing the ball up in front and ahead. (2) With players in single file, the teacher throws the ball to each player. Each player catches, cradles, and runs around the gymnasium. (3) Four players, one at each corner of the gymnasium, begin cradling on signal and then throw to the person diagonally opposite. She catches and returns the throw. Practice continues with the walk increasing to a trot and then to a run.

Shooting. Hang gymnasium mats on the wall or move portable goal inside. Players are in two lines—one to the front and one to the side. They alternately approach, shoot, and move to the other line.

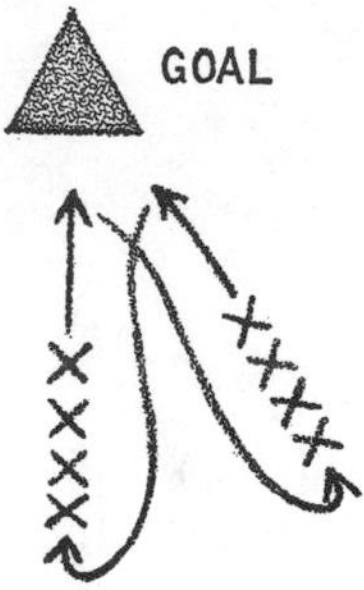

Dodging and Body Checking. Four players are on the floor. Each couple has half of the floor. One partner body checks the length of the floor as the other partner attempts to dodge. Reverse actions as the couples return to starting position.

Waiting turn

3 4

1 2

TEACHING PROGRESSION

The following unit is designed for beginners in 50 minute periods. Throughout the unit, emphasis should be given to footwork and skill drills that approximate a game situation.

Lesson I

1. Nature and purpose of the game
2. Facilities and equipment
3. Grip
4. Cradle

Lesson II

1. Review of cradle
2. Picking up
3. Overarm throw

Lesson III

1. Extensive review of cradle, pick-up, overarm throw
2. Catching
3. Game of keep away

Lesson IV

1. Review of skills
2. Simulated game situation on the field
3. Short discussion of position and rules

Lesson V

1. Review
2. Dodging and body checking
3. Game situation

Lesson VI

1. Marking
2. Full game situation (stress skill and strategy of stand, throw-in, and free position)

Lesson VII

1. Draw
2. Shooting
3. Goalkeeping

Lesson VIII

1. Game
2. Strategy of attack and defense
3. Crosse checking (introduce crosse checking only if players have confidence in the control of their crosses and cradle)

Lesson IX

1. Practical evaluation through tournament play

Lesson X

1. Written evaluation
2. Complete tournament

SKILL DIFFICULTIES AND THEIR CORRECTION

Grip

Difficulty	*Correction*
a. Collar hand slides down, resulting in poorly balanced crosse and lack of control and accuracy	a. Review grip, emphasizing the importance of the top hand at the collar for stick control
b. Failure to place "V" of right hand between stick and player's face when stick is in vertical position, thereby making cradling difficult	b. Review entire procedure for proper placement of hands

Cradling

Difficulty	*Correction*
a. Arms are stiff and shoulders immobile, preventing a smooth running style	a. Have the student overswing and exaggerate arm movements until the shoulders relax. Later suggest practice with back against the wall to get proper arm movement

b. Bottom hand grip slips to the front so the wrist cannot extend enough to turn the stick head; and, as a result, the ball falls	b. Review grip and emphasize the importance of the butt hand in controlling crosse movement
c. Lower hand drops below wrist level; lower arm becomes frozen to the side	c. Experience a "full" swing with few restrictions while stretching away from an opponent. Sit on the floor, forcing the lower hand up while cradling
d. Elbow of lower arm pushes forward, lowering the crosse or altering the cradle arm so that ball flies from the crosse	d. Back to a wall and cradle to left and right. The knuckles of both hands should touch the wall simultaneously. Crosse should not touch the wall
e. Failure to twist and pull stick away from opponent when body checked	e. Practice twisting from the waist, putting the right or left shoulder forward, and moving the butt hand around to right or left so swing continues in a rhythmical pattern. Practice small cradling action on right and left

Pick-up

Difficulty	*Correction*
a. Player fails to bend to pick up the ball	a. Stress flexion in the knees and body lowering
b. Player scoops the ball with butt hand high so that it rolls out as player rises or head of stick catches on the ground	b. Bend the knees, get under the ball with knuckles of the lower hand brushing the ground, and begin cradling immediately
c. Loss of speed and momentum as the pick-up is completed, leaving the crosse and player vulnerable to a body check	c. Accelerate on the pick-up rather than slowing down
d. Stick is too flat to catch ball rolling toward a player	d. Remind the student this pick-up is like an upside down catch in which the crosse head is down on contact. Ball enters crosse opposite the forward foot and is cradled immediately

Catching

Difficulty	Correction
a. Grip changes when catching, thus hands are in poor position for cradling or passing	a. Insist that beginner meet the ball with the movement of her body rather than hands. Run to a position for a proper catch
b. Ball is batted as it is caught, as the result of poor reach and initiation of the cradle too early	b. *Reach* for the ball. Imagine the crosse is an extension of the catching hand and the open face the palm of the hand
c. Failure to cradle or pass after catching	c. In drills, the catch should be followed immediately by a pass or by cradling—both while running

Passing and Shooting

Difficulty	Correction
a. Pushing with the upper arm, shoulder and top hand, resulting in little power and accuracy	a. Practice overarm softball throw mimetically. Progress to throw with crosse held in upper hand only. Add butt hand for direction and power
b. Consistently inaccurate passes	b. Teacher should explain that all accurate passes must run along the wood and off at the angle. The whole stick directs flight

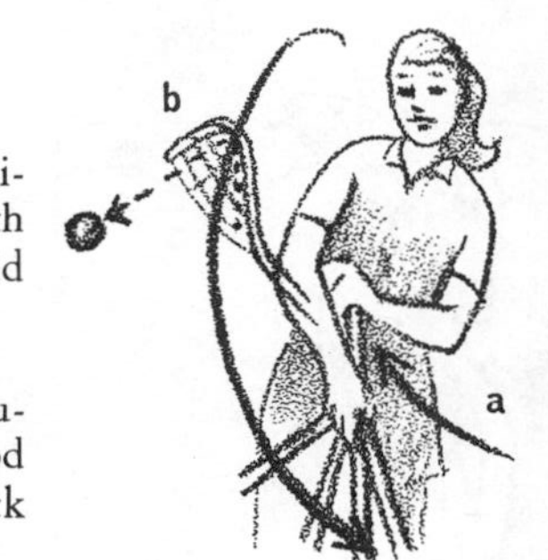

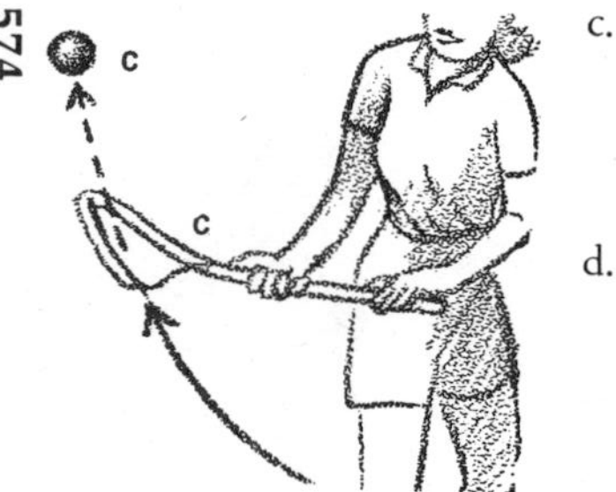

c. Losing the ball on the take-back due to a wide, sweeping, preparatory movement	c. Stress control of the crosse with the lower hand. Stand several feet in front of a wall so the take-back is limited
d. High, slow, ineffective underarm passes caused by high finish of the crosse head	d. Student should experiment with a lower finish and move forward with the entire body, rather than upward, follow-through

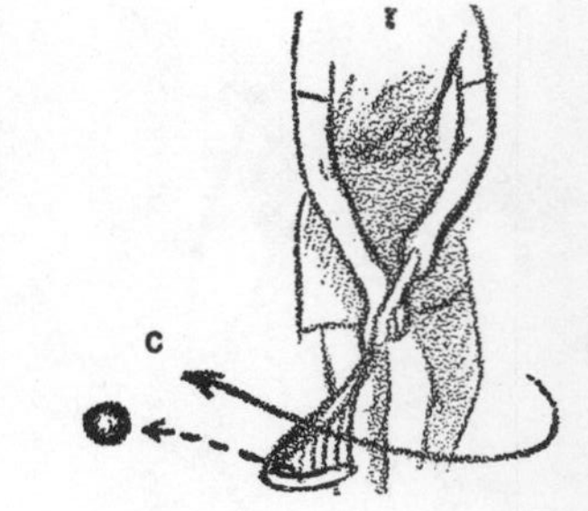

Marking, Body Checking, and Crosse Checking

Difficulty	*Correction*
a. Failure to move effectively with an opponent	a. Practice guarding techniques of basketball, using neat, small, agile steps. Pick up a crosse and continue the same technique until body movement becomes more natural and easy, then *follow the opponent's crosse with your own* as body stays between the goal and opponent
b. Slipping top hand down to extend for a crosse check often results in a foul or dangerous hit	b. Control is important. Teacher can demonstrate that a player off balance or unable to control her crosse is ineffective in a pick-up, run, and pass, even if she dislodges the ball with a crosse check

EVALUATING THE RESULTS

AAHPER Lacrosse Skills Tests offer varied tests of individual skills with test norms available for girls in grades 5 through 12. The tests are intended to measure the execution of fundamental skills. They are not intended to be predictive of total playing ability, therefore, they should be regarded as practice tests intended to be used by players as a means of improving fundamental game skills. These tests are the first comprehensive lacrosse tests to receive wide circulation.

General skills in lacrosse can be measured, but the individual's ability as a team member is difficult to evaluate. The following suggestions are helpful in understanding the total class progress:

1. Keep progress charts to record scores on skills tests including cradling, pick ups, catching, passing, shooting, marking, and dodging.
2. Use rating scales, by teacher and pupils, to evaluate an individual's team ability, understanding, and skill as an offensive and defensive player.
3. Give written tests to evaluate knowledge of rules, officiating, and strategy.
4. Use an incident chart to record the skills successfully performed and the errors committed during a game.

TERMINOLOGY

Body checking—Placing one's body between an opponent and her objective so that the opponent's progress is impeded.

Cradling—The action of the body and the rhythmical swing of the crosse that keeps the ball under control in the netting.

Crease—A circle 8½ feet in radius surrounding each goal. It serves as a restraining line when shooting for a goal.

Crosse checking—Controlled tapping of the crosse of an opponent in an attempt to dislodge the ball.

Cutting—Movement into a specific location to receive a pass.

Dodging—Getting past an opponent while maintaining possession of the ball.

Draw—The method of beginning play between opposing players at each half and after each goal.

Free position—A position awarded a player when an opponent has fouled. The player is given the ball in her crosse and may run, shoot, or pass. All other players must be at least 5 yards away.

Holding down—Holding an opponent's crosse by one's own crosse—either in the air or on the ground. Unlike legal crosse checking, holding is a foul.

Marking—Guarding an opponent by staying close by and moving as she moves.

Stand—A stationary position all players must hold, unless otherwise directed by the umpire, when the umpire suspends play.

Stick—Another name for the crosse.

Stickwork—Any and all techniques of controlling the ball and stick.

Tackle—Approaching an opponent for the purpose of body checking or crosse checking to take the ball or impede progress.

Throw-in—Putting the ball in play by having the umpire throw it between opposing players. Used when both players were equidistant from the ball as it went out of bounds, and following a double foul.

DISCUSSION QUESTIONS

1. Explain defense interchange. What happens when the third home is attacking free and unmarked?
2. What skills must a wing attack possess? What of the cover point and second home?
3. Describe the parts of the crosse. How do you take care of this stick?
4. Trace the historical development of the game of lacrosse.

SELECTED AUDIOVISUAL AIDS

Lacrosse Film Loops 1961. (8 mm. & 16 mm., 9 loops with notes, silent, b & w.) Guy Butler, Harbledown, Little Hadham, Herefordshire, England.

Lacrosse, Lacrosse. (16 mm., 18 min., sound, color.) USWLA Association. Sterling Films, 600 Grand Avenue, Ridgefield, New Jersey, 07657. (Purchase and rental)

Let's Play Lacrosse, 1968. (16 mm., 23 min., sound, color.) USWLA Association. Sterling Films, 600 Grand Avenue, Ridgefield, New Jersey 07657. (Purchase and rental)

USWLA Technical Materials. (Bulletin board materials, 21 bulletins including skills and coaching notes.) Available from the Technical Materials Chairman, USWLA (see current NAGWS *Guide*).

SUGGESTED READINGS

Boyd, Margaret: *Lacrosse Playing and Coaching.* Rev. ed. Nicholas Kay Ltd., London, 1971.

Delano, Anne Lee: *Lacrosse for Girls and Women.* Dubuque, Iowa, Wm. C. Brown Co., 1970.

NAGWS. *Field Hockey-Lacrosse Guide.* Washington, D.C., AAHPER, Published every 2 years.

Newhof, Carol (ed.): *Selected Field Hockey-Lacrosse Articles.* AAHPER, DGWS, 1201 16th Street, N.W., Washington 6, D.C., 1955.

Poindexter, Hally B. W. and Mushier, Carole L.: *Coaching Competitive Team, Sports for Girls and Women.* Philadelphia, W. B. Saunders Co., 1973.

Reeson, Joan: *Know the Game—Lacrosse.* Write Gertrude Hooper, 242 Highland St., Milton, Massachusetts 02186.

Stewart, Harriet (ed.): *Selected Field Hockey and Lacrosse Articles.* AAHPER, DGWS, 1201 16th Street, N.W., Washington, D.C., 1971.

PERIODICALS

Crosse Checks. Yearly publication of the United States Women's Lacrosse Association. Available from Second Vice President USWLA (see current NAGWS *Guide*).

Lacrosse. Published several times yearly by All-England Ladies Lacrosse Association. Write Gertrude Hooper, 242 Highland Street, Milton, Massachusetts 02186.

CHAPTER 17

SOCCER, SPEEDBALL, AND SPEED-A-WAY

Soccer. Since the origin of soccer is attributed to such widely separated places as Ireland, Greece, England, and Rome, it is likely that the game developed in several localities at about the same time. The ancient sport of *Harpastrum*, in which a crudely shaped ball was either hit with the hands or kicked, later became *feetballe*, a rough and rugged kicking game played as a mob sport. An inflated animal bladder covered with leather was moved by sheer force through alleys and streets and out into vacant fields between goals often located miles apart. Even though many English monarchs, including Edward II, Elizabeth I, and James I, passed edicts forbidding their subjects to play this bloody, brawling sport because of the many complaints of damaged property from shopkeepers, the game somehow survived through the centuries. The nobility looked down upon this degrading contest as being for the lowly, rugged commoners. Therefore, it is ironic that it was an Englishman from the upper class, J. C. Thring, who drew up the rules and gave the game respectability. He made soccer safer to play and introduced it into the private schools and adult clubs of England.

Even though the game was played in America during early colonial times and in an intercollegiate match for men between Princeton and Rutgers as early as 1869, it did not gain popularity until after World War I. A modified game for women was first introduced at Bryn Mawr College in 1919, and the first official women's rules appeared in the form of modified men's rules in 1927. Soccer is a popular instructional and intramural sport, and women's participation is increasing in interscholastic and intercollegiate competition. As an international game soccer has no equal, for it is the national sport of 53 countries. Truly, the sun never sets on the game of soccer.

Speedball. Speedball was created by Elmer D. Mitchell at the University of Michigan in 1921 for use in the men's intramural program. Although girls and women started playing the game shortly thereafter, it was not until 1930 that the National Section on Women's Athletics (now NAGWS) made the necessary rule changes which popularized the game and tailored it to the specific needs of women instructors and students.

Speed-a-way. Speed-a-way,* was copyrighted in 1950 by Marjorie A. Larsen as an uncomplicated lead-up game to hockey. It utilizes many of the skills of speedball and serves a need expressed by many girls—to play a game that includes basic football skills.

NATURE AND PURPOSE OF THE GAMES

Soccer, speedball, and speed-a-way are active running, kicking, and passing field games played by two teams of 11 players each. Speedball and speed-a-way combine basketball passing skills with the drop kick of football and the dribble of soccer. Although scoring methods differ, the object of the games is to advance the ball down a field 100 yards long and 60 yards wide and score. The team with the larger score at the end of playing time is declared the winner. The five forward line players—center forward, right and left inners, and right and left wings—are primarily responsible for scoring. The duties of the left, center, and right halfbacks include guarding their opponents and passing the ball to their forwards, as well as scoring themselves. The left and right fullbacks have duties similar to those of the halfbacks except that they play a more vital defensive role. The goalkeeper's primary task is to prevent the opposing team from scoring.

SIMPLIFIED RULES AND SCORING**

Rules Basic to All Games

1. A team consists of 11 players. Any number of substitutes may enter or reenter the game unless disqualified.
2. A game is made up of four 8 minute quarters. There is a 2 minute rest period between quarters and a 10 minute rest between halves.
3. The winner of the toss has the choice of either taking the kick-off or selecting the goal her team defends.
4. Play is started with a place kick by the center forward. On a kick-off, the ball must travel at least the distance of its circumference into opponent's territory. Thereafter, the team scored against kicks off, except at the beginning of each quarter, when teams alternate kick-offs. Goals are changed at half time.

---

*For official rules and film write Marjorie Larsen, 1754 Middlefield Road, Stockton, California.

**For complete rules and scoring see the current NAGWS *Soccer-Speedball Flag Football Guide.*

Rules for Soccer

1. The ball may be volleyed, blocked, trapped, kicked, dribbled, and passed with the feet, body, and head. Only the goalkeeper (in the penalty area) may use her hands.
2. A player is *off-side* when she is ahead of the ball in the opponent's half of the field and nearer to the goal than any three opponents.
3. A *throw-in* is taken when the ball is kicked over the sideline by a member of the opposing team.
4. A *corner kick* is awarded an attacking player when the ball is sent out of bounds over the endline outside the goal posts or over the crossbar by a defending player. A place kick from the endline is made from a point 5 yards from the nearer corner.
5. A *defense kick* is taken by a defending player when any member of the attacking team causes the ball to go over the endline outside the goal posts or over the crossbar. The ball is place kicked from any point on the quarter circle.
6. A *roll-in* results when two opponents cause the ball to go wholly over the side or goal line outside the goal posts. The umpire rolls the ball between the opponents as they stand 5 yards in and directly opposite the point where the ball left the field. If the cause of the roll-in occurs within 5 yards of the goal, the roll-in is taken 5 yards from the goal.
7. A *free kick* is awarded to opponents for a foul or rule infringement. It is a place kick taken at the spot of the infringement. A direct free kick (one from which a goal may be scored directly) is awarded for a foul committed outside the penalty area by either team, a foul committed by the attacking team inside the penalty area, and a foul resulting in player disqualification. An indirect free kick is awarded to opponents when a team improperly takes a corner kick, kick-off, penalty kick, defense kick, free kick, or roll-in. A free kick is also awarded for infringement of goalkeeper's privileges and for off-side.
8. A *penalty kick* is awarded the attacking team from the penalty kick mark when the defending team commits a foul or rule infringement within the penalty area.
9. A *foul* is called when a player trips, kicks, strikes, holds, pushes, or jumps at an opponent, uses unnecessary roughness, or handles the ball.
10. A *field goal* is scored when the ball passes over the endline between the goal posts and under the cross bar. A field goal scores 2 points. A penalty goal scores 1 point.

Rules for Speedball

1. A ball may be advanced with the feet, head, or body when it is a ground ball. An aerial ball may be air dribbled, passed, punted, drop-kicked, volleyed, blocked or headed. Ground balls may be converted to aerial balls by a lift-up to oneself or another player. Aerial balls become ground balls as soon as they touch the ground.
2. Balls going out of bounds over the sideline are put back in play by a throw-in by an opposing team member opposite the spot where the ball went out. When the ball is sent out of bounds over the endline, it is put back in play by an opposing team member by a punt, place kick, drop kick, or throw-in opposite the spot on the goal line where the ball went out.
3. A *tie ball* results when two opponents catch the ball at the same time, cause it to go out of bounds, or commit a double foul. The umpire tosses up the ball

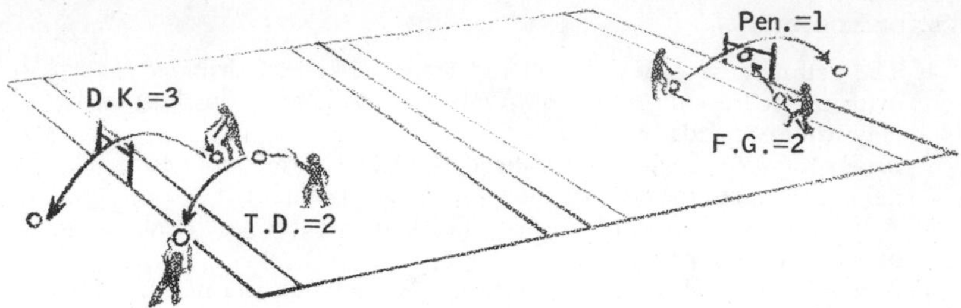

Figure 17–1 Methods of scoring in speedball.

between the players at the point of infraction or 5 yards from the boundary on out-of-bounds balls.

4. A *free kick* is awarded to an opponent when a foul is committed by a player outside her penalty area during the play of a ground ball. A free throw is awarded if the foul was made during play of an aerial ball.
5. A *penalty kick* (drop kick behind penalty kick mark) is given to an attack player when the defense commits a team foul or an individual foul within its own penalty area or behind the goal line.
6. The following are individual fouls: blocking, charging, drop kicking for goal, or attempting a forward pass for touchdown within the penalty area; delaying the game; touching a ground ball with hands or arms; holding, tripping, pushing or tagging an opponent; snatching a ball from an opponent; unnecessary roughness; threatening the eyes of a player; air dribbling more than once; traveling with the ball and holding the ball more than 5 seconds on the field or out of bounds; and taking more than 10 seconds for a penalty kick.
   Team fouls are as follows: taking more than three time-outs, having more than 11 players on the field, and making illegal substitutions.
7. The methods and point values given for scoring in speedball are as follows:
   Field goal—2 points, made when the ball is advanced across the goal line between the goal posts and under the crossbar.
   Touchdown—2 points, made when the ball is thrown by an attack player outside the penalty area in the field of play and is caught by a teammate behind the opponent's goal line excepting the area between the goal posts.
   Drop kick—3 points, made by dropping the ball and kicking it after it strikes the ground; it must be kicked outside the penalty area, and it must pass over the crossbar and between the goal uprights.
   Penalty kick—1 point, made by drop kicking the ball from behind the penalty kick mark; the ball must pass between the uprights and over the crossbar.
   A goal cannot be scored directly from a kick-off, throw-in, or a ball caught directly from a toss-up play.

Rules for Speed-a-way

1. Players may advance to any point on the field. There is no offsides rule.
2. After a kick-off, a *ground ball* may be advanced by dribbling, kicking, shouldering, or otherwise volleying with the body, or by a lift-up.
3. An *aerial ball* is one caught on the fly or after one bounce, if kicked. It may be advanced by a pass, run, punt, drop kick, or volley.
4. Any rule infringement is considered a foul. Fouls result when:
   a. Any player except the goalkeeper picks up a ground ball.
   b. A player holds an aerial ball longer than 3 seconds without passing or running.

c. A player tags an opponent who is receiving or who has possession of a ball before 3 seconds elapse.
d. Two or more players guard an opponent in possession of the ball so that she cannot successfully run, pass, kick, or otherwise play the ball.
e. A player trips, shoves, pushes, charges, or strikes an opponent. Only an opponent running with the ball may be tagged.
f. A player knocks or snatches a ball from an opponent's hands; a player kicks an opponent or kicks the ball dangerously into an opponent.
g. A player stands closer than 5 yards to a player taking a penalty corner, throw-in, or a free kick.
h. A player executing a throw-in or a penalty kick plays the ball again before it is played by another person.
i. A player receiving a ball from a penalty corner or from a throw-in taken between the goal line and the 25 yard line passes or runs for a touchdown. There must be three passes before a touchdown is scored.
j. A player scores directly from a free kick, toss-up or throw-in.

5. Penalties for fouls vary according to the place of the foul and the player fouled.
   a. When any foul occurs outside the striking circle, a free kick is awarded an opponent at the spot of the infringement.
   b. When a foul by a member of the attacking team occurs in the striking circle, a free kick is awarded the defending team at any point inside the circle.
   c. When the defending team fouls in the circle, the attacking team is awarded a penalty corner.
   d. A double foul results in a toss-up between the two offenders on the spot unless it is within 5 yards of the goal or sidelines. In such a case, it is brought to a place opposite the spot of the foul and 5 yards from the side or end line.
   e. A tie ball results in a toss-up at the point of the tie, if more than 5 yards from goal or side lines. Otherwise it is moved 5 yards in from the line.
6. The following rules govern *out-of-bounds balls:*
   a. Balls passing over the sidelines are thrown in by an opponent of the player last touching the ball. On a throw-in the player stands outside the sideline and throws in any manner. The ball may be played as a ground or aerial ball.
   b. Balls sent over the end line outside the goal posts (and not scoring) by either attacker or defender shall be awarded to an opponent at a point on the endline, 15 yards from the nearer goal post, where the circle bisects the endline. The person may put the ball into play by a throw-in, punt, place kick, or drop kick.
   c. When a forward pass is intercepted by a defensive player behind the goal, the defending team is awarded an endline out of bounds.
   d. If the ball is thrown between the goal posts, out-of-bounds rules are enforced.
   e. If the ball goes out of bounds off the bodies or hands of two opponents, the ball is tossed up at a point 5 yards from the sideline or endline opposite the spot where the ball went out.
   f. If a drop kick initiated *outside* the circle passes below the goal crossbar, out-of-bounds rules apply.
7. The methods and point values given for scoring in speed-a-way are as follows:

   Field goal—3 points, scored when an attacking player kicks a ground ball or executes a drop kick from within the striking circle so that the ball travels across the goal line between the goal posts and beneath the crossbar.

Touchdown – 2 points, scored by a player running across the goal line outside of the goal cage area. Also scored by completion of a forward pass from an attacking player in the field to a teammate behind the goal line, but *not* behind the goal cage or post area.
Optional scoring rule – when soccer, speedball or football goal posts are used, and the crossbar is higher than that used in hockey, a drop kick from any place on the field that passes over the crossbar and between the goal posts scores 4 points.

NEEDED FACILITIES AND EQUIPMENT

The field should be a level, grassy area no larger than 100 yards in length and 60 yards in width. The minimum for high school play is 80 by 40 yards. The field is divided by a *halfway line*, and the center of this line is marked. For soccer and speedball, a restraining line is laid five yards on each side and parallel to the center line.

Specific Soccer Markings. The goal posts are 6 yards apart and joined by a crossbar that is 8 feet above the ground. Fifteen yards in front of

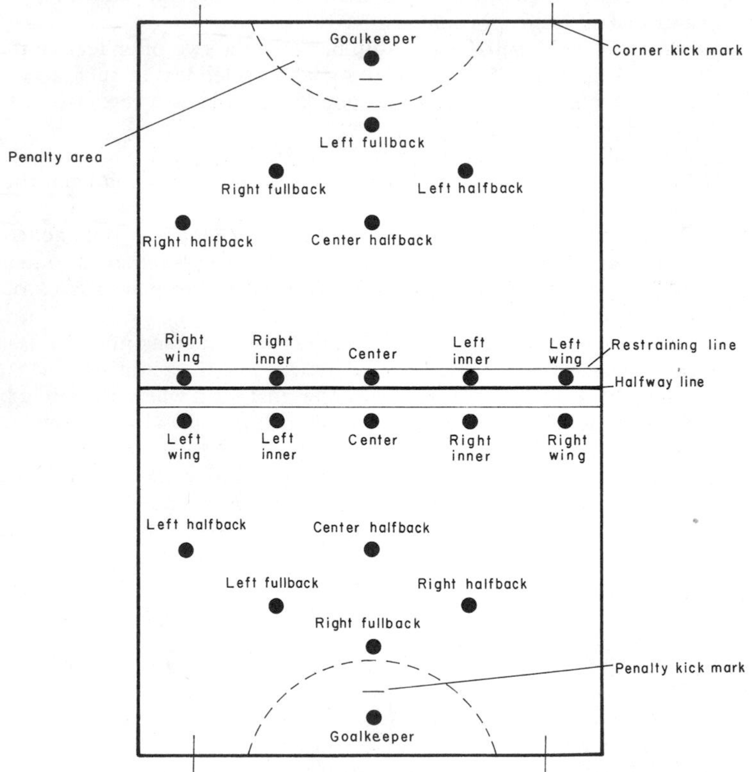

Soccer field and offensive and defensive playing positions on kickoff.

each goal line, a line 4 yards long runs parallel to the goal. From this line, quarter circles are drawn which measure 15 yards in radius from a point 1 yard inside the goal post on the goal line. The penalty area includes the lines and space in front of each goal made by these quarter circles. The penalty kick mark is a line 2 feet long, parallel to the goal line, and 12 yards from the center of the goal. Corner kick marks are lines 3 feet long that are marked across goal lines at a point 5 yards from each corner (Figure 17–1).

Specific Speedball Markings. A line, called the five-yard line, is drawn across each end of the field at a point 5 yards from each goal line (Figure 17–2). The space enclosed by the goal line, sidelines, and five-yard line is called the penalty area. Penalty kick marks are the same as the soccer markings. The distance between the goal posts and the height of the crossbar are the same as for soccer, but the posts are 20 feet high.

Specific Speed-a-way Markings. The field is divided into four parts by the center line and two lines 25 yards from the end lines. Five yards inside and parallel to the sidelines is a broken line running the length of the field. The space between the five-yard line and the sideline is called the alley.

A striking circle is marked at both ends of the field. The circle includes the area described by a 4 yard line parallel to the goal line and 15 yards from it. Using the goal posts as the center, two quarter circles are drawn from the

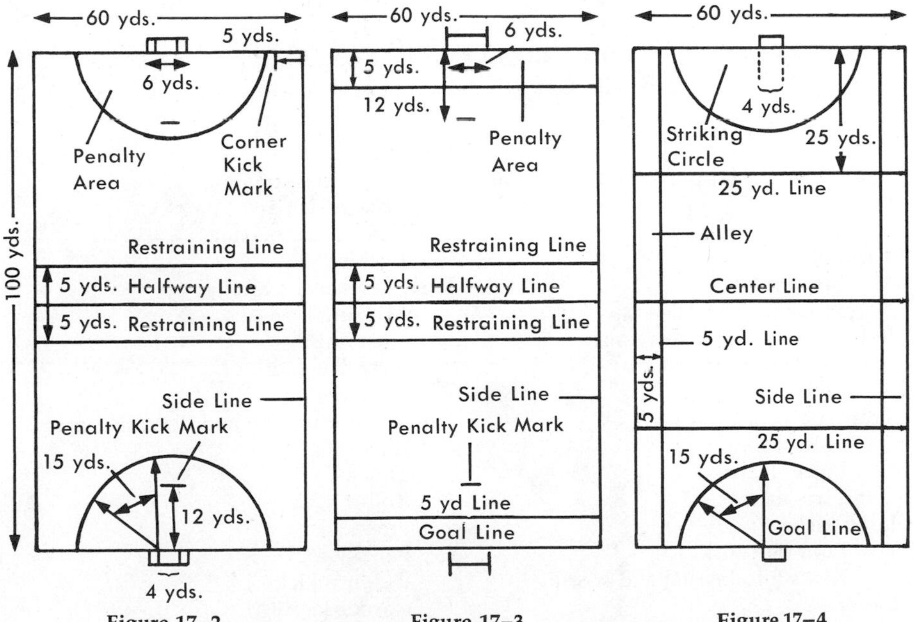

Figure 17–2 Figure 17–3 Figure 17–4

Figure 17–2 Soccer field and markings.
Figure 17–3 Speedball field and markings.
Figure 17–4 Speed-a-way field and markings.

ends of the 4 yard line to a point 15 yards from the goal posts on both sides (Figure 17–3).

At the center of each goal line is a goal 4 yards wide. Two 7 foot goal posts, 4 yards apart and joined by a crossbar 7 feet from the ground, mark the goal mouth. Four feet behind the goal, other posts and crossbars are joined to the goal posts and covered with wire or netting.

Basic Equipment. The ball should be a regulation leather-covered soccer ball measuring 27 to 28 inches in circumference. Rubber-covered balls serve on humid days on damp ground. An official speed-a-way ball of different texture and greater rebound ability is available, although a soccer ball is acceptable. Balls should be thoroughly dried and then stored after use.

The seasonal activity costume of shorts and shirts, tunics, or warm-up suits is appropriate dress. Teams should wear distinguishing colors. Smooth soled shoes with canvas or leather tops are suitable for beginners, with rubber cleated soccer or hockey shoes preferred by more advanced players. Shin guards are helpful for protection and confidence for beginners.

Cloth strips tucked in the belt of each player may be a helpful teaching aid for beginners in speed-a-way. To avoid the shoving that often comes in tagging a player, the one tagging must snatch the streamer of the ball carrier.

TEACHING UNITS

Suggested topics for a *soccer unit* include the following materials. The order of presentation will vary with the age and readiness of each group.

Beginners

- Short history and purpose of the game
- Safety rules
- Dribbling
- Tackles
  - Straight on
  - Hook
- Passing (long, short, diagonal)
  - Inside of foot
  - Outside of foot
- Trapping
  - Sole of foot
  - Lower-leg trap
  - Two-leg trap
- Long kicks
  - Punt (instep kick)
  - Kicks for clearing and scoring
- Dodging
- Elementary volleys
  - Knee
  - Shoulder and hip
  - Heading
- Basic offensive strategy
  - Triangular pass
  - Directional passing
  - Rushing
- Basic defensive strategy
  - Marking
  - Covering
  - Interchanging
  - Intercepting
- Situational offensive and defensive play
  - Kick-off
  - Throw-in
  - Roll-in
  - Free kicks
  - Penalty kick
  - Defense kick
  - Corner kick
- Position play
  - Selected positions (forwards, backs, etc.)
  - Elementary goalkeeping skills
- Evaluation (skill and knowledge tests)

Advanced

Review of fundamental skills
Review basic strategy
Advanced passes
- Heel pass
- Sole of foot

Pivot instep kick
Variations of trapping
- Inside of thigh

Blocking with chest, thighs, and abdomen
Split tackle
Feinting and evading
Volley and half volley kicks
Advanced game strategy
Advanced situational play
- Penalty kick
- Defense kick

Techniques of officiating
Skill and knowledge evaluation

Rainy Day Material

Movies and filmstrips
Inside novelty games
Indoor practice (trapping, feinting, blocking, tackling)
Rules
Chalk-board strategy
Officiating techniques

Suggested topics for a unit in *speedball* include:

Beginners

Brief history, nature, and purpose of the game
Safety rules
Soccer skills
- Dribbling
- Instep kick
- Passing
- Kicking with the inside and outside of the foot
- Punting
- Tackling
- Body traps and blocks
- Sole-of-foot, one-leg, two-leg trap
- Evading an opponent
- Kicking for a goal
- Drop kick

Basketball skills
- Catching and passing (chest, underhand, one-hand, shoulder)
- Air dribble
- Pivoting
- Guarding

Speedball skills
- Pick-up with one foot on a moving ball, on a stationary ball, with two feet, with one foot over a moving ball
- Lifting the ball up to pass
- Guarding

Rules
Strategy
Situational play
Evaluation

Advanced

Review of the nature and purpose of the game
Review of all fundamental skills
Advanced soccer skills
Advanced basketball skills
Advanced speedball skills
Variations of body traps and blocks
Variations of the leg trap
Position play
Advanced strategy
Officiating
Evaluation

Speed-a-way was designed to be played without extensive practice of techniques or study of rules. As played, it is a passing and running game, rather than a kicking game, and little emphasis is needed on advance techniques of soccer. The suggested unit varies somewhat from the usual pattern. The unit for *beginners* is designed for those who have little background in soccer, speedball, or basketball; the advanced unit assumes players have some background in hockey, soccer, speedball, and basketball.

Beginners

Nature and purpose of the game
Basic body control: running, starting, stopping, dodging, evading
Ball handling skills: guarding, catching, passing
Scoring techniques: running, kicking
Drop kick; punting
Playing ground balls
Playing aerial balls
The running game
  Tagging (safety factors)
Rules
Strategy (beginning)
Evaluation

Advanced

Review of nature and purpose
Review of advanced basketball skills
Review of advanced soccer skills
Intensive review of selected speedball skills
Stress development of accuracy and distance of the punt and the drop kick
Situational plays
Running strategy
Officiating
Evaluation

SOCCER FUNDAMENTALS

Soccer fundamentals include skills necessary for controlling, moving, and gaining the ball, as well as scoring. The techniques involved are often referred to as ball-handling skills, although the goalkeeper is the only player who may actually handle the ball. Soccer requires endurance and balance, and a conscientious player should strive to develop stamina, speed, and skill through a planned conditioning program.

Advancing the Ball with the Feet. Kicking is the basic technique for moving the ball and for passing and shooting for goals. It is also the primary defense technique of the goalkeeper. Players should strive to become versatile in the use of both feet in as many kicking skills as possible.

Instep Kick. The instep kick is basic to all kicking skills. It is used on both moving and stationary balls as a short pass, a long kick, or a shot for goal. It is generally preceded by several running steps. The nonkicking foot

Figure 17–5 The instep kick.

Figure 17–6 The pivot instep kick.

supports the body weight slightly behind the ball. As the kicking leg swings backward from the hip, the knee bends and the toe points toward the ground. The arms are away from the body and the body is inclined forward for balance. Watch the ball constantly. The leg swings forward, and as the knee comes in line with the ball, the leg straightens. The toe remains pointing downward so that the ball is met below center by the top of the instep (shoe laces). The knee remains straightened, and the leg and foot extend, thus lifting the ball up and away from the body. A forceful kick will often result in the supporting foot leaving the ground for a moment on the follow-through. A simple instep kick has backspin and remains low. If more height is needed, the kicking leg should be straightened quickly and completely at the moment of ball contact.

Pivot Instep Kick. The pivot instep kick is effective as a place kick and in sending a moving ball in a direction other than the one in which it is traveling. The nonkicking foot is placed 12 to 16 inches behind the ball on the side of the ball in which direction it is to be kicked. The backswing is similar to the simple instep kick, but, on the forward movement, the leg swings in a circular motion from the hip, and the body leans slightly backward and *in the direction* in which the ball is to be kicked. The body pivots on the nonkicking toe as the ball is contacted on the instep of the other foot. The ball follows the direction in which the kicking foot points on follow-through.

Outside-of-the-foot Kick. The outside-of-the-foot kick is made in a manner similar to that of the instep kick. The difference is that the toe of the kicking foot is turned in so that the ball is contacted by the side and little toe of the foot. For a right-foot kick, the ball is met at the center or to the

Figure 17–7 The outside-of-the-foot kick.

Figure 17–8 The volley kick.

left of the body. The mechanics are described in more detail in the discussion of the outside-of-the-foot pass (see page 591).

Toe Kick. The toe kick is recommended only for skilled players who are wearing hard-toe shoes. It is used most often for a place kick on a stationary ball. The body mechanics of the kick are similar to the instep kick except that the toe is parallel to the ground and points toward the ball. The toe contacts the ball below center, and the follow-through is in the direction of ball flight.

Volley Kick. The volley kick is an advanced skill used less frequently by women than men. It is used to kick a ball while it is in the air, either before or after it bounces. The ball must be watched carefully so the kick can be properly timed. The kicking leg is bent and swings from the hip. Allow the ball to drop to about knee level before contacting it with the instep. A ball contacted at too high a point is usually kicked by an extended leg. This results in a skied ball, which offers little control of direction. A *knee volley* may be used on high balls, but control and power are often lost.

Drop Kick. The drop kick is actually a half volley kick which is used to contact a ball the instant it bounces from the ground. In soccer, the drop kick is a goalkeeping skill, but in speedball and speed-a-way, it is needed by

Figure 17–9 The drop kick.

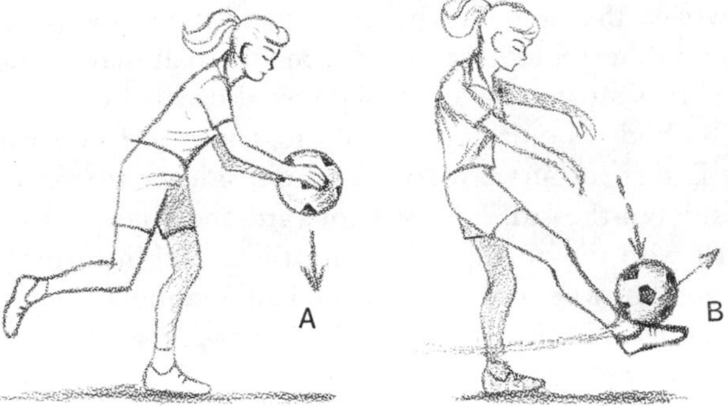

Figure 17–10 The punt.

all players for penalty kicks and scoring. The ball is held at arm's length in front of the body and slightly to the side of the kicking leg. It may be dropped from one or both hands. The kicking leg swings forward, toe pointing toward the ground, and the knee extends as the instep contacts the ball just as it bounces from the ground. The leg follows through forward and upward.

Punt. The soccer goalkeeper and all speedball and speed-a-way players use the punt. The ball is held at about waist level at arm's length in front of the body. It is held in this position as a step or weight shift is made to the nonkicking foot. The ball is dropped as the kicking foot begins its forward swing, and the ball is kicked by the instep as it reaches a point just off the ground. The higher the point at which the ball is met in the air, and the higher the follow-through, the higher the ball flight will be.

Dribbling. Dribbling is the skill by which a moving player maintains control and possession of the ball. It is simply a series of well controlled and timed kicks. A dribble should be used when no opponents are near or when no teammate is clear to whom the ball may be passed. The ball is tapped or pushed along the ground by alternating short kicks which contact the ball below center. Each impetus should move the ball about 10 to 12 inches

Figure 17–11 The dribble.

forward; however, the speed of the runner and the threat posed by the opponents should determine how far in front the ball may be tapped.

The dribble is most easily controlled by alternate taps with the *inside* of each foot. The body is quite erect and the arms are free for balance. The kicking foot is turned outward so that the inside of the foot contacts the ball. This results in the ball having a forward and slightly diagonal path.

Dribbling with the outside of the foot is useful in turning quickly and in keeping one's body between the ball and an opponent. The foot is rotated inward, and the toe is pointed diagonally downward so that contact is made on the outside of the instep.

When moving diagonally across the field or in a circular fashion, the dribbler may alternate an outside tap and an inside tap.

Dribbling with the toes or with the top of the instep with toes forward is a useful skill when running rapidly; however, a "loose" dribble results in a ball that is difficult to control and easily intercepted because of the distance it moves from the dribbler's body. To execute this dribble the toes are pointed forward. Each contact is made with the toes slightly under the ball so that backspin is created and control is maintained.

Short Kicks (Passes). Short kicks, directed with proper power and accuracy, are used for passes, dodges, and goal shots.

Instep Kick. The instep kick was described earlier (see page 586). As a short pass, it is most effective when it is deceptively used. That is, the opponents are led to believe a long kick is to be anticipated, but instead a controlled short pass results from less force and limited follow-through.

Inside-of-the-foot Kick. This push pass is accurate but rarely deceptive. The ball is met with the inside of the instep (between the large toe and the heel) and can be directed sideward or forward.

The kicking leg swings diagonally backward and outward. It then swings forward and across the body to contact the ball, which is close to and in front of the body. The knee of the kicking leg straightens, and the ball is swept out and away from the body. The supporting leg is bent to maintain balance and allow an easy swing of the kicking leg.

Figure 17–12 The inside-of-the-foot kick.

Figure 17–13 The outside-of-the-foot pass.

Outside-of-the-foot Pass. The outside of the foot is used for short, deceptive passes and goal shots. Little power is possible because of the limited backswing. The kicking leg swings across and away from the body and passes in front of the bent supporting leg. The knee straightens as the ball is contacted in front of and slightly to the outside of the supporting foot.

Heel Pass. The heel pass is a more skillful pass. The heel is used to prevent a ball from going out of the boundary lines or for a deceptive pass following a feint. The body weight is supported on one leg as the kicking leg, knee flexed, swings backward from the hip. The leg extends slightly as the heel of the kicking foot meets the ball below its center. The knee again flexes to assume the body weight on the follow-through.

Sole-of-the-foot Pass. This skillful maneuver can be executed either from a dribble or on the run. The sole of the foot is placed lightly on the ball and force is exerted by quick flexion of the knee so that the ball is rolled backward. If the passer is running, she may jump, leave the ground, and execute the movement while in the air.

Figure 17–14 The heel pass.

Controlling or Advancing the Ball with the Body. A ball may be trapped by the body or rebounded from the body in order to bring it under control or change its direction.

Trapping. Trapping is the technique for bringing the ball under control. It may result in stopping a ball, bringing it to the ground, changing its direction, or slowing it down. No matter how the ball is to be trapped, the player keeps her eyes on the ball and maintains a relaxed body during performance of this skill so that she is ready for the next play after the ball is controlled.

Sole-of-the-foot Trap. This is a simple and effective trap for low bouncing or slowly rolling balls. It becomes less effective as running speed and ball speed increase. As the ball approaches, the trapping leg extends forward, the foot is 4 or 5 inches off the ground, and the heel is downward. At the moment the ball touches the foot, pressure is exerted, and the ball is pinned between the foot and the ground.

Side-of-the-foot Trap. The ball may be trapped by either the inside or the outside of the foot. This trap is not recommended for the goalkeeper, for a misplay could deflect the ball toward the goal. Flex the knee of the trapping leg and raise the foot several inches from the ground. If the ball is to be deflected by the outside of the foot, turn the toe in and downward (pigeon-toed); if the inside of the foot is used, turn the foot out and let the ankle remain loose and relaxed. The ball will rebound slightly as the body leans in the direction in which the ball is to go.

Inside-of-the-thigh Trap. Trapping with the inside of the thigh is an excellent way of gaining control of a low-flying or rebounding ball. The body weight is shifted to the nontrapping leg. The trapping leg bends at right angles to the line of flight. The foot is several inches off the ground. As the ball strikes the fleshy part of the thigh, the leg "gives" slightly to absorb the impact and allow the ball to fall near the feet.

One-leg Trap. The player prepares to stop the ball by lining up directly in its path. For a right-leg trap the left leg moves forward, flexes, and carries the body weight down and slightly forward. The right knee bends.

Figure 17–15 Trapping with the sole of the foot.

Figure 17–16 Inside-of-the-thigh trap.

The shin contacts the ball and forces it to a stop in the wedge formed by the leg and the ground.

Two-leg Trap. The feet are close together. As the ball approaches, the knees bend. The body is inclined slightly forward and balanced on the balls of the feet. The arms are held out for balance as the ball is trapped between the ground and the shins of both legs. Rise quickly and continue play.

Blocking or Trapping with the Abdomen or Chest. These traps are used when the ball is traveling above the ground. As the ball moves to the player, she "gives" or jumps back slightly as she bends forward at the waist. At the moment the ball drops, the body is poised and ready to play the ball. For the abdomen trap, the arms may be extended for balance, but on the chest block, the arms are folded across the chest for protection. The arms and hands must remain in contact with the body throughout the block if they touch the ball.

Volleying. A ball can be rebounded legally from any part of the body except extended hands and arms. Skills of volleying are useful for intercepting or changing the direction of a ball.

Figure 17–17 The two-leg trap.

Figure 17–18 The chest block.

Foot Volley. The volley and the half volley kicks are used when a ball has a low trajectory in the air either before or after it bounces. The half volley is performed *just* after the ball strikes the ground (see drop kick).

Knee Volley. The knee volley is used to play a ball descending from a high flight that cannot be played by the more efficient foot volley. The ball must be carefully watched as a step is taken to the supporting leg and the other leg is bent and raised so that the knee contacts the ball from underneath and behind. If the ball is hit directly underneath, it will be skied ineffectively.

Hip and Shoulder Volleys. These volleys are used on balls too low for heading. To execute the shoulder volley, watch the ball flight carefully. Turn the hitting shoulder toward the ball and hold the arm close to the body. As the ball approaches, jump and extend the body to meet the ball with the side and top of the shoulder. The head tilts away from the hitting shoulder.

In executing the hip volley, the arms are away from the body, and the side is turned toward the oncoming ball. The ball is met off the top of the

Figure 17–19 Heading.

Figure 17–20 Two hand throw-in.

hip, and the body moves laterally to follow through in the direction of ball flight.

Heading. Volleying with the head is an advanced technique used for bringing the ball under control or to the ground and as a method of passing or scoring a goal. With eyes on the ball, place the head so the ball will be met by the forehead. The ball is met by jumping toward it; the neck is stiffened, and contact is made at the hairline on the front of the head.

To head the ball to the side, meet the ball with the side of the forehead and move the head sharply to the side in the direction of intended ball flight.

Throw-in. After the ball goes out of bounds over the sideline in soccer, it is put in play by a *throw-in.* It is usually taken by a side halfback, and this is the only time the ball may be legally handled by a player other than the goalkeeper. The ball may be thrown-in by one of several passes. The two-handed pass (Figure 17–20) is recommended for direct, well placed balls. The one hand sidearm and the overarm throws cover greater distance and are relatively less accurate.

In speedball and speed-a-way, *all* players may pass aerial balls.

Speedball Fundamentals

Many of the fundamental skills of speedball are the same as those of soccer and basketball. All soccer skills and all skills for ball handling in basketball except the bounce to oneself and the dribble may be used. Emphasis should be placed on the drop kick, but the only skills peculiar to speedball are those of converting a ground ball to an aerial ball.

Figure 17–21 Lifting to a teammate.

Lifting to a Teammate. The player lifting is about a foot behind the stationary ball. Weight is on the left leg, and the right leg is forward. The knee of the right leg is flexed and the toe is toward the ground. The instep contacts the ball and lifts it by a rapid leg movement, an extension of the knee, and a toe lift. The leg follows through in the direction of the receiver. The lifting of moving balls requires increased speed and accurate timing.

Kick-up or Lift to Self

One-foot Lift of Stationary Ball. Standing behind the ball, the player puts the sole of her lifting foot on top of the ball. Applying pressure, she pulls it back toward herself and quickly slides the toes of the same foot under the ball to lift it upward. The toes of the lifting foot turn slightly upward as the knee bends outward to allow the body and arms to move forward to catch the ball.

Lift of a Moving Ball. The player awaits the moving ball with one leg slightly extended. Her heel is off the ground, and her toes are pointing down. As the ball rolls up and over the toes, the leg is quickly lifted, the knee bends outward, and the body leans forward to catch the ball as it rises off the instep.

Figure 17–22 One-foot lift of stationary ball.

Figure 17–23 Lift of a moving ball.

Kick-up with Both Feet. The ball is held between the player's feet by the inside of the feet and ankles. With body weight equally distributed on the outer portion of the feet, the player jumps and bends knees outward to pull the ball up within reach of the hands.

Speed-a-way Fundamentals

The unique aspects of speed-a-way are those of combining passing, catching, and running for touchdowns. Otherwise, all the skills of soccer, speedball, and basketball (except the bounce, bounce pass, and dribble) are used. Refer to Chapter 14, Basketball, and the preceding sections of this chapter for detailed analyses of catching and passing with the hands, blocking, tackling, trapping, dribbling and passing with the feet, kicking, lift-up and kick-up.

Running and Dodging. All players are responsible for moving rapidly, positioning themselves for a pass or kick and for marking and guarding an opponent. Dodging is necessary to avoid being tagged while running with the ball. A high level of fitness, gained through conditioning exercises and distance and obstacle running, develops the stamina for effective play.

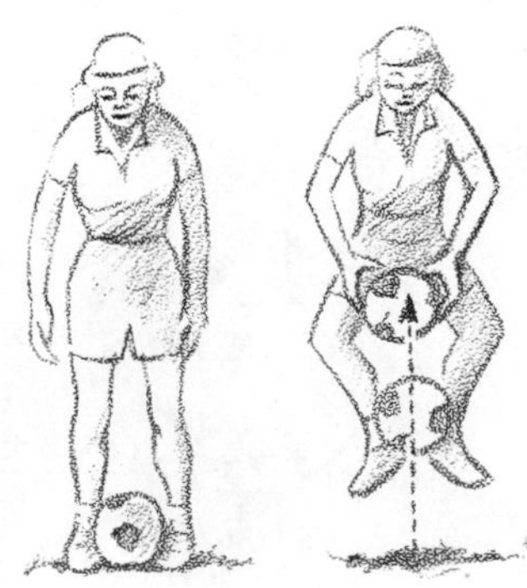

Figure 17–24 The kick-up with both feet.

Running with the Ball. Hold the ball securely with both hands or cradle it in an arm, pulling it against the body. Run when the field is open and no pass receivers are clear.

Tagging. Tagging a runner with the ball gives the tagging team possession of the ball. Using one or both hands, the tagger approaches the runner from the side or rear. If awaiting her from the front, the tagger watches for a dodge and change of direction, and then steps to the side for the tag. While maintaining running balance to avoid pushing the runner, the tagger makes a quick striking movement and recovers to avoid following through with her weight on her opponent.

Techniques Common to All Three Games

Tackling. The tackle is a technique for taking the ball from an opponent by using the feet. A tackle is considered successful if it causes a dribbler to make a poor pass, overrun the ball, or otherwise play the ball so that her opponents gain possession or have an opportunity to set up a better defense. Tackling requires accuracy and correct timing, for the tackler must play the ball, not the player, and body contact must be avoided.

Front, or Straight, Tackle. This is used against an opponent who is dribbling. Just after the dribbler contacts the ball, the tackler reaches with one foot, body weight on the other, and places the sole of the foot on the ball. She holds it as the opponent overruns; then the tackler attempts to maintain possession and avoid a tackle back by her opponent.

Side, or Hook, Tackle. This tackle is effective for most field situations. The tackler is positioned to one side of her opponent. Her body weight is supported by the leg away from the ball. As the opponent approaches, the stationary leg bends deeply, allowing the leg near the opponent to extend. The ankle is flexed and the side of the foot is turned toward the ground. The ball is hooked and pulled toward the tackler as the stationary leg straightens.

Figure 17–25 Tackling.

Figure 17–26 The front or straight tackle.

As tackling skill develops, players should initiate the tackle from a straight-on position in order to delay relaying their intention to the dribbler as long as possible. When time permits, plan to tackle from the most advantageous position. For example, if the opponent dribbles straight ahead or taps the ball every step, hook the ball to the side of the dribbling foot. The dribbler will find it difficult to tackle back because her weight will be transferred to the foot near the ball. When the dribbler uses a diagonal kick or a skip-foot dribbling pattern, attempt to hook the ball on the side of the dribbler's receiving foot in order to avoid body contact.

Split Tackle. This is a desperation, or "spoil," play much like the left-hand lunge in hockey. The opponent is almost out of reach as the tackler drops to one knee and extends the other leg and foot toward the ball. If the ball is blocked, the tackler must regain playing position quickly.

Feints and Dodges. Individual ability is greatly improved if a player develops some deception in her play. *Feints* are deceptive moves and tactics which tend to confuse opponents. When possible, passes should be preceded by a feint in order to draw the opponent off balance or out of position. A few common feints are as follows:

1. Feint with the knees in one direction and pass in the other. This is most effective from a stride stand position with the ball in front of and near the feet. Bend the knees, look in one direction and pass suddenly in the other.

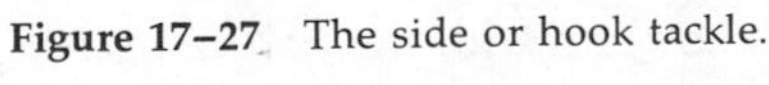

Figure 17–27 The side or hook tackle.

2. Feint to pass with the inside of the foot, but stop just before kicking the ball. This is effective on stationary or moving balls.
3. Feint to pass with the inside of the foot, but bring the foot over the ball and pass in the opposite direction with the outside of the foot. It is effective on stationary balls or while dribbling with the inside of the foot.
4. Feint an instep kick but stop or allow the foot to pass over the ball. If the foot passes over the ball, it may be followed by a heel- or sole-of-the-foot pass.

Dodges are individual techniques used by a player with the ball to avoid a tackler. The ability to dodge to either side of an opponent is important. The elements of surprise and speed are important in dodging. The direction of the dodge is determined by the opponent's position 2 strides away. If her next step will be on the left foot, the dodge should be made to the dribbler's left, as the opponent will be weighted on her right foot and less able to play a ball on her right. The ball is quickly pulled to the left with the right foot. The right foot then takes a long cross-step to the left. The left foot regains control of the ball.

When an opponent approaches before a dodge can be executed, the evasion dodge may be attempted. Push the ball to one side, step to the other side and out of the opponent's path, and quickly return to the ball. The speed and momentum of the opponent may carry her out of the play momentarily.

Marking and Interchanging. Marking and interchanging are basic defense tactics. Marking is the ability to stay close enough to an opponent to intercept her passes or tackle the ball. Interchanging is the technique used by the defensive players in changing positions with one another. It is used when an opposing forward evades the defensive player marking her and is moving down the field unguarded. (See Field Hockey for discussion of defense tactics.)

GAME STRATEGY—SOCCER AND SPEEDBALL

The basic factor in successful and winning strategy is the blending of skillful individual play into a united team effort. If this is to be accomplished, position play is a must. This seems to be a difficult concept for girls and women to grasp, for the problem of players bunching around the ball is one most common in beginning soccer and speedball.

The basic individual skills necessary for team play are accurate ball handling, skillful blocking and trapping, quick and accurate passing, dodging, marking, and interchanging.

Basic Offense. "Only the team with the ball can score" is a concept which should be instilled in both offensive and defensive players. As the players try to gain control of the ball and pass it to their forwards for a scoring attempt, they should remember the following tenets:

1. Once in possession of it, try to keep the ball. Protect the ball with the body as much as possible.

2. Generally pass ahead of an intended receiver and out to the sidelines until nearing the opponent's goal.
3. Play your own position and avoid bunching near the ball. When interchanging with a teammate, do so quickly, endeavoring to throw the opponent off guard.
4. Look for weaknesses in the opponent's skill and strategy and capitalize on them.
5. Pass to open spaces that can be reached by a moving teammate. Avoid passing to a closely guarded teammate, and never pass *across* your own goal. An interception gives the opponents an immediate scoring opportunity.
6. Master the skills of playing a *long-pass game* out to fast forwards (this is good in soccer when the field is wet); a *short-pass game* quickly, endeavoring to throw the opponents off guard; and a *triangular-pass game*, using any three players (usually a wing halfback and two forwards) to zigzag the ball downfield quickly. Change from one style of attack to another often enough to keep the opponents guessing.
7. Conserve energy whenever possible. Take advantage of "breathers" when the ball is elsewhere on the field and playing it is someone else's responsibility.
8. Be sure all forward line players *know* to whom the ball will be passed and the opponents *do not know* for certain.
9. Take free kicks and throw-ins quickly, before the defense can get organized.
10. Take advantage of wind and all other environmental factors.
11. Be ready to change quickly from offensive to defensive play.

Specifics for Soccer

1. Rush for a goal in the penalty area.
2. Have the wing take a corner kick while her forward line teammates form a semicircle between her and the far side of the goal. Attempt to kick high so that the receiver can get the ball directly in front of the goal and kick it quickly.
3. On a free kick or throw-in, it is best to have the forward line ahead of the ball (but on-side), and for a right or left halfback to take the kick or throw-in.

Specifics for Speedball

1. Usually an aerial-pass game will move the ball downfield more quickly. Occasionally vary the aerial attack by advancing the ball down the *center* of the field. Pass quickly toward the sideline to score a touchdown.
2. Attempt to have two tall forward players who are adept at ball passing and tall enough to catch a ball thrown over the endline players' heads for a touchdown.
3. Plan and practice situational plays from kick-off, free kick, out of bounds, and toss-up.
4. Quick changes from aerial play to ground play keep defense shifting and often open more scoring opportunities.
5. Know the game score at all times, and when behind, work toward making the type of goal which will give the most points.

Basic Defense. Basic tactics are as follows:

1. Always keep opponents not playing the ball well marked and be alert to intercept passes.

2. The player with the ball should always be tackled or guarded by the nearest defensive player.
3. Plan and practice a plan for interchanging positions.
4. Attempt to keep two strong lines of defensive players plus the goalkeeper between the oncoming attackers and scoring area.
5. Anticipate what a play will be before it becomes a reality.
6. On the kick-off, one fullback should move up near the restraining line to intercept if possible.

Specifics for Soccer

1. On a penalty kick, the halfbacks should stand near the forwards they are marking; the fullbacks stand at the outer edge of the penalty area and on each side of the goal posts. The goalkeeper is on the endline, and at the moment of the kick, she defends against the kick with the help of the fullbacks. The halfbacks mark to prevent a rush on the goal.
2. On the corner kick, the two fullbacks should be in the goalkeeper's cage. Two halfbacks should be on the same side of the goal as the ball. The third halfback should be in the opposite area. The forward line should be halfway down the field on their respective sides.
3. On the throw-in, one halfback should mark a wing, the center halfback the inner, and the other halfback the center forward.
4. The goalkeeper must always keep her eye on the ball. She usually stands about 6 feet in front of and slightly left of the center of the goal.

Specifics for Speedball

1. Defensive players must be able to shift from ground defense to aerial defense quickly. Basic soccer defense is used for ground play. Aerial play demands a man-to-man or zone defense similar to basketball.
2. On a penalty kick, defending players should stand behind the endline opposite their opponents and rush out to mark their players as the ball is kicked.

GAME STRATEGY—SPEED-A-WAY

Many of the strategies of soccer and speedball are applicable to speed-a-way; however, skillful play tends to be more offensive than defensive and more of an aerial game than a ground game. The strategies of the passing and running game are emphasized below.

Basic Offense

1. A good offense begins with a successful kick-off. An example of such a play follows. The center forward lifts to an inner who catches the ball on the fly or after the first bounce. The inner passes to the halfback, who has moved forward. The halfback punts to the wing, who has moved well into the opponent's field. The wing receives the ball on the fly or after the first bounce and runs or passes the ball to the other wing for a touchdown. Many options exist once the wing receives the ball. She may pass the ball toward center field for a field goal attempt by the center forward or pass to either inner for a score.
2. It is often wise to have one or more players over the goal line waiting to receive a pass. Forwards should vary their attack to divert the defense. As

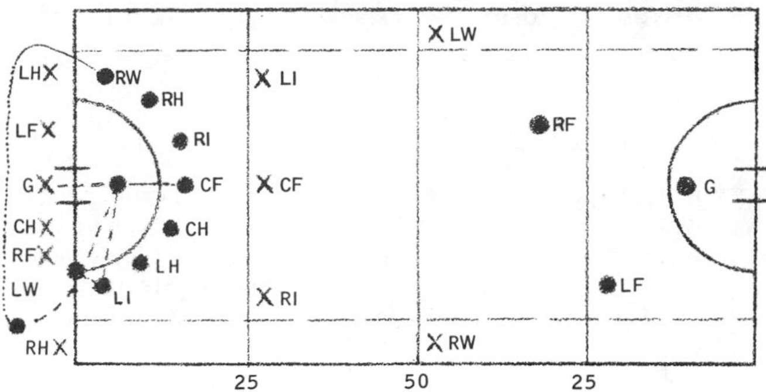

Figure 17–28 Scoring from a penalty corner in speed-a-way.

forwards approach scoring position they can expect to be guarded more closely and therefore must become more accurate with short direct passes. More success is gained if the ball remains or is converted to an aerial ball. If positioning is good for a field goal, the ball may be dropped and kicked.

3. Penalty corner plays can often result in a score. For example, the left wing (LW) lifts the ball to her left inner (LI) or left halfback (LH); then, that person passes to the center forward, who may kick the ball through the goal or throw the ball to the right wing, who has come over the goal line for a touchdown pass. The ball could be passed to the LW if she is not too closely guarded.
4. As backfield players gain possession of the ball, they pass or kick to the wings, preferably away from the center of the field to avoid interception. Occasionally, diagonal passes upfield are used to keep the defense spread.

Basic Defense

1. The forwards are the initial line of defense as they attempt to intercept during the kick-off. Once play begins, forwards rarely drop back into their own half of the field.
2. A defending player attempts to stay between the goal and the player she is marking. Ground attack strategy is similar to that of soccer. Player-to-player defense may prove ineffective with an aerial and running attack. A zone defense is recommended.
3. Using a zone, the center halfback guards the center of the field in front of the goalkeeper; left and right halfbacks guard the area from the sidelines 15 yards in; the fullbacks are deeper, guarding the areas between wings and center. If the forwards on the defending team are fast, they may move in to mark the halfbacks. It is rarely necessary for the inners to go back too deeply to guard offensive actions of their fullbacks. Defending fullbacks and goalkeeper must be alert to their wings' moving upfield and kick and clear to them.

DUTIES AND SPECIFIC SKILLS OF PLAYERS

Goalkeeper. The goalkeeper plays near the goal, usually within the penalty areas in soccer and approximately 4 feet in front of the endline in speedball. She leaves her position to attack an opposing forward *only* if the goal area is protected by a fullback.

Skills and Duties

1. Primary responsibility is to keep opponents from scoring.
2. Must possess ability to move quickly at all space levels and in all directions.
3. Must possess alertness and judgment in anticipating players and ball flight.
4. Must possess ability to punt, drop kick, and throw for distance.
5. Must not be easily upset or panicked by pressure of onrushing players and close play.

Strategy

1. Clear the ball down the sidelines.
2. Place the ball as close to own forwards as possible.
3. Take advantage of all the privileges of ball handling and moving allowed the goalkeeper.
4. Take the defense kick if a fullback covers the goal.

Fullbacks. In defensive play, each fullback plays primarily in one half the width of the field around the penalty area. In offensive play, one fullback moves near the restraining line and one remains near the goal.

Skills and Duties

1. Mark opposing inners.
2. Must be skillful at anticipating the movement and speed of both players and oncoming balls. Move to intercept or tackle quickly.
3. Must be skillful at trapping, volleying, blocking, passing, and intercepting.
4. Must be bold when it is necessary to tackle near the goal area in order to prevent scoring.
5. Must have the ability to execute long kicks when clearing from the goal area or from a defense kick.
6. In speedball and speed-a-way, must be effective in lifting the ball to a halfback.

Strategy

1. Avoid crowding the goal and avoid obstructing the view of the goalkeeper.
2. Be ready to interchange with halfback near the goal if necessary.
3. Be quick to take defense kick (in soccer) if halfbacks are not ready.
4. On offense, one fullback plays near the restraining line to intercept a clear or defense kick. Quickly return to defensive position if opponents get the ball.

Halfbacks. As both attacking and defensive players, the halfbacks cover the entire field. In defensive play, they mark the opposing center forward and wings (the right and left halfbacks may be responsible for opposing inners on kick-off or when play is in the center of the field). In offensive play, they follow 6 to 10 yards behind their own forwards.

Skills and Duties

1. On defense, marks opposing players. On offense, works the ball to the forward line.
2. Must have endurance, and be able to run fast, dribble, tackle, lift, kick, punt, and pass accurately. They also must interchange on defense. They intercept ground and aerial balls and create aerial balls in speedball and speed-a-way.
3. Must be alert to the occasional opportunity to shoot and score a goal.
4. Must have a working knowledge of their duties and the ability of their own forwards. Must know when to change from offensive to defensive players and the correct playing position to take at all times.
5. Center halfback must have good judgment and the ability to direct the play of her teammates.

Strategy

1. Be alert and ready to take throw-ins, free kicks, and an occasional defense kick.
2. Must be able to make accurate kicks and passes to the sidelines and to openings created so that forward line players gain quick possession.

Forward Line. The forward line is made up primarily of attack players who generally play from their own halfback area to the opponents' goal.

Skills and Duties

1. Must be made up of fast runners and accurate dribblers and passers. Players must be aggressive and deceptive. Players should have the ability to play the ball with either foot, pass and catch under pressure, and kick, shoot, and trap. They must be alert and quick to convert a ground ball to an aerial ball in speedball and speed-a-way.
2. Players must be skilled in taking advantage of and creating spaces for passes by rapid and deceptive moves.
3. Players must be able to feint and dodge effectively.
4. Players must be able to change from offensive to defensive tactics and tackle back quickly and effectively.
5. Center forward is the pivot of the forward line and directs much of the attack. She must be skilled at the kick-off and directed passes.
6. Inners spread the defense to open scoring opportunities. They have many chances to score and intercept balls.
7. Wings must be decisive players who move quickly downfield. They are the skilled catchers of touchdowns in speed-a-way. They keep the defense spread and must be effective on penalty kicks.

Strategy

1. Short passes toward the sidelines are generally the best method of moving the ball toward opponents' goal; however, the center forward often uses long passes to the wings.
2. Center the ball for most shots to the goal in soccer.
3. In speedball and speed-a-way, be alert to the *best* scoring opportunity at the moment. That is, if the defense is out of position, attempt a field goal; if a single defensive player marking the player with the ball is slow in responding or out of position, a drop kick may be attempted. When the defense moves

out to mark a play closely, a forward player should break for the endline and a touchdown pass may be attempted.

4. Never miss an opportunity to kick for goal. Follow each kick.
5. Rush the goalkeeper when the ball is in scoring position.

CLASS ORGANIZATION

When there is only one instructor, it is wise to introduce the entire class to skills by explanation and demonstration. Initially beginners may practice the same skills at the same time under close teacher supervision to check movement patterns and skill execution. As skills are developed, squads directed by student leaders may be led through rotational warm-ups in which all basic skills are used. This pattern enables the teacher to keep an eye on the whole class and be on the lookout for those in the group who most need help. Squads should be composed of no more than eight players, and each squad should have at least one ball. Self-testing in skill development is an incentive to practice and improve play. A suggested plan by Thorpe should be noted.*

Team play should begin as soon as the class acquires the basic concepts of the game and enough skill to enjoy play safely. When the class is large, squad leaders may continue drills along the sidelines while the game progresses (see Figure 17–29). The first attempts at game play should be stopped occasionally at teachable moments, for this is an ideal time to teach rules and strategy. If bunching continues to be a problem, it may be wise to divide the field lengthwise, either actually or imaginatively, into five alleys. By this method, players may be taught to stay in their own areas.

*JoAnne Thorpe: Self testing in soccer skills, *Soccer-Speedball Guide,* DGWS, 1966–1968, pp. 25–29.

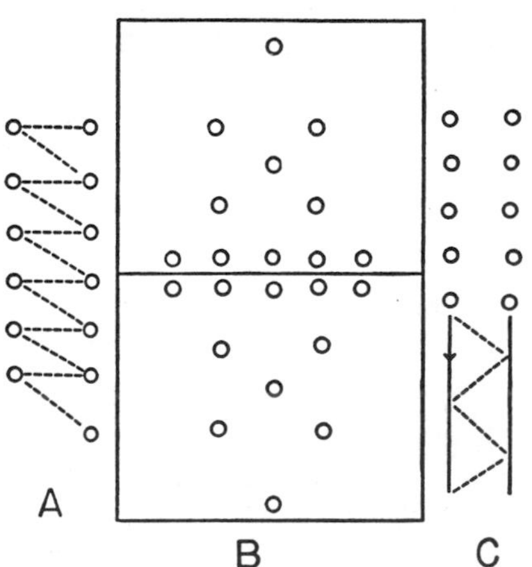

Figure 17–29 Class organization for 45 students. Twenty-two students are involved in team play *(B)*; the others are practicing dribbling *(A)* and passing and trapping *(C)*.

Suggested class organization for specific drills follows:

The Dribble. Arrange group in two or more lines. Dribble from the center of the field to the endline and back, using the feet alternately. For speedball, dribble forward, convert to self, and turn and kick ball to player next in line.

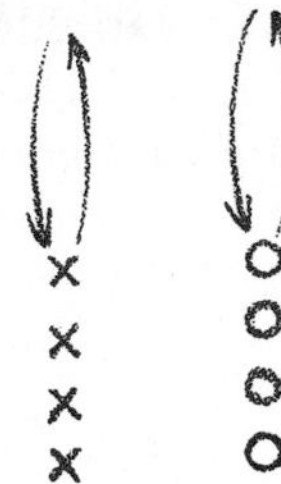

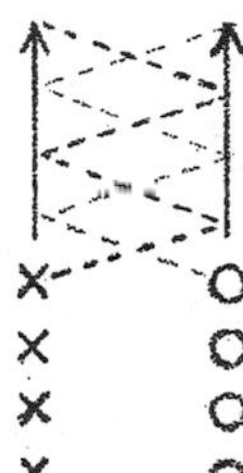

Dribble Pass. Arrange players in two lines. Players in each line work as partners. They dribble the ball and pass it diagonally in front of each other from the center of the field to the endline and back.

Have players in each squad weave in and out of players stationed 5 yards apart.

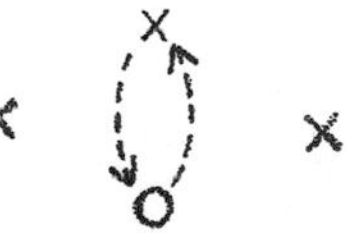

Heading. Make a circle formation with one player in the center. The ball is tossed to the center player by those making up the circle. The center player heads it back. Each player takes a turn in the center.

The player in the center then throws the ball clockwise to each person to head it back to her.

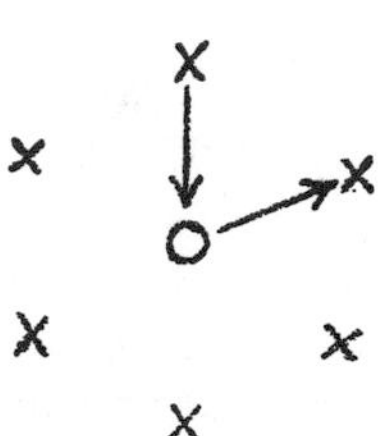

Trapping. Make a circle formation with one player in the center. Each outside player kicks the ball into the center player. The center player traps it and kicks it back to the next player, who traps it before kicking it back to the center. Each takes a turn in the center. Practice one-foot trap, lower-leg trap, two-leg trap, thigh trap, and body trap.

Dribble, Pass, Trap, Dribble, and Pass. Arrange players in two lines that are 30 feet or more from the center of the field. Players in each line work as partners. The first player in the first line dribbles the ball and passes it diagonally to the first player in the second line. The first player in the second line traps it, dribbles it, and then passes it diagonally back to the first player. In this manner, they progress up the field, turn at the end, and dribble back.

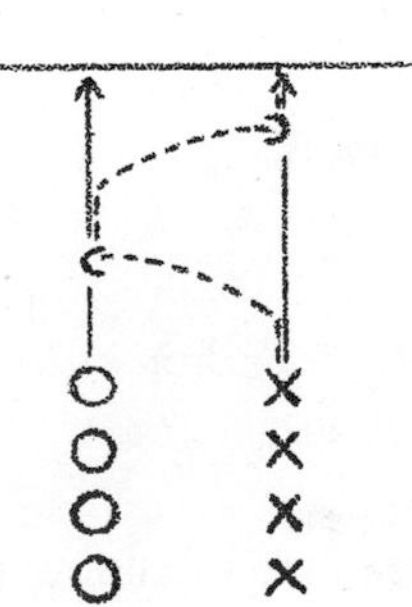

Dribble and Shoot. X's try to dribble through to shoot. The O's, as defensive players, clear the ball. X's halfbacks feed the ball up to the forward line.

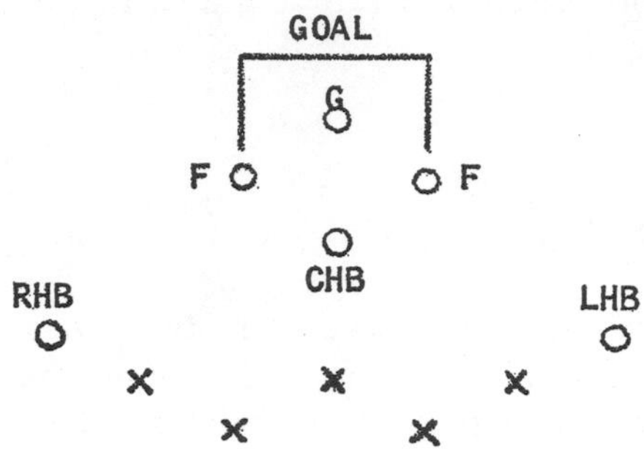

Passing and Tackling. Two lines 10 feet apart. The first two in each line advance, dribbling and passing the ball toward a player who is stationed about 15 feet out. She attempts to tackle while the two try to avoid being tackled. This formation may be used as a passing drill for speedball. A player in one line converts a ground ball to her partner. Her partner then runs downfield to receive a pass, avoiding the would-be interception.

Tackling. Double line formation 15 feet apart. One player in line A slowly dribbles the ball to opposite player in line B, who tackles her. Next have one couple in line A advance to tackle as their passes go from one to the other. Rotate positions.

Punting and Drop Kicking. Players in a double line 20 yards or more apart punt to each other. Combine punting or drop kicking with trapping, dribbling, and passing.

Line A

Punts or drop kicks

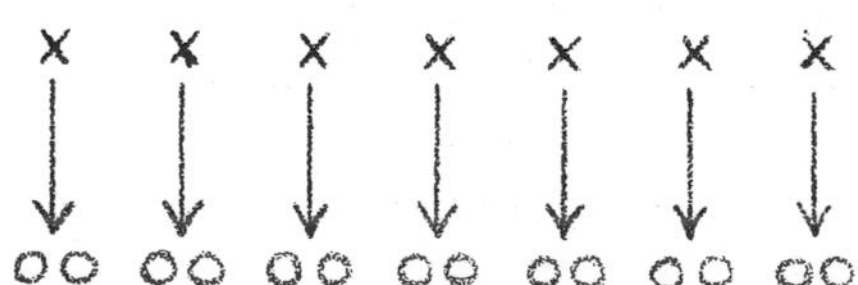

Line B
One traps, couples dribble and pass up to line A

Speed-a-way skills should be practiced by combining the basic skills of soccer and speedball with running techniques. The following drills serve as examples:

1. Place kick (or drop kick or punt), catch, run, and pass.
   X_1 place kicks from the 25 yard line; X_2 catches the ball on the fly or after the first bounce, then runs and makes a forward pass to X_3. X_3 then place kicks and the drill continues. The initial kicker follows the ball and goes to the end of the opposite line. If a player fails to catch the ball, she should lift the ball to herself and continue play.

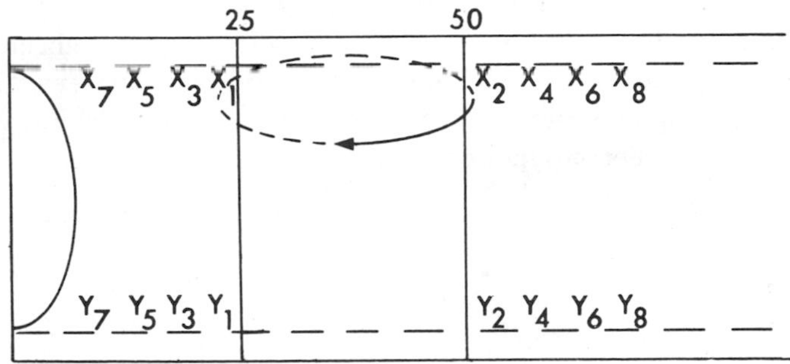

2. Dribble, lift to a teammate, run and pass.
   X_1 begins dribbling the ball as her forward line moves forward with her. X_1 lifts to X_2, who catches the ball and passes forward to any one of her teammates who runs over the goal line. There are numerous variations possible: (a) alternate aerial and ground balls with the last player attempting a field goal if a ground ball or throw a touchdown pass if an aerial ball; (b) lift up to a teammate as soon as possible and pass downfield to a player awaiting an opportunity to drop kick.

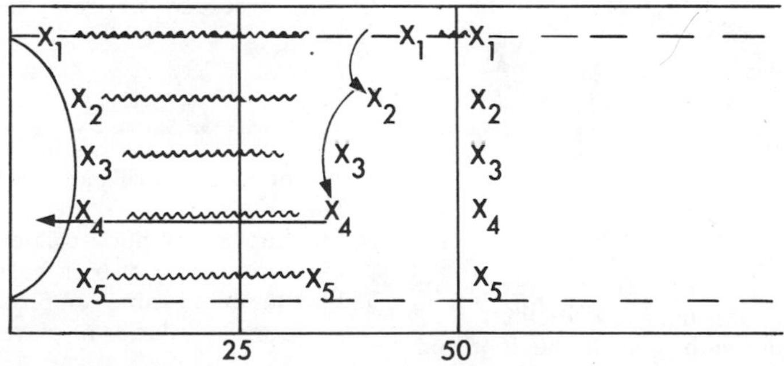

3. Running drop kick for score.
   Players line up on the 25 yard line. Each has a ball. Each runs a short distance toward the goal area and attempts a drop kick over the crossbar. The player then returns to the end of her line or replaces a retriever behind the goal.

Position Play. Station players as they should be on the field. Walk through a play taking the ball downfield at normal running speed. Encourage skill execution and play to be practiced at the speed they will be used in a game.

The mechanics of game skills can be practiced in the gymnasium on rainy days. Position play, the duties of each player, and offensive and defensive strategy can often be grasped more readily by beginners if a magnetized board or an illustrated blackboard talk is used.

Each person should learn to play several positions before choosing the one on which to concentrate. Homogeneous grouping is best for teaching offensive and defensive teamwork, and those with superior skill should play against a team made up of players who are equally adept. Advanced players will enjoy learning the intricate techniques of good game strategy. They will also enjoy developing timing, coordination, speed, and the ability to *think while playing* in a keen competitive situation.

TEACHING PROGRESSION

A suggested unit of 10 lessons for soccer beginners includes:

Lesson I

1. Short history of the game
2. Safety precautions
3. Warm-up exercises (stress running, changing direction, and balanced starts and stops)
4. Kicking and passing (long, short, and diagonal)
   Instep
   Outside of foot
   Inside of foot
5. Dribbling
6. Relays and drills

Lesson II

1. Warm-up exercises and review of kicking, passing, and dribbling
2. Trapping with sole of the foot and the lower leg
3. Watch a quarter of a game played by highly skilled players or a movie. Discuss the use of field positions and basic skills
4. Drills and relays

Lesson III

1. Warm up by reviewing skills (stress increased speed and control when dribbling and passing)
2. Two-leg trap
3. Goal shooting (stress rushing to goal and shooting with sides of foot and instep)
4. Goalkeeping skills of punt and drop kick preceded by two steps or a bounce

Lesson IV

1. Warm up with drills and relays
2. Dodging
3. Straight-on and hook tackles
4. Brief discussion of basic rules
5. Play modified game (emphasize field positions and duties of players)

Lesson V

1. Review previous game play. Chalk board presentation of field positions and players' duties

Lesson V *Continued*

2. Four minute game following warm-up. Discuss rules and situations at teachable moments. Emphasize kick-off position and play
3. Shoulder, hip, and head volleys
4. Relays (stress use of dribble, review tackles, and explain and encourage tackle back)

Lesson VI

1. Individual skill practice and warm-up
2. Review of rules
3. Ten minute game (stress offensive playing patterns)
4. Situational play demonstrating throw-in, roll-in, and free kick

Lesson VII

1. Warm up (stress offensive playing patterns)
2. Game situation (stress marking, covering, and intercepting)
3. Evaluate game situation; have question and answer period
4. Review skills selected by class

Lesson VIII

1. Warm-up drills
2. Demonstrate and explain penalty kick, defense kick, and corner kick
3. Game play

Lesson IX

1. Warm up
2. Skills tests (rotate stations while others participate in game situation)
3. Game (stress rules and situational play at appropriate times)

Lesson X

1. Written evaluation
2. Game as time permits

A suggested unit of 10 lessons for speedball beginners follows. The plans are based on the assumption that the students have some background and skill in soccer and basketball techniques.

Lesson I

1. Brief history and nature and purpose of the game
2. Safety rules
3. Warm-up exercises
4. Soccer skills
   - Dribbling
   - Instep kick
   - Kicking with the inside and outside of the foot
5. Watch a short film on game

Lesson II

1. Warm-up exercises
2. Review of soccer skills from the previous lesson
3. Trapping
4. Tackling
5. Punting
6. Evading an opponent
7. Kicking for goal
8. Short test on skills

Lesson III

1. Warm-up exercises
2. Review of soccer skills from previous lessons
3. Basketball skills
   - Pivoting
   - Catching and passing
   - Guarding
   - Air dribble
4. Continue tests

Lesson IV

1. Warm-up exercises
2. Review of basketball skills of the previous lesson
3. Speedball skills
   - Drop kick
   - Kick-up to self (stationary ball)
   - Lift to a teammate (stationary ball)
   - Punting
4. Practice time given for testing improvement

Lesson V

1. Warm-up exercises
2. Review of speedball skills of previous lesson
3. Additional speedball skills
   - Lift-up with one foot (moving and stationary ball)
   - Lifting a moving ball to a teammate
4. Chalk or magnetized board talk on player positions
5. Brief rule discussion

Lesson VI

1. Warm-up exercises and skill drills
2. Drill review of the most difficult skills of soccer, basketball, and speedball
3. Play at least half a game, stopping the game at teachable moments (stress rules and strategy)

Lesson VII

1. Warm up by drill review of specific speedball skills
2. Play two quarters (stress rules and strategy)
3. Work on situational plays such as kick-off, out of bounds, free kick

Lesson VIII

1. Warm-up drills
2. Play the entire period (stress techniques of scoring)
3. Brief class evaluation of the game, with suggestions for improving team play

Lesson IX

1. Warm-up exercises
2. Play an entire game (stress game strategy and situational play involving out of bounds, over the endline, and penalty kick)

Lesson X

1. Evaluation (paper-pencil knowledge test and skill test). Continue game play if skill evaluation has been ongoing

TEACHING PROGRESSION

A suggested unit of 10 lessons for speed-a-way beginners might include:

Lesson I

1. Brief history and purpose
2. Safety precautions
3. Basic body control and movement fundamentals: running, starting, stopping, dodging, evading
4. Tag and ball-carrying games of tag

Lesson II

1. Practice running, tagging, evading
2. Ball handling skills (basketball skills): catching, passing (one-hand shoulder, two-hand chest)
3. Kicking skills: punt, place kick
4. Speed-a-way film: discussion and explanation of play

Lesson III

1. Review rules and play as introduced by film
2. Review ball handling and kicking skills
3. Dribbling
4. Drop kick
5. Lift up of stationary ball to self; lift up of stationary ball to teammate
6. Play a ten minute game

Lesson IV

1. Intensive practice using drills similar to those suggested in Class Organization section (p. 566). Stress combining skills with running techniques
2. Two-hand overhead pass, one-hand underhand pass
3. Introduce guarding; review tagging
4. Lift up of moving ball
5. Ten minute game

Lesson V

1. Review techniques of converting ground ball; lift up to self and teammates of stationary and moving balls
2. Discussion and explanation of defensive strategy
3. Volleying and trapping
4. Play a game as time permits, stopping at teachable moments for rule and strategy explanation

Lesson VI

1. Review and question-and-answer period on rules
2. Introduce situational strategy explanation of kick-off, free kick, etc.
3. Game situation

Lesson VII

1. Offensive strategy—stressing scoring techniques
2. Review skills that show up as obviously needing practice
3. Practice specific situation and position play (i.e., privileges and duties of goalkeeper, forwards, halfback, fullbacks)

Lesson VIII

1. General skill review—dribbling, ball handling, and kicking. Stress drop kicking skills
2. Squad practice of individual and team skills in preparation for interclass game

Lesson IX

1. Warm-up period
2. Interclass game

Lesson X

1. Evaluation—written
2. Discussion of further technique and skill development needed for effective play

SKILL DIFFICULTIES AND THEIR CORRECTION – SOCCER

Dribbling

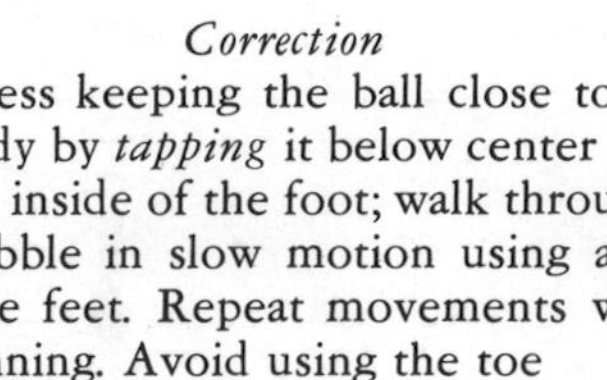

Difficulty	*Correction*
a. Kicking the ball too far in front; using the feet incorrectly	a. Stress keeping the ball close to the body by *tapping* it below center with the inside of the foot; walk through a dribble in slow motion using alternate feet. Repeat movements while running. Avoid using the toe
b. Dribbling when it would be better to pass	b. Be sure player understands *why* and *when* to dribble or pass. Dribble only when no opponents are near or no teammate is clear for a pass

Kicking

Difficulty	*Correction*
a. Missing the approaching ball	a. Have the player watch the spin of the ball as it comes toward her. Be sure the ball is within reach before kicking it

b. Lack of control and power	b. Review skill description. Be firm in leg swing and decisive on follow-through
c. Hurting foot and toe	c. Stress instep kick for punts. Avoid using toe. Keep foot and ankle firm on inside, outside, and instep kicks
d. Kicking with the toe; throwing the ball in the air for a punt instead of bending over it as it drops from the hands	d. Have student kick with toe, then kick correctly in order to get the feel of doing it correctly and gain insight into *why* the instep is better to use. Demonstrate how to get closer to the ball by dropping it and kicking it mimetically. Do this in counts. Next use the counts and the ball
e. Lack of control before kicking the ball	e. Combine kicking, passing and trapping drills. Say "trap, control, then kick" until student knows the meaning of the phrase and can put it into practice
f. Ability to kick or dribble well with only one foot	f. Practice to develop the weaker foot. Stress drills and relays using weaker foot

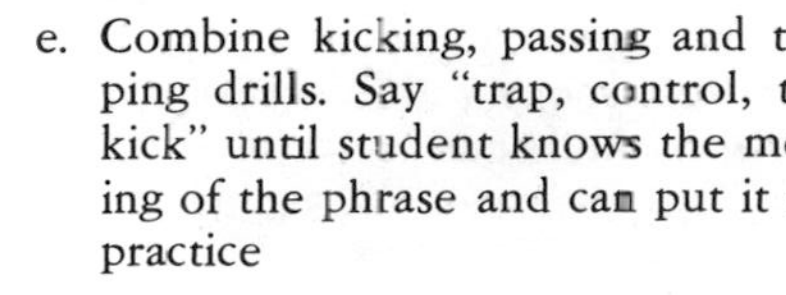

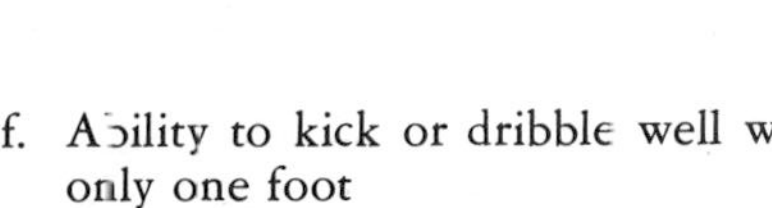

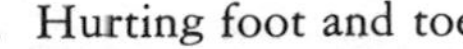

Trapping

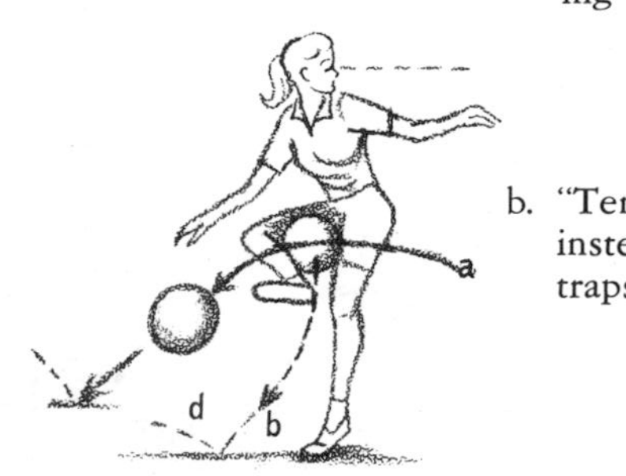

Difficulty	*Correction*
a. Missing the ball. Pressing down on ball in leg traps, resulting in "shooting" the ball from the leg	a. Practice without opposition. Stress "watch the approaching ball." Practice with opposition first at slow then at normal speed. Various traps. Practice until the proper amount of pressure feels right
b. "Tensing up" and "fighting" the ball instead of "giving" with it on body traps	b. Be sure student masters simple traps before going on to more advanced ones. Start with thigh trap and advance to the two-leg trap. Demonstrate how one "gives" when contacting a ball; show how this also occurs in trapping and stress why
c. Using the wrong trap in a game situation	c. Develop the ability to do all kinds of trapping through drills with and without competition between squads or teams

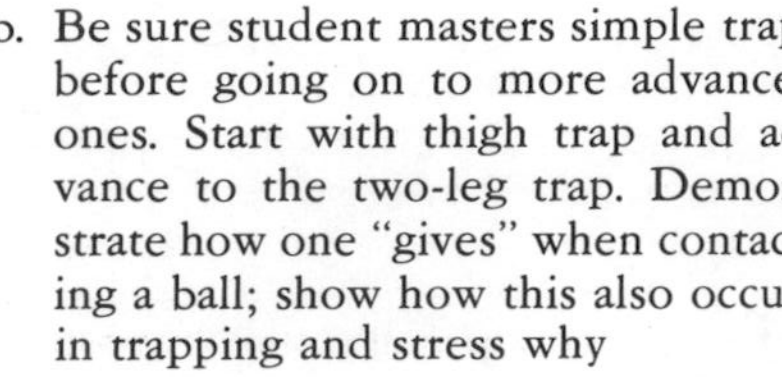

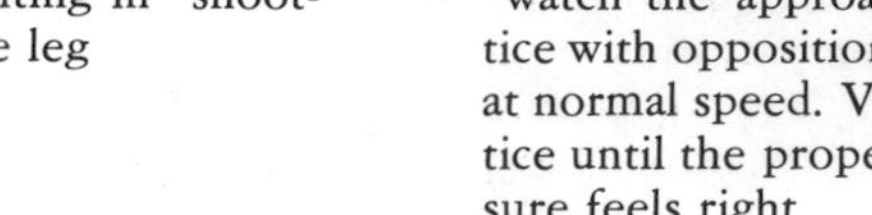

Difficulty	Correction
d. Letting the ball get too far away from the body after trapping or failing to recover to normal position to play the ball	d. Practice maintaining control of the ball until it can be passed off to another player. Show ways the body can bend and twist for doing so. Stress drills requiring immediate dribbling or passing after a successful trap

Heading and Blocking

Difficulty	*Correction*
a. Fear of heading or body blocking	a. Toss easy balls at close range until player gets the idea that heading cannot hurt her. Have partner toss easy balls to practice hip, shoulder, and chest volleying and blocking
b. Closing the eyes	b. Stress keeping the eyes on the ball until it meets the hairline in front of the head
c. The ball hitting the top of the head, or too low on the head	c. Use a competitive drill with two players scoring one point each time the ball is headed in the correct position. Stress watching the ball. Use suggestion *b* above

d. Heading with both feet on the ground	d. Have student jump to head. Be sure she understands the advantage of doing so

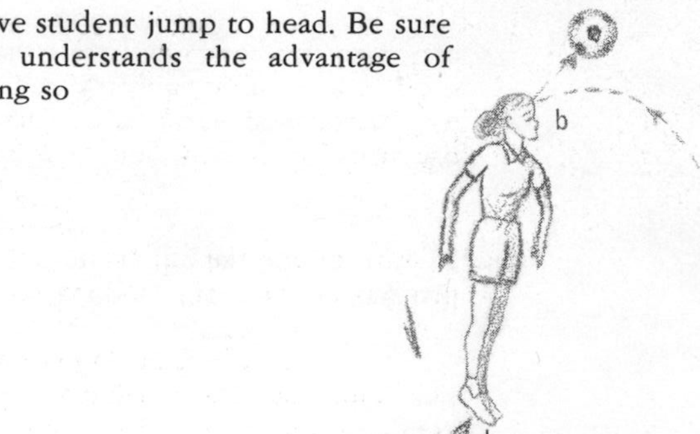

Tackling

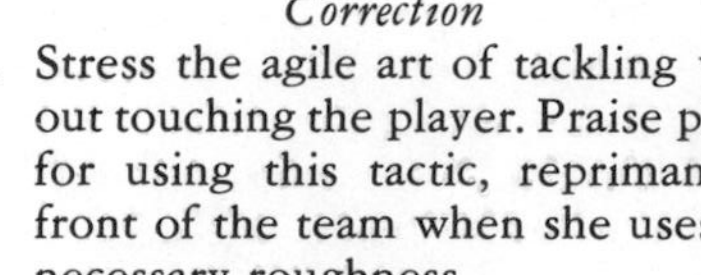

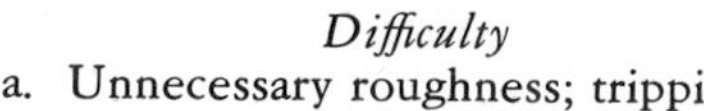

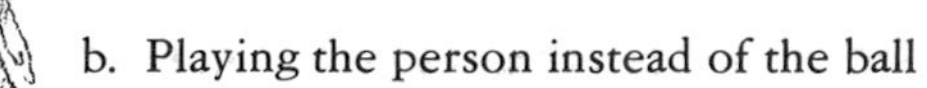

Difficulty	*Correction*
a. Unnecessary roughness; tripping	a. Stress the agile art of tackling without touching the player. Praise player for using this tactic, reprimand in front of the team when she uses unnecessary roughness
b. Playing the person instead of the ball	b. Teach that the object is to get the *ball* away from the player and not to get the player

Game Strategy

Difficulty	*Correction*
a. The show-off who wants to "star"	a. Stress the value of team play. Avoid praising just one player or letting the team or spectators do so
b. Bunching	b. Use a magnetized board and chalk talks to stress correct position play. Have a person assigned to watch each player and record the number of times in each quarter the player was offside or bunched. Review individual responsibility for field area, and marking. Emphasize play at the sides of the field to keep players spread
c. Trying to use too many set plays which fail	c. Use the M or W forward line formation mostly when in scrimmage; also use triangular pass
d. Fighting hard to gain or regain the ball only to lose it by using foolish strategy	d. Coach all to keep any opposite team player from getting the ball. Stress "*get* the ball, *control* the ball, *keep* the ball, and *score!*" Stress fundamentals

SKILL DIFFICULTIES AND THEIR CORRECTION—SPEEDBALL

The Kick-up with Both Feet

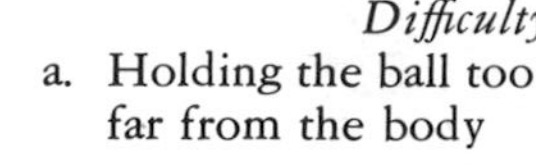

Difficulty	*Correction*
a. Holding the ball too close or out too far from the body	a. Too close—be sure the arms are fully extended; too far—show how the body should bend only slightly forward before action is started, and that one need not strain too far forward
b. Letting the ball rise too high before catching it	b. Bend to catch the ball before starting foot action; watch the ball and practice to gain the correct timing
c. Failing to catch the ball as it rises from the feet	c. Watch the ball closely. Practice several times doing it with eyes closed in order to get the "feel" of the body movement and the place in space where the ball is usually caught

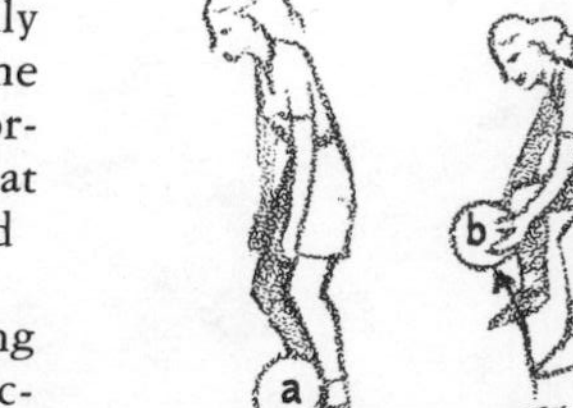

The One-Foot Lift to Self

Difficulty	*Correction*
a. Failing to get the foot securely enough under the ball (lifting before it gets on the instep)	a. Move so that the body is directly in line with the ball, extend foot so toes are depressed until the ball feels securely balanced, and then flip the foot up sharply

Difficulty	Correction
b. Standing too erect during lift-up	b. Incline body forward so hands are free to catch the ball
c. Losing control of the ball on the lift; hitting ball against the knee	c. Be sure the ball is controlled before movement starts. Practice by using a heavier flat object placed on the foot long enough to get the "feel" of the movement. Then use the ball. Practice to develop proper timing, and turn knee outward when it is flexed and foot is lifted

Kick-up of a Rolling Ball

Difficulty	*Correction*
a. Missing the ball; kicking it up too high or too low	a. Practice to gain timing with a ball rolled at a slow, medium, and fast speed. Look toward the area in which the kicked-up ball should land, and aim for it each time rather than just kicking the ball

Kick-up of a Stationary Ball with One Foot to Teammate

Difficulty	*Correction*
a. Not letting the ball roll far enough up the toes, thus kicking it instead of lifting	a. Turn the toes slightly up and flip the ankle up quickly. Be sure that the toes are completely under the ball before the motion begins
b. Reaching for the ball with extended leg	b. Wait for the ball; extend the knee *after* the ball is on the instep
c. Kicking the ball up too far instead of lifting it; jabbing at the ball	c. Get the feel of the movement by doing it several times, first mimetically, then with the ball. Aim for the place the ball should land. Watch the ball!

Drop Kick

Difficulty	*Correction*
a. Kicking with the leg instead of the top of the foot	a. Step as the ball is dropped and watch ball carefully so it is kicked *just* as it rebounds
b. Kicking with toes, thus losing control	b. Point toes downward; leg swings from hip with knee extension
c. Poor release and uncontrolled ball drop	c. Release the ball by pulling hands apart; avoid throwing ball up or casting it down

SKILL DIFFICULTIES AND THEIR CORRECTION—SPEED-A-WAY

For correction of skill errors of ball handling, see basketball; for dribbling, kicking, passing, and ground ball conversion, see above sections. Suggestions below relate only to ball carrying and tagging skills.

Difficulty	*Correction*
a. Inability to evade an opponent or position for pass or receipt of kick.	a. Practice feints, dodging, and evading. Have a positive attitude about ability to outmaneuver an opponent; do not fear tag. Maintain speed or increase it as a dodge is accomplished

b. Tagging an opponent who is receiving the ball or who has not held it 3 seconds	b. Review rules; try to wait patiently, properly positioned for the tag or play
c. Inability to control a tag, so rough tactics result with the possibility of falls and injuries of opponents	c. Maintain balanced control as you reach with one or both hands to tag a moving opponent with the ball. Do not lunge or fall toward the opponent
d. Body contact resulting when players try to gain an aerial ball	d. Practice running and dodging. A player should *move* to create a space where her teammate can throw or kick the ball. Avoid standing still and waiting for opponents to surround you. Move away from opponent and toward anticipated ball position
e. Failure to take advantage of best scoring opportunity	e. Review scoring tactics and point value. Use simulated situations for mental rehearsal; *think* while playing

EVALUATING THE RESULTS

Each player should be tested for her knowledge of the background, rules, and strategy of the game. The results of this written examination should be coupled with those of a skill test if a final grade is to be given for the soccer, speedball, or speed-a-way unit.

Rating scales for subjectively classifying players during game play can be devised. These should be based upon criteria established for players of average, below average, and above average ability.

Soccer skill tests which may be used in evaluating both soccer and speedball performance are as follows:

The Soccer Dribble Test. Set four posts in a straight line as in Figure 17–30. On "go" the player dribbles the ball from the starting line and weaves around the posts as shown. When passing the first post coming back, she kicks the ball across the starting line. If she loses control of the ball, she must regain it and complete her dribble. Record the amount of time taken from the word "go" to the ball's crossing the starting line. Record the best of three trials, and award a grade from those curved recorded times of the best scores made by each in the group.

Soccer Dribble for Speed and Left-Foot Pass for Accuracy. Mark the area as shown in Figure 17–31. On a signal, the player dribbles the ball from point B to any point along line AB between X and Y. At some point between X and Y, the player kicks the ball through the goal.

Timing commences with the word "go" and is stopped when the ball crosses the goal line. It should be recorded in seconds and tenths.

The contestant must kick the ball toward the goal from some point between X and Y, and she must not be nearer to the goal than the 6 yard line when the kick is made; if this rule is violated, no score is recorded. The player may try until she scores. Three trials are recorded, and the best of the

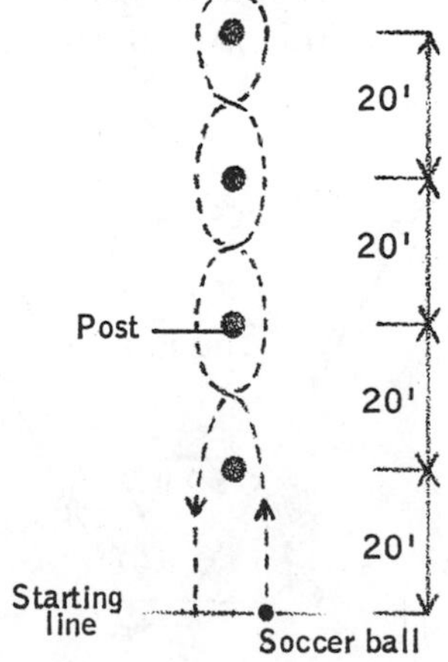

Figure 17–30 Field arrangement for soccer dribble test.

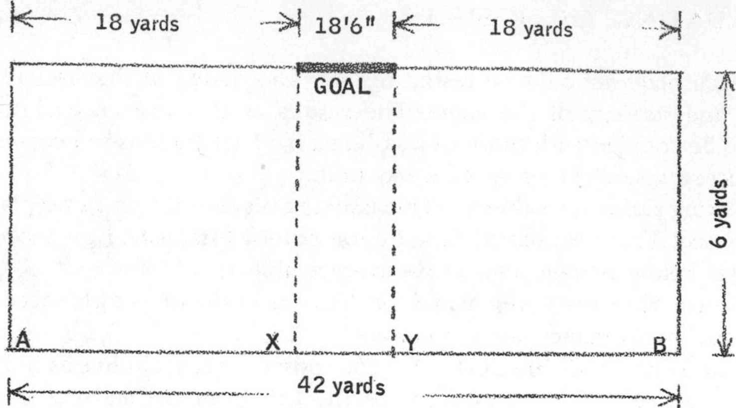

Figure 17–31 Field markings for soccer dribble and left-foot pass tests.

three is curved along with those other best recorded tries by each in the class.

Soccer Dribble for Speed and Right-Foot Pass for Accuracy. Use the same diagram and directions given in the previous test. In this test the player starts from point A and kicks with the right foot.

Soccer Punt for Distance. Equipment needed includes several balls, three pointed marking sticks, a 100 foot tape, and a timer. The area should be marked as shown in Figure 17–32. Each player has three trials. Without stepping over the line, she takes several steps and punts the ball as far as she can. One student places a marker where the ball first lands and returns all balls to the kicking line. Two others measure and mark the distance, having the zero end of the tape in the field. The instructor should read and record all measurements made and supervise the placement of the markers.

Trapping Test. The instructor kicks the ball or passes it to the player from a point 30 feet away. The number of times she successfully traps it out of 10 tries is recorded. A variety of traps should be used, or the test can be

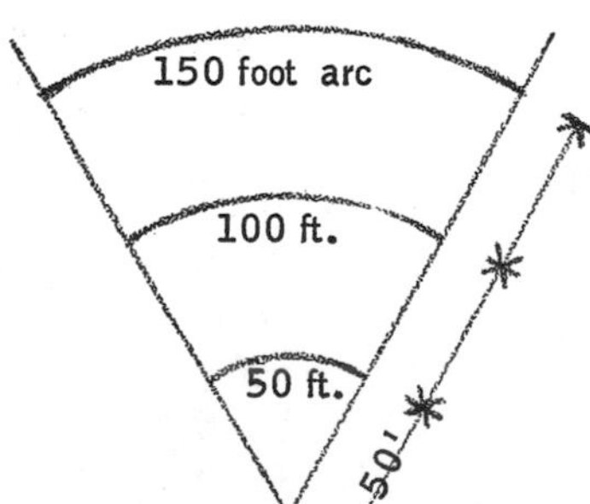

Figure 17–32 Field markings for soccer-punt-for-distance test.

run 10 times for each type of trap. The test should measure the ability to adjust to a moving ball as well as the ability to trap.

Kicking for Accuracy. The player stands 30 yards away from five concentric circles and attempts in five tries to kick the ball into the center circle. She receives 10 points if the ball hits on the line or in the center circle, 8 for the next, etc., with the last circle worth 2 points. No point is scored if all circles are missed. The total number of points made in the five attempts is totaled.

Achievement Practice Tests for Speedball Beginners. This is an ideal test for players of varying skill, for it is a good motivator for learning. Each student should be given two tries and may keep an improved score, if made after practice.*

1. Dribble the ball 30 yards in 6 seconds or less. (Record the exact time taken.)
2. A two-legged kick-up to oneself at least five times in 30 seconds. (Only lifts done correctly count. Half of the group counts and records while the other takes the test; reverse roles.)
3. Kick-up to oneself a ball rolled from 10 yards at least five times without missing. (Score only the greatest number done correctly.)
4. Lift a moving ball to a receiver 5 yards away at least five times without missing. (Score only the greatest number done correctly.)
5. Kick a ground ball 20 yards with either foot at least five consecutive times. (Use an instep kick with either foot, and score only those done correctly.)
6. Punt a soccer ball 20 yards at least five consecutive times. (Score only those done correctly and going 20 yards.)
7. Kick a rolling ball on the ground under the crossbar and between the goal posts at least five times without missing. (Score the greatest number done correctly.)
8. Catch five basketball-type passes in succession thrown by a passer 10 yards away. (Score the greatest number caught correctly.)
9. Drop kick a ball from a distance of 12 yards over a crossbar between the goal posts five times without missing. (Score the greatest number kicked correctly.)
10. Volley the ball five times consecutively with the foot or knee when tossed 5 yards away. Volley it back to the thrower so that she can catch it without moving more than one step. (Score the greatest number of volleys done correctly.)

Miller** developed and compiled suggested tests for both indoor and outdoor testing. The suggested indoor battery consists of three tests—foot pass to wall, kick-up to self, and speed toss. The recommended outdoor battery includes speed toss and dribble time.

---

*Adapted from Dr. Mary Buice's article, Selected achievement standards as a practice test for beginners, *Official Soccer-Speedball Guide,* AAHPER, DGWS, 1956–1958, pp. 84–86. Also available in Ruth Sevy (ed.): *Selected Soccer and Speedball Articles,* AAHPER, DGWS, 1963.

**Shirley B. Miller: Speedball skill tests, *Soccer-Speedball Guide,* AAHPER, DGWS, 1962–64. (See also *Selected Soccer-Speedball Articles.*)

Harrison developed a four item test for skill evaluation of beginners which requires little equipment and limited time to administer. The basic skills of dribbling and two foot kick-up; one foot kick-up; passing for accuracy and the drop kick are tested.*

Knowledge tests covering rules, strategy, and player responsibilities should also be given.† The results of these examinations, coupled with those of a skill test, should be considered if a final grade is recorded.

Evaluation of speed-a-way may be designed for specific skills or general playing ability. Skill test items are noted in the basketball, soccer, and speedball sections for such skills as dribbling, volleying, lift-up, punting, etc. The following items are designed to judge those skills unique to speed-a-way.

1. Kick-up to oneself of a ball rolled from ten yards and run twenty-five yards for the goal line. Repeat three times and record the best time.
2. Lift a moving ball to a receiver five yards away; the receiver returns the ball with a basketball-type pass; the original player runs fifteen yards. Repeat three times and record the best time.
3. Catch five basketball-type passes thrown by a passer ten yards away in succession. Score the number correctly caught.
4. Drop kick a ball from a designated point within the penalty area under the crossbar. Repeat five times and record the number that would have scored.
5. Catch a pass twenty yards from the goal line and drop kick over the crossbar. Repeat five times and record the number of effective scoring kicks.

TERMINOLOGY

Soccer

Blocking—Using any part of the body except the arms and hands to change or direct the progress of the ball.

Clearing—A throw or kick by the goalkeeper after she has stopped a ball in the vicinity of the goal.

Corner kick—Place kick taken on the goal line by attacking team 5 yards from the nearer corner. It is awarded when the ball is sent over the endline or crossbar by a defending player.

Defense kick—Place kick awarded defending team when the attacking team sends the ball out of bounds over the endline not between the goal posts or over goal posts.

Direct free kick—A free kick from which a goal may be scored directly.

Dribble—Short series of foot taps used to move the ball.

Drop kick—Dropping the ball and kicking it as it bounces up from the ground.

Free kick—Awarded to the opposing team when a foul or rule infraction is committed (see rule explanation).

Indirect free kick—A free kick from which a field goal may not be scored directly.

Kick-off—Taken by the center forward, who kicks the ball forward or to the sides, at the beginning of the game, at each quarter, and after each goal is scored.

---

*See JoAnn Harrison: Selected Speedball Skills Test, *Soccer-Speedball Flag Football Guide.* Washington, D.C., DGWS, AAHPER, 1972–1974.

†For speedball examinations see Phyllis Roney's A written knowledge examination for speedball, *Soccer-Speedball Guide,* 1958–1960, pp. 91–94, and Rosabel Koss's Speedball quiz, *Soccer-Speedball Guide,* 1964–1966, pp. 100–105.

Marking—A back remains sufficiently close to the opposing forward for whom she is responsible in order to intercept a pass, to tackle—should the forward gain possession of the ball—or to prevent the execution of a pass.
Off-side—An infringement that occurs when a player is nearer the opponent's goal line than the ball and fewer than three opponents between the player and the goal. It occurs only in the opponent's half of the field.
Penalty kick—A place kick taken on the penalty kick mark 12 yards from the center of the goal. It is awarded when any member of the defending team fouls in the penalty area.
Place kick—Kicking the ball from a stationary ground position without touching or picking it up with the hands.
Punt—Dropping the ball and kicking it with the top of the foot before it touches the ground.
Tackle—Method of getting the ball away from an opponent without body contact.
Throw-in—Method of putting the ball in play after it has gone out of bounds over the sideline.
Trapping—Stopping and gaining control of the ball by use of a foot, one or both legs, or the body.
Volleying—Kicking, kneeing, or otherwise contacting the ball while it is in the air.

Speedball

Aerial ball—A ball raised into the air by a kick with one or both feet or a thrown ball that has not touched the ground.
Attackers—The team having possession of the ball.
Defenders—The team members who seek to gain possession of the ball.
End goal—A ball that crosses the endline not between the goal posts. It does not count for a score in girls' rules.
Foul—A rule infraction for which a free or penalty kick is given.
Ground ball—A moving or stationary ball on the ground. It may be converted to an aerial ball only by the use of the feet.
Intercept—Catching a pass, a drop kick, or dribble, or getting a passed ball intended for a player on the opposing team.
Kick-off—The way the game is started at its beginning, at each quarter, and after each scored goal. It is done with one foot and is a pass to another player.
Passing—Advancing the ball downfield as in basketball.
Trapping—Stopping a moving ball with the body, or one or both feet.
Volley—Playing the ball with the head or any part of the body except the hands, forearms, and feet before it touches the ground. This does not convert a ground ball into an aerial ball.

Speed-a-way (additional or expanded definitions of soccer and speedball)

Aerial ball—A ball that may legally be played in the air. It may be passed, run with, kicked, or reconverted to a ground ball. An aerial ball results from a kick, punt, drop kick, or kick-up caught on the fly or after the first bounce.
Drop kick—A ball dropped by a player and kicked as it strikes the ground. An optional method of scoring 4 points when soccer or football goals are used.
Field goal—A score of 3 points made by any attacking player kicking a ground ball or executing a drop kick from within the striking circle so that the ball passes between the goal posts and below the crossbar.
Holding the ball—Maintaining possession of an aerial ball for more than 3 seconds without running or advancing the ball.
Penalty corner—Awarded to the attacking team when the defending team commits a foul in its own striking circle. The ball is put into play by a wing of the attacking team from a point on the goal line 15 yards from the nearer goal by a throw-in, punt, place kick, or drop kick.
Tagging—A defending player places one or both hands on the back of an attacker who is carrying the ball. A legal tag results in a free kick for the tagging team.
Tie ball—A ball caught and held simultaneously by two opponents. A toss-up results.

Touchdown—A score of 2 points gained by (1) an attacking player's running over the goal line outside the goal cage area, or (2) a successful pass from the field of play to a teammate across the goal line.

DISCUSSION QUESTIONS

1. Make a chart with three headings to show the qualifications, specific duties, and areas of the field each should cover for all players on a soccer, speedball, or speed-a-way team.
2. Draw sketches to show your coaching suggestions for a penalty kick formation, a kick-off play in speedball, a line-up of players for a corner kick, and an out of bounds over the endline in speedball.
3. Some girls are reluctant to play goalkeeper. How would you go about "selling" them on the advantages of playing this position?
4. Officiate an intramural game. Write a brief report of the strong and weak points of your officiating ability and the playing styles and weaknesses of both teams.

SELECTED AUDIOVISUAL AIDS

Beginning Soccer, 1962. (3 filmstrips, sound, color.) The Athletic Institute, 805 Merchandise Mart, Chicago, Illinois 60654. (Purchase and rental)

Soccer. (Series of 11 films) The Athletic Institute, 805 Merchandise Mart, Chicago, Illinois 60654.

Soccer for Girls, 1962. (11 min., sound, b & w.) Coronet Instructional Films, 65 East South Water Street, Chicago, Illinois 60601.

Soccer—Girls', 1969. (6 filmstrips, sound.) Athletic Institute, 805 Merchandise Mart, Chicago, Illinois, 60654. (Purchase from Association Instructional Materials, 600 Madison Avenue, New York 10022, or rental)

Soccer: The Universal Game. (10 min., sound, b & w.) Hollywood Pan-American Films, 5356 La Mirada Avenue, Hollywood, California 90028. (Purchase and rental)

Speed-A-Way. (b & w.) Marjorie S. Larsen, 1754 Middlefield Road, Stockton, California 95204. (Purchase and rental)

Speedball for Girls, 1948. (16 mm., 11 min., sound, b & w and color.) Coronet Instructional Films, 65 East South Water Street, Chicago, Illinois 60601. (Purchase and rental)

The Great Game: Soccer. National Soccer Coaches Association of America. (Rental)

SUGGESTED READINGS

Bailey, C. Ian, and Teller, Francis L.: *Soccer.* Philadelphia, W. B. Saunders Co., 1970.

Csanadi, Arpad: *Soccer.* Budapest, Hungary, Corvine Press, 1965. 2 vols.

DiClements, C. L.: *Soccer Illustrated for Coach and Player.* 2nd ed., New York, The Ronald Press, 1968.

Larsen, Marjorie S.: *Speed-A-Way Guide Book*, 1754 Middlefield Road, Stockton, California 95204.

Mott, Jane A.: *Soccer and Speedball for Women.* Dubuque, Iowa, Wm. C. Brown Co., 1973.

Sevy, Ruth: *Selected Soccer and Speedball Articles.* second ed. AAHPER, DGWS, 1201 16th Street, N.W., Washington, D.C. 20036.

Soccer-Speedball Flag Football Guide. Current ed. AAHPER, NAGWS, 1201 16th Street, N.W., Washington, D.C. 20036.

CHAPTER 18

SOFTBALL AND SLOW PITCH SOFTBALL

Like other truly American sports events, softball just "growed" like Topsy. Softball, so popular with youth and adults in schools and on playgrounds, is a direct descendant of Abner Doubleday's game of baseball. A game of indoor baseball was originated in 1887 by George W. Hancock of the Farragut Boat Club in Chicago. Originally played with a broom as a bat and a boxing glove ball, the game drew on the skills of barn ball, rounders, and one old cat. As the game attracted enthusiastic followers, Hancock devised rules and provided a large softball and a small-headed bat.

Variations of the game were played under the names of mush ball, pumpkin ball, and kitten ball. Recreation groups moved the sport outdoors under the title of playground ball, and here it gained its greatest popularity as a sport suitable for men and women in an area smaller than that required for baseball.

Softball was officially adopted in 1933 after the first national tournament in Chicago. Walter A. Hakanson of the Denver YMCA is credited with naming the present-day game. Since 1927, when the American Physical Education Association adopted softball rules for girls as drawn up by Gladys Palmer, the National Section for Girls' and Women's Sports, now the National Association for Girls and Women in Sport, has continued its interest in rule development. The official game is governed by the International Joint Rules Committee on Softball, and the rules are published every two years by NAGWS. The Amateur Softball Association of America is the primary governing body in this country. The ASA* promotes

---

*Amateur Softball Association, 4515 North Santa Fe, Oklahoma City, Oklahoma 73118.

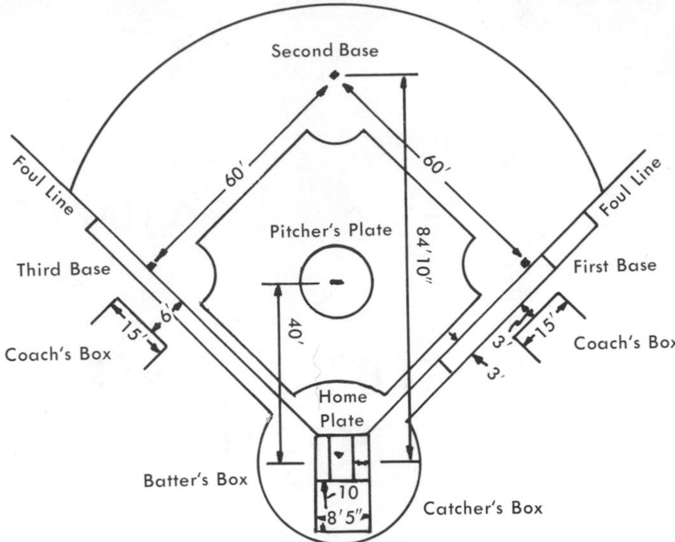

Figure 18–1 Official softball field according to NAGWS specifications.

clinics, offers information services, sponsors tournaments, and encourages the growth of softball as an international activity.

Softball is one of the few team games that readily lend themselves to informal, corecreational settings. Played at picnics, playdays, backyard gatherings, and in competitive leagues, the game is satisfying to both men and women of all skill and experience levels. The small area needed for play, the flexible rules, and the carry-over value make it the ideal team sport for girls and women.

NATURE AND PURPOSE OF THE GAME

Like baseball, softball is a game using the throwing, batting, catching, and running skills of two opposing teams on a diamond-shaped field. Each team of nine players alternates turns at bat and in the field throughout a regulation game of 7 innings. Teams remain in the offensive (batting) position until the defending (fielding) team succeeds in getting three of the team members out. Each team member has a specific position to play when on the defense. They are the catcher, pitcher, first baseman, second baseman, third baseman, shortstop, right fielder, center fielder, and left fielder. Each position is primarily responsible for covering a specific area of the field (see Figure 18–2).

Game play begins with one team in fielding position and the other team at "home," one member preparing to bat. The pitcher, in preparation for delivering the ball, stands squarely facing the batter. She has both feet in contact with the pitcher's plate and holds the ball in front of the body in

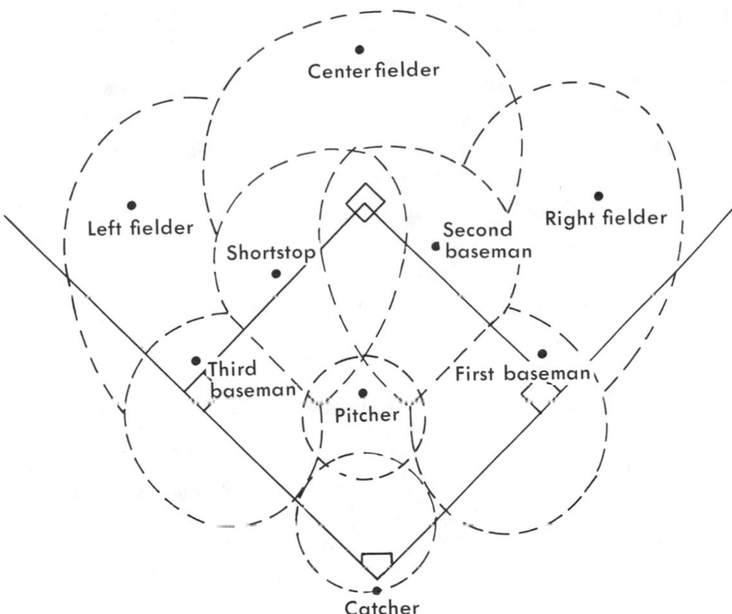

Figure 18–2 Playing positions and areas of play.

both hands. The ball is delivered toward the batting area with an underhand motion so that the hand is below the hip and the wrist no farther from the body than the elbow. The pitcher may take one step toward the batter during the delivery.

The batter attempts to hit the pitched ball with the bat so that the ball travels into the fair territory of the diamond or outfield area. The pitcher attempts to throw the ball so that it is difficult to hit or, if hit, is easily fielded by her defending teammates. Defensive players are positioned in the field to catch the ball on the fly, bounce, or roll and get the batter out.

A player in batting position is "out" if she swings and misses three times, fails to hit after three called strikes, bunts foul after the second strike, hits a fair or foul ball that is caught, or is put out at first base. When the ball is hit foul (and is not caught), the batter may remain at bat.

If the batter is successful in hitting the ball into fair territory, she attempts to run to first, second, third base, and home to score a run. She does not have to run all the bases on her own hit, but may stop safely at any of the first three bases and await a teammate's hit to drive her forward. The defensive team tries to tag the baserunner or get the ball to a base ahead of the runner in order to force her out. Players who advance around the bases score runs and further the real team objective of winning the game by scoring more runs than the opponents.

SIMPLIFIED RULES*

An official game consists of seven innings. A full seven innings need not be played if the team second at bat has more runs in six innings or before the third out in the seventh inning. A game tied at the end of seven innings shall continue until one team has more runs at the end of a complete inning or until the team second at bat has scored more runs.

Each team of nine players may have substitutes. Once a player is removed she may not reenter the game as a player.

The following simplified rules cover the the most frequent situations:

Strike. This is called when one of the following situations occurs:

1. A batter swings at a legally pitched ball and misses.
2. A legally pitched ball is delivered over home plate between the top of the knees and the armpits of the batter.
3. A fly ball goes foul and is not caught, and the batter has less than two strikes.
4. A foul tip that remains lower than the batter's head is caught by the catcher when the batter has less than two strikes.
5. A batter with less than two strikes is hit by her own batted ball.
6. A batter strikes at and misses the ball, which then touches her.

Ball. A ball is any of the following:

1. A pitched ball that does not go over the plate in the strike zone and at which the batter does not swing.
2. A ball that touches the ground before reaching home plate.
3. An illegally pitched ball.

Fair Ball. This is a legally batted ball that:

1. Settles or is touched on fair ground in the infield.
2. Bounds past first or third base on or over fair ground.
3. Touches first, second, or third base.
4. Touches the person or clothing of an umpire or player while on or over fair ground.
5. Lands in the outfield in fair territory between the extended lines from home to first and home to third.
6. Lands behind a fence or in a stand at a distance of more than 200 feet from home plate after traveling on or over fair ground (considered a home run).

Foul Ball. A batted ball is foul if:

1. It settles in foul territory between home and first base or between home and third base.
2. It first touches on foul ground beyond first or third base.
3. It bounds past first or third on or over foul ground.
4. It touches the person or clothing of an umpire or player, or is blocked, while on or over foul ground.

---

*For details of rules and scoring, see the current NAGWS Softball Guide.

Batter Out. Batter is out when:

1. The third strike is caught by the catcher.
2. She has three strikes, there are less than two outs, and first base is occupied.
3. She swings at and misses the third strike and the ball touches her.
4. She bunts foul after the second strike.
5. A foul ball is legally caught.
6. She hits an infield fly with baserunners on first and second or on first, second, and third with less than two outs. (This is the *infield fly rule.*)

Baserunner Out. She is out when:

1. The catcher drops the third strike but the runner is touched with the ball by a fielder before touching first base.
2. The ball reaches first base and is caught and held before the runner reaches base.
3. She is tagged with the ball before reaching first base or at any time when not in contact with a base.
4. Her fly ball is caught.
5. She interferes with a fielder trying to field a ball.
6. When running to any base, she runs more than 3 feet outside a baseline unless umpire deems she moved to avoid a fielder attempting to field a batted ball.
7. She is forced out at base.
8. She passes a baserunner.
9. She fails to touch the intervening base or bases in order.
10. She leaves her base before the ball leaves the pitcher's hand.
11. She fails to return to her base before the ball reaches the baseman following a fair fly that is caught.
12. She is hit by a fair batted ball while off base before it is touched by or passes a fielder.

SCORING

Use of an official scoresheet in class and during a game improves one's knowledge of the game of softball and gives accurate records of individual and team play. When one's own team is at bat, it is charted for offensive play and the opponents' defensive acts are recorded; with the opponents on offense, charting is identical. Players are numbered by position; that is, (1) pitcher, (2) catcher, (3) first baseman, (4) second baseman, (5) third baseman, (6) shortstop, (7) left fielder, (8) center fielder, and (9) right fielder.

An example of scoring three innings of play is reproduced from Poindexter and Mushier, pp. 196–197.

The *official scorer* has a unique responsibility in softball. She has the authority to make all decisions involving judgment on a play as long as there is no conflict with the official playing rules or the umpire's direction. Her duties and use and interpretation of the box score and game summary are delineated in DGWS *Softball Guide,* 1972–74, pp. 142–147.

Lee, centerfielder, hits a long fly ball to left field. The count was two and one. Out number one is recorded.

Patterson, second baseman, pops up to the pitcher. Two outs are now recorded.

Walker, left fielder, gets a hit driving the ball past the second baseman into right field.

Garrison, third baseman, pops up to the third baseman with a full count of three balls and two strikes. The side is retired.

In the second inning, Fowler, first baseman, takes first base on balls.

Wilson, shortstop, sacrifice bunts to the first baseman who throws to the second baseman covering first for the out. Fowler advances.

Glazner, catcher, hits the pitch delivered for a double to deep right field. Fowler comes home.

Barnes, right fielder, gets a hit past the second baseman to right field. Glazner scores.

Meffert, pitcher, pop flies to short right field. The second out is recorded.

Lee hits to the shortstop who throws to first on a fielder's choice for the third out of the inning.

Patterson leads off in the third inning. She pop flies to the shortstop for the first out.

Walker hits a long fly ball to the center fielder for the second out.

Garrison hits a home run beyond the left fielder.

Fowler hits to the shortstop who throws to first for the third out.*

Abbreviations on the right side of the player's box of each inning indicate the method of getting on base. A mark through the appropriate symbol is all that is required of the scorekeeper. It is helpful in later evaluation of a player's placement or opponents' defensive strengths and weaknesses to draw a line from home in the direction and approximate distance of the hit. A base on balls, sacrifice hit or hit by a pitched ball does not count as times at bat in statistical tabulation.

Strikes and balls are recorded on all batters in the small frame in the player's box. An out made by the batter is recorded to indicate the way it was made and the player or players who were involved. For example, F4 indicates a fly to the second baseman. The type of fly ball, pop-up or long ball, may be indicated by an arc over the play recorded—pop-up, F9 or a long fly F9. An unassisted play, such as the first baseman fielding a ball and stepping on base, is recorded as 3U.†

---

*From Hally B. W. Poindexter and Carole L. Mushier: *Coaching Competitive Team Sports for Girls and Women.* Philadelphia, W. B. Saunders Co., 1973, p. 197.

†*Ibid.*, p. 194.

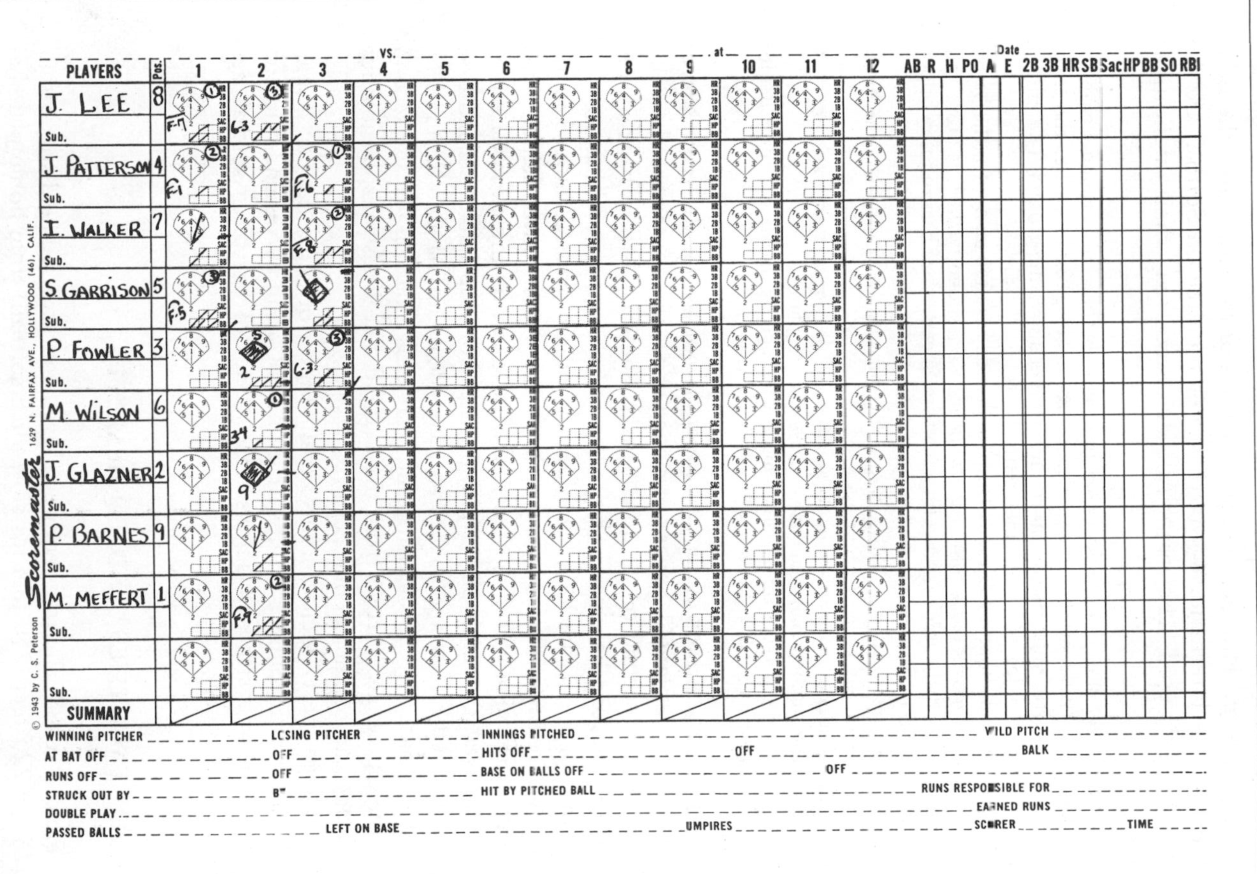

Figure 18–3 Sample scoresheet. (From Poindexter, Hally B. W., and Mushier, Carole L.: *Coaching Competitive Team Sports for Girls and Women*. Philadelphia, W. B. Saunders Co., 1973, p. 196.)

SLOW PITCH SOFTBALL

Slow pitch softball has gained popularity among those players who appreciate the shift of skill emphasis from pitching to strategic hitting and fielding. Although there are several variations of the basic rules, the rules adopted by the International Joint Rules Committee on Softball are the most commonly used. The major rule differences and their implications follow:

1. The pitcher must deliver the ball with moderate speed underhand, below the hip, with a perceptible arc of at least three feet before it reaches the strike zone. The ball must rise no more than 10 feet above the ground. The umpire is the sole judge of compliance with the rule.
2. Bunting and chopping at the ball are illegal and result in an out for the batter. The batter must take a complete swing and consequently there is more "hitting" of the ball which is traveling at a slow speed, more baserunning opportunity, and more reliance on fielding skills.
3. If the pitcher wishes to walk a batter, she informs the umpire and the batter is automatically awarded first base.
4. Baserunners are not allowed to steal bases. A runner may leave her base when the pitched ball reaches or passes home plate.
5. There are *ten* players on a team. This tenth player is the short center fielder and may play as an infielder, outfielder, or rover.

If the hitting power of the opponents is not strong, the tenth player makes a five player infield. She is positioned about three feet behind second base and covers second on all infield plays. She can learn to back up the shortstop or second baseman and then move to cover second base.

If the opponents are long ball hitters, the tenth player is moved to the outfield where she is placed to the right or left of the center fielder. Such defensive patterning will give up a single hit to cut off the extra base hits.

As a rover, the tenth player plays to the shortstop side of second base on right-handed batters and to the first base side on left-handed batters. The short center backs up the shortstop and second baseman on plays to second and double plays and throws from the outfield. She is also responsible for closing any gap behind second base.

Although the 12 inch official softball is most often used, a larger ball may be used with younger groups or teams not using gloves and mitts on defense. The offensive and defensive strategies of fast pitch softball are basically unchanged.

NEEDED FACILITIES AND EQUIPMENT

Field. A softball game requires a level, unobstructed field area within a radius of 225 feet (250 feet for slow pitch softball) from home plate between the foul lines. There should be at least 25 unobstructed feet between

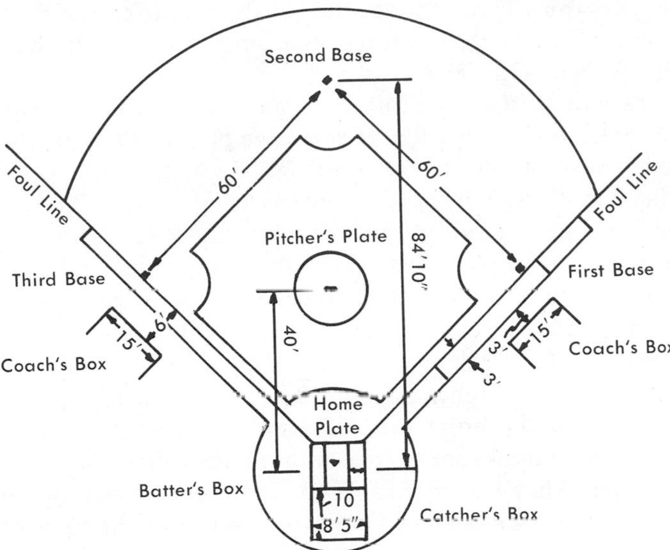

Figure 18–4 Softball diamond layout.

home plate and the backstop and outside the foul lines. The diamond has 60 foot baselines with a pitching distance of 40 feet (46 feet for men). The field should be free from rocks and holes and the diamond should be placed so that the players do not have to look directly into the sun.

Figure 18–4 shows the basic layout of the diamond with:

1. The three foot line, parallel to and 3 feet from the baseline, is drawn from a point halfway between home and first base.
2. The batter's box, each side measuring 3 by 7 feet, on each side of home plate.
3. The catcher's box, 10 feet in length and 8 feet 5 inches wide.
4. The two 15 foot coaches' boxes.

Balls. Although 14 to 16 inch balls may be used indoors and for slow pitch softball the official softball must be between 11⅞ and 12⅛ inches in circumference. It may weigh not less than 6¼ ounces nor more than 7 ounces. The exterior is smooth horsehide or cowhide smoothly seamed with concealed stitches. The center is kapok or cork and rubber covered with yarn. The hide cover is glued over the round ball. Rubber covered balls are "harder" than leather and although ideal for play on damp ground in early morning classes may not be appropriate for beginners.

Bats. Official bats are made of solid hardwood, laminated wood or metal (generally aluminum) and must be no longer than 34 inches or more than 2⅛ inches in diameter at the largest part. Weight is a matter of player preference. A safety grip, at least 10 inches long and of cork, tape, or composition material should not extend more than 15 inches from the small end of the bat. A plastic cap may be attached to the handle end of the bat, but it shall not extend more than two inches from the top of the bat. The bat should be marked "Official Softball."

Gloves and Mitts. A protective hand covering that aids in skill development is recommended for all defensive players. Only the catcher and first baseman are allowed to wear mitts (gloves without separated fingers). The catcher's mitt is heavily padded and has a deep pocket. The inflexibility of this mitt encourages skillful catchers to use the first baseman's mitt. The first baseman's mitt (often called the *claw*) is less padded and more flexible and designed to trap the ball. Fingered gloves worn by all other players should be of soft horse, cow, or elk hide. No top lacing, webbing, or other device between the thumb and body of a fielder's glove or first baseman's mitt can be more than 4 inches in length.

Masks and Body Protectors. These must be worn by the catcher and plate umpire. Wire masks are padded with sponge rubber or hair covered in smooth leather. They are adjustable for all players. Body protectors are usually made of kapok and a dark canvas or check covering so that the ball is visible against the background. Leg protectors should be worn by catchers during instruction and competitive play.

Figure 18–5 Softball equipment.

Shoes. Canvas-topped or leather-topped shoes with smooth soles or soft or hard rubber cleats may be worn. Metal sole and heel plates may be worn if they do not extend more than 3/4 inch from the sole or heel. Beginners find regular physical education class footwear appropriate for instruction.

Plate and Bases. Home plate is a five-sided figure, made of rubber or comparable material, that measures 17 inches across the edge facing the pitcher. When laid, the 8½ inch sides are parallel to the inside lines of the batter's box. The sides of the point facing the catcher are 12 inches long.

The pitcher's plate is a 24 by 6 inch section of wood or rubber which is placed level with the top of the ground. The front of the plate is 40 feet from the outside corner of home plate.

First, second, and third base are 15 inch padded squares of hair or felt covered by heavy canvas. Each base has a strap underneath to hold it securely to the ground.

Care of Equipment. Softball equipment is easily maintained and stored. Bats should be wiped and rough edges should be sanded and treated with linseed oil prior to storage. Grips should be repaired or replaced with canvas composition material or cork. Store in a dry room at constant temperature.

Leather balls should not be used on damp ground, as they absorb water and become misshaped when hit. Both rubber- and leather-covered balls should be stitched immediately when split.

Gloves, masks, and body protectors should be hung for rapid drying. All leather surfaces should be cleaned and treated with leather conditioner to prevent hardening and cracking.

The pitcher's plate and home plate should be pulled from the ground and stored in a cool place. Canvas covered bases should be removed after every game to prevent water damage. After brushing and reshaping, they should be stored flat to insure longer life.

TEACHING UNITS

The following suggested units are designed for players who have some skill and experience in throwing, catching, and batting. In all cases, a brief review of the basic skills is helpful for improving team play.

Beginners

- Nature and value of softball
- Review of basic skills
  - Use of a glove
  - Underhand and overarm throwing
  - Catching flies and grounders (thrown and batted)
  - Batting

Advanced

- Complete review
- Game situation
- Individual skills
  - Sidearm throw
  - Underarm whip throw
  - Base stealing
  - Sliding

Brief history of game
Care and use of equipment
Individual skill development
- Pitching
- Bunting
- Throwing to bases
- Base running
- Fielding

Knowledge and rule understanding
- Pitching
- Fair and foul balls
- Batting
- Strikes and balls
- Outs and forced outs
- Infield fly rule
- Third strike rule

Game situation
Beginning game strategy
- Stealing bases
- Placing hits
- Pitching strategy
- Hit and run
- Backing up and covering
- Positioning fielders and relaying

Beginning officiating and team management
Evaluation
- Skills tests
- Written and demonstrated knowledge and skill, and team and individual strategy
- Officiating and scoring
- Class tournament

- Pitching
  - Fast ball
  - Curves
  - Slants

Team strategy
- Offensive—hitting, bunting, signals, double steal, and squeeze play
- Defensive—player placement on field

Tournament play
Perfect scoring techniques
Develop umpiring skill
Evaluation
- Individual skills test
- Written test of rules, tactics, officiating, and scoring
- Demonstration of officiating ability

Observation of playing skill

BASIC SKILLS

Softball skills require strength, quick reaction time, agility in fielding, accuracy in throwing and hitting, and speed in running. These skills are developed in many activities but are refined for the game of softball only through practice and playing the game.

Catching. The player should be mentally and physically alert, so she can quickly position herself for the catch. The catching position depends on both the height and speed of the ball and the throw the fielder wants to make. In all defensive positions, proper use of the glove should be emphasized. The fingers should be inserted in the glove so the base of the fingers at the fleshy portion of the hand is approximately at the center of the glove palm. Individuals adjust this position to assure finger flexibility to control the glove and extend the arm and hand reach.

The catching player moves to meet an approaching ball. If the ball is going over the fielder's head, she turns and runs with her back to the ball, looking over her shoulder. (This is faster than running backwards.) The height at which the catch is made determines the direction of the fingers. Both hands reach for the ball. The fingers and arms are relaxed and the hands slightly cupped. As the ball hits the glove hand, the fingers squeeze and the free hand closes on the top so that the ball is trapped. The ball is caught in the glove pocket, slightly to the thumb side. The hands and arms "give" with the impact of the ball, cushioning the catch.

If possible, the ball should be caught above the waist to facilitate throwing. The fingers point upward and the thumbs are together. For catches below the waist, fingers point downward and the little fingers are together.

Throwing. Throwing is one of the essential skills for a softball player.

Overarm Throw. This should be a basic skill of all players, as it is the fastest, most accurate form of ball propulsion. For the right-handed player, the ball is held in the right hand with the first two fingers on top of the ball, the third and fourth fingers spread comfortably to the side, and the thumb supporting under the ball. Do not allow any part of the palm to touch the ball.

With the feet in stride position, the weight equally distributed, and left foot forward, the left shoulder turns toward the target, moving the body at right angles away from the target. As the right arm moves back to a position behind the head about ear level, the weight shifts to the rear leg. The elbow points away from the body with the upper arm parallel to the ground. The wrist is cocked backward. The release is indicated as the forward leg extends in the direction of the target, the shoulders turn parallel to the target as the body rotates, the hips move forward, and the arm is brought forward in a semicircular motion. The hand passes forward past the ear, the elbow straightens, wrist uncocks, and the ball rolls off the first two fingers. The power of the swing carries the arm down and across the body, rotating the body so that the shoulder of the throwing arm points toward the target.

Figure 18–6 The overarm throw.

Underarm Whip Throw. The underarm and sidearm throws are used most often by infielders for quick throws when there is little time to stand or take a full backswing after fielding a grounder. The ball is held with the thumb on top. The first and second fingers are under the ball, and the third and fourth fingers are on the side. The body is crouching more than for the overarm throw, and the ball is held below shoulder level. The arm swings back, bent elbow restricting backswing, forearm below a line parallel to the ground, wrist cocked. The forward foot extends, and the arm swings across the body at waist level as the body follows around.

The *sidearm throw* has similar action with the forearm parallel to the ground during execution.

Pitching. The well controlled delivery of a ball into the strike zone is one of the highly individualized skills of softball. The pitcher places the heel of her throwing arm side on the front edge of the plate and the toe of the other foot on the back edge. A comfortable stride of ten to fourteen inches is desirable. *She stands with both feet on the plate and shoulders facing the batter with the ball held in both hands. She must remain motionless for a minimum of one and a maximum of twenty seconds before removing one hand for delivery. She may use either a slingshot or a windmill delivery.**

Basic Pitch. The ball may be held in a tripod grip with the tips of the thumb, index, and middle fingers over the seams or it may be held with all four fingers and thumb. Younger, less strong players with small hands prefer the grip and control of all fingers. The ball is pushed forward above waist level as the trunk rotates to allow a full backswing of the arm as it circles downward and backward. At the top of the backswing, the throwing arm is fully extended, the wrist is cocked back as far as possible, and the body is

*Italicized sections paraphrase rules that determine skill execution.

Figure 18–7 The basic pitch with slingshot delivery.

rotated toward the pitching arm. The downward and forward motion of the arm is preceded by a step forward and the forward rotation of the body. The pitching arm is pulled downward and swings forward parallel to the body line. The arm follows through in line with the pitch, elbow straight, as the ball leaves the fingertips last. Power is gained from a full arm swing, elbow extension, wrist snap, and body rotation. *While delivering the ball the pitcher may take only one step, which must be toward the batter and taken as the delivery is made. The ball must be delivered with an underhand motion, the release and follow-through forward, beyond the straight line of the body.** "The hand shall be below the hip and the wrist not farther from the body than the elbow."†

On the follow-through, the foot of the throwing side moves parallel with the other foot in a side stride position. The pitcher is positioned for defensive play.

For a *windmill delivery,* the pitching arm makes a complete circle, beginning either in front of the body or on the side. The arm moves rapidly forward, passing straight overhead, then downward away from the batter, and finally forward in the direction of the batter. As the throwing arm moves forward, initially body weight is shifted to the foot on the pitching arm side; as the ball passes overhead, the right-handed pitcher lifts her left foot slightly in preparation for a step forward. Stepping forward on the left foot braces the body as the pitching arm is thrust forward for the release. The point of release is determined by velocity of the delivery and angle of wrist cock at the point of release. The right leg pushes against the rubber to transfer weight and add momentum to the swing.

Once the straight, fast pitch is mastered, the pitcher should learn other deliveries. Either the slingshot or windmill windup may be used, but it should be consistent to conceal the delivery as long as possible. The grip, wrist, and finger actions determine the type and the amount of spin, which result in a change-of-pace, drop, curve, or rise ball.

Change-of-Pace Pitch. The ball is held loosely by the knuckles of a player with large hands or by the finger pads and nails of one with smaller hands. The ball is released by all fingers and the thumb simultaneously and moves to the batter with little or no spin. The deception is in its slow "floating" action when a faster working ball is expected.

Drop Ball. The ball is held by a right-handed pitcher with the thumb to the right, first three fingers to the left, and the little finger back. The palm faces the batter on delivery, and the ball is released with an upward motion of the hand. The ball rolls off the three fingers imparting a forward spin. The ball breaks downward at the plate.

Rise Ball. The ball is held with the thumb underneath, first and second fingers on top, and third and fourth fingers slightly to the left. On delivery the knuckles are forward. The wrist snaps upward, the fingers pull, and

*Rules which determine skill execution.
†NAGWS *Softball Guide.* 1974–76, p. 142.

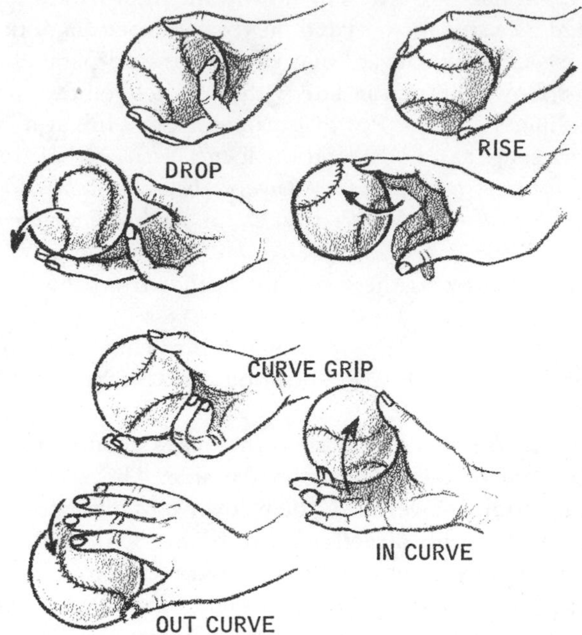

Figure 18–8 Hand positions for deliveries.

the thumb pushes. This results in a backspin on the ball. When this pitch is properly executed, the ball rises near the plate.

Outcurve. The palm is turned toward the left by a right-handed pitcher as the ball is held in a triangle formed by the thumb and the first and second fingers. Upon release the second finger is away from the ball. The wrist is snapped sharply to the left, thrusting the ball out of the little finger side of the hand. The ball curves from right to left—*away* from a right-handed hitter.

Incurve. This pitch curves *toward* a right-handed batter. The ball is gripped between the thumb and the first two fingers. On release the wrist is snapped from left to right.

Fielding. Fielding involves the basic skills of catching and throwing. At the "crack" of the bat, the fielder watches the ball and moves from a waiting position to the anticipated ball path. She moves as quickly and as close to the oncoming ball as possible to cut fielding time. Once the velocity and trajectory of the ball are determined, she positions herself behind, and in line with, the oncoming ball. With her feet in a side stride, the weight is evenly distributed on the balls of the feet, and the knees and hips are slightly bent. (See Figure 18–9.)

Fielding Ground Balls. With the upper body nearly erect, the fielder bends her knees to get down to the ball. The hips are low and weight is over the feet until the ball is scooped up by the fingers and wrists. If the ball is

Figure 18–9 Fielding a ground ball.

bouncing, the catch is made as the ball rises. The finger tips should be touching the ground ready to rise with the bounce. The palm of the glove hand is at a right angle to the path of the ball; the throwing hand is next to it and the little fingers are together. The throwing hand snaps over the glove hand to hold the caught ball, and the natural "give" of the fielding action starts the backswing for a throw.

Fielding Fly Balls. Whenever possible, flies should be caught about head high. A catch at this level saves time in making the catch and prevents the fielder from blocking her own vision. She is in a position for a rapid throw. The fielder tries to position herself so that she will be *standing* (not running) when the catch is made. The fingers are pointed up, thumbs together, and the palm of the glove hand is facing the ball. As the fly is caught, the hands, arms, and body give backward and are the beginning motion of the backswing preceding the throw. While awaiting the fly, the feet point in the direction of ball flight, and as the ball is caught, the trunk turns to the right and the right leg moves back to take the impact. The weight then shifts to the left foot as the throw is made.

Batting. This is an individual's basic offensive skill. Understanding

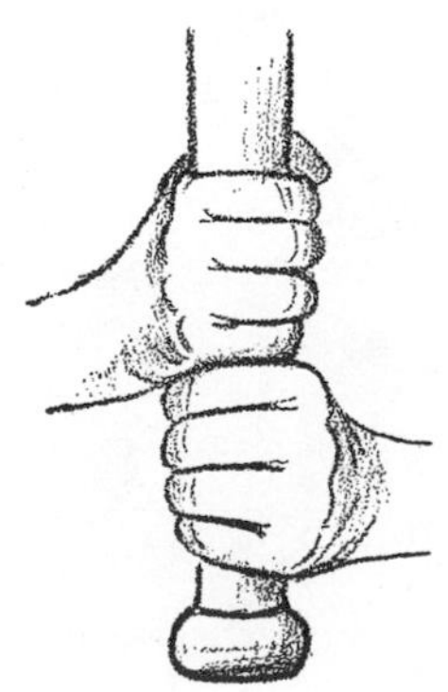

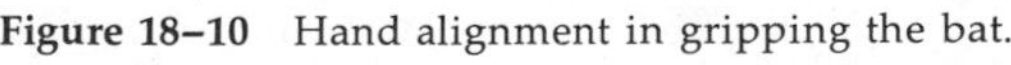

Figure 18–10 Hand alignment in gripping the bat.

the basic grip, stance, stride, and swing is fundamental to developing one's own style.

Grip. The standard grip is used by most players. A right-handed player places her left hand around the bat several inches above the end. The right hand is placed above the left and touches it. The natural grip is firm to avoid recoil and loss of power, but not tense. The second joints of the fingers of the top hand are aligned with the knuckles of the lower hand. Batters attempting to power hit often use the end grip, in which the hands are brought as far down the bat as possible. For more accurate and less powerful hits, a player may move her hands up the handle of the bat or spread her hands slightly. This is particularly useful to a player who swings late because of weak arms, wrists, and shoulder strength.

Stance. A comfortable, natural stance is taken in the batter's box. The batter must stand within the three feet by seven feet box when hitting. The distance from the plate is gauged by the individual's reach and swing. Feet are comfortably spread, and the knees are relaxed to support the upright trunk, which is facing home plate. The rear foot points toward the plate and the forward foot is turned slightly toward the infield so the body is angled slightly to view the pitcher. The bat is held up and back by an almost straight left arm and a bent right arm. The elbow of the right arm is pointing toward the ground and away from the batter. The wrists are cocked. The batter looks over her forward shoulder toward the pitcher. The position of the head adjusts from pitch to pitch to get the best and longest look at the ball.

Stride. As the ball is released by the pitcher, the batter slides her forward foot toward the pitcher. The stride should be short to avoid locking the hips and falling away from the ball. The stride initiates the rotary action of the body.

Swing. The body rotates powerfully and dramatically in effective hitting. The hips begin the the motion while the shoulders remain stationary or rotate slightly backward to overcome the inertia of the bat and increase the arc of the swing. The shoulders and hips are level, and the head stays relatively level throughout the swing. The pivot opens the hips, and as the hips

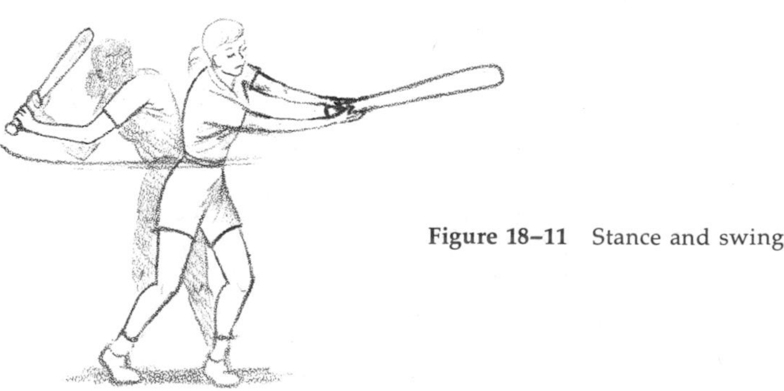

Figure 18–11 Stance and swing.

Figure 18–12 Bunting.

come around, the arms and hands follow, with each successive member of the body increasing in speed. As the bat reaches the hitting area in a horizontal plane, the lead arm is straight, and the wrists are square and unbroken; the wrists impart power and roll after the ball is contacted by the bat. Near the completion of the follow-through the hands are completely over (for right-handed batter the back of the right hand uppermost) and the right foot, free of body weight, moves toward first base.

Bunting. A bunt is a well placed ball that is tapped into the infield, usually along the first or third base line. Even when a player is willing to be put out executing a sacrifice bunt, the hit should be deceptive; therefore, the batter should keep her regular batting stance as long as possible. As the pitcher delivers, the batter pivots from her normal stance so that her body and toes turn toward the pitcher. A batter who crowds the plate should pivot by placing her lead foot to the outside and bringing her rear foot parallel to it. Feet are spread well apart. The batter who stands away from the plate pivots by turning the lead foot and bringing the rear foot parallel. Simultaneously, she slides the top hand up and behind the middle of the bat as it is brought across the body. (Some batters can bunt effectively with their hands remaining in a "choked grip" position.) The bat is in front of the player and parallel to the ground so that the incoming ball is blocked by the bat. There is *no* swing as the head of the bat is turned in the direction of the bunt.

To execute a "drag" bunt, the batter runs for first base *the instant* the ball is contacted. An attempt is made to place the ball down the third base line, but a well placed first base line bunt is often successful.

Running. A batter takes her first stride toward first base as the ball is hit. Short strides and vigorous arm action lead her into a full stride as she crosses first base. Once on base, the runner may stand with one foot on base in a sprinter's start, ready to leave when the ball is pitched. A player can observe the action of the game better if she places her left foot on base and faces the infield. With her feet in side stride position, she is slightly crouched with her weight over the right foot. The runner's arms hang freely down and away from the body to aid in balance and shift of body weight. As the ball leaves the pitcher's hand the runner takes two or three strides from the base in anticipation of a hit, wild pitch, or catcher's error. If none occurs she returns to base and assumes the starting position. (For a more complete treatment see section on offensive strategy.)

Stealing. Stealing bases is a way a baserunner may advance on weak defensive plays. Steals most often occur as the ball is missed by the catcher, overthrown at a base, or held too long by a fielder or as a play is made at another base. Stealing should be done in the interest of team play rather than as a spectacular individual feat.

Sliding. Sliding is a skill for *advanced players* who are properly dressed in long pants or long socks. Sliding helps runners evade a tag at second or third base and home and serves as a method of stopping to avoid overrunning second or third base. Once a slide is begun, it must be completed for the safety of the player. The three most common slides are the straight, bent leg, and hook. Basically, all slides are initiated the same way. The take-off is approximately two body lengths from the base with the direction of the slide determined by the take-off foot and the side of the body on which the slide will be executed. The body lean is away from the base with weight supported by one leg and the other lifted toward the base. The arms are thrown up to get full body extension. The weight-bearing foot slides along the ground as the body becomes horizontal.

Straight Slide. Beginning from a full stride, the weight-bearing leg bends, lowering the body, as the top leg extends directly toward the base. The lower leg skids along the ground, and the knee bends to avoid injury. The toe of the extended leg touches base.

Bent Leg Slide. The bent leg slide is used when the baserunner feels she will be safe and wants to regain her footing quickly in an attempt to gain extra bases. The slide begins nearer the base than the straight-in slide and the backward fall is limited so that recovery can be rapid. Executed much as is the straight slide, the nonsliding leg is flexed, and as soon as the sliding leg touches base, the arms are thrust forward and weight is shifted to the flexed top leg for a rapid recovery to running position.

Hook Slide. The hook slide is considered an "all purpose" slide but is frequently used when the runner is aware that the baseman has the ball and is waiting for a tag. The side to which the runner slides is determined by the direction of the throw to the infielder making the tag and the tagging position of the infielder. The baserunner may go wide, rather than directly to the base. The body leans in the opposite direction from the take-off foot; the runner lands on her buttocks and turns so the slide is on one side. The toe of the extended leg contacts and hooks the base as the knee bends and the upper part of the body and the sliding leg are twisted away from the infielder.

Figure 18–13 The hook slide.

STRATEGY*

The mental concentration and preplanning involved in softball strategy make the game more than a hitting-pitching contest between two teams.

Offensive Strategy. This is built around batting and baserunning skills of individuals combined to make a team contribution. Team work is enhanced by the use of base coaches as players become more skillful and respond to assistance in determining when they should advance, hold, or leave a base. Competitive players rely on coaches to determine the batting plan and to relay the play to baserunners.

1. The order of batting is one of the first strategic moves a team plans. There are several theories, but the following suggestions are offered as a basic plan. Generally, the lead-off batter is one who can get on base; the second, a fair hitter and bunter; third, a consistent hitter; fourth, the strongest and longest hitter, who can advance baserunners. Number four is the "clean-up" batter and clutch hitter; number five should be a long ball hitter; and number six should be an adequate clutch hitter. The weakest hitters hold the seventh, eighth, and last positions.
2. Place hitting is more important to a team offensive than inconsistent, spasmodic hits. Generally a low ball placed straight away through second base serves as a hit. This "spot" is not advised if a runner is on first base, as a weak hit is a perfect set-up for a double play.
3. Bunts and sacrifice flies serve to advance players to scoring position, but both usually result in an out for the hitter. The sacrifice bunt is used when runners are on first or first and second and there are no outs. The hitter places the bunt down the first or third base line and tries to "beat it out" to first.
4. Baserunners must be alert to the positions of all other runners and to any plays called for runners. A few simple guides help the player anticipate her moves. She should run as fast as possible for first base, touching it and overrunning it along the right field line. If she can advance more than one base on her hit, she moves into foul territory before reaching first, touches base on the infield corner, and moves quickly toward second base. The runner must not overrun second or third base. Some teachers suggest the slide for close

*For more extensive discussion of strategy see Hally B. W. Poindexter and Carole L. Mushier: *Coaching Competitive Team Sports for Girls and Women.* Philadelphia, W. B. Saunders Co., 1973, pp. 175–190.

plays; however, it should be avoided if players' legs are not protected. Players learn to "pull up short" from a rapid pace without abrupt muscle jerks.

Runners must not lead off bases until the pitcher releases the ball.

On fly balls, other than with two outs, runners advance a safe distance toward the next base so they can return to their original bases if the ball is caught, or be ready to advance if the ball is dropped. When a fly is hit deep and the runner has time to advance after the ball is caught, she may hold near her base, touch, and then advance. Runners should advance on wild pitches, overthrown bases, and balls dropped by the catcher.

These additional plays are helpful for a basic team offensive:

1. *Stealing.* An important offensive tactic which is effective against a pitcher with poor technique or a weak catcher. The runner starts quickly as the ball leaves the pitcher's hand.
2. *Double steal.* Attempted with runners on first and third with two out. The runner on first starts a steal. If the ball moves to second base, the runner pulls up and acts as a decoy as the runner on third tries for home. If no play is made at second base, the runner from first advances.
3. *Hit and run.* Used to move a first base runner and avoid a double play. A signal from the coach or batter indicates that an attempt will be made to hit the next pitched ball and the baserunner thus has additional seconds to run to the next base. The batter protects the runner by swinging at the pitch.
4. *Squeeze play.* An attempt to score a runner from third by giving the runner a signal indicating a bunt down the first base line. The base runner moves toward home with the pitch.

Defensive Strategy. The defense must be prepared to handle the offensive team maneuvers of hitting, bunting, and baserunning. The defensive units are the battery, infield, and outfield. Some general considerations concerning their play follow:

1. The pitcher's knowledge and skill in pitching the ball where it cannot be hit is the first line of team defense.
2. The position of the infield and outfield is dependent on the throwing range of individual players, the batter's style and skill in hitting, and her running ability. The infield plays shallow with first and second bases occupied and when there is a runner on third with fewer than two outs (Figure 18–14).

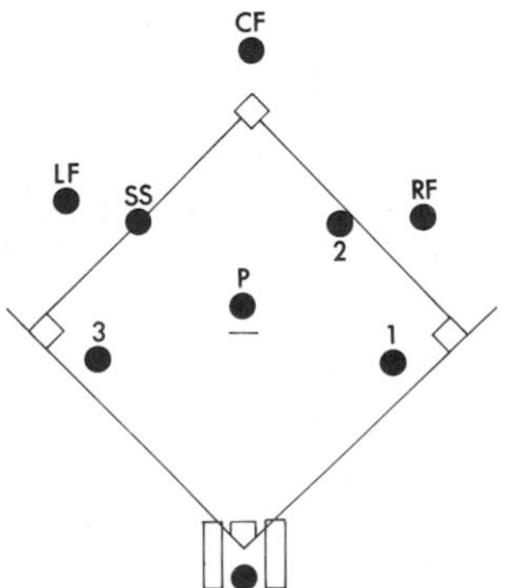

Figure 18–14 Shallow defensive position of the infield. (From Poindexter, Hally B. W., and Mushier, Carole L.: *Coaching Competitive Team Sports for Girls and Women.* Philadelphia, W. B. Saunders Co., 1973, p. 187.)

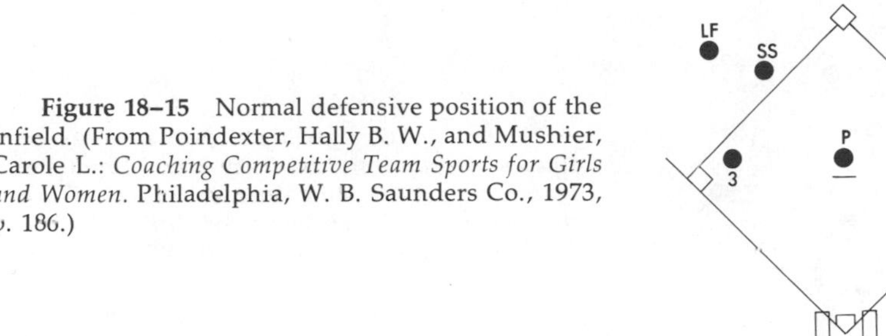

Figure 18–15 Normal defensive position of the infield. (From Poindexter, Hally B. W., and Mushier, Carole L.: *Coaching Competitive Team Sports for Girls and Women.* Philadelphia, W. B. Saunders Co., 1973, p. 186.)

The regular, deeper position is played with no one on base or with two outs, regardless of runners on base (Figures 18–15 and 18–16).

3. Infielders serve as cutoff and relay players for the outfield. Cutoff player to home plate should be the third baseman on balls hit to left and center field and the first baseman in all other situations.

When a ball is hit deep to the outfield, and a throw to base is too long to be successfully made by the outfield, a relay is necessary. The infielder runs toward the outfield and becomes the middle player in the relay. The shortstop relays when the ball is hit to left, left center or center field; the second baseman relays on balls hit to right or right center field.

4. Outfielders have the responsibility of backing up and covering infielders and other outfielders to protect against a missed ball or a misplay.

Further defensive hints include the following:

1. If possible, put out the runner who is closest to home plate.
2. Make the third out at the nearest and surest point.
3. Consider walking a strong batter when runners are on base and a weak hitter follows.
4. When a runner leaves the base before a fly is caught, attempt a double play by throwing to the base the runner just left. If the runner leaves the base after the fly is caught, throw the ball to the base toward which the runner is advancing.

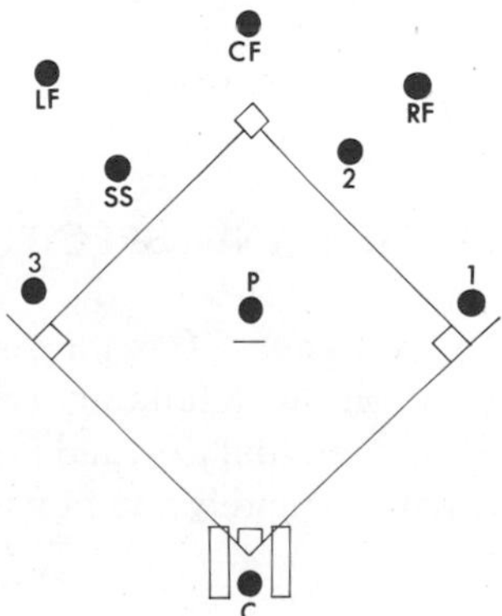

Figure 18–16 Deep defensive position of the infield. (From Poindexter, Hally B. W., and Mushier, Carole L.: *Coaching Competitive Team Sports for Girls and Women.* Philadelphia, W. B. Saunders Co., 1973, p. 187.)

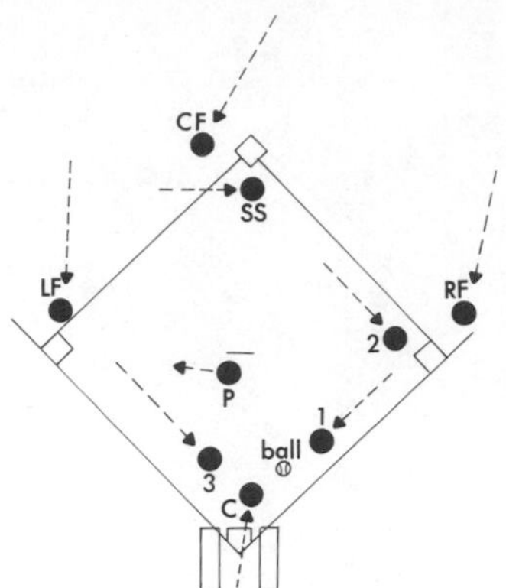

Figure 18–17 Infielders' positions for bunt defense with runner on first base. (From Poindexter, Hally B. W., and Mushier, Carole L.: *Coaching Competitive Team Sports for Girls and Women.* Philadelphia, W. B. Saunders Co., 1973, p. 188.)

5. When a runner is on third base, the catcher should not throw the ball to second in order to catch a runner who is stealing. The runner on third may score if the ball is thrown.

One of the best techniques for developing defensive strategy is by simulating actual game situations. The following serve as examples:

1. Normal positioning (Figure 18–15) is assumed when there are no base runners and a straight-away hitter is at bat. The fielders shift to the right for a left-handed batter.
2. With a runner on first base, the first baseman, third baseman, and catcher move in to field the bunt. Pitcher fields only if the ball is deep down the middle. Shortstop covers second base, and the second baseman covers first base. The pitcher and left fielder cover third base if the ball is fielded by the third baseman (Figure 18–17).
3. With runners on first and second base (or on second only), the first baseman covers the bunt on her side and the third baseman on her side. The catcher protects home, shortstop moves to cover third base, center fielder covers second base, and second baseman covers first base. Catcher verbally directs the throw.
4. Double play positioning with a runner on first brings the first baseman closer to the first base line as second and third basemen move toward their bases, and shortstop moves several steps toward the batter.

DUTIES AND SPECIFIC SKILLS OF EACH PLAYER

Catcher. Catching is one of the most important and demanding positions on the defending team. The catcher must be able to catch all varieties of pitches, foul tips, and pop flies. She must also be able to move quickly and throw accurately and rapidly to all bases. The catcher is important if pitching signals are used. She evaluates the batter's ability and characteristics and signals for the pitch.

In preparation for the pitch, the catcher assumes a semi-erect position directly behind the plate as close to the batter as is possible for safety. The body bends forward, feet parallel. The mitt hand is up as a target for the pitcher, and the right hand is close and ready to close over the ball as it hits the glove. Like all basemen, when making a play at the plate, she moves one foot to the corner and stretches to meet the ball so as not to interfere with the runner. The catcher should back up plays at first and third base as the situation demands.

Pitcher. The pitcher must master delivery of a well controlled ball. Her deliveries should include fast balls, curve balls, and slow balls which effectively cross the plate in an area approximately 2 feet above the ground, 3 feet high, and 17 inches wide. Aside from fielding hits, she should cover home on a wild pitch or passed ball when runners are on base and cover first or third on hits to these basemen when a baserunner is moving toward the base. Pitchers soon learn to throw fast balls to late swinging batters, inside curves to batters crowding the plate, outside curves to those standing away or stepping into the swing, and balls above the waist to batters attempting a bunt.

First Baseman. A tall player with a good reach and an ability to catch all types of throws is descriptive of a potential first baseman. She must play off base and field balls with general infield ability, and then place a foot on first base and reach for throws. She must develop a quick pivot and throwing motion to all other bases for effective double plays.

Second Baseman. She must move rapidly and throw accurately to all bases from many fielding positions. She is responsible for the area toward first base, as well as covering second base on attempted steals and most hits.

Shortstop. The shortstop must be a versatile player of unusual speed. She is positioned between second and third base and receives many hits from right-handed batters. She backs up the pitcher on hits to the box and third base on throws from the outfield. She also covers second base when the baseman is fielding.

Third Baseman. The third baseman plays slightly toward second base and is responsible for bunts, flies, fouls, and hits in that area. She must be able to throw accurately and fast to first base and recover her position quickly.

Outfielders. An outfielder must be able to move rapidly to field balls and throw far and accurately. The center fielder has more territory and should move faster than the left and right fielders. The fielders back up the bases when ground hits come in front of them. The center fielder backs up both other outfielders; the left fielder backs up the infield on hits to the left of the diamond; the right fielder backs up the center fielder and infielders to the right.

CLASS ORGANIZATION

Softball can be taught effectively to large groups. It is advisable to divide the class into teams of 11 or 12 players and have additional team members serve as coaches and officials during game play. Whenever possible, allow teams to play a game or a novelty game early in the unit to help maintain interest and give purpose to skill drills.

A certain amount of skill practice is basic to developing individual playing ability. Drills and practice situations should be executed at the speed and in a setting of game play. Confidence is gained rapidly under these circumstances. One of the easiest formations for throwing and catching involves two teams. Teams face one another and each girl throws and receives from a partner on the other team. If gloves are not available for all players, the gloveless players should receive ground balls. If there is not an adequate supply of balls for each twosome, groups of four may practice together.

Batting practice may be accomplished either through the game of pepper or in a game-like situation. In pepper, a semicircle of players faces the batter, who is 35 to 40 feet away. The first player on the semicircle pitches the ball to the batter, who hits it to another player. That player then tosses it back, and so on.

Fielding is practiced by "fungo" hitting, wherein the batter throws the ball and hits grounders or flies to the awaiting players in the field.

One of the best ways of teaching game play is by situations. The situation should first be explained and then enacted by the players. The following is an example of a set situation:

Runner on first, one out, fly ball hit to center field.

1. Team in the field.
   a. Fly caught by center fielder and ball thrown immediately to first base to catch runner from first who started for second when ball was hit.
   b. First baseman covers first and tags base before runner returns.
   c. Second baseman covers second base.
   d. Shortstop backs up second baseman.
   e. Pitcher backs up first baseman.
2. Team at bat.
   a. Batsman becomes baserunner immediately after hit and starts toward first.
   b. Runner on first should wait until fly is caught or missed before advancing to second base.

TEACHING PROGRESSION

The following lessons are suggested for beginning players with basic skills of catching and throwing:

Lesson I

1. Nature and value of softball
2. Equipment—wearing a glove, face mask
3. Review basic skills
   Overarm throwing
   Catching flies, grounders (thrown), and direct throws
   Batting

Lesson II

1. Throwing relays
2. Review batting
3. Pitching
4. Situation drills

Lesson III

1. Review pitching
2. Fielding practice—batted grounders and flies (use selected students who hit fungo style)
3. Scrub

Lesson IV

1. Filmstrip or chalk talk (stress positions on field and safety precautions and have brief rules discussion)
2. Three inning game covering rules in game situation

Lesson V

1. Baserunning
2. Infield practice
3. Discussion and demonstration
   Relaying throws
   Backing up
   Covering
4. Game situation

Lesson VI

1. Review
2. Bunt
3. Scrub (stress use of the bunt)

Lesson VII

1. Review bunt
2. Batting practice (stress placement of hits)
3. Game situation—stress defensive strategy

Lesson VIII

1. Brief explanation of officiating techniques and scoring
2. Game situation—stress offensive strategy

Lesson IX

1. Game situation
2. Class discussion of effectiveness of team play

Lesson X

1. Evaluation
   Brief written examination
   Begin skill tests

Lesson XI

1. Complete skill tests

Lesson XII

1. Review written examination
2. Brief discussion and evaluation of the unit
3. Game as time permits

SKILL DIFFICULTIES AND THEIR CORRECTION

Catching

Difficulty	*Correction*
a. Tense hands and fingers cause loss of control of the ball	a. Teacher stresses relaxation. The use of gloves gives players more security
b. Failure to "give" with the body as the ball is caught	b. Practice mimetically and demonstrate the relaxed "give" as the ball comes to the hands
c. Incorrect positioning of the hands—thumbs up below the waist and little fingers down above the waist result in inability to hold ball	c. Demonstrate proper catching technique; exaggerate improper manner. Student should practice throwing and catching at close range to stress form without concern for hard delivery
d. Ball rebounds from the glove	d. Use throwing hand to squeeze the ball in the glove *after* impact

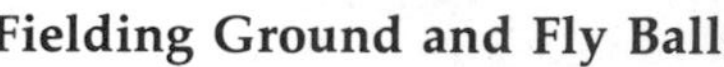

Fielding Ground and Fly Balls

Difficulty	*Correction*
a. Awaiting a ground ball in an erect position with arms at sides causes delay and a miss in stopping the ball	a. Demonstrate "ready" postion, feet spread, hips and knees bent, eyes on ball, hands in front of the body and relaxed. Player moves to play the ball as soon as it is hit

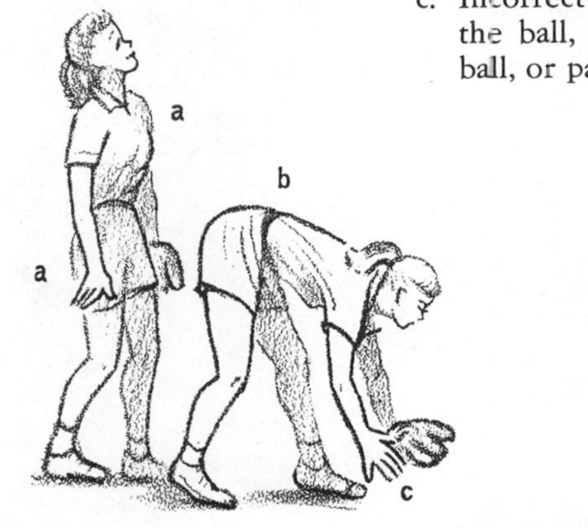

b. Bending at waist with knees stiff to field grounder as ball passes through legs	b. Move the body down through knees and hips so weight is low. If necessary, drop to one knee to block a hard-rolling ball
c. Incorrect hand position. Slapping at the ball, fingers spread toward the ball, or palms facing	c. Review technique of catching below the waist
d. Inability to judge velocity, trajectory, and descent of fly ball, resulting in overrunning or underrunning the ball	d. Watch the ball carefully on upward flight – the angle of descent is similar to the angle of rise. If the ball is in front, run forward, stop, and wait for the ball. If the ball is hit over player's head, turn and run, watching the ball flight over the shoulder

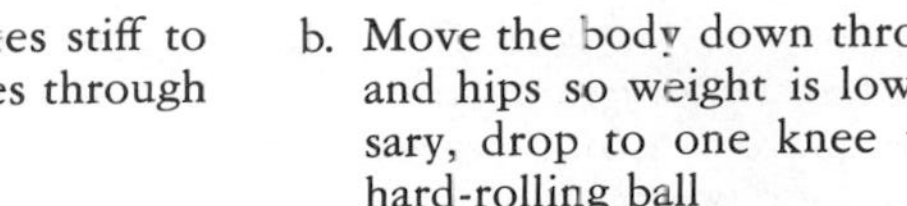
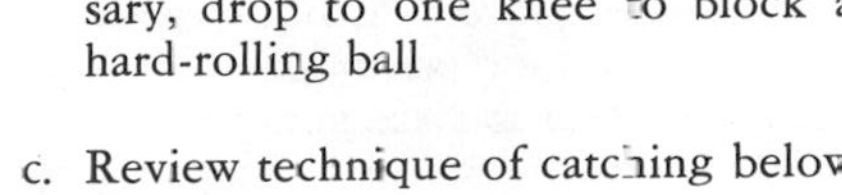
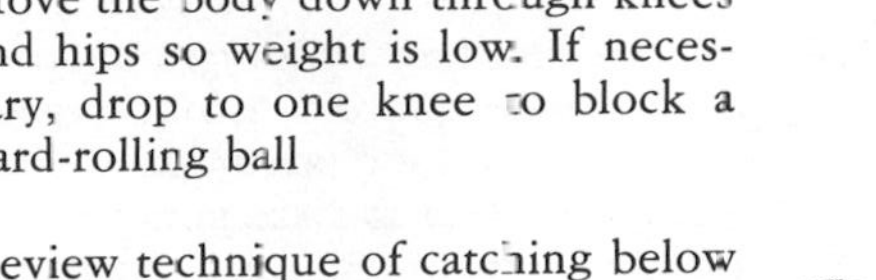

Throwing

Difficulty	*Correction*
a. Loss of power resulting from holding the ball in the palm of the hand so that a throw becomes an uncontrolled push	a. Review grip for overarm and underarm whip. Finger touch is the key to softball "feel"
b. Throwing off wrong foot	b. Review principle of opposition – right arm moves forward with left leg
c. Throwing stiff arm with no wrist or finger snap, resulting in loss of power and accuracy	c. Relax the arm and keep the elbow out from the body. Wrists cock and then flex on delivery. Stress wrist flexibility by waving the hand
d. Failure to use the body. Standing with the shoulders and hips facing the target – feet in side stride position	d. Practice throwing mimetically. In slow motion teacher may say, "body rotates, arm back, body and shoulder rotate, throw through, and follow through." *Check for body rotation*

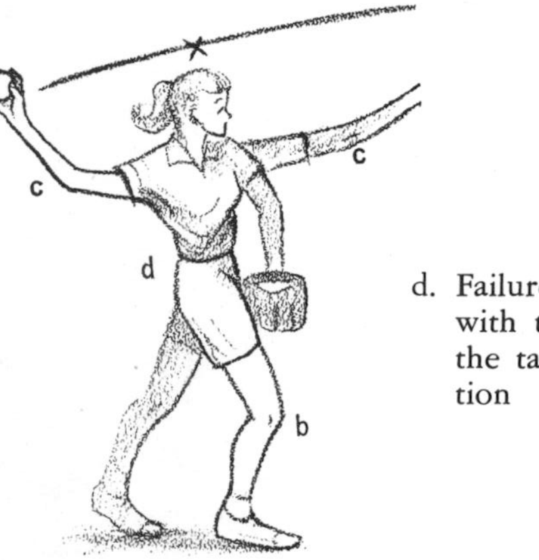

e. Releasing ball too early (a high, looping throw) or too late (throwing it into the ground)	e. Review grip. Ball is probably palmed or clutched in fingers on a late delivery. Correcting a stiff arm throw often remedies early release
f. Restricted backswing resulting in a "push" of the ball with limited body action and poor accuracy	f. Move freely and use a bold backswing and throwing arc. Shoulders and hips move forward and around prior to the forward motion of the arm

Pitching

Difficulty	*Correction*
a. Illegal pitching motion or balks	a. Review rules and give an accurate demonstration of the stance, backswing, delivery, and follow-through
b. Throwing wildly so that ball goes into the dirt, over the catcher, or hits the batter	b. The pitcher should review her delivery motion and be certain her forward step is consistently timed and spaced. Check grip to avoid causes of early or late release
c. Lack of power due to incomplete body rotation, arm extension, and wrist snap	c. Conscientious and consistent practice emphasizing free flowing pitching action

Batting

Difficulty	*Correction*
a. Separating or crossing hands at the grip, resulting in poor balance of the bat and inconsistent swing	a. Review the standard grip with hands comfortably placed two inches from the end – right above the left hand. Suggest a lighter bat if the player feels unsure
b. Placing feet too close together, resulting in poor balance and a leg slide or lift as the swing is made	b. Practice swing mimetically until foot position is comfortable and body is balanced. Teacher may chalk suggested foot marks as a guide for beginning batters
c. Arm swing without body rotation, which results in inconsistent and weak hits, often "pulled"	c. Review batting technique, emphasizing practice with weight shift forward, powerful hip and shoulder rotation that brings the bat to hitting area.
d. Crowding or pulling away from the plate, resulting in balls hit off the handle or tip	d. Use a batting tee so that each batter can find her best batting position
e. Resting bat on shoulder in preparation for delivery, resulting in late swing	e. Constantly remind student that the bat is up and the body alert in the "ready" position. Explain the loss of time involved in lifting the bat
f. Failure to swing the bat in an arc parallel to the ground. The ball is chopped downward or batted skyward	f. Player should set a swing pattern by working on the batting tee; analyzing why balls follow the flight path

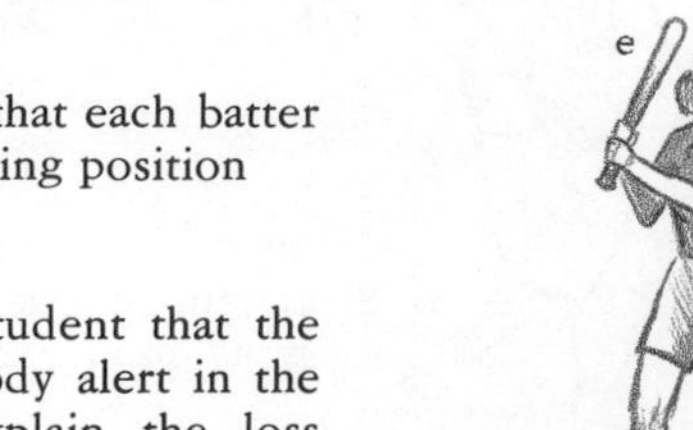

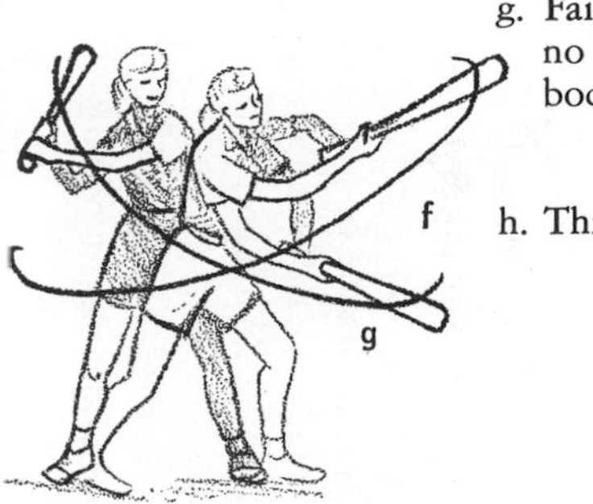

Difficulty	Correction
g. Failure to use wrist snap, resulting in no follow-through and power or in a body whirl	g. Stress relaxation and suggest that student pretend she is driving nails into a board 3 feet from the ground with a bat
h. Throwing the bat	h. Stress the safety factor involved and insist that the player *put* the bat on the ground or carry it to first base

Base Running

Difficulty	*Correction*
a. Failure to begin running as the ball is hit	a. Player must avoid watching her hit and train herself to "go for first" on every hit
b. Slowing down before crossing first base and incorrect approach to proceed for extra bases	b. Review technique of direct run to first or arcing out, touching infield corner if moving to second base
c. Overrunning second and third base	c. Review rules and demonstrate running form
d. Forcing a teammate because of inattention to other baserunner's position	d. Stress the importance of *team awareness* (see section on offensive strategy)
e. Failure to watch batter or coach for play signals	e. An occasional reminder may be all that is necessary
f. Incorrect slides resulting in outs and minor injuries	f. Discourage sliding by inexperienced player. When sliding is taught, stress relaxation and proper execution. Practice slides at speeds approximating game execution

EVALUATING THE RESULTS

Measuring individual skill in softball is difficult, and there is some question as to whether or not an isolated skill is a true measure of playing ability as a team member.

The AAHPER Softball Skills Tests offer varied tests of individual skills, and test norms are available for girls in grades 5 through 12. The tests are intended to measure execution of fundamental skills. The tests are not intended to be predictive of total playing ability; therefore, they should be regarded simply as practice tests used by players as a means of improving game skills.

The following suggestions are helpful in planning a program for measuring total class progress.

Skill Tests. There are test batteries for softball and selected baseball tests which are adaptable for measuring individual skill. When using skill tests for accuracy in pitching, throwing, or batting some allowance must be made for the style, type, and speed of delivery.

Pitching Targets. A rectangular area representing the strike zone may be painted, chalked, or taped on the gymnasium wall or tennis backboard. A wooden or rope frame, further divided by colored ribbon, is helpful in judging pitching ability to the "corner" areas.

For general throwing, players should be encouraged to throw 60 feet or more to a target area made up of three concentric circles. The center of the circles should be 5 feet from the ground, and circles of 1½ feet, 2¼ feet, 3 feet, and 4½ feet in diameter should be inscribed to show the reach of a teammate.

Baserunning for Speed. Record the time it takes each player to run from the batter's box to home plate. The runner must touch all bases.

Batting Tests. Although tests for accuracy have been devised for use with a batting tee, a situational test is advisable for most classes. If possible, the same pitcher should be used for all students tested. With the batter using good form, she attempts to hit the first five balls into left field and the next five into right field. Called strikes should count as trials. The student is evaluated on the number of fair and foul hits made.

Throw for Distance. This is one of the most valuable skill measures. With 10 foot intervals marked from home to first and 40 feet beyond, and from third to second base and 40 feet beyond, each student takes three trials. Her best distance is recorded.

Pepper. An informal measure of fielding ability is the game of pepper, or flies and grounders. The ball is batted to the fielders, who are lined up in the infield or outfield awaiting a turn to play the ball and return it to the batter.

Rating Scales. Use of rating scales by the teacher and pupils is a means of evaluating an individual's ability and understanding of offensive and defensive strategy.

Incident Chart. Use of an incident chart during a game to record errors, assists, hits, putouts, etc.

Written Examinations. Use of written examinations to evaluate knowledge of the rules, officiating, and strategy. Situational examinations are very valuable, as the student must solve the problem by strategy which would apply during the actual game.

TERMINOLOGY

Appeal play—A play upon which an umpire cannot make a decision until requested by a player. The appeal must be made before the pitcher's next delivery.

Assist—A credit awarded each player who handles the ball in a series of plays which results in a baserunner's being put out.

Base on balls—A walk. The batter is allowed to take a position as a baserunner on first base when four balls are called before she hits, strikes out, or is put out.

Battery—The pitcher and the catcher.

Batting average—A percentage which indicates a batter's effectiveness at hitting. It is determined by dividing the number of hits by the number of turns at bat.

Double—A two base hit.

Double play—A defensive play that results in two outs.

Earned run—A run scored by a player who reaches first base in any legal manner other than an error made by the defending team.

Error—A misplay on a ball which the scorer rules as avoidable. It results in the advancement of a baserunner or prolonged life of the batter.

Fielder's choice—An option which a fielder has in playing a ball in which he may retire the baserunner rather than the hitter.

Fungo hitting—Batter tosses the ball and hits it to fielders for practice.

Hot corner—Third base.

Infield fly—A fly to the infield which is caught or, in the opinion of the umpire, could easily be caught by an infielder.

Inning—One of seven sections of the game in which teams alternate offensive and defensive turns.

Interference—The act of hindering a batter by a defensive player; or an act by an offensive player which impedes or hinders a defensive player who is executing a play.

Keystone sack—Second base.

Line drive—An aerial ball batted sharply and directly into the field.

No hitter—A game in which one team was unable to make a safe hit.

Obstruction—An act by a fielder not in possession of the ball or in the act of fielding a batted ball which physically impedes a baserunner.

Pass—A walk or a base given by delivering four balls.

Sacrifice—A bunt, fly, or hit intended to advance the baserunner. It results in an out for the hitter.

Single—A one base hit.

Squeeze play—Bringing a player home from third base on a bunt.

Stolen base—A surprise advance to a base closer to scoring position made by a baserunner unaided by a hit, error, or putout.

Texas leaguer—A fly ball that drops between the infielders which cannot be successfully fielded by either.

Triple—A three base hit.

DISCUSSION QUESTIONS

1. Discuss the way in which softball developed. What are its major contributions as a team sport for women?

2. As manager of an intramural team, how would you determine who would be the first four batters?
3. Plan a "chalk talk" on strategy. Use game situations to explain the use of (a) a bunt, (b) a double steal, and (c) hit and run.
4. Safety is extremely important in softball. Explain safety precautions that apply to (a) dress and equipment of players, (b) batting, (c) baserunning, and (d) fielding.
5. Explain the infield fly rule. What is the reason for such a rule?

SELECTED AUDIOVISUAL AIDS

Fundamentals of Softball Pitching. (16 mm., 12 min., silent, b & w.) United World Films, Inc., 1445 Park Avenue, New York, New York 10029. (Purchase and rental)

Girls, Let's Learn Softball. (16 mm., 20 min., sound, b & w.) United World Films, Inc., 1445 Park Avenue, New York, New York 10029. (Purchase and rental)

1969 Open Slow Pitch National Tournament. (16 mm., 20 min., sound, b & w.) Amateur Softball Association, 4515 North Santa Fe, Oklahoma City, Oklahoma 73118. (Free loan)

Softball Fundamentals. (16 mm., 12 min., sound, b & w.) Young America Films, Inc., 18 East 41st Street, New York, New York 10017. (Purchase and rental)

Softball: Skills and Practice. (16 mm., 12½ min., sound, color.) University of Southern California, Division of Cinema, Film Distributing Section, University Park, Los Angeles, California 90007. (Purchase and rental)

Women's World Championship Games. (Selected films 1961–1965.) Amateur Softball Association, 4515 North Santa Fe, Oklahoma City, Oklahoma 73118. (Free loan)

SUGGESTED READINGS

Amateur Softball Association: *Official Guide.* 4515 North Santa Fe, Oklahoma City, Oklahoma 73118. Published annually.

Brace, David K.: *Skills Test Manual: Softball for Girls.* Washington, D.C., AAHPER, 1966.

Felshin, Janet and O'Brien, Catherine (eds.): *Selected Softball Articles* (3rd ed.). Washington, D.C., AAHPER, DGWS, 1970.

Kneer, Marian, (ed.): *Selected Softball Articles.* Washington, D.C., AAHPER, DGWS, 1962.

Kneer, Marian, and McCord, C. L.: *Softball.* Dubuque, Wm. C. Brown Co., 1966.

National Association for Girls and Women in Sport: *Softball Guide.* Washington, D.C., AAHPER. Current edition.

Poindexter, Hally B. W. and Mushier, Carole L.: *Coaching Competitive Team Sports for Girls and Women.* Philadelphia, W. B. Saunders Co., 1973.

Shick, Jacqueline: "Battery of Defensive Softball Skill Tests for College Women," *Research Quarterly.* Washington, D.C., AAHPER. Vol. 41, No. 1, pp. 82–87, March, 1970.

CHAPTER 19

VOLLEYBALL

Volleyball, an increasingly popular national and international team sport, originated in the United States in 1895. The original game, called *Mintonette,* was devised by William C. Morgan while he was a student at Springfield College. After graduation, Morgan became a YMCA physical director at Holyoke, Massachusetts, where he introduced his game to a group of mature businessmen seeking an indoor activity that was less strenuous than basketball. Using combined rules of tennis, handball, and baseball, a basketball bladder was air dribbled, batted, and hit so that it crossed from one team to the other over a tennis net stretched across the gymnasium at a height of 6 feet, 6 inches. Each team could have as many players as it wished and an unlimited number of hits on each side of the court. A game was nine innings in length with each team allowed three outs per inning.

The game was well received, and at a demonstration for YMCA physical directors in 1896, it was renamed *volleyball.* Morgan published the rules in 1897, and A. G. Spalding and Brothers Company manufactured the regulation net—lighter than a tennis net—and a more suitable regulation ball. The sport has always had the enthusiastic endorsement of the YMCA, and largely through the efforts of leaders in this organization and in the armed forces, volleyball has been carried throughout the world.

The United States Volleyball Association (USVBA), founded in 1928, was formed from the members of the Volleyball Rules Committee of the YMCA and directed by Dr. George J. Fisher. Today, this volunteer organization includes representatives from the NCAA, the NAIA, the AAHPER, the NFSHSAA, and fifteen other agencies and organizations interested in the development of volleyball. The USVBA establishes and coordinates rules on a national basis, qualifies officials, and sanctions open, college men's, college women's, senior, and YMCA regional tournaments, and national championships. The USVBA is recognized by the United States Olympic Committee (USOC) as the governing body for volleyball in the United States. In addition to rules published by the USVBA, the National Federation of State High School Athletic Associations (NFSHSAA) publishes official rules for boys and girls for use in competition sponsored by member schools. The National Association for Girls' and Women's Sports (NAGWS), an association of the American Alliance for Health, Physical Education, and Recreation (AAHPER), publishes rules for girls and women which are used by selected schools, colleges, and recreational teams. All international competitive play, national play in other countries, and Olympic competition is conducted under rules of the International Volleyball Federation (FIVB). Although minor differences still exist among rules established by the FIVB, the USVBA, the NFSHAA, and the NAGWS, it appears that each year the rules draw closer together. This is obviously advantageous to the player learning skills and strategy and striving for high level competition.

National championships have been sponsored by the Amateur Athletic Union (AAU) since 1925, by the National Association of Intercollegiate Athletics (NAIA) since 1969, by the National Collegiate Athletic Association (NCAA) since 1970, by the Association for Intercollegiate Athletics for Women (AIAW) since 1970, and by the National Junior College Athletic Association (NJCAA) since 1974. The AIAW sanctions collegiate women's regional tournaments and a national intercollegiate championship. The Volleyball Committee of the United States Collegiate Sports Council (USCSC) was formed to select men and women student athletes and coaches from colleges and universities to compete in the World University Games. The Men's and Women's Olympic Volleyball Committee of the USOC selects players, coaches, managers, and officials to participate in the Pan American and Olympic games.

Although girls and women began playing a modified version of volleyball soon after it was devised, special rules were not published until 1926. During that year they were published in the Red Cover Series of the Spalding Athletic Library. The National Section on Women's Athletics, at that time a division of the American Physical Education Association, set about establishing rules for girls and women that were in keeping with the association's current standards and principles of sports and competition. The "two-volley" game, with a maximum of six contacts, lenient interpretation of the term "volley," and the underhand service technique, reflected the thinking about strenuous sports for women at that time.

Recognized as an Olympic event for women in the 1964 games in Tokyo and won by the host nation's skilled players, volleyball captured the interest of American sportswomen. Interestingly, the United States, where volleyball originated, has won neither Olympic medals nor a large number of international events. Perhaps the reason for this lies in volleyball's heritage and development as a nonstrenuous, deliberately paced, game in the United States. Among Europeans and Asians however, it developed as a power game of quickness, stamina, offensive power plays, and daring defensive tactics. Although the USSR and Czechoslovakia have dominated men's international competition, and the USSR and Japan have dominated the women's competition, new standards of training, strategy, and performance which assure a more competitive international position have emerged in the United States.

Among the 60 million players in the United States and millions of others in 110 countries throughout the world are participants in two-player beach volleyball, players in sex-limited or coeducational recreational play, and millions of competitors in high school, collegiate, open, and international competition. In the United States, volleyball is unquestionably the most popular and fastest growing participant team sport. Extensive television coverage, films, and competitive touring teams have provided greater visibility and understanding to assure the rapid growth of volleyball as a spectator sport.

NATURE AND PURPOSE OF THE GAME

The game is played by two teams of six players each; each team is placed in its own half of the rectangular court (60 feet by 30 feet). The court is divided into halves by a net 7 feet, 4¼ inches from the floor. Members of a team play the volleyball across the net and into the opponents' court using skilled placement of shots in an attempt to make the ball touch the opponents' area. The opponents attempt to prevent this by playing the ball up and back across the net.

Play begins when a server directs the ball across the net with her hand

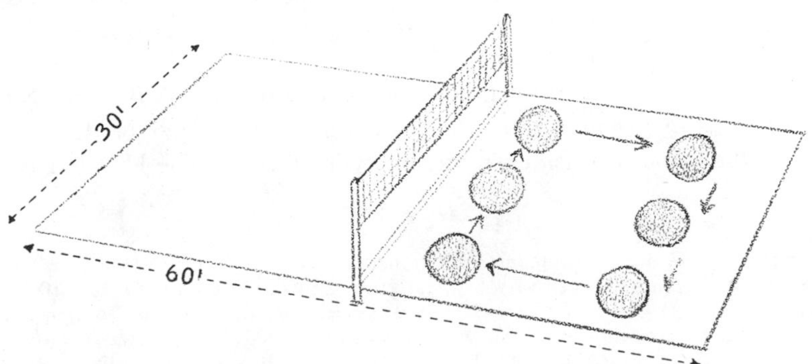

Figure 19–1 Volleyball rotation pattern and court dimensions.

or forearm from a position behind the endline of her own court side. Each server continues serving until she commits a fault or her team fails to return the ball to the opponents and score a point. Only the serving team can score points.

During play, the ball may be hit in any direction with one or both hands or forearms. The ball may be hit three times on each side of the net, but it may not be hit two consecutive times by any one player. The ball may be played as soon as any part of it crosses the net. In play, the ball may be recovered from the net and play continued.

GAME RULES AND SCORING*

Although minor differences still exist, it appears that each year the rules of the IVF, the NAGWS, the USVBA, and the NFSHSAA become more similar. The following rules will point up the major differences that presently exist.

The Game. A game is completed when one of the following occurs:

1. One team scores 15 points and has a 2-point advantage over the opponent.
2. A team leads by at least 2 points at the end of 8 minutes of playing time.
3. At the end of 8 minutes, if the game is tied or there is only a 1 point difference between opponents, play continues until one team has a 2-point lead.

A match is won by the team that first wins two of three games. At the end of each game of a match, teams change courts. In the middle of the third game, teams change after one team has scored 8 points or the first time the ball becomes dead after 4 minutes of play, whichever occurs first.

The captain of the team winning the coin toss may take either the first service of the first game or have a choice of court. The remaining choice goes to the other team. In subsequent games the team that received first in the previous game will have first serve in the following game.

Players, Substitutes, and Court Positions. Six players constitute an official team. Under USVBA and NAGWS rules if a team is reduced to fewer than six by injury or disqualification, the game is defaulted. NFSHSAA rules state that a team shall continue play with fewer than six players, but it must begin with six.

Players may enter the game three times under USVBA and NFSHSAA rules; a player may enter the game only twice under NAGWS rules. Starting the game is considered one entry in all cases. The USVBA limits a

---

*For complete rules and rule interpretations refer to: (1) *Official Volleyball Rules and Reference Guide of the United States Volleyball Association.* USVBA Printer, P. O. Box 109, Berne, Indiana 46711; (2) *Volleyball Guide.* National Association for Girls and Women in Sport, AAHPER, 1201 Sixteenth St. N.W., Washington, D.C. 20036; (3) *Volleyball Rulebook.* National Federation of State High School Associations, P. O. Box 98, Elgin, Illinois 60120.

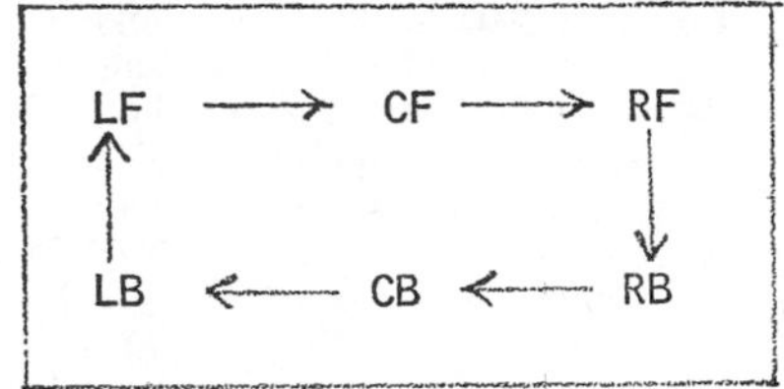

Figure 19–2 Playing positions and rotation path.

team to twelve substitutions during a game. A substitute must take the position and place in the serving order of the player for whom she is substituting. A player re-entering the game takes her original position in the serving order and in relation to her teammates.

Players assume court positions of left forward, center forward, right forward, right back, center back, and left back. At the time of service, no player's position may overlap that of the player immediately in front (or back) of her or adjacent to her. NAGWS rules state that the *feet* of all players must be clearly beside the people in adjacent positions on the same row or clearly in front or behind the feet of respective front- or back-line players. USVBA and NFSHSAA rules state that *no part of the body* (hands, etc.) may overlap. The server is the only player allowed outside the court at the moment of service.

Service. Play begins with a serve by the player in the right back position. Thereafter, the player continues to serve as long as her team scores points. After the loss of service a "side-out" is called and the ball passes to the opposing team. (Under NAGWS and NFSHSAA rules the team does not rotate when ball is received for the first serve after opponents have served; under USVBA rules the team rotates when the ball is received for the first service following the loss of serve by opponents.) Each player has only one term of service until the serving order is repeated. Players rotate in a clockwise manner to gain serving position. The following rules govern the serve:

1. A serve may be hit with one or both hands, open or closed, or the forearms. The ball may be held or tossed in the air but must be clearly hit, not thrown.
2. The server stands behind the endline and within the serving area. She may step on or over the endline *after* the ball is hit.
3. A service fault occurs when a player fails to be within her own serving area, when the ball touches the top of the net, when the ball goes into or below the net, when the ball fails to reach the net, when the ball lands outside the court boundaries, or when the ball hits an object over the court, even where ceiling height does not conform to the rules.

Conduct of the Game. During play the following rules govern the game. If a member of the serving team violates a rule, a side-out is called and the serve passes to the opposing team. If a member of the receiving team is the offender, the serving team is awarded a point.

1. The serve must be legally executed.
2. The ball must be clearly hit with one or both hands (open or closed), forearms, or

any part of the body above and including the waist. Contacts with two hands or forearms must be simultaneous.

3. The ball may be volleyed only three times on a side. A player may not have two successive hits; however, USVBA and NFSHSAA rules state that successive contact is permissible when playing a hard-driven, spiked ball if the contacts constitute one attempt to play the ball. (NFSHSAA states that such successive contacts are allowed only when the ball has not been played by a teammate and only when the ball rebounds from one part of the player's body to another, *excluding* forearm or hand-to-forearm or hand.) If two or more players contact the ball simultaneously it is considered only one play, and players involved may participate in the next play. If more than one player forms a block and any of the players is contacted by the ball, any one of the players is eligible to make the next contact (this contact would be considered the second team contact).
4. When players of opposing teams simultaneously contact the ball at the net, the contact is not considered one of the three volleys for either team.
5. Any ball, except a serve, that strikes the net and crosses over is still in play.
6. A ball in play that is not a serve may be recovered from the net if the player makes no contact with the net.
7. A player may not touch the net when the ball is in play. Net supports and net antennae may not be contacted. If the ball is driven into the net by an opponent and causes the net to touch a player of the opposing team, no foul is called and the ball continues in play. When the play occurs on the third contact, the ball is dead.
8. A player may not reach under the net to touch a ball or a player of the opposing team. A player participating in a play in which the ball becomes dead must complete the play without touching the floor beyond the center line and without touching the net.
9. A ball may be played as soon as any part of it crosses the net.
10. A player may leave the court to play a ball.
11. A ball touching a boundary line is good.
12. A player must be in the proper position in relation to her teammates on the serve. Once the ball is served she may assume any position on the court; however, a back-line player may not come to the net to spike or participate in a block.
13. A back-line player who is forward of the 10 foot line when returning a ball across the net must contact the ball from below the level of the top of the net. A back-line player behind the 10 foot line may contact the ball above the top of the net (spike attempt) if her takeoff is clearly behind the line.
14. A team is allowed two time-outs (not to exceed one minute each in NAGWS and NFSHSAA rules and 30 seconds in USVBA rules) for rest during a game when the ball is dead. Additional time-outs result in a side-out or loss of point.
15. A team is penalized by a side-out or by awarding a point to the opponents when a player delays the game by (a) slow preparation for playing or serving; (b) delayed recovery of an out-of-bounds ball; (c) slow rotation; or (d) taking more than two time-outs or unnecessary delay for substitution (more than 15 seconds under NAGWS and no designated time under other rules) after the team has used its two allotted time-outs.

Double Foul. A double foul occurs when opposing players or sides foul simultaneously. The play is repeated when a double foul is called.

Scoring. Scoring techniques and official score sheets vary slightly, depending upon the rules under which a team is playing. Refer to the specific rule book for more details. NAGWS suggests the following scoring methods.

At the beginning of each game the names of the players are entered according to serving order. Each player's position or number is indicated. Points scored are tallied on the team's running score and also next to the

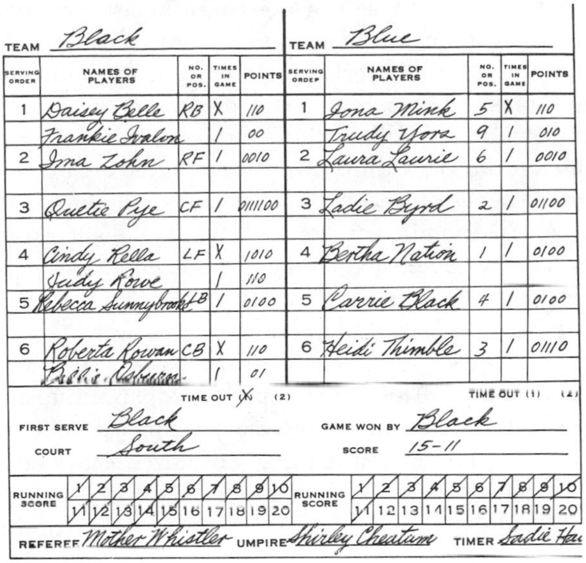

TEAM	Black				TEAM	Blue			
SERVING ORDER	NAMES OF PLAYERS	NO. OR POS.	TIMES IN GAME	POINTS	SERVING ORDER	NAMES OF PLAYERS	NO. OR POS.	TIMES IN GAME	POINTS
1	Daisey Belle	RB	X	110	1	Iona Mink	5	X	110
	Frankie Avalon		/	00		Trudy Yora	9	/	010
2	Ina Zohn	RF	/	0010	2	Laura Laurie	6	/	0010
3	Quetie Pye	CF	/	0111100	3	Ladie Byrd	2	/	01100
4	Cindy Rella	LF	X	1010	4	Bertha Nation	1	/	0100
	Judy Rowe		/	110					
5	Rebecca Sunnybrook	LB	/	0100	5	Carrie Black	4	/	0100
6	Roberta Rowan	CB	X	110	6	Heidi Thimble	3	/	01110
	Bobbie [illegible]		/	01					

TIME OUT (1) (2)   TIME OUT (1) (2)

FIRST SERVE Black   GAME WON BY Black

COURT South   SCORE 15–11

RUNNING SCORE 1 2 3 4 5 6 7 8 9 10 11 12 13 14 15 16 17 18 19 20   RUNNING SCORE 1 2 3 4 5 6 7 8 9 10 11 12 13 14 15 16 17 18 19 20

REFEREE Mother Whistler UMPIRE Shirley Cheatum TIMER Sadie Ha[illegible]

Figure 19–3 Score card. (Adapted from DGWS *Volleyball Guide*, 1967–69.)

server's name. A zero (0) indicates the completion of a term of service. A diagonal line (/) drawn through a point indicates that it has been officially removed; an (×) over the point indicates that the scorer has made an error.

A substitute's name is entered below that of the person she replaced in the serving order. When a player leaves the game and another enters, this is indicated in the column headed "Times in Game." When a player re-enters, it is indicated with a "2". If she again leaves the game, the "2" is crossed out. This indicates that she cannot enter the game again.

Time-outs are tallied in the area indicated on the score sheet.

Information pertaining to first team serving, court area, total score, and victor should be attested to by the officials at the end of the match.

NEEDED FACILITIES AND EQUIPMENT

Court. The rectangular playing court is 60 feet by 30 feet overall bounded by a 2-inch line, with at least 6 feet of unobstructed area extending outward from the boundary lines. A center line (2 inches in width under NAGWS rules and 4 inches in width under NFSHAA and USVBA rules) divides the court into two equal playing areas. A line, known as the spiking line or ten-foot line, is drawn 10 feet from the center line and parallel to the endline on each half of the court. Measurement of the line is from the middle of the center line to the middle of the ten-foot line.

A height of 30 feet of overhead clearance is recommended.

Serving Areas. The serving area for each court is a minimum of 6 feet in depth behind the endline within ten feet of the imaginary extension of the sideline on the right third of the court. This area is marked by two lines, each six inches long and two inches wide. One line is drawn behind the endline and perpendicular to it, beginning eight inches from the endline, serving as an extension of the right sideline; the other line is ten feet to the left of the first line. In smaller gymnasiums the serving area extends into the court to provide minimum service area.

Net. A regulation net is made of 4-inch square mesh of black or dark brown linen twine. The net is bounded, top, bottom, and sides, with 1/4-inch Manila rope. White or orange canvas, 2 inches wide, is sewn at the top of the net. It is recommended that galvanized cable (aircraft) be run through both the top and bottom of the net. Two-inch vertical tape markers are placed over the net, directly above and vertical to each sideline.

Fiberglas, plastic, or other flexible *net antennae* are placed 8 1/2 inches outside the vertical tape markers to assist officials. The antennae are fastened securely to the top and bottom of the net and extend at least 2 1/2 feet, but no more than 3 1/2 feet, above the net. The antennae are no more than 3/8 inch in diameter with alternating 4 to 6 inch white and orange or red bands.

Ball. The ball is spherical with a laceless leather cover of 12 or more panels of uniform light color. It is 25 to 27 inches in circumference, weighs from 7 to 9 ounces, and should be inflated with 5 to 7 pounds of air pressure. A rubber cased ball is acceptable for outdoor use if it meets other specifications of the leather ball.

Scoring and Timing Devices. Visible scoring and timing devices should be part of the equipment for official competition. Both timing and scoring devices should be visible to the teams and spectators.

Uniforms and Accessories. An official gymnasium costume or attractive shorts and shirts are appropriate for most game situations. During interscholastic or intercollegiate competition all team members should be in attire of similar design and uniform color. Each player must be identifiable by displaying a number, not less than 6 inches high on the back of the shirt and not less than 3 inches high on the front of the shirt. Numbered pinnies serve in class situations.

Tennis type shoes or those specifically designed for gymnasium wear should be worn with socks that cushion the feet and prevent blisters. Knee guards are advisable for beginning competitive play.

For an official match an official rule book, scorebook, and an appropriate number of whistles should be provided.

TEACHING UNITS

The topics suggested are content units for beginners and advanced students in volleyball. Whenever possible, drills should simulate game situations and actual play should be encouraged as often as possible.

Beginners	*Advanced*
Brief history and nature and purpose of the game	Review of skills, strategy, and rules
Conditioning	Advanced training techniques
General conditioning	Backset
Jump training	Digs
Serve	One hand
Underhand (younger players)	Two hand
Overhand floater and spin	Net recovery
Passing	Roundhouse serve
Overhand	Spin
Forearm	Floater
Set	Review and establish good overhand floater
Attack skills	Screw under set
Spike	Rolls (Japanese full)
Off speed spike	Dive (Russian)
Dink	Attack patterns
Blocks	Two player
Individual technique	Three player
Two-player block	Short set
Dig—basic technique	Strategy
Strategy	Offensive 6–0, 6–2 patterns
Offensive 4–2 and 5–1 patterns	Player up defense
Defensive serve reception	Player back defense
Defensive positioning	Block
Half roll	Three player
Rules	Officiating
Beginning competition	Competitive play
Evaluation	Evaluation

BASIC SKILLS

Serve

The serve is a team's first offensive move and the one time in the game when a single player is in complete control of the action of the ball. In power volleyball the serve is more than a means to put the ball in play—it is an important offensive skill.

There are three basic planes from which serves are executed—underhand, sidearm, and overhead—with varying hand positions and spins that may be imparted in each plane. Two specific serves, the floater and the roundhouse, are commonly used skills at all levels of play.

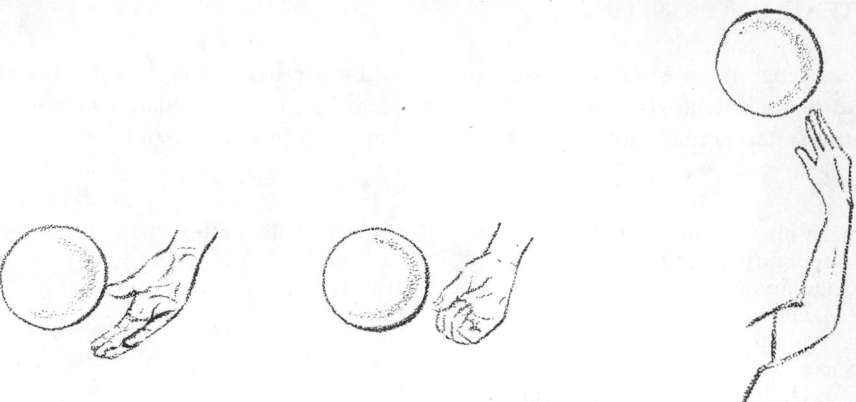

Figure 19–4 Hand positions for three basic serves.

In executing any of the basic serves the ball may be struck by the hand, fist, or forearm by the server from the right third of the court behind the endline. One of the two hand positions described can be developed for effective use. In the *open hand position,* the fingers are extended and firm and the hand is slightly cupped. The impetus may be given the ball by the lower palm and heel of the hand with the fingers used for direction and control. The entire hand contacts the ball in executing the roundhouse spin serve. The basic open position is most commonly used.

Greater force is given at ball impact by a *closed hand position.* The fingers are closed forward and in contact with the palm. The ball is contacted by the heel of the hand or by the knuckles and the heel of the hand simultaneously. The semiclosed fist position reduces the striking surface and consequently results in loss of control and direction.

Figure 19–5 The underhand serve.

The *underhand serve* is the easiest serve for youngsters and beginners to execute. It is easy to learn and to control but lacks the force and power of other serves. Standing in the legal service area, the right-handed player faces the net with her feet in stride position, left foot forward, knees bent, shoulders square to the net. The ball rests in the palm of the left hand with the supporting fingers pointing to the right and the thumb directed toward the net. The left arm is extended low across the body and forward toward the right sideline. As the right hand and arm swing backward and upward in a long backswing arc, the elbow is slightly flexed. The trunk of the body rotates to the right to allow for the backswing as the body weight shifts back to the right foot. Additional length and height in the backswing result in more power at contact. The right arm and hand swing firmly through to contact the ball below its midline as body weight transfers to the forward foot. Contact is with the heel if the hand is open, and with the heel and knuckles in a closed hand position. The ball is lifted from the stationary left hand and the right arm follows through in a straight line in the direction of the intended ball flight. The underhand serve is not a strong offensive weapon, but a soft underhand spin or floater may gain an occasional point against a deep defense.

The *sidearm serve* is similar in basic body positioning and timing to the underhand serve; however, the right-handed player stands with her left shoulder toward the net and her feet pointing toward the right sideline. The left foot is slightly ahead of the right in stride position. The ball is held in the palm of the left hand with the fingers of the hand directed toward the right sideline. The thumb of the supporting hand is directed toward the net. The left arm is fully extended about shoulder level and aligned so that the ball is beyond the left foot.

The extended right arm swings back at shoulder level and parallel to the playing surface. During the backswing, hips rotate and weight shifts to the right foot. The open hand or closed hand position may be used as the right arm swings through to contact the ball near center and drive it from the holding hand. Body weight shifts to the left foot as the contact arm swings forward. The right arm follows through past the left shoulder. This serve is difficult for opponents to judge because of its spinning or floating action and its angle of entry into the court.

The *overhand serve* requires movements similar to those of the tennis serve or overarm softball throw. Once mastered, the spin serve results in a fast dropping action. The right-handed server faces the net. The left foot is forward, and the right foot is back and angled toward the right sideline. Weight is equally distributed. The ball is tossed by the left hand 3 or 4 feet above and in front of the right shoulder; the right arm, with open hand, cocks behind the head; and the shoulders rotate back as the weight shifts to the right foot. As the ball begins its descent, the shoulders turn forward, the body opens to the net, and the elbow leads the arm into the

Figure 19–6 *A,* The overhand serve. *B,* The overhand floater serve.

striking area. The arm straightens as the heel of the cupped hand contacts the ball, the wrist flexes, and the hand rolls over the ball, imparting spin to it. The ball may be contacted on its right or left side to produce a curve in addition to the spinning action. The follow-through is in the direction of the ball flight.

The *overhand floating serve* is most commonly used by competitive players because of its accuracy and unpredictable flight. Recognized as a deceptive serve after its effective use by the Japanese women in the 1964 Olympics, the floater does not spin, but ducks and weaves in flight, similar to a knuckleball in baseball. This results in an erratic path that frequently finds the receiver unprepared. The server's body faces the net with feet in forward stride position and weight equally distributed. The ball may be held high or "lifted," with no spin imparted, about 3 feet above and in front of the right shoulder. As the ball begins to drop, body weight transfers forward (a short step forward is used by some players for additional power), and the striking arm extends from its cocked position. The elbow leads and the heel of the open hand (or closed fist) contacts the inert ball several inches below its midline. The elbow may be fully extended or slightly flexed upon contact, depending upon the player's height and the intended trajectory of the serve. The wrist of the hitting arm is firm, and there is limited follow-through after contact.

The weaving action of the floating serve seems to be related to application of force and resulting ball compression in relationship to the location of the valve stem. The ball usually breaks in the direction of the valve. That is, if the valve is pointed toward the center of the opponent's serving area, the ball will break from side to side; if the valve is pointed up toward the opponent's court, the ball will travel a greater distance; and if the valve stem is low, the ball drops more rapidly.

The *roundhouse serve* was popularized by Europeans. Although the traditional roundhouse results in a powerful, spinning ball, its flight is predictable. The *roundhouse floater* produces a hard driven, fast, floating serve with a dropping, side-to-side movement that is highly unpredictable. It is a singularly effective serve which is being developed by American players.

The right-handed server faces the sideline with feet in a forward stride position; shoulders are perpendicular to the net. The ball is tossed approximately 3 feet in the air slightly in front of the forward shoulder. During the toss the body bends backward as knees flex. The hitting arm swings upward from the right knee in an extended windmill fashion. The torso twists forward, and weight shifts forward as the knees and legs extend. As the ball descends directly above the right shoulder the hand contacts the ball. For the *spin* serve the ball is struck with the entire hand, which is cupped in a manner similar to that in the overhand spin service. Contact for the *floating* serve is made only with the heel of the hand. At the moment of contact the body is balanced on the forward foot and the server then pivots on that foot and prepares to move to her defensive position.

The Pass

The pass is the controlled movement of the ball from one player to another. The type of pass used—the *overhand* or the *forearm*—is dependent upon the speed and position of the ball to be played. The pass is used for serve and spike reception, and it is the first contact of the ball by the offense. The primary purpose of the pass is to control the ball and place it so that it can be set for an attack play above the level of the net. However, any pass technique can be used as a set for an offensive play if necessary, and can be used as a defensive return to opponents as well.

Correct body positioning and movement to the ball are essential for effective passes. The player must anticipate the flight of the ball and quickly position her body in its path before contact. The body position may be high, medium, or low, depending upon the type of pass to be executed; however, the medium position is an excellent *ready position* from which a player moves. The player's legs are apart in a forward stride position with knees flexed. The body weight is forward over the balls of the feet and the toes, with weight distributed through both legs. A player on the right side of the court should advance the right leg; on the left side of the court, she should advance the left leg, so that her body is open to the court and a pass can be directed easily to other players. Ankles and knees are flexed to carry the hips lower as the body leans slightly forward with the back straight. In anticipation of a forearm pass the arms are low and extended; for an overhead pass the body is more erect, and the arms and hands are carried higher.

Often the body must be realigned at the last moment to play a ball with an erratic flight path. After moving to the proper court depth so that the ball can be contacted with the forearms slightly above the waist, the player may use a *slide step* to get her body into the path of the oncoming ball. The legs never cross and the player keeps her head and body facing the ball throughout the shift. The shift is initiated by a long sideward stride, knees flexed to support body weight, toward the desired direction. The other leg is quickly brought parallel in a comfortable side stance.

Overhand Pass. The *overhand pass* is used primarily as a set on the second play of an offensive series, but it is also used for receiving easy, lofting balls from the opponents or as a technique for returning the ball to opponents when a power attack is not possible. The overhand pass should not be used to receive serves or hard-driven attacks, for they are frequently judged illegal hits. The temptation to use the overhand pass on serves and spikes is lessened if one remembers that if front court players

Figure 19–7 The overhand pass.

are positioned properly at a depth of 12 to 15 feet from the net, balls passing above the waist level can be received more efficiently by back court players. If back court players are properly aligned, balls above waist level travel out of bounds.

The player moves to a *ready position* to await the ball. Her feet are apart in a slight stride stance with weight supported on the balls of the feet. The heel of the forward foot remains in contact with the floor as the knees flex and lower the body to a semicrouch position. The trunk is inclined slightly forward and the hips remain under the body. The hands are at face level with a triangle formed between the index fingers and thumbs of both hands. The thumbs point slightly toward the nose. The wrists are flexed and the arms are in front of the body. The elbows are flexed and elevated and spread slightly beyond shoulder width. The player's hands are 3 to 5 inches from the forehead before contact with the ball. The head is slightly back, and the eyes follow the flight of the oncoming ball through the triangle formed by the hands. The ball contacts the thumbs and pads and second joints of the index and middle fingers; the hands give slightly (avoid contact with palms of the hands), and the arms and legs begin to extend through the ball with hands firm but relaxed. Extension of the body is slightly upward. The wrists extend as the body and arms follow through in the direction of the pass.

Forearm Pass. The *forearm pass,* often called the "bump," increases the time a player can follow the ball's trajectory, increases player range, and eliminates ball handling violations of open-hand techniques below the waist. This pass should be used to receive serves, spikes, net recovery, or any ball which must be played at waist level or lower.

Figure 19–8 The forearm pass.

The player's hands should be comfortable and result in effective alignment of the forearms. Beginners find the *clenched fist* a natural and comfortable technique. One fist is clenched and the other hand encircles the fist with thumbs parallel and on top of the index finger of the inside hand. The wrists and hands should be lowered to allow outward rotation of the forearms.

The *hand in heart* or curled fingers position is most frequently used by women's competitive teams. To assume proper hand position the palms of both hands face upward; the back of one hand is placed in the palm of the other, and it is firmly clasped with fingers of both hands curled. Thumbs are close together, parallel, and on top of the hand.

The *thumb over palm* position allows greater forearm rotation, but the open hands should not be allowed to contact the ball. The thumb of the bottom hand is placed in the palm of the top hand at the base of the fingers. During the pass, hands point toward the floor, resulting in wrist extension and outward forearm rotation.

Proper *arm position* and use is important to a successful pass. Ball contact should be on the forearms between the wrists and elbows. Contact by the hands, although usually legal, results in less control and often reflects poor timing on the play. Two popular styles of arm use deserve consideration – the elbow lock and the elbow snap.

The *elbow lock,* the most popular technique, dictates that arms remain rigid and locked before and during ball contact. Movement of the arms is directed by shoulder action, and power is imparted to the ball by body extension and arm lift.

The *elbow snap* is a newer technique and requires excellent timing in execution. Prior to contact the elbows are flexed and relaxed. Just before contact the elbows rotate inward and extend, and wrists and forearms are brought close together.

When using either arm position, the hands are together, and the thumbs are parallel. Thumbs and wrists point toward the floor so that con-

Figure 19–9 The one-hand dig.

tact is made on the inside portions of the forearms. The player must keep her eyes on the ball to assure equal contact with both arms as she judges the velocity of the oncoming ball. The greater the velocity of the ball, the less arm and body action that is needed to get the ball into the air.

The *lateral pass* is a modification of the two-arm forearm pass. It is used when the player has not had enough time to position herself behind the ball. With arms extended forward and the ball approaching from the side, the shoulder toward the oncoming ball dips to turn the forearms toward the ball path. The player leans with weight borne by the forward leg nearer the ball.

The *one-arm pass,* or "dig," can be effective for net recovery and the handling of powerful spikes that are hit to the side of a player and too far away to contact with the two-arm lateral pass. Whenever possible, the forearm is used to contact the ball. If the ball must be hit by the fist, contact may be with the heel of the hand or with the knuckles and the heel.

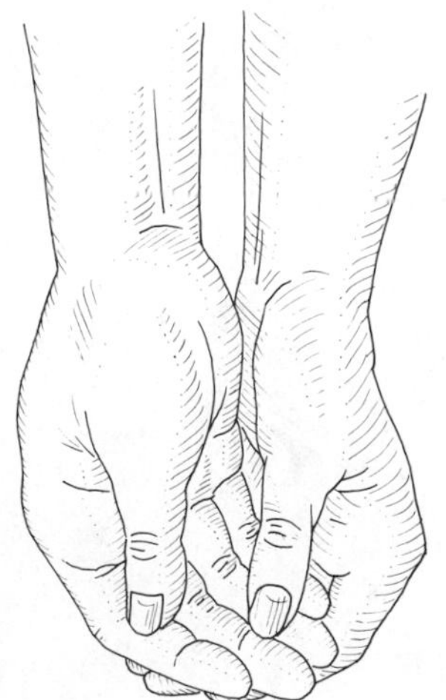

Figure 19–10 Hand position for two arm, underhand volley. (From Poindexter, Hally, B. W. and Mushier, Carole L.: *Coaching Competitive Team Sports for Girls and Women.* Philadelphia, W. B. Saunders Co., 1973.)

The extended arm is near the playing surface, and the hand is directly under the center of the ball. As the ball contacts the hand, the arm swings upward to counteract the force of the ball and lift it in the air.

A *backward pass* is used frequently by a player to recover poor passes, hits off the block, or for a defensive return to opponents. The player turns her back, runs to position and meets the ball high with a locked elbow position. At the instant of contact, the shoulders shrug and the player leans backward in the direction of intended ball flight.

The Set

The set is an overhand or forehand pass that is designed to place the ball in the best possible position for an effective spike. The overhand pass is used whenever possible, for it affords more precise control and allows the spiker an opportunity to analyze the ball in flight. A highly skilled setter will effectively place the ball at any height at any spot along the net. Such setters know their spikers' preferences and soon learn to take advantage of the weaknesses of the defense. The beginning setter should develop the normal set which travels in a high arc to either side of the court at the corner of, and approximately 2 feet from, the net. For a front set the player's feet should be pointed in the direction of the intended set. This position encourages simultaneous contact on the ball with both hands.

The *back set* is executed to deceive opponents who are preparing a blocking defense against an obvious set and spike. For example, a setter faces a spiker to her left, but sets the ball over her head and backward to a

Figure 19–11 *A*, The set. *B*, Body and arm position when setting. (From Poindexter, Hally B. W. and Mushier, Carole L.: *Coaching Competitive Team Sports for Girls and Women.* Philadelphia, W. B. Saunders Co., 1973.)

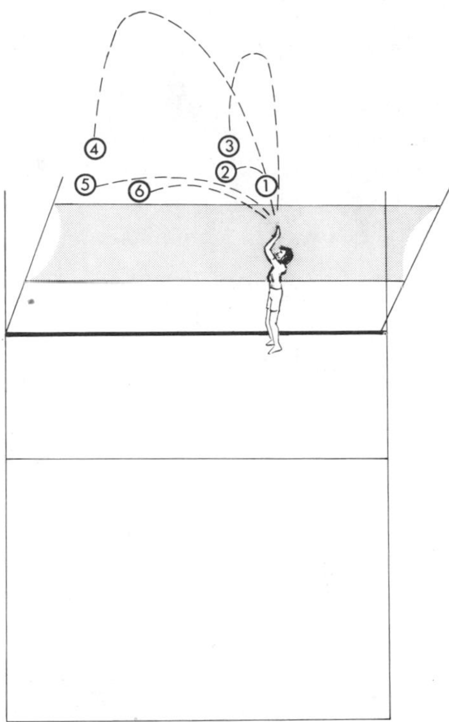

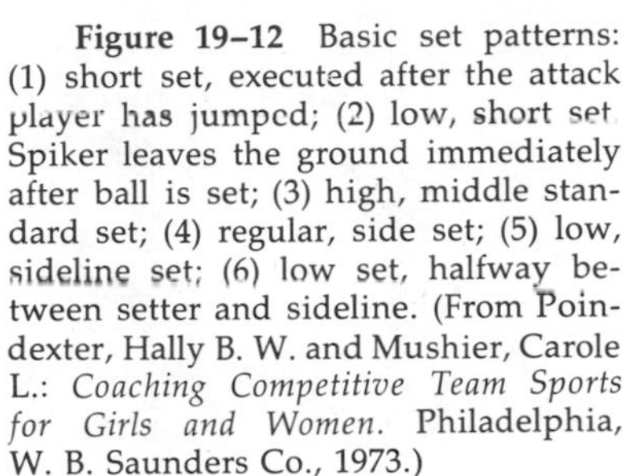
Figure 19–12 Basic set patterns: (1) short set, executed after the attack player has jumped; (2) low, short set. Spiker leaves the ground immediately after ball is set; (3) high, middle standard set; (4) regular, side set; (5) low, sideline set; (6) low set, halfway between setter and sideline. (From Poindexter, Hally B. W. and Mushier, Carole L.: *Coaching Competitive Team Sports for Girls and Women.* Philadelphia, W. B. Saunders Co., 1973.)

spiker to her right. The initial body, hand, and arm positions are the same as for the front set. The hands contact the ball above the forehead and extend upward and slightly backward. The back arches, allowing the ball to pass overhead, and the head remains up as the arms follow through.

The *lateral set* is used effectively by experienced setters only. The technique is used increasingly in international play. The movement of the arms is to the side, rather than forward or backward. The ball is set over the side of the body with the body and arms extending up and sideward toward the direction of the intended set.

The *jump set* is another advanced technique used by a player to feign an attack and confuse the block, to save a pass that would hit the net, or to save a pass from traveling over to the opponents' court. The body extends, as in a basketball jump shot, and the set is executed from this extended position.

Attack Skills

An attack is an attempt to play the ball in such a manner that the opponent cannot return it, and a point or side-out results. The hard spike is a forceful attack. The off-speed spike and dink are less forceful, yet are often deceptive and effective as attack skills.

Figure 19–13 Spiking.

The Spike. Execution of the spike is highly individualized, and there are many variations in approach, takeoff, and hand position at contact. Japanese women players use a hop takeoff in their fast offensive play, but the *step-close takeoff* is used most frequently by Americans.

The spiker begins her *approach* 10 to 15 feet from the net. The initial step is directional to position the body in proper relationship to the ball. The approach leads to the takeoff. In the *step-close takeoff* the spiker takes a long last step, jumping forward and contacting the floor with the heel; the trailing foot quickly closes to the lead foot with weight on the heel. The legs flex, body upright or slightly backward, as the arms swing forcibly backward and the heels contact the floor. The arms then swing forward and upward above the shoulders as the weight transfers to the toes and the legs and body extend upward. The entire purpose of the approach and takeoff is to get the striking hand as high as desirable or possible, consequently the technique of converting horizontal momentum to vertical force must be mastered. The jump must reverse the direction of the approach, and the vertical or slightly backward angle of the jump increases vertical height. If the approach speed is great, a true vertical jump may not reverse the forward momentum enough to prevent fouling at the net or center line.

As the arms are raised, the knees bend backward to aid body elevation; the back arches slightly. The right-handed spiker will throw the left arm up over the left shoulder as the right arm, elbow bent, moves above and behind the right shoulder with the hand cocked behind the head. As the body extension is reached, the body twists toward the attacking arm with the left shoulder turning toward the net. The right elbow leads the arm forcefully and the left arm drops, reversing the shoulder angle. The legs snap forward and downward, creating a slight body pike.

The right arm extends upward to contact the ball above and in front of the right shoulder. The ball is contacted by the heel, or heel and palm, of the open or firmly cupped hand; contact by the base of the fingers and pads quickly follows if a wrist snap or turn is used to impart spin or place the ball. The striking arm usually continues down and across the body for a hard-driven spike, but the elbow may bend and pull the arm from the follow-through path.

The recovery is made by a cushioned landing on both feet with the spiker turned toward the ball and prepared for immediate play.

Angle hitting is used to hit inside, around, or over the block when there is enough court to angle. It is also used to "wipe out," that is, to hit off the outside blocker's hand when the block is set wide and the ball rebounds out of play. To accomplish an *outside hit* by a right-handed player, the left arm pulls down and back, causing shoulder rotation. The hand contacts the ball slightly to the right. The more angle needed, the more wrist that must be used. To hit *inside the block* that is set for the crosscourt power shot, the left arm pulls downward and across the body, limiting shoulder rotation. The left shoulder dips and the right moves back. The hand contacts the ball left of center, and the wrist snaps to the right.

The *short vertical spike* is most effective, for it does not give opponents time to set a proper block. It requires cooperation and coordination between the setter and the spiker. The set must be close to the spiker, as she sets the ball vertically from a low ready position. The set should rise just above net level and the spiker, who has anticipated the set, jumps before the ball is set. The suspended spiker hits the ball as it rises or at the moment its upward flight has ended.

The Dink. The dink is a soft spike, a passive attack technique, directed to the open court or to a defender who is prepared to return a spike. The approach and arm position are similar to the spike, but the forward arm swing is slower and the ball is contacted with the fingertips. The wrist is held stiff. The dink strategy is effective on high sets when the ball can be tipped just over the block or when it can be put into the arms of a blocker in such a way that it is trapped by the blocker and rolls down her body to the floor.

The closed-fist dink is used by less skillful players above net level and by all when punching the ball over the net when the ball has dropped below the top of the net. Once below net level, the play is defensive and lacks deception.

Blocks

The block is intended to counteract the efficiency of the power attack. It is a defensive play by one, two, or three front line players. Recent rules permitting the block to be set across the net have resulted in strong offensive blocks. Good blockers set the defensive pattern of the team. Individually or in multiple blocks (two player is the most common pattern), players shift quickly in response to the opponents' strategy.

Individual blocking skill varies according to the reach and vertical jumping ability of the player. The block is usually preceded by a short run and a lateral or oblique shift. Facing the net, the blocker squats to the position of leg flexion which gives the best possible power to achieve her highest vertical jump. She leaves the ground from both feet, arms extended upward to aid in achieving height by their upward and forward thrust. A short blocker needing additional jumping power may begin with hands below the waist which then move past the chest and face to a full extended position at the height of the jump. Tall blockers with superior jumping ability may crouch with hands at shoulder level. This initial high

Figure 19–14 Blocking.

hand position allows added body control for last-moment body position adaptation. Blockers jump shortly after the spiker leaves the floor on normal sets but delay the takeoff when the set is farther from the net. The distance between the hands must be less than the diameter of the ball.

As the blocker descends, her arms draw back from the net and toward the body. Landing is on toes and then heels over flexed knees which absorb the landing shock. The player should be ready to return to game action immediately.

The *attack block* is an attempt to intercept the ball prior to crossing or just at the net. Rules forbid blocking contact until the opponent has attempted to hit the ball. The attack block is used when the set is close to the net or on an off-speed spike. The blocker's jump is timed so that she is descending as the ball is spiked. Reaching over the net with firm arms pressed downward from the shoulders, the hands and wrists are tilted forward with fingers firm. Ideally the ball is contacted by the heels of the hands but may rebound from the hands, fingers, wrists, or forearms.

The *soft block* is used when the ball is set away from the net. It is effective in rebounding a ball to the opponents' court with less angle and speed than that of an attack block. It is also used to deflect the ball to one's own teammates. The jump comes later than in an attack block and is timed an instant after the jump of the spiker as she is attacking the ball. The ball is contacted by the blocker at the height of her jump. The hands and arms are parallel to, or slightly over, the net. Hands and wrists are firm and extended upward more than forward, and the ball is contacted on the palms or fingers rather than on the heels of the hands.

Multiple blocks are those using two or three front line players. The two player block is used most commonly, for it allows one front line player to be free for short court defensive duties. When two players are blocking, the outside player is termed the *end blocker* and the inside player is called the *middle blocker.* The end blocker positions herself opposite the attacker, and the middle blocker shifts to align herself with the end blocker. They stop momentarily at the spot from which they will jump and then rise simultaneously in vertical jumps. It is important that the blockers' hands are tilted so that the rebounding ball will go into the opponents' court rather than ricocheting off their hands and out of bounds for a "wipe out."

As a general rule when there are two blockers, the inside hands are parallel to the net, and the outside hands face inward. In a three player block the hands of the inside player and the inside hands of the outside players are parallel to the net; the outside hands are turned inward.

Net Recovery. Often a ball, poorly delivered on a set or a misjudged spike, hits into the net. Different plays are called for, depending on whether the ball was driven into the net on the first or second contact. A ball going into the net on the third contact is dead. If two contacts remain for the ball, the recovery player goes into a deep crouch facing the ball and

Figure 19–15 Net recovery.

the side of the court. As the ball drops free of the net she executes a dig, preferably using both arms for control. If the ball rises in the back court, a player delivers the ball deep to the opponents' court; if a high recovery near the net is possible, a spike or dink by a front court player may follow.

When there is only one contact remaining, the net player attempts a defensive save. Usually a one-arm dig is called for as the ball falls from the net. As it nears the floor, the hand and arm rotate away from the net and contact the ball on the upswing. This stroke imparts upward and forward momentum to the ball.

Players should be alert to the position of ball contact with the net. Balls hitting high on a taut net fall down the net and close to the center line; those hitting at center or lower on the net tend to rebound farther into the court.

Rolls. In order to play difficult serves and attacks, it is often necessary to thrust the body into an unbalanced position that demands a speedy recovery to playing position. For some years Europeans have used a partial roll to get the midline of the body in line with the oncoming ball. The Japanese introduced the full roll as an important defensive technique.

The *partial roll,* frequently called the "screw under," because of the pivoting motion of the body as it falls, is used with an overhead pass or as a player extends a thrust or squats for a dig. The sequence begins with a body extension, pushing from one leg to a flexed support leg. As the ball is contacted, the support leg turns inward with toes pointing away from the direction of the body motion. The player sits down on the hip of the fully flexed support leg and rolls to her back. Rapid recovery follows by snapping the legs downward as the body rolls forward.

The *back roll* generally follows an overhead pass taken from a full squat position. The player sits down as she completes the pass and completes a partial roll on her back. Recovery is similar to the partial roll.

The *complete roll* is accomplished at high speed, usually following a wide lateral move. If the ball is relatively close to the body and lateral speed is slow, the early movements are similar to those of the partial roll. If the player has gone to her right to play the ball, she twists to her left, rolling to her buttocks, rounded back, and left shoulder. The feet and legs snap over and down with the left knee and toe making first floor contact. As the speed of lateral movements is increased, there may be no time for the support leg to screw under the body. The knee, thigh, and lower back of the squat leg touch the floor. The roll and recovery bring the player to a low ready position.

The *dive* is a forward thrust of the body to save a ball coming in front of a player when there is no time to shift to the ball, or when the ball changes directions suddenly. Only the highly skilled player should attempt this technique. The dive is taken from a low position with the front foot bearing the body weight. The body is thrust horizontally with arms outstretched. The hit may be with one or both hands or arms and immediately after contact, the player touches the ground with the palms of the outstretched hands and arms, easing the body down. The head is held back as the body is lowered to chest, abdomen, and thighs prior to recovery.

GAME STRATEGY

As in all team sports, players have both offensive and defensive roles. The roles change in volleyball each time the ball crosses the net. Rules dictate a rotation pattern in which all players eventually play each court position. Ideally, all players should develop the basic skills of passing, setting, spiking, dinking, digging, blocking, and net recovery and further develop the specialties of offensive and defensive skills. The opportunity for interchange of two or more players allows them to use their special skills in specific positions and strategic patterns.

Offensive Strategy. The offense begins with the service and is reinstated each time the ball crosses the net from the opponents. To benefit from a team's first offensive weapon each team member should develop effective, controllable serves. The following points should be emphasized:

1. Be certain to deliver a legal, playable serve. Avoid sacrificing a playable ball for one of more power but less reliability.
2. Observe opponents on serve reception and identify weak and strong receivers. Serve to the weakest receivers.

3. Serve deep if back court players are up; serve short and to the corners if receivers are deep.
4. If receivers interchange, serve to the area of change to benefit from players' movement and possible confusion.
5. Serve to the setter if she is pulled off the net to confuse their attack pattern.
6. Serve across court from the strong spiker to force a long pass to the setter.

The basic concept of pass, set, and attack is fundamental to all offensive systems. Various systems have been developed to utilize the combined talents of team members in effecting the power play.

Four-two. The numbering system indicates that four players are attack players and two are primarily setters. This offensive system is standard for high school and collegiate teams where players do not have equal ability as attack players. Differences in height, agility, jumping power and aggressiveness may dictate this system. There is a minimum of exchange in positions, and slower teams find this system results in fewer ball handling errors. Four players are attack and two are setters. All must have passing, digging and serving capabilities.

"The rotation order places an attack on each side of a set, with two attacks between the sets. There is always a setter on the front line and if she is in left forward or right forward position, she switches into center forward position as the ball is served. Her teammates always try to pass to the center position so she can direct the attack from that point. The system is not deceptive and its success is dependent on the individual skill of setters and the attacks' ability to find weak spots in the defense. If the attacks are unusually tall and strong, the lack of a deceptive offense is minimized.

"The four-two lends itself to covering attack players and switching from offense to defense easily.

"Two basic formations are used to receive serves from the four-two. Both protect the setter from receiving the serve.

"1. Star and crescent. The set is positioned near the net and the five remaining defenders assume a bowed line position about midcourt. The pattern assumes players can move forward and backward more easily than they can move laterally. It is most effective against straight, hard serves with consistent midcourt depth. If a weak receiver is in the line-up, she may be protected close to the net or deep in the court. The four strong receivers assume more lateral responsibility (Fig. 19–16).

"2. W-formation assumes there will be a variety of serves, and players have the ability to move laterally as well as forward and backward. The setter is at the net and three receivers are approximately 15 feet in the court and the two deep receivers are about six feet in the court. Short receivers do not take serves above the waist or to the sides. The deep players have more time to adjust for receipt.

"When the W is deepened—that is, the front receivers pull back ap-

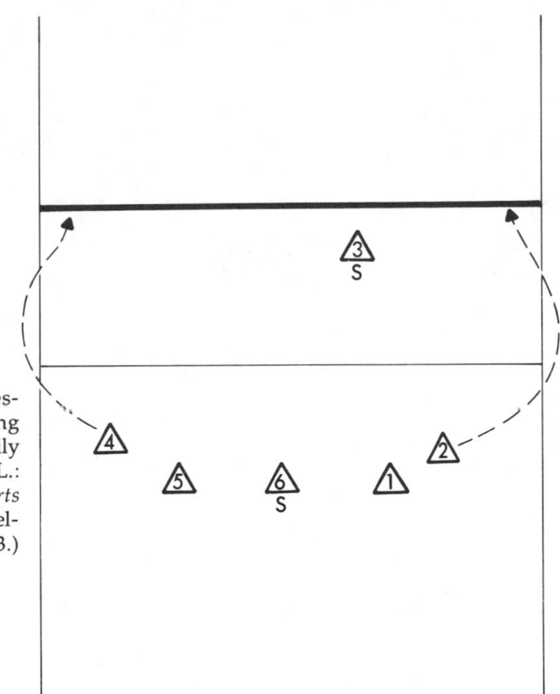

Figure 19–16 Star and crescent formation; (4-2) receiving serve. (From Poindexter, Hally B. W. and Mushier, Carole L.: *Coaching Competitive Team Sports for Girls and Women.* Philadelphia, W. B. Saunders Co., 1973.)

proximately three feet—more protection is offered against deep serves and hard floaters, but it is vulnerable to a short serve (Fig. 19–17)."*

Five-one. The five-one offense utilizes five attack players and one setter. It has the advantage of using three attack players at the net when the setter is in the back row. She moves from her back row position into the front court near the center as the ball is served. A four-two pattern is used when she has rotated to the front row. She may interchange across the front so she can be in the center front for setting. In this offensive pattern it is important that the setter be protected from receiving the serve.

Six-0. The six-0 system demands that all players have good skills and attacking ability. The individual skills of passing and mobility must be outstanding. The advantage of the system is that all three front court players can be potential attackers with the set coming from the back court. The attack patterns can be deceptive with frequent use of the short vertical set. Return to four-two is always possible if deception is unwise or unnecessary.

Six-two. The six-two implies that all players are capable of playing

*From Poindexter, Hally B. W. and Mushier, Carole L.: *Coaching Competitive Team Sports for Girls and Women.* Philadelphia, W. B. Saunders Co., 1973, pp. 221, 222.

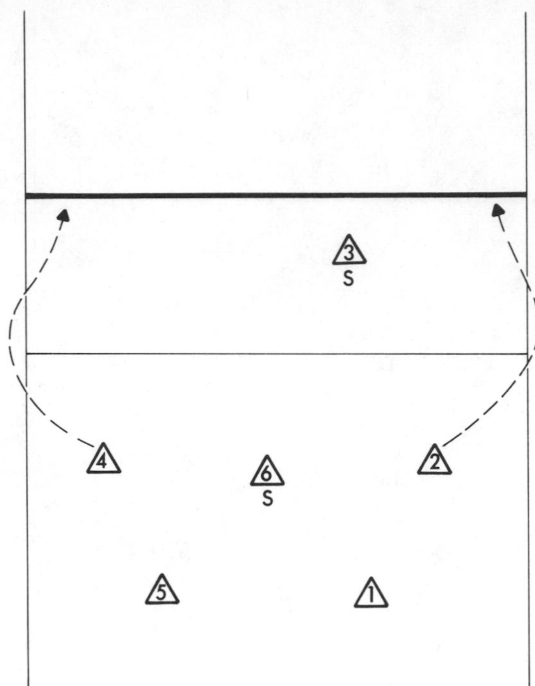

Figure 19–17 W-Formation; (4–2) receiving serve. (From Poindexter, Hally B. W. and Mushier, Carole L.: *Coaching Competitive Team Sports for Girls and Women.* Philadelphia, W. B. Saunders Co., 1973.)

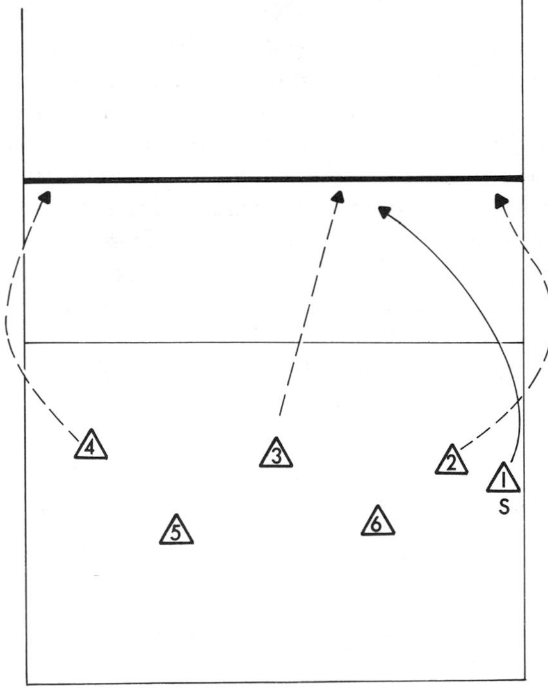

Figure 19–18 Serve receiving position for 5-1 or 6-0 with setter in right back position. (From Poindexter, Hally B. W. and Mushier, Carole L.: *Coaching Competitive Team Sports for Girls and Women.* Philadelphia, W. B. Saunders Co., 1973.)

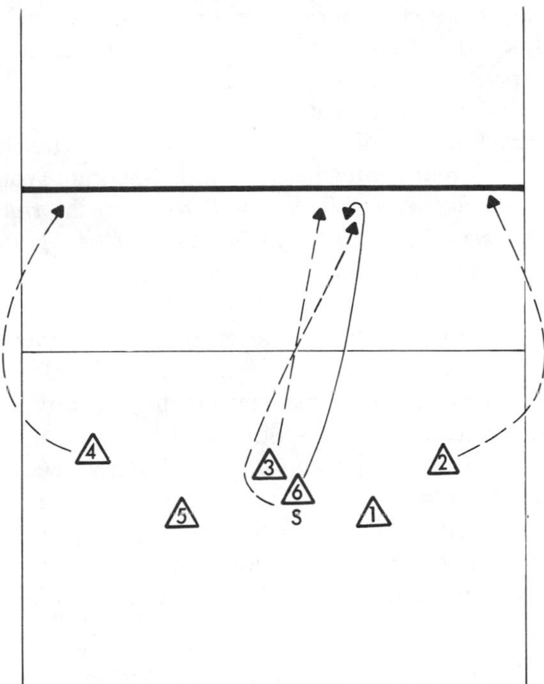

Figure 19–19 Serve receiving position for 5-1 or 6-0 with setter in center back position (line receiving pattern). (From Poindexter, Hally B. W. and Mushier, Carole L.: *Coaching Competitive Team Sports for Girls and Women.* Philadelphia, W. B. Saunders Co., 1973.)

attack positions, but two are designated setters. The system works much as the six-0, and a multiple attack can be used with the setter coming from the back row.

Multiple Offensive Patterns. The intent of multiple offenses is to deceive the defense by having three attackers at the net. This results in blockers' having to cover three areas until the last moment and frequently produces delayed or poorly formed blocks. Several offensive options are commonly used.

"1. The center forward (CF) moves on the pass and prepares for the short set at the net in midcourt. If the block does not form, the setter executes a 12 to 16 inch vertical set as the attack jumps. The attack must jump as the ball is set, not knowing if she will receive the ball. The other attacks (LF, RF) move in anticipation of a regular set.

"2. Left front attack runs to center for a short set and center front goes outside to the side line. Play continues as above.

"3. Setter moves toward right side. Center front comes forward for short set. Right front moves to the left of CF. Center front jumps and a low set to RF or higher set to LF are possible.

"The five-one and six-0 serve receiving formations are similar when the setter of five-one is in the back court. When the setter is in the back row she is shielded from receiving the serve. She moves to front court as the serve is contacted. Her position will vary depending on the pass; ideally she sets from right of center court to at least two 'on hand' spikers. A left-handed attack directly behind her in the front court presents a very strong offense.

"From the right back position, the setter moves outside the right front attack to a position about ten feet from the right side line.

"From center back position she cuts around the CF who shields her from the serve. She attempts to go to the right of CF, but may pull left if the serve is traveling in her path. When going left, she may receive the pass with her back to her LF and CF attacks and a back set may be necessary.

"Another option exists to assure proper positioning of the set. The CF stays close to the net and CB pulls close behind. The serve defense remains with four players but the set moves easily into position and the CF is in excellent position for the short set.

"The left back position presents the most difficult position from which to move. The setter moves as directly as she can, but frequently has to go left before hastening to the right front position. A high pass can give her additional time for positioning. Many six-0 offenses will not have the setter move from the LB position, but will have another player move from

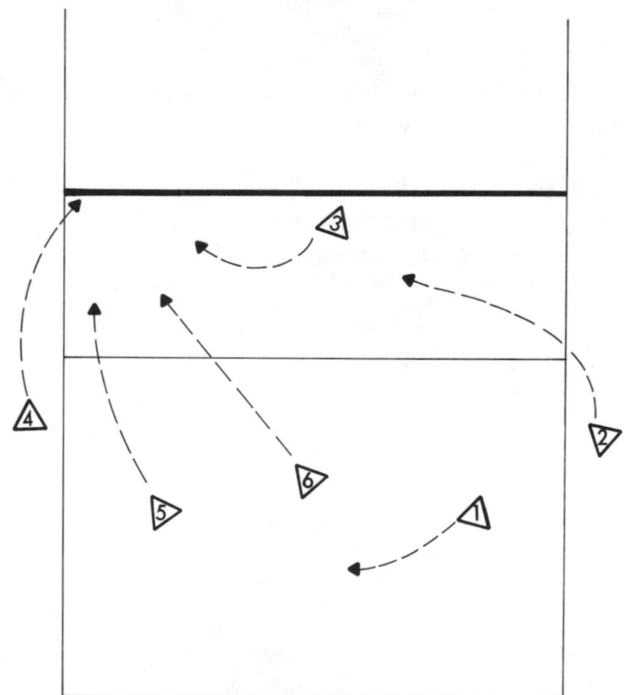

Figure 19–20 Covering the left side attack (4–2 offense). (From Poindexter, Hally B. W. and Mushier, Carole L.: *Coaching Competitive Team Sports for Girls and Women.* Philadelphia, W. B. Saunders Co., 1973.)

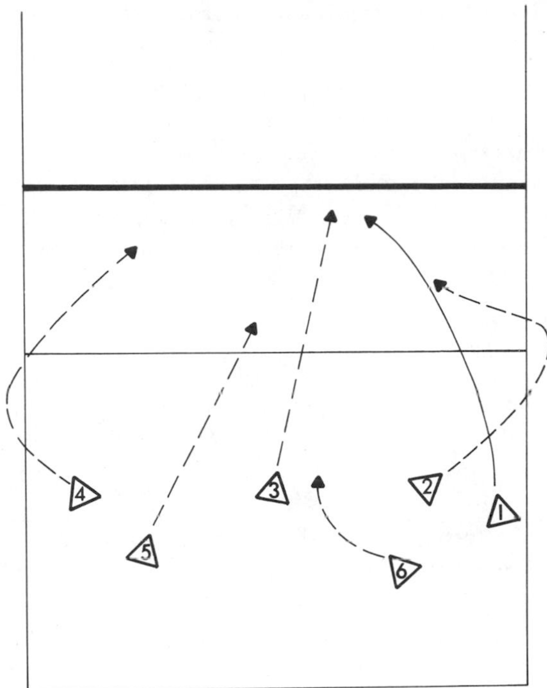

Figure 19–21 Covering center attack (6–0; 5–1). (From Poindexter, Hally B. W. and Mushier, Carole L.: *Coaching Competitive Team Sports for Girls and Women.* Philadelphia, W. B. Saunders Co., 1973.)

right back position if three attacks are used. Obviously a team using this pattern must have two setting specialists.

"Serve receiving positions are illustrated in Figures 19–18 and 19–19.

"*Covering the attack* is designed to recover the ball if it is successfully blocked by opponents and returns to the attacker's side of the court.

"In a four-two offense, players position around the spiker and within ten feet of the net. Figure 19–20 illustrates players moving to protect a left side attack. Right side coverage is reversed.

"1. Right back moves to her left to assume responsibility for the entire back court. A ball coming to this area is rarely hard driven.

"2. Right front sees the set is not coming to her; she turns to cover the area vacated by the setter and to recover a rebounding block.

"3. Center front follows her set and positions herself three feet from the net about five feet from the spiker. She plays sharp rebounds coming to the inside.

"4. Left front is the attacker who should recover quickly to play a ball that comes directly back.

"5. Left back pulls directly behind and inside the attacker. She is responsible for balls rebounding in back of the attacker and toward the outside of the court.

"6. Center back moves between left back and center forward, seven or eight feet from the net.

"When using five-one offense, court position to cover the attacker is the same as four-two if the setter is a front court player; it is similar to six-0 when three attack players are used.

"The six-0 affords numerous possibilities for covering the attacker. When a feint or short set is used, Number 3 is unable to cover the court. A back line player is at the net as setter, leaving only two players in the back court (Fig. 19–21).

"Number 1 is setter.
"Number 3 is spiker.
"Number 2 pulls behind and to the right of setter, six to eight feet from net.
"Number 4 pulls to left of attacker, six to eight feet from net.
"Number 5 follows the spiker and is directly behind her, approximately ten feet from the net.
"Number 6 remains at midcourt to cover deep balls."*

Defensive Patterns. Defensive strategy should be developed for (1) serve reception and (2) offensive attacks of the opponents. Many variations exist in each situation and all must be countered with sound skill, strategy, and the mental attitude that "no ball will touch the floor."

Basic patterns for serve reception are noted in the preceding discussion of offensive patterns. Serve reception begins the offensive play.

The first line of defense against an offensive attack is the block; the second is the back court players. Normally, a two player block is used with the blockers protecting the strongest spiking area and trying to force the attacker to hit around the block to the middle of the court, to hit down the sideline where a defensive player is awaiting, or to hit over the block to the middle of the court. The players not involved in the block should be positioned and coordinated in relationship to the blockers. Their individual readiness, as well as position, are based upon the knowledge of their own blockers' abilities and of their opponents' speed and style of attack. Players learn to assume defensive responsibilities for specific court areas.

"The following patterns illustrate defense of a two player block against a right side and middle attack. Defensive positions for a left side attack are a reverse of the right side.

"This defense (Fig. 19–22) is successful against teams that do not dink or use off-speed spikes. It is frequently used when attack players are taller hitters than the blockers. The back court players must be skilled in executing digs, and blockers must go for the attack block.

"For middle attack, Number 2 and Number 5 are responsible for dinks and half-speed spikes (Fig. 19–23). Player Number 1 covers the cut-

---

*From Poindexter, Hally B. W. and Mushier, Carole L.: *Coaching Competitive Team Sports for Girls and Women.* Philadelphia, W. B. Saunders Co., 1973, pp. 223, 225, and 226.

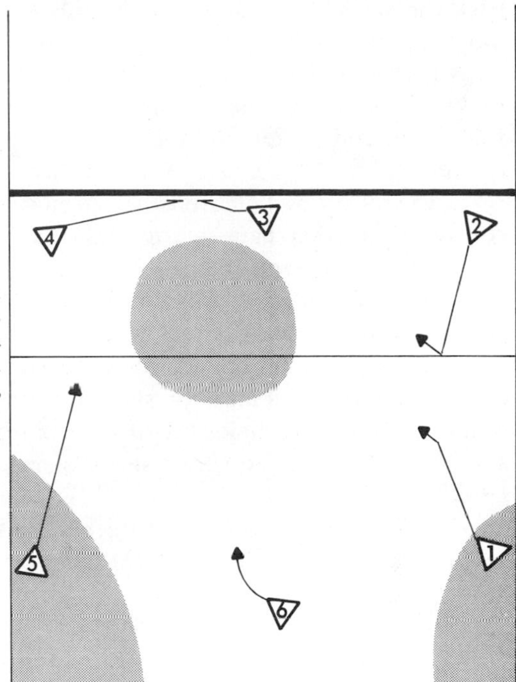

Figure 19–22 Two-player block and player back defense positions against middle attack (shaded area indicates vulnerable court area). (From Poindexter, Hally B. W. and Mushier, Carole L.: *Coaching Competitive Team Sports for Girls and Women.* Philadelphia, W. B. Saunders Co., 1973.)

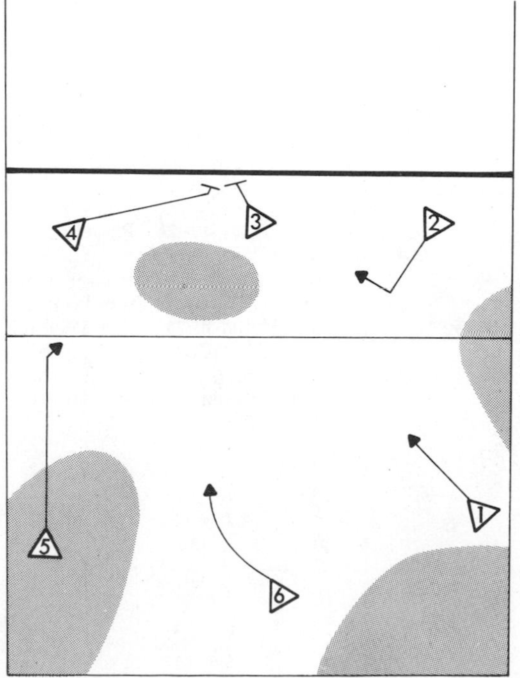

Figure 19–23 Two-player block and player back defense positions against middle attack. (From Poindexter, Hally B. W. and Mushier, Carole L.: *Coaching Competitive Team Sports for Girls and Women.* Philadelphia, W. B. Saunders Co., 1973.)

back and straight attack. Player Number 6 covers a ball deflected off the block or passing through a poorly formed block.

"For right side attack, Number 1 and Number 4 are responsible for dinks and off-speed spikes. Player Number 5 defends against a straight inside spike, and player Number 6 covers a deflection or missed block as above.

"The following defense is used against teams that vary the attack. It is considered a good pattern for hiding one weak defensive player if the blockers are good and the other defense players very quick.

"Blockers set area blocks to protect the middle of the court. Player Number 6, the weakest defensive player, is responsible for dinks and short balls off the block. In middle attack, Number 2 is responsible for off-speed attacks or outside spikes. In side attack Number 4 has these responsibilities for covering dinks, off-speed and inside spikes. Players Number 5 and Number 1 must be very fast and alert to an attack over the block (Fig. 19–25).

"If there is no need to protect a weak defense player, player alignment (see Figs. 19–26 and 19–27) serves to defend the same relative court areas.

"A three player block can score very effectively or can give up points rapidly to dinks and off-speed attacks in the vulnerable front court. This

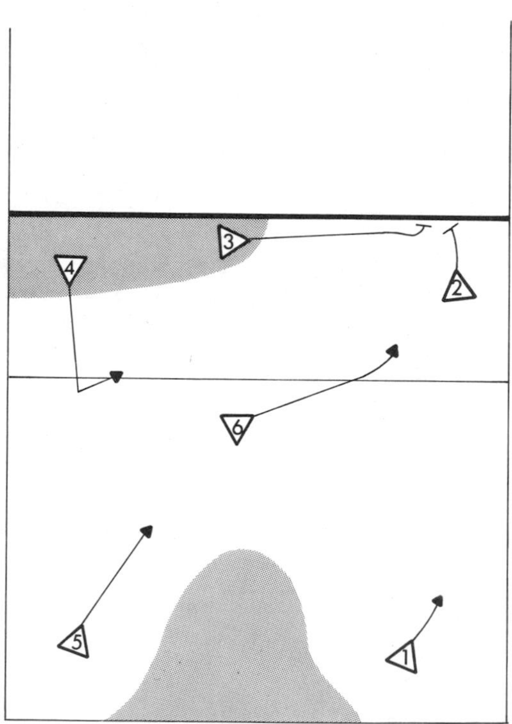

Figure 19–24 Player up defense and two-player block on side attack; used to hide weak defensive player. (From Poindexter, Hally B. W. and Mushier, Carole L.: *Coaching Competitive Team Sports for Girls and Women.* Philadelphia, W. B. Saunders Co., 1973.)

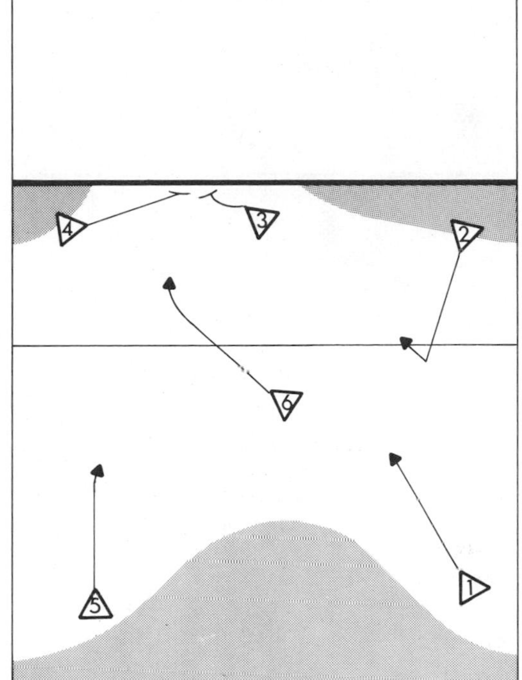

Figure 19–25 Player up defense against middle attack. (From Poindexter, Hally B. W. and Mushier, Carole L.: *Coaching Competitive Team Sports for Girls and Women.* Philadelphia, W. B. Saunders Co., 1973.)

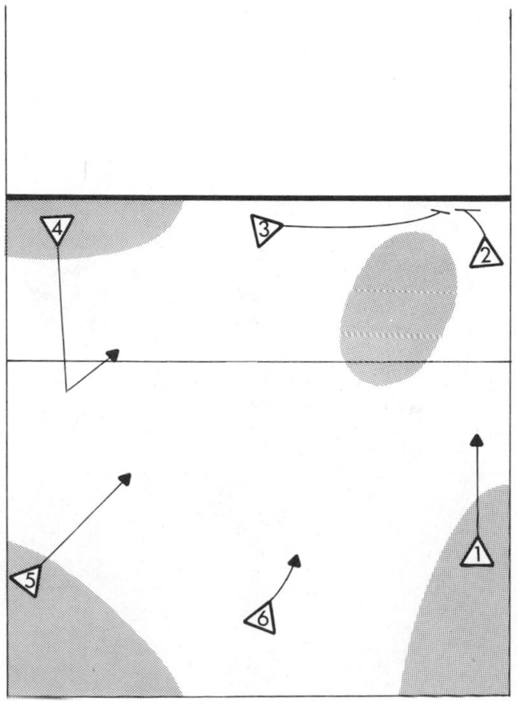

Figure 19–26 Defense and two-player block of side attack; strong defensive back court. (From Poindexter, Hally B. W. and Mushier, Carole L.: *Coaching Competitive Team Sports for Girls and Women.* Philadelphia, W. B. Saunders Co., 1973.)

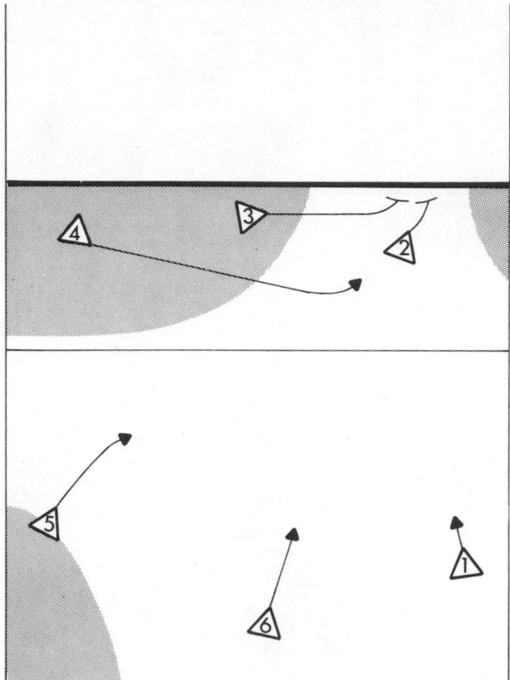

Figure 19–27 Defense of side attack; strong defensive back court. (From Poindexter, Hally B. W. and Mushier, Carole L.: *Coaching Competitive Team Sports for Girls and Women.* Philadelphia, W. B. Saunders Co., 1973.)

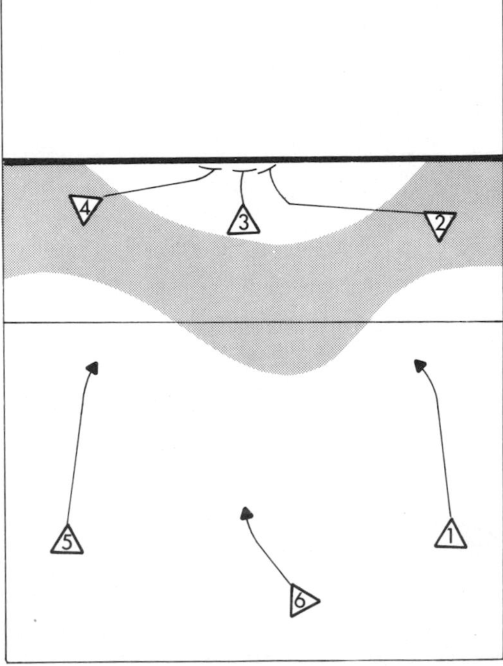

Figure 19–28 Three-player block—middle attack. (From Poindexter, Hally B. W. and Mushier, Carole L.: *Coaching Competitive Team Sports for Girls and Women.* Philadelphia, W. B. Saunders Co., 1973.)

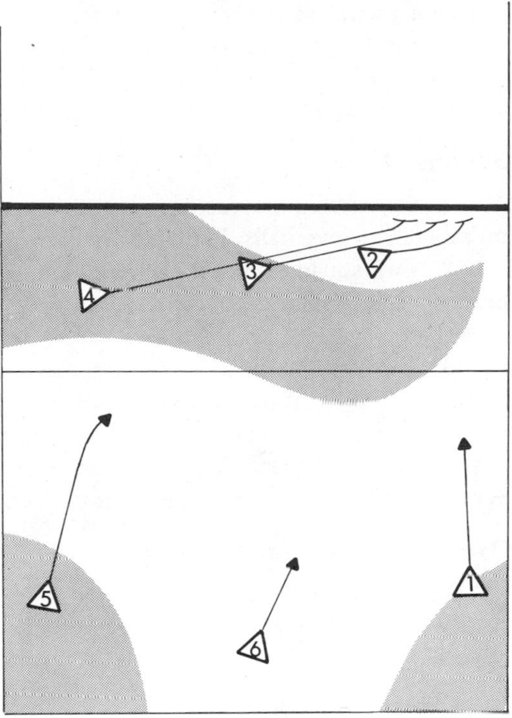

Figure 19–29 Three-player block—side attack. (From Poindexter, Hally B. W., and Mushier, Carole L.: *Coaching Competitive Team Sports for Girls and Women.* Philadelphia, W. B. Saunders Co., 1973.)

pattern is successful with predictable setting and attackers who do not vary the speed and angle of their shots (Figs. 19–28 and 19–29)."*

A *free ball defense* is used when it is obvious that the opponents will pass the ball over the net, rather than attempt a power attack. The court coverage is basically the same as in receiving a serve. Front row players pull back, leaving the setter at the net to protect her so that she may play the second ball. She may have to cover a possible dink or soft volley. The back row players move to defensive positions in the middle of the court.

A similar defense is used when the opponent's set is placed inaccurately, and a *no block defensive pattern* can be established. The spiker has no opportunity for a strong attack and must drive the ball deep, dink, or place a short return volley in the front court.

CLASS ORGANIZATION

Carefully planned drills are essential for teaching fundamental techniques and preparing students for game situations. Squads of six to eight players may be directed by student leaders as they practice. Competitive relays and "minigames" are valuable teaching devices if the competition

*From Poindexter, Hally B. W. and Mushier, Carole L.: *Coaching Competitive Team Sports for Girls and Women.* Philadelphia, W. B. Saunders Co., 1973, pp. 227, 228, and 231.

does not overshadow the focus on technique. Drills should be kept simple so that the focus is on techniques of volleyball, rather than on mastery of the complexity of the drill. Whenever possible, drills should be performed at the speed and tempo required in game play.

Serving Drills

1. Four to six players on a squad line up on the endline. Other squad members retrieve balls. Players serve a minimum of twenty balls.
2. Two squads, one on each endline, serve a minimum of 25 balls per player. Players should concentrate on style of service—floater or spinning overhead.
3. Place a rope three feet above the net and have players serve so that ball passes below rope and above net to encourage low trajectory.
4. To improve serving placement, mark receiving area with point values and have players place five consecutive serves in designated areas. Scoring systems can be devised if intrasquad competition is desired.

Overhead Passing and Setting Drills

Pass to self and partner passes are basic drills. If balls are available as a class enters the gymnasium, much practice can take place before class begins.

Group Drills

1. Floating circle—designed to keep the setter alert to shifting for the set. In groups of six to eight, players are positioned as illustrated. Number 8 begins by setting the ball to Number 2 and leaving the circle between Numbers 1 and 7. Number 2 sets the ball to the center of the circle. As soon as Number 2 *contacts* the ball, Number 1 moves to the center of the circle to receive the ball and sets to Number 3. Number 3 sets to the center, and Number 2 moves to set the ball to Number 4. Pattern continues. The player in the center exits on the side of the circle away from the set. She returns to her original position.

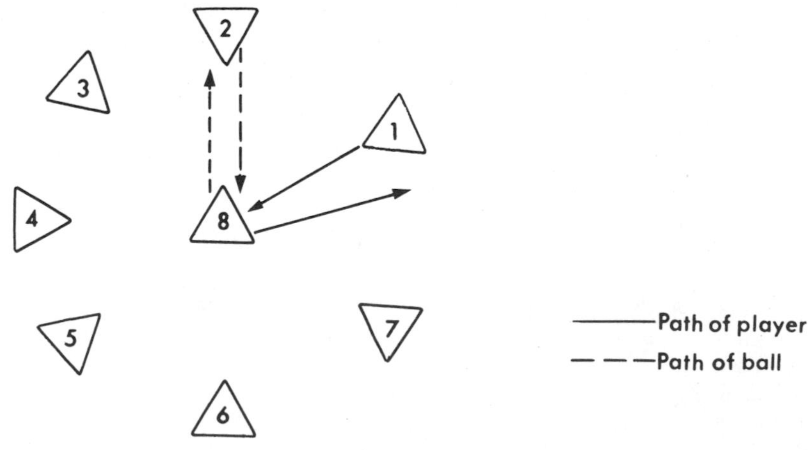

2. Shuttle drill—in groups of seven or eight players, one player (Number 8) faces the others in line. The drill begins with Number 1's setting to Number 8, who then sets to Number 2 and follows the set, continuing to the end of the line. As Number 8 touches the ball, Number 1 moves to replace her and receives Number 2's set. Number 2 sets to Number 3 and then goes to the end of the line. The pattern continues.

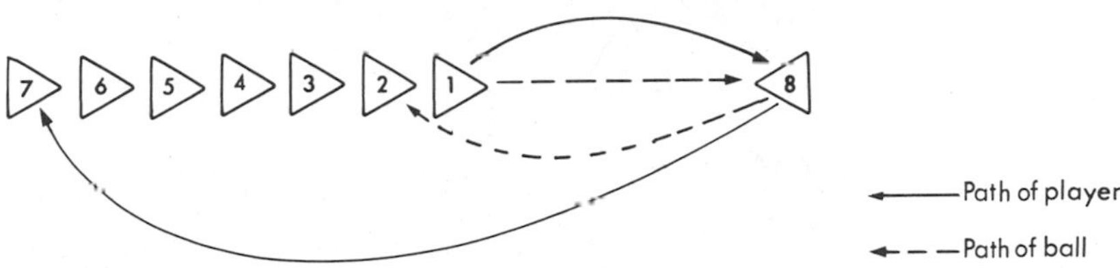

3. Back set and set—designed to improve the back set. Number 1 sets to Number 2 who sets back to Number 1. Number 1 returns set and Number 2 *back sets* to Number 3. Number 3 sets to Number 2 who sets back to Number 3. Number 3 returns set to Number 2 who *back sets* to Number 1. Pattern continues. Each back set is preceded by three sets.

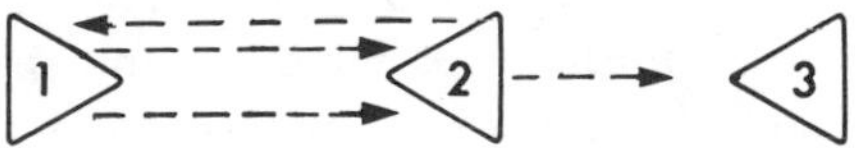

Forearm Pass and Digging Drills

A large portion of time should be spent in developing techniques of the forearm pass. Many of the partner drills and overhead pass and set patterns may be used.

Group Drills

1. One player with many balls throws to players in defensive positions. The balls are thrown with increasing speed so that players move from high to medium and low body positions.

2. Use the above pattern but direct the ball to one side of the player so that a one hand and arm dig results. Add a roll as players' skill level improves.

3. Teacher or squad leader stands on a table and throws above net level at players at midcourt from side to side. Alternate dinks and spikes. Players should pass and roll.

4. Balls are served to defensive players who pass to potential setter positioned near the net in center court. Serves should be placed and varied in style and speed.

Net Recovery Drill

Players are in groups of three with Numbers 1 and 3 in a line and Number 2 forward as shown. Numbers 1 and 3 alternate throwing the ball into the net, varying the position of net contact and speed of throw. Player Number 2 recovers and passes to either Number 1 or Number 3, who has moved toward the net for a possible attack play.

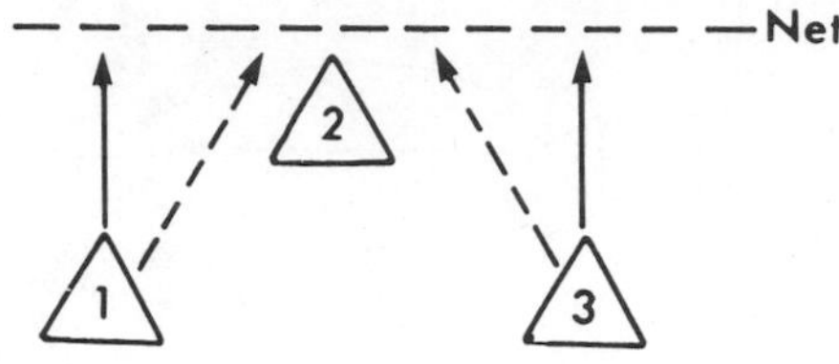

Pass, Set, Spike, and Block Drill

This combination drill should be practiced after drilling on spiking and blocking techniques with individuals. Spiker-setter drills should be a part of every practice and warm-up before a game. Blockers may drill mimetically without an opposing spiker when first learning the techniques of positioning and takeoff, but later should use the spiker-setter drill as an opportunity to practice blocking.

Arrange players into groups of six. O throws the ball to X who passes back to O, who sets to Y. Y spikes the ball as any one or two A players block it. Repeat several times alternating dinks and spikes. Change player positions. Use the same basic pattern for crosscourt sets, front and back sets. Defensive player A not involved in the block should back up the play.

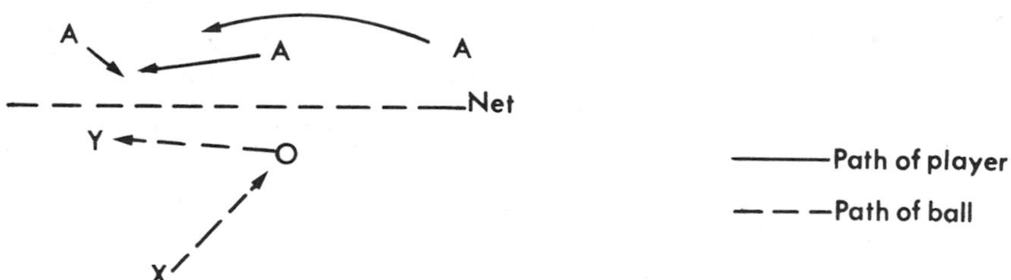

Plan for Drilling a Class of 40 Students

Large classes often present a problem to the teacher who is inexperienced in planning ways to take care of many students but who is aware that all in the group should be as active as possible during the instructional period. The following plans showing how a class of 40 students can be arranged should prove helpful. In each, a skilled squad leader works with the group, and the teacher is free to give individual help to those needing it most.

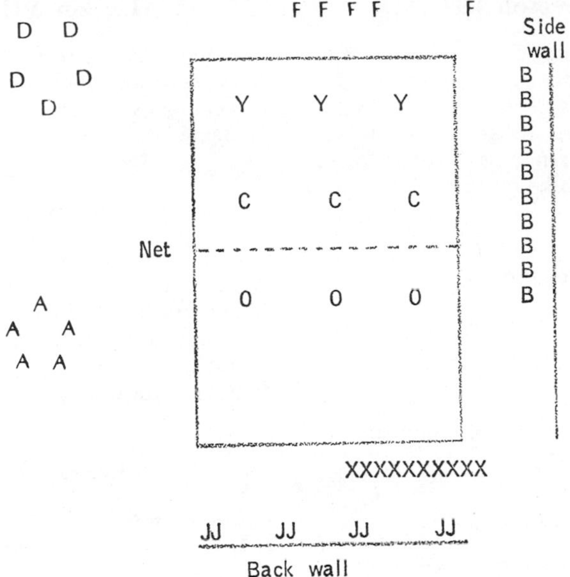

X's—Servers
Y's—Receivers
C's—Spikers and setter
B's—Volley and spiking practice at the side wall
J's—Forearm pass practice in pairs at back wall
A's—Passing and setting drills
D's—Passing and setting drills
F's—Shuttle drill for sets and back sets

TEACHING PROGRESSION

A suggested unit of 12 lessons of 40 minutes each might include the following:

Lesson I

1. Brief history; nature and purpose of the game
2. Forearm pass—demonstration and partner drills
3. Serve and rules of serving

Lesson II

1. Review forearm pass and serve
2. Combined practice of serve and forearm pass
3. Overhand (face) pass

Lesson III

1. Review passing and serving
2. Discuss overhand pass as set
3. Setting drills
4. Combination drills—return of service by forearm pass to setter for set
5. Introduce spike techniques

Lesson IV

1. Review passing, setting, and serving
2. Explain basic offensive and defensive positions
3. Spiking drills
4. Introduce blocking techniques

Lesson V

1. Pass-set-spike drills
2. Blocking drills
3. Game play

Lesson VI

1. Practice spike-block drills
2. Introduce off-speed spike
3. Introduce dink
4. Short practice game

Lesson VII

1. Game situation drills
2. Work on dinks
3. Introduce two- and one-arm digs
4. Net recovery

Lesson VIII

1. Practice floater serve for placement
2. Explain and demonstrate officiating techniques
3. Game situation

Lesson IX

1. Review general offensive and defensive play
2. Discuss and practice covering
3. Combination drills—serve, pass, set, spike, and block
4. Begin skill testing

Lesson X

1. Continue skill testing
2. Brief written examination

Lesson XI

1. Begin class tournament
2. Use student officials and student evaluators
3. Discuss success of offensive and defensive patterns

Lesson XII

1. Complete tournament
2. Discuss evaluations and skill and written tests
3. Show film of advanced play (or have competitive team demonstrate) to encourage students to continue development

SKILL DIFFICULTIES AND THEIR CORRECTION

Serving

Difficulty	Correction
a. Hitting the ball into the net on the underhand serve	a. Check to see if the ball is being held high enough before it is hit; hit with a higher follow-through; control the ball by hitting it more with an open hand position below center
b. Hitting the ball too high over the net on the underhand serve	b. Bend more at the waist; check and improve the follow-through; lower the ball position and extend left arm. Hit the ball just below center. Keep arm firm
c. Hitting the ball out of bounds	c. Review basic skills of specific serve. Stress hand position for ball control. Pick a spot on the opposite court near the net and aim for it; develop a smoother, more controlled swing

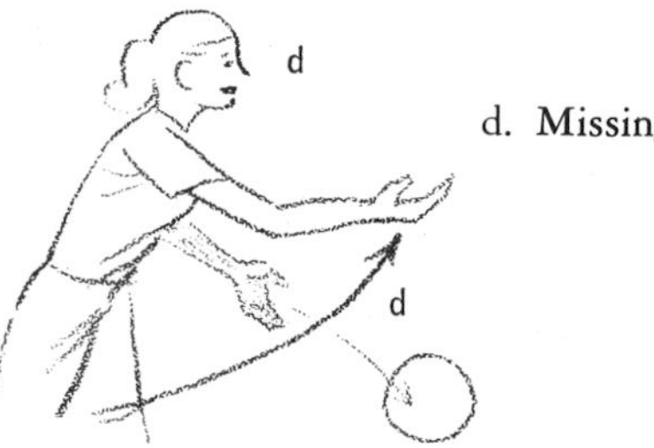

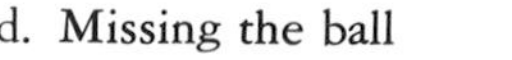

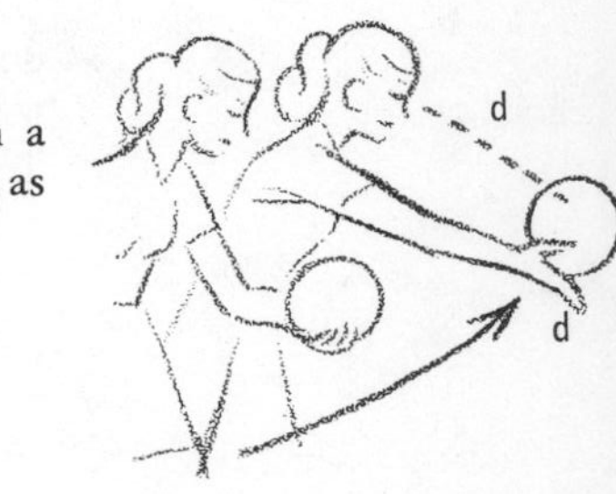

d. Missing the ball	d. Do not toss the ball; hit it from a stationary position; watch the ball as you hit it
e. Ball fails to cross net on overhand serve	e. On spin serve be certain toss of ball is forward of hitting arm. Hit with a firm arm and follow through in the direction of ball flight. On a floater, "punch" firmly and take a short step forward for additional power
f. On overhand serves ball travels too deep out of bounds	f. On spin serves hit more to center or top of ball—not below center—and follow through downward. On floater, contact *slightly* below center
g. Poor placement and erratic flight to left or right of court	g. On spin serve be sure hand does not contact ball too much to the side. Follow through in line of intended flight. On floater check position of the ball valve, for the ball breaks in the direction of the valve on contact

Forearm Pass

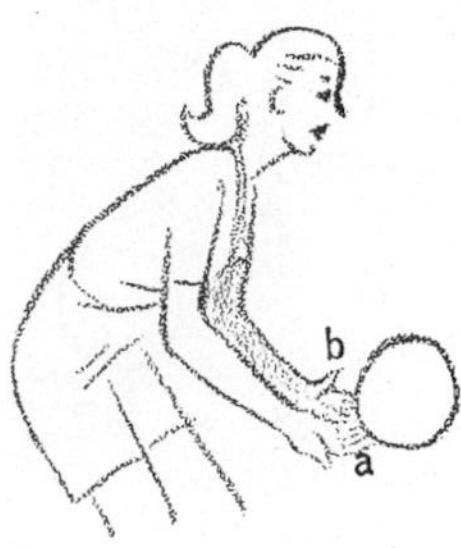

Difficulty	*Correction*
a. Constantly being called for lifting and holding	a. Eliminate open-hand underhand volleys. Review and practice hand, arm, and body position for forearm pass
b. Inability to get under the ball	b. Anticipate flight of the ball and position accordingly. Be prepared to dig, crouch, or dive to get forearms under the ball
c. Ball rebounds erratically off one or both arms or wrists	c. Get body in line with oncoming ball and be prepared to move if ball changes direction. Check arms to be certain forearms are parallel and flat, elbows firm and extended, on contact

Overhead Pass and Set

Difficulty	*Correction*
a. Slapping at the ball with the palms, resulting in poor ball control and illegal hits	a. Check ready position of hands. Concentrate on meeting the ball with the fleshy parts of fingers and thumbs; follow through with entire body in an upward arc. "Give" with the ball, control it, then use fingertips more for passing in a sharper, more refined movement

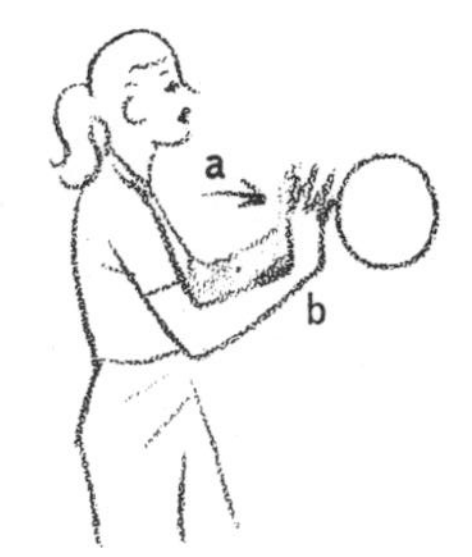

b. Receiving the ball too low	b. If below the waist, use a forearm pass. Bend to a deep crouch if an overhead pass is used. Meet the ball at forehead level
c. After contact, ball flies backward off the fingers	c. Meet the ball at forehead level in front of the body. Point thumbs toward the nose. Wrists are flexed, arms flexed and in front of the body
d. Inaccurate direction of the pass	d. Get body in line with oncoming ball. Watch for ball through the hands. Feet should be turned in the direction of intended ball flight, or directly away for a back set. Be certain both hands are controlling the pass or set
e. Passing too low or high	e. Concentrate on aiming; know where and how you want the ball to arc; bend knees more if the ball is going too low; watch the follow-through in all cases

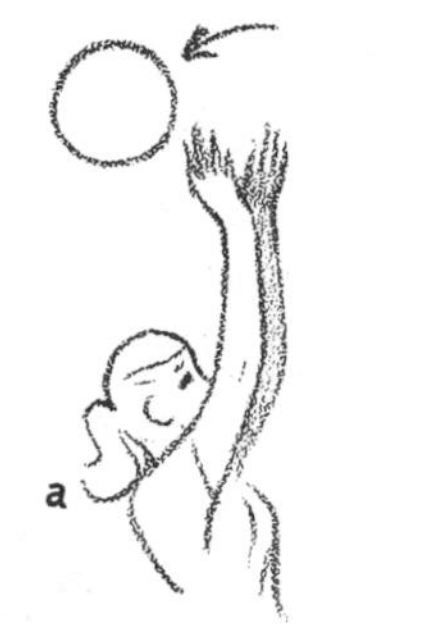

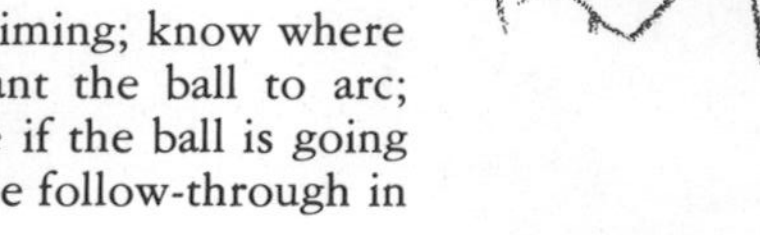

Setting

Difficulty	*Correction*
a. Setting too close to the net	a. Move closer to the net in order to make a more vertical set; check body position and follow through as the ball is contacted
b. Setting the ball too low for the spiker	b. Get the ball up 10 to 12 feet from the floor, about 2 feet from the net until skill of spikers warrants a short set

Spiking

Difficulty	*Correction*
a. Hitting the net with the body while spiking	a. Work on technique of vertical jump. Bend the body slightly backward on jump takeoff to stop forward momentum
b. Inability to get above net level for an effective spike	b. Strengthen legs so more power can be exerted in the jump. Raise arms and bend knees slightly to aid elevation
c. Hitting at the side or under the ball consistently	c. Concentrate on timing and height of the jump; attempt to strike the top of the ball with an extended arm. The ball is hit in front of the shoulder of the hitting arm
d. Hitting the ball deep and out of bounds	d. Hit the ball in a sharper downward motion; always make contact on top of the ball with an extended arm

Blocking

Difficulty	*Correction*
a. Missing the block	a. Failure to time takeoff after spiker's jump. Hurry to takeoff position and wait for the proper moment
b. Holding a blocked ball	b. Emphasize meeting the ball at the net; do not tilt hands backward
c. Trapping a spike or a dink with forearms or body and the net	c. Arms must be extended toward the net so there is not enough space for the ball to be "caught" on blocker's side of the net
d. Allowing ball to pass through the blocker's hands or arms	d. Concentrate on spreading hands but keeping the distance between hands and arms less then the diameter of the ball

Recovery of the Ball from out of the Net

Difficulty	*Correction*
a. Missing the ball	a. Quick reaction time is necessary and must be developed for success; bend body more; anticipate where the ball will fall; keep eyes on the ball
b. Driving the ball back into the net	b. Player crouches with side to the net and faces the falling ball. The dig recovery should be upward and slightly backward or upward and forward

EVALUATING THE RESULTS

There are a number of independent skills that contribute to successful play in the game of volleyball. Although a degree of efficiency in each of these skills can be measured, the test scores cannot be used as predictors of success in actual performance, for the actual game involves more than isolated skill execution. Evaluation is further complicated by the fact that volleyball techniques have changed to keep pace with the development of the game, and the older tests have less value in technique assessment than do the newer ones.

The Research Council of the AAHPER published the Volleyball Skills Test,* designed to assess volleying, serving, passing, and setting. Norms for both girls and boys are available. Volleying is measured as the subject volleys the ball against a wall as many times as possible in one minute. The wall is marked with a line 11 feet above the floor and 5 feet long with vertical lines extending upward from each end of the line.

Serving is assessed by the server's executing 10 trials into a court zoned into areas of designated point value. The server is rewarded for deep back court or sideline serves. Serves are executed 30 feet from the net; children under 12 serve from 20 feet.

Passing. A thrower tosses a high pass to a subject standing in a designated area. She attempts to execute a legal pass over an 8-foot rope into a designated and marked court area. Twenty trials are allowed, and a point is awarded only if the pass goes cleanly over the rope and into the 4′ × 6′ target area.

Setting. A thrower tosses a high pass to the subject who executes a set over a rope 10 feet high and into the 4′ × 6′ target area. Ten trials are given with the set going to the right, and ten are given with the set going to the left target area.

There are other skills tests that are recommended for use, but the tests must be carefully examined for reliability and validity for girls and women. Among those which should be considered are the following:

*Volleyball Wall Volley** (Kronquist and Brumbach, 1968). Similar to the AAHPER volley test but utilizing a U-shaped target, 5 feet wide and 4 feet long, painted on a smooth wall. The five-foot line is 11 feet above and parallel to the floor. A student is scored on the number of balls clearly volleyed into the target in three 20-second time trials.

*Brumbach Volleyball Service Test.** Designed to measure the student's ability to

---

*AAHPER *Skills Test Manual: Volleyball.* Clayton Shay, Test Consultant. Washington, D.C., AAHPER, 1969.

Johnson, Barry L. and Nelson, Jack K.: *Practical Measurements for Evaluation in Physical Education.* 2nd Ed. Burgess Publishing Co. Minneapolis, 1974.

†See Baumgartner, Ted A. and Jackson, Andrew S.: *Measurement for Evaluation in Physical Education, Review and Resource Manual.* Boston, Houghton Mifflin Co., 1975, for further description.

serve low and deep into the opponents' court. A rope is stretched four feet above the volleyball net, and point value is assigned to court areas. Scoring is based upon the path of the ball between the net and the stretched rope (or over both) and the area in which the served ball lands.

Volleyball Pass† (Liba and Stauff, 1963). Although designed to measure the accuracy of a volleyball chest pass, it is applicable to the overhand pass. Using a self-toss, the student attempts to pass the volleyball in such a manner that it clears a rope stretched 13 feet (12 feet for junior high school girls) high and lands in the highest scoring area painted on a two-foot wide canvas target.

Rating scales, individual evaluation charts,* and tournament results are valuable in assessing an individual's ability to combine individual techniques into a total game.

Objective knowledge tests and strategy concept assessments can be teacher designed, stressing the knowledge felt important for the age and skill level of the students tested.

TERMINOLOGY

Back court spike—An offensive play in which a back court player spikes the ball after initiating her takeoff from behind the 10-foot spiking line.

Back line players—The three players who, in normal rotation at the time of service, are behind front line players.

Back set—A ball set backwards over the head of the setter to an attack player behind her.

Block—A defensive play in which one or more front line defensive players attempts to interfere with the flight of the ball from the offense. The ball may be returned to opponents or into the defenders' court.

Covering—The process of "backing up" a player by taking a position behind her to play a serve, block, spike, or hard offensive ball which might glance off the first person playing the ball.

Cross court hit—A ball hit diagonally from one side of the attackers' court to the opposite side of the opponents' court.

Dead ball—A ball temporarily out of play.

Dig—A defensive play using one forearm and hand or both forearms to save a hard-driven attack ball.

Dink—A soft spike which is lobbed over, or to the side of, the hands of the blockers.

Dive—A forward thrust of the body to save a ball coming in front of a defensive player.

Double foul—Faults committed on the same play by members of opposing teams. Results in a replay.

Floater—A served ball which ducks and weaves in an erratic flight path.

Forearm pass—A pass in which the ball is contacted and controlled by simultaneous contact of both forearms. Contact is usually from arms extended below the waist.

Foul—A fault for which a point or side-out is awarded.

Freeball—An opponent's return which is easily played and controlled.

Front line players—The three players who, in normal rotation position at the time of service, are in front of the back line players.

Interchange—The intentional switching of positions with another player at the time of service to gain advantage in playing the ball.

---

*See Poindexter, Hally B. W. and Mushier, Carole L.: *Coaching Competitive Team Sports for Girls and Women.* Philadelphia, W. B. Saunders Co., 1973, pp. 236–237, for example and use of individual evaluation charts.

Jump set—Execution of a set while the setter is in an extended jump position off the ground.

Offensive patterns—A system of arranging players to utilize their best offensive talents (4-2: four spikers and two setters; 5-1 five spikers and one setter; 6-0: six spikers and six potential setters; 6-2: six spikers and two designated setters).

Overhead pass—A basic pass in which the ball is played from a position in front of and above the forehead.

Overlapping—Illegal positioning of one or more players at the time of service. A player may not overlap a player immediately in front (or back) of her or adjacent to her.

Own court—The playing area occupied by one's own team.

Rolls—Technique of positioning the body for rapid recovery after playing a difficult serve or spike.

Rotation—Process of shifting positions in a clockwise direction.

Roundhouse—A style of serving which can produce either a spinning or a floating serve.

Serving order—Serving sequence of a team's players.

Short set—A set which rises only slightly above the level of the net and which is spiked by a player who is already in the air as the ball is set.

Spike—A ball, other than the serve, which is hit forcibly from a position above the level of the net.

Time-out—Temporary suspension of the game for substitution, rest, injury, or at the discretion of the officials.

DISCUSSION QUESTIONS

1. Describe and demonstrate the forearm pass. Include a description of body position and hand and arm position. Explain the various situations in which this skill would be used.
2. Discuss the techniques of individual blocking. Diagram and explain the defensive positions of each team member for a two player block at (1) left front position and (2) middle court position.
3. Explain the use of the dink. Explain and demonstrate its execution.
4. Explain the overlapping rule. Diagram the relationship of adjacent players in each position on the court. Explain the value of interchanging when playing a 4–2 offense.
5. Select and administer volleyball skills tests to four teammates. Explain the tests, testing procedures, and results.
6. Make up an objective volleyball test of 20 items for advanced players. The test should involve five true-false, five matching, five multiple choice, and five fill-in questions. Check to avoid duplication and overly simplified statements.

SELECTED AUDIOVISUAL AIDS

Beginning Volleyball. (4 slidefilm units, color, recordings.) Society for Visual Education, 1345 Diversey Parkway, Chicago, Illinois 60614. (Purchase)

Fundamentals of Volleyball. (10 min., 16 mm., sound, b and w.) All American Productions, P.O. Box 91, Greeley, Colorado 86031.

Power Volleyball. (Super 8 loop films; series of 5, color.) Athletic Institute, Merchandise Mart, Room 705, Chicago, Illinois 60654. (Purchase)

USA vs. Russia: (1966). (16 mm., 34 min., silent, color.) Roger C. Burton, Midway YMCA, 1761 University Avenue, St. Paul, Minnesota 55104.

Volleyball. (Instructional super 8 loop films; series of 6, silent, color.) NCAA Films, P.O. Box 2726, Wichita, Kansas 67201.

Volleyball for Intermediate Grades: (1970). (16mm., 24 min., sound, color.) Universal Educational Visual Art, 221 Park Avenue South, New York, New York 10003. (Purchase, rental)

Volleyball Drills and Techniques. (16mm., 14 min., sound, color.) All American Productions, P.O. Box 91, Greeley, Colorado 80631. (Purchase)

Volleyball, U.S.A.: (1967). (16mm., 17 min., sound, b and w.) Association Instructional Materials, 600 Madison Avenue, New York, New York, 10022. (Rental, purchase)

Women's Power Volleyball. (super 8 loop films; series of 7, color.) Athletic Institute, Merchandise Mart, Room 705, Chicago, Illinois 60654. (Purchase)

Technique Charts

Pictorial Volleyball for Women. Creative Sports Books, P.O. Box 2244, Hollywood, California 90028. (Series of 26 photographs illustrating skills and positioning with printed descriptions of skill execution. Black and white.)

SUGGESTED READINGS

American Alliance for Health, Physical Education and Recreation: *Proceedings of the Fourth National Institute on Girls' Sports.* AAHPER, 1201 16th Street, N.W., Washington, D.C., 1968.

Boyden, E. D., Burton, R. G., and Odeneal, W. T.: *Volleyball Syllabus.* United States Volleyball Association, Berne, Indiana.

Bratton, Robert D.: *Power Volleyball for Player, Teacher and Coach.* Canadian Volleyball Association Publication, Scarborough, Ontario, 1968.

Cherebetiu, Gabriel: *Volleyball Techniques.* Creative Sports Books, P.O. Box 2244, Hollywood, California 90028, 1969.

Cohen, Harlan: *Power Volleyball Drills.* Creative Sports Books, P.O. Box 2244, Hollywood, California 90028, 1966.

Egstrom, Glen H., and Schaafsma, Frances: *Volleyball.* 2nd Ed. Dubuque, Iowa, Wm. C. Brown Co., 1972.

Keller, Val.; *Point, Game and Match!* Creative Sports Books, P.O. Box 2244, Hollywood, California 90028, 1968.

Liba, Marie R., and Stauff, M. R.: Test for the volleyball pass. *Research Quarterly 34*:56–63, March, 1963.

McGown, Carl M. (ed.): *It's Power Volleyball.* Berne, Indiana, United States Volleyball Association, 1968. (Available from Albert Monaco, Jr., 557 Fourth Street, San Francisco, California 94107.)

McManama, Jerre L., and Shondell, Donald: *Volleyball.* Englewood Cliffs, New Jersey, Prentice-Hall Inc., 1971.

National Association for Girls and Women in Sport: *Volleyball Guide.* Published every two years, AAHPER, 1201 16th Street, N.W., Washington, D.C. 20036.

Poindexter, Hally B. W., and Mushier, Carole L.: *Coaching Competitive Team Sports for Girls and Women.* Philadelphia, W. B. Saunders Co., 1973.

Sandefur, Randy: *Volleyball.* Pacific Palisades, California, Goodyear Publishing Co., 1970.

Scates, Allen E.: *Winning Volleyball.* Boston, Allyn and Bacon, Inc., 1972.

Scates, Allen E., and Ward, Jane: *Volleyball.* Boston, Allyn and Bacon, Inc., 1969.

Schaafsma, Frances, and Heck, Ann: *Volleyball for Coaches and Teachers.* Dubuque, Iowa, Wm. C. Brown Co., 1971.

Shick, Jacqueline: Effects of mental practice on selected volleyball skills for college women. *Research Quarterly 41*:88–94, March, 1970.

Singer, Robert N.: Sequential skill learning and retention effects in volleyball. *Research Quarterly 39*:1, March, 1968.

Slaymaker, Thomas, and Brown, Virginia H.: *Power Volleyball.* Rev. Ed. Philadelphia, W. B. Saunders Co., 1975.

Thigpen, Janet: *Power Volleyball for Girls and Women.* 2nd Ed. Dubuque, Iowa, Wm. C. Brown Co., 1974.

Trotter, Betty J.: *Volleyball for Girls and Women.* New York, Ronald Press, 1965.

Veronee, Marvin D. (ed.): *Official Volleyball Rules and Reference Guide of the United States Volleyball Association.* Berne, Indiana, P.O. Box 109 46711, USVBA, printer.

Welch, J. Edmund (ed.): *How to Play and Teach Volleyball.* New York, Association Press, 1969.

IV

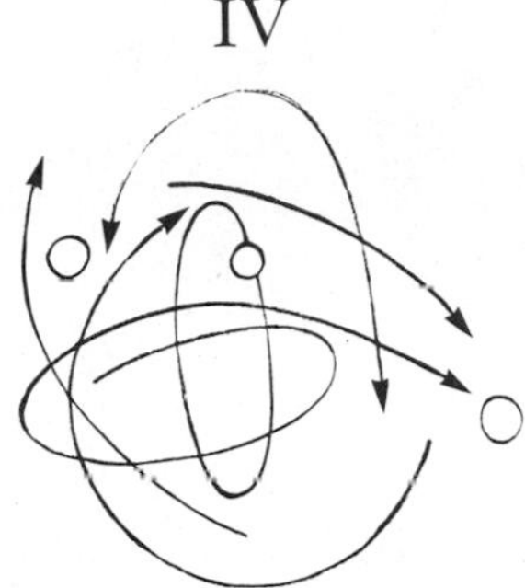

PART IV

EXTENDING THE PROGRAM

"If education is a means of developing personality, equipping the mind, strengthening the body, learning skills, building character, and creating an appreciation for beauty, then recreation has enormous educational values."

...Charles Brightbill and Harold Meyer

CHAPTER 20

STANDARDS IN SPORTS FOR GIRLS AND WOMEN

Standards in the conduct of sports for girls and women as devised, endorsed, and promoted by the many outstanding leaders in the National Association for Girls and Women in Sport of the AAHPER, the National Federation of State High School Athletic Associations (NFSHSAA), and the Association for Intercollegiate Athletics for Women (AIAW) have given both great impetus and strong guidance to the rapidly growing sports programs for females throughout the nation. At first there were no such guiding groups; highly organized competitive games for girls and women were introduced cautiously and slowly in selected eastern women's colleges. The first women's game of basketball was played at Smith College in 1899, followed shortly afterwards by hockey as introduced by Constance Applebee in 1901, then by swimming and track and field events.

The first attempt to guide women's sports on the national level was in 1907, when the Women's Basketball Guide of that year announced that a Women's Rules Committee had been formed. From this group developed the Women's Athletic Committee, which later became the National Section for Women's Athletics. In 1957 it became the Division for Girls' and Women's Sports, and in 1974 it became the National Association for Girls and Women in Sport of the American Alliance for Health, Physical Education and Recreation. The purpose of this association is to foster the development of sports programs for girls and women. This is accomplished through developing and publicizing principles and standards, publishing and interpreting rules, cooperating with other sports organizations, encouraging and disseminating research relating to females in sports, providing means for training, evaluating, and rating officials, and providing leadership training for teachers and coaches.

The present position of NAGWS is both realistic and idealistic. It recognizes the increased interest in intercollegiate and interscholastic competition as well as recognizing many of the problems attending this growing interest and participation. However, it maintains that comprehensive guidelines can be developed to insure competitive programs which protect the welfare of the individual participants. NAGWS and other supportive organizations for girls' and women's sports believe in a sound and inclusive instructional program which should be augmented by a broad intramural program and supplemented by an extramural program.

The following selected standards, deemed important for guiding competition in these programs are adapted from *Philosophy and Standards for Girls' and Women's Sports.**

Leadership. Administrators, teachers, coaches, and officials should provide competent leadership to assure desirable outcomes of the sports program. Players have an obligation to perpetuate fair play while gaining skill development and personal satisfaction from sport.

1. The administrator is directly responsible for:
   a. Selecting qualified persons to direct the program
   b. Providing facilities, equipment, and finances to carry on the program
   c. Providing equal use of facilities and equipment for boys and girls
   d. Providing health safeguards
   e. Guiding publicity to emphasize the educational and recreational values of the program
2. The teacher or coach is responsible for:
   a. Having a thorough knowledge of the games and their rules and strategy
   b. Providing opportunity for all girls to play
   c. Encouraging skillful play for full enjoyment of the game
   d. Emphasizing the importance of health examinations
   e. Developing intelligent leadership and wise following among the players
   f. Conducting activities on a sound competitive basis
   g. Exemplifying through her behavior those personal and professional qualities which influence high ideals and standards in others
   h. Providing opportunities for player participation in planning, conducting, and evaluating the sports program
3. The official is responsible for:
   a. Assuming authority during competitive play
   b. Thorough preparation through knowledge of the rules and regulations governing play
   c. Demonstrated ability in the use of officiating techniques

*Adapted from DGWS: *Philosophy and Standards for Girls' and Women's Sports,* 1973. Presently under revision by NAGWS. See current edition for complete standards and guidelines.

   d. Acceptance of recognized philosophy and standards of sports for girls and women
   e. Conduct before, during, and after a game reflecting the highest professional standards
4. The player is responsible for her own conduct as shown through:
   a. Intelligent health practices
   b. Courtesy, fair play, and good sportsmanship
   c. High quality leadership within her own group reflected by her understanding of the duties of group leaders, captains, managers, and officials
   d. Emotional control in all game situations
   e. Playing to the best of her ability

Health. Provision must be made for careful supervision of the health of all players.

1. Participants must have periodic health examinations.
2. After serious illness or injury, permission from a physician should be required to resume participation.
3. First aid supplies should be available at practices and games.
4. Participation during the menstrual period should be determined on an individual basis.
5. Equipment and facilities should be hygienic and safe.
6. Players should be removed from activity if they are injured or overfatigued, or show evidence of emotional instability.
7. Adequate health and accident protection for participants should be provided.

Financing. The financing of the sports program should be included in the budget of the school, college, or recreational program. Funds may include gate receipts and student fees, but the program must not be fully dependent on fluctuating income.

Publicity. A planned program of publicity should present interesting information on the program, its standards, aims, and outcome. The publicity should be carefully interpreted to newswriters, telecasters, parents, community leaders, the players, and their associates. Publicity should stress the educational and social values of sports. Constructive public relations considers the best interests of the participants as it develops a sound public attitude, an understanding of goals, and an appreciation of the efforts of the players.

THE PARTICIPANTS

Individual interest and participation in the sports program develop because of a soundly based instructional program. This program begins when the student first enters school and continues throughout her high school and college years. The elementary school program provides experience and skill development in basic movements and fundamental sports skills. Intramural sports and some selected extramural events are desirable for fourth, fifth, and sixth grades. Careful supervision and conduct of these programs is imperative. Instructional, intramural, and extramural programs expand throughout high school and college augmented by programs of community agencies, recreational clubs, sports clubs, and social groups. A general review of the interests and needs of elementary, high school, college, and adult age groups aids in planning the competitive program.

10 to 12—Pre-adolescent. Formative stage, seeking peer status and approval, influenced by media coverage of sports, interest moves from simple team games (dodgeball, kickball) to organized sports, likes informal groups for biking and hiking. Suggest sex segregation as little as possible, except when there are marked differences in strength and endurance.

13 to 15—Early Adolescent; 15 to 18—Late Adolescent. Making up the junior and senior high school, this group increases in height and weight rapidly, inaccuracy of movement decreasing, becoming sexually mature, seeking freedom and adventure yet needing surrounding cluster of gang friends. Awkwardness decreases with age, as does insecurity with successful experience, greatly needs approval, understanding, likes team and individual games requiring increasing skill, needs the opportunity for many coeducational game experiences.

19 to 24—Young Adult. Slower, more refined development, period of high physical efficiency, begins to participate more in community life and feels personally more responsibility to society, takes part in more service projects, has multiplicity of interests, prefers coeducational activities.

24 and Over—Mature Adult. Increasingly aware of responsibilities to self and others, now matured with fairly definite motor patterns well fixed, vigorous activity is satisfying. Willing to learn new, socially acceptable skills, needs diversified activities in many areas, wants to keep fit, plays mostly for exercise and fun, will seek out places to play.

THE PROGRAM

Suggested Types of Activities
10 to 12 years

- Ball games
  - Softball types
    - Liberty bat ball
    - Schlag ball
    - Long ball
    - Tap baseball
    - Softball
  - Basketball types
    - Dodgeball
    - Endball
    - Captain ball
    - Basketball
- Field types
  - Flag football
  - Line soccer
  - Corner kickball
- Net games without rackets
  - Newcomb
  - Volleyball
  - Ring or deck tennis
  - Cageball
- Net games with rackets
  - Paddle tennis
  - Table tennis
  - Badminton
- Track events
  - Running
    - Dashes (50, 75, 100, 220, 440 yds.)
    - Relays (220, 440 pursuit; 220 yd. shuttle)
    - 1 mile cross country
    - Hurdle (50 yd., 2′6″)
  - Long jump: standing, running
  - Running high jump
  - Throwing
    - Basketball
    - Softball
    - Shot put (6 lbs.)

THE PROGRAM *(Continued)*

Suggested Types of Activities

10 to 12 years

- Swimming
  - Individual events
  - Relays
  - Strokes for form
  - Water games
  - Simple diving
- Tumbling and gymnastics
- Miscellaneous
  - Rope jumping
  - Hiking
  - Bicycle riding
  - Roller skating
  - Coasting
  - Ice skating
  - Bowling
  - Shuffleboard
  - Tetherball
  - Aerial darts

13 to 18 years

- Ball games
  - Softball types
    - Schlag ball
    - Hit pin baseball
    - Soccer baseball
    - Softball
  - Basketball types
    - Dodgeball
    - Endball
    - Captain ball
    - Pinball
    - Nine court basketball
    - Basketball
  - Field types
    - Corner kickball
    - Fieldball
    - Soccer
    - Speedball
    - Field hockey
    - Lacrosse
    - Flag football
    - Speed-a-way
  - Net games without rackets
    - Newcomb
    - Giant volleyball
    - Ring or deck tennis
    - Volleyball
  - Net games with rackets
    - Paddle tennis
    - Table tennis
    - Badminton
    - Tennis
  - Wall games
    - Handball
    - Squash
    - Racquetball
- Track events
  - Running
    - Dashes (50, 100, 220, 440, 880 yds.)
    - Relays (220, 440, 880 yd. pursuit; 880 yd. medley) (1 mile relay)*
    - Hurdles (50 yd., 80 yd., 2′6″) (100 meter, 2′9″,* 200 meter, 2′6″*)
    - 1 mile cross country
    - 1½ mile cross country
    - 2 mile cross country*
    - 1 mile or 1500 meter run
    - 2 mile or 3000 meter run*
  - Jumping
    - Running broad jump
    - Standing broad jump
    - Running high jump
  - Throwing
    - Basketball—distance
    - Soccerball—distance
    - Softball—distance
    - Shot put (8 lb.)
    - Discus throw*
    - Javelin throw*
- Swimming
  - For speed (50, 100, 200, 400 yd. freestyle; 50 and 100 yd. breaststroke;

---

*Not recommended for junior high school girls.

THE PROGRAM *(Continued)*

Suggested Types of Activities

13 to 18 years

- 50 and 100 yd. backstroke;
- 50 and 100 yd. butterfly;
- 100 and 200 yd. individual medley;
- 200 yd. medley relay;
- 200 and 400 yd. freestyle relay)
- Strokes for form
- Diving (1 meter)
- Water games
- Lifesaving events
- Tumbling and gymnastics

Miscellaneous
- Hiking
- Skating (roller, ice)
- Coasting
- Horseshoe pitching
- Bowling
- Shuffleboard
- Horseback riding
- Archery
- Golf
- Bicycle riding
- Fencing
- Skiing

19 to 24 years

Ball games
- Softball types
  - Hit pin baseball
  - Softball
- Basketball
- Field types
  - Soccer
  - Fieldball
  - Speedball
  - Field hockey
  - Lacrosse
  - Flag football
- Net games without rackets
  - Ring or deck tennis
  - Giant volleyball
  - Volleyball
- Net games with rackets
  - Paddle tennis
  - Table tennis
  - Badminton
  - Tennis
- Wall games
  - Racquetball
  - Handball
  - Squash

Track events
- Dashes
- Relays
- Distance events
- Hurdling
- Jumping
  - Running long jump
  - Running high jump
- Throwing
  - Basketball
  - Softball
  - Shot put
  - Discus throw
  - Javelin throw

Swimming
- As recommended above plus 400 yd. medley relay and 200 yd. freestyle
- Water games
- Diving (1 meter and 3 meter)
- Lifesaving events

Tumbling and gymnastics

Miscellaneous
- Hiking
- Skating (roller, ice)
- Coasting
- Horseshoe pitching
- Bowling
- Shuffleboard
- Horseback riding
- Archery
- Golf
- Fencing
- Bicycle riding
- Boating
  - Sail
  - Ice
  - Canoeing
- Skiing

The sports program is an integral part of school and college life, and the program of activities should be scheduled when students are available to participate. Many facilities are open at odd hours so that any spontaneously formed group—such as two would-be badminton players, or a single individual looking for companionship and an opportunity to exercise for fun—can be served. Fortunately today more and more schools are opening their facilities and furnishing or renting equipment and providing supervisors or teachers for after work or after school fun.

Leadership is the real key to the success and value of any physical education or recreation program, whether it be furnished by a school or any other organization. The real test of the program is in the enjoyment and benefit the participant receives from taking part in it. The sports program should be broad, varied, and planned for participants of differing levels of skill. Each should have the opportunity to participate, improve, and excel in a sport of her choice.

DISCUSSION QUESTIONS

1. Why should teams composed of girls or women players be coached by women? Support your answer by giving five, well-thought-through answers you would endorse as an educator. What are the advantages and disadvantages of a male coach for an all female team?
2. Review federal legislation which deals specifically with equality of competitive opportunity for men and women. Discuss your findings in view of policies relating to financing, coaching, and publicizing women's sports. Discuss the pros and cons of "separate but equal" teams for men and women, and coeducational competitive teams.
3. Look through any official NAGWS Guide. Review or critique three articles in it designed to help in instructional techniques, presentation, and interpretation of research or improvement of coaching skills.
4. List the personal and professional qualifications a teacher of girls' and women's sports should possess. List the personal and professional qualifications of a coach. Cite the differences and similarities between the two jobs.

SUGGESTED READINGS

AIAW Handbook of Policies and Operating Procedures. Current Ed. Washington, D.C., AAHPER.

D.G.W.S.: "Guidelines for Intercollegiate Athletic Programs for Women." In *Philosophy and Standards for Girls' and Women's Sports.* Washington, D.C., AAHPER.

D.G.W.S.: "Guidelines for Interscholastic Athletic Programs for High School Girls." In *Philosophy and Standards for Girls' and Women's Sports.* Washington, D.C., AAHPER.

D.G.W.S.: "Guidelines for Interscholastic Athletic Programs for Junior High School Girls." In *Philosophy and Standards for Girls' and Women's Sports.* Washington, D.C., AAHPER.

D.G.W.S. Research Reports: *Women in Sports.* 1971.

D.G.W.S. Research Reports: *Women in Sports.* 1973.

Gerlser, Ellen W., Felshin, Jan, Berlin, Pearl, and Wyrick, Waneen: *The American Woman in Sport.* Reading, Massachusetts, Addison-Wesley Publishing Company, 1974.

Leavitt, Norma, and Price, Hartley: *Intramural and Recreational Sports.* 2nd Ed. New York, The Ronald Press, 1958.

NAGWS: *Philosophy and Standards for Girls' and Women's Sports.* Current Ed. Washington, D.C., AAHPER.

Poindexter, Hally B. W., and Mushier, Carole L. *Coaching Competitive Team Sports for Girls and Women.* Philadelphia, W. B. Saunders Co., 1973.

The First National Institute on Girls' Sports. Washington, D.C., AAHPER, DGWS, 1965.

CHAPTER 21

COMPETITION

Under proper conditions and with sound leadership, sports competition for girls and women can be a rich, educational experience. "Competition is a term which describes the concerted efforts of two or more individuals striving toward a desired goal. It is true competition when (1) the individual recognizes her opponent or rival as one who is equal, or nearly equal, in potential ability and intent to accomplish the task and attain the common goal, and (2) the participants are, in fact, capable of, and highly motivated toward, obtaining the desired goal in less time, and in better fashion or with greater or fewer points than their opponents. Competition against one's self to better one's performance also fulfills these criteria."*

The values of competitive sport can be gained through participation in intramural and extramural sports; all who wish to compete should be allowed the opportunity at their own levels of competence. *Intramural* competition involves participation from *within* the *same* school, club, community group, institution, or organization; whereas *extramural* competition involves participants *from two or more* schools, colleges, centers, or other organizations. Forms of extramural competition include *sports days* in which each school or team competes as a unit, and *play days* where teams are composed of members of all invited units. *Telegraphic meets* involve the conduct of competitions at a number of home grounds or central locations. The results are then forwarded by mail or wire for determination of winners. *Invitational events* include symposiums, games, or matches to which a school or sports group invites one or more teams or persons to participate.

---

*See *Philosophy and Standards for Girls' and Women's Sports.* Washington, D.C., DGWS, AAHPER, 1973, p. 7.

Interscholastic, intercollegiate, or *interagency programs* in which groups or individuals who are trained and coached, play a series of scheduled games or tournaments with teams from other schools, cities, or organizations are other forms of extramural competition.*

GUIDELINES FOR INTERSCHOLASTIC ATHLETIC PROGRAMS FOR JUNIOR HIGH SCHOOL GIRLS†‡

Principles

During the junior high school years, girls should have the time and opportunity to explore a great variety of sports. Because of growth and development patterns, this is an age when many goals can be accomplished through team sports and a time when skills of individual sports should also be sampled and developed. Therefore, the junior high school sports program for girls should involve opportunities to participate in many kinds of sports and in a variety of sports situations.

It is also recognized that some girls with high skill potential will wish to extend their training and competitive experiences under competent leaders outside the jurisdiction of the school.

A wide variety of activities should be offered and made available to all students in the school instructional and intramural programs. Opportunities for interschool competition may be provided in the form of a limited number of sport days at the end of the intramural season. The following guidelines are recommended:

1. Competitive sports opportunities for junior high school girls should be planned as a program separate and different from the program of competitive athletics for senior high school girls, whether or not the state high school athletic organization includes the junior high school level.
2. Sports competition should be planned for the values offered to the participant rather than as a spectator sport or as a training program for senior high school teams.
3. Extramural programs may be a valuable supplement to broad instructional and intramural programs, provided sufficient time, facilities, and personnel are available for these programs.
4. The responsibility for leadership of the local girls' interscholastic program should be delegated to the women physical education teachers. The school administration should delegate to them the major responsibility for planning, organizing, coaching, and supervising the program with the understanding that the ultimate authority remains in the hands of the administration.
5. The program, based on the needs and interests of the girls, should include those individual and team activities for which qualified leadership, financial support, and adequate facilities are available.
6. The entire financing of the girls' sports program should be included in the total school budget. Any monies collected should go into the general fund.
7. DGWS§-recommended guidelines should be used in all sports. It is strongly recommended that DGWS rules be used in those sports in which DGWS publishes rules.
8. The administration should provide a healthful, safe, and sanitary environment for all participants.

---

*It is anticipated that the interpretation and implementation of Title IX of the Educational Amendments Act of 1972 will result in extensive changes in guidelines and programs for girls and boys.

†Although the pattern differs, "junior high" is used here to include grades 7 through 8 or 9.

‡Material reprinted from *Philosophy and Standards for Girls' and Women's Sports.* Washington, D.C., DGWS, AAHPER, 1973, pp. 39–41.

§Now NAGWS.

Programs

1. Sports days following the end of the intramural season may, in most cases, give enough breadth to the opportunity for student competition in sports at this age.
2. Interscholastic programs may be desirable at this level. Where they exist, the length of the season will vary according to locale and the sport and should not interfere with the primary educational objectives for the student or the total program.
3. The wide variation in growth and development within this age grouping necessitates equating of competitors with reference to skill level, age, and/or size.
4. All-star teams are not appropriate for girls' sport programs.

Standards

The following standards are recommended for participants, leaders, and administrators of programs. Within each state, additions or modifications may be made by the regulatory body.

Participants

1. Participants must be bona fide students of the school which they represent. Students under temporary suspension or probation for disciplinary reasons should not be allowed to participate.
2. Participants must have amateur standing in the interscholastic sports in which they participate.
3. Written permission of the parent or guardian is required for all participants.
4. A physician's certification of a girl's fitness for participation shall be filed with the administration prior to the first practice in a sport. The examination must have been made within the time period specified by local regulations. Written permission by a physician should be required for participation after a serious illness, injury, or surgery.
5. Participants should carry some type of accident insurance coverage that protects them during athletic competition.

Leaders

1. The interscholastic program should be directed, coached, and officiated by qualified women whenever possible. No program should be expanded past the ability of the girls' department of physical education to direct it.
2. All coaches should be certified teachers employed by the local board of education. If teachers other than trained women physical educators are used to coach, they should be qualified and work closely with the girls' department.
3. A woman faculty member appointed by the principal should accompany and supervise girls' teams at all contests.
4. Officials should hold a current DGWS rating in the specific sport and should be registered with the appropriate administrative or regulatory bodies.
5. A doctor should be on call for all contests, and someone who is qualified in first-aid procedure should be in attendance.
6. In case of question as to fitness for play, the official has the right to overrule the coach for the protection of the girl.

Administrators

1. All games and contests in which school teams participate must be under the direct sponsorship and supervision of the schools involved. No postseason games for teams or individuals should be permitted.
2. A girl should participate on only one competitive team during a season. Participation on more than one competitive team includes participation on an additional team within an institution or participation on an additional team outside an institution. In unusual circumstances such participation may be permitted provided it contributes to the welfare of the participant and does not place excessive demands and pressures upon her.

3. Awards, when given, should be inexpensive tokens of a symbolic type, such as ribbons, letters, or small pins. The giving of other types of awards, as well as fund-raising for expensive or elaborate awards is considered a violation of this guideline.
4. Travel should be kept to a minimum by competing only with other schools in the vicinity. Travel should be in school buses or with bonded carriers.

The interest in and growth of interscholastic and intercollegiate competition justifies consideration of desirable guidelines for the conduct of competition.

GUIDELINES FOR INTERSCHOLASTIC ATHLETIC PROGRAMS FOR HIGH SCHOOL GIRLS*

Principles

Competitive sports are an important part of the total physical education program for high school girls. A program of intramural and extramural participation should be arranged to augment a sound and inclusive instructional program in physical education. The interscholastic program should not be promoted at the expense of the instructional or the intramural programs.

As the interscholastic program is expanded, the State High School Athletic Association will be the regulatory body for its member schools. For schools that are not members, a regulatory body may need to be formed. The State Department of Education should be involved.

1. Existing legislative and administrative bodies for interscholastic athletic programs will retain ultimate control of the new program for girls within the state. However, a women's advisory board composed mainly of women high school physical educators should be formed to propose policies to these administrative and legislative groups and to review policies approved by them.
2. Total responsibility for the administration and supervision of the local interscholastic athletic program is vested in the local school administration and the appropriate persons designated by the administration.
3. The responsibility for leadership of the local girls' interscholastic program should be delegated to the women physical education teachers. The school administration should delegate to them the major responsibility for planning, organizing, coaching, and supervising the program with the understanding that the ultimate authority remains in the hands of the administration.
4. The program, based on the needs and interests of the girls, should include those individual and team activities for which qualified leadership, financial support, and adequate facilities are available.
5. All-star teams are not appropriate for girls' sports program.
6. The entire financing of the girls' sports program should be included in the total school budget. Any monies collected should go into the general fund.
7. DGWS-recommended guidelines should be used in all sports. It is strongly recommended that DGWS rules be used in those sports in which DGWS publishes rules.
8. The administration should provide a healthful, safe, and sanitary environment for all participants.

Standards

The following standards are recommended for participants, leaders, and administrators of programs. Within each state, additions or modifications may be made by the regulatory body.

**Ibid.*, pp. 43–45.

Participants

1. Participants must be bona fide students of the high school which they represent. They shall not have attended high school for more than eight semesters after entering the ninth grade. They must be successfully carrying full academic loads. Students under temporary suspension or probation for disciplinary reasons should not be allowed to participate.
2. Participants must have amateur standing in the interscholastic sports in which they participate.
3. Written permission of the parent or guardian is required for all participants.
4. A physician's certification of a girl's fitness for participation shall be filed with the administration prior to the first practice in a sport. The examination must have been made within the time period specified by local regulations. Written permission by a physician should be required for participation after a serious illness, injury, or surgery.
5. Participants should carry some type of accident insurance coverage that protects them during athletic competition.

Leadership

1. The interscholastic program should be directed, coached, and officiated by qualified women whenever and wherever possible. No program should be expanded past the ability of the girls' department of physical education to direct it.
2. All coaches should be certified teachers employed by the local board of education. If teachers other than trained women physical educators are used to coach, they should be qualified and work closely with the girls' department.
3. A woman faculty member appointed by the principal shall accompany and supervise girls' teams at all contests.
4. Officials should hold a current DGWS rating in the specific sport and should be registered with the appropriate administrative or regulatory bodies.
5. A doctor should be on call for all contests, and someone who is qualified in first-aid procedure should be in attendance.
6. In case of question as to fitness for play, the official has the right to overrule the coach for the protection of the welfare of the girl.

Administration

1. All games and contests in which school teams participate must be under the direct sponsorship and supervision of the schools involved.
2. A girl should participate on only one competitive team during a season. Participation on more than one competitive team includes participation on an additional team within an institution or participation on additional teams outside an institution. In unusual circumstances, such participation may be permitted provided it contributes to the welfare of the participant and does not place excessive demands and pressures upon her.
3. Competition should be limited to a geographical area which will permit players to return at reasonable hours. Safe transportation should be assured.
4. The length of the season will vary according to the locale and sport and should not be so long that the educational values for the student in terms of the total program are jeopardized (approximately 10 to 14 weeks). This season should include conditioning and instruction. An extended season should be limited to a postseason tournament which should not exceed the area or state level.
5. Interscholastic competition should be limited to those sports for which DGWS publishes rules and standards, and they should be used in administration of the program.
6. Awards, when given, should be inexpensive tokens of a symbolic type, such as ribbons, letters, and small pins. The giving of other types of awards as well as fund-raising for expensive or elaborate awards, is considered a violation of this guideline.
7. Teams for girls should be provided for those who desire competitive athletic experiences. While positive experiences for the exceptional girl competitor may occur through participation in boys' or men's competitive groups, these instances are rare and should be judged acceptable only as an interim procedure for use until girls' programs can be initiated.

GUIDELINES FOR INTERCOLLEGIATE ATHLETIC PROGRAMS FOR WOMEN*

Many colleges and universities with intercollegiate programs may be members of the AIAW or its regional branch and will be governed in their intercollegiate competition by these bodies. The following guidelines are recommended for all programs.

Administration

The intercollegiate athletic program(s) should be specifically designed for women, and its administration and organization should be the responsibility of the women in physical education. It is also the responsibility of the physical education faculty women to recommend and formulate policy for the expanded program to be submitted to the appropriate policy-approving authority of the institution.

Budget

The budget for women's intercollegiate athletics should be part of the budget of the institution so that the program is assured. A separate budget item should be specifically designated for this program. (This does not preclude the use of state monies, student fees, gate receipts, and other sources of income, but the program should not depend solely on fluctuating sources of income.) The budget should be administered by the appropriate personnel in women's physical education.

Financial Assistance

Success of financial assistance programs is dependent upon the quality of administration. To foster appropriate administrative procedures. the following guidelines are recommended:

1. The enrichment of the life of the participant should be the focus and the reason for athletic programs.
2. Adequate funding for a comprehensive athletic program should receive priority over the money assigned for financial assistance. A comprehensive athletic program provides adequate funding for:
   (a) A variety of competitive sports which will serve the needs of many students
   (b) Travel using licensed carriers
   (c) Appropriate food and lodging
   (d) Rated officials
   (e) Well-trained coaches
   (f) Equipment and facilities which are safe and aid performance
3. The potential contribution of the "educated" citizen to society should be the motive for financial aid rather than the contribution of the student to the college offering the scholarship.
4. Staff time and effort should be devoted to the comprehensive program rather than to recruiting.
5. Students should be free to choose the institution on the basis of curriculum and program rather than on the amount of financial aid offered.
6. When financial aid is to be given, participants in certain sports should not be favored over those in other sports.
7. Students should be encouraged to participate in the athletic program for reasons other than financial aid.

Since financial aid programs for athletes in the past have resulted in conditions where abuses frequently outweighed benefits, initiation of such programs should be approached with caution. Colleges which are not currently providing financial aid for athletes are encouraged to

---

*See the current *AIAW Handbook for Policies and Procedures.* AAHPER, 1201 16th Street, N.W., Washington, D.C. Material reprinted from *Philosophy and Standards for Girls' and Women's Sports.* Washington, D.C., DGWS, AAHPER, 1973, pp. 47–50.

adhere to their current philosophy and, in fact, some colleges may choose to discontinue all financial assistance aid programs for athletes. A college considering the use of a program of financial aid for athletes should be cognizant of potential abuses.

Scheduling

Contests should be scheduled among schools having players of comparable ability in order to equate competition. In order to make this possible, scheduling in each sport need not be with the same institutions each season.

Scheduling with collegiate institutions is recommended. However, when budget is inadequate for travel, limited scheduling with outside organizations (i.e., church, industrial leagues, etc.) in the local areas may be desirable. Scheduling should allow opportunities for participants of intercollegiate teams to meet on an informal social basis.

Health and Safety

Adequate health and insurance protection should be provided by the institution for all members of athletic teams. First-aid services and emergency medical care should be available during all scheduled intercollegiate athletic events.

Awards

Awards are not necessary. However, if awards are given they should be of a symbolic type rather than elaborate awards of a costly nature. The giving of expensive awards as well as fund-raising for this purpose is considered a violation of DGWS* standards. All-star teams are not appropriate for women's sports programs.

Leaders (Teachers, Coaches, and Officials)

1. Good leadership is essential to a desirable sports program. The qualified leader meets standards set by the profession through an understanding of (a) the place and purpose of sports in education, (b) the growth and development of children and youth, (c) the effects of exercise on the human organism, (d) first aid and accident prevention, (e) specific skills, and (f) sound teaching methods. It is desirable that, when possible, leaders of women's sports have personal experience in organized extramural competition. The leader should demonstrate personal integrity and a primary concern for the welfare of the participant.
2. The program should be under the direct supervision of the appropriate personnel in women's physical education. Qualified women should teach, coach, and officiate wherever and whenever possible, and in all cases the professional background and experience of the leader must meet established standards of the physical education profession.
3. It is strongly recommended that an official's rating be considered a prerequisite for coaching in order to enhance the coach's understanding of the official's role.
4. Intercollegiate events should be officiated by DGWS state or national officials. In those sports where DGWS does not rate officials, an equivalent rating is acceptable.
5. If a nonstaff member is teaching or coaching, a woman member of the physical education faculty should supervise the participants. Cooperative institutional efforts should be devoted toward preservice and in-service programs and clinics for leaders and teachers.
6. DGWS-approved rules should be used in the conduct of all intercollegiate sports events.

Participants

1. Intercollegiate participation should not interfere with primary educational objectives.
   (a) A girl should participate on only one competitive team during a season.
   (b) Participation on more than one team includes participation on an additional team within an institution or participation on an additional team outside an institution.

---

*Now NAGWS.

In unusual circumstances such participation may be permitted provided it contributes to the welfare of the participant and does not place excessive demands and pressures upon her.

2. The athletic schedule should not jeopardize the student's class and study time.
   (a) The length of the season and the number of games should be established and agreed upon by the participating schools.
   (b) The length of the season will vary according to the locale and sport and should not be so long that the educational values for the student in terms of the total program are jeopardized (approximately 12-14 weeks). This season should include conditioning and instruction.
   (c) The season may be lengthened to include opportunities for participation in state, regional or national tournaments or meets for which individuals or teams qualify.
3. Teams for girls and women should be provided for all who desire competitive athletic experiences. While positive experiences for the exceptional girl or woman competitor may occur through participation in boys' or men's competitive groups, these instances are rare and should be judged acceptable only as an interim procedure for use until women's programs can be initiated.
4. Any woman who is presently enrolled as a full-time undergraduate student in a college, junior college, or university, and who maintains the academic average required for participation in all other major campus activities at her institution shall be eligible to participate.
5. Transfer students are immediately eligible for participation following enrollment in the institution.
6. Students may not participate in the same annual event for more than four years.
7. All participants must have amateur status. Amateur status is maintained in a sport if a player has not received and does not receive money, other than expenses, as a participant in that sport. A participant may receive money from her own school to pay for housing, meals, and transportation providing such funds do not exceed actual costs. For open or international competition governed by the respective sports governing body, a student may lose amateur status if she receives remuneration in excess of her expenses for playing, coaching, or officiating. Scholarships allowed by AIAW will not jeopardize a student's amateur status for DGWS-AIAW competition.
8. A medical examination is a prerequisite to participation in intercollegiate athletics. This examination should be given within the school year prior to the start of the sport season. Where health examinations are done by the family physician, a covering letter explaining the program of activities and an examination which would include the information needed are suggested. Written permission by the physician should be required for participation after serious illness, injury, or surgery.

TYPES OF TOURNAMENTS

There are many plans for organizing competitive events for individual and team participation. The type of tournament selected depends upon available facilities, time allotted to complete the competition, and the number of competitors. The most frequently used plans include:

1. Group and individual event meets
2. Single and double elimination tournaments
3. Round robin schedules; round robin leagues followed by a play-off:
   a. Leagues followed by single elimination play-offs
   b. Leagues followed by double elimination play-offs
   c. Leagues followed by championship play-off series
4. Ladder tournament
5. Pyramid tournament
6. Ringer tournament
7. Special events

Group- and Individual-Event Meets. Meets involving individual and team events which utilize a cumulative point scoring system to determine the winner are often popular in track and field, swimming, physical fitness testing, gymnastics, and field days. Points are scored on the basis of places; for example, a plan where six places are recognized in the event would be to award seven, five, four, three, two, or one point to the respective places. At the end of the tournament the points are totaled to declare individual or team winners.

Elimination Tournament. Single elimination tournaments are the most direct route to a team or individual championship. Their greatest weakness lies in the fact that one defeat eliminates a competitor. A consolation bracket or tournament may be added to a single elimination tournament to accommodate those teams or individuals eliminated in the first or first and second rounds of play.

Double elimination tournaments prevent the quick elimination of a team and assure each player of at least two competitive encounters. No team or individual is eliminated until it has lost two games or matches. Winners work to the right of the bracket and upon the first loss go to the left. The attempt then is to work one's way to the left side of the bracket, for another loss results in elimination. If the winner of the first elimination (right side) loses to the winner of the left side, she has lost but once and still another game or match must be played before a winner is declared.

Single and double elimination tournaments are easily drawn up by using the perfect power of two, if the number of contestants is 4, 8, 16, 32, etc. However, when there are more than the perfect power of two, byes are added until this is reached. The number of byes should equal the difference between the number of competitors and the next higher power of two. When 15 are entered, there will be one bye (16 − 15 = 1), etc.

If more than 25 players are entered, two tournaments are recom-

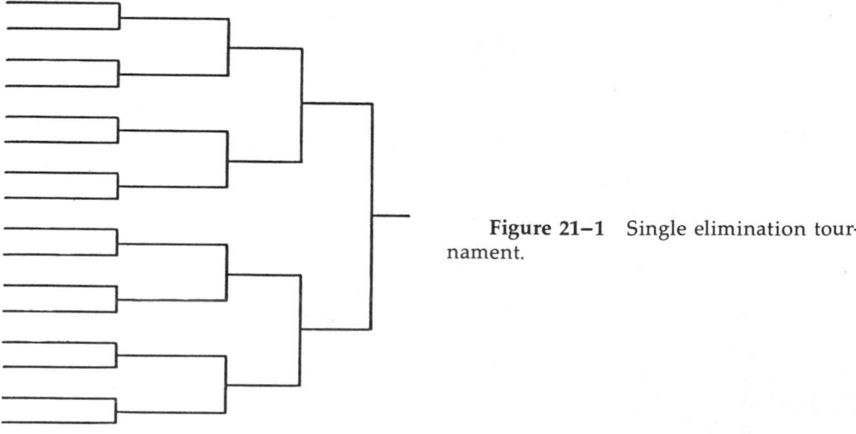

Figure 21–1 Single elimination tournament.

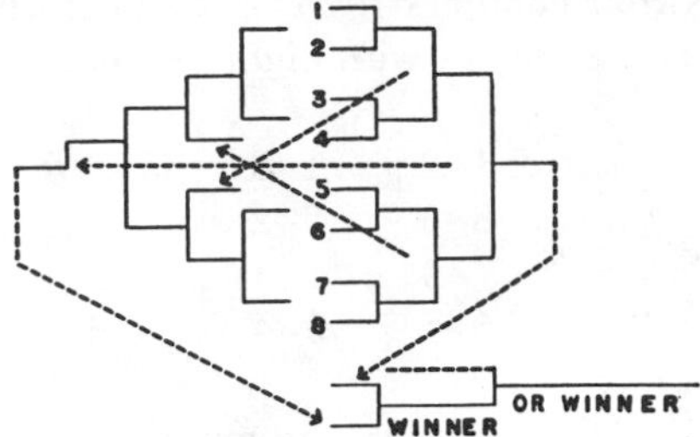

Figure 21–2 Double elimination tournament.

mended rather than one. The best players should be seeded, but not more than one player should be seeded for every eight entries. If two are to be seeded, numbers 1 and 2 shall be drawn by lot with the first drawn placed at the top of the upper half of the bracket and the second at the bottom of the lower half. If four are to be seeded, numbers 1 and 2 are treated as above; numbers 3 and 4 are drawn by lot with the first drawn placed at the top of the second quarter and the second placed at the bottom of the third quarter.

Round Robin Tournament. Several types of tournaments utilize round robins. A round robin may be conducted in which each team or individual plays every other team or individual once or twice with the final standings determined on a win percentage basis. Round robin leagues followed by play-offs are a popular method of organizing team sports. Play-offs following league play can be single or double elimination or another round robin schedule of league champions.

The following formula will apply to any number of teams, whether the total is odd or even. With an odd number of teams there is the same number of rounds; with an even number of teams there is one less number of games than teams.

For an Uneven Number of Teams. Assign each team a number and then use only the figures in drawing the schedule. For example, in a league with seven teams, start with 1 and put figures down in the following order:

7	6	5	4	3	2	1
6–1	5–7	4–6	3–5	2–4	1–3	7–2
5–2	4–1	3–7	2–6	1–5	7–4	6–3
4–3	3–2	2–1	1–7	7–6	6–5	5–4

Note that the figures go down on the right side and up on the left. Number 7 draws a bye in the first round, and the others play as indicated. With an odd number of teams, all numbers revolve, and the last number each time draws a bye.

For an Even Number of Teams. With an even number of teams, the plan is the same except that the position of 1 remains stationary, and the other numbers revolve about it until the original combination is reached. For example, with eight teams:

1–2	1–8	1–7	1–6	1–5	1–4	1–3
8–3	7–2	6–8	5–7	4–6	3–5	2–4
7–4	6–3	5–2	4–8	3–7	2–6	8–5
6–5	5–4	4–3	3–2	2–8	8–7	7–6

Only two things must be remembered: (1) with an even number of teams, 1 remains stationary, and the other numbers revolve; (2) with an odd number of teams, all numbers revolve, and the last number each time draws a bye.

Ladder Tournament. This is an excellent plan for small competitive groups or for use as "challenge matches" to determine positions on a team such as tennis or badminton. The tournament is self-operative once the calendar dates for challenges and termination are established. It is often called a perpetual tournament for it may run throughout the school year. Although there are several plans which involve seeding players, the most common method of determining ladder positions is by random selection or lot. A player may challenge the person directly above her and if she defeats her opponent, they change positions on the ladder. The winner is the person achieving the top rung of the ladder at the close of the tournament.

The Pyramid. This tournament is a form of ladder tournament and again, several types are in use. In one plan players are placed in the spaces by random selection. A player may challenge any other player in her own horizontal row and if she is successful, she may challenge anyone in the row above. If she is successful again the two players change places up and down.

In a second plan, the number of spaces on the bottom line should be equal to half the number of contestants. In the beginning, no contestant has a position on the pyramid: she gains a position by challenging another to a match. The winner then takes a place on the lowest pyramid. The loser must challenge another contestant and win before she can gain a position on the pyramid. Contestants advance to the next highest level by

TEAM 1
TEAM 2
TEAM 3
TEAM 4
etc.

Figure 21–3 Ladder tournament.

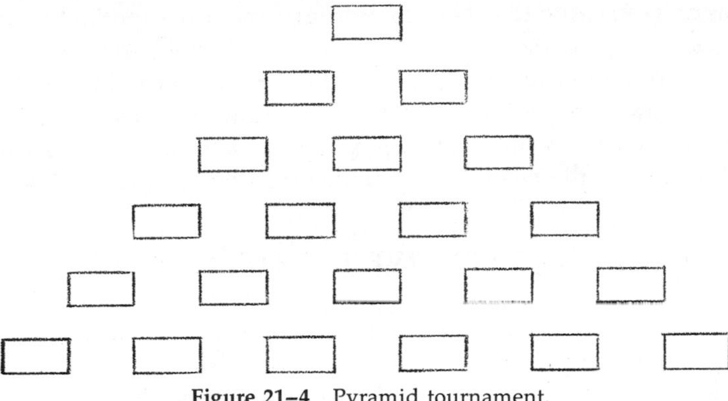

Figure 21–4 Pyramid tournament.

winning a match from someone on the same level. Losers change places with the winners. Advancement can be made only when there is a vacant spot on the next higher level (or, if there are no vacant spots on that level, by challenging to the next higher level). The winner is the one who arrives at the top first or stays there longest.

The Crown Tournament. The crown tournament is made up of several pyramids, each of 10 spaces at different levels. Challenging is vertical within each pyramid and horizontal among pyramids. The winner is the first to advance to the top of the highest pyramid. Players may gain their needed first position at the bottom of the horizontal pyramids by lot, by challenging another, or by assignment, with the better players placed there.

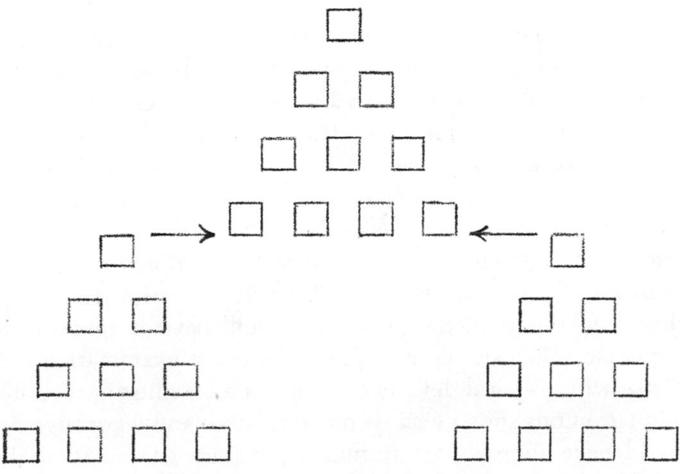

Figure 21–5 Crown tournament.

Ringer Tournament. The ringer tournament is a method of arriving at the season's low score. It is successfully used in golf, archery, and other individual scoring events. For example, during the golf season each player records her lowest score for every hole each time she plays the course. (A minimum or maximum number of games may be established.) At the end of the tournament the champion is determined by the lowest total score.

PLANNING FOR COMPETITIVE EVENTS

The conduct of *extramural* competition, including game rules, player eligibility, financing, and awards, is usually established by high school athletic federations or by college, university, or agency regulating bodies. These guidelines and rules should be known to all athletic coaches and administrators. The conduct of *intramural* competition is largely in the hands of the local school, agency, or college. Consequently, each should determine its own policies to assure equitable competition and to protect the welfare of participants. Consideration must be given to player eligibility, financing, leadership, officiating, coeducational competition, and awards.

Player Classification. Contestants may be classified according to age, height, weight, class level, club sorority, dormitory, skill level, fitness level, or other meaningful ways of grouping. Care must be taken to assure that players are as equally matched as possible and that every safety precaution has been taken in assigning groups to compete against each other in specific areas. In coeducational events policies should be established concerning special rules of play as well as the number of players of each sex participating. Intramural teams should select their own captains.

Point System. A simple system should be devised for keeping points. It should be accurate and not time consuming. Winners should receive the greatest number of points with runners-up the second most. Each participant may be given entry points for playing in one or more tournament games. The system should be kept on a yearly basis, and will, when used cumulatively over a longer period of time, increase participation. All records might well be kept by elected student intramural managers under close teacher guidance and supervision.

Eligibility Rules. Although each organization should draw up its own eligibility rules, such a group working on this project should be aware that rules (1) are primarily for the protection of the players and (2) cover participation eligibility (for girls as well as boys on coeducational teams), health requirements, forfeits, penalties for rule infractions, and player conduct. All who take part in the program should have permission to do so from a physician. They should also have a physical examination before entering. Those with physical defects or other defects must not be allowed to compete in strenuous sports against more capable and vigorous opponents. They should have their own intramural program geared to their limitations. Such a program might include table tennis, shuffleboard, archery, or other similar types of noncombative sports.

Awards. If awards are given at the completion of a season, semester, or school year, they should be simple and inexpensive, for the major portion of any intramural budget should be spent on equipment rather than on costly cups, charm bracelets, or other awards. In granting the awards, it should be remembered that every student should have an equal opportunity to earn one. Rotating trophies or plates with winners' names printed on them has value, and using them is one way to keep the cost of awards down. A sportsmanship trophy may be given and be as valued, or even more so, among the players as the first place trophy. An awards banquet honoring both the men and women is often the climax of a successful intramural and extramural year. Colored slides or action films taken during the season when shown at such a banquet add greatly to program interest, and do much to acquaint the school president, deans, principal, and teachers with the importance, scope, and value of the program. A student committee under the guidance of a selected representative and the instructor should plan the awards banquet around a unique yearly theme, and it should become an occasion that is eagerly looked forward to by every player.

DISCUSSION QUESTIONS

1. Discuss the place of intramurals in the total physical education program and in the total educational program of the school.
2. Design a program of coeducational intramural activities for a senior high school. What criteria guide the selection of activities, rules of the games, and eligibility of participants?
3. Plan on paper an intramural program for a group of 30 girls on the senior high school level who have physical or other defects which prohibit them from taking part in the regular program.
4. A play day is built around a specific theme and all activities are renamed in light of it. Plan on paper a play day in detail for eight senior high schools in your city or community.
5. Review a current issue of *Women Sport* or *Sportswoman.* How many sports were mentioned in which women participate? Review an article about an outstanding sports personality.

SUGGESTED READINGS

AIAW: *Handbook of Policies and Operating Procedures.* Current Ed. Washington, D.C., AAHPER.

Bunn, John et al.: *The Art of Officiating Sports.* Second Ed. Englewood Cliffs, N.J., Prentice-Hall, 1957.

Kirk, Robert: Practical aspects of coeducational intramural activities. *The Physical Educator,* Vol. 20, No. 4., December, 1963.

Kleindienst, Viola, and Weston, Arthur: *Intramural and Recreation Programs for Schools and Colleges.* New York, Appleton-Century-Crofts, 1965.

Means, Louis, E.: *Intramurals: Their Organization and Administration.* Englewood Cliffs, N. J. Prentice-Hall, 1963.

Mueller, P. T.: *Intramurals: Programming and Administration.* 4th Ed. New York, Ronald Press, 1971.

N.A.G.W.S.: *Philosophy and Standards for Girls' and Women's Sports.* Current Ed. Washington, D.C., AAHPER.

INDEX

Note: Page numbers in *italics* refer to illustrations.
Page numbers followed by (t) refer to tables.

A

C

D

E

F

G

M

N

O

P

Q

R

S

T

U

V

W

Z